A HISTORY OF AUSTRALIA

VOLUME II

A History of Australia I

Select Documents in Australian History, 1788-1850
Select Documents in Australian History, 1851-1900
(Angus & Robertson)

Sources of Australian History
(Oxford University Press)

A Short History of Australia
(Mentor and Heinemann)

Meeting Soviet Man
(Angus & Robertson)

THE YOUNG WENTWORTH

Drawing at Vaucluse House, Sydney

C. M. H. CLARK

A HISTORY OF AUSTRALIA

II

NEW SOUTH WALES AND
VAN DIEMEN'S LAND
1822–1838

MELBOURNE UNIVERSITY PRESS

LONDON AND NEW YORK: CAMBRIDGE UNIVERSITY PRESS

First published 1968

Printed in Australia by
Brown Prior Anderson Pty Ltd
5 Evans Street, Burwood, Victoria 3125
for Melbourne University Press, Carlton, Victoria 3053

Registered in Australia for transmission
by post as a book

75636

Dewey Decimal Classification Number 994
Library of Congress Catalog Card Number 63-5969
Aus 67-2021

Text set in 11 point Caslon type

To
Keith Hancock and Max Crawford

Some men, like bats or owls, have better eyes for
the darkness than for the light.

Charles Dickens: Pickwick Papers

The land, boys, we live in.

Anniversary Dinner, Sydney. 26 January 1825.
W. C. Wentworth, President.

PREFACE

THE FIRST VOLUME attempted to describe the coming of European civilization to Australia. This volume attempts to tell the story—or rather part of the story, for no man can hope to tell it all—of what happened in New South Wales and Van Diemen's Land in the years from the departure of Macquarie at the end of 1821 to 1838. The history of South Australia, Western Australia, Port Phillip and Moreton Bay, the events in the United Kingdom which affected the Australian colonies during these years, and surveys of land, immigration and education will be attempted in the third volume, which will end during the decade of gold.

The material for this volume has been collected in London, Dublin, Glasgow, Edinburgh, Auckland, Norfolk Island and in the public libraries of Australia. I would like to thank Dr Watson of the Department of History, Duke University, North Carolina, for making it possible for me to spend part of my time in their great university reading the London *Times* for 1821–38. I would like to thank Merval Hoare for her help in Norfolk Island, and Judith Egerton for her help in London. I would like to thank, too, Dr and Mrs Parnaby for helping me to see the Marsden country in New Zealand. I would also like to thank the Rector of Canisius College for permitting me to read the Therry Papers, and J. A. Dumaresq for allowing me to read the Dumaresq Papers at Mount Ireh. As before my great debt is to the National Library in Canberra, and in particular to the head of the Australian Section, Pauline Fanning, J. L. Cleland, and Jennifer Strickland in the Manuscript Section. My other great debt is to the Tasmanian State Archives, and their excellent staff, led by the late P. R. Eldershaw and G. T. Stilwell. It was also my great good fortune to have the help of A. J. and Nancy Gray, and Dr Charles Currey, all three of whom gave generously of what they knew. Simon Proctor drew my attention to much useful material. As before, too, there have been many people with whom it was useful to exchange ideas. Two men helped me more than I can say. They were Keith Hancock and Ken Inglis. Some found time to help me with their knowledge, and in other ways. They were Laurie Gardiner, Kathleen Fitzpatrick, Don Baker, Bruce Grant, James McAuley, Judah Waten, Noel McLachlan, Ian Turner, Sandy Yarwood, Allan Martin, Ann Moyal, Alison Priestley, Bede Nairn, Macmahon Ball, Daphne Gollan, David Campbell, Keith Sinclair and Michael Roe. I was lucky also to have at different times three excellent helpers—Barbara Penny, Rima Rossall, and Lyndall Ryan. Pat Romans typed the manuscript with great efficiency. I am grateful to the Trustees of Vaucluse House for permission to reproduce the pen and ink drawing of W. C. Wentworth, and to Lady Stanham for permitting me to reproduce the portrait of James Macarthur. I would like to thank the Trustees of the Public Library of New South Wales for allowing me to use the illustrations of Gellibrand, Truganini and Mannalargenna, Robinson, Forbes, Lang, McLeay, Bourke and Vaucluse; the National Library for permission to reproduce the portrait of Arthur; and the National Portrait Gallery, London, for permission to reproduce the portrait of Molesworth. And I would like to thank H. Hennig of the Bureau of Mineral Resources for drawing the maps. It has been my great good fortune to have the help of Dymphna Clark and the staff of the Melbourne University Press in editing the manuscript; to both my debt is greater than would suit a man to say. The students at the Australian National University helped me to believe one ought to try to tell the story of how we became what we are—even though no matter how much one gave to it, that story never could be told as it ought to be, and, indeed deserves to be, by anyone.

M. C.

CONTENTS

ILLUSTRATIONS

PLATES

MAPS

ABBREVIATIONS

C.M.S.	Church Missionary Society
C.O.	Colonial Office
C.S.O.	Colonial Secretary's Office (Hobart, Tasmania)
Encl.	Enclosure
H.R.A.	*Historical Records of Australia*
H.R.N.S.W.	*Historical Records of New South Wales*
Hist. Studies	*Historical Studies, Australia and New Zealand*
M.L.	Mitchell Library, Sydney
MS.	manuscript
n.d.	no date
N.S.W.S.A.	New South Wales State Archives
NAT. L.	National Library of Australia, Canberra
P.D.	British *Parliamentary Debates*
P.P.	British *Parliamentary Papers*
R.A.H.S., *J. & P.*	Royal Australian Historical Society, *Journal and Proceedings*
S.P.G.	Society for the Propagation of the Gospel
T.H.R.A., *P. & P.*	Tasmanian Historical Research Association, *Papers and Proceedings*
T.S.A.	Tasmanian State Archives
V. & P. (L.C. N.S.W.)	*Votes and Proceedings* of the Legislative Council of New South Wales

I

DARKNESS

SOME WHO CAME to man's estate in the cities and country districts of the British Isles in the decade between 1820 and 1830 who knew the defeat of good, the success of evil, the physical pain and the mental anguish considered that the human race was out of joint with the purpose of its creator. From the East End of the great city of London right to the outskirts of Westminster, unwashed, unshaven, squalid and dirty men constantly raced to and fro ankle deep in the filth and mire.[1] In that mass of dirt, gloom and misery drunken tramps jostled with the rich and the titled. Men and women craving for booty, their bellies filled with beer and gin, committed crimes for which they were hanged by the neck until they were dead after which their bodies were cut down and given to their friends.[2]

In Vauxhall Gardens, orgies of lust and drunkenness prevented the industrious in the neighbourhood from sleeping, and the dying from departing in peace.[3] In the streets, ragged and half-starved starved Flemish boys importuned females, and thrust forth from under their coats disgusting monkeys, to terrify the women.[4] In the courtyard at the Old Bailey men were publicly whipped.[5] Women gave birth to children in public places, because of their extreme misery and degradation.[6] Multitudes of Irish loitered in the vicinity of St James's Palace from dawn till dusk in the infatuated delusion that the royal family would assist them, only to learn in the law courts the consequences of pestering people in high places.[7] Virtuous young girls, deceived by the fair promises of men and then betrayed by their paramours, swallowed poison, and died bewailing their cruel fate and the callousness of their destroyers.[8]

Bishops, priests, and deacons laboured to explain to all and sundry that the filth, the violence, the savagery, and the cruelty were the consequences of human depravity. As punishment for that offence in the Garden of Eden all creatures great and small were condemned to live in a vale of tears for the term of their natural lives. Men who dreamed dreams of the life of man without God, or of the happiness, the joy, the pleasure and the enrichment to be achieved by dropping that jealous Jehovah and his savage laws were hounded

---

[1] The point was made by John Henry Newman in his *Apologia pro Vita Sua*, first published in 1864; see World's Classics ed. 1964, pp. 251-2. Newman was born in February of 1801. Three of the novels of Dickens explore the response of an innocent boy when confronted with the great darkness of the decade. They were *Oliver Twist*, first published in book form in 1838, *David Copperfield*, first published in book form in 1850, and *Great Expectations*, first published in book form in England in 1862. Dickens was born in February of 1812.

[2] For example, see *The Times*, 20 August and 11 December 1828.

[3] Ibid., 21 May 1828. [4] Ibid., 29 May 1828. [5] Ibid., 5 November 1824.

[6] Ibid., 29 January 1828. [7] Ibid., 4 June 1824. [8] Ibid., 18 November 1828.

by the gaolers of mankind as common criminals. In June 1823, a young man of nineteen, his heart hot within him for the moral improvement of mankind, published Thomas Paine's *Age of Reason*. For publishing such libellous and blasphemous passages, as well as for exceeding the bounds of common decency during the proceedings in the Court, he was sentenced to three years in Newgate Gaol, after which he was to enter into a bond of £100 to be of good behaviour for life.[9]

The courts of criminal law were a stage designed to incite terror, but not pity, in the breasts of all the players in the drama of life. At Guildford Assizes at the end of July 1828 two men and three women were found guilty of assaulting and robbing a foreigner in a house of ill fame. When the judge solemnly put on the black cap the prisoners screamed and sobbed dreadfully. Before the judge had uttered ten words one of the women fell down in strong hysterics, which set off her companions again into such screams of violence that the judge ordered them to be removed. He then announced that he would spare the lives of the women. To renewed screams from the men the judge went on to inform them that so long as human nature remained the same men would be likely to be led astray by the allurements of females. All men who plundered those who were led on by sexual passion must suffer the extreme penalty of the law. He sentenced them to be hanged by the neck until they were dead, adding the wish that God would have mercy on them, for they could expect no mercy from one of their kind.[10]

Even though the evil imagination of man's heart exposed him to the torments of his own kind in this world and the eternal bonfire of his creator in the next, the great consolation was held out to the dying thieves and murderers that God pitied and loved them. On the evening of their last day on earth, in all the gaols of the United Kingdom, prison chaplains preached in the chapels in which the coffins destined to contain the bodies of those set down for execution were visible from the pew reserved for those about to die. On 21 November 1824 at Newgate Gaol the Reverend Mr Cotton told an unhappy youth to be of good cheer for God would have pity on him, just as he, God's servant, pitied him from his very soul. The service left the unhappy youth in such an exhausted condition that he needed restoratives to enable him to return to his cell. Early next morning he walked out of his cell to those words about resurrection and life and climbed the scaffold erected in the public square, while from every window in Newgate Street drunken spectators yelled and mocked as the victim, clinging to life to the last in his wild despair, dropped into the silence. For they had converted what their masters had designed for their instruction and terror into a ghastly sport. In the meantime, in the church on the other side of that square, a few touched by the image of Christ went down on their knees and asked God to forgive them all, and read again in letters of gold on the board

[9] Ibid., 9 June 1823.
[10] Ibid., 2 August 1828; see also the case at Bury in *The Times* of 28 March 1828 when three men charged with stealing knelt down and begged for mercy in the most piteous accents, but the learned judge, after warning them not to entertain the least hope that their lives could be spared, passed upon them the awful sentence of the law after a suitable exhortation.

beside the altar those commandments of God, which men transgressed at their peril.[11]

In Newgate Gaol the women were the usual products of material neglect and a life of vice. They were so deaf to all attempts to appeal to their good feelings that the words of the reformers, the charity workers, the philanthropists, the clergy and the improvers of mankind were greeted with indifference or contempt. They talked of hunger and the streets, beggary and whipping, the ginshop, the pawnbroker, and the men paid to lag all those who lacked the guile, the cunning, and the smiles of dame fortune to look after 'Number One'. In one portion of Newgate was a school for the education of the boys committed for trial on charges of pocket-picking. It was said there was not one redeeming feature amongst them—not a glance of honesty, not a wink expressive of anything but the gallows and the hulks. Their great pride was in their life of crime in which coming to Newgate was a grand affair: to the sentiments of shame and contrition they were perfect strangers. Every boy seemed to behave as though he had done something very meritorious in getting to Newgate. On the table in this room lay a Bible, but there were no signs that it had ever been taken into use.

It was the same with the men. For them Newgate was the nursery of future crime where the old instructed the young in the career of thieving. There men learned once again what they had first heard outside in the lodging houses of St Giles, the low parts of Westminster, and both parts of White-chapel in those gathering places for thieves, that robbery or blackmail and preying on humanity were the only means of continuing to enjoy a life in which they could gratify sensual passion, and remain drunk forever without working. There, too, the Bible had curious uses. One man who always attended chapel with an air of great devotion, and generally snatched up a Bible whenever any official was likely to observe him, had for years been a corrupter of the boys of Houndsditch, showing them gold at their lodging houses to seduce them into bringing stolen goods to him.[12]

In the provinces of England, in the towns as well as in the countryside, the outrage of human sensibilities, the bestiality and the cruelty were as commoplace as in the metropolis of London. At Poulton near Blackpool in July 1823 yeomanry wandering round aimlessly in search of a 'lark' one Sunday afternoon found a Methodist 'ranter' praying to his dear, kind God to forgive sinners, approached him with a tumbler of wine and forced it down his throat, to the no small amusement of the rabble who drove the preacher out of town.[13] One Saturday early in March 1828 a man brought his wife with a halter round her neck to Axbridge market, where he sold her to his brother for a shilling.[14] In the midland towns technological changes left in their wake material and spiritual wrecks. Large bodies of unemployed roved the streets of the weaving towns, searching for work. Men and women were called on to

---

[11] Ibid., 22 November 1824.

[12] Based on Charles Dickens, *Sketches by Boz*, (2 vols, London, 1836), ch. 25 'A Visit to Newgate'; E. G. Wakefield, *Facts relating to the Punishment of Death in the Metropolis* (London, 1831), pp. 16-27; for a description of Old Newgate by a contemporary see also *Birmingham Journal*, 18 September 1839.

[13] *The Times*, 8 July 1823.   [14] Ibid., 5 March 1828.

B

face hardships they could not understand or reconcile with their ideas of desert.[15]

In the country districts landowners displayed more zeal for the preservation of that rural tyranny symbolized by the old game laws than for any schemes for the greater glory of the English, or the betterment of their people. The poachers were brutalized by the very evil they were attempting to evade. In Berkshire one shiny Sunday night early in January of 1828 some poachers knocked down a bailiff with a gun, and beat him most brutally. When the bailiff recovered sufficiently to get back on his feet, they yelled 'Shoot the cursed bastard; curse his eyes, shoot him'. And they pursued him and again knocked him down, and beat him with their guns as he lay on the ground till he was senseless, and then they stripped him of his clothes and went away. On being brought to trial at Reading they hollered outside the court and pointed to their necks, intimating that they expected to be hanged.[16]

Surrounded by such darkness, brutality, filth and squalor in their daily lives, some of those who probed the nature of God and man were attracted to a religion which offered an explanation for the savagery and brutality by which they were surrounded. They found no difficulty in assenting to the proposition that the imagination of man's heart was evil from the start: that men drank iniquity like water for their deeds were evil. So in a decade of darkness some turned to that jealous God who had promised that he could still the madness of the people, and sang of their hope that in the chaos and confusion, the terror, the brutality, and in all the changing scenes of life the God of Jacob would be their refuge.

A few with the strength to brush away the mist before their eyes looked at the horror and the agony Blake had caught in the face of King Nebuchadnezzar at that moment when, after hearing the sounds of the cornet, flute, harp, sackbut, psaltery and dulcimer, and all kinds of music, and having fallen down and worshipped the golden image, he had been driven from men, and had eaten the grass as oxen, and his body had become wet with the dew of heaven, till his hairs had grown like eagles' feathers, and his nails like birds' claws.[17] John Keats, frail of body, a fiery particle, yet quite unable to stand up to the mockers and the fault-finders, wrote of what he saw in the core of an eternal fierce destruction, where men preyed on each other like the creatures in the sea where the mouth of the greater fed on the lesser for evermore.[18] The young Carlyle, hot of heart, stormy, buffeted by great gales of passion when the ways of the world affronted his innocent heart, came down from Scotland to London Town, and recoiled in horror at that huge, dead, immeasurable steam engine, rolling on, in its dead indifference, to grind him from limb to limb, and cried out in his anguish and despair: 'O, the vast, gloomy solitary Golgotha, and Mill of Death'.[19]

[15] Ibid., 31 January 1828.   [16] Ibid., 16 July and 4 February 1828.

[17] W. Blake, 'Nebuchadnezzar', 1795—Tate Gallery, London; Book of Daniel, iii. 10 and iv. 33; see also Songs of Experience, The Tiger, the Marriage of Heaven and Hell, in *The Poetical Works of William Blake*, ed. by J. Sampson (London, 1913).

[18] For the ideas of Keats see A. Ward, *John Keats: The Making of a Poet* (London, 1963), pp. 158, 172 and *passim*.

[19] T. Carlyle, *Sartor Resartus* Book 2, ch. 7; see also B. Willey, *Nineteenth Century Studies* (London, 1949), ch. 4, 'Thomas Carlyle'.

Some, later, setting aside the explanations of the parsons and priests as an opiate exploited by the oppressors to distract men from the true cause of their misery, asked whether the darkness, the savagery and the brutality were but the symptoms of a change in the relations of productive forces, which were in turn the result of changes in the methods of production. By reducing the workers' needs to the barest and most miserable level of physical existence men had been deprived of the need for both activity and enjoyment. The workers were gradually being converted into insensible beings who only wanted to work to earn enough to meet the needs of a savage. The poor house in the industrial city was man's regression to the life of a cave-dweller where he shared his crudest needs, not in love and charity with his neighbour, in that communion with others of his kind, but alienated from him, just as he was alienated from the product of his labour. Man was being alienated from tenderness and pity just as he was being alienated from the fruits of his labour. Industrial society was ushering in a new age of barbarism in which some men, like bats or owls, had better eyes for the darkness than for the light.[20]

In Scotland it was the same. Glasgow and Edinburgh were cities where half-naked savages drew knives and daggers against each other, or threw vitriol in each other's eyes, like the citizens of an Italian state.[21] The inhabitants of the gaols corrupted each other in the practice of every villany; the streets were rendered unsafe to property by swarms of pickpockets, and unsafe to virtue by unceasing offers from prostitutes. By day and night the unwary were exposed to the begging of half-starved, ill-clad savages from Ireland. Each Sunday the ministers preached of that peace of God which passed all understanding, to men and women whose only experience of life was the constant excitement, commotion and uproar of the streets.[22] In the villages, while the preachers thumped the pulpit boxes and thundered that God would punish dancers, drinkers, fornicators and all unclean livers with hell-fire, in taverns nearby to the music of the bagpipe, men and women, lightly clad, the breasts of the women shaking in the general merriment, sang, danced and shouted in drunken sprees. So some were full of love divine, and some were full of brandy.[23]

While the ministers implored mankind to renounce the pomps and vanities of this wicked world and all the sinful lusts of the flesh, and those who slept in the Glasgow necropolis waited for their Lord's reviving call, the law aimed to deter from crime by terror. The hangman's noose, the whip, outlawing and transportation were the punishments of those who were driven by some folly or madness to seek desperate remedies for their desperate situations. For house-breaking in January of 1823 a lad of seventeen was launched into eternity, after being told by his judge that, though he could not expect mercy

[20] Based on K. Marx, *Economic and Philosophic Manuscripts* (Moscow, 1961), no. 115; Charles Dickens, *Pickwick Papers* (Oxford ed., London, 1948), p. 799; for the response of the young Dickens to the period between 1821 and 1840 see E. Johnson, *Charles Dickens: His Tragedy and Triumph* (2 vols, London, 1953), vol. 1 *passim*.

[21] *The Times*, 8 October 1823.

[22] Based on the *Glasgow Herald* and *Correspondent* (Edinburgh) for the decade 1821-31.

[23] *Correspondent* (Edinburgh), 27 May 1822; see also the collection of sketches on the way of life of the period by R. Bryden in the Burns Museum, Alloway, Ayrshire, Scotland; see also Robert Burns, 'The Holy Fair'.

in this world, yet for a heartfelt repentance, God might forgive him: for corrupting the minds of the young a schoolmaster was outlawed: for petty theft two men were publicly whipped. Some beseeched God to give them patience in all their sufferings, and a happy issue out of all their afflictions: and some sought comfort and oblivion in the wine-cup: and some were tormented and brought to derision.[24]

In Ireland the same savagery and brutality darkened the land. Haunted by their own melancholy history, and preserving in their folk songs and ballads the memory of an ancient wrong committed against their people, some blamed their misfortunes on the English who had trampled on their ancient laws, had confiscated every acre in Ireland, destroyed the political institutions of the country, and then stripped the altars and melted the chalices and sacred utensils of her venerable church, but could not destroy their ancient and holy faith.[25] Then in the decades after the Napoleonic Wars another darkness began to descend on that stricken people. As the population increased from 4,753,000 in 1791 to 6,802,000 in 1821, and 7,767,000 in 1831 the demand for labour decreased, mainly because of subdivision of farms and the absence of demand for the labour of the evicted tenant farmers in the cities. By 1831 at least one-fifth of the population was pronounced redundant. In addition to the gypsies, fortune-tellers, strumpets and thieves who had always roved the countryside in search of prey, droves of poor now wandered from farm to farm, and village to village, seeking work, and begging for food. Poverty became one of the wrongs of Ireland.[26]

Uproar and outrage broke out through the length and breadth of the country. Rural Ireland began to furnish a fearful catalogue of deeds of terror, intimidation and violence. Horses were cruelly disabled by hocking: traitors and informers were waylaid and mangled or savagely murdered: evicting landlords were threatened to have their coffins ready. The priests played their trump card of terror—the threat of excommunication. The English Parliament contributed its own brand of secular terror, punishing such outrages with whippings, transportation, or death. But the outrages continued undiminished despite the priests' warning about damnation, and the savage criminal code.[27] At Mallow, near Cork, in the autumn of 1823 a crowd assembled to hear one victim of the criminal law urge his erstwhile companions to take an example from his awful fate, and turn from their evil ways of terror and out-rage, and fear God. As the lad dropped into the silence people screamed and wailed, and hurried off to their rude cabins, nursing in their hearts not that

[24] See the plaque for John Bowman in St Mungo's Cathedral, Glasgow; *Glasgow Herald*, 17, 27 and 31 January 1823.

[25] See, for example, the speech by D. O'Connell in *The Times*, 1 September 1828.

[26] Report of the Select Committee on the State of the Poor in Ireland; being a Summary of the First, Second and Third Reports of Evidence taken before that Committee, *P.P.*, 1830, VII, 667, p. 4; evidence of J. Doyle to Committee, ibid., pp. 399-416; see also K. H. Connell, 'Land and Population in Ireland', *Economic History Review*, vol. 3, 1950, p. 278.

[27] Evidence of M. Barrington to the Select Committee on the State of Ireland, *P.P.*, 1831-2, XVI, 677, pp. 11-15, Appendix p. 5 et seq.; *The Times*, 27 August 1823, report from Kilkenny; *The Times*, 8 July 1823, for an example of tithe collecting; for an example of a priest urging the people to forswear their foolish ways, see *The Times*, 6 September 1823; the emergency legislation passed by the Parliament of the United Kingdom is conveniently summarized in the Report of the Select Committee on the State of Ireland, *P.P.*, 1831-2, XVI, 677, pp. 21-2.

advice about their own folly, but an implacable hatred of those enemies of their people who had brought a comely youth to an untimely and cruel death.[28]

Such scenes confirmed the Irish conception of the English as the men who had converted the most beautiful island under the sun into a land of skulls or of ghastly spectres. The English had stolen their land, barred them from the professions, reduced justice to a mockery and a farce, and plotted the destruction of their holy faith. The Protestant had his nightmare too—the nightmare that a Catholic Ireland would enslave the mind, reduce all and sundry to grovel before an ignorant and superstitious priesthood, and drag everyone down to the level of those semi-savages who crawled over the countryside or eked out a filthy existence in stinking mud hovels. So while the men of God reminded the faithful that charity and universalism should distinguish the behaviour of all the followers of the Galilean fisherman, a Catholic in desperation knocked down an Orange leader with a sledge-hammer and the Orangeman, in retaliation, fired on the Catholic demonstrators. That was in September of 1823.[29]

On the walls of their churches, in their graveyards, and other public places they erected memorials in which they expressed the sentiments and aspirations by which they hoped to be guided in their daily lives. In all the Protestant churches of Ireland tablets of stone testified to posterity of the faith by which they lived: 'Mark the perfect man, and behold the upright man. For the end of that man is peace'. The law of kindness was on their lips, and the love of God and man was in their hearts.[30] The Catholic, overwhelmed with a sense of man's impotence to replenish the earth and subdue it, cried out in his anguish to the Holy Mother of God: 'O Mary: Conceived without sin: Pray for us: Who have recourse to thee'. They erected pitiful memorials to remind them of their melancholy history, and keep alive that love of old Ireland, and their holy faith.[31] By contrast, in the market place, the tap-room, the snug, the farm-house, and the fields, they were surrounded by a different life—a life of terror, of treachery, of cruelty, bestiality, darkness and vileness.[32]

Some of the men and women who were driven to transgress the laws of God or the laws of man were transported to New South Wales and Van Diemen's Land. Between 1821 and 1830 21,780 convicts were transported to New South Wales, and 10,000 to Van Diemen's Land. Of those sent to New South Wales 19,280 were men and 2,500 women; to Van Diemen's Land were sent 8,382 men and 1,618 women. Of them, two in three had been tried in England, about one in three in Ireland, and a few in Scotland.

---

[28] *The Times*, 6 September 1823.

[29] J. Doyle, *Letters on the State of Ireland: addressed by J.K.L. to a friend in England* (Dublin, 1825), pp. 85-6, and 175-9; Report of the Select Committee on the State of the Poor in Ireland; being a Summary of the First, Second and Third Reports of Evidence taken before that Committee, *P.P.*, 1830, VII, 667, pp. 377-9, 408, 505 and 531; *The Times*, 8 and 23 July 1823, 13 August and 12 December 1828; O. MacDonagh, 'The Irish Clergy and Emigration during the Great Famine', *Irish Historical Studies*, vol. 5, 1946-7, p. 292.

[30] Examples taken from the memorial tablets in St Mary's Church of Ireland Cathedral at Limerick for persons who died between 1821 and 1831.

[31] See, for example, the shrine to the Virgin in Galway, and the memorial in Sligo to 'the valiant Irish and French soldiers who fought here for dear old Ireland'.

[32] For other aspects of the Irish contribution see vol. I of this history, pp. 103-7.

One-half and probably two-thirds had formerly been punished, two-thirds were Protestant, and one-third was Roman Catholic.[33]

All sorts and conditions returned from the law courts of London to Newgate, or from the courts of Scotland to Leith, or from the courts of Ireland to the depots at Dublin and Cork, to await transportation to New South Wales and Van Diemen's Land. Chance played its part in deciding who should leave their country for their country's good and who should stay behind. In March 1828, as the kind-hearted Mr Croker was walking in the streets of London with his friend Holmes, the latter caught a man pickpocketing him. As the poor devil had no spirit and was very humble and penitent Holmes, just as kind-hearted as his friend, decided to let him off. So one pickpocket dropped back into the anonymous history of that immense city. Five years earlier a constable saw with his own eye one Nicholas Bullock, a well-known member of the fraternity of thieves, lift up the coat of a man and caught him and said to him, 'Nick, I want you', to which Bullock replied blandly, 'What for, George?', and took him before the Recorder who sentenced him to transportation for life. So Bullock became part of the history of Australia.[34]

Some mocked their judges, and reviled them, and swore at them. Some wept: some laughed: others bragged, and strutted in their dock. A boy of thirteen spoke with pride of his distinguished career in crime which he had begun at the age of seven when he was instructed in how to rob everybody that came his way. In six years in the profession of crime he had been arrested half a dozen times, privately whipped once, and tried three times at the Old Bailey. For the past year he had kept a girl whom he had called in the language of the fraternity of thieves his 'old woman'. At least one very pretty boy of thirteen years was transported for seven years for stealing a handkerchief. For the law at least attempted to enforce that one event unto all, so that a boy, his face painted by nature's own hand like a woman's, had to endure the same punishment as those on whom chance or nature had practised a cruel joke.[35]

Some were caught in that great net by one deed of folly. George Foyles, for seventeen years a brave soldier in the service of the East India Company but sometimes addicted to the evil of taking a drop too much, after which he was incapable of being master of himself or responsible for his engagements, committed bigamy, for which the judge sent him on the long journey across the oceans. So a man of passion, but not endowed with the strength to resist the clamour of a dark, undying source of pain, was called on to expiate his folly in forced labour.[36] Some were the victims of a dark side of the human heart. In September 1828 one Anne M'Gee, driven not by want or need, but by some demon within her with an insatiable appetite for the subterranean satis-

[33] For the discussion of numbers see L. L. Robson, *The Convict Settlers of Australia* (Melbourne, 1965); see also R. M. Martin, *History of Austral-Asia: Comprising New South Wales, Van Diemen's Land, Swan River, South Australia, &c.* (London, 1836) and W. D. Forsyth, *Governor Arthur's Convict System: Van Diemen's Land, 1824-36* (London, 1935).

[34] L. J. Jennings (ed.), *The Croker Papers: The Correspondence and Diaries of the Right Honourable J. W. Croker* (3 vols, London, 1885), vol. 1, p. 409.

[35] For example, see the reports of trials in *The Times*, 22 September and 30 October 1823, 20 April 1829.

[36] *The Times*, 8 January 1828; Charles Dickens, *Oliver Twist* (3 vols, London, 1838).

faction, enticed a girl from her house, and stripped her of her clothing. For this she received a sermon from the judge on her infamy, and transportation beyond the seas for the term of her natural life.[37] At Lewes, in Sussex, a man who had extorted money from another man by threatening to denounce him as a sodomite was transported for life, the people in the court room gasped in horror at the disgusting narration of a man driven on by greed to such a deed of darkness.[38] For giving his wife 'what cheer' with such violence that she died from his beatings, James Clegg was called on to expiate his offence by forced labour for the term of his natural life.[39]

Some committed their crimes deliberately to promote their own personal happiness, or material advancement. One woman convict in New South Wales wrote to her lover far away in York in England passionately beseeching him to commit a felony as a means of transporting him to her arms. He stole a pair of breeches and, in due course, received his prize—a passage to Botany Bay and the embraces of his lover.[40] The advantages of transportation to New South Wales or Van Diemen's Land were estimated so highly amongst the lower order of society that some soldiers and others committed crimes to ensure transportation. In May 1828 some soldiers of the 46th Regiment, who had served in New South Wales, and then transferred to Madras, had committed the crime of coining in that latter place to ensure transportation.[41] Second offenders for theft were generally transported: first offenders were often whipped at the scene of the crime. So the professional lag sailed away to the comparative affluence of Botany Bay, while the casual criminal received a public whipping after which he returned to that savage struggle for survival which had first driven him to covet his neighbour's goods. Life for the men was a fearful lottery.

It was the same for the women. Many were in liquor when they committed their offence, and had no memory of what they had done. Early in 1831, for the pleasure of it as well as to keep out of the cold, Ann Gower drank two quarterns of gin with Jeremiah McGurrin in an inn in the great city of London, and staggered out into the street where, after much fumbling with each other, she found herself outside Mr McGurrin's house. There, overcome like many a man before and since by contradictory impulses, McGurrin decided he must get away from her, or so he told the court, hoping pitifully that those upright men would detect that the man of principle had not been drowned by the quarterns of gin, or that drive to know the wonder of a man with a maid. Besides, he added, he was worried because he was not certain what his wife would make of him coming home drunk with a woman of the streets. So he bolted for the door, but the woman chased him and slipped his handkerchief out of his pocket. For this Ann Gower went to New South Wales for fourteen years, and Jeremiah McGurrin went back to his wife.[42]

---

[37] *The Times*, 30 October 1821.   [38] Ibid., 16 April 1828.   [39] Ibid., 22 September 1828.
[40] Ibid., 23 December 1823; see also the trial of Henry Phelp at the Old Bailey on 29 October 1824 for stealing a gold snuff box. In his cruelty he had stolen the worldly goods of a Spanish army officer, and then endeavoured to fix upon Rodriguez a crime of an odious nature. He was sentenced to be transported for seven years, *The Times*, 30 October 1824.
[41] Ibid., 3 September 1828.
[42] Ibid., 24 May 1828, quoting the *Yorkshire Chronicle*.

Some, driven to desperation by poverty and suffering, pinched some trifle, for which they were sent over the oceans for their transgression of the divine command: thou shalt not steal. Mary Corbett, with one son dead, two children at home starving, and no husband to act as provider, stole two books, and found herself in a convict ship with women who had sold their bodies for mere tots of gin, and the opportunity to pick the pockets of the lecherous.[43]

Some of the women belonged to families who depended for their livelihood on crime. When Sarah Stanhope was found guilty at the Hull Sessions early in 1828 of stealing, the Recorder, after some observations on the enormity of her crime, informed the court that she was a relation of the notorious Snowden Dunhill Bounders who for their daring and extensive crimes had earned the infamous title of the Rob Roys of the East Riding. Her father had been transported in 1813, returned to Hull and been re-transported in 1825. One of her sons had been executed in Hobart Town, another had been transported, and her daughter had been gaoled for stealing. The two husbands of that daughter had been transported, as had the three husbands of Sarah Stanhope. Here, indeed, the Recorder continued, was a depth of infamy to disgrace a family, so stained by such an aggregate of guilt as to leave all their numbers irreclaimable by human endeavour. He, the Recorder, proposed to send her to places where she could do no further harm, and where those at large were checked not by any appeal to better sentiments, but by terror of the consequences of transgression. To check such an infamy, degradation of the victim was quite permissible.[44]

Yet when James Hawkins, who had been previously transported, was again sent overseas for the term of his natural life, the press in London wrote of him not as a man irredeemably marked by his infamy, but with a brazen pride. For Hawkins was a prize-fighter, who had observed the code of honour men demanded from the weak as well as from the strong, and refused ever to practise any cruelty either in the prize ring or in the dens of thieves which swarmed beside the banks of those troubled waters. The members of the Snowden Hill family were hounded all their lives by the consequences of their own infamy until their bodies were cased, unwept, unloved, unsung as manure for the soil of a harsh land, while James Hawkins and men of his kind went down to the grave, not only enjoying the respect and esteem of their goalers, but nursing that great stroke of fortune that they were neither loathed nor derided by their fellowmen on account of their infirmities.[45]

Some had no connection with the criminal classes. In 1831, 464 men, farm-labourers, reapers, mowers, milkmen, herdsmen, shepherds and stable boys, the men whose legs were calfless from half-starvation and whose shoulders were sloping from hard labour, were transported for burning hayricks and threshing machines. In the severe winter of 1830-1 a bad harvest and high prices drove them to demand higher wages from their local

[43] Ibid., 29 May 1828.
[44] See, for example, the reports of the trials of W. Saunders, an incorrigible little rogue, and E. Greyson, a fine youth of fifteen, in *The Times*, 3 September 1828.
[45] *Sessions Papers*, First Session held at Justice Hall in the Old Bailey, 24 February 1831, p. 356 (London, 1830-1); for another example see ibid., pp. 420-1.

landlords who refused. Some then burnt haystacks, broke threshing machines,
and set fire to houses. When brought before the courts the judges urged juries
not to be moved by pity or compassion, as the law in its wisdom punished such
transgressions severely, not in the interests of the landlords but to preserve
the security of the kingdom. The judges, too, lost no opportunity to remind the
men of the enormity of their offence: 'You will leave the country all of you',
Mr Justice Alderson said to three young machine-breakers, 'you will see your
friends and relations no more . . . the land which you have disgraced will see
you no more: the friends with whom you are connected will be parted from
you forever in the world.' Just to make sure the lesson had been absorbed
by the farm-labourers, some of them were called on to witness an execution
before leaving for the colonies. There they watched one of their kind
stagger and roll so painfully towards the scaffold while they wept in the
felons' yard, or buried their faces in their smock frocks, or wrung their hands
convulsively, or leaned for support against the walls of the yard quite unable
to cast their eyes upward to that place where another human being was
uttering the last deep and heavy sobs before he paid the supreme penalty for his
crime. For some this was their last picture of a life at the heart of which
there seemed to be a great darkness.[46]

Some had suffered much between the detection of their crimes and the
departure of the convict ship. William Jones, a literary dandy, who had supplemented his income by forgery, was detected in 1828 and brought to trial.
For him the whole universe suddenly turned to a mighty stranger: his mistress
turned informer: his mother died of a broken heart: the judge sentenced him
to death. But then family influence stepped in to save him from his fate: his
mistress repented of her treachery, and visited him in Newgate Gaol: the death
sentence was commuted to transportation for life. So Jones, who had lived
through all that anguish in his days of confinement, was taken from Newgate
Gaol one spring morning to board the convict ship at Chatham.[47]

Thieves, fences, receivers of stolen goods, forgers, prostitutes, Jews who
had stolen silver instruments from the synagogue, agricultural labourers who
had shot at gamekeepers with intent to do bodily harm,[48] the professionals and
the casuals from Scotland were brought together at Newgate to prepare to be
sent to a country in which they would do no harm to their fellow-countrymen.
As sailing day drew near a chaplain told them not to wallow or rejoice in
their past, which was gone beyond recall, but rather to set forth with joy in
their hearts, relying on the promises of Christ.[49] A woman with a calm, Ma-

---

[46] For a description of the riots see the reports by the special correspondents of *The Times*
September 1830-January 1831; see also Mr Justice Parker's charge to the jury at Reading, *The
Times*, 28 December 1830; see also *The Times*, 24 December 1830 and 17 January 1831; for
other accounts see F. O. Darvall, *Popular Disturbances and Public Order in Regency London*
(London, 1934); for other accounts see E. G. Wakefield, op. cit.; see also the excellent article by
G. Rudé, ' "Captain Swing" and Van Diemen's Land', T.H.R.A., P. & P., vol. 12, 1964-5, pp.
6-24.
[47] *Sessions Papers*, First Session held at Justice Hall in the Old Bailey, 21 February 1831, p.
311 (London, 1830-1).
[48] *The Times*, 24 January and 29 August 1828.
[49] T. Reid, *Two Voyages to New South Wales and Van Diemen's Land* (London, 1822), pp.
103-16.

donna-like face visited the women under sentence of transportation, opened the Bible, and read to them in a most sweetly solemn manner. She encouraged them in their needlework, their knitting and their rug-making, and by the love of Christ in her heart won over some of the women to the prospect of changing their life of vice for one in which from day to day they strengthened their feeling for virtue. She was Elizabeth Fry.[50]

On the night before the women were removed from Newgate to the convict ship they all went mad: they got drunk, tore things up, broke and set fire to all they could, and then scratched and spat at the turnkeys who tried to put on irons to restrain them. It was the same with the men. Rejecting every religious or serious reflection, they, too, began a glorious Bacchanal at the end of which they tore down everything within their reach, destroyed their beds, broke the windows, and set up a hideous clamour which was only ended when they were ironed for the journey to the convict ship, at which they arrived looking more like wild beasts than human beings. There while the few were suffering from the pangs of impending exile, and the many were suffering in mind and body from a quite different cause, with unwitting irony, a chaplain or surgeon-superintendent, often selected on account of their itch to improve mankind, reminded them that those who were heavy-laden might come unto Christ: that virtuous actions tended infinitely more to promote their happiness in this world than the most successful career of vice, and that their separation from their previous haunts of infamy might prove to be the greatest benefit that heaven could bestow, for neither fornicators, nor idolators, nor thieves, nor drunkards, nor revilers of mankind would inherit the kingdom of God.[51]

In Ireland the professional criminals, and the casuals, those driven to crime by Ireland's wrongs, or their own folly, those with an aversion to labour, the idle and the disorderly who had corrupted and depraved the innocents were gathered at Cork to be transported beyond the seas to expiate their crimes by forced labour, and deter others of like mind and disposition, by such an example. With them there was the usual sprinkling of bizarre characters. One man had told his judge he would thank his lordship if he could transport him, as he was now anxious to leave his regiment, seeing there was not a single gentleman in it.[52] Some women had been treated as sport for the judges during their trials. Biddy Regan of Tralee had been asked by the judge in August of 1828 to take her wig off so that he could have a good look at her, and had stood there in the dock while judge and jury, learned counsel, the gentlemen of the press, and the spectators in the visitors' gallery tittered and guffawed, and giggled at her in her agony and confusion.[53]

[50] *The Times*, 17 October 1828; F. Cresswell, *A Memoir of Elizabeth Fry* (London, 1886), pp. 86-7; J. Whitney, *Elizabeth Fry. Quaker Heroine* (London, 1953), pp. 210-11; Evidence of Mrs Fry to the Select Committee on Secondary Punishments, *P.P.*, 1831-2, VII, 547, p. 559; Original Diary or Visiting Book of the Rev. H. S. Cotton, Chaplain of Newgate, from 1823 to 1836 (MS. in NAT. L.); Elizabeth Fry, *Observations on the Visiting, Superintendence and Government of Female Prisoners* (London, 1827) pp. 51-2.

[51] T. Reid, op. cit., pp. x-xii; see also E. G. Wakefield, op. cit.; Evidence of A. B., a discharged convict, to the Select Committee on Secondary Punishments, *P.P.*, 1831-2, VII, 547, p. 559 et seq.; for the women see E. Fry, op. cit.; James Tucker, *Ralph Rashleigh*, ed. by C. Roderick (3rd impr., Sydney, 1953), pp. 49-50.

[52] *The Times*, 13 August 1828.   [53] Ibid., 13 August 1828.

The tone of the departure of a convict ship from Cork was set as much by the melancholy history of old Ireland as by the dissipations, the oaths and blasphemies of the hardened criminals. When thirty-six convicts were moved one flowery May day in 1828 from the county gaol at Cork to the harbour at Cobh they were followed a part of the way along the leafy enamelled banks of that noble estuary by their relatives and friends who sobbed, shrieked and howled as the convict conveyances wended their way along the lane. As they drew near the ship one of the convicts was ordered to restore his own child, which he was holding tenderly and passionately in his arms, to his wife. It was too much for him: 'Oh God', he cried out in his anguish, 'my heart is broken'. And he fell down and died. Later at the end of the inquest into his death the coroner pronounced the solemn verdict that he had died by the visitation of God. The Irish would not, indeed could not, accept that verdict. How could they expect the truth from the law courts of their eternal foes? Such events at the departure of a convict ship symbolized the tragic destiny of their people. As they wept, and wailed and lamented the departure of relatives and friends, they were weeping too, for Ireland and her tragic history.[54]

In the meantime the men in high places in London had decided to encourage the migration of free settlers to the colonies of New South Wales and Van Diemen's Land. Staggered by the enormous burden of running the colony of New South Wales, which, in the year 1822, had cost the British taxpayer £450,000, swayed by rumours trickling back to London of the moral evils of building a society from the dregs of mankind, and influenced too by rumours that transportation had ceased to arouse anything like the appropriate degree of apprehension and terror in the minds of the criminal classes, they decided to encourage settlers to proceed to the colony when, in return for employing convicts, they would receive a grant of land in proportion to their capital. At the beginning of the decade the Colonial Office had drafted a letter to intending settlers.[55] The rumour ran through London Town and all over the British Isles that the adventurous, the needy, the failures and the misfits could start afresh in New South Wales or Van Diemen's Land. Irishmen who wanted with God's help and their own best endeavours to achieve a livelihood, Chelsea pensioners anxious to help their little ones, the limbless from the wars in Spain, those who had voted for the return of the government for which they believed they were entitled to ministerial favours, clergymen who lacked the wealth with which to support their large families, the wife of Thomas Davey, one time Lieutenant-Governor of Van Diemen's Land, because of her many privations and her husband's claim to be the first person to land at Port Jackson on that 26 January 1788 when the European began to plant his civilization in Australia, wrote for permission to proceed to New South Wales or Van Diemen's Land, only to be told in the best prayer-book, off-

[54] Ibid., 21 May 1828.

[55] Macquarie to Bathurst, 28 November 1821, *H. R. A.*, I. x. 568-9; Instructions to Sir Thomas Brisbane, 5 February 1821, ibid., I. x. 600; for an example of a prospective settler presenting the benefits of such a policy see T. Potter MacQueen to Bathurst, Park Lane, 21 July 1823, C.O. 201/147, p. 23.

putting prose of the Colonial Office that for those who had no capital beyond their head and their hands no directions in regard to a grant of land could be given to the Governor. On the other hand, those who had funds sufficient to cultivate a large portion of land, as well as testimonials to their respectability, had their letters marked promptly 'Grant'.[56] Unto those that had, it was given.

Some, too, who were apprehensive lest developments in England should deprive them of their expectations then turned their minds towards the prospects of New South Wales. James Henty, merchant and manager of a family bank in Worthing, Sussex, and a member of a family which had belonged for centuries to the class of gentlemen farmers in those majestic Sussex downs, put down on paper in August of 1828 the reasons why a gentleman should entertain the idea of forsaking such a heritage and environment. He had come to the conclusion that New South Wales would do more for his family than England ever would. Like so many of the gentry they could only stay in England if they chose to descend many steps in the scale of society, which their feelings could not stand. They would not only be wealthier in New South Wales; they would be placed in the first rank in society—and thus avoid the humiliation of the second rung of the ladder, which would be their eternal fate in England.[57]

In January of 1822 Mr James, his wife and three children and a manservant, Mr Hugh Murray, his wife and five children and a manservant, Mr James Thomson, his mother, two brothers and one sister, Mr Thomas Young, his brother and sister, Mr David Murray, his wife and child and a manservant, Mr James Hume and his wife, and Mr William Oliver, each head of a family having proved he was possessed of a capital of at least £500, chartered a vessel and set out from Leith in Scotland for Van Diemen's Land, taking with them all their worldly possessions. They planned to transplant the way of life of the gentry, the gracious living in the great house, with its elegant furnishings, its library, and surrounded by park land. They took with them that loyalty to altar and throne, that fervour for the revolution settlement and the Protestant ascendancy, as well as horror of the industrial civilization of cities with their grime, their dirt, their ugliness, their mobs, their radicalism, and their tendency to degrade everyone down to the level of the brutish members of society.[58]

By contrast one young man, with a private hell in his heart, brought on, according to his own confession, by having no fixed sentiments on moral subjects, which had led him to look on the excesses of the bottle and the bed without any pangs of conscience, enlisted in the Horse Guards. Here not enjoying being lectured on his poor performances as a button-polisher, he decided, impulsively, that the life of the common soldier was not for him, just as this doffing of the cap, this continual saluting affronted his sense that he

[56] For examples of such applications to the Colonial Office see C.O. 201/112, pp. 474 and 529; C.O. 201/190, pp. 13, 30, 38 and 73; C.O. 201/170, pp. 239, 267 and 324; for examples of two applicants recommended for grants see W. Gibson to Bathurst, 5 October 1825, C.O. 201/170, p. 264, and J. Dulhunty to Bathurst, 23 and 24 August 1825, C.O. 201/170, pp. 223-5.

[57] James Henty to William Henty, August 1828, quoted in M. Bassett, *The Hentys: An Australian Colonial Tapestry* (London, 1954), pp. 34-6.

[58] See, for example, the letters of Edward Dumaresq to his mother, Ann Dumaresq (Dumaresq Papers).

should touch the hat to no man. He deserted, and took ship for New South Wales as an emigrant mechanic. There he was to be caught up in that quest for a comforter to replace the life of the world to come, and found it, or believed for a time he found it, in mateship. There too he was consumed by that thirst to believe, which brought him face to face with the conflict between revelation and enlightenment, between God's grace and man's justice, between belief and unbelief, and the debate on religion and morality, and the life of man without God which became the subject of subjects for the serious-minded in the bush shanties of New South Wales and Van Diemen's Land, just as much as in the coffee houses and the taprooms of London and Edinburgh, the snugs of Dublin and Londonderry, and the common rooms of Oxford, Cambridge, Edinburgh, Glasgow, and Trinity College, Dublin; indeed wherever two or three were gathered together who wanted to be there when everyone suddenly understood what it had all been for.[59]

There were the wives and children who made the long journey over the oceans to be reunited with husbands and fathers. There was Johanna Casey of Garryfine in Ireland who reached Cork one day hoping to see her husband once again before the convict ship sailed only to find that he had gone. Months later when she received a letter from her husband from far away New South Wales, she burst into tears. The poor children were at her every day to take them to their father and she replied to her husband:

> Be assured that unless I perish in the attempt that neither water, fire, or tempest will prevent me of going to you, O that I cannot fly to you, it's then I would not sigh for you, your Children would not cry for you, and we would all cease to moan ... sending you my Blessing and the blessing of God may attend you and remain your ever loving Consort, Johanna Casey.

So Johanna Casey and other wives and their families, having satisfied the Colonial Office that nothing could be said against their characters, and that their appearances were extremely decent, set out on their long journey to join the men and women who were beginning to see New South Wales and Van Diemen's Land not as English park-land where the gentry could build their manors with cheap convict labour, but as a land which belonged to them and their remotest posterity.[60] They were beginning to see it as a land where the darkness of the old world which had exposed them and their kind to the oppression and derisions of their gaolers might one day give way to light. They were going to a land which had hitherto responded with a vast indifference to all the efforts of their predecessors to scratch a mark on its harsh interior. Some were making the long journey over the oceans as exiles not only from their families, and their country, but also from God's world, and yet strangers to any faith of what they and their kind could achieve once they had discarded the talk of priest and parson on human vileness, and darkness in their hearts and reached for the light.

In 1821, 320 arrived free in either New South Wales or Van Diemen's

---

[59] *The Secrets of Alexander Harris*, ed. by A. H. Chisholm (Sydney, 1961), pp. 55-61.

[60] Johanna Casey to William Casey, Garryfine, 13 May 1825 (Therry Papers); see also the petition of Robert Hensen, 30 November 1823, C.O. 201/147, pp. 160-1.

Land, 875 in 1822, 543 in 1823, 780 in 1824, 485 in 1825, 903 in 1826, 715 in 1827, 1,056 in 1828, 1,005 in 1829, and 772 in 1830.[61]

[61] Returns of the number of Persons who have Emigrated from the United Kingdom to any of the Colonies of Great Britain in each year since 1820, *P.P.*, 1830, XXIX, 650, p. 435; Report of the Select Committee on Immigration, *V. & P.* (L.C. N.S.W.) 1835; Report of the Select Committee on Immigration in Van Diemen's Land, C.O. 280/42; see also R. B. Madgwick, *Immigration into Eastern Australia 1788-1851* (London, 1937), pp. 49-54.

2

THE SETTING IN NEW SOUTH WALES

ONE DAY IN August 1822 the Reverend Samuel Marsden sat down in his study at Parramatta to write to two of his brothers in Christ in London. He had cause, he believed, to be thankful for many striking interpositions of divine providence in his favour. God had highly exalted him from the lowly station of son of a blacksmith and small farmer to minister before Him in holy things as the principal chaplain of the colony of New South Wales. God had blessed him and had given him all things richly to enjoy. He, the blacksmith's son, now owned 4,500 acres of land at Parramatta and many cattle, sheep, pigs and horses. God, too, had blessed him with a beloved wife and a quiver full of children.

Anxious as ever for the eternal welfare of the souls committed to his care, no man was more alive than he to those evils which tended to the ruin of his people. Every night he went down on his knees to ask the father of mercies to crown his feeble efforts in New Zealand for the evangelization of the Maoris, adding with fervour his hope that all Christian societies might unite in love and in one body against the prince of darkness. But as for the Wesleyan missionaries it was intolerable that they should ever presume an equality with him. They must be kept in their proper place. They should go out into the highways and hedges to collect the lost sheep of Christ: it was unchristian of them to set themselves up in opposition to a priest of the established church. Besides, it pained him to add, though some of them were humble and pious, some were under the influence of anger, and jealousy and other evil passions, and some were ignorant and proud, and some were very fractious: some were very wise in their own eyes, and some, it grieved him to say, were very immoral.

On 28 July he had turned fifty and was beginning to approach that time of life when honour, the respect of his fellow-men, and recognition of his achievement should have been his. Instead he was aware of those curses not loud but deep which his past had kindled in the hearts of his enemies. For the Reverend Samuel Marsden had never gained the good will or the affection of those with whom he had had to deal. There had been dark days of persecution under Macquarie when his name had been so defamed in every part of the globe that he had wanted to escape, in the words of the psalmist, like a bird out of the snare of the fowler. There was such depravity in New South Wales that even in the room where the dead were lying, debaucheries were going on.

Twenty-seven years in the colony of New South Wales had brought him to the melancholy conclusion that those convicts who had not received the precious gift of God's saving grace could only be rescued from their wickedness by severity of punishment. Twenty-seven years had convinced him that anyone who urged mankind to turn from their wickedness could only earn their undying hatred and contempt. So the Reverend Samuel Marsden lifted up his eyes to his heavenly father, and beseeched Him to give His faithful wretch that prize he had looked for in vain from his fellow-men.

He was hoping for much from the new Governor. This time he was determined not to give offence, believing that at long last God had delivered him from the hands of his enemies. But it was too late. Face and gesture were beginning to mirror the outrage, humiliation and insult he had endured for twenty-seven years as God's instrument to impart the means of grace and improve the morals of the inhabitants of the colony of New South Wales and its dependent territories. The great bulbous eyes were more and more startled by memories of terrible moments in the past, which came up from inside him to mock his days so that he cried in anguish to his Lord: 'O spare me a little . . . before I go hence and be no more seen'. The lips were more and more often seen to move, though no intelligible sound was heard by those near to him. The pious believed they were moving in silent prayer, but those with an eye of pity knew these mumbles were but one of the many signs of an increasing uproar in his soul. The Reverend Samuel Marsden was beginning to walk into the night.[1]

At Parramatta, John Macarthur was also approaching the season of the sere, the yellow leaf. He turned fifty-five on 3 September 1822. When he had arrived back from London in September of 1817 he had written to his dearest best beloved wife that her sons, James and William, would hasten to her the moment they could procure a conveyance, while he would follow at a slower pace. For those passions which had driven him both to glory and damnation with his own kind were calming down. He waited till the heat of the day was over, and then set out in his carriage for Parramatta.[2] His ideas for the promotion of his private interests and the welfare of the colony of New South Wales were still in the grand manner. By 1821 his ideas on New South Wales and Van Diemen's Land as colonies for the growth of fine wool were gaining a wide currency in London among those who were unhappy about the dependence of the British manufacturer on the fine wools of Spain, Saxony and Austria. No serious disease had been prevalent amongst his own sheep. The whole emphasis was on improvement. He had planted olive trees for oil to rub on the fleece to improve its quality.[3]

He had ideas on the type of society which ought to be developed in New South Wales. He wanted the landed proprietors to become powerful as an

---

[1] Based on S. Marsden to J. Taylor and R. Watson, Parramatta, 15 August 1822 (Bonwick Transcripts, Box 52, p. 1126 et seq.); S. Marsden to Secretaries of Wesleyan Missionary Society, 4 August 1821 (Bonwick Transcripts, Missionary, vol. 3, pp. 845-55); Bigge Appendix, C.O. 201/123, document D.36; T. Kendall, Journal of proceedings during a voyage from Port Jackson to New Zealand, and T. Kendall to England, 13 February 1815 (Kendall Papers, MS. in M.L.); S. Marsden to W. Wilberforce, 5 February 1818 (quoted in Journal of Mary Reiby or Reibey, MS. in M.L.); S. Marsden to the Reverend J. Pratt, 2 July 1825 (Bonwick Transcripts, Box 53).

[2] John Macarthur to Elizabeth Macarthur, Tuesday morning 7 o'clock, September 1817 (Macarthur Papers, vol. 2, p. 345).

[3] Transcriptions of the Society of Arts 1823 (Bonwick Transcripts, Box 61, pp. 113-15).

aristocracy, a development which, he knew, would excite the envy and even the hatred of the multitude, as a pernicious democratic feeling had taken deep root in the colony in consequence of the absurd and mischievous policy pursued by Macquarie. But Macarthur hoped for great things from the new Governor, as well as from those ideas he had planted in the mind of Mr Commissioner Bigge and people in high places in London on how a plantation society would promote subordination, correct the vicious habits of the convicts, redeem the expenses of government, and reduce the price of wool for the manufacturer.

He had visions of a race of sober, industrious, and moral agricultural labourers growing up in the country districts of New South Wales under the paternal and kindly eye of titled proprietors of the soil. He was proud of his own record of humanity, proud that only two convicts had ever been punished on his estates, proud that no convict had ever petitioned to be released from his service, nor caused any commotion which indicated that the storm centre of the public life of New South Wales had ever employed cruelty or unnecessary rigour on his convict servants. His one great object in cultivating grapes on his estates was to put down the taste for spirits amongst the democratic multitude, and to create temperate, cheerful and thrifty habits among the people. Lying tongues in Sydney and Parramatta scoffed at him as a brazen hypocrite, who was using the juice of the grape to distil brandy, because it was well known in Sydney that a case of brandy put the Governor in a good mood when he had to consider requests from John Macarthur for more convict servants. But what else could one expect from a convict rabble, except this swinish assumption that the motives of the élite were as low and carnal as their own? When he had proudly emblazoned a coat of arms for his family on the landau in which he drove through the streets of Sydney, the envious and the malicious had mocked, and shouted it was meant to obscure his low birth. They also whispered that he was an expert stay-maker and his wife a humble mattress-maker.[4]

In the golden glow of the autumn of his life he began to unfold his vision of the role of his family in New South Wales. He spoke of erecting a manor at Camden which would be worthy of their position as the doyens of the new nobility of New South Wales. He spoke of how, for his part, he would prefer chaste and simple lines, no baroque splendours, or extravagances, but a building cut from stone, something to stand against wind and rain, earth and sky, as an austere symbol both of his worldly grandeur, and of his claim to distinction for his person and his class. In politics he was proud to belong to the school of Pitt. For his ideal of a man he looked to the heroes of classical antiquity, to Coriolanus and to Scipio Africanus. God and the consolations of religion were not mentioned in his conversation or his correspondence, which were pervaded with the stoic virtues of courage, honour and the strength to endure. When the world cheated him of the prizes he desperately coveted he

[4] Based on John Macarthur, Memorandum for Commissioner Bigge, 19 December 1821, and John Macarthur to J. T. Bigge, 7 February 1821 (Bigge Appendix, C.O. 201/118); John Macarthur, Suggestions relative to the employment, discipline and ultimate reformation of the convicts in New South Wales, Memorandum to Sir Thomas Brisbane, January 1822 (Macarthur Papers, vol. 1, pp. 72-4); W. C. Wentworth, Lampoon on John Macarthur (D'Arcy Wentworth Papers, Item 24).

C

consoled himself by calling on the virtues of patience and the will to endure rather than call on the gods or his fellow-man to vindicate his helpless plight, or look to some compensation, some atonement in any life of the world to come for all his sufferings in this world. Life, as he saw it, was a dance, and a fearful lottery. In the world a few artful knaves led a multitude of fools. He had decided to turn his back on the world, to retire to his estate where undisturbed by the vices of the modern Babel, he could enjoy the pursuits of a country gentleman, sowing wheat, lambing, growing corn, tending the ewes, buying and selling stock, the love and affection of his family, and savour those passages in Shakespeare, Milton, Byron, Scott, Crabbe, and Hudibras which he quoted to them so freely with such skill and passion.

But there were dark moments. By 1822 he was beginning to spend more and more of his time in bed, a victim of gout, and of an obscure melancholy, during which strange visions and queer thoughts came up from inside him. In the beginning he treated it all with good humour, telling his wife that just as the cat would mew, the kitten play, and every dog would have his day, so he would revenge himself on all doctors, and uphold the cause of all unhappy convalescents on them all. For even in sickness or when joking there was with him always that sense of an Ishmael whose hand was raised against every man, and who believed every man's hand was raised against him. For him life at times had been a vaudeville of devils. Now the past was beginning to haunt him, reminding him of what he had done to all who had stood in his way, how he had crushed them, and rejoiced at their humiliation and punishment. Here he was in the fifty-fifth year of his life, the proprietor of 7,065 acres of land, the pioneer breeder of fine wool in New South Wales, the man with a vision to see how a sordid gaol would be metamorphosed into a plantation society, the man who under the new governor must surely receive some public recognition, some mark of the sovereign's favour for his achievement, haunted and hunted by his past—throwing, as his dearest love put it rather delicately, an accumulated gloom round the family.[5]

For she had her anxieties—anxieties over her husband's health, over the hostility to which the family, and possibly all the gentry, had been exposed by the violence of his passions, and the consequent lack of sympathy to which it would expose all of them in the coming days when her dearest love, her own darling John, walked into a night where she could no longer comfort or relieve him. The society she had known in the old days was fast changing, as numbers of strangers began to arrive. Things would be all right, she believed, if people were contented with bread, milk, meat, vegetables and fruit, but, alas, in New South Wales, even the servants had begun to demand tea, and sugar, and other imported luxuries, which many of them, she was sure, had never been accustomed to in their former lives. Happily she knew that she and all mankind were under the superintendence of an Almighty Ruler. From such a faith, as well as the courage, the resilience, and the toughness with which she had been endowed by nature, she would draw the strength to resist any temptation to

[5] Based on James Macarthur to R. Therry, Camden Park, 24 February 1859 (Macarthur Papers, vol. 1, pp. 229-31); John Macarthur to J. Mitchell, 18 December 1824 and 1 April 1825 (Papers of James Mitchell, MS. in M.L.).

bitterness of spirit, and praise the Lord always, for He had done wondrous things. He had given her dearest love the gift of Midas, and He had given her that precious gift of a loving heart. The Lord was her shepherd: therefore she could lack nothing.[6]

Besides she found much to delight her in the trivial round and the common task. She loved the occasions when two or three hundred aborigines gathered for a corroboree near Parramatta. They painted their bodies and decked themselves with green boughs and performed grotesque dances while others sat apart and chanted a sort of wild song. They always held corroborees on bright moonlight nights when the number of small fires gave an air of brilliance and mystery to the surrounding woods and lit up the faces of the blacks. The purpose of a corroboree was to do honour to and entertain strangers, whom the aborigines called Myall. So what did it matter if the white man's social gatherings left much to be desired: what did it matter if nothing like the splendour and gaiety of a ball in England could be exhibited in New South Wales for many years to come, when they had their own sources of pride, and joy, and wonder, and mystery?[7] With God in His heaven, what did it matter who was governor of New South Wales: what did it matter who was in, and who was out in that coterie of little men who shouted and fretted on the stage of that little world of Sydney?

Chance had brought to the high office of Captain-General and Governor-in-Chief in and over the colony of New South Wales and its dependent territories a man who was indifferent to the dreams of a Macarthur, the hopes of a Marsden to be delivered from his enemies like a bird out of the snare of the fowler, the hopes and convictions of the convicts that the wealth created by the labour of their hands belonged to them and their descendants, and the perception of the aborigine that the white man's invasion spelt a doom and destruction for his people which he was impotent to avoid. Thomas Brisbane, who was born in that year 1773 when Cook dropped anchor in Adventure Bay in Van Diemen's Land, and was educated by tutors and at the University of Edinburgh, where he developed a lasting interest in mathematics and astronomy, entered the army as a profession where in 1812 in the Peninsula Wars he formed a firm and lasting friendship with Arthur Wellesley, later Duke of Wellington. In November of 1819, he was united by marriage to a lady in every respect worthy of him, one Anna Maria Makdougall, who became a source of exquisite gladness to him, for she had that elegance of manners and appearance to delight a vain man, as well as being possessed of a refinement of taste and a vigour of intellect which were ennobled by a benevolent disposition grounded on the rock of Christian principle. From the earliest days, Brisbane had lifted up his eyes away from the world towards the heavens in more senses than one. Those who judged by appearances, and what a man gave out about himself, took him as a Christian, a scholar and a gentleman.

[6] Elizabeth Macarthur to Eliza Kingdon, 21 September 1822, June 1824 and March 1827 (Macarthur Papers, vol. 12, p. 59).

[7] Elizabeth Macarthur to Eliza Kingdon, 4 February 1826 (Macarthur Papers, vol. 12, pp. 62-3); for a different reaction to a corroboree, see W. Walker to R. Walker, 26 November 1821 (Bonwick Transcripts, Box 52, pp. 1041-2).

But Wellington knew his man. One day in Paris in 1815, as his grace was walking arm-in-arm with Brisbane, he began to converse on the idleness to which many of them would be doomed when the army was reduced to a peace establishment. When Brisbane volunteered the remark that he would gladly serve His Majesty in New South Wales the Iron Duke, with that eye of his for the heart of the matter, quipped that my lord Bathurst would be looking for someone who could govern not the heavens but the earth in New South Wales. But Brisbane persisted, and Wellington used his good offices and enormous prestige with my lord Bathurst with such skill that by November Under-Secretary Goulburn wrote to Macquarie to inform him that Sir Thomas Brisbane had been selected, and would proceed to the colony as soon as the preparations necessary for his departure could be made.[8]

The discerning few shook their heads, or shrugged their shoulders at the folly of the men from Vanity Fair. Sir Thomas, they feared, was rather more addicted to star-gazing than was quite compatible either with his own comfort, or with the well-being of those who lived under his control. Had they peeped into Brisbane's private journal their misgivings might have been strengthened. For his mind was set on the heavenly prize, for that peace which the world could neither give nor take away. His great interest in life was that when the actions of all men were weighed in the balance of eternal doom, his would not be found altogether wanting. Every Sunday he received the memorial of his Saviour's dying love. In order that he might be a worthy partaker of the sacrament, each week he renewed his covenant to be the Lord's to all eternity before he approached the holy table. For him an immortal soul was the unspeakable object of value in human life.[9]

When he landed in Sydney from the *Royal George* early in November of 1821 with his wife, that source of exquisite gladness to him, the civil and military officers and all the respectable people warmly welcomed them. The full band of His Majesty's 48th Regiment played soothing and martial airs on the lawn in front of Government House. The gates of that august house were thrown open to the Australian public who, in a cheerful mood of gratitude to the governor-elect, romped all over the domain. At the ceremony to commission him as Captain-General and Governor-in-Chief in and over the colony of New South Wales and its dependents his predecessor, Macquarie, justly proud of his achievement but still not able to ignore his critics, spoke at inordinate length of how he was buoyed above the fear of calumny, vindictive slander and malicious reproach by the consciousness of a long life of upwards of forty years' service spent in favourable pursuits, and stained with no action which could give him remorse, and how he confidently anticipated not only the approbation of his sovereign, but also the applause of posterity for the purity of his motives and rectitude. Brisbane, not sensing then what life in New South Wales could do to a man, spoke very briefly, confining himself to the an-

---

[8] Based on *Reminiscences of General Sir Thomas Makdougall Brisbane* (Edinburgh, 1860) pp. 3-37; Memoir of the Duke of Wellington, *The Times*, 15 and 16 September 1862; Goulburn to Macquarie, 10 November 1820, *H.R.A.*, I. x. 371.

[9] J. Stephen to Arthur, 31 July 1826 (Papers of Sir George Arthur, vol. 4, Correspondence with James Stephen); see also the extract from the diary of Sir Thomas Brisbane, quoted in *Reminiscences of General Sir Thomas Makdougall Brisbane* (Edinburgh, 1860), pp. 47-8.

nouncement that a number of prisoners would be released from the gaols to commemorate the day. For that lived in him too, that hope that if he freely forgave, then he, through the merits of Jesus Christ, would be as freely forgiven for all the sins of his life.[10] And when the clergy, civil officers, magistrates and landholders presented him with an address in which they expressed their hopes that he would heal all divisions and reconcile all parties, he replied a week later that though he might cede the literary crown to a Voltaire, for he was a man who went in for those self-deprecating jokes which were designed to inspire the flattery he craved, yet, he went on, he would yield to no man in purity of intuition. His maxim being, *Nil desperandum, auspice deo*, he hoped to give satisfaction to all classes and see them reconciled.[11]

Hopes were running high. When divine service was celebrated for the first time in St James's Church on 6 January of the following year, the Reverend Samuel Marsden, sensitive as ever to the whims and vanities of the rulers of this world, chose an appropriate text for his sermon: 'Arise, shine; for thy light is come, and the glory of the Lord is risen upon thee': the *Sydney Gazette* was delighted. Such occasional intelligence as this, they wrote, would render Australia increasingly beloved and respected by her ever kindly considerate parent—Great Britain.[12]

Marsden had his own private reasons for delight that day as he knelt at the altar of his Lord. Brisbane had offered to restore him to the high office of a magistrate on the bench at Parramatta. Repressing the memory of his previous trials and tribulations as a magistrate, brushing aside the warning that no convict was likely to listen to his reverence on divine love on Sundays if he could sentence him to be flayed alive on Mondays, sensing like most men only his present desperate need that being a magistrate once again was a sign that my lord Bathurst and Sir Thomas Brisbane did not believe the cruel charges Macquarie had laid against him in *A Letter to the Right Honourable Viscount Sidmouth* in 1821, he accepted the offer as a balm to his injured pride. Once again he took his seat on the bench of magistrates at Parramatta, not pausing for a moment to reflect on whether nature had endowed him with the gifts for that office or the strength to endure the taunts and jibes of his enemies, knowing at that moment only the satisfaction of vindicating himself before the public against the malicious attacks of Macquarie. Besides, he added characteristically, by accepting he would neither offend the Governor, nor stand in the way of his glorying in the gospel of Christ—two things very dear to his heart. It was music in his ears to hear Brisbane say he was back again on the bench because he, Brisbane, was anxious to get the bench of magistrates as respectable as possible.[13]

Macarthur was also pleased. At long last it seemed that there was to be

---

[10] *Sydney Gazette*, 10 November and 1 December 1821; *Reminiscences of General Sir Thomas Makdougall Brisbane* (Edinburgh, 1860), p. 47.

[11] *Sydney Gazette*, 15 December 1821.   [12] Ibid., 11 January 1822.

[13] Marsden's appointment as a magistrate was announced in the *Sydney Gazette* on 1 March 1822; for Marsden's motives in first accepting the office of magistrate, see S. Marsden to the Reverend M. Atkinson, 16 September 1796, in J. R. Elder (ed.), *The Letters and Journals of Samuel Marsden 1765-1838* (Dunedin, 1932), pp. 29-31; for his motives in 1822 see ibid., pp. 50-1; see also L. Macquarie, *A Letter to the Right Honourable Viscount Sidmouth* (London, 1821); Brisbane to Bathurst, 27 February 1822, *H.R.A.*, I. x. 624-5.

public recognition for his achievement. Brisbane, impressed by Mr Macarthur's stake in the country, and his exertions for the improvement in fine wool, and entertaining a high opinion of some of Mr Macarthur's family, decided he was a fit person to be named for the commission of the peace. Macarthur was delighted. But his past cheated him of this prize. For Judge Advocate Wylde and Mr Justice Field promptly reminded Brisbane of the part Macarthur had played in the rebellion against Bligh, adding that good terms so little, if at all, prevailed between Mr Macarthur and the other magistrates. So Brisbane informed Macarthur on 31 January that since making the first offer under the influence of Macarthur's talents, useful pursuits and character, he had discovered that divisions, which unfortunately existed in the colony, had placed him under the painful necessity of declining to receive Macarthur's assistance in the magistracy.

Macarthur was incensed. He told Brisbane it was a public degradation, which nothing but the consciousness of the rectitude of his own conduct and honourable intention would enable him to support. It was so deep a wound that he solicited no favour but that of being permitted to defend himself against the marked attacks of his enemies as that had become indispensable for the relief of his injured feelings and the support of his honour. The man was looking for an opportunity to crush the Botany Bay 'worthies', who had dared to stand between him and the recognition of his life's work. When roused to revenge an insult to his pride or his honour the man's self-destroying drives took over. Reckless of what damage such behaviour could do to his reputation, that it could prove the very point his enemies were making against him, the cup of revenge had to be drained to the last dregs. While he was thus musing on his subject of revenge, blind as ever when possessed by that evil spirit to the warning that that way madness lay, Sam Marsden, all unaware of the hell in Macarthur's heart, thinking, indeed, only of how he must answer one day before the judgment seat for those who caused the least of the little ones to stumble, obliged by kindling the faction fires of their world.[14]

On the night of 31 July Dr Hall, one-time surgeon on convict ships, a man who had heard in his own ears the divine command to urge sinners to turn from their wickedness and live, called on the Reverend Samuel Marsden in Sydney, and told him that he had heard that day from the lips of Ann Rumsby, a convict girl who had arrived in Sydney in the *Mary Ann* on which Hall had served as surgeon-superintendent, that her employer, Dr Douglass, had lifted her petticoat and attempted to seduce her. Marsden, driven, as ever, by that fear that through his neglect souls may suffer the torments of hell fire, driven, too, by that fear that he, through indifference or coldness in such matters, may be scorched too by those flames, and driven, too, by his own pleasure in hounding the lecherous, listened greedily to all that Hall had to say, and agreed to join with Hall and Sir John Jamison in an open letter to Ann Rumsby, to be read to her by one of the footmen in the house of Dr Douglass at Parramatta,

[14] Based on Brisbane to Bathurst, 27 February 1822, *H.R.A.*, I. x. 624-5; Judge Advocate Wylde and Judge Field to Sir Thomas Brisbane, 19 January 1822, encl. in ibid., pp. 625-6; for the original of this letter see the Macarthur Papers, vol. 1, pp. 84-5; Copy of a message delivered by Frederick Goulburn Esq., Colonial Secretary, to Mr Macarthur, with his reply, 31 January 1822 (Macarthur Papers, vol. 1, pp. 76-9).

in which Ann would be urged to scream for help if anyone attempted her violation.

Then, remembering the warning of the Apostle Paul that it was better to marry than burn, Sam Marsden beamed with satisfaction when he published the banns of marriage at St John's, Parramatta, between Ann Rumsby and a convict named Bragge, and twice urged Douglass to send Ann back to the Female Factory, saying, in the full flush of his own righteousness, that he had very strong reasons for giving that hint. Once again, the faithful servant of the commandments of God was blind to the promptings of the human heart. For Ann Rumsby, when asked to exchange the creature comforts of the Douglass home for the frugality and coarseness and licentiousness of the Female Factory, began to say, maybe, Sam Marsden was plotting her ruin, meaning by that something quite different from what Marsden understood by ruin.[15]

Others were prepared to use Marsden for their own purposes. For ever since Douglass had arrived in the colony in May of 1821 he had irritated, and provoked the exclusive coterie, centred as they were in Parramatta, by openly fraternizing with the convict party in New South Wales. Douglass was a man of liberal and independent principles. As a distinguished doctor he was a member by birth of the professional classes of the Protestant ascendancy in Dublin. Born in 1790, and admitted to membership of the Royal College of Surgeons in London and the Royal Irish Academy in Dublin before he had reached the age of thirty, he had had the audacity to treat lags, old hands, and currency lads and lasses on a footing of equality with the members of the ancient nobility of New South Wales. Marsden, smarting under the rebuke from Brisbane that he was guilty of daily neglect of the spiritual exercises of his parish for the sake of attending to his own multitudinous temporal affairs, and so anxious to show himself to Brisbane in the role of the stern champion of female morals, offered up Douglass for sacrifice.[16]

The exclusives of Parramatta snatched greedily at the opportunity to show the public that men such as Dr Douglass who were loose in their politics were also lax in their morals. On 16 August, while Ann Rumsby, still fearful of being sent to the Factory, was solemnly assuring Brisbane that she had no complaints against Douglass, the magistrates of Parramatta assembled and resolved that inasmuch as the said Dr Douglass had taken Ann Rumsby knowing she was about to be summoned as a witness, they would not associate with or act with Dr Douglass as a magistrate. The following day they re-assembled, and ordered Ann Rumsby to the Female Factory where she refused to go, and then resolved to inform Douglass that the charges against him by Hall would be heard on 19 August.

On that 19 August Douglass declined to attend lest his presence might exercise an undue influence over the evidence of Ann Rumsby. She promptly

[15] Brisbane to Bathurst, 6 September 1822, *H.R.A.*, I. x. 744-50; J. Hall to Bathurst, 29 May 1823, C.O. 201/146; Brisbane to Bathurst, 31 August 1822, *H.R.A.*, I. x. 725.

[16] N. J. B. Plomley, 'Some Notes on the Life of Doctor Henry Grattan Douglass', *Medical Journal of Australia*, 1961, vol. 1, pp. 801-7.

denied on oath every particular in the affidavit by Hall. The bench of magistrates with Sam Marsden carried away by abhorrence for the ways of the wicked, and Hannibal Macarthur, the Palmers, and John Blaxland, sensing the opportunity to humiliate a man tainted with political radicalism, passed a panegyric on Hall, declared that Ann Rumsby had been guilty of wilful and corrupt perjury, and sentenced her to be imprisoned until such time as she could be sent to Port Macquarie.

Then Brisbane took action. Impressed by the integrity of Douglass, and irritated by the posturings of Marsden, and the animus of the exclusives, he informed the bench of magistrates, through his Colonial Secretary, Goulburn, that if they persevered in their resolution not to act with Dr Douglass, they might adopt the alternative of transmitting their resignation. That was on 21 August. On the following day the magistrates again assembled, and decided to inform Brisbane that they adhered to their determination to act no longer with Dr Douglass. The next day, 23 August, a general meeting of the magistrates took place at Parramatta, attended by the Judge Advocate, Wylde, the judge of the Supreme Court. These gentlemen expressed in very warm terms their approval of the conduct and character of their brother magistrates. But again Brisbane stood firm. The bench of magistrates at Parramatta was dismissed, and the punishment of Ann Rumsby remitted.[17]

So, once again, that service of Caesar ended in public humiliation for Marsden. Filled with a sense of his own righteousness, comforting himself once again with the words of the psalmist that the faithful servant of the Lord must endure such odium, he sat down in his study at Parramatta, and wrote to two of his friends in London, and told them that it had ever been his anxious wish to spread the Gospel by every means in his power, but he knew there would be opposition, that pride, avarice, lust, anger and every evil passion would be used in the service of the prince of darkness to thwart the man of God. God would carry on the work. He sat down to write to Kendall, the lay missionary in the Bay of Islands, to warn him against any nefarious traffic in muskets and powder with the natives. His heart was still set upon the civilization and evangelization of the inhabitants of New Zealand, but that, he must warn Kendall, would not be achieved by using carnal weapons such as muskets and gunpowder, which would bring a curse and not a blessing upon all who were involved.[18]

While the vulgar, the profane, and the men without the eye of pity for what came up from inside a man to lead him on to his damnation mocked him as a creep, a prier, and an unctuous hypocrite who hounded drunkards and fornicators, while feathering his own nest to the tune of many thousands of acres, one Thomas Hassall, who had arrived as a babe in arms in Tahiti in the mission ship *Duff* in February 1797 with his father, Rowland Hassall, and his mother, and then moved with them to New South Wales, wrote to ask for

[17] Brisbane to Bathurst, 6 September 1822, *H.R.A.*, I. x. 744-50; J. Stephen to Horton, 2 September 1824, *H.R.A.*, IV. i. 556-67.

[18] S. Marsden to J. Taylor and R. Watson, 15 August 1822 (Bonwick Transcripts, Box 52, p. 1126 et seq.); S. Marsden to T. Kendall, Parramatta, 1822 (Marsden Papers, vol. 1, pp. 65-6).

the hand of his daughter Ann in marriage. Marsden replied with a dignity and tenderness strangely lacking in his public life:[19]

Dear Thomas,

I received your Letter in which you solicit my permission to pay your Addresses to my daughter Ann. In reply, I need only say you have my Approbation to do so as she is at Liberty to please herself in a matter in which her own future Happiness is so Nearly interested.

I am, Yours Truly, S. Marsden.

But that was not his subject, for marriage as a coming together of true minds, or as an example of how two people made in the image of God could tear at each other like wild beasts, touched him not at all. His one all-consuming self-destroying passion was female morals. Tell him a story of seduction, a story of men behaving like insects to whom God had given sensual lust, and he became like a man possessed with a devil—just as reckless of his honour and his reputation as was John Macarthur when possessed by his own demon of vengeance. So when James Hall, possibly influenced by the pro-Douglass role that Colonial Secretary Goulburn had seemed to play in the Rumsby affair, began spreading stories that the Colonial Secretary, wishing to reduce the amount of sodomy amongst the convicts on government farms, had sent women convicts to the Emu Plains establishment, and solemnly drawn up a time-table prescribing the maximum number of men they could take on in an hour, once again the huge bulbous eyes of the stern champion of female morals began to dance not with merriment, or tenderness, or pity, but rather with a wild glee which reminded the discerning in that little world that there was madness in men's hearts while they lived.[20]

At the same time disturbing reports reached the parsonage at Parramatta about the behaviour of the Reverend Thomas Kendall in the Bay of Islands. The Reverend Mr Kendall had written to Marsden to explain how, while prying into the obscene mysteries of the natives so that he might ascertain their notions respecting the Supreme Being, his own natural corruptions had been so excited, and his vile passions so inflamed that he had fallen into their vices. He had begun to practise their own lascivious customs, and had had a child by a Maori woman. Or so Kendall explained what was to him a wee lapse. But Sam Marsden would have none of such queer justifications. Kendall's behaviour might be summed up in the words of Eve: 'The Serpent beguiled me, and I did eat'. Kendall had changed the glory of the incorruptible God into an image like unto corruptible man, and to birds, and four-footed beasts, and creeping things. Besides he had expressed no contrition for his crimes, no humility of mind, no wish to return from his back-slidings. So Marsden, ignoring that question about the one without sin, for on questions of morals and behaviour his teachers were those stern prophets of the Old Testament, and their divine hounder of mankind, rather than that One who

[19] S. Marsden to T. Hassall, 13 November 1822 (Hassall Papers, vol. 2, p. 453).
[20] James Hall to Sir John Jamison, 15 September 1822, and Sir John Jamison to James Hall, 20 September 1822, C.O. 201/169.

knew what was in man, took up his stance, and expelled Kendall from Christ's church.[21]

Through all this sound and fury one man remained deeply pleased with himself. That was Brisbane. He knew he was surrounded with foes because he had not allowed people to fatten in idleness on Treasury Bills, but he could, he believed, exultingly state at the end of that year in the face of the colony, and of the world at large, that no human being could accuse him of an unjust, illegal, cruel, harsh, or even an improper act. His scientific pursuits had been no less crowned with success than those of the gubernatorial order, as nothing had escaped him that had been worthy of a record. He had observed a great variety of eclipses and occultations, which would form the basis of his catalogue of all the stars of the hemisphere. True, slander and malevolence were constantly stalking abroad—but, for himself, he proposed to steer clear of favouritism, and not be identified with any party. Of any improper act of his during that year his internal monitor fully acquitted him.[22]

Apart from observing the stars, and private communings with his internal monitor, the other inexpressible satisfaction Brisbane had enjoyed that year was to spare the lives of fellow-creatures, and reduce the punishments of the convicts. At Windsor early in the year he had announced one of these amnesties. With a fulsome display of humanity, he had remitted the second part of the sentence of James Ring, who had arrived in Sydney in 1816, and been sentenced to a flogging and transfer to Port Macquarie in November of 1821. So Ring, after being appropriately flogged, was assigned as a servant to the Reverend Samuel Marsden where, on weekdays, he worked in the garden, and on Sundays he sang in the choir those hymns about love divine, all loves excelling and decided he might even risk marriage—an estate on which he had received many wholesome homilies from the Reverend Samuel Marsden.[23]

In May of 1823 Elizabeth Marsden, wife of the Reverend Samuel Marsden, a stranger to that naughtiness of heart which tormented her beloved Sam, and all unaware of the plots of his enemies to enmesh him in the world's great net, became so exasperated by the never-ending quarrels of her gardener, Graham, and her husband's servant Ring, that she took them before the bench of magistrates, hoping a reprimand would end their wrangling. By chance Douglass was on the bench that day with Macleod. So when in the course of the investigation Ring was asked if he was the person who had exhibited a sign over his door as a painter and glazier, and he replied that he was, and added that his master had allowed him to employ himself about the town for

---

[21] S. Marsden to J. Pratt, 19 April 1823 (Marsden Papers, vol. 2, pp. 64-5); for Marsden's account of what he was trying to achieve see *Sydney Gazette*, 8 December 1823; see also Eric Ramsden, *Marsden and the Missions* (Sydney, 1936) pp. 1-19; The Letters of Henry Williams in the Hocken Library, Dunedin; H. M. Wright, *New Zealand, 1769-1840; Early Years of Western Contact* (Cambridge, Mass., 1959); see for example (quoted in Wright, p. 41) the letter of William Hall to the London Missionary Society, 6 April 1822: 'Mr Stockwell that convict that Mr Kendall brought to N. Zealand with him was cohabiting with Mrs Kendall, well known to all the Settlement except Mr Kendall, self, and she actually brought forth a Son by Stockwell nothing like any other part of Mr Kendall's family . . . And since he [Kendall] came home from England he took a native girl into his house and sleeps with her in preference to his own wife, publicly known to both settlements.'

[22] Sir Thomas Brisbane to Mr Bruce, Parramatta, 13 December 1822 (Brisbane Papers, Box 1).

[23] Brisbane, Forbes and Scott to Bathurst, 10 August 1825, *H.R.A.*, I. xi. 717.

his own advantage, Douglass saw his chance to take his own vengeance on the Mahomet of Botany Bay. Perceiving Marsden's behaviour to be a breach of government orders, the two magistrates ordered Ring to be committed to gaol for further investigation and summoned Marsden to appear before them.

On 17 May Marsden, the principal chaplain of the colony of New South Wales, had to appear before the bar of justice. Douglass and Lawson, finding him guilty of a breach of government orders, fined him 2s 6d for each day his servant had been permitted to employ himself for his own advantage. Marsden refused to pay, and when Brisbane announced on 21 May that he saw no reason to interfere with the case, Marsden again refused to pay and threatened action in a higher court. When the magistrates sat again on 31 May Marsden attended and delivered a written paper protesting against the illegality of the fine and intimated an intention of appealing to a higher court. Douglass then lectured Marsden warmly for presuming to question the legality of the fine. Marsden, finding the lecture very insulting and galling to his feelings, and resenting the humiliation before the surrounding multitude, shouted back at Douglass, who, becoming warmer, shouted in reply that Marsden was driven by private spleen. Whereupon Marsden rose again from his seat, and began to speak, but before he could do so, the Reverend Thomas Hassall rose up hastily to restrain him, and Marsden went away.

Early in June, with Marsden still not having paid the fine, the magistrates issued a warrant of distress against him. Whereupon the constables entered the parsonage at Parramatta on 9 June, made an affray therein which disturbed Marsden, and seized his pianoforte which he valued at £100. Marsden then promptly took action for trespass in the Supreme Court, and questioned the legality of the fine. The Court awarded him damages, and found the magistrates incorrect in imposing the fine as Marsden had not violated the regulations.

In the meantime, Ring who had been committed to the barracks in Sydney, began to despair. He burst into tears, and told a soldier that as now his sentence would never be mitigated, nor would he be permitted to marry, he would abscond and take ship for New Zealand after contributing his mite to the great storm which was brewing between the convict party and the ancient nobility of New South Wales. For during the legal arguments other issues began to emerge. Marsden put round stories that Douglass was a drunkard. Douglass countered with stories that Marsden and his fellow magistrates had used flogging to extract confessions. The ancient nobility began to paint a picture of their opponents as a drunken rabble, composed of convicts, publicans, Jewboys, drunkards, fornicators and liars who would subvert the very foundations of society, and usher in a period of anarchy and savagery. Their opponents retorted that their aim was to rescue mankind from some of the cruelties and insults inflicted by those practising social exclusion of ex-convicts. So Ring took ship just as faction fighting, back-biting and slander began to be the characteristics of the public life of New South Wales.

In New Zealand he heard that 'Greatheart' was once again bringing the gifts of divine love to people who were enslaved to the prince of darkness.

Ring, in great alarm, took to the bush, till such time as he could jump an
American whaler, after which he disappeared from the pages of Australian
history, having quite by chance scratched his name on the sections which deal
with the origin of the tendency of the men in public life to turn on an
opponent and savage him. When Marsden heard that Ring did not dare to
meet him he was much concerned, as all Ring's sufferings and distress were,
he believed, unmerited. So Marsden in New Zealand began to ask himself if
he was justified in seeking justice for himself at the cost of great anguish to an
innocent man. But this was a question he had neither time nor opportunity to
put to himself when the excitement of the public life of New South Wales
stirred up the madness in the blood.[24]

By chance, just as the muddiers of mankind were moving on to the centre of
the stage in New South Wales, another Ishmael appeared on the scene. He
was the Reverend John Dunmore Lang who arrived in Sydney from Glasgow on 23 May 1823. He began as a man speaking with the tongue of an
angel, and having charity. He told his congregation in the school-house in
Castlereagh Street, it was delightful to hear in those valleys where the wild
beasts of the forest had once roamed the bleating of sheep and the lowing of
oxen. But in the controversy with his fellow-men he was proud of his ability
and his pleasure in returning scurrilous abuse with interest—to exact an eye
for an eye and a tooth for a tooth. He told them of his triumphant pleasure in
marking the progress of an enlightened liberality, and how he rejoiced that
the days of bigotry were passed. Yet in public he behaved as though the mantle
of the prophet had descended on him to warn the innocents of the new world
of the corrupting and degrading influence of the modern whore of Babylon—
the Church of Rome. He told them that only those of a humble and a contrite
spirit who trembled at God's word would get into heaven. Yet all his life he
behaved as though the storm of God's wrath was about to burst upon the heads
of mankind in one irresistible torrent of devouring fire and everlasting
burning. In his eyes, it had been ordained from the beginning that few were
honoured to be called the sons and daughters of the Lord Almighty: the great
majority would be licked for all time by the flames of hell, to much weeping,
wailing and gnashing of teeth.

Glasgow and Calvinism fashioned him as a man. He was born in Greenock,
near Glasgow, on 25 August 1799. He grew up in that city where amid the
swirling mists, the filth and the degradation masses lived in wynds and Gorbals,
overrun with those half-human half-beast Irish migrants who practised a degrading superstition. But Lang was nurtured not in any hope of better things
for mankind, of their liberation from their gaolers and their oppressors, but
trained rather for a ministry in a church which accepted poverty, and filth and

[24] Based on Bathurst to Governor of New South Wales, 3 January 1825, *H.R.A.*, I. xi. 462-3,
and Brisbane, Forbes and Scott to Bathurst, 10 August 1825, *H.R.A.*, I. xi. 717-26; S. Marsden
to Sir Robert Peel, 28 January 1824, C.O. 201/163; Evidence of James Elder before the Inquiry
held at Government House, 20 July 1825, C.O. 201/163; *Australian*, 11 August 1825; S.
Marsden, Letters addressed to the Governor and the Magistrates (ms. in Hocken Library,
Dunedin); for James Ring in New Zealand see J. R. Elder (ed.), op. cit., pp. 53-4; S. Marsden
*Statement, including a correspondence between the Commissioners of the Court of Enquiry, and
the Rev. Samuel Marsden* (Sydney, 1828) pp. 47-53.

degradation as evidence that the whole of mankind must go on to the end of time suffering the consequences of that aboriginal calamity when the serpent tempted Eve. As a young man he sat not at the feet of the teachers of Enlightenment but at the feet of Dr Chalmers, listening in mingled awe and delight as he painted those horrifying pictures of the torments of the damned. So Lang became the preacher of an avenging Jehovah—a harsh faith for a harsh society, a stranger to that remark of the blessedness of the meek, and how they would inherit the earth, for the potter had so fashioned his clay that it was pleasing to him to smite sinners, and humiliate the proud. Another wild boar had strayed into the vineyards of the Lord in New South Wales.[25]

In the first weeks he told his congregation of the mortification at having to share the schoolroom with Catholics, in which their incense stank in his nostrils, and the ringing of the sanctuary bells offended his ears. He decided to appeal to government for funds to build a church. But when the Colonial Secretary, acting on instructions from Brisbane, refused to grant such assistance because he was not convinced that Presbyterians wanted to keep the unity of the spirit in the bond of peace, Lang replied so offensively that Brisbane, as a rebuke to the young Ishmael, removed his name from the list of subscribers to the Presbyterian church building fund. Whereupon Lang, with that daring and energy which sustained him to the end of his days, announced he would go to London to defeat the eternal enemies of his church and his people. Privately, Brisbane wrote off to a friend in England, to say he knew the Presbyterian faction was very angry with him, but, dammit man, he explained, if he gave in to the kirk party he would soon have the Jews down upon him for a synagogue![26]

Heaven knows, for Sir Thomas, it was bad enough to have to stomach giving assistance to the Catholics. Ever since his arrival in the colony the Catholic chaplain, Father Therry, had been trying to interest him in his dream to build a church to the greater glory of God, and the honour of his holy faith. The Colonial Secretary, Goulburn, was so well disposed that for years Therry seldom approached the altar of his God without making a memento of Goulburn as his principal temporal patron. The Protestant community responded generously in the new spirit of liberality. But the funds lagged behind the grandiose ideas Therry entertained. Lying tongues whispered that his reverence could save souls, but not the mites he had collected to build the church. In December 1822 with the funds exhausted, and the unfinished church a standing reproach to Therry's incompetence with the money-changers, he appealed again to the well-known benevolence of the Governor, reminding him of the moral and political importance of the undertaking, and adding that a judge and twenty-six magistrates were amongst his recommenders. Therry knew that Brisbane was more sensitive to the minds of the

[25] *John Dunmore Lang: Chiefly Autobiographical 1799 to 1878*, ed. by A. Gilchrist (2 vols, Melbourne, 1951) vol. 1, pp. 1-22; J. D. Lang, *Aurora Australis; or Specimens of Sacred Poetry, for the Colonists of Australia* (Sydney, 1826); J. D. Lang, *A Sermon preached in the Hall of the National School Institution* (London, 1823).
[26] *Sydney Gazette*, 4 August and 24 September 1823; *H.R.A.*, I. xi. 922, n. 80; 'Ignotus' in *Sydney Gazette*, 16 October 1823; 'Scaevola' in *Sydney Gazette*, 23 October 1823; Sir Thomas Brisbane to Mr Bruce, 31 December 1823 (Brisbane Papers, Box 2).

respectable than the preposterous claims of this deluded Irishman to be one of Christ's vicars on earth. Brisbane offered to pay a sum equal to what was raised by donation. In 1823 the tongues began to wag again as the financial situation resumed its traditional mess, with Therry not able to sort out what came from government, what came from his private income, and what were donations.[27]

His problem was how to protect the souls of the faithful from perdition in a Protestant-dominated society. Catholic convicts were compelled to attend Protestant religious services on pain of being punished. This placed Therry in a dilemma. On the one hand he applauded the motives of the magistrates who inflicted such punishments, if they were only trying to maintain discipline, subordination and peace, and to prevent theft by designing and ill-disposed persons. He believed that altar and throne were never so respectively secure as when reciprocally and mutually supported by each other. But should such support be at the expense of conscience? The Governor surely never contemplated that by enslaving conscience he would render more nauseous the already bitter cup of exile and bondage. For the church prohibited absolutely the attendance of its members at the religious rites and ceremonies of all other creeds and persuasions.

What Therry wanted was the provision of a church for Catholics which would protect them from the violation of their consciences within the existing social system. He was not concerned with criticizing the existing social order or values, or condemning all the abominations of the convict system, the floggings, the solitary confinements, and the tyrannies of masters over men. His radicalism was the product of the religious disabilities of Catholics, and did not extend to any concern for their political rights as men. He was respectful to and even obsequious to authority except when it acted for or promoted Protestant interests at the risk of the eternal perdition of a Catholic.

His great nightmare was the Protestantizing of the whole colony. He beseeched wealthy Catholic friends in Ireland to send out cheap prayer-books and religious tracts because the country abounded with books of a different description which were distributed gratuitously. He campaigned against the partial, impolite and unjust system of forcing children in the Orphan School whose parents were Catholic to receive religious instruction from the Protestant chaplains. He asked government to allow these children to be instructed in the rites of their own religion and to be exempted from conforming to Protestant forms of worship. He implored the Colonial Secretary to conceive of the situation of a parent about to depart this life whose children must then go into an orphanage and so sacrifice a religion which the dying parent cherished as something far more precious than property or even than life. Surely their plight was worth a sympathetic ear.

For the same reason he pushed ahead with schemes to build schools for the education of Catholic children. For though his faith taught him that his church would continue until the consummation of the ages, experience of the Protestant ascendancy both in Ireland and New South Wales fed the dark

[27] Based on J. J. Therry to H. Goulburn, 3 and 6 December 1822; J. J. Therry to Mrs W. Redmond, 18 September 1824; Memo. of J. J. Therry on his finances, 16 August 1823 (Therry Papers).

suspicion that Protestants were plotting shipwreck for the faith of the simple people committed to his care.[28]

Brisbane saw it as a problem of law and order, rather than the correct way to salvation. Since his arrival in the colony he had found that every murder or diabolical crime had been committed by Roman Catholics who were so bereft of every advantage that could adorn the mind of man that soon there would be nothing but the shade of their skin to distinguish them from the aborigines. He had hoped they would dwindle away or become ingrafted with the Protestants, but as they seemed to cherish their faith as dearly as their lives, and as their priest counselled obedience and subordination with the same zeal as the Protestant chaplains, he had agreed reluctantly to contribute to the building of a church for them. To his disgust Therry had proceeded to draw up plans which included the tinsel and show appropriate for a rich and populous city rather than the dregs of Irish slums and bogs. So while Therry dreamed of the greater glory of God, Brisbane shook his head over these craven slaves to a vulgar superstition. That was in October 1824.

When my Lord Bathurst got round to replying to Brisbane in June of 1825, he told him he agreed there was a case for sending more priests as the Catholic religion was a handmaiden to the morality appropriate to a convict society. He also agreed that the Catholics should have a church, but he was not prepared to pay for all that ornamentation which the Catholic wished to place between the worshipper and his God. If they must have statues, and gorgeous vestments, they must pay for such extravagances themselves.[29]

While Father Therry laboured to win souls for heaven, and beat his breast each day and recited the words Lord I am not worthy that Thou shoulds't enter under my roof, the Wesleyan missionary, the Reverend W. Walker, was labouring to tell the aborigines the glad tidings that there was a home for little children above the bright blue sky. He had promised his God to convert the aborigines to Christianity. After he had arrived in Sydney in 1821 he had found much that had caused him pain. Duty had compelled him to attend the corroborees, but he had been a most uneasy spectator at scenes which were too shocking, too unseemly and too disgraceful to describe. 'To a sensible and susceptible mind', he had told his missionary brothers in London in November of 1821, 'it is sufficient to say, they were naked. For the sustenance of the indelicate I have no descriptive food'. To his disgust he had seen with his own eyes an Englishwoman enjoying one of these obscene assemblies. What was worse, he had seen the Catholic priest, Father Therry, gabble Latin prayers to gaping black children, sprinkle them with holy water,

[28] See, for example, the draft letter of J. J. Therry to the Colonial Secretary, 10 June 1824; J. J. Therry to the Colonial Secretary, 8 December 1822 and 31 August 1824; J. J. Therry to Mrs Redmond, 18 September 1824; J. J. Therry to Bishop Slater, 13 November 1824; see also the material in the Therry Papers on the Catholic School Committee for the district of Parramatta, begun on 12 January 1825; the main contributors to the Catholic chapel in Sydney were: Sir Thomas Brisbane, the late Major-General Macquarie, Chief Justice Forbes, Major Goulburn, Captain Piper, D'Arcy Wentworth, Alexander Berry, Sir John Jamison, J. T. Campbell and John Mackaness; on Therry's opposition to the proselytizing of Catholics in the Orphan School see draft letter of Therry to the Colonial Secretary, 19 July 1825 (Therry Papers).

[29] Brisbane to Bathurst, 28 October 1824, *H.R.A.*, I. xi. 382-3; Bathurst to Brisbane, 20 June 1825, ibid., 670-1.

and then have the effrontery to claim them as members of Christ's mystical body, the church.

For the men who believed the aborigines were indispensable heirs to the same eternity as all other men, and that their happiness in this life, as well as hereafter, depended chiefly upon those who possessed the means to promote and carry into effect those heavenly designs, there was much to ponder over. At the end of each year the Governor and a considerable number of people of the gentry attended the annual conference of the aborigines at Parramatta. With the tables groaning with grog and mutton, the aborigines performed their dances, and the children from the mission school displayed their progress in reading and writing. In the towns the aborigines eked out a living as degraded wretches who cadged alcohol and tobacco, and provided blood sports for the white men, while their women washed bottles in the white man's kitchen. In the bays and harbours along the coast where the sealers and whalers called for water and timber, ex-convicts and absconders themselves scarcely one remove from the savage, used aboriginal women as their mistresses, and peggers-out of their skins. In drunken rages, brought on by disappointments in the chase, or, at times, by some darkness in themselves, they tied these women up, and flogged them in the most cruel manner, for God had given men other hungers than the hunger for food.

In the country districts terrible scenes of degradation occurred. The convict workers, the ticket-of-leave men, lags and old hands, in the absence of white women, bartered with the aborigines for the use of their women, and when the aborigines took offence, or retaliated for some breach of their own way of life, of which the white remained blandly ill-informed, the white men hit back. So the aborigines speared the sheep and cattle of the invaders of their land, the robbers of their hunting fields, and violators of their women. As atrocity followed atrocity more and more settlers lost patience with the official policy of amity and kindness, and demanded that troops be sent to pacify the country, and terrify the aborigine into submission. The aborigines began to despair: 'Black man die fast since white man came', one of them told the Reverend Mr Mansfield at the end of 1821: 'Old black men nigh all gone. Soon no blackman, all whitemen'. The Reverend Mr Walker, in grief and shame, wondered whether his society in London should not also send missionaries to the white man.[30]

While the Reverend Mr Walker was thus musing on his mission station near Parramatta on why God's creatures should drink iniquity like water, far away in London my lord Bathurst decided to accept most of Commissioner Bigge's recommendations on the future of the colony of New South Wales. In May of 1823 he instructed Brisbane to remove the convicts capable of being reformed from the towns and assign them to settlers in the country districts where they would be free from the contagion arising from evil associations and connections. In this way the cost to government would be reduced.

[30] Based on W. Walker to R. Watson, 26 November 1821 (Bonwick Transcripts, Box 52, pp. 1041-2); J. Nobbs to W. Bedford, July 1824 (Papers of W. Bedford, MS. in M.L.); *Sydney Gazette*, 8 January 1824; the conferences were begun by Macquarie, see vol. I of this history, pp. 346-7; R. Mansfield to Genl. Commissioner, 23 November 1821 (Bonwick Transcripts, Box 52).

He also told Brisbane that settlers with capital were to be encouraged to migrate to New South Wales and Van Diemen's Land in return for employing corrigible convicts. So settlement was to spread—and the aborigine to be doomed, but the mind of my lord Bathurst was not on those men with their feet on the lowest rung of the ladder of human life. The incorrigible were to be sent to penal settlements at Port Macquarie and Moreton Bay.[31]

All those elements in the old convict system which had aggravated ill-feeling between the emancipists and the exclusives during the era of Macquarie were to be dropped. Land grants to ex-convicts were abolished. Brisbane was reminded that if he drew no distinction socially between the emancipists and the free migrants, he would disgust the better half of the community. He was instructed not to appoint an emancipist as a magistrate, until that man had proved himself by the meritorious discharge of other civil employment, and until such times as Brisbane had been able to form a full estimate of his private character. It was to be as difficult for the emancipist to win office or social preferment as for that camel to walk through the eye of the needle, or that rich man to enter into the kingdom of heaven. The Simeon Lords and the Samuel Terrys could store up for themselves treasures on earth, but they must not expect to break bread at the Governor's table or hold high office in the colony of New South Wales.[32]

In the middle of 1823 my lord Bathurst had written to T. H. Scott, the rector of the parish of Whitfield in Northumberland, to seek his advice on the future of religion and education in the colony. Scott, a man of pleasing manners and mild address, belonged by birth to a parson's family. By natural inclination and deep conviction he had come to accept the Burke dictum that a decent, regulated pre-eminence, a preference, though not exclusive appropriation, given to birth, was neither unnatural, nor unjust, nor impolitic. For him the aristocracy was that giant oak under whose shade all lesser mortals gathered for their comfort and protection. Scott believed that the diversity of poverty and riches was the order of Providence, that just as the oak towered in grandeur to heaven, while the shrub at its base was trodden under foot, so neither vain regrets, nor still vainer discontent could change the course of nature. The brief experience in the colonies of New South Wales and Van Diemen's Land as secretary to Mr Commissioner Bigge had convinced him that colonial society desperately needed such oaks to rescue it from the age of sophists, economists, publicans, Jew-boys, and anarchists who would bring everything to ruin. The England he knew on his return from New South Wales, the England of Peterloo, the incipient violence of a society rocked by material changes, and the ideals of a world revolution, only served to confirm those views on society he had found he enjoyed in common with John Macarthur in New South Wales.

So when Bathurst wrote to him he had no hesitation in recommending that the clergy of the Anglican church should be given land grants large enough to support their position as social and spiritual leaders of society. In each parish

---

[31] Bathurst to Brisbane, 30 May 1823, *H.R.A.*, I. xi. 83-6; for the recommendations of Bigge and the detailed instructions by Bathurst see vol. I of this history, pp. 367-72.

[32] Bathurst to Brisbane, 29 July 1823, *H.R.A.*, I. xi. 91-2.

D

he recommended there should be a school under the control of the Church of England vicar. In these schools the children should be grounded in the rudiments of reading, writing and the four simple rules of arithmetic, and then sent to another establishment where they were to be instructed in agriculture or trades before being apprenticed out. In each county there should be a central school for those who could pay as well as for a number of orphans who had distinguished themselves by their diligence in the primary schools, for Scott wanted both the career open to talent as well as that main pre-eminence conferred by birth to exist side by side in his society. In one of these central schools an academy should be organized to lay the foundations of a university in which students would proceed to degrees in classical, scientific and general subjects. Until such time as the university was founded the gifted pupils should be sent to Oxford or Cambridge at the expense of government as King's Scholars. This, he believed, would strengthen the ties between the colony and the mother country by implanting English habits and opinions amongst the educated members of the community.

Scott wanted to sow the seeds of Christian humanism in the minds of the gifted sons of the native-born, not only to rescue them from the vicious and irreligious habits of their parents, but to prepare them to serve God in church or state. He wanted men to grow up as liberals in religion, tolerant and broadminded on questions of doctrine, but Tories in politics. The cultivated English country gentleman, a gentle Sir Roger de Coverley rather than the boisterous Squire Western or an amoroso of a Tom Jones, was the model Scott recommended for the currency lads and lasses of Botany Bay.[33]

My lord Bathurst was very gracious. In the following year he accepted Scott's ideas, promised to establish a Church and School Corporation for the colony of New South Wales, and offered Scott the position of Archdeacon and head of the church at a salary of £2,000 a year, and a seat in the new Legislative Council. Scott was pleased to accept. So a man with the talents and urbanity of manner to adorn a plantation society was to give a lead in a colony where all previous ministers of God had been used as moral policemen for a gaol and a whorehouse. My lord Bathurst went on to explain that whatever qualms he had entertained in passing over Samuel Marsden had been silenced by Barron Field's assurance that ecclesiastical office played no part in the ambition of that worthy man, who would rejoice much more over one sinner that repented than all the pomps and vanities of ecclesiastical rank.[34]

Well before then Bathurst and the Colonial Office had introduced important changes in the administration of New South Wales. In August of 1823 my lord Bathurst informed Brisbane that an Act had been passed in the last session of

---

[33] L. Macquarie, The Governor's Diary and Memorandum Book, 1 July 1818 to 28 January 1820, Entry for 27 September 1819 (ms. in m.l.); T. H. Scott to Wilmot Horton, 4 September 1823, C.O. 201/157, pp. 343-53; T. H. Scott to Bathurst, March 1824, C.O. 201/157, pp. 156-68; T. H. Scott to Bathurst, 30 March 1824, C.O. 201/157, pp. 170-85; Bathurst to Brisbane, 21 December 1824, *H.R.A.*, I. xi. 419-22; E. Burke, *Reflections on the Revolution in France* (London, 1790); P. O. Thatcher, *A Charge to the Grand Jury of the County of Suffolk* (Boston, 1834), p. 17; A. M. Schlesinger, *The Age of Jackson* (London, 1946), p. 14; see also B. Willey, *Nineteenth Century Studies* (London, 1949), ch. 1, 'Samuel Taylor Coleridge'.

[34] Bathurst to Brisbane, 21 December 1824, *H.R.A.*, I. xi. 419-22; Barron Field to S. Marsden, London, 28 June 1824 (Marsden Papers, vol. 1, pp. 412-13).

Parliament to form a Supreme Court of Judicature, and to acquaint him that Francis Forbes, Esq., had been appointed to the office of Chief Justice in the new court, and would immediately proceed to Sydney to enter upon the duties of his office. As Judge Advocate Wylde and Mr Justice Field were to be recalled, Brisbane was to provide a passage for themselves and their families to England.[35]

Forbes had been a child prodigy, a man born to that complex fate of being endowed with intellectual and imaginative gifts which far exceeded the range to which he could aspire either by virtue of his birth or his strength of character. It was to be his fate in life to serve men who were his inferior in ability, but never to question the great gulf fixed between merit and desert in his society. As a child he had represented his fate as a man in nursery charades. He was fond of miming a wrestling match between a judge and the devil, in which he, the boy of promise, rescued the judge from destruction. There was in him from the start the makings of a great judge: nature had given him that precious gift of the headpiece clever: nature had endowed him with a great fondness for the intellectual games in which lawyers excel: chance and circumstance though had planted in him the devil of ambition as well as that devil of using his great talents to serve, to become the attendant judge, the talents to see the way forward for mankind, but not the strength in a crisis to resist those who stood in its way.

He had been born in Bermuda in 1784, the son and grandson of doctors in a family which had migrated from Scotland after the disaster at Culloden in 1745. Educated for the bar in London he had returned to Bermuda in 1811 to take up office as Attorney-General, and practise in the law until 1816. In that year he had taken up office as Chief Justice of the Supreme Court of Newfoundland—having married a doctor's daughter in London in 1813. In Newfoundland he had clashed with the governor, one of those naval officers on whom superior birth had conferred a higher office, but not those powers of intellect to draft legal proclamations. So Forbes had a lawyer's feast of nulling and voiding until 1822, savouring to the full that delight of the prodigy in exposing the stupidity of a dunderhead, but never using his great intellectual powers to satirize the Lord Verisophts or the Sir Mulberry Hawks of the post-war era, nor posing to himself fundamental questions on the right or expediency of such persons to exercise power. Deep down, Forbes was not moved by any hope of better things for mankind, but rather by that hope that one day he would receive preferment from his masters in London. So when ill-health had forced him to resign in 1822 he had repaired to London, and had heard, to his delight, that my lord Bathurst wanted his advice on drafting an Act for the better administration of justice in the colonies of New South Wales and Van Diemen's Land.[36]

---

[35] For the passing of the Act for the better Administration of Justice in New South Wales and Van Diemen's Land, 4 Geo. IV, c.96, see vol. I of this history, pp. 374-5; *Statutes at Large*, vol. 9; Bathurst to Brisbane, 4 August 1823, *H.R.A.*, I. xi. 102.

[36] For the life of F. Forbes, see the excellent article by Dr C. H. Currey in *Australian Dictionary of Biography*, vol. 1; see also C. H. Currey and J. H. Plunkett, *The Australian Magistrate* (Sydney, 1935); A. H. Maclintock, *The Establishment of Constitutional Government in Newfoundland* (London, 1941); Memorial of Francis Forbes to the Right Honourable Earl

In a convict society the case for concentrating legislative and executive powers in the Governor was very strong. But, granted that, how then could the king's loyal subjects be protected from the evils of arbitrary power? Was not the division of powers the supreme example of that English political genius, which had enabled them to develop a constitution which provided order without arbitrary power, and liberty without licence? It was a question on which Forbes could employ his great intellectual powers. In January of 1823 Forbes came up with a solution to the New South Wales problem. He recommended the creation of a Legislative Council with power to make rules and ordinances which were not repugnant to the laws of England.

In the course of long discussions in London he also suggested that the Chief Justice to be appointed under the Act should have the power to decide whether rules and ordinances were repugnant to the laws of England. The Act accepted the substance of Forbes' proposals. The Chief Justice was to be a member of the Legislative Council, and to be given the power to certify that no proposed law was repugnant to the laws of England, but was consistent with such laws, so far as the circumstances of the said colony would admit. Here was a clause which promised much intellectual sport in which Forbes could excel. In London it pleased him to pose such a question as: could one man be both a legislator and a judge of the meaning and intention of laws he had assisted to draft? The repugnancy power, too, was quite pleasing to his vanity: 'I suppose', he wrote later, 'I am the Lords House', implying that he, as Chief Justice, was expected to be the second house, or house of review. He never asked himself then whether supposing he were to assume a place of prominence, even eminence on the stage of public life, would he be taking his stand on the entrenched ground of the laws of God, or the rights of man, or would it just be once again that odd mixture of the elements in his being, that veneration for the majesty of the law, that reverence for all men as God's creatures living side by side with a basic delight in enmeshing a dunderhead in the nets of legal sophistry and pedantry, a delight in opposition which he would abandon at the first whisper that his masters in London were not amused, or were even displeased? The fiery furnace in New South Wales would give him the opportunity to display to the full his great powers of intellect and then expose dramatically, even cruelly, that deep division in him between passion and reason—that great cause of self division for Francis Forbes.[37]

Bathurst, Bermuda, 10 March 1813, C.O. 37/70, pp. 32-3; Letter Book of Dr Francis Forbes, St George's Historical Society, Bermuda, and microfilm in NAT. L.; W. Territ to F. Forbes, 3 June 1822 (Forbes Papers); C. H. Currey, 'The First Three Chief Justices of the Supreme Court of New South Wales', R. A. H. S., *J. & P.*, vol. 19, 1933-4, pp. 74-110; R. Therry, *Reminiscences of Thirty Years' Residence in New South Wales and Victoria* (London, 1863), p. 333 et seq.; Forbes Papers.

[37] Memorandum by F. Forbes, 1 January 1823, C.O. 201/146; F. Forbes to C.O., 15 May 1823, ibid.; F. Forbes to C.O., 1 June 1827, C.O. 201/188; see also A. C. V. Melbourne, *Early Constitutional Development in Australia: New South Wales 1788-1856* (London, 1934) *passim*; Section 29 of the Act 4 Geo. IV, c.96, 19 July 1823, *Statutes at Large*, vol. 9, 'And be it further Enacted, That no Law or Ordinance shall by the said Governor or Acting Governor be laid before the said Council for their Advice or Approbation, or be passed into a Law, unless a Copy thereof shall have been first laid before the Chief Justice of the Supreme Court of *New South Wales*, and unless such Chief Justice shall have transmitted to the said Governor or Acting Governor a Certificate under the Hand of such Chief Justice that such proposed Law is not repugnant to the

In the meantime all the respectable people of New South Wales were delighted with the news from London, as all the people who had interviewed Forbes in London had expressed themselves highly satisfied with his gentlemanly disposition. Here, at last, they believed, was a high-minded man with such a fine conscience that he spent a restless night every time he believed he had passed an erroneous judgment, a man to illustrate by his example on the bench the majesty and dignity of British institutions. So, after the inspiring landing at Sydney Cove in March 1824, followed by the pomp and ceremony at the opening of the Supreme Court on 17 May the *Sydney Gazette* once again enthused over the number of respectable and distinguished people who had crowded into the court-room on that day to witness the valuable extension of their privileges.[38]

Soon after on 15 July the ship, *Alfred*, arrived at Sydney town with four men on board with an abundance of talent and some of the motives to rock the established order in New South Wales. There was William Redfern, a surgeon who had been transported for his part in the mutiny at the Nore in 1797, returning now from London after presenting successfully the case for the legal rights of the emancipists. Redfern was a man whose character had been defamed by one of the architects of the new plantation society as guilty of participating in the most foul and unnatural conspiracy that had ever disgraced the pages of English history.[39] There was Robert Wardell, Doctor of Laws of the University of Cambridge, who had been born in 1793 into a gentleman's family. He was slight of build, a man with a Roman nose, who looked out on the world with a relentless eye, a man who might in an earlier age have become a grand inquisitor, but now in a more secular age he was the intellectual child of Byron's Vision of Judgment, the stern judge of the way of life of the Lord Verisophts and the Mulberry Hawks: as such, certain to hold up to ridicule and contempt any attempt to transplant the society of the Verisophts to Botany Bay, or any talk by the parsons of analogies between the vegetable world and human society. In February of 1823 he had applied unsuccessfully for the position of Attorney-General of New South Wales.[40] There was John Mackaness, Sheriff elect of the colony of New South Wales, a man not lifted up by any righteous desire to take down the mighty from their seat, and send the rich empty away, but a boon companion, a jolly fellow, who could be provoked to laugh out of court anyone who boasted of the eminence of his birth.[41] There was William Charles Wentworth, who told all and sundry that there were yellow snakes in the colony whom he would deprive of their venom and their fangs. The *Sydney Gazette*, edited by a man

Laws of England, but is consistent with such Laws, so far as the Circumstances of the said Colony will admit'.

[38] *Sydney Gazette*, 20 February 1823 and 20 May 1824.

[39] For the association of Redfern with the emancipists, see vol. I of this history, pp. 337-8 and 357-60.

[40] Norton Smith Legal Papers, Wardell's Heirs (MS. in NAT. L.); *Admissions to Trinity College, Cambridge*, vol. 4, p. 68; Tablet to Robert Wardell, LL.D., St James's Church, Sydney; above the inscription there is a head in profile of Wardell; Extract from a book of admissions to the Middle Temple, 16 April 1817, in Norton Smith Legal Papers; R. Wardell to Bathurst, 28 February 1823, C.O. 201/47, p. 540.

[41] *H.R.A.*, I. xiii. 744-5.

whose father had come to Sydney Cove as a convict, was delighted not only with the arrival of this group of learned gentlemen, but took pride in reminding their readers that Mr W. C. Wentworth was an Australian. The native son had returned to the land of his birth.[42]

42 *Sydney Gazette*, 22 July 1824.

3

THE RETURN OF THE NATIVE SON

WENTWORTH was thirty-four years old when he stepped ashore from the *Alfred* that July of 1824. There was about him the air of one of the gods who was mixing with mortals. His head was leonine, his language had a brilliance befitting a scion of the Whig aristocracy, and his ambitions a grandeur to match the promise of his appearance and his words. The man seemed likely to fulfil his great hope not to be outstripped by any competitor. Appearances were perhaps deceptive. For those who looked more closely there were blemishes: there was the slight cast in the eye, the walk was clumsy, the features coarse. This scion of the Whig aristocracy lapsed at times into the language of a coarse brat. This man who hoped to take his place at the top of society had a long record of savaging the very people who alone could confer that distinction on him.[1]

There was enough in his past to explain these contradictions. First and foremost there was the great gap between his father's and his mother's world. The father D'Arcy Wentworth was a distant relative of Earl Fitzwilliam, head of one of the great Whig families in the English aristocracy. He saw himself and his child as belonging to a long line of illustrious progenitors. Born in Portadown in Ireland he had qualified as an assistant surgeon in London in December of 1785.[2] There in an evil hour for himself he had sat down at the gaming tables, and mixed with low company. In 1787 and 1789 he had been charged with highway robbery. In 1787 he was found not guilty. In 1789 he was discharged on the understanding that we would take up a position as a superintendent of convicts at Botany Bay, where he was promised work as an assistant surgeon as soon as a vacancy occurred. He sailed for Botany Bay in the *Neptune* in January 1790, determined to expiate his folly, and repay the confidence the head of his family had placed in him.[3]

The mother was Catherine Crowley, a young woman of twenty or twenty-one who had been sentenced to transportation for seven years at the Stafford Assizes on 30 July 1788. She, too, boarded the *Neptune* for the long journey across the oceans during which, or some time before, she began with D'Arcy

[1] For W. C. Wentworth's own ideas on his father and his family, see, for example, W. C. Wentworth to H. G. Bennet, Temple, London, 12 February 1819 (Wentworth Papers, Letters from W. C. Wentworth).

[2] Court of examiners holden at the Theatre, the first day of December 1785, Examination Book in the Library of the Royal College of Surgeons, London.

[3] Blacker Manuscripts, vol. 3, p. 130 (ms. in m.l.); for a report of the trials of D'Arcy Wentworth see the transcription in the Macarthur Papers, vol. 109, pp. 2-36; W. Fitzwilliam to W. C. Wentworth, 9 February 1821 (Wentworth Papers, Letters to W. C. Wentworth); text of testimony to D'Arcy Wentworth, *Australian*, 26 May 1825; *H.R.A.*, I. i. 779; Charles Bateson, *The Convict Ships 1787-1868* (Glasgow, 1959), pp. 110-11.

Wentworth a coming together, the memory of which will survive as long as men attach importance to the coming of European civilization to Australia. The child born from their union who first appeared on the stage of that history as William Crowley, a name in a convict victualling list, became known in time as William Charles Wentworth. So his parentage cast him for membership of either of the two factions in the colony; the father's illustrious family qualified the boy for the exclusives with their hopes of a plantation society headed by a colonial aristocracy; the mother's place in society qualified him to join the convict party in New South Wales, with their egalitarianism and their levelling.[4]

Then there were the five and a half years as a child at Norfolk Island. At the end of July 1790 D'Arcy, Catherine Crowley and William sailed from Sydney in the *Surprize* for Norfolk Island where they arrived on 7 August. There that gap between the father and the mother was plain for all to see; the father was victualled as an officer; the mother and her children (there were three by the end of their stay) were victualled as convicts. On Norfolk Island, nature was lavish in her bounty and her beauty but men behaved so vilely to each other that an earthly paradise became the hell of the Pacific. Just as John Macarthur's early experience persuaded him that life was a fearful lottery, and the Reverend Samuel Marsden came to sum up life as the darkness of human depravity, so this early experience possibly turned William Charles Wentworth into an Ishmael, a wild man, who raised his hand against every man because deep down he feared every man's hand was raised against him.[5]

There was also the early death of the mother. For Catherine Crowley, who had left Norfolk Island in February 1796 with D'Arcy Wentworth and her three children, died at Parramatta in 1800, and was buried there by the Reverend Samuel Marsden, who was not to know that the child of this woman would one day write all manner of evil things against him. But on that wound, on that loss, and its meaning for him, Wentworth said not a word. Years later he gave his contemporaries one peep behind that curtain of his past, when he wrote of those

> Scenes, where my playful childhood's thoughtless years
> Flew swift away, despite of childhood's tears;[6]

[4] For Catherine Crowley see the Victualling Book, Norfolk Island, 1792/6, Per *Surprize*, No. 229 Cath° Crowley, Despatched 19 February 1796 by *Reliance* for Port Jackson (MS. in M.L.); see also List of Convict Children per *Surprize*, 7 August 1790, No. 42. William Crowley; see also Convicts Children, Dorset Crowley 23 June 1793, Mattw. Crowley 13 June 1795, ibid.; see also copy of tombstone for Catherine Crowley found in Parramatta in 1949 (typescript in M.L.); D'Arcy Wentworth named 13 August 1791 as the date of the birth of his son; see D'Arcy Wentworth to Earl Fitzwilliam, 30 November 1811 (microfilm in M.L. of Fitzwilliam Papers in Sheffield City Library); compare this with Victualling Book, Norfolk Island, which suggests the boy was born before the *Surprize* reached Norfolk Island on 7 August 1790.

[5] P. G. King to Nepean, Norfolk Island, 23 November 1791, *H.R.N.S.W.*, vol. I, pt 2, p. 564, and P. G. King to Phillip, Norfolk Island, 29 December 1791, ibid., p. 575; impressions of Queensborough from visit there in September 1965; W. C. Wentworth to D'Arcy Wentworth, 3 August 1819 (Wentworth Papers, Letters from W. C. Wentworth).

[6] For Wentworth's reference to his being born in Australia see his poem, *Australasia* (London, 1823): 'Land of my birth!'; for the return to Sydney from Norfolk Island see Victualling Book, Norfolk Island; see also entry under Catherine Crowley in ibid. The reference to his childhood is in W. C. Wentworth, *Australasia*, p. 2, lines 5-6.

Finally, there was the shock of discovering when he came to man's estate that his father had not taken that place in colonial society to which his birth entitled him. To prepare his two sons, William Charles and D'Arcy junior, to mix in the top ranks of society, D'Arcy had sent them to England to receive the education appropriate for gentlemen. Even then a Mrs Cookney noticed a cast in the eye which did not always lead him to the object he intended.[7] He returned in 1810 to find his father excluded from the drawing rooms of the self-styled gentry of New South Wales. Rumour had it that the circumstances of his private life were the cause of this affront to his father's pretensions. William Charles retaliated by savaging in words the very families whose regard and esteem he was coveting. He circulated a lampoon round Sydney in which he mocked at the Macarthurs as a family who would have lifed by their needles and their scissors to eternity.

> Had not aspiring John McArthur
> In a propitious, lucky hour
> Thrown whalebone, thimble, tapes away
> And bent his course to Botany Bay.[8]

A scion of the Whig aristocracy seemed to have joined the convict mockers of Botany Bay. Three years later in 1814, still flaunting his solidarity with social outcasts, he acted as witness to the marriage of the wealthy emancipist, Simeon Lord.[9] Two years after that he again took up his pen to ridicule the opponents of the pro-emancipist policy of Governor Macquarie.[10]

But there was more to the man than this superb use of vulgar spite against the competitors who threatened to outstrip him. When in company with Blaxland and Lawson he had found a way across the Blue Mountains in 1813, one of his companions had spoken of the achievement in that dreary, unimaginative and materialist way which was said to be characteristic of colonials. Gregory Blaxland had spoken of grass for his sheep and his cattle. The other, 'Ironbark' Lawson, had distinguished himself by his silence.[11] Wentworth alone had an eye for the majesty of the occasion. For him it was like one of those moments when

---

[7] For Wentworth at school near Bletchley see W. C. Wentworth and D'Arcy Wentworth jr to D'Arcy Wentworth, Bletchley, 24 July 1804 (Wentworth Papers, Letters from W. C. Wentworth). For the cast in the eye, see the postscript, J. Cookney to W. C. Wentworth to D'Arcy Wentworth, 11 August 1805 (Wentworth Papers, Letters from W. C. Wentworth).

[8] Bigge Appendix, C.O. 201/142, p. 336 et seq.: 'yet I think it also my Duty to state that the circumstances of his private life are such as to afford ground for serious reproach. He has lived for some time in a state of concubinage with the wife of a Free Person at his Houses in Sydney and Parramatta, and with another Female at a House situated between those places. By one of these women he has several Children, in addition to another family that he had by a Female with whom he cohabited during his residence in Norfolk Island. It is in consequence of the circumstances of his Domestic Life that Mr Wentworth has very rarely mixed in the Society of New South Wales altho' he has always been distinguished by propriety of demeanour when invited to partake of it and has been observed to shun rather than to court attention'. The lampoon of W. C. Wentworth against John Macarthur is in D'Arcy Wentworth Papers, Item 24.

[9] Certificate of marriage of Simeon Lord and Mary Hide, St Philip's Church, Sydney, 27 October 1814 (Lord Papers, ms. in m.l.).

[10] The pipes against Molle and the officers (Wentworth Papers, Miscellanea).

[11] For Gregory Blaxland and William Lawson, see vol. I of this history, pp. 277-8.

a meteor shoots athwart the night,
The boundless champaign burst upon our sight,
Till nearer seen the beauteous landscape grew,
Op'ning like Canaan on rapt Israel's view.[12]

Three years later in March of 1816, being then twenty-six years old, he set sail for England to study law, actuated, as he put it, by a desire of better qualifying himself to perform the sacred duties his birth had imposed. By acquainting himself with all the excellence of the British constitution he hoped to advocate at some future period the right of his native land to a participation in its advantages. He entertained, too, the proud hope that, by the very excellence of his services in the law, he would be considered not unworthy of the name of Fitzwilliam. The man who had poured scorn on souls attached to filthy pelf had begun to conceive of his own destiny on a grand scale.[13]

He enrolled at the Middle Temple on 5 February 1817, as the eldest son of D'Arcy Wentworth of New South Wales Esquire, for the past again cast its shadow when he had to tell those men in black who he was.[14] He had decided against going to Christ Church or Oriel College at Oxford because, as he told his father, at Oxford he would not be able to live in a style which would prevent noblemen and gentlemen of fortune preserving a distance from him as one of the vulgars—and that was a fate he did not propose to endure. He would bow the knee to no man—and would never degrade the dignity of his nature by turning parasite. He had other schemes for his own personal aggrandisement. He hoped to marry a daughter of John Macarthur. For a brief season he wrote as though without her his universe would turn to a mighty stranger, in a singular testimony to his need for another person, wondering then whether a man of ardent character, rebel wits and wild passion, driven as he knew himself to be with a sacred fervour for his country's cause, with a Byronic scorn of tyrants and a love of equal laws, could know anything but wounded pride in his relations with women. Besides the union would contribute to the respectability and grandeur of his family. Happily, too, John Macarthur senior, one of the objects of his witty lampoons, who was about to return to the colony, had given his blessing to the union, and his son John had urged him to write a work on the colony of New South Wales.[15]

So, while pacing to and fro on polished floors, or walking along those galleries lined with portraits of his own and other people's ancestors, or sitting on the satin-covered chairs, or chatting gaily under the candelabra, it seemed as though the great dream his father had planted in his heart was within his grasp. In the flowering time in his life he began to conceive for himself a destiny, and a mission to match the splendour of his worldly ambition. He had no intention of abandoning the country that gave him birth: he was conscious of

12 W. C. Wentworth, *Australasia* (London, 1823), p. 13.

13 W. C. Wentworth to Earl Fitzwilliam, 18 December 1816 (Wentworth Papers, Letters from W. C. Wentworth); see also W. C. Wentworth to D'Arcy Wentworth, Paris, 25 May 1818, ibid.

14 Certificate for W. C. Wentworth from the Middle Temple (Wentworth Papers, Miscellanea); see also *Register of Admissions to the Middle Temple*, vol. 2, p. 438: 'Feb. 5, 1817: William Charles Wentworth, eldest s. of D'Arcy Wentworth of N.S.W., esq., called 8 Feb. 1822'.

15 W. C. Wentworth to D'Arcy Wentworth, London, 1817 (Wentworth Papers, Letters from W. C. Wentworth).

the sacred claims it had upon him. To perform the duties his birth had imposed he calculated upon acquainting himself with all the excellence of the British constitution, hoping at some future period to advocate successfully the right of the country of his birth to a participation in its advantages. That year he began to roister by night with other bosom cronies who were reading law at the Middle Temple, and to read the poetry of Lord Byron, and go each Sunday against his will to that church in the Middle Temple where, through the dreary, if edifying, prayers and sermons, he could read cut in gold letters those words on the tablet behind the Lord's table, that law of God, the violation of which had cheated his father of his place in society—'Thou shalt not commit adultery'. But as he sat there in the church he never believed that either God or man could come between him and the fulfilment of his great dream; he was never anxious lest the past which had sent his father to Norfolk Island, and those throws of chance which had presided at his birth to coarsen his features, and endow him with a rancour and malevolence in his heart towards all who stood in his way, would or could cheat him of the prizes he coveted.

In 1817 he moved to Paris to acquire a language so generally known that it was a reflection in a gentleman to be ignorant of it. There, too, he pushed on with the writing of his book. In the intervals between work he spent lavishly, searching in a life of wild gaiety for 'precious metal in the dirt'. When his creditors became pressing he appealed for accommodation from Earl Fitzwilliam and John Macarthur junior who both refused—minor hurts to his pride which caused him to reproach his father: 'I hope you will in future take care', he wrote to him after he returned to London for the winter of 1818–19, 'that I need not the assistance of any man'.

That was but the mood of a moment—a brief gust of passion. That winter he had other things on his mind. His pamphlet on New South Wales had grown into a book. He began with a profession of modesty. His only aim in obtruding this hasty production on the public was to promote the welfare and prosperity of the country which gave him birth. But then, impatient as ever, he rushed on to uncover his vision of how his native land, which had hitherto been considered more in the light of a prison, might be rendered one of the most useful and valuable appendages of the empire by diverting from the United States of America to the shores of New South Wales and Van Diemen's Land some of the vast tide of emigration which was then flowing thither from all parts of Europe.

His remedy was simple: grant the colonists the enjoyment of those rights and privileges from which they ought never to have been debarred; remove the unmerited and absurd restrictions on their trade; replace the present arbitrary system with a free government, or else the colony would degenerate into what he called a 'vast stye of abomination and depravity'. He looked forward to the day when oppression was hurled from the car in which it had driven triumphantly over prostrate justice, virtue, and religion; he looked forward to the day of 'retired pursuits of unobtrusive industry' when men were no longer victims of the ambitious candidates for power and distinction. For it was the moral and high-minded Wentworth who poured himself into this book, using magnificently, if somewhat extravagantly, the language of post-war London where it was a commonplace that British institutions preserved both the rights of conscience and those rights of political and civil liberty which had allowed England to escape the evils of revolution and arbitrary power. It was also a Wentworth who had a vision of what Australia might become once it was freed from the oppressor and the 'convicts' clanking chains'. He had a vision of men living in the colony as though they were in Arcady, of gay innocents who had not been tainted by power, or the pursuit of filthy material gain. He ended with a quotation from a poem which summed up his great dream for the future of humanity in his native land.

> The lifted axe, the agonizing wheel,
> Luke's iron crown, and Damien's bed of steel,
> To men remote from pow'r but rarely known,
> Leave reason, faith, and conscience all our own.[16]

While his heart was still hot with this picture of a brave new world in the land of his birth, he was cut to the quick to read in a pamphlet by a member of the House of Commons, one H. G. Bennet, that his father had been arraigned at the bar of justice on a criminal charge. His first impulse was to demand that the author of this infamous calumny should wash out the foul stain he had cast upon his father's character with his blood. But on second thoughts he decided to tell Bennet how his father had sought to efface forever the memory of an unjust accusation by exile to a distant shore. So one bitter day in February of 1819 Wentworth was ushered into Bennet's study, where he began to berate him with a torrent of words. Startled by the wild talk of washing away the stain of the infamous calumny with his own blood, Bennet changed colour, and showed other signs of agitation. But nothing would satisfy Wentworth short of an ample public apology. This Bennet undertook to give. A few days later, on 18 February, Australia's native son sat proudly in the visitor's gallery in the House of Commons, while Bennet told the members that the gentleman he had mentioned in his pamphlet was not a convict, and he went on to say he understood the gentleman in question had conducted himself with the utmost propriety during the whole of his residence in the colony. As reparation he had decided to stop the circulation of the pamphlet. There, for Bennet, the matter ended, but not for Wentworth. For him, the rancour and the desire for revenge lived on. Someone must be punished for his humiliation and pain. So he told his father he had no doubt 'you have to thank that dark villain Samuel Marsden (heaven requite him one day or other according to his deserts) for this most unpleasant occurrence'.[17]

[16] W. C. Wentworth to Earl Fitzwilliam, Holborn, 15 August 1817 (Wentworth Papers, Letters from W. C. Wentworth); for Wentworth in Paris see W. C. Wentworth to D'Arcy Wentworth, Paris, 25 May 1818; W. C. Wentworth to John Macarthur jr, Paris, 29 July 1818; W. C. Wentworth to D'Arcy Wentworth, London, 18 November 1818 (Wentworth Papers, Letters from W. C. Wentworth); W. C. Wentworth, *A Statistical, Historical, and Political Description of The Colony of New South Wales, and Its dependent Settlements in Van Diemen's Land* (London, 1819). A second and enlarged edition was published in 1820.

[17] For this episode see W. C. Wentworth to H. G. Bennet, Temple, London, 12 February 1819 (Wentworth Papers, Letters from W. C. Wentworth); W. C. Wentworth to D'Arcy Wentworth, Elm Court, Temple, 13 April 1819, ibid.; see also the speech of H. G. Bennet in the House of Commons on 18 February 1819 on motion for appointment of a committee to inquire into the transportation system, *P. D.*, 1st Series, vol. 39, col. 471.

But that was precisely what Wentworth could never achieve in life: that detachment and restraint, and humility to allow God to repay. While he was still fuming Jeffery Hart Bent, one-time judge in the colony of New South Wales, and no friend to the pro-emancipist sympathies of Governor Macquarie, repeated in London the lying slander about D'Arcy. Once again Wentworth shouted in anger that he would either wipe out the stain with Bent's blood, or shed the last drop of his own blood in the effort.[18]

That spring of 1819 in London his world seemed to be crumbling around him. In the middle of all the hurry to get out his book he heard from Sydney that John Macarthur senior would not grant him permission to marry his daughter. Again Wentworth snatched at the idea of vengeance: 'as soon as I get over the hurry of my work, I will pay him off in his own coin', he told his father. So that book, which had been suggested to him by young John Macarthur, came out by chance at a time when Wentworth was consumed with an implacable hostility towards the Macarthurs. Of all the dreams he had entertained in 1817, that hope of making great and powerful connections, that happy union of heart and pocket in marrying into the Macarthur family, only the ambition remained. 'You may rely', he told his father that August of 1819, 'that I will not suffer myself to be outstripped by any competitor and I will finally create for myself a reputation which shall reflect a splendour on all who are related to me'. Eminence was now the master-mistress of his passion.[19]

Yet, even though one part of him cast hungry eyes towards the great Whig houses, circumstances had driven him again into association with the pro-convict party in New South Wales. Shortly after Wentworth was called to the bar at the Middle Temple on 8 February 1822 Bigge published his report on the state of the colony of New South Wales in which he dropped some measured words on the stormy career of William Charles as a writer of lampoons. Wentworth immediately accused him of wilful misrepresentation of evidence, and of misrepresenting his father: he demanded satisfaction by ten the next morning. Once again Wentworth shouted that he would have vengeance. As he wrote to his father in 1822:

> Depend upon it if he [i.e. Bigge] will only venture his life in support of these infamous calumnies, that the existence of one of us is nearly at a close. Which of the two is to fall is of course yet in the womb of time; but were inevitable death staring one in the face, I should not hesitate an instant in the performance of my duty; but should ever rejoice in having the power to convince you that I have a proper feeling and due sense of what is due from a child to an affectionate father.

Not being a man for death with honour, Bigge promptly expressed his concern for attributing authorship of the pipe to Wentworth on the last page of

[18] For the Bent episode see W. C. Wentworth to D'Arcy Wentworth, London, 6 December 1819 (Wentworth Papers, Letters from W. C. Wentworth).

[19] W. C. Wentworth to D'Arcy Wentworth, Elm Court, Temple, 13 April 1819; W. C. Wentworth to D'Arcy Wentworth, London 5 or 8 August 1819; W. C. Wentworth to D'Arcy Wentworth, 1 May 1820, ibid.

his report on the judicial establishments of New South Wales and Van Diemen's Land.

Wentworth, unlike Hamlet, that other man driven to avenge evil done to his father and himself, wanted darker satisfaction than just the changing of a paragraph in a report to the House of Commons. In collaboration with Edward Eagar, an ex-convict, who had been befriended in his early days in New South Wales by the respectable Reverend Samuel Marsden, and was now in London to present a petition praying for the restitution of the legal rights of emancipists, he arranged to publish a third edition of his book on New South Wales, in which he exposed the unctuous hypocrisy of the Mahomet of Botany Bay, Samuel Marsden, and ended with a passionate call for British institutions in the land of his birth. John Macarthur who had not been happy about the first edition, finding its tendency to be highly mischievous, was not surprised to hear from his son that Wentworth was bound to offend grossly.[20]

Early in the new year, as an indication to posterity of the contradictory gusts flowing through him, he applied to Dr Redfern, like Eagar, an ex-convict who had come to London with the emancipists' petition, for financial assistance to go to Peterhouse, Cambridge, the college which had received copious benefactions from the Fitzwilliam family. This college had been originally founded for those studiously engaged in the pursuit of literature, and in that, after all, Wentworth had been endowed with great gifts. For him, as ever, there was that other reason. There was, he told his father, a good deal in the 'name' of having been at a college. So he signed the book of admissions on 27 February 1823. Shortly afterwards he had a chance to distinguish himself in a way which would also minister to his delight. He could submit a poem for the Chancellor's Medal and, if he won, he would distinguish himself more in a month than John Macarthur junior could contrive to do during the four years he resided there. The subject that year was Australasia. He had to accept the mortification of gaining second place.[21]

In the poem he had risen to the occasion magnificently. On the title page he called himself an *Australasian*. In the preface he wrote of his fervent prayer that Macquarie might receive his due recognition from those who had 'Aus-

<hr />

20 For the relations between Wentworth and Bigge see W. C. Wentworth to D'Arcy Wentworth, n.d., imperfect copy in Wentworth Papers, Letters from W. C. Wentworth; Bigge to Bathurst, 29 July 1822, Bigge Appendix, C.O. 201/142, and Bigge to Bathurst, 3 August 1822, Bigge Appendix, C.O. 201/142; for Bigge on the Wentworth pipe against Molle see J. T. Bigge, *Report of the Commissioner of Inquiry, on the Judicial Establishments of New South Wales,* p. 148, *P.P.,* 1822, XX, 448; for Bigge on D'Arcy Wentworth see ibid., p. 101, and Bigge Appendix, C.O. 201/142, p. 336; for the text of Wentworth's pipes against Molle and the officers see Wentworth Papers, Miscellanea; for Eagar's part in the third edition of Wentworth's book see E. Eagar to R. W. Horton, 5 June 1824, C.O. 201/255; for Bigge's retraction see the *Report of the Commissioner of Inquiry, on the Judicial Establishments of New South Wales, and Van Diemen's Land,* p. 90, *P.P.,* 1823, X, 33.

21 W. C. Wentworth to D'Arcy Wentworth, 18 March 1823 (Wentworth Papers, Letters from W. C. Wentworth); for the admission of W. C. Wentworth to Peterhouse, see *Admissions to Peterhouse or S. Peter's College in the University of Cambridge,* comp. by T. A. Walker (Cambridge, 1912), p. 417: Die xxvii^{mo} Gul^{mus} **Carolus Wentworth** juris consultus et Londinensis apud nos ad mensam Sociorum admittitur.; for Wentworth at Cambridge see *Alumni Cantabrigienses,* comp. by J. A. Venn, pt 2, vol. 6, p. 405, which states that he was born at Norfolk Island on 26 October 1793, and that his mother's name was Catharine Parry; see also Burke's *Colonial Gentry;* the article on W. C. Wentworth in the *D.N.B.* says he was admitted to Peterhouse in 1816.

tralasian hearts'. For the poem was in part a song of praise for Macquarie: it was dedicated to Macquarie, and given a special Wentworth twist in the preface in which he attacked the few dastardly and privileged calumniators of the Major-General, for that dark shadow in his heart fell across even this great hymn of praise. 'Land of my birth!' he began. And he went on to ask:

> Dear Australasia, can I e'er forget
> Thee, Mother Earth?

He loved it all from the rich pastures, where the wild herds strayed, to the desolate, stunted woods where eagles brooded, and torrents roared. He loved the people: he loved especially the women—

> Thy blue ey'd daughters, with the flaxen hair,
> And taper ankle, do they bloom less fair
> Than those of Europe?

For that tempest lived in him, too, and that wonder of a man with a maid had already brought him great pleasure, and great anguish to those who ministered to his delight.

In the land of his birth there was one great darkness: the felon's shame stilled the voice and clouded the opening fame of the country of his heart. He sang of his hope that this early blot would soon be forgotten, and then the convicts' clanking chains would no more deform the wilds or stigmatize the plains of his beloved Australasia. He hailed the future when, freed from the convict taint, the native-born dedicated themselves to science, taking the teachers of Greece and Rome as their models, for he was no groveller at the shrine of grace, no God-botherer, but rather a recoiler from the Judaic-Christian whine about human depravity and unworthiness. For him the Greeks and the Romans were the fountains of human wisdom: celestial poesy was his spiritual food. He looked to the day not when all men cried out aloud, thou art just, O Lord, for thy ways are revealed, but rather to that day when an Austral Shakespeare, or an Austral Milton, or an Austral Pindar would soar with daring like an eagle in the sky—as though men could and should steal fire from heaven. His theme was man's glory, and pride and honour—not God's. He looked forward to that day when Australasia would

> float, with flag unfurl'd,
> A new Britannia in another world.[22]

---

[22] *Australasia: A Poem. Written for the Chancellor's Medal at the Cambridge Commencement, July 1823*. By W. C. Wentworth An Australasian; Fellow-Commoner at Saint Peter's College (London, 1823); at the end of the preface Wentworth made the following observation: 'The author feels that his poem would have been much more perfect, if some allusion had been made in it to the religious improvement which has been effected in Australasia, and particularly to the great missionary efforts which are now in progress in the Polynesian Archipelago. An allusion of this nature, as a friend has justly observed to him, naturally belongs to the subject; and its omission too was the less excusable, as it may be considered a species of *ascriptio glebae* to the ancient and religious manor [*sic*] from which the subject sprung. He can only plead in apology the hurry in which his poem was written; little more than three weeks having elapsed between its commencement and completion. Had he joined the University a month sooner, both the argument and execution of the poem would have been very different.'

No wonder the *Sydney Gazette,* the currency lads and lasses, and the supporters of the convict party welcomed him with pride and pleasure when he stepped ashore from the *Alfred* in July of 1824. Yet from the start the man behaved in ways which bewildered his companions and angered his enemies. There were the blemishes in the appearance—the cast in the eye, the clumsy walk and the coarse features, suggesting not so much one favoured by the gods, but rather one mocked by them. It was as though the gods had planted in him great talents and fatal flaws for their sport. There were all the contradictions in his behaviour, for, at one moment, he gave out in a drunken boast that he would scotch that yellow snake, John Macarthur, or expose that dark villain, Samuel Marsden, and, at the next, he was bragging about his great connections. Soon the tongues of the gossips were wagging. It was said there were great drunken carousals in a house in Castlereagh Street, and much bawdy conversation. The *Sydney Gazette,* which had welcomed him as a hero, began to drop hints that Australia's native son was a prodigal and a wanton.

For in place of that conflict between good and evil, that conception of man in the Christian view of the world, Wentworth began to put forward the Byronic hero, the great soul who defied destiny, and pursued pleasure even at the price of his eternal damnation. He had nothing but contempt for those mean souls, those God-botherers, who cringed every Sunday before their jealous Jehovah, not forgetting to cock an eye over their shoulder to see whether the Governor and all the respectable people of Sydney town were observing their deed of piety. He was too much in love with life, too swept on by pride and arrogance to conceal his loathing and contempt for cringers and knee-benders. He would how the knee neither to man nor God. For there was about him that air of a man in whom once again the battle between damnation and impassioned clay would be played to a finish. There was within him that power to dream a great dream, and to conceive a great future for himself and his country. Fate had also endowed him with the talent to achieve his ambition but had planted inside him passions which would snatch it from him at the very moment when it was within his grasp.[23]

He had come back not as the prodigal son to beat his breast, and tell his father he had sinned against heaven and was no more worthy to be called his son, but rather as the native son, the currency lad with the ambition and sense of the opportunity to make great and powerful connections. For a season he had to content himself with great expectations, as happily during his absence in England, his beloved father had waxed fat in the land to which he had voluntarily been banished to expiate the follies of his youth. From grants of land in the Parramatta district, from the profits made from the rum hospital contract, and the business partnership with Simeon Lord for trade in the

---

[23] Based on the letters to his father up to 1822, the poetry he had written, and especially the poem *Australasia.* See also John Macarthur to John Macarthur jr, 12 September 1816 (Macarthur Papers, vol. 3, p. 134b); for Wentworth's attitude to the Christian religion some light is thrown in his moving letter to his daughter Thomasine, n.d. (Parkes Correspondence, vol. 18, MS. in M.L.): Doubtless this Belief is desirable and Comfortable wherever it prevails, and a Source of hope and Consolodation at our latest hour.

If my Faith in Christianity is not so fervent as your own, do not therefore imagine that I am altogether an unbeliever. . . .

Do not despair that we may meet again in futurity however soon we may be separated in time.'

Pacific, D'Arcy had become very rich, and William Charles knew, and so did some of the gossip mongers of Sydney, that most of this wealth would pass to his beloved son.[24]

With the promise of that grandeur and that freedom from being tied to any man which such riches would bestow, Wentworth prepared to walk on the stage of public life in the colony of New South Wales. It was a propitious moment. On 25 August, just one month after he had stepped ashore from the *Alfred,* the first session of the Legislative Council began in the Court House in Sydney.[25] Neither Brisbane nor the members lingered over the significance of the occasion. Brisbane asked them whether they wished to proceed in the absence of the Lieutenant-Governor, and when they replied in the affirmative, he announced that as there was no further business the Council stood adjourned.[26]

Three weeks later, on 10 September, Wentworth made his first appearance on the stage of public life. In company with Wardell he appeared before the Supreme Court to be sworn in to act in the character of proctors, attorneys and solicitors in the said court. Wardell then moved, seconded by Wentworth, that the attorneys should show cause why they should not immediately retire from the bar. Wentworth spoke for nearly two hours, in the course of which, as the *Sydney Gazette* put it, considerable ardour and talent were pressed into service.[27]

The following month, again in partnership with Wardell, his old boon companion from his student days at the Middle Temple, Wentworth published the first edition of a newspaper for which he used the name of the country he loved best in all the world: he called it the *Australian.* When he and Wardell announced their intention to publish the paper Brisbane decided to try the experiment of the full latitude of freedom of the press. Howe then applied for removal of all government restraint on the *Sydney Gazette,* and applied successfully. A free press, Wentworth and Wardell told the readers of the first issue of 14 October, was the most legitimate, and at the same time, the most powerful weapon that could be employed to annihilate the influence of individuals, frustrate the designs of tyranny, and restrain the arm of oppression. The joint owners introduced a note of gaiety and gusto in their paper. They told their readers they liked fairs because they promoted good fellowship, and brought the lads and lasses together. The sin, the smut, and gloom of darkness of the parsons were to be spirited away on gales of laughter and ridicule.[28]

A week later lists of the persons eligible to sit as jurors in civil cases were nailed to the doors of the churches and other places of worship in Sydney. The name of every person who had not come free to the colony had been omitted. Wentworth, sensing the influence of his implacable enemies, the Macarthurs,

[24] For the wealth of D'Arcy Wentworth see the text of the will of D'Arcy Wentworth, trustees, J. T. Campbell, W. Lawson, W. Redfern, and W. C. Wentworth (Documents of Titles etc. Miscellaneous, Minter and Simpson & Co., MS. in M.L.); see also D'Arcy Wentworth Papers 1821-27, pp. 275-7.

[25] *V. & P.* (L.C. N.S.W.) 25 August 1824; *Sydney Gazette,* 26 August 1824.

[26] *Sydney Gazette,* 26 August and 2 September 1824.   [27] *Sydney Gazette,* 16 September 1824.

[28] *Australian,* 14 October 1824; Brisbane to Bathurst, 12 January 1825, *H.R.A.,* I. xi. 470-1; Brisbane said in this despatch that the measure had been productive of more benefit than disadvantage to the public.

E

in this decision, denounced it as a sweeping act of exclusion. If trial by jury was to be modified in this way, he wrote in the *Australian*, then instead of becoming a bond of union, and a common medium for the amalgamation of two discordant and heterogeneous classes, it would keep them more aloof, and apply to those fatal feuds which had already sprung up and threatened one day or other to cleave the society to its centre, a new rancour and inveteracy.[29] The native son, it seemed, had donned the mantle of a tribune of the people. The opposition to the exclusives had acquired a leader.

Again the following month when news of the death of Macquarie reached Sydney, Wentworth wrote his article on the late General Macquarie as a party man. He praised Macquarie for gradually and silently undermining that colonial oligarchy, to whose avarice and ambition the public weal had till then been systematically prostituted. Yet in the very same issue Wentworth marked the death of another man just as close to the passions of his heart—the death of Lord Byron:

'Where art thou, man of might, thou grand in soul', he asked, and answered, not like the parsons with their story of a home for little children above the bright blue sky, but with a becoming grandeur and courage:

> But thou hast past the bourne we cannot pass
> In mortal vest; and whether weal or woe
> Be now thy portion, we know not:—alas!
> We only know that of the sons of earth,
> The wayward Harold, with his eye of pride,
> The outlaw'd Conrad, Juan's soul of mirth,
> Liv'd each his life intense, and early died![30]

By the end of that month it was well known in Sydney that Wentworth was living 'his life intense' with a magnificent disdain for the parsons' gloomy talk about 'man's sure inheritance of woe'. Women were there to minister to his delight, not to comfort and forgive him for what he had done, because in life he travelled alone—proud, defiant, ruthless, looking neither to man nor to God for forgiveness. He was one of those sons of earth, who with the eye of pride and soul of mirth would live life intense, and loathe and despise any man who wanted to be washed clean 'in the blood of the lamb'.[31]

For the native-born were beginning to sense that they too could steal that fire from heaven, and increase and replenish the earth of their native land and subdue it. When Brisbane wanted to ascertain whether any large and navigable rivers flowed over the territory to the south of the Goulburn Plains to the oceans on the east or south coasts of New South Wales, Hamilton Hume volunteered to lead the expedition, 'presuming myself', as he put it, '(altho' an Australian) capable from experience of understanding such an expedition'. Hume was twenty-seven years of age, having been born near Parramatta, the

---

[29] *Australian*, 21 and 28 October 1824.   [30] Ibid., 11 November 1824.
[31] Baptismal register, Christ Church St Lawrence, Sydney: Henry Eagar, born 4 November 1830, son of W. C. Wentworth, gentleman, and Jemima Eagar, Castlereagh St Sydney (T. D. Mutch index in M.L.); Jemima Eagar, like Wentworth, was native-born, the daughter of John McDuel (various spellings) and Margaret Moloney in 1796; she had married Edward Eagar in July 1815.

son of an English migrant who had laboured in vain to raise his family to the level of society to which they had belonged in the United Kingdom. W. H. Hovell also volunteered to take part in the expedition. Now Hume was a currency lad, and Hovell belonged to the sterling, those men who believed that the accident of place and station of birth had conferred on them a superiority of character and talent over the currency lads and lasses.[32] So an expedition designed to increase man's knowledge of a harsh and elemental land developed into a trial of strength between a currency lad and a bloody immigrant.

They set out from Appin near Sydney with their six pack-horses, a tent of Parramatta cloth, two tarpaulins, and three convict servants each, for Lake George which they reached on 13 October 1824. Soon after the trial of strength between the dinkum Aussie and the Jimmy began when they reached the banks of the Murrumbidgee River near Yass. To the mingled scorn and delight of Hume and Thomas Boyd, a convict member of the party, Hovell, the Englishman, became faint of heart and despaired of ever crossing the river. The Australian-born knew no such temptation. With magnificent cheek and effrontery Hume taunted Hovell on the banks of the Murrumbidgee in that south country where courage and resource rather than the accident of birth or the inheritance of wealth become richer than all the jewels of Araby: 'If you think you can't, you may go back, for I mean to go on'. Hovell, bewildered by the role his companion had thrust on him as the representative of the civilization of the old world, could only register his surprise that such a vulgar and groundless feeling of envy should have awakened in the mind of a man whom he preferred to think of as his companion in adventure.

On 29 October they crossed the Tumut River, after which Hume, once again claiming for himself the sagacity of the native-born to find his way in the Australian bush, insisted they should strike south-west towards the rolling plain country, and so avoid the passage of mountains. Following this course, on 16 November, they came upon a noble stream to which Hume gave his own surname in memory of his father, but in this fate cheated the native-born of his attempt to bequeath the name of his family to posterity. Five years later Charles Sturt, an Englishman, a man of vision and faith and a stranger to the passions swirling in Hume's heart, reached the same river lower down and called it the Murray after His Majesty's principal Secretary of State in the Colonial Office.

After crossing this river they pushed south over dreary plains which induced such a state of depression in the men that the leaders promised to turn back if they did not soon sight the sea. Then on 13 December Hume, impatient as ever, having pushed on ahead, came to the top of a big hill, where he cheered so long and loud that the other men rushed towards him, Mr Hovell being amongst them. In one of the rare moments of companionship on that long journey, the Australian and the Englishman looked down from the top of that hill over a plain where in time men would attempt to plant British civiliza-

[32] For the early life of H. Hume see vol. I of this history, third impression, pp. 251-2, 352-5; H. Hume to Bathurst, 20 April in Hay to Darling, 22 October 1826, *H.R.A.*, I. xii. 655-6; for W. H. Hovell see *Australian Dictionary of Biography*, vol. 1.

tion in that alien soil. Within three days they were camping on the shores of Corio Bay on the edge of the country where the gentry would raise their mansions of stone as supports of civilization and refinement in a great sea of barbarism.

No such vision was vouchsafed to either Hume or Hovell on that day. On 18 December they set out on their return journey, vying with each other to be first in Sydney with the news. Hovell broke camp at Gunning to steal a march on his precocious companion but Hume, not to be outdone, caught up with him at Berrima, and they entered Sydney together late in January. Hume, brash and boastful as ever, quickly laid claim to the success of the expedition: 'It was I', he said, 'who took him to Hobson's Bay, and brought him back'. But Brisbane would not listen to the preposterous and noisy boasts of the currency lads. With a becoming dignity he thanked them both for their work, issued instructions for both of them to receive grants of land as a reward for their labours, and wrote off to London with a characteristic detachment that a new and valuable country extending from Lake George towards Western Port (in error for Corio Bay) had been discovered by two young men, Hovell and Hume, the latter colonial, who seemed to have performed their duty well. By contrast the *Australian*, possibly influenced by Wentworth, sensing the significance of the occasion for posterity, hailed the achievement with a characteristic piece of rhetoric. Hume and Hovell, they wrote, had rescued a large part of Australia from the stigma of Oxley who had branded the inland as uninhabitable and useless for all the purposes of civilized man. Soon a tide of settlement would move into the new lands.[33]

By the year 1824 Brisbane's detachment reflected not just the mind of a man for whom star-gazing and personal salvation enjoyed pride of place over such mundane subjects as the government of men, but also the mind of a man who had turned away from the human scene in disgust. He had come to the melancholy conclusion that such a society as New South Wales had not existed since the introduction of Christianity into the world. He had lived, he said, to discover that expectations from the world were fallacious: from now on he would seek his rewards not from man, nor put his trust in princes, but would look for it from God, the rock on which alone he relied for his ever-lasting inheritance. Human behaviour in New South Wales reminded him of that passage in the third chapter of Romans: Their throat is an open sepulchre; with their tongues they have used deceit; the poison of asps is under their lips. Besides, all through 1824 his administration suffered from the protracted delays and the ungracious reception he and all others had to endure from that most honourable man, who alas did not possess the best of tempers, the Colonial

---

[33] Based on W. H. Hovell, Journal kept on a Journey from Lake George to Port Phillip, 1824-1825 (ms. in m.l.); *Australian*, 10, 17 February and 21 July 1825; H. Hume, *A Brief Statement of Facts in connection with an Overland Expedition from Lake George to Port Phillip, in 1824* (Sydney, 1855); W. H. Hovell, *Reply to 'A Brief Statement of Facts, in connection with an Overland Expedition from Lake George to Port Phillip, in 1824,'* published in May last, by 'Hamilton Hume' (Sydney, 1855); Brisbane to Horton, 24 March 1825, *H.R.A.*, I. xi. 555; H. Hume to Brisbane, 24 January 1825, Encl. in Darling to Bathurst, 10 October 1826, *H.R.A.*, I. xii. 643-4; W. Bland, *Journey of Discovery to Port Phillip, New South Wales, by Messrs W. H. Hovell, and Hamilton Hume: in 1824 and 1825* (Sydney, n.d., 2nd ed. 1837); E. Scott, *Hume and Hovell's Journey to Port Phillip* (Sydney, 1921).

Secretary, Major Goulburn.[34] So he turned more and more to his God for comfort, and away from the world of men. While Hume and Hovell were wrangling during their long walk, Brisbane was thankful to reflect that he had made progress in the divine life. All through 1824 he had suffered many internal conflicts, and been exposed to many dangers from wicked men. He knew that these trials were sent by God to try his faith, that it was just as necessary to suffer as to do the will of God in whose constant presence he proposed to spend his life, and at death resign himself into God's merciful disposal. That was his world.[35]

By contrast the currency lads and the emancipists were turning, noisily, exuberantly and boisterously to embrace the world they knew. On the night of 26 January 1825 a party of them, with Wentworth as president, and Redfern as vice-president, met at Hill's hotel to celebrate the thirty-seventh anniversary of the colony. The drank toasts to many things—to the king, to the memory of Governor Phillip, and of Macquarie, to Sir Thomas Brisbane, who believed that all human striving was vain, to trial by jury, to a house of assembly, to freedom of the press, to commerce and agriculture, and to the currency lasses, for Wentworth was a man. There was much merriment, and much shouting when Robinson, an effective writer of doggerel verse for such occasions, called on them to drink the toast: 'The land, boys, we live in'.[36]

A few months later copies arrived of the third edition of Wentworth's book on the colony of New South Wales. The emancipists hailed him as their historian and their advocate, a worthy native son of 'the land, boys, we live in'. John Macarthur was not greatly alarmed. The rhodomontade and the savage invective only confirmed what he had been telling himself for a long time about Wentworth—namely, that the man would offend grossly.[37] But Marsden was deeply hurt. Wentworth, and his collaborator, Edward Eagar whom he, Marsden, had befriended in his early days of the colony, had held him up to public ridicule and contempt as a turbulent and ambitious priest, who had set his face against every philanthropic project. They had taunted him as an unctuous hypocrite whose reverence for the Lord's day was not such as to permit a windmill of his, which stood in full view of the very sanctuary where he officiated, suspending its profitable gyrations even during church time. They had written that he was as conversant with the points of a pig, a sheep, an ox, or a horse, as with the contents of the sacred volume which it should be the peculiar study and occupation of his life to inculcate. And, they had continued, 'tell it not in Gath, publish it not in the streets of Askelon', he had long been a private vendor in any quantity from a pint to a puncheon of those very spirituous liquors against which he had so righteously declaimed.[38]

[34] Sir Thomas Brisbane to Mr Hepburn, January 1824 (Brisbane Papers, Box 4); the passage in the Bible to which Brisbane refers is in Romans iii. 10-18; Sir Thomas Brisbane to Mr Butterworth, 28 April 1824 (ibid., Box 2).

[35] See extracts from the diary of Sir Thomas Brisbane for the year 1824 in *Reminiscences of General Sir Thomas Makdougall Brisbane* (Edinburgh, 1860) pp. 47-9.

[36] *Australian*, 3 February 1825.

[37] For this point about Wentworth see for example, the letter by John Macarthur jr to Elizabeth Macarthur, 12 April 1825 (Macarthur Papers, vol. 15, pp. 419-21).

[38] For these and other charges by Wentworth against Marsden see W. C. Wentworth, *A Statistical Account of the British Settlements in Australasia* (3rd ed., 2 vols, London, 1824), vol. 1, pp. 367-77.

From far away in London Barron Field wrote to urge him to take legal advice and bring Wentworth before the law courts as the man had called him a hypocrite over and over again. Marsden asked his solicitor to write to Wentworth to ask whether he acknowledged authorship, but when Wentworth declined to furnish the information, Marsden decided to let the matter drop. He then turned once again to his God for that comfort and consolation of which the world seemed so bent to deprive him. Gross falsehood, he told himself, could do him no harm: he would never covet the good opinion of the ungodly. He proposed to trust God with all he had. Or so he mused in May of 1825 after the correspondence with Wentworth.[39]

Perhaps he had forgotten, for memory no longer held the door wide open for him on his own past, that just over twelve months earlier he had written a letter to His Majesty's principal Secretary of State for Home Affairs, Sir Robert Peel, to seek redress, and possibly even vengeance against a young man, Dr Douglass, who had insulted, galled and degraded him in the eyes of the surrounding multitude of the colony, and alleged, with characteristic recklessness on such questions, that Douglass was a notorious drunkard who had ordered convicts to be flogged to extort confessions from them. Two months later one Bradley deposed five examples of unseemly behaviour by Douglass to illustrate his drunkenness, his use of the torture of flogging to extort confessions, and his soliciting females in the streets of Sydney when in a drunken state.[40] Peel passed on the letter to Bathurst, who wrote to Brisbane for an explanation. Perhaps Marsden had forgotten that all through 1824 he had been corresponding with Barron Field, nudging him, coaxing him to tell Bathurst the truth about Dr Douglass.[41] Now, once again, this mad, fond hope he had always entertained that it was possible to fish in such waters without being caught in the world's great net, was to torment and pain him in ways he was least able to bear.

After the arrival of Thomas Hobbes Scott in May 1825 to take up his duties as Archdeacon of New South Wales, relations between the factions warmed up. With his usual flair for exposing pompous parsons Wentworth poked fun at him in the *Australian* as his 'Venerability'. Scott winced, but, after all, what else could he expect from a society where senior officials roistered each night with fornicators, liars and thieves? The very week before he was to deliver his charge to all the members of Christ's church the paper owned by Wentworth and Wardell, both notorious toss-pots, and freethinkers, was telling its readers, with its usual vulgar colonial cheek, that His Majesty's ministers of state in London had discovered the happy method of

[39] Barron Field to S. Marsden, 21 November 1824 (Marsden Papers, vol. 1, pp. 428-31); W. C. Wentworth to S. Norton, 23 May 1825 (Wentworth Papers, Legal Letter-Book); S. Marsden to D. Coates, 17 March 1825, and S. Marsden to J. Pratt, 2 July 1825 (Bonwick Transcripts, Box 53).

[40] S. Marsden to Right Honorable Robert Peel, 28 January 1824, Encl. in Report in the Case of James Ring by Sir Thomas Brisbane, Chief Justice Forbes and Archdeacon Scott, C.O. 201/163; the Marsden letter to Peel is also printed in *H.R.A.*, I. xi. 307-10; for the deposition of Bradley see Encl. in Bathurst to the Governor of New South Wales, 3 January 1825, *H.R.A.*, I. xi. 463-5.

[41] See examples in the Marsden Papers, vol. 1; see especially Barron Field to Marsden, 21 November 1824, 28 June 1824 and 27 February 1826.

exactly fitting the resources of colonies to the measure of their male friends' breeches pockets, or to the exact dimensions of ladies' reticules.[42]

Scott, nettled and flustered by such scurrilous buffoonery, began his charge to the clergy at St James's Church on 14 June with some dignified remarks on the peculiar excellence of the doctrine, discipline and ritual of the Church of England, and then railed against the infidelity and corruptness in the public press of New South Wales. He was pleased to announce that as a counter to the forces of anarchy and moral slackness, the church was to receive large areas of land in both New South Wales and Van Diemen's Land to provide the wealth for its divine mission of social order and salvation. Again, the *Australian* admonished him for inveighing against the great bulwark of British civil and religious liberties—the freedom of the press, and cracked a joke at his expense. Why, they asked, should a settler pay in advance by temporal losses of land here for his spiritual comfort hereafter? To Scott it was no laughing matter that altar and throne were mocked each week in the paper owned by Wentworth and Wardell to titillate the malice and envy of the convicts and other low-born persons. He decided to set up house in Parramatta, where he could enjoy the society of the ancient nobility of New South Wales far from the vulgar madding crowd in Sydney.

Marsden was delighted. He found Scott was a very friendly man, and a true liberal on all questions of religion. Besides, by July, he had other reasons for cultivating the friendship of his 'Venerability', the Archdeacon, as in that month it was announced that there was to be an inquiry into the allegations of drunkenness against Douglass, the deposition of Bradley, and the use of flogging by Douglass to extract confessions from convicts, before the Governor, Sir Thomas Brisbane, the Chief Justice, Francis Forbes, and the Archdeacon, Thomas Hobbes Scott. The tongues of Sydney and Parramatta were beginning to wag. Brisbane, it was said, was a vain star-gazer and God-botherer, and did not count. Forbes, according to the gossips, tossed pots and swapped bawdy jokes with Wentworth, and Scott was in the bag, it was said, for the Macarthur faction. Excitement ran high, if only because the subjects of the inquiry had always exercised a fatal fascination for mankind—drunkenness, lechery, and cruelty by men in high places.[43]

Marsden once again faced his enemies with all his incurable optimism. That kind Providence, he believed, which had always watched over him would continue to do so. Besides, Barron Field, he believed, had had the ear of my lord Bathurst all through the discussions about that drunken seducer, Dr Douglass, in London. Vain hope, for my lord Bathurst had already decided not to give any additional trust or authority to Mr Marsden, as he considered him to be a very turbulent priest, with somewhat more than malignancy in his character to allow him ever to be quiet, or let other persons be so.

Brisbane, too, approached the inquiry with something less of his usual sublime confidence. To his mortification he had just heard that far away in London my lord Bathurst had passed judgment on him too. My lord Bathurst,

[42] *Australian*, 16 June 1825; *Gleaner*, 19 April 1827.
[43] *Australian*, 16 June 1825; Bathurst to the Governor of New South Wales, 3 January 1825, H.R.A., I. xi. 462-3.

having come to the conclusion that Brisbane was occupying himself too much with the stars and leaving worldly affairs to his Colonial Secretary, had decided that Brisbane, honourable and excellent man that he was, nevertheless was very unfit to be governor of a colony, and had instructed Horton at the Colonial Office to draft a very short letter of recall, saying: 'that it has been expedient to relieve your Excellency and to appoint a Successor'. So Brisbane, never believing that he would one day be tried in that balance and found wanting, opened a despatch from London and read those fatal words: 'I am commanded by the King to signify to you that His Majesty is pleased to relieve you from the exercise of the Government of New South Wales'. Goulburn was recalled in a despatch written on the same day.

The three commissioners began by asking Marsden to substantiate the charge that Douglass had sentenced convicts to be flogged to extort a confession. Marsden replied blandly that he was not the accuser of Douglass, nor did he ever wish to be. That was on 15 July. The very same day he told them by letter that he had in the meantime recalled a conversation in a public street on the matter in question, and it was just possible he had mentioned it to to my lord Bathurst. The court of inquiry then pressed him for proof. By 30 July Marsden told them he was ready to produce proof—but they ruled they were not instructed to inquire into that case. So on 11 August they sent off their findings to London: exonerating Douglass from the charge of drunkenness, rejecting the charges made by Bradley in his deposition, and dismissing the charges of the use of flogging to extract confessions from convicts. Brisbane had no hesitation in confirming Douglass in his position as Clerk of the Council.[44]

All up and down Sydney town and Parramatta the mockers and the malicious whooped for joy when the news leaked out that Marsden, the flogging parson and the Mahomet of Botany Bay, was also a brazen liar. Marsden tried to console himself with the quibble that the court had not exonerated Douglass, but had merely found the charge not proven. But, deep down, it was quite clear what had happened: once again he had placed his trust in man, and man had let him down. As in all the crises of his life, he looked to holy scripture for an explanation of this patent miscarriage of justice. He found it in the story of John the Baptist. 'I believe', he wrote to Horton in London, 'that spirit by which Herod and Herodias were governed was never more manifest than in these settlements'. But then, what else could he expect from his fellow human beings, but that just as in earlier times, the rulers of this world had cut off the head of John the Baptist, so here they were after his head. As ever, the divine promises were his comfort, and God would, he was sure, make all things good for them that loved him—Or was he so sure? Would it not be wise to put down on paper his case against his enemies, against all those men who had slandered him, against Macquarie, Wentworth and Douglass, so that posterity might be able to judge his motives and his

[44] S. Marsden to J. Pratt, Parramatta, 2 July 1825 (Marsden Papers, vol. 1); W.M. to Sir Thomas Brisbane, 3 January 1825 (Brisbane Papers, Box 1); Bathurst to Wilmot Horton, Cirencester, 20 December 1824 (Letters of Lord Bathurst, MS. in M.L.); Bathurst to Brisbane, 28 December 1824, *H.R.A.*, I. xi. 429; Brisbane, Forbes and Scott to Bathurst, 11 August 1825 and Enclosures, ibid., 782-807.

behaviour as a preparation, or an overture, as it were, to that day he clung to with more desperation when the judge of all the Earth would do right to all God's faithful children?[45]

By contrast Brisbane conducted himself with a becoming dignity. He cordially submitted to the recall if thereby the public interest should be benefited, as he had the interests of the country much at heart. He held out to Goulburn a forgiving hand which, to his delight, was warmly received, for with that eye as ever on the heavenly prize, and much loving kindness in his heart, Brisbane, unlike Marsden, found it easy to heed the divine command that men should agree with their adversaries quickly. He spoke with pride of his achievements in the colony, of his astronomical observations of that virgin sky, and his removing the censorship of the press. He gloried in having given the colony this inestimable privilege, and asked, with unwanted prescience, whether his successor would be bold enough to remove that palladium. For he had the vain man's concern for historical significance and spiritual grandeur. It was outside his range to see that the getters and spenders, the men concerned with things as they are, and not as they look at the end of a telescope, or *sub specie aeternitatis*, those concerned with the government of men rather than their salvation, were already telling the men in black that freedom of the press was a silly measure in a convict colony. To have freedom of the press in a vast penitentiary, it was said, was like allowing a radical newspaper in Newgate.[46]

In the colony of New South Wales the opponents of the exclusives were hailing him as their hero. The *Australian* wrote on 20 October that the days when the Nimrods of the colony dominated convicts, emancipists, and free men alike, and trampled on men's rights, and used the cat-o'-nine-tails to cow people into obedience were drawing to a close. Now, thanks to Brisbane, New South Wales was no longer a penal settlement: a British public inhabited the territory, and enjoyed a free press.[47] The following day people flocked to the Court House to consider the propriety of addressing the Governor on his approaching departure. Some spoke with the voice of moderation, but Wentworth, sensing the chance to settle some scores with his arch enemies, shouted that now was their chance to put an end to those snug coteries, and annihilate the yellow snakes of the colony, and deprive them of their venom and their fangs. He urged them to include in the address a reference to the urgent necessity of the immediate establishment in the colony in all their plenitude of those two principles of the British constitution, trial by jury and taxation by representation. This was carried triumphantly.[48]

The exclusives were not discouraged. They decided to forward their own reply to the wild ideas of Wentworth and the drunken rabble who had

[45] S. Marsden to W. Horton, Parramatta, 25 September 1825, C.O. 201/169; for the decision to put pen to paper see S. Marsden to D. Coates, Parramatta, 27 September 1825 (Marsden Papers, vol. 2) and S. Marsden, *Statement, including a correspondence between the Commissioners of the Court of Enquiry, and the Rev. Samuel Marsden* (Sydney, 1828).

[46] Brisbane to Bathurst, 15 May 1825, *H.R.A.*, I. xi. 589; Brisbane to Mr Crawfurd, 13 May 1825 (Brisbane Papers, Box 3); Barron Field to S. Marsden, 13 March 1827 (Marsden Papers, vol. 1, pp. 460-3).

[47] *Australian*, 20 October 1825.   [48] *Australian*, 27 October 1825.

shouted themselves hoarse applauding the Wentworth malice. For themselves they were alarmed lest a licentious pro-convict press should disseminate doctrines which tended to inflame the worst passions of the lower orders, and incite a spirit of animosity towards the upper classes. They suggested the creation of an executive council, an increase in the number nominated to the Legislative Council, and an extension of trial by jury, which would not necessarily exclude all ex-convicts.[49]

To help my lord Bathurst make up his mind on the pro-convict group Macarthur wrote down some short character sketches of his opponents. The Wentworths were too well-known to require description; Dr Bland had agreed simply to avoid offending his patients; Solomon Solomons was a Jew publican, who had been deprived of his licence for keeping a disorderly house. The others were renegade Jews, shopkeepers, American adventurers, and a man who had married a convict woman—the notorious Tambourine Sal who had once made a living singing and dancing at country wakes and fairs.[50]

In the meantime, all those who believed that Brisbane had made many a widow's heart dance for joy, had befriended the orphans, and succoured the distressed, and all those who believed that a broken-down oligarchical faction who worshipped wool freight, and dollars, could not continue for long to occupy the centre of the stage in New South Wales, gathered in strength on 1 December 1825 at Sydney Cove to farewell Brisbane and his family who were about to sail out on to the high seas to London. They were not to know that seven months earlier John Macarthur junior had sat down on a large sofa at the University Club in London with Wilmot Horton, and discussed the vanity of Brisbane and the weakness of his character. They were not to know that the men in high places in the Colonial Office were talking the language of the ancient nobility of New South Wales. They were not to know that they had decided in future only to transport those convicts who were capable of labour, and certainly not those who would swell the number of republicans, or the amount of immorality in the towns. They were not to know either, as they called out over the water their fond farewells to Brisbane, that by their own madness and folly they would push his successor into the arms of the gentry of New South Wales.[51]

[49] The Address of the Landed Proprietors, Merchants, and other Free Inhabitants of New South Wales to the Right Honourable Earl Bathurst, Sydney, December 1825, Encl. in John Macarthur jr to W. Horton, 11 July 1826, C.O. 201/179.

[50] John Macarthur sr, Names of Persons who voted the address to the Governor at the Meeting held in Sydney, 21 October 1825, Names of Party who gave the Governor a public dinner and of the Guests invited, Parramatta, 7 November 1825, Encl. in John Macarthur jr to W. Horton, 11 July 1826, C.O. 201/179.

[51] *Australian*, 1 and 8 December 1825; *Sydney Gazette*, 28 November and 1 December 1825; John Macarthur jr to John Macarthur, 12 Suffolk Street, London, begun on 12 April and continued in May 1825 (Macarthur Papers, vol. 15, pp. 419-21).

4

THE NATIVE SON OFFENDS GROSSLY

ON THE MORNING of 20 December 1825 a procession led by Francis Forbes in the full robes of the Chief Justice of New South Wales, followed by the Archdeacon in full canonical dress and then the new Governor, Lieutenant-General Ralph Darling, reached Government House in Sydney. The band of the 40th Regiment then struck up the tune: 'See the conquering hero comes'. Hope and confidence were in the very air men breathed that morning. Upon a glimpse of His Excellency's person satisfaction lit up every countenance. For His Excellency had a dignity of bearing, a composure of the face which betrayed an inner tranquillity of mind, and a firmness which would not become overbearing in time of stress. He had too a noble brow which was becoming to the austere features of the man.

John Macarthur was delighted to meet such a sensible and dignified man who, he was sure, would promote the sales of wool and so make everything very smooth. The Reverend Samuel Marsden rejoiced in the parsonage at Parramatta, detecting, as ever, the hand of a benevolent providence in the auspicious choice of the General. Chief Justice Forbes had his own reasons for being pleased. Darling was one of those cautious, reflecting men whom the Chief Justice admired. Besides, over the first few weeks Darling lived with Forbes, and turned to him for comfort and counsel, and Forbes was pleased to find that his counsels carried a greater weight than those of any body of persons. But Mrs Forbes, who saw the General at close range during those early days in Sydney, found him somewhat forbidding in appearance. His manner, too, she found inclined to be overbearing, and he seemed, even at their first meeting, to be very dictatorial. Was the man, perhaps, a martinet? So while her husband was enjoying to the full that puff to his vanity of being the chief counsellor to the Captain-General and Governor-in-Chief of the colony of New South Wales and its dependent territories, she sensed a coldness of the heart beneath the correct, off-putting exterior. One other man who met Darling a year or so later wrote down his impressions. 'The Governor appeared to me', he wrote in his diary, 'a cold, stiff, sickly military person. He had none of the frankness and ease of a soldier, and I absolutely froze in his presence'.

From far away in England too, John Macarthur junior had written to his father to warn him that Darling's manners were so cold and repulsive that it would be difficult to become intimate with him. But, he added, he had one great merit: he would entertain great jealousy towards the convict party. On this subject, happily, the General had considerable anxiety, for knowing that

Wentworth might well be troublesome, he had wondered in London whether he would have the power to silence him. Thank God, John Macarthur junior added, Darling was a soldier, with a sense of the importance of obedience, and so would carry out orders from London. As for Wentworth, they should let him alone as the man was certain sooner or later to offend grossly. He added, it might be a good idea if his father presented His Excellency with a grey horse.[1]

At the swearing-in ceremony that December Darling expressed his hope that it would be possible to see justice impartially administered to all. His object, he said, was to combine the purposes of a penal colony with the welfare of the free classes of the inhabitants. These two aims, he believed, were neither inconsistent nor impracticable. In his very first proclamation on 20 December he urged all and sundry to display a spirit of concord.[2] He was then in his fiftieth year. Born in 1775 the son of an army officer, he had followed his father's footsteps, and served with both heroism and distinction at Corunna where he and his fellow officers left Sir John Moore alone with his glory. In 1819, at a loss like other professional soldiers in days of peace for suitable employment, he had accepted an appointment as commander of the troops in the colony of Mauritius where, while acting as Governor, he had defended the slaves on the sugar plantations against all the bluster and threats of the owners. For this he caught the eye of the men in the Colonial Office who offered him in 1824 the position of Governor of New South Wales and Van Diemen's Land with the promotion to the rank of Lieutenant-General. They thought they had the right man for the job, an honourable man who possessed a sound and just understanding, but with little reach of thought or variety of knowledge. They saw him as a man who, memorably stiff though he was in his manners, and a great formalist in civil business, as well as a perfect martinet in military affairs, would nevertheless do what he was told, and not take sides. They saw him as a man who would stand firm when the world rocked. They, indeed, had a high regard for a man who was concerned with the efficient working of things as they were, and who was not bothered by any abstract thoughts or moral twinges on how things might or should be.[3]

By contrast his wife was a woman of parts. Eliza Darling was the daughter of Ann Dumaresq, the widow of an army officer who had died during the Napoleonic Wars in March of 1804, leaving her, her three sons, Henry, William and Edward, and two daughters, Eliza and Marianne, to lament his connubial virtues, his paternal tenderness and affection. Her mother was a

[1] Based on *Sydney Gazette*, 22 December 1825; *Australian*, 22 December 1825; John Macarthur to Elizabeth Macarthur, Sydney, [1825] (Macarthur Papers, vol. 2, pp. 368 and 460-3); F. Forbes to W. Horton, 7 March 1826, C.O. 201/178; Lady Forbes, Sydney Society in Crown Colony Days, ed. by G. Forbes (being the personal reminiscences of the late Lady Forbes, typescript in M.L.); J. Dowling, Journal, 25 February 1828 (MS. in M.L.); John Macarthur jr to John Macarthur sr, 12 June 1825 (Macarthur Papers, vol. 15, pp. 297-9); *Sydney Gazette*, 5 January 1826.

[2] Darling to Hay, 10 December 1825, *H.R.A.*, I. xii. 82-3; *Sydney Gazette*, 26 December 1825.

[3] J. Stephen to G. Arthur, 4 January 1825 (Papers of Sir George Arthur, vol. 4, Correspondence with James Stephen); Charles Wolfe, 'The Burial of Sir John Moore after Corunna', in A. Quiller-Couch, *The Oxford Book of English Verse* (Oxford, 1939), pp. 712-13; see also A. Bryant, *The Age of Elegance 1812-1822* (London, 1950), ch. 1; *Sydney Gazette*, 16 January 1826; E. Riley, Journal of a Voyage to New South Wales with Saxon Sheep (MS. in M.L.).

woman of great strength, and strong opinions. She never wearied of telling the children to keep God's injunctions, to use the talents God had given them, and never become a mountain of misery, and then they would all become 'ripe for glory' as she put it. Eliza inherited the strength, industry, and religious zeal of the mother. As a young girl in 1815 she had written a long story called *Lascelles* in which a moral of an improving kind was drawn for the reader. She had also written verse in which she wagged a censorious disapproving finger at pleasure-seekers:

> What! shoot little birds, with a great, long, big gun,
> Poor dear little things! And they say, it's all 'fun'.

When later a lady asked her to account for the scarlet fever being brought into her family, Eliza Darling recommended her to repeat each day the words: 'Lord we are vile—humbled in dust we fall. Thou hast not dealt with us, as we must own we have deserved'. Her great hope, which she shared with her mother and her brothers, was that after death she and all those whom she had loved would join the spirits of just men made perfect, and sit down with Abraham, Isaac and Jacob in the kingdom of heaven. Like her mother she had married an army officer, Ralph Darling, but in that close family he seemed to always remain the eternal outsider: mother and daughter wrote of him always as the general, and never with that deep affection with which they addressed each other and their God.[4]

The General was composed of quite different clay. It was characteristic of the man that on the day he took the oaths of office he spoke not the language of any political party, nor the language of either the moral improver or the aspirant for a seat with Abraham, Isaac and Jacob, but rather the language of the man whose own passion in life was administration. He announced the members of the Legislative Council would be the Governor, the Lieutenant-Governor, W. Stewart, the Chief Justice, F. Forbes, the Archdeacon, T. H. Scott, the Colonial Secretary, A. McLeay, J. Macarthur, R. Campbell and C. Throsby. He also announced the creation of an executive council. The *Sydney Gazette* was delighted. Here at last was a cabinet for Australia which illustrated the English genius of giving the Governor the benefit of collective wisdom without weakening his power which must, they insisted, remain strong in a predominantly convict society. When Darling proceeded to apply a new broom to the unwieldy administration in New South Wales the *Sydney Gazette* once again wrote with enthusiasm on the spirited and energetic way in which the new government was comporting itself.[5]

But Robert Howe, the editor of the *Sydney Gazette*, with an eye for heaven, and another for hints on how not to offend the men in high places, had no eye left for the great storm that was brewing in the colony that summer. Two months earlier, on 27 November 1825, the agent of the Australian Agricul-

---

[4] Based on material in the Dumaresq Papers; see especially the copy of the memorial plaque to Lieutenant-Colonel Dumaresq, Worcester Cathedral; see also the letters of Ann Dumaresq to Henry and Sophia Dumaresq and Eliza Darling 1823-32; Eliza Darling to Edward Dumaresq, 20 August 1827.

[5] *Sydney Gazette*, 5 and 9 January 1826; *Monitor*, 19 April 1826.

tural Company, R. Dawson, had arrived in Sydney with sheep, cattle and choice plants, and servants to select land for the company. That day the servants told him that had they known what New South Wales would be like they would never have left their homes. As long ago as July of 1824 my lord Bathurst had informed Brisbane that a company had been formed with a view to the purposes of agriculture generally, but more particularly for the rearing of flocks of sheep of the purest and finest breed. He had written of the advantages to New South Wales of the impact of huge capital and agricultural skill. He had told Brisbane that the plan of the company corresponded almost exactly with the recommendation by Mr Commissioner Bigge for the future advancement of agriculture in the colony. He added that the number of convicts employed by the company would tend to decrease most materially the great expenditure which their maintenance annually caused to the public.

Similar points were made in the preamble to the Act for granting certain powers and authorities to a company to be called the Australian Agricultural Company which had been passed in June of 1824. Divers waste lands in the colony, it was said, might be cultivated to advantage if sufficient capital were available. There were a number of convicts at present maintained at the public expense who might be employed in the cultivation of such lands. Under the terms of the charter issued by Bathurst in November the company was to receive large areas of land in New South Wales, in return for its investment of £1,000,000 of capital.

In October of 1824 the principals of the company in Sydney, James Macarthur, James Bowman and Hannibal Macarthur, had sent a circular to the prominent citizens such as John Macarthur, Francis Forbes, John Piper, and the Reverend Samuel Marsden inviting them to take shares in the company as evidence of their patriotic exertions, as well as their hopes for material gain. A. Berry, J. T. Campbell, R. Campbell, F. Forbes, S. Marsden, John Macarthur, H. Macarthur, C. Throsby, J. Oxley, Archdeacon Scott, and E. Wollstonecraft, to mention some of the public figures of the day, bought shares.[6]

From the day of the arrival of Dawson in the colony with his menservants, his sheep, his oxen, and his asses, the *Australian* cast a disapproving eye over the whole venture. Ministers, they wrote, on 18 November, must have been hoodwinked or duped by artful men. The company, they said, would raise up a monopoly. A week later they opened up on the Macarthur interest in the company—It was, they said, a case of 'my son, my son-in-law, or my nephew's

[6] *Sydney Gazette*, 12 and 16 January 1826; for the text of the address and the reply to Darling on 19 January 1826 see the two Enclosures in Darling to Bathurst, 1 February 1826, *H.R.A.*, I. xii. 144-8; R. Dawson, *The Present State of Australia* (London, 1830); Bathurst to Brisbane, 13 July 1824, *H.R.A.*, I. xi. 305-6; An Act for granting certain Powers and Authorities to a Company to be incorporated by Charter, to be called 'The Australian Agricultural Company' 5 Geo. IV, c.86, 21 June 1824, *Statutes at Large*, vol. 9; Charter of Incorporation for the Australian Agricultural Company 1 November 1824, *H.R.A.*, I. xi. 563-8; James Macarthur, James Bowman, and H. H. Macarthur to prominent citizens of New South Wales, 30 October 1824 (Correspondence of the Australian Agricultural Company 30 October 1824–11 April 1826, Papers of the Australian Agricultural Company, Archives of The Australian National University, Canberra); Circular letter to the shareholders, 10 June 1825, ibid.; Brian Fitzpatrick, *British Imperialism and Australia 1783-1833* (London, 1939), p. 248.

brother-in-law . . . so snug a corner in which to form family contacts'. It would enable, they said, the Macarthurs to bring their sheep to a very good market.

Then just as Dawson set out from Sydney to select a suitable site for the company near Port Stephens, only to find the captain of his ship, one Captain Charlton, attempting to molest one of his maidservants, Miss Elizabeth Barnes,[7] Robert Howe, displaying that inadequate awareness of the seekers after righteousness for the ways of the mischievous, urged the native youths to attend a meeting at the Court House at Sydney on 12 January of 1826 to draft an address of welcome to Darling, as they and their future were likely to be intimately involved in the proceedings.[8]

But on that day the spirit of concord was rudely shattered. Wentworth, sensing an opportunity to use the native-born in his own vendetta against the Macarthurs, reminded them that not they but the free immigrants were getting their 'filthy paws' on all the good land in the colony. The solution to this state of affairs was obvious, he told them. They must put down the faction which was keeping them in a state of vassalage. Nothing short of a legislative assembly and unlimited trial by jury would be sufficient for the present wants of the colony or would in fact satisfy the wants of the colonists.

At that point prudent men might have stopped. But Wentworth, tempted to satisfy the passions he had aroused in the crowd by feeding them with something from the dark side of his own heart, went on to savage the Australian Agricultural Company—not objecting to the concentration of wealth in the hands of the few, for he was careful never to be guilty of any giddy, radical nonsense about the distribution of wealth. Then, swept on to greater recklessness by the drunken shouts of approval his superb oratory had aroused, he let slip some vulgar abuse about Darling for his unpopularity in Mauritius. The *Sydney Gazette* was prepared to excuse him for this offence. Everyone, they wrote, who was acquainted with the veneration that the 'Australian Counsellor' naturally entertained for his country, would make allowance for his warmth of expression. But for Darling this was the first evidence of the truth of the young John Macarthur's warning that as a demagogue at the head of the convict party, Wentworth was certain to offend grossly. So when Darling received the address of the delegates from the meeting of 12 January, he explained to them with a characteristic frosty formality and dignity of bearing he always presented to the outside world, that as he had not as yet had the opportunity to form an opinion on the points made, he must abstain from making any observations in reply. He could only assure them that he would put His Majesty's ministers in possession of the sentiments, and they would doubtless give every due consideration to the address.[9]

By chance that month another man had arrived in Sydney who seemed destined both by his own past and the elements in him to goad Wentworth to further displays of vulgar abuse of the administration of Governor Darling. In

[7] *Australian*, 18 and 25 November 1825; T. L. Harrington to A. McLeay, 27 March 1826 (Correspondence of the Australian Agricultural Company, 30 October 1824–11 April 1826, Papers of the Australian Agricultural Company).

[8] *Sydney Gazette*, 12 January 1826.

[9] *Australian*, 26 January 1826; Darling to Hay, 6 March 1826, *H.R.A.*, I. xii. 210-11.

January Alexander McLeay had arrived to take over from Goulburn the office of Colonial Secretary. McLeay was then an elderly gentleman of fifty-eight years of age, who had been for many years head clerk in the Transport Board in London, from which he had retired on a pension of £750 a year to take up more thoroughly his great passion for zoology. In Wentworth's eyes he was a pensioner who had exploited 'clerk influence' in the Colonial Office to get what he, Wentworth, had so far failed to achieve— namely, a public office in New South Wales. McLeay was yet another example of using the resources of colonies to fill the breeches pockets of the friends of ministers. But there were other elements in McLeay to excite Wentworth's great gifts for mockery and cruelty. McLeay was a Scot with the values of an English Tory, a man with the pretensions and aspirations of the gentry, and the appearance of a decent shopkeeper of a Scottish Royal Burg. His carriage was ungentlemanly and discouraging. He uttered the Tory sentiments on throne and altar in a broad Scots dialect. Nature, too, had left him with two marks to attract the traffickers in human savagery: he was bald-headed; he also had that woman's gentle face, that suggestion of being created for a woman, till nature, as she wrought him fell a-doting. He had too about his very being that indefinable something which incited the madness in the blood of a Wentworth. With it there was also that impotence to stand up to the men with the Wentworth hungers in their hearts. In a sense it was unnecessary for my lord Bathurst to tell McLeay that he was to have no pretension to control the judgment or direct the decisions of the Governor in any particular case, for McLeay was a server, a clerk to the men in high places, and a man who understood Darling's conception of authority, as well as his values.[10]

As evidence of what to expect from the convict party just on one hundred sat down to dinner at Mrs Hill's Hyde Park tavern on 26 January to celebrate the anniversary of the foundation of the colony, with Wentworth once again in the chair, and Redfern assisting him. Once again they drank the toasts so close to the interests of Wentworth's heart. They toasted their heroes Phillip and Macquarie; they toasted trial by jury, and a house of assembly, a toast which Wentworth did not let pass without some jokes about the Legislative Council running amok—as though the frosty Darling, the clerk-like McLeay, or the pompous Forbes would succumb to the madness in the hearts of other men. Then they toasted the currency lads and lasses just as the drinks had ripened them to raise their glasses and shout: 'Hail to Australia'. Several of them remained over their cups to an early hour in the morning, till they dispersed with all the confidence of men buoyed up with the delusion that all that stood between them and their dreams of landed wealth and the appropriate political institutions to serve such appetites, was that pompous 'Venerability', the Archdeacon, or that efficient clerk, McLeay, or that madman, John Macarthur.[11]

10 For some comments on A. McLeay by his contemporaries see J. Stephen to G. Arthur, 4 January 1825, and 9 October 1826 (Papers of Sir George Arthur, vol. 4, Correspondence with James Stephen); Journal of James Dowling 1827-8 (ms. in m.l.); for the arrival of McLeay see *Sydney Gazette*, January 1826 *passim*; for the appointment of McLeay see Bathurst to Darling, 14 July 1825, *H.R.A.*, I. xii. 18-19.
11 *Sydney Gazette*, 28 January 1826.

THOMAS BRISBANE

Portrait by Robert Frain, engraved by Frederick Bromley
From a print in the Public Library of New South Wales

RALPH DARLING

Portrait by J. Linnell, engraved by J. Richardson Jackson
From a print in the Public Library of New South Wales

Scott, with his usual fear of the mob, asked Darling to protect him against the impertinent and irritating articles in the *Australian*. Darling refused, because the articles had not reflected on Scott's conduct as a member of the government. John Macarthur called at Government House to appeal for protection against the slanders on his family in the *Sydney Gazette*. Darling refused. Macarthur boasted that he would destroy Howe, just as he had crushed every man who ever dared to thwart his will. Darling took the opportunity to offer some worldly wisdom to Macarthur, telling him that the fruits of past surrenders to the passion to destroy opponents had cheated him of that position at the head of society which his talents and achievements would have otherwise earned. But no man could offer advice to Macarthur on how to live in love and charity with all men. He retired to his estate: he stayed away from the Legislative Council: he began to talk of visiting his native land to tell them the truth about the convict party, and their sham talk about trial by jury and a house of assembly: he began to talk of a visit to China, or to South America to improve the breed of asses in the colony. He began to spend more and more of his time at home, brooding over plans to destroy his enemies, chattering away like a wayward child. Some laughed: some with more charity began to wonder why a man of such gifts had brought himself to destruction. With that courage which she always displayed in the face of adversity, his wife turned more and more to the Mighty Ruler of the universe to give her strength to endure the last days.[12]

At the same time the Reverend Samuel Marsden had taken up the pen to reply to the scandalous reproach of his enemies that for years a barbarian had presided at the head of the church in New South Wales. He had finished his pamphlet, *An Answer to certain calumnies in the late Governor Macquarie's pamphlet, and the third edition of Mr. Wentworth's Account of Australasia*, and had chosen London as the centre in which to publish it. In it he wrote of his motives for opposing Macquarie's measures to bring bond and free down to one common level, contrary to those arrangements of nature which reflected so correctly the divine plan. He defended himself against the charge of lust for filthy material gain: he had entered a country which was in a state of nature, and was obliged to plant and sow, or starve. After all, he had only copied the example of St Paul, who had administered to his own wants in a cultivated nation, while he, Marsden, had used his own hands to minister to his wants in an uncultivated one. He had been accused of severity as a magistrate. He was not a severe magistrate: he was a strict magistrate because strictness alone, he had discovered, could so operate on the mind of a delinquent as to rescue him from a state of vice and profligacy. Strictness was the only answer to human depravity. He had been accused of trafficking in spirits by Mr Wentworth when he published that false, scandalous, and malicious libel upon his character. That charge he easily disproved. He had been further accused of throwing cold water on the institution for the education and civiliza-

[12] *Australian*, 17 June 1826; *Sydney Gazette*, March and April 1826 *passim*; Darling to Hay, 1 May 1826, *H.R.A.*, I. xii. 253-7; John Macarthur to J. D. Lang, 1 May 1826 (Lang Papers, vol. 6); Darling to Hay, 2 September 1826, *H.R.A.*, I. xii. 522-4; Elizabeth Macarthur to Eliza Kingdon, March 1827 (Macarthur Papers, vol. 12, p. 63).

F

tion of the aborigines, and of refusing to supply the Sunday School at Parramatta with Bibles. He could only reply with the words used by over three hundred people when they presented him with an address: your sanctity, philanthropy, and disinterested character, they had written, would ever remain an example to future ministers. When the Reverend Samuel Marsden went down to the temple to pray he went as the Pharisee who thanked his God he was not as other men.[13]

Scott, too, was bothered by living in a colony whose population, he had found, was composed of the worst and most malignant convicts and of free people who were little better. The editor of the *Sydney Gazette* which enjoyed the confidence of the government was the most infamous of a bad lot as he pretended religion when everyone knew he had lived a life of profligacy and robbed his own father.[14] John Macarthur, in lucid moments between the mad fantasies which were providing more and more perverse delight for him and an undying anguish for his wife, cast a cold eye on the unprincipled, profligate characters who roistered every night in the rooms of Mr Wentworth.[15] He had reason to be confident that autumn and winter, as the society for which he had dreamed his great dream was beginning to take shape before his eyes.

Darling had directed that free men should replace convict clerks in the government service. Under an Act of the Legislative Council to furnish further means of supplying settlers with servants and labourers for their farms, five hundred convicts were removed from the penal settlement at Port Macquarie and offered for assignment to the settlers.[16] In August the executive council agreed that it was inexpedient in any view of the case even to raise the question whether persons who had been convicted of felony or other infamous crimes and transported here should be eligible to serve as jurors in cases before the Supreme Court—that for such jurors property in land or stock to a considerable extent should become the criterion.[17]

At the same time Darling accepted the recommendations of Scott on how to raise the children of the convicts from barbarism to civilization. Most of them instead of attending school were being instructed by their parents in the vices of thieving and drunkenness. From lack of schoolmasters and clergymen they went through the cycle of birth, mating and death ignorant alike of the divine commands, and of their duties to God and man. With more parsons and teachers the lower orders would live soberly and quietly, and the men of talent would be trained to serve their Maker either in church or state.[18]

[13] S. Marsden, *An Answer to certain calumnies in the late Governor Macquarie's pamphlet, and the third edition of Mr Wentworth's Account of Australasia* (London, 1826); *Australian*, 10 October 1826.

[14] T. H. Scott to the Reverend A. Hamilton, 27 January 1827 (Extracts from the S.P.G. records, typescript in M.L.).

[15] John Macarthur to John Macarthur jr, 12 September 1826 (Macarthur Papers, vol. 3, p. 134b).

[16] Darling to Bathurst, 20 July 1826, *H.R.A.*, I. xii. 366-7; Darling to Bathurst, 31 August 1826, ibid., 513-14; Darling to Bathurst, 1 September 1826, ibid., 515-16.

[17] Extract from Minute no. 17 of the Proceedings of the Executive Council, 15 August 1826, Encl. in Darling to Bathurst, 2 September 1826, *H.R.A.*, I. xii. 519.

[18] Report on the Church and School Establishments by T. H. Scott, 1 May 1826, Encl. in Darling to Bathurst, 23 May 1826, *H.R.A.*, I. xii. 309-16.

A year earlier, fearful lest the system of granting land might contribute to an age of barbarism in New South Wales, my lord Bathurst in January of 1825 had told Brisbane of the injury to society when land remained in a barren state from either the lack of capital or a disinclination to employ it. The settlements of the richer or more enterprising colonists became separated from each other by intervening tracts of the original wilderness. It must be remembered, said my lord Bathurst, that it was anomalous for ex-convicts to become landowners. What was needed were settlers who either possessed or had the command of capital. There were, he believed, two classes who proposed to become cultivators of the soil. There were those who were capable of purchasing extensive tracts of waste land, and there were those who needed the bounty of the Crown to be placed in possession of land. To expedite the sale of land to persons of the first class, my lord Bathurst invited Brisbane to appoint three commissioners, of whom the Surveyor-General was to be one, to report on how the land of the colony should be divided into counties, hundreds and boroughs for the purpose of such sale.

By May of 1825 Oxley, the Surveyor-General, had submitted his report. But it was not until September the following year that Darling, after consulting the members of his executive council, was ready to publish the new regulations for the granting and purchasing of land. Applicants who had satisfied the Governor of their character and respectability would receive grants at the rate of one square mile for every £500 of capital invested, the maximum grant to be 2,560 acres. Persons wishing to obtain more could purchase up to 9,900 acres by tender. To confine settlement within an area convenient for administrative and financial purposes, such grants and purchases were to be held within a boundary bounded to the north by a line from Cape Hawke due west to Wellington Valley, then due south to the Lachlan River, thence due east to Campbell River, and then south-east to the latitude of Bateman's Bay which was to form the southern boundary.[19] With an unerring eye for the drift of events the *Australian* groaned at the ineptitude and folly of their rulers in London, who, they argued, had taken one further step to prevent a class of small proprietors from coming into existence, and would favour the rich land monopolists.[20]

Scott, a bachelor, a prey to those fears and phantoms which torment the minds of the lonely, thought he heard in the roars of protest from the native-born and the convict party the barrackers for a terror in Sydney, and warned Darling the day might come when blood would flow in the streets of Sydney. Saxe Bannister, the Attorney-General, was suffering too from a strange nightmare. He kept whispering to Darling in the corridors of Government House that the aborigines were assembling to overthrow white domination in New South Wales. But Darling, with iron control, told them both not to be silly: there was, he assured them, no great convulsion at hand in Australia.[21]

[19] Bathurst to Brisbane, 1 January 1825, *H.R.A.*, I. xi. 434-44; Brisbane to Bathurst and the enclosed letter of J. Oxley to Major Ovens, 31 July 1825, ibid., 691-7; for the text of these regulations see *Sydney Gazette*, 6 September 1826.
[20] *Australian*, 13 September 1826.
[21] Darling to Hay, 1 May 1826, *H.R.A.*, I. xii. 256-7; Darling to Hay, 25 July 1826, ibid., 445-6; Darling to Hay, 2 September 1826, ibid., 522-4.

That August his own indomitable confidence began to snap. In that month he wrote to the Catholic chaplain, Father Therry, to ask if it was true that he had married Protestants according to the rites of the Church of Rome after the Protestant chaplains had refused. Therry replied in an extremely offensive and insulting letter. So Darling suspended him as a chaplain. Then doubts and fears began to assail him. What if Therry began to poison the minds of those priest-ridden, ignorant, and bigoted Irish convicts against government? Would it not be prudent for government in England to send an English priest who might at least rescue the Irish Catholics from dangerous political delusions even if he could not be expected to cleanse their minds of their vulgar and degrading superstition? Would inflammatory language in the popular press incite the lower orders to tumult and sedition? Was it prudent in a convict colony to allow the editor of the *Monitor*, E. S. Hall, to describe the large landowners of New South Wales as monsters of cruelty, and the magistrates as men who had excited horror and disgust all over the world?[22]

Hall was the pot-house companion of all the turbulent and disaffected. He had come to the colony on 10 October 1811 as a lay missionary, a denouncer of human depravity who trafficked in all those extravagances of the malicious and the cruel. During the governorship of the late Major-General Macquarie Hall had turned from things spiritual and begun to covet the prizes of land and wealth with the same zeal with which he had lifted his eyes up to heaven. He had taken up land at Bringelly but had failed as a settler and then moved to Sydney town where he took up work with the Bank of New South Wales and later with the merchants Jones & Riley. On 19 May 1826 he published the first issue of the *Monitor*. In this paper he announced only the language of sense and moderation would be permitted to secure a place in his columns.[23] The disappointment over land, however, soon lent a rancour and a bite to his words. At all previous public performances he had spoken with such vituperation and slander against the exclusives that the *Sydney Gazette* had omitted his speeches.

Now he had his own columns in which to urge the native-born not to sit idly by while the exclusives, the Australian Agricultural Company, those well-known friends of ministers in London, stole from them that land which was their inheritance. On 8 September he let fly most mischievously against the new land regulations, ending, after more gross misrepresentations, with a solemn warning to all gentlemen in England and Scotland not to emigrate. Darling decided to take action because people might even be prevented by such mischief from coming out to the colony. But Hall, who saw himself as a firm friend to legitimate freedom, a man willing to suffer damage in defending the rights of mankind, was confident that justice would be done to a man who had used his pen for the noble purpose of drawing attention to those conditions which demoralized mankind. This, surely, was not sedition.[24]

---

[22] Darling to Bathurst, 6 September 1826, *H.R.A.*, I. xii. 543-4.

[23] For the career of E. S. Hall see *Australian Dictionary of Biography*, vol. 1 and *Monitor*, 19 May 1826; Darling to Hay, 12 September 1826, *H.R.A.*, I. xii. 579-80; for Hall's speech at the public meeting of 12 January 1826, see *Australian*, 19 January 1826.

[24] See, for example, *Monitor*, 22 September 1826.

A convict servant grew warm in an argument with Charles Macarthur about rations and threatened to take revenge in lambing time. Charles Macarthur promptly charged him with insolence and insubordination before the magistrate of the district, his brother Hannibal Macarthur, and other magistrates who sentenced him to be flogged and to be transported to a penal settlement for life. As Hall saw it the men who persecuted their convict servants were the same men who controlled the Legislative Council of New South Wales, the same men who opposed a house of assembly and the extension of trial by jury. If they could, they would use their numbers in the Legislative Council to send the editors of journals who criticized their policies to a penal settlement for seditious libel. Or so Hall argued that September—as though severity, repression and censorship were the exclusive prerogatives of the conservatives of New South Wales.[25]

In November two soldiers of the 57th Regiment, Joseph Sudds and Patrick Thompson, committed a theft to ensure a sentence to transportation which would confer on them the blessing of release from the tedium and oppression of military service in New South Wales. Darling, fearful lest others of like mind might be tempted into conduct unbecoming to good order and discipline in the army, had the trial transferred from the Court of Quarter Sessions to a military court which sentenced the two to be drummed out of their regiment and worked in chains. At a military parade their uniforms were stripped from the two men, the yellow clothing of convicts was substituted, irons were placed on their legs, and iron collars locked round their necks, after which the two culprits were drummed off the parade ground to the tune of the Rogue's March. The *Australian* said that this was carrying severity too far, as the men could not even lie down to sleep when yoked with such monstrous collars.[26]

When Sudds died on 27 November the popular press set up a great howl. A man who was a mass of tumour from head to foot, and who was approaching his last mortal struggle, had had his neck and heels enclosed in iron shackles. A dying man had been tortured by the believers in severity. The deed which occasioned his death would rebound on its perpetrators, who could only be saved from the hangman's rope by royal clemency. With infinite patience and tact McLeay showed them the facts did not substantiate such sweeping charges. No responsible official in Sydney, he pointed out, had known of the gravity of Sudds' illness before the irons had snapped shut around his neck. But the hue and cry had gathered too much momentum to be swayed by the voice of sweet reasonableness. In the heat and passion of the day truth, like Sudds, became an early casualty. Darling, unmoved as ever, cast a cold eye over the affair. It could hardly be supposed, he wrote, that a man who could deliberately commit such an act with so base an interest, could possess any sense of shame or really feel the degradation to which he had wantonly and wilfully subjected himself.[27]

[25] Ibid.

[26] *Australian*, 25 November 1826; Darling to Bathurst, 4 December 1826, *H.R.A.*, I. xii. 716-25.

[27] Based on the *Australian*, 6, 13 and 27 December 1826; see also *Monitor* for November and December 1826 *passim*; for the efforts of McLeay to inform the public on the facts, see the letter by A. McLeay to the editor of the *Australian*, 1 December 1826, in the *Australian*, 2 December 1826; for the attitude of Darling see Darling to Bathurst, 4 December 1826, *H.R.A.*, I. xii. 716-17.

How different for Wentworth. The death of Sudds, he said, would have softened any heart not made of stone. The use of irons on a dying man was proof, strong as holy writ, of the existence in Darling of a most wicked, depraved and malignant spirit. So up and down Sydney town the 'Australian Counsellor' told all and sundry that Darling had now joined the ranks of the greatest monsters of antiquity. On 15 December he wrote to my lord Bathurst of the universal feelings of horror prevailing in Sydney, adding he would write later at greater length as soon as he had decided whether Darling should be charged with murder or a high misdemeanour.[28] After collecting the required twenty-four signatures, he asked the Sheriff, John Mackaness, his old travelling companion on the *Alfred*, to call a public meeting at the Court House on Anniversary Day, 26 January.

There before all the landholders of wealth in the colony, with only a few notable exceptions, and in an atmosphere remarkable both for the extreme decorum displayed as well as the perfect unanimity, Wentworth presented a petition to the king and the two Houses of Parliament for trial by jury and a house of assembly. With heavy sarcasm, he made some happy allusions to the pious labours of the clerical brethren who were about to render them the most moral people in the British dominions. They roared with laughter. But why, he asked, should they not also have those safeguards which would shelter them from oppression—those bulwarks of the constitution—trial by jury and a house of assembly? Was not New South Wales in the same situation as America in 1776? Might it not be forced to shake off the yoke? Again they roared their approval, and accepted the petition unanimously after some observations from Sir John Jamison, Mr Gregory Blaxland, Mr D'Arcy Wentworth, Dr Wardell, and Mr Hall.[29]

This wild talk of shaking off the yoke alarmed Darling. The extravagant behaviour of Wentworth during the Sudds affair had convinced him that he was a vulgar, ill-bred fellow, utterly unconscious of the civilities due from one gentleman to another. Now he wondered whether Wentworth would become a 'man of the people', join hands with Hall, Father Therry and the Reverend William Walker to incite the lower orders to sedition, and pollute the minds of the infatuated and deluded Irish convicts, and of the convict rabble in Sydney and Parramatta with his irresponsible talk about shaking off the yoke.[30] In response to the abuse of government in the popular press and at public meetings, vulgar upstarts such as Solomon Levy and Daniel Cooper, presuming a power and importance far above their proper station in life, were writing insolent letters to the officers of his government. Scott, that great sleeve-plucker in the corridors of Government House, kept whispering in his ear that the press would continue to sow the seeds of discord and sedition so

[28] W. C. Wentworth to Bathurst, 15 December 1826, C.O. 201/179; see also Miles (pseud.), *Governor Darling's Refutation of the Charges of Cruelty and oppression of the Soldiers, Sudds and Thompson. At Sydney, New South Wales, November 26th, 1826* (London, 1832), p. 12.

[29] For a report of the meeting see *Australian*, 27 January 1827; for the text of the petition see ibid.; for the Wentworth point on shaking off the yoke, see Darling to Hay, 6 February 1827, *H.R.A.*, I. xiii. 81-2.

[30] Darling to Bathurst, 4 December 1826, *H.R.A.*, I. xii. 716-17; Darling to Hay, 6 February 1827, *H.R.A.*, I. xiii. 81-2.

long as it was allowed to be licentious. Was not Hall, the editor of the *Monitor*, the drinking companion of that very Mackaness, the Sheriff, who had presided at that public meeting where those alarming words about shaking off the yoke, and the coarse jokes against the high officers of the government in New South Wales had met with such a disturbing response? Was it not notorious that Hall and Mackaness mingled freely with the convict classes in Sydney?[31]

For months past Darling had been wondering whether the time had not come to take up the suggestion my lord Bathurst had made as long ago as July of 1825 that government should issue licences to newspapers, to be forfeited if the proprietor or publisher were found guilty of a blasphemous or seditious libel. The difficulty was that this would need a change in the law, and no law could be passed through the Legislative Council of New South Wales unless the Chief Justice issued a certificate that such a proposed law was not repugnant to the laws of England, but was consistent with such laws, so far as the circumstances of the said colony would admit. Time was when he and the Chief Justice could exchange mind with mutual confidence and respect, but a great coolness had developed between them ever since Darling had heard, possibly from John Macarthur or from Scott, or from the general gossip of Sydney town, that the Chief Justice was one of the men who tossed pots and swapped bawdy jokes with that ill-bred fellow, Wentworth, and other vulgar and seditious people at an hour when all respectable people should be sleeping virtuously in their beds. Darling had also heard that the editor of the *Australian*, Robert Wardell, attended these carousals at which the Chief Justice, it was said, had talked all too freely about those very confidences of government he had solemnly sworn to betray to no man.[32]

Forbes, caught between conflicting voices in his mind—one which urged him to stoop for the sake of his career, the other which encouraged him to take a stand on principle and so win the approval of his contemporaries, and possibly also of the historians, decided to act on that excellent advice of Polonius to all attendant judges—that he should beware of entrance to a quarrel. He played for time. He told Darling he had some sympathy with the arguments to repress the licentiousness of the press. But with Wentworth telling him over the brandy and water that Darling could be likened to the monsters of antiquity, and even the respectable people saying there must be an extension of trial by jury and a house of assembly, Forbes informed Darling that different and even contrary opinions might be entertained on whether an act should prohibit newspapers being published without previous licence from the Governor. That was in December of 1826.[33]

Then a naughty article in the *Australian* and a chance remark by a judge in the following March set off a chain of events which stiffened the attitude of Forbes to the Darling proposals. On 17 March under the heading of 'How

---

[31] Darling to Hay, 6 February 1827, *H.R.A.*, I. xiii. 81; T. H. Scott to the Reverend A. Hamilton, 27 January 1827 (Extracts from the S.P.G. records, typescript in M.L.).

[32] Bathurst to Darling, 12 July 1825, *H.R.A.*, I. xii. 16-17; John Macarthur to John Macarthur jr, 12 September 1826 (Macarthur Papers, vol. 3, p. 134).

[33] F. Forbes to Darling, 1 December 1826, Encl. no. 2 in Darling to Hay, 4 December 1826, *H.R.A.*, I. xii. 727-9.

to live by plunder' Robert Wardell told his readers how Robert Howe filled the pages of the *Sydney Gazette* by the aid of gin and bribing the journalists of the *Australian*. Howe was posing at that time as a one-time drunkard and a philanderer who had been miraculously saved by the blood of the lamb. Wardell told his readers that these transgressions with the gin bottle were doubtless remembered on Sunday when Howe went to his temple to pray: they were doubtless remembered at each Wesleyan 'love feast' by an additional number of up-liftings, not shop-liftings, nor calf-liftings, nor news-liftings. They should write a new commandment for Howe: Thou shalt not covet thy neighbour's news. The readers rocked with laughter. One man, however, was not amused. He was Henry Dumaresq, whose sister Eliza had married Governor Darling. Wardell had told the readers of the *Australian* that if any one else in Sydney wanted to live by plunder, they should think of the colonel. Dumaresq promptly challenged Wardell to a duel. Shots were fired—neither party happily being wounded. Dumaresq lived on to pester his brother-in-law not to give an inch to those rascally, democratic Sydney newspaper men. Now between Forbes and Dumaresq there had been a great coolness ever since the former had dropped remarks about Darling's family coterie. For his part Dumaresq had always eyed Forbes as an example of the new professional men who were taking over the administration of the colonies from that navy and army officer class to which he belonged.[34]

Then a chance remark by Mr Justice Stephen in March of 1827 further stiffened Forbes' attitude to the Darling proposals. Stephen had announced from the bench that the rights of prisoners were as sacred in the eye of the law as those of free men. Darling, alarmed lest sedition had poisoned the mind of a judge who, alas, like other men he could name, was temperate neither in his language nor his drinking habits, wrote off to ask Stephen whether he had used the words. Stephen did not reply. After Darling wrote a second time, Stephen explained that he objected to the original request for an explanation because it implied that the government could teach the justices of the peace what to do. Here, indeed, was food for the Chief Justice. Was the head of the executive in New South Wales about to tamper with the independence of the judiciary? Was this Newfoundland all over again—the only difference being that here it was a military and not a naval governor? Did Darling want to reduce the Supreme Court to the status of a military court martial? Was this proposal to control the press part of some plan by a humane, well-intentioned soldier for whom the checks and balances of British institutions were an obstacle to his own plans for peace and good government? The Chief Justice was proud of his own rectitude: 'The same clean hands', he wrote to his friend Horton in London, 'that received His Majesty's Commission shall be preserved to lay at the foot of the throne. I rest with firmness upon the consciousness of rectitude.'[35]

[34] *Australian*, 17 March 1827; article on H. Dumaresq in *Australian Dictionary of Biography*, vol. 1; H. Dumaresq to Ann Dumaresq, 25 March 1827 (Letters of Colonel Henry Dumaresq, 1825-1838, ms. in m.l.); for the attitude of H. Dumaresq to Forbes see extracts from H. Dumaresq's letter to General Darling, 3 July 1833, ibid.

[35] Darling to Hay, 27 March 1827, *H.R.A.*, I. xiii. 206-10; F. Forbes to W. Horton, 22 March 1827, *H.R.A.*, IV. i. 703-17; for James Stephen on Forbes see C.O. 201/195, p. 420 et seq.

While Forbes was thus musing on the motives of Darling the Governor became convinced the time had come to put an end to the licentiousness of the press of New South Wales. All through that month Hall in the *Monitor* kept accusing him of drawing the cords of their slavery tighter than ever.[36] Neither Dr Wardell nor Mr Hall were known in society in Sydney. Besides, the men and women to whom he turned for advice were all clamouring for action. Mrs Macarthur, he knew, believed their greatest annoyance to be a licentious press, which published so much trash, and abused every person and everything respectable. John Macarthur kept telling him that the stamp duty was the one way to diminish the circulation of fire-brand papers. Henry Dumaresq and his sister Eliza, Darling's own wife, kept hammering away that a licentious press agreed as well with a convict society as god with the devil, and how a kind providence wanted no harm done to man's dwelling in New South Wales. The Reverend Samuel Marsden reminded him, as if he did not know already, that Hall was a hypocrite, and Wardell a self-declared free-thinker, and as such an enemy of the source of all true morality, and revealed religion. Scott, no more able now than earlier to ignore the mockers, and the unjust charge about priest-craft and tyranny, pestered him day in, day out, to do something about the corrupters of youth and the disturbers of law and order.[37]

So on 11 April Darling introduced two bills into the Legislative Council to control the press.[38] He asked Forbes for an opinion whether the bills were re-pugnant to the laws of England, pointing out that in his opinion the penal character of the colony overruled any such repugnancy, and adding, good soldier and sound administrator that he was, that surely good order and dis-cipline must take precedence over liberty. Delay, he pleaded, was pregnant with danger, adding again as evidence of the panic in his own mind, that private feelings must yield to the exigencies of the times. Duty was an un-gracious but stern commander, which he, for himself, proposed to obey. But Forbes, a judge, and deep down a stranger to, even hostile to, the soldier's talk about duty, replied that the laws of England had always been found sufficient to restrain the licentiousness of the press.[39]

That was on 16 April. At the end of that month and all through May, the Legislative Council debated the contentious second bill. John Macarthur, for-

---

[36] *Monitor* for March 1827 *passim*, see especially the article on hardships and absurdities on 16 March 1827; Darling to Hay, 23 March 1827, *H.R.A.*, I. xiii. 178-80.

[37] Darling to Hay, 23 March 1827, *H.R.A.*, I. xiii. 180; H. Dumaresq to C.O., 6 November 1827, C.O. 201/187, p. 432 et seq.; Eliza Darling to Edward Dumaresq, 20 August 1827 (Dumaresq Papers); Elizabeth Macarthur to Eliza Kingdon, March 1827 (Macarthur Papers, vol. 12, p. 63); John Macarthur sr to John Macarthur jr, 27 May 1827 (Macarthur Papers, vol. 3, pp. 162a-5b); T. H. Scott to the Reverend A. Hamilton, 21 May 1827 (Extracts from the S.P.G. records, typescript in M.L.).

[38] No. 2. An Act for preventing the mischiefs arising from Printing and Publishing News-papers, and Papers of a like nature, by persons not known, and for regulating the Printing and Publication of such papers in other respects, and also for restraining the abuses arising from the Publication of blasphemous and seditious libels; No. 3. An Act for imposing a duty upon all Newspapers and Papers of a like nature, printed to be dispersed and made public. *V. & P.* (L.C. N.S.W.) 24 April 1827.

[39] For the exchange of letters on repugnancy between Darling and Forbes, 2-16 April 1827, see Darling to Forbes, 14 April 1827, and Forbes to Darling, 16 April 1827, Enclosures in Darling to Bathurst, 8 May 1827, *H.R.A.*, I. xiii. 277-82.

getting his earlier rebuke by Darling turned up regularly as evidence of his conviction that Darling was right: delay was pregnant with danger. So did Scott, McLeay, Robert Campbell and Charles Throsby, all supporters, not only of press censorship, but also of exclusion of the low-born from society in New South Wales. Forbes stayed away from the debates in the Legislative Council, pleading pressure of judicial business as his excuse, but Darling, who was beginning to chafe and fume under the man's exasperating insolent assumption that the Chief Justice was the colonial house of lords, concluded that Forbes was just waiting to see which way the popular wind blew.

On 1 May, Forbes at last set out in dignified and measured language his reasons for not granting the certificate prescribed by the Act of 1823. The bill (he meant the second of the two bills) was repugnant to freedom of the press, as by law established, as every man had an undoubted right to lay what sentiments he pleased before the public. In the proposed bill this right had been confined to such persons only as the Governor should deem proper. To vest such a discretionary power in the head of the executive was repugnant to the principles and practice of English law. The press might be licentious, but that did not, and indeed could not, justify the proposed restraints on the freedom of the press. The law of England provided adequate remedies against such licentiousness, and if the law should be found inadequate, the remedy was to change the law of England.[40]

Darling, with that eye of the soldier for the coward in the civilian, concluded that Forbes was just too pusillanimous to risk his popularity and low enough to take advantage of his situation as a defender of a licentious press. The *Monitor* and the *Australian* hailed Forbes as the champion of freedom, and their ally in the coming struggle for the extension of trial by jury, and the creation of a house of assembly, all unaware of the feet of clay of their popular idol, for how were they to know then that the Francis Forbes who had refused to bow the knee to a coterie of alarmists and fuss-pots in Sydney town would stoop before his masters in London? How did they ever come to think that a Tory government in England would lend a sympathetic ear to the political policy of a group tainted with republicanism, and wild talk about casting off the yoke, a group of free-thinkers and radicals? How could a Tory government place the least confidence in such a body of men? Besides, had not John Macarthur junior been telling the men in black in Downing Street that the opposition to General Darling was a motley of publicans and Jew-boys, who were led by a man who was bound sooner or later to offend grossly?[41]

While Wentworth, Hall, Jamison, and their supporters were toasting Forbes in their midnight carousals in that house in Castlereagh Street as the defender of the freedom of the press, and hailing Wentworth as the Thomas Jefferson of all those with Australian hearts, the men in high places in London

---

[40] Darling to Bathurst, 29 May 1827, *H.R.A.*, I. xiii. 374-9; *V. & P.* (L.C. N.S.W.) 24 and 25 April, 2, 3 and 31 May 1827; for the correspondence between Darling and Forbes in May 1827, see the Enclosures in Darling to Bathurst, 30 May 1827, *H.R.A.*, I. xiii. 383-5.

[41] Darling to Hay, 30 May 1827, *H.R.A.*, I. xiii. 386-7; *Monitor* and *Australian* for June 1827 *passim*.

had already taken decisions calculated to promote the interests of those exclusives who had already got their filthy paws on all the good land in the
colony. In February, just as the controversy over the press was warming up,
Darling issued instructions to the superintendent of convicts to give preference
to up-country settlers in the distribution of convicts.[42] On 16 March Darling
ordered convicts assigned in Sydney to be sent to persons up-country so that
they might be placed out of reach of those pleasures which corrupted and
corroded their souls in the towns. At the same time he announced his intention
to enforce a more strict discipline at the penal settlements, as though to
illustrate the argument Hall never wearied of repeating to his readers in the
Monitor—that all moves to promote the material interests of the large landowners also tightened the iron bonds of slavery round the necks of the poor
unfortunate convicts.[43]

That summer of 1826-7 D'Arcy Wentworth had opened a letter from his
sister in Ireland which reminded him that he was going fast down the stream
of time into the great ocean of eternity, where the pleasures of sin would soon
be gone, and leave nothing but a sting. For herself she would ever pray that
she and D'Arcy might meet beyond the grave to praise redeeming love. A few
months later, on 7 July 1827, D'Arcy died. Two days later, on a wet dismal
day, forty carriages and gigs and a large number of horsemen assembled at
Homebush to follow the coffin to St John's, Parramatta, for D'Arcy had enjoyed in abundance the regard of his fellow-men. There the son who had
found his father's love to be wonderful to him, passing that of woman, and the
woman whom D'Arcy had loved, now big with child by him, shed their tears,
as the Reverend Samuel Marsden recited the words which summed up
D'Arcy's earthly pilgrimage 'My heart was hot within me'. Then the
mourners, conducting themselves with great steadiness and propriety, moved
on foot to the burial ground of St John's, where all that was mortal of his
wayward, vagrant spirit was committed to the earth of his adopted country,
after which the mourners adjourned to Walker's in Parramatta to drink one
toast in silence: 'The memory of our departed friend'.[44]

In gratitude to his father whom he had loved with much ardour, William
Charles arranged for the remains of Catherine Crowley to be placed next to
those of his father, and put up a simple gravestone on which was cut the words:
'Here lie the Mortal Remains of D'Arcy Wentworth Esquire . . . Also of
Catherine his Wife . . . In my Father's House are many Mansions. John
14.2'[45] No religious symbol decorated the stone, for William Charles entertained no such hopes, no such comforter, though the stone still breathes that
spirit of tragic grandeur, that spirit of a man who had asked in his poem on
Byron: 'Where art thou, man of might, thou grand in soul?' Deprived of the
one man he had loved in life, who had planted in his heart that ambition for

[42] Darling to Bathurst, 8 May 1827, *H.R.A.*, I. xiii. 277-87.

[43] Government Order, 16 March 1827, Encl. in Darling to Bathurst, 17 March 1827, *H.R.A.*,
I. xiii. 166-8.

[44] Martha Johnston to D'Arcy Wentworth, Lurgum, Ireland, 3 February 1826 (D'Arcy Wentworth Papers, Supplementary, 1785-1826); *Gleaner*, 14 July 1827; *Monitor*, 12 July 1827; *Australian*, 13 July 1827; *Sydney Gazette*, 11 July 1827.

[45] Inscription on tombstone of D'Arcy Wentworth, cemetery of St John's Church, Parramatta.

making great and powerful connections, he began to climb to that top place in society he had always set for himself. The father had bequeathed him one great instrument to fulfil his ambitions. He had left him a rich man. With his new wealth he bought Vaucluse, an estate in a bay on the south side of Sydney Harbour. He began in time to surround himself with the worldly grandeur, the pomp and ceremony he had known in the houses of the great Whig families in London. He began to develop the Britannia of the Fitzwilliams beside the green waters of Sydney Harbour.[46]

At the same time that other fire began once again to kindle in his heart, that fire of vengeance against colonial yellow snakes, and all toadies such as Bowman and McLeay. Within a month of his father's death he began to savage Darling with all the ferocity of a wild boar who had strayed into the vineyards of human society. He urged my lord Bathurst to file a bill of impeachment against the General for his crimes against humanity.[47] In September he spoke wildly in the Supreme Court about the oppressive and tyrannical government which was paralysing the energies of the colony, and indulged in an orgy of abuse for Darling, calling him a tyrant, a monster, and a scoundrel. The *Sydney Gazette* asked nervously: 'When will all this end?' Eliza Darling, believing, as she did, that it was good for a man to be troubled, nevertheless wrote off to her brother in Van Diemen's Land that the General was far from well, and no wonder as the poor man had had enough to wear him out in mind and body. But Wentworth, cheered on by Wardell and Hall, continued as one possessed by an evil spirit to muddy the waters of human life.[48]

In September he and his friends decided to hold a Turf Club dinner at which they proposed to honour Governor Brisbane for presenting a gold cup as a prize for a horse race. Darling, sensing Wentworth and Wardell might exploit the occasion to his own pain, declined to attend. By then he was beginning to see the point of Brisbane's remark that not even an angel from heaven could get on in the colony of New South Wales.[49] On the night of 9 November forty members of the Turf Club sat down at Cumming's Hotel. The very air seemed charged with that spirit of drunken bravado and recklessness which followed Wentworth wherever he went. What he muddied, stayed muddied for life. Wentworth himself spoke to the toast of the former Governor Brisbane, who, he said, had been 'one of us'. By contrast, the present Governor had not even condescended to dine either with a gentleman, or with the members of any public body. When the time came to drink the toast to Darling a very convivial party had gathered round Dr Wardell. With his usual flair for the moment of mischief, Wentworth asked the band to play a tune appropriate to the object of their toast. One wit called for 'There's nae

[46] For the text of the will of D'Arcy Wentworth see Documents of Titles, etc. Miscellaneous, Minter and Simpson & Co. MS. in M.L.; for W. C. Wentworth and Vaucluse see the *Australian*, 27 June 1827; W. C. Wentworth to John Piper, 30 May 1828 (Piper Papers, MS. in M.L.); W. H. Ifould, Notes on Vaucluse House, April 1913 (typescript in M.L.); and C. H. Bertie, *The Story of Vaucluse House and Sir Henry Browne Hayes* (Sydney, 1918).

[47] W. C. Wentworth to Bathurst, 4 August 1827, C.O. 201/189.

[48] *Monitor*, 17 September 1827; *Gleaner*, 17 September 1827; *Sydney Gazette*, 19 and 21 September 1827; Eliza Darling to Edward Dumaresq, 20 August 1827 (Dumaresq Papers).

[49] Quoted in Darling to Goderich, 1 November 1827, *H.R.A.*, I. xiii. 587.

luck aboot the Hoose', and they laughed heartily. Then Wardell, carried away by the tendency of the tipsy to drag the mighty down to their own level, shouted 'No, not that . . . play 'Over the hills and far away'. And they roared with laughter, and rose to their feet and swayed and emptied their glasses while the band played merrily that tune which summed up their attitude to General Darling—that this would be a much better place when that bloody Englishman went over the hills and far away.[50]

By chance in the following month Wentworth took part in a scene which strengthened Darling's conviction that his reviler, this man who aspired to the top place in colonial society, was a drunken and irresponsible philanderer. On the night of 16 December Wentworth, when a little intoxicated, was stopped by a sentry at the back of the residence of the Colonial Secretary. For Wentworth this was just another proof that here was a government which permitted the liberty of one of His Majesty's subjects to be wantonly outraged. He proposed to bring the matter before a tribunal to determine a question of such vital importance to the colonists at large. Darling saw the incident in quite a different light. The posting of sentries was essential to produce good order and tranquillity. As he saw it, an ill-bred fellow, drunk and turbulent as usual, and probably about to seek some guilty pleasure in the arms of a woman whose husband he had cruelly wronged, had bellowed like a little child when deprived of his lollipop.[51]

Besides, Darling knew, and so did everyone in Sydney for whom muckraking and vilification of the eminent were the one low entertainment in their Vanity Fair, apart from the cock-fighting, the baiting of aborigines, and bare-fisted fights to a finish, that on the following week the Supreme Court would once again be converted into a stage, on which Robert Wardell, a great colonial mocker, would once again perform. For on 22 December Dr Wardell was to be tried for a seditious libel inasmuch as on the preceding 25 May he had published in the *Australian* a letter signed 'Vox Populi', in which he had likened Darling's press bill to that Stamp Act, which Darling knew, and Wardell knew, had played such a notorious role in the decision of the Americans to cast off the yoke. When the action began Wardell, who conducted his own defence, dwelt at length on the benefits of a free press, and asked the jury to consider whether the motive for his prosecution had not been vindictive and political. As soon as the chairman of the jury pronounced the words 'not guilty' on the first two counts, loud expressions of triumph reverberated through the streets of Sydney. When the jury announced a few days later that it had not been able to agree on the third count, again the shouts of victory broke out in Sydney town, and wafted up to the very doors of Government House.[52]

By the time the bells rang out that Christmas their promise of peace and good will on earth the tumult and the shouting had dropped to a whisper. It was known in Sydney town that Darling had already dismissed the Sheriff Mackaness because of his association and intercourse with certain factious

---

[50] *Australian*, 14 and 23 November 1827.

[51] Darling to Hay, 19 January 1828, *H.R.A.*, I. xiii. 727-9; W. C. Wentworth to Darling, 19 December 1827, Encl. in above, ibid., 729-30.　　　　[52] *Australian*, 26 December 1827.

individuals, who in the most open and wanton manner had endeavoured to degrade the government in the eyes of the public, and to create discord between it and the people. It was known too that Douglass had been suspended until such time as His Majesty had pronounced on the propriety of a member of the government downing a bumper toast while the band played that disrespectful air: 'Over the hills and far away'. Now, on the eve of the season of good will, the rumour flew around Sydney town that Darling has written a peremptory note to Foster, the Solicitor-General, to ask him whether he had ever spent a night in Wentworth's house.[53]

Immediately the timid and the cautious, the career men, and all those dependent on the patronage of the Governor for either land or assigned servants, or just for a good word dropped in the right place in London, took fright. When the patriots, the men with Australian hearts, gathered for the dinner to commemorate the foundation of the colony on 26 January of the new year, 1828, Mackaness, bound by deep ties of conviction to what he thought Wentworth stood for, proposed a toast to their absent friend the 'Australian Counsellor'. An uneasy silence descended on the gathering. The men kept their places. There was one, an Australian by birth, who despising the conduct of the elders, stood up alone, and drank to his fellow-countryman's health, and then left the company. While the patriots were displaying their political prudence when untouched by the extravagant, brilliant oratory of Wentworth, Darling was putting down on paper his ideas on the future constitution of New South Wales.[54]

[53] Darling to Goderich, 14 December 1827, *H.R.A.*, I. xiii. 638-9; *Australian*, 28 November 1827; Darling to Hay, 17 December 1827, *H.R.A.*, I. xiii. 652-4.
[54] *Monitor*, 31 January 1828.

5

TOWARDS A COLONIAL GENTRY

IN THE MIDDLE of December 1827 John Macarthur called on Darling at Government House to enquire about the bill for better administration of justice in New South Wales and Van Diemen's Land. The man with the dream of establishing a colonial gentry and the Major-General found they had much in common. On the qualification of jurors, they both prayed that the question should be settled at home, as any decision in Sydney would be bound to cause some embarrassment. As for the legislative assembly, as they saw it, the colony was by no means prepared for such an institution. The idea was absurd in the extreme. It would unsettle the people and divert them from the necessary attention to their business, and would render many individuals who were then peaceable and well-disposed, troublesome, if not insolent, as they gained power and importance. The people were in general quite indifferent to the matter except for the few who had been worked on by Wentworth's inflammatory speeches, and the radical articles in the *Monitor* and the *Australian*. This was, they knew, also the view of the directors of the Australian Agricultural Company, and if His Majesty's government was to be guided by the friends of that company, then the colonists would not be boasting of any great extension of their privileges, and it was altogether better that it should be so.[1]

Darling and Macarthur had already taken their own steps to guide His Majesty's government into their way of truth. As long ago as June of 1827 Darling had sent his private secretary who, by a happy coincidence, was also to be his brother-in-law, to London to present his views in Downing Street. Henry Dumaresq lost no time in reminding the men in the Colonial Office of the equivocal virtue of emancipists such as Edward Eagar, who were also pressing their views. John Macarthur knew full well that, thanks to his son John Macarthur junior, the men in power in London had been told time and time again that the supporters of a house of assembly and the extension of trial by jury were led by that gross and notorious father of bastards, William Charles Wentworth, and a motley mob of ex-convicts, publicans, shopkeepers, and Jews, who earned their living by buying and selling, which disqualified them from the title of gentleman.[2]

[1] Extract from General Darling's letter to James Stephen, 17 December 1827, *H.R.A.*, I. xiii. 656-8.
[2] Darling to Hay, 10 June 1827, *H.R.A.*, I. xiii. 417; H. Dumaresq to F. L. Gower, 29 April 1828, C.O. 201/197; John Macarthur sr to John Macarthur jr, 27 May 1827 (Macarthur Papers, vol. 3, pp. 162a-5b); John Macarthur jr to John Macarthur sr, 18 January 1826 (Macarthur Papers, vol. 15, pp. 339-50).

By an odd irony the chief target of attack, William Charles Wentworth, did not seek to present his case to the Colonial Office. All through that summer in Sydney he had threatened to send off to London a bill for the impeachment of Darling, but he dithered and procrastinated, at one moment boasting in his cups that he would bring the tyrant down, at another blaming his natural indolence for his delay. Just as the divisions deep within the man had caused that gap between desire and performance in taking revenge against his father's vilifiers, so that same conflict between his father's and his mother's world, led him slap up against that question which he had such deep reasons for ducking— namely, what did he mean by a house of assembly? For a man whose aim in life was to make those great and powerful connections to which he was entitled by his ancestry, deep down his only objection to John Macarthur's list of renegade Jews, shopkeepers, and American adventurers, was that his name appeared on it.[3]

Forbes, too, had his reasons for taking a stand against the Macarthur-Darling conception of what should be written into the bill for the better administration of justice in New South Wales and Van Diemen's Land. Ever since he had sat on the enquiry into Dr Douglass in July of 1825 he had been cut by all Mr Macarthur's followers, and no Macarthur had since set foot within his house.[4] Up to the press bill controversy he had experienced a little soreness with Darling, but no more. Forbes had thought it inexpedient and unbecoming, and had even detected a want of grace in two brothers-in-law being seated at opposite ends of the council table, one as the King's representative, the other as a clerk. He believed Henry Dumaresq had pushed Darling into the Stamp Act, and that in his heart Darling was not otherwise than glad that Forbes had provided the opportunity to suspend what would have been a most unpopular measure.[5]

At the height of that controversy rumours came back to Forbes which wounded him in his tenderest place. It was being said in Sydney that he had a secret connection or understanding with the conductors of the press. The retailers of gossip whispered to him that the head of government had condescended to receive insinuations under the pledge of secrecy. The representations of his political enemies had infected the ear of the Governor. So as Darling leaned more heavily on John Macarthur for ideas on the future institutions of New South Wales, and began to say openly that he for one would not favour any great extension of their privileges, a different vision began to take shape in the mind of the Chief Justice. He began to detect a higher purpose in placing a colony of thieves at Botany Bay in 1788: for him it was the planting of a young and ambitious colony of Europeans in the heart of Asia; the education of England's giant son in a manner suited to his illustrious birth, and fitted to perpetuate in this eastern clime, to the end of time and the earth's duration, the glorious institution of England's laws, the beautiful productions of England's literature, and the moral fire of England's genius.[6]

3 For Wentworth's reference to his 'natural indolence of disposition', see W. C. Wentworth to Murray, 1 March 1829, Encl. in Darling to Murray, 1 March 1829, *H.R.A.*, I. xiv. 801.

4 Forbes to Horton, 20 September 1827, *H.R.A.*, IV. i. 741.

5 Forbes to Horton, 14 June and 5 September 1827, C.O. 201/188.

6 Forbes to Horton, 20 September 1827, *H.R.A.*, IV. i. 732.

FRANCIS FORBES

Portrait by an unknown artist in the Mitchell Gallery, Sydney

JOHN DUNMORE LANG

Drawing by Charles Rodius in the Mitchell Library, Sydney

So on the night when Wentworth, Wardell, Hall, Mackaness and Douglass tightened the Macarthur embrace on Darling by their horseplay at the Turf Club dinner Forbes had sat down to write to the Colonial Office his own ideas on the next steps in the political history of New South Wales. He earnestly prayed that the Chief Justice might be relieved from that most invidious and responsible duty of certifying every proposed law. As for trial by jury he believed the colony was fit for that mode of trial. He suggested a high property qualification for jurors who had been transported to ensure some approach to that respectability which he had found most commonly accompanied the acquisition of landed property. As for a house of representatives he argued for some middle estate between the unpopular existing body and the house of assembly clamoured for by the opposition. With a legislative body having some points of contact with the people, a cabinet, composed of the heads of the higher departments, and an executive, guiding itself by the rule of leaving every office to its own details, and holding the head of it responsible for its own performance, New South Wales, he believed, might be made one of the most happy as it was one of the best disposed of all the English colonies.[7]

For Forbes knew that in arguing for checks and balances against Darling's plea for concentration of power because of the peculiar features of a convict dominated society, he would have strong supporters in the Colonial Office. One of these was James Stephen who believed that power could never be rendered safe in the hands of men, except by being divided. One of the difficulties in the Australian colonies was that there would not be enough men among whom to divide it.[8] Born in 1789 into a family which believed that the religion of Jesus Christ afforded the only plausible solution to the great mystery of human life and the only foundation for any lofty or consolatory thoughts, he had taken up his official business as a salaried legal counsellor in the Colonial Office in 1825 from a sense of duty rather than necessity. He thought of Benthamism then as a subtle enemy of Christianity. He looked down with disdain on men who were corrupted by careless amusements. He had once smoked a cigar, but decided not to repeat the experiment because it had afforded him so much pleasure. With Forbes he had in common an interest in the West Indies, a contempt for aristocratic frivolity, and opposition to all systems of slavery. His own problem was how to overcome the prejudice of men of the world against the aspiration of his own Clapham sect to saintship. He believed the government of men should conform to the fatherhood of God, rather than to any notions of abstract human rights. He had the tendency of the man of superior intellect to infer that God had entrusted the government of men to the few rather than the many. The promise of 1789 of better things for mankind touched him not at all: what concerned him was the abolition of all those evils which prevented men perceiving the divine plan for their eternal salvation.[9]

[7] Forbes to Hay, 12 November 1827, *H.R.A.*, IV. i. 747-51.

[8] J. Stephen to Arthur, 29 April 1825 (Papers of Sir George Arthur, vol. 4, Correspondence with James Stephen).

[9] L. Stephen, *The Life of Sir James Fitzjames Stephen* (London, 1895); C. E. Stephen, *The Right Honourable Sir James Stephen* (London, 1906); P. Knaplund, *James Stephen and the British Colonial System 1813-1847* (Madison, 1953); J. Stephen to Arthur, 9 October 1826 (Papers of Sir George Arthur, vol. 4, Correspondence with James Stephen).

G

So when he came to put down on paper on 8 March 1828 his ideas on the future government of New South Wales he wrote as a man who believed the *summum bonum* to be what encouraged men to live in love and fellow-ship with each other rather than what were their lawful rights as men. Trial by jury should not be conceded, because if emancipists were included they would avenge the affronts which they had sustained from their opponents. On the other hand if the emancipists were excluded, this triumph for their opponents would excite rancour and malice in their hearts. This political quietism, this concern to avoid all causes of stirring up envy, jealousy, malice or pride in the hearts of God's chosen people pervaded his whole memorandum. The duty of the Chief Justice to issue a certificate certifying a bill was not repugnant to the laws of England so far as the circumstances of the colony permitted it, he knew, had caused much contention and jealousy between the Governor and the Chief Justice. Happily the increase in the size of the Legislative Council would remove the need for such a check on the absolute power of the Governor. On control of the press he wrote too as one concerned with promoting public safety and welfare, rather than the liberty of the press as a bulwark of human liberty. Was it safe in a convict society to permit the Governor to be the object of unremitting hostility of the popular press? Any analogy with England was delusive partly because there an edition of a newspaper was corrected and kept in check by an opponent, and partly because there, unlike New South Wales, two-thirds of the population were not convicts or the relatives of convicts. But this, happily, was a question of public policy which was for parliament, and not for one of His Majesty's humble servants to discuss.[10]

On 1 April 1828 Mr Secretary Huskisson explained in a brief speech to the House of Commons that because of the peculiar situation in which the population of New South Wales was placed, about two-thirds of the population having forfeited their civil rights, His Majesty's government had decided to continue the existing system of administration, provide a system of justice suited to the nature of the population, and provide for the introduction of British institutions as soon as circumstances permitted. Because of the peculiar composition of their society, New South Wales was not ready for a legislative assembly. His Majesty's government proposed to increase the number of members of the Legislative Council to twelve or fifteen members, and charge them with the responsibility for the peace, order and good government of the colony until such time as circumstances favoured the establishment of institutions similar to those in the country from which the inhabitants had sprung.[11]

Seventeen days later Sir James Mackintosh presented the petition, drafted by Wentworth, and signed by some of the gentry, the merchants, landholders, yeomen, traders, and other free inhabitants of the colony of New South Wales, praying that the members of the House of Commons would bestow on all His Majesty's loving subjects: those inherent birthrights of the British constitution of trial by jury and an elected assembly. When the second reading debate on the bill to provide for the administration of justice in New South Wales and

10 Memorandum by James Stephen on the New South Wales Bill, 8 March 1828, C.O. 201/195.
11 *P.D.*, 2nd series, 1828, vol. 18, cols. 1430-1; see also *The Times*, 1 April 1828.

Van Diemen's Land and for the more effectual government thereof came on in the House of Commons, Spring Rice, a friend of Richard Bourke, destined to be Darling's successor, urged the government to deal with New South Wales as a society of free and unpolluted men who were not subject to the legislation appropriate to a penal colony. But Huskisson, speaking for a Tory government, replied to him with that argument with which conservatives have resisted change down the ages—namely, that the time was not ripe, though he for one looked forward to that day when the glorious institutions of England were not alien to the habits and feelings of the convicts. As evidence both of his hope and his goodwill he was prepared to confer on the Legislative Council of New South Wales the power further to extend and apply the form and manner of proceeding by grand and petit juries in the trial of all crimes, mis-demeanours, issues, matters and things properly cognizable by juries. The bill then passed on to the House of Lords for a token debate, and received the royal assent on 25 July.[12]

This Act to provide for the Administration of Justice in New South Wales and Van Diemen's Land and for the more effectual Government thereof, introduced some important alterations in the judicial and legislative constitution of the colony. Although the general constitution of the Supreme Court and the mode of trial in civil and criminal cases established by the Act of 1823 were retained, the local legislature was empowered to draft all details respecting the constitution of juries. In the despatch to Darling on these alterations he was instructed that one of the earliest duties of the new Legislative Council would be to report to His Majesty on the expediency of altering the law on the composition of juries. The appeal from the Supreme Court to the Governor was abolished and replaced by an appeal direct to the King in Council, it being deemed incongruous to permit an appeal from three professional judges to a Governor uninstructed in the law.

The Act provided for an increase in the members of the legislative body to a minimum of ten and a maximum of fifteen, partly because of the increase in population, and partly because the small number provided for in the Act of 1823 could not exercise great powers without exciting serious discontent and jealousy in society at large. By so adding to the number of members of the Legislative Council from the more intelligent, wealthy, and respectable mem-bers of the commercial, agricultural and professional bodies of the colony, it was hoped that the legislature would represent the various interests of colonial society, and both receive a salutary influence from public opinion, and exercise a wholesome control over it.

The repugnancy power of the Chief Justice was revoked, because it had been found from experience to occasion disputes between the executive and judicial authorities. To preserve a greater harmony between the judges and the legislature, while retaining provision to protect colonial law against repug-nancy, the Act provided that every law should within seven days of passing the legislature be transmitted to the Supreme Court for enrolment. During that period the judges could transmit their opinions on any supposed repugnancy to the Legislative Council, which would then consider these opinions. If the

[12] *P.D.*, 2nd series, 1828, vol. 19, cols. 1564-7, cols. 1456-63.

Legislative Council should adhere to the terms of the original act, then that Act would take effect until such time as the royal pleasure should be known.

The power conferred on the Governor in the previous Act to pass laws in opposition to the advice of the members of the Legislative Council was withdrawn. The power of the Governor of New South Wales to issue tickets-of-leave or to withdraw assigned convicts from their masters being deemed so essential to the good government of the colony, the Act had placed it beyond dispute. The government had not been prepared to include a clause for the restraint of the press, because, as the Secretary of State put it to Darling in his covering letter, they would not fetter a privilege which, in its legitimate exercise, was so highly conducive to the welfare of society.[13]

By this decision not to concede an elective assembly, or the immediate extension of trial by jury the exclusives had won an important victory over those landholders, merchants, shopkeepers and American traders who believed in the inherent birthrights of the British constitution to preserve their liberty and promote their material advantage. Yet by one of those odd ironies in human affairs, when the news of the new Act reached Sydney the architect for the grandeur and power of the gentry of New South Wales, John Macarthur, was consuming his energies crushing a small landholder who had dared to stand in his way. Wentworth, restless as ever whenever opportunity offered to score off the man who had despitefully used him, accepted the brief from the victim of Macarthur's rancour—one John Raine. In the case before the lower court Macarthur shouted at Wentworth and Wardell as bottle-holders. Wentworth retaliated by scoffing at the son of a stay-maker putting on airs of a gentleman.[14]

At the beginning of April, while his eldest son John was whispering in the ears of the men in high places that supporters of an elective assembly and trial by jury were radicals and republicans, and that excellent man Henry Dumaresq was telling them too that emancipists and other loud-mouthed agitators for the birthrights of Englishmen had equivocal virtue, John Macarthur invited his friends to a dinner to farewell his son James on the eve of his departure for London. It was a dinner where toasts of an official-like character were drunk. While at the notorious Turf Club feast at the end of 1827, coarse jokes against the Governor delighted the diners, here John Macarthur, sober, and upright as ever, his reputation unblemished by any breath of scandal, rose to his feet and asked them to drink to the toast 'May our youth be taught that Liberty is a fallacy, unless founded on the fear of God, and a loyal devotion to the King'. The editor of the *Monitor* was enraged. In the next issue of the paper he reminded his readers that those gaolers of mankind, the supporters of political servility, had always basely used the fear of God, and dragooned those advocates of superstition, the priests and the parsons, into the service of their evil ambitions.[15]

While John Macarthur was thus raging and celebrating, Charles Throsby, a

---

[13] An Act to provide for the Administration of Justice in New South Wales and Van Diemen's Land and for the more effectual Government thereof, and for other Purposes relating thereto. 9 Geo. IV, c.83, 25 July 1828, *Statutes at Large*, vol. 11.

[14] *Monitor*, 4 February, 29 March and 12 April 1828.   [15] *Monitor*, 12 April 1828.

member of the Legislative Council, oppressed by melancholy and debts, put an end to his existence. Darling wondered whether there was something peculiar in the climate, something produced by the sudden transition from heat to cold, which affected the spirits and excited extraordinary depression. Others pointed to other manifestations of how New South Wales or the climate or the environment were shaping human behaviour. It must be allowed to be, one writer said that April, a most pugnacious colony—the very centre of jealousies and fears, of squabbles and contentions, of libel and litigation. The love of whisperings and back-bitings, and a certain innate pleasure in prying into the thoughts and actions of other people, instead of looking at home were the dominant features of the inhabitants.[16]

Yet that July one man at long last acquired the wisdom and the grace to turn from such wickedness and live. That was the Reverend Samuel Marsden. He was happy to say he had lived in great peace and quietness since General Darling's arrival, which, he added ruefully, was a new thing for him. The spirit of wickedness was as great as ever, but now it was more directed against the Archdeacon and the Governor. As the man within had calmed down, he had heeded more and more that last appeal by the holy voice on that green hill without a city wall—'Father, forgive them; for they know not what they do'. The man who in his early days in the colony had thanked his God he was not as other men, and had refused in 1810 to commit to the earth the body of a man who had cohabited with a woman who was not his wife, had in July 1827 committed to the grave the body of D'Arcy Wentworth, and had shaken hands with William Charles Wentworth on whom in his darker moments he had plotted to seek vengeance in the law courts of New South Wales.

In July of 1828 when he published his *Statement, including a correspondence between the Commissioners of the Court of Enquiry, and the Rev. Samuel Marsden, relative to a charge of illegal punishment preferred against Doctor Douglass*, it was said in Sydney that he was a man who could not but descend to the latest posterity in the annals of Australian fame as the one who had done everything for the civilization of the savages of New Zealand. Forbes said publicly that he respected Marsden as an old and zealous minister of religion. For the first time, men gave him their regard. With pride, and some surprising tenderness for his fellow-man, he wrote to London that the publishing of his last pamphlet had produced a very extraordinary effect in the colony in his favour, amongst all ranks. An air of dignity and tragic grandeur began to descend on him as he went about God's business—comforting and relieving the sick, giving patience in their sufferings to the dying, preaching God's holy word, freed at long last from the meshes of the world's great net, just at that moment when desire began to fail.[17]

[16] Darling to Huskisson, 5 April 1828, *H.R.A.*, I. xiv. 118-19; *The Australian Quarterly Journal of Theology, Literature & Science*, July 1828, p. 246

[17] Based on S. Marsden to D. Coates, 3 August 1827 (Bonwick Transcripts, Box 53); Forbes to Darling, 2 October 1828, Encl. in Darling to Murray, 8 November 1828, *H.R.A.*, I. xiv. 430; S. Marsden, *Statement, including a correspondence between the Commissioners of the Court of Enquiry, and the Rev. Samuel Marsden, relative to a charge of illegal punishment preferred against Doctor Douglass* (Sydney, 1828); S. Marsden to D. Coates, Parramatta, 14 October 1829 (Bonwick Transcripts, Box 53); Marsden Papers, vol. 1, pp. 482-5.

That same July, while high-minded men in London were looking forward to the day when the glorious institutions of England would not be alien to the habits and feelings of the inhabitants of New South Wales, Hall, the editor of the *Monitor*, believing Archdeacon Scott had turned the house of God into a counting-house, and a stepping-stone for the seekers of worldly rank, forced his way into a pew in the Church of St James, and lifted his daughters in. When the Archdeacon threatened to prosecute him for trespass, Hall wrote with anger and bitterness of Scott as a paid hireling of the exclusive faction, or ridiculed him as a wine merchant in gaiters.[18]

During that July and the succeeding months of August and September the Legislative Council acted as a committee to regulate the affairs of a pastoral society employing convict labour. They passed Acts to authorize the impounding of cattle, to establish yards and enclosures for the inspection of horses, cattle and sheep at certain places in the colony of New South Wales, to prevent the nuisance occasioned by the great numbers of dogs at large in Sydney; Acts to prevent persons from purchasing or receiving clothing, bedding or rations from convicts, for the better regulation of servants, labourers and work people; and Acts to regulate the dividing fences of adjoining lands, to regulate the licensing of auctioneers, to regulate places of exhibition and entertainment.[19]

While John Macarthur and Robert Campbell were drafting laws and regulations to convert New South Wales into a sheep-walk for the profit and pleasure of the gentry, the aborigines continued to present their own ineffectual resistance against the invaders of their land. When white men encouraged black boys in the towns to mangle each other with great waddies while white men, and women, roared with drunken laughter, one aborigine refused to allow his daughter to return to the whites on any consideration whatever. In the country districts aborigines whose tribal lands had been stolen from them, or whose women had been infected with venereal disease, sought vengeance in raids on the white man's huts or stock. Near Wellington in August of 1828 the commandant, exasperated by the very serious annoyance to the settlers, offered a reward to any soldier who captured an aborigine, hoping thereby to conciliate the natives. When his soldiers attempted to capture an aborigine, the natives slung their spears, the soldiers fired their rifles, killing a woman and two children, and wounding one man so badly that a soldier shot him to relieve him from further senseless suffering. Darling, unperturbed as ever, thought the event was much to be deplored, but could see no point in prosecuting the soldiers.[20]

When the news reached Sydney, no cry of horror rent that city: there the voice of conscience was still. The men who had heard the call to bring the gifts of divine love to the savages of New South Wales were deeply divided. There was one Lancelot Edward Threlkeld who had been born in London in that year in which the aborigines of Port Jackson had set up their horrid howl, and brandished their spears in anger as the men from the First Fleet landed at Sydney Cove. His conscience had been awakened as a boy, when he had first

18 *Monitor*, 5 and 12 July 1828.
19 *V. & P.* (L.C. N.S.W.) 16 and 17 July, 2 August and 11 September 1828.
20 *Gleaner*, 12 April 1827; Darling to Huskisson, 28 August 1828, *H.R.A.*, I. xiv. 350-1.

known that joy of being called to begin life anew. He had arrived in Sydney in 1817. After missionary labours in New Zealand and the Society Islands, where he gave the first indication of the officiousness, the self-opinionatedness and pessimism that tainted the whole of his missionary activities, he began a mission to evangelize the Australian aborigines at Reid's Mistake, on the shores of Lake Macquarie, it being hoped that being alone in the woods of New South Wales he would have no one to quarrel with. This site was selected on 20 January 1825.

Within three years Threlkeld was back in Sydney quarrelling with Scott about money, and with Marsden about status, for Threlkeld, when faced with discipline by Scott and Marsden, replied that he conducted his life in conformity with Him who had said respecting ministers assuming superiority one over the other that 'so it shall not be among you'. And when he had become warm with Marsden about bills and status, Marsden, in the prim, confident tone of a man but recently converted to the command to agree with his adversaries quickly, had replied: 'I shall not notice any other observations which you have made, though they appear to me intended to be personal'. So God's servants tangled with each other in Parramatta and Sydney town on the meaning of Christ's words and the mission to evangelize the aborigines of New South Wales languished until such times as Christians could at least agree with if not love one another.[21]

Late in September the Attorney-General opened the Crown's case for criminal libel against E. S. Hall for writing and publishing an article in the *Monitor* of 5 July in which he had held up Archdeacon Scott to public ridicule and contempt as a greater enemy to the liberties of New South Wales than Mr Macarthur himself. He argued Hall had uttered libel of an aggravated character because of the rank of the party libelled, and the sacred office which Scott held as a church dignitary, a person who of all others was bound to stand high in the public esteem for morals and character, and who was therefore entitled to peculiar protection at the hands of the law. Hall, who conducted his own defence, asked the members of the jury to throw off their military character and judge him as settlers of New South Wales. It was, he pleaded, lawful to ridicule the Archdeacon in his public capacity. His raillery, he insisted, had been playful and mild, and calculated to provoke a good laugh and that was all. That was not the view of the seven military officers who, sensitive as ever to all talk about rank and dignity, promptly agreed with the Attorney-General, and brought in a verdict of guilty.[22]

The ensuing gaol sentence stung Hall into reckless attacks on Darling and his senior civil officers. In the *Monitor* and in a letter to the Secretary of State he accused Darling of gross abuse of the power of patronage, of nepotism in public appointments, and such lavish land grants to immigrants and civil officers

---

[21] Based on L. E. Threlkeld, *A Statement chiefly relating to The Formation and Abandonment of a Mission to the Aborigines of New South Wales* (Sydney, 1828); B. W. Champion, 'Lancelot Edward Threlkeld: His Life and Work, 1788-1859', R.A.H.S., *J. & P.*, vol. 25, 1939-40, pp. 279-330, and 341-411; for the correspondence between Marsden and Threlkeld between October and December of 1827 see L. E. Threlkeld, op. cit., p. 35 et seq; J. D. Lang called Threlkeld 'theatrical, improvident and self-righteous', *Colonist*, 31 March 1836.

[22] *Monitor*, 4 October 1828.

that the native-born received none.[23] Darling, assuming rather rashly that Wentworth was also fanning such radical flames with his own grotesque ideas on the government of men, wrote off to London that all colonial radicals, such as Wentworth, were Americans at heart who should be rooted out of the land, or they would triumph.[24] To strengthen the gentry against the colonial radicals he had decided to grant land as a marriage portion or dowry to the daughters of clergymen and other daughters in large families to encourage the sons of the gentry to ask for their hands in marriage, as that could not fail to prove in every point of view beneficial to the colony and the community in general. Darling, who lacked that art to read the mind of a man in his face, was quite unaware that what he was planning for ladies and gentlemen otherwise without prospects could be twisted for base purposes. Life, as John Macarthur was fond of saying, was a fearful lottery—and not without its odd ironies.[25]

Towards the end of that long trying summer in Sydney, that season of storms and southerlies, Wentworth at last overcame his natural indolence of disposition, and sent off thirty thousand words to the Right Honourable Sir George Murray, K.C.B., His Majesty's principal Secretary of State for the Colonies, about Darling's act of atrocity against Sudds. He wrote of Darling's wicked, depraved and malignant spirit: he likened him to the greatest monsters of antiquity: he accused Darling of a series of fraud, tyranny and corruption such as had never occurred before in the history of colonial government: he wrote of him as a man guilty of a system of misdemeanours, of which murder itself glared at the centre: he wrote of him as a man who might run amok against the expression of universal feeling in the colony: and ended by asking whether it was fitting, whether it was decent, whether it would not in fine be an outrage on the feelings and opinions of all His Majesty's loyal subjects in the colony to suffer any one who stood thus guilty and degraded in their estimation, to fill any longer the dignified office of His Most Gracious Majesty's representative among them.[26]

By contrast when Hall wrote to Sir George Murray he raised a great question. The root of the matter, as he saw it, was that the good land of New South Wales had been picked and occupied by twenty-nine persons only, and a large portion of it by four families, the Macarthurs, the Macleays, the Berrys, and the Throsbys who were closely allied to the executive. Great families by their being magistrates and civil officers thus formed a strong chain of political power in the colony. As he saw it, the faint distant cry of the poor people seeking land, if it should happen to penetrate to Government House in Sydney (which was not very probable) would have to break through the clamour and misrepresentations of a host of wealthy, interested and greedy men. These men, Hall continued, were on terms of friendship

[23] Ibid., 22 and 29 November 1828.

[24] Darling to Murray, 8 November 1828, *H.R.A.*, I. xiv. 445.

[25] Darling to Huskisson, 4 September 1828, *H.R.A.*, I. xiv. 385; Darling to Murray, 22 December 1828, ibid., 534-5.

[26] W. C. Wentworth to the Right Honorable Sir George Murray, K.C.B., His Majesty's Principal Secretary of State for the Colonies, Sydney, New South Wales, 1 March 1829, Encl. in Darling to Murray, 28 May 1829, *H.R.A.*, I. xiv. 800-59.

with the members of the closed Legislative Council, who were the makers of those laws by which the poor of New South Wales were now being every day sacrificed to the rich.[27]

That question of the distribution, let alone deeper issues of the ownership of wealth, played no part in the exchange between Darling and Wentworth. When a group of landed proprietors and merchants, headed by John Macarthur, Robert Campbell, Richard Jones, John Jamison, and 111 others, presented Darling on 4 July 1829 with an address in which they expressed their regret that every measure of His Excellency's had been grossly vituperated in a manner calculated to inflame the minds of the lower orders of the community, and to produce discontent and insubordination among the prisoners of the Crown, Darling told them the Wentworth impeachment was a gross and absurd compound of base and incredible calumnies, which carried with it its own antidote, and furnished ample means of judging of the character and motives of the author. In a private letter to London he told the Colonial Office that Wentworth and his party were not countenanced by one respectable individual. For it meant much to Darling that the political opinions of the opposition were not countenanced by any man of character or respectability. This approval of the respectable far outweighed any disappointment he had experienced from the attempts of infatuated incendiaries to assail his character.[28]

Darling had the mind of the server. When Murray wrote to him on the evils of the mutual jealousy and ill-will which had been permitted to take possession of the minds of the colony's principal officers, and warned him that should such dissensions continue he would feel himself called upon humbly to advise His Majesty to recall the judges, and at the same time to relieve Darling of his command. He received the despatch with feelings of infinite pain and disappointment, but promptly proceeded to compose his differences with Forbes.

Forbes, too, as soon as he heard of the wishes of his masters in London, hastened to tell Darling that it would be his constant care to meet His Excellency with all those feelings of confidence, good will and conciliation which had been so energetically impressed upon them both.[29] Only Wentworth held out against this pressure from London for conciliation and harmony. He was fighting, not for those hopes for better things for mankind proclaimed in the declaration of the rights of man, or for that divine promise of the day when men should neither hurt nor destroy, but rather for revenge against Darling. He stigmatized the address by the landholders and merchants to Darling as a heartless sycophantic effusion. Happily, as he saw it, there was

---

[27] E. S. Hall to Sir George Murray, 2 May 1829, Encl. in Darling to Murray, 6 July 1829, *H.R.A.*, I. xv. 61-7.

[28] The Address of the Landed Proprietors and Merchants of New South Wales to His Excellency Lieutenant General Darling, Governor in Chief, etc. etc. etc., *H.R.A.*, I. xv. 71-2; His Excellency's Reply to the Landed Proprietors and Merchants of New South Wales, 4 July 1829, ibid., 73; see also the Address from the Land holders and Resident Proprietors of the Lower District of the River Hunter, and the reply by Darling 6 July 1829.

[29] Murray to Darling, 30 August 1828, *H.R.A.*, I. xiv. 356-65; Darling to Murray, 21 April 1829, ibid., 714-15; F. Forbes to Darling, 18 April 1829, ibid., 715.

still in Sydney a torrent of public indignation which would denounce Darling as the man who had tortured and murdered Sudds.[30]

That August the torrents of indignation began to swirl around a discussion of the membership of the new Legislative Council, and the first contentious subject before it, the qualifications of jurors in actions at law before the Supreme Court. When the members of the Legislative Council subscribed to their oaths on 21 August, the *Australian* asked why was the old guard of Macarthur, Robert Campbell, and A. Berry still so firmly entrenched: why not a Wentworth, a Jamison, a Jones, or a Wardell, they asked?[31] Soon the question of membership of the Legislative Council gave way to the debate on the qualification of jurors. On this the council was divided. The old guard, led by Macarthur and the Archdeacon, clung to their belief in a sweeping exclusion—an exclusion of all persons who had arrived in the colony of New South Wales under the sentence of the law. The moderates suggested a high property qualification. Others, anxious not to offend the susceptibilities of the emancipists advocated a qualification based on good repute.[32] Once again a priest of Christ's church had spoken in public like a hireling of the ancient nobility of New South Wales: behind the cassock and the gaiters of his 'Venerability' there lived, it was said, a director of the Australian Agricultural Company.[33]

This time Scott could afford to smile at such vulgar abuses. Happily for him the day was at hand for his embarkation on a ship for England where once again he could shelter from the glare of the vulgar under the abundant shade cast by those great oaks, the aristocracy. In the eyes of the Governor he was a most excellent man. Marsden touched him by letting him know that he was approaching his last dinner with Scott with a pang. But to the people at large, to all those men and women to whom he had solemnly vowed to preach the message of divine salvation, he remained a person so devoid of feeling that he could pass in his carriage another clergyman on foot and not deign to offer him a lift. So when a man, at the request of E. S. Hall, still languishing in gaol for that playful and mild raillery against Scott, rushed down to the ship on 20 October and served a summons on Scott for that act of trespass in locking Hall out of the pews in God's Church of St James, the mockers and back-biters savoured to the full the discomforture of a man who had looked down on all their disquiet not with the eye of pity, but with a timid, possibly even frightened, disdain.[34]

By chance on the same day as Scott was receiving this lasting memorial of colonial vindictiveness, Wentworth went down on his knees at the fatal rails in St Philip's Church, and swore before Almighty God that he, the Don Giovanni of Botany Bay, would now forsake all others, and love, honour and cherish Sarah Cox until death did them part. He was then thirty-nine years of age. It was not the consummation of any of those hopes intertwined round

[30] W. C. Wentworth to Murray, 7 July 1829, C.O. 201/209.
[31] *Australian*, 26 February 1829.
[32] *V. & P.* (L.C. N.S.W.) 2, 11, 15, and 24 September, and 9 October 1829.
[33] *Sydney Gazette*, 27 October 1829.
[34] S. Marsden to D. Coates, 14 October 1829 (Bonwick Transcripts, Box 53); Memorandum Book of McGarvie, 29 October 1829 (MS. in M.L.).

his heart in those days in London when the fires of love and ambition had so convinced him that existence without a woman would be an insupportable burden to him. It was not like that earlier passion which he had hoped would confer happiness on him and promote the future respectability and grandeur of his family. Like him, she was one of the native born; like him one of her parents, Francis Cox, had been a convict; like him, she had been born out of wedlock. But she was fifteen years his junior, having been born in January of 1805. There was about her enough of the Rachel to inspire Wentworth once again to write love poetry:

To Sarah

For I must love thee, love thee on,
Till life's remotest latest minute;
And when the light of life is gone,—
Thou'll find its lamp and *mee* within it.

There was about her, too, that strength to endure, that patience to put up with terrible outrages to her pride. Over three years before the wedding she had borne a child to Wentworth. Within a year of her becoming the wife of Australia's greatest native son, rumours were flying round Sydney town that another woman had just borne a child to her husband. It was all very well, it was said, for her to enjoy her husband's jokes at Sam Marsden as the Mahomet of Botany Bay, but what would she do when she found that her husband's idea of behaviour on earth was the prophet's picture of man's pleasures in paradise? It was not given to her to know that Dionysian frenzy of the heart which drove her husband on to glory, and damnation.[35] It was given to her to live with a man who on all questions of the heart lived as though men of his great gifts were beyond good and evil.

That spring of 1829 another man had stood on the deck of a ship as it entered Sydney Harbour, and experienced a mysterious feeling of wonder and thankfulness, but at the same time a chill in the heart on finding the land dreary and cheerless. As for human beings, there was, he feared, no one in the whole of New South Wales whom he would wish to see. He was William Grant Broughton, who had arrived in September to take over from Scott the high office of Archdeacon of the colony of New South Wales with a seat in the Legislative Council. He was just forty years of age when the Duke of Wellington offered him the position in October of 1828, having been born in the year the European arrived at Sydney Cove. In point of pecuniary advantage, as he put it to his mother, it was a most noble offer, as well as an opportunity to exert the abilities God had given him. On the other hand, to go to such a distant country, to separate from all that they knew and loved, was a sacrifice neither he nor his wife could make without breaking their hearts. The Duke had offered the vicar of the Church of St Andrew in Farnham, on

---

[35] For Wentworth's early attitude to marriage, see W. C. Wentworth to D'Arcy Wentworth, London, 10 April 1817 (Wentworth Papers, Letters from W. C. Wentworth); Extract from St Philip's Register of Marriages, 1829 (Wentworth Papers, Miscellanea); for the poem 'To Sarah' see the *Australian*, 23 September 1829; on 4 November 1830 Mrs Jemima Eagar gave birth to a son by Wentworth, see extract from Baptismal Register of Christ Church St Lawrence in T. D. Mutch index in M.L.; Sarah Cox, card in MS. cat. in M.L.; Baptismal Records of St Philip's Church (MS. in M.L.).

a pittance of a stipend and fees from baptisms, marriages and funerals, and gifts of game from the local squires, the stupendous salary of £2000 a year. The Duke knew his man. In a parish church, the walls of which were cluttered with memorials to men belonging to ancient families, and all those who had departed this life in the hopes of a better one, Broughton had proclaimed Christ's church as the rock on which the levelling tendencies of his age, and the new barbarian, Mr Money-Bags, would founder. Broughton had gone over to Strathfieldsaye, the seat of the Duke, and prayed with him in that chapel designed to extol the Roman virtues of discipline, courage and endurance rather than glorify God, and told the Duke he believed it was God's will that he should go to New South Wales. The next day he told his mother that if he had rejected this opportunity to protect his own ease he would never have been satisfied with himself again.[36]

During the journey on the convict transport *John* he asked himself how he could acquire an influence with the convicts. He answered his own question: he would draw their attention to the terrors of the Lord in the strongest language provided by holy scripture. He spent some time too studying the life of Bishop Heber in Calcutta whom he censured for spending his time writing hymns about the heathen in their blindness bowing down to wood and stone, as though such vulgar idolatry and superstition were but the effects of environment, and not the fruits of errors which must be rooted out.[37] This uncompromising dedication to truth was to characterize all his work in a colony where the tendencies of the age were running counter to the vision which sustained him.

When he delivered his charge to the clergy of the archdeaconry of New South Wales in St James's Church on 3 December he spoke as a man sustained by a lofty vision of his mission. He told them that the great purpose of the gospel he proclaimed was to bring man back to God. He conjured them to prevent that general relapse into atheism and infidelity. He urged them to use the parochial schools to nurture the minds of the young in the admonitions of their Lord, for the real greatness and security of Australia depended, he believed, on its religious character. He told them to work for the reformation of the convicts, reminding them they were accredited ministers to One who came not to call the righteous but the sinners to repentance. He told them that as they had been commanded to preach the gospel to every creature, they must labour for the recovery of all those unhappy people, the aborigines. Above all, they must strive to promote those things which were true and lovely and of good report, and turn men to righteousness so that they might shine in the hereafter. It was the duty of the clergy to teach men how to gain this heavenly prize.[38]

[36] Based on W. G. Broughton, Diary of a voyage to New South Wales on the *John* Transport 1829 (Broughton Papers); W. G. Broughton to his mother, Farnham, 27 October and 4 November 1828 (Broughton Papers); see also the Baptismal Registry kept in St Andrew's Church, Farnham; visit to the Church of St Andrew, Farnham, and the chapel at Strathfieldsaye, 15 June 1964.

[37] W. G. Broughton, Diary of a voyage to New South Wales on the *John* Transport 1829, 13 and 26 June 1829.

[38] W. G. Broughton, *To The Reverend Clergy of the Archdeaconry of New South Wales, This Charge* (Sydney, 1829).

Believing that revealed religion should form the basis of education, Broughton immediately drew up a scheme for training up the rising generation and
all succeeding generations in the colony for ever in the faith of Jesus Christ,
the redeemer of the world, and in a firm assurance of the sufficiency of His
atonement for the salvation of mankind. To encourage and maintain piety
and virtue, and a holy, sober and religious character among all classes of the
community, he suggested the creation of a King's School for fee-paying day
scholars in the town of Sydney and one in Parramatta for fee-paying
scholars and boarders, in which pupils would be instructed in every department
of useful and polite learning and science. Broughton hoped that by attending
such schools the inheritors of the large properties, who were hereafter to take
the lead in society and to occupy a station of importance in the country,
would no longer be destitute of the acquirements which should qualify
them for such a situation. He hoped also that in these schools the pupils
would not be so elevated in their opinion of their own powers, and their
memory so cultivated at the expense of their judgment, that they would be
prone to contravene all established opinions, to despise the authority of all
former times, and to decide without any hesitation upon points which had
exercised the minds of the most reflective men down the ages.[39]

To rescue the lower orders of society from such vices of transportation as
adultery, drunkenness and theft, Broughton urged Darling to build more
churches in which the adults could be instructed in the precepts of that
religion which alone could restrain their vicious propensities, and to erect more
schools in which the children could imbibe those same religious principles
which alone could amend their lives.[40] He shared with the Reverend J.
Dunmore Lang and other divines a conviction that an institution of higher
learning in Sydney would also reduce that reckless depravity so alarmingly
characteristic of the lower orders of Sydney. When Chief Justice Forbes laid
the foundation stone of the Sydney College for the vigorous and pious promotion of polite literature and liberal arts among the sons of Australia in
January of 1830, he expressed the hope that the native youth, trained up in
the principles of virtue and religion, and enlightened by the blessings of
liberal education, would emulate the virtues which so nobly characterized the
British people. He, after all, was using the same language as Broughton. Dr
Lang, speaking as one who believed his God had condemned a large portion
of mankind to eternal damnation, with that mien of mingled awe and terror,
and divine wrath, shouted to them: 'Except the Lord build the house, they
labour in vain that would build it. Except the Lord keep the city, the watchman
walketh but in vain'. Broughton, who would have said a loud Amen to that
sentiment too, was not there to hear these words.

To him the Sydney College scheme smelt to high heaven of liberalism in
questions of religion, that monstrous error of religion without doctrine which

[39] W. G. Broughton, Plan for the Formation and Regulating of the King's Schools Prepara-
tory to the Institution of a College in New South Wales, 25 January 1830, and other Enclosures
in Darling to Murray, 10 February 1830, *H.R.A.*, I. xv. 356-67.
[40] W. G. Broughton to Darling, 19 June 1830, Encl. in Darling to Murray, 20 September
1830, *H.R.A.*, I. xv. 725-8.

perverted the minds towards unbelief and indifference to religion. So he stayed away from the ceremony. Was not obedience to principle a higher duty than seeking the applause of the multitude? Was it not his high duty to bear witness to the truth in this dreary and cheerless land, to take his stand on the rock of Christ's church against which, his divine master assured him, the gates of hell would not prevail? How could those puny manifestations of human error, how could the levelling tendencies of his age, survive before such a witness? Or so he mused that January.[41] By then the men and women of New South Wales had begun to judge Broughton as a man. Elizabeth Macarthur, who believed all men to be under the superintendence of an Almighty Ruler, found him chilling, so different from Mr Marsden who said such nice things about the attentive demeanour of all the convict servants on the Macarthur estates, and spoke like a man who was at the very heart of the church.[42]

Events that December and January of 1829-30 only strengthened Broughton's conviction that in this dreary, cheerless land of levellers, adulterers, drunkards and thieves, some restraint should be placed on human passions. As Darling was leaving St James's Church on the morning of 20 December J. D. Shelly, a gentleman in dress and manners, shouted at him: 'You are a damned scoundrel, sir'. Darling, with the coolness he always could call on in moments of danger, turned to the horror-struck, over-anxious McLeay and said calmly: 'The man is mad', just as the attendants uncovered a murderous carving knife under Shelly's coat. In the days that followed the *Monitor* described Shelly as a victim of an oppressive administration which had driven him to use desperate remedies to combat the favouritism and despotism of Darling in the granting of land. Darling, they said, had converted a gentleman into a madman.[43]

By contrast, Darling, encouraged by the alarmist McLeay, with Broughton dropping his own icy truths on religious terror as the only effective antidote to depravity, and John Macarthur shouting once again that in that fearful lottery of human life, the babel of Botany Bay, gentlemen needed protection, asked McLeay to introduce a bill into the Legislative Council to restrain the publication of libellous matters in colonial newspapers. Some applauded this move to curb the fire-brands of disaffection and anarchy, and some sneered that for the hundreds of wicked Pharisees, sycophants and crawlers it was the appropriate scourge. The *Monitor* came out in mourning, its pages edged with a thick black border, and on its editorial page the drawing of a coffin to symbolize the strangling of the liberty of the press by the government of Ralph Darling on 29 January—and adding, with defiance: 'I shall rise again'.[44]

[41] *Sydney Gazette*, 28 January 1830; W. G. Broughton to J. D. Lang, 16 January 1830 (Lang Papers, vol. 16); J. D. Lang, Outline of a Prospectus of an Academical Institution which it is proposed to establish in Sydney, N. S. Wales, Encl. in Goderich to Darling, 12 January 1831, *H.R.A.*, I. xvi. 23-4.

[42] Elizabeth Macarthur to Edward Macarthur, 23 March 1832 (Macarthur Papers, vol. 10).

[43] *Monitor*, 26 December 1829; *Sydney Gazette*, 5 January 1830; Darling to Twiss, 22 December 1829, *H.R.A.*, I. xv. 299-301.

[44] *V. & P.* (L.C. N.S.W.) 29 January 1830; *Sydney Gazette*, 19 January 1830; *Monitor*, 16 January and 20 February 1830.

In anger and dismay the opposition and the disaffected came together to dine on Anniversary Day, 26 January 1830. G. R. Nicholls, an emancipist who had risen to a position of affluence and respectability, spoke with considerable animation of his determination to oppose tyranny whether exercised in the colony or in the mother country. After an angry tirade against the colonial government and much sympathy for such victims of its misrule as E. S. Hall, which provoked loud expressions of sympathy from his listeners, he asked them to drink the health of William Charles Wentworth, the single-handed patriot of Australia. The cheers with which this announcement was received were absolutely deafening.[45]

As this tumult and shouting rose to its crescendo and then died away, a party of men was struggling heroically to return to Sydney town after a journey in which they had uncovered part of the mystery of that harsh land over which men were wrangling in the centres of civilization. The leader of this expedition was Captain Charles Sturt. He had been born in India in 1795, the son of a judge in the East India Company, educated privately and at Harrow, and had entered the army. Like so many of his fellow officers in the Australian colonies, he had served for a time in Spain, in the army of occupation in France and then in that other army of occupation, the English army in Ireland where he had developed an unspeakable distaste for all those who put intercessors, statues or idols between themselves and their God. In May of 1827 he arrived in Sydney with a detachment of his regiment. He was a man on whom the gods seemed to have smiled as he was both monstrous handsome and lovable. Indeed there was about him all his life the bearing of an upright man, who happened to keep into his days of manhood that most precious gift of innocence of heart. He was a transparently simple and straightforward man, guileless in his own motives, and quite unsuspicious of others. A simple faith sustained him through all the changing scenes of life: he had found that neither in rigorous observance nor within convent walls was happiness to be found. By one way only was peace to be found, and that was by prayer. For no treasure on earth would ever persuade him to give up the inestimable comfort of pouring forth his feelings before God in the silence of his chamber. Prayer was his comforter. In many a scene of danger, of difficulty, and of sorrow he had risen from his knees calm and confident. A man relieved did not need any human mediator between himself and the Almighty. How could any man, himself sinful, presume to forgive others their sins? It was a faith for a man to whom much had been given.[46]

During that severe drought of 1826 and the succeeding two years the surface of the earth became so parched that minor vegetation ceased upon it, and it almost appeared as if the sky of eastern Australia was never again to be traversed by clouds. General Darling, sensing that now was the time to send an expedition of discovery into that interior from which Oxley had been obliged to retire in 1819 because of its wet and swampy state, asked his military secre-

---

[45] E. O'Shaughnessy, Holograph statement respecting the conduct of G. R. Nicholls at the anniversary dinner of the Australian Society, 26 January 1830 (MS. in M.L.).

[46] Mrs Napier George Sturt, *Life of Charles Sturt* (London, 1899), *passim*; Minute of Sir John Barrow on Sturt's proposal to cross Australia from South to North (Sturt Papers, microfilm in NAT. L.).

tary, Captain Charles Sturt, to lead an expedition into the interior to ascertain the course of the Macquarie, and the nature of the country to the westward. With him he was to take Hamilton Hume, the currency lad who had over-landed with Hovell in 1824 from Sydney town to the shores of Corio Bay, and a party of eleven other men. They set out from Sydney on 10 November 1828 on a journey which Sturt believed would be of dubious issue, travelled to Wellington and examined the course of the Macquarie, the Bogan, and the Castlereagh Rivers, traversing a large and sun-blasted plain on which the sun's rays fell with intense heat, and on which there was but little vegetation. He then pushed west until the party came on a river flowing south-west on which he conferred the name of the Darling. Then he turned for home, and at journey's end reported that it was a matter of mystery whether the Darling made its way to the south coast, or ultimately exhausted itself in feeding a succession of swamps, or fell into a large reservoir in the centre of the island. He came back, too, to tell them what they already feared, namely that no beneficial consequences would immediately follow from what he had seen, which had only confirmed that cry of anguish of Oxley on first seeing the dreary, inhospitable character of the country to the westward of Bathurst.[47]

There was one gleam of sunshine over that extensive melancholy landscape. There was still the veil of mystery over the channel of the Darling. Did those waters flow into a country where the flint stone he had seen on its banks had been turned into a springing well, and an Englishman's green and pleasant parkland delighted the eyes, as well as the nostalgic hearts of her exiles rather than those dreary plains, where even the vegetation disappeared off the face of a wind-cracked and sun-scarred earth, and men suffered from intense heat? To answer this question in November of 1829 General Darling sent Sturt on another expedition to the Murrumbidgee to see whether that river flowed into the Darling, or emptied itself into the sea on the southern coast of the colony. This time he took with him George Macleay, and not Hume who was suffering from asthma as a result of the privations on the previous journey, and so lost the chance to keep his name for the noble river along which Sturt was destined to travel. All told fourteen travelled in his party.

They came to the Murrumbidgee near Jugiong in that countryside of surpassing beauty where in time Flash Jack from Gundagai will be all among the wool shearing for old Tom Patterson on the one tree plain, where Sturt lifted up his eyes onto the hills and praised his God that He had done such wondrous things. And they moved down river from those lovely hills into a broad plain where by day not a cloud covered the dome of that very vast sky, and at dusk, as darkness came down over the plain, a golden collar lingered on the horizon, and with the nip in the air, and wonder in his heart, Sturt again thanked his Maker that He had done such wondrous things. And the men, warming to a man with such astonishment of heart, such lack of guile, such innocence, such enthusiasm, looked at each other, with some of

---

[47] Darling to Murray, 19 November 1828, *H.R.A.*, I. xiv. 471-2; Darling to Murray, 24 April 1829, ibid., 721-3; C. Sturt, *Two Expeditions into the interior of Southern Australia* (2 vols, London, 1833), vol. 1; see especially ch. 1 and 5 and appendix 5 for the letters of Sturt to the Colonial Secretary written during the expedition.

that still laughter which lived so abundantly in the heart of their leader. Then they came to a country where it was impossible to describe the dreariness of the view. The plains were still open to the horizon, but here and there a stunted gum tree, or a gloomy casuarina, seemed placed by nature as mourners over the surrounding desolation. Neither beast nor bird inhabited these lonely and inhospitable regions, over which the silence of the grave seemed to reign. Sturt's native boy deserted him: the natives who visited their camp came to pilfer. They were an ill-featured race. But Sturt did not despair. Concluding that the horses and the drays could make but slow progress through the swamps, he decided on the bold and desperate measure of building a whale-boat, and sending home the drays. Then in January of 1830, as the morning mists blew over their heads, and the sun funnelled through, Sturt and his party of seven men embarked on the bosom of the Murrumbidgee, and made rapid progress between its gloomy banks till the afternoon of 13 January when one of the party, Hopkinson, called out that they were approaching a junction, and in less than a minute afterwards they were hurried into a broad and noble river. They were on that high road Sturt believed he would find, either to the south coast, or some important outlet.

They proceeded down this river till 22 January when they came upon a river entering their own from the north, which Sturt rightly determined to be the Darling. The natives who had evinced hostile intentions changed miraculously from anger to curiosity, for as soon as the white men landed, their wrangling ceased, and they swam towards Sturt's party like a party of seals. For Sturt this was yet another example of the merciful superintendence of that benevolent providence to which they had humbly committed themselves. In pride at his achievement, Sturt directed the Union Jack to be hoisted, and they all stood up in the boat and gave three cheers. It was, Sturt thought, an English feeling, an ebullition, an overflow which their circumstances and situation alone could excuse—but very pleasing. The eye of every native had been fixed upon that noble flag, to Sturt at all times a beautiful object, and to them all there in the heart of a desert.

After inspecting the course of the Darling they re-entered the capacious channel of the new river, which Sturt named the Murray in compliment to the distinguished officer, Sir George Murray, who then presided over the Colonial Office, not only in compliance with the known wishes of General Darling, but also in accordance with his own wishes as a soldier. For in the channel of a river encumbered with an alien timber, and banks of sand of unusual size, and dreary inhospitable plains on which beasts of the field could obtain neither food nor water, a love of English things so overwhelmed Sturt that the name of the currency lad, that Australian son who had first crossed the noble stream further up river in 1824, disappeared off the map.

In the succeeding days of January and February they continued their journey down stream searching for the outlet where this great river emptied itself into the southern ocean, and came into a more promising country at a bend in the river where it began to run away to the south. The traces of kangaroos were numerous. They began to see signs that the sea was not far away from them: seagulls flew over their heads, and one of the party raised his gun

H

to fire at them, but Captain Sturt prevented him. The gulls, he said, should be hailed as messengers of glad tidings, and not be greeted with that grim messenger—death. And they began to pull the boat against the heavy swell that rolled up the river from the south seas, stroking the oars with the elation of men for whom the tang of the sea in their nostrils, the gulls wheeling overhead, the sand-hills and the stiff breeze blowing, all conveyed the promise of their impending victory.

When it came, it was not quite that for which their captain was prepared. On 9 February their whale-boat shot into the waters of a beautiful lake, a fitting reservoir for the noble stream that had led them to it, and now ruffled by the sea breeze that swept over it. And the captain wondered whether the lake had any practicable communication with the sea—whether this noble stream emptied the waters of all those inland rivers, the Lachlan, the Murrumbidge, the Darling, not into a harbour which man could use, but into a lake surrounded by a sandy and sterile country. The hopes of the captain began to be damped on being confronted at journey's end with the ruffled water and the dreary sterile land which so mocked his conception of the fitness of things. The following day the sound of the sea came gratefully to their ears, and they promised themselves a view of the ocean on the morrow. On that day the captain stood on the shores of Encounter Bay, as the thunder of the heavy surf shook the ground beneath him, and broke with increasing roar upon his ears. The voices of the aborigines echoed through the bush, as the men enjoyed the cockles they had boiled.

As the captain began to examine the quantities of food they had left, he found to his dismay that their circumstances were really critical. His men were weak from the poverty of the diet, and their great bodily fatigue, as well as their bitter disappointment at not being picked up by a boat passing on that huge green sea which thumped and roared and hissed its indifference to their destiny. Sturt knew it was their fate to contend against the united waters of that river with diminished strength and, in some measure, with disappointed feelings. It was as though God's creation mocked man's idea of the fitness of things. Sturt drew back from the abyss of his own despair by his faith in the bounty of divine providence, knowing in his heart that its merciful superintendence would protect them from evil, and would silently protect them where human foresight and prudence had failed. As though to answer the faith in his heart, the river showed to advantage as they re-entered it on 13 February, and the scenery was really beautiful in his eyes and the land on the west bank was of the very richest kind, with hundreds of thousands of acres available which might be used.

As the boat ceased to be aided by the breeze from the sea, and the men were called on to pull harder at the oars, and the heat of the interior of that continent of iron became more and more oppressive every day they moved away from the sea, the spirits of the men dropped. Sturt humoured them as best he could. By the time they had reached the junction of the Murrumbidgee and the Murray their provisions were running very short, the men tired, and the natives threatening. But Sturt had the strength to endure. In the midst of all their adversities Macleay preserved his good humour, and lightened Sturt's task, and cheered the men as much as possible. On 11 April, with their provisions nearly consumed, Sturt sent two men forward on foot to the depot at Pondebadgery. On the very day when their provisions were exhausted, these two men came back with more. McNamee, who had been sullen and silent for days, received uncommon satisfaction from the sight of those drays, and Clayton gorged himself. But Sturt, Macleay and Fraser could not at first relish the meal placed before them. Life is immense. By 12 May they were at Yass Plains, and reached Sydney by easy stages on 25 May.[48]

He had much to tell. He told them of the horrid occurrence which was still fresh in his mind. He had heard, he said, out on the Yass Plains that a blackfellow had killed his infant child by knocking its head against a stone, after which he threw the child on the fire, and then devoured it. He told them the aborigines of the interior were almost in a state of starvation, having been deprived of most of the means of subsistence by European settlers, and so had been driven in too many instances to that inhuman and shocking practice of cannibalism. He told them the great point with the aborigine was not to alarm their natural timidity, to exercise patience in intercourse with them, and to treat them kindly, but eye them with suspicion. He told them of aboriginal women of such loathsome condition and hideous countenances that they were a complete antidote to the sexual passion. He spoke with pride of the behaviour of his men, of how, despite their privations, and their arduous labours, they had not murmured, though one of their number had, it must be said, been sullen and silent. He told them, monstrous handsome as he was, and lovable, and, like King Duncan, a gentleman who built an absolute trust in other gentlemen, how a wish to contribute to the public good had led him to undertake those two journeys which had cost him so much, how his path among a large and savage population had been a bloodless one, and how although the effects of the exposure had impaired his sight, he had owed his deliverance, not to human foresight or human prudence, but to the guidance and protection they had received from that good and all wise Being to whom they had committed themselves. So Sturt at journey's end went down on his knees, and with tears of joy offered his thanks to Almighty God. Darling, impressed by such zeal and such important services recommended that the captain receive promotion as a mark of royal favour to a man who had won that most precious prize of eternal honour and glory.[49]

The word soon passed round Sydney that the captain had laid open a boundless extent of excellent well-watered country to the south of the colony: that he had found districts to which the tide of migration could flow, and a noble river whose banks would one day be studded with settlements. Southward, the womb of the country was neither dry nor sterile. But that news fell not so much on deaf ears, as on ears not ready to be distracted from the political tumult of Botany Bay. For Sydney town was still humming with

[48] C. Sturt, ibid., vol. 2, Expedition down the Morumbidgee and Murray Rivers, in 1829, 1830 and 1831.

[49] Ibid., pp. 177-8, 126, 5-6; see also Report of the Reverend Joseph Orton on missions, 20 January 1836 (Bonwick Transcripts, Missionary, Box 54, p. 1971); Darling to Goderich, 14 April 1831, *H.R.A.*, I. xvi. 242-4.

stories both grave and gay about the Jane New case as the gallant captain, his cheeks still caked with inland clay, came back to tell them what he had seen. Jane New, a convict from Van Diemen's Land, raised questions which went to the heart of all the faction-fighting in Sydney. On the serious side, there was the question whether the Governor had the power to revoke an assignment, with the not unexpected side wind that General Darling's use of the power had been both illegal and tyrannical. On the lighter side, Jane New was a loin-stirrer, who had driven John Stephen, great friend of humanity, to furnish her with two certificates, and put up a shooting box where Jane could live in hiding from the minions of the law who wanted to shut her away.

In March of 1830 Wentworth appeared as counsel for Jane New before the Supreme Court of New South Wales in that role which allowed him to indulge his great passions in life—his campaign against the tyranny of Governor Darling, and his anger with the men and the system which perverted power to the base use of allowing the beauty of women to be consumed away in the dungeons of New South Wales. Once again Wentworth raised his voice against the insolent language of the tormentors of Jane New, against their contempt of law, and their succumbing to the dictum of some secret and controlling power.[50]

GOVERNMENT NOTICE.

Colonial Secretary's Office, 30th July, 1827.

AN Individual, whose servants had been returned to Government by an Order of one of the Benches of Magistrates, having expressed a doubt as to the power of the Bench to remove his servants, the Governor, in order to prevent any misunderstanding on a point of so much importance to the Inhabitants and the Prisoners of the Crown, avails himself of this opportunity to state that it has been signified by the Right Honorable the Secretary of State for the Home Department 'that the 8th Section of the 5th Geo. 4, chap. 84, neither precludes or was intended to preclude the local Government from making any Regulation, which may be necessary respecting the re-assignment of the service of Convicts,' and further 'that the Governor, who is empowered to assign that service, is fully competent to modify his assignment in such manner as justice and good policy may require'.

His Excellency, therefore, desires it to be understood:

1st. That Persons receiving Prisoners of the Crown will continue liable, according to established practice, to be deprived of the service of any such *Prisoners* by order of any Bench of Magistrates, on proof of any such Prisoner being insufficiently fed or clothed, or otherwise improperly treated, or being allowed to work out, or to be at large.

2nd. That no Person is to assign to another a Prisoner of the Crown from the Governor, until he or she shall have obtained His Excellency's sanction.

3rd. That the Governor still reserves to himself the right of granting Tickets of Leave or other indulgence to the well conducted Prisoners in the service of the Settlers and Inhabitants.

In thus adverting to the conditions, under which Prisoners of the Crown will continue to be assigned, and which will be considered binding on all persons receiving them, His Excellency is desirous to state that, with a view of accommodating and relieving the Settlers and Inhabitants, the Government will, under the conditions of Assignment above specified, receive as hitherto such of their servants as they may be desirous of returning to the Public Service.

By His Excellency's Command,

ALEXANDER McLEAY.

[50] Darling to Murray, 29 June 1829, *H.R.A.*, I. xv. 28-33; *Sydney Gazette*, 18 March 1830; for a discussion on the legal power of the governor to re-assign a convict see 5 Geo. IV, c. 84, section 8; see also Bathurst to Darling, 19 February 1827, *H.R.A.*, I. xiii. 115-16; see also *Australian*, 3 August 1827 for Wardell's opinion; see also section 9 of the Act 9 Geo IV, c. 83 and *H.R.A.*, I. xv. 463-4 and 822-4; for Darling's proclamation of 30 July 1827 see *H.R.A.*, I. xiii. 488-9:

Outside the court Hall once again echoed the cry of tyranny and favouritism. In May he sent off to London a letter in which he charged Darling with fourteen offences against mankind, including an unequal, unfair, and impolitic assignment of the Crown lands, and Crown servants, and with having proposed and caused to be passed, laws contrary to the laws of England; and intimidating opposition in the Legislative Council to consent to his measures by the use of menacing language.[51] Wentworth, stirred to anger by Darling's public reference to his impeachment letter as a gross and absurd compound of base and incredible calumnies, sued Ralph Mansfield, the editor of the *Sydney Gazette*, for publishing the words. Wardell, as counsel for Wentworth, asked the court to decide whether it was to be endured that a person was to be held up to the gaze of mankind, as capable of committing such acts as those attributed to the defendant, namely that he was guilty of telling lies. Roger Therry, the counsel for Mansfield, expressed surprise to see Wentworth as the prosecutor of press as he understood Wentworth had gained a reputation for himself in its defence. It only showed the people, Therry argued, that the vaunted champions of the press really adored the god of their idolatry.[52] But the time had not yet arrived when that mask of a champion of the liberties of the people could be ripped off the face of Wentworth.

On 15 October a long contemplated marriage in colonial high life was celebrated at St James's Church between William Dumaresq, the brother-in-law of General Darling, and Christiana Susan, a marvellous, discreet, pious, bulky woman, a daughter of Alexander McLeay the Colonial Secretary. To the *Australian* and the *Monitor*, and all the General's critics, this was just another outward and visible sign of the great truth about the colony—namely that a few families close to the General, the Colonial Secretary, and the Macarthurs had grabbed the best land, and the best-paid positions. But to Darling and the members of his family this grossly misrepresented the situation. Henry Dumaresq was not a man to take such criticism lightly. Born in 1792, he had entered the army just before he turned sixteen and gone on to serve with heroism and distinction at Waterloo where he had been severely wounded. His sister, Eliza Darling, was absolutely reverenced by every description of person. She was the ornament of New South Wales. As for himself and his own wife they had endured all the hardships and humiliations of a convict society to raise New South Wales from a wilderness to park-land for the English gentry. In this odious country his wife had found she could trust no one. The servant they had brought with them had left to grow disgustingly rich selling millinery. Their convict housemaid was fonder of the brandy bottle than work. The climate was detestable. The lower orders were depraved, and the country was dull, heavy and gloomy in the extreme. Why should they have to put up with the abuse and insults of the rabble in the press? Darling, who was becoming philosophical with the passage of time, thought such

[51] E. S. Hall to Murray, 19 May 1830, Encl. in Darling to Murray, 27 July 1830, *H.R.A.*, I. xiv. 628-32.

[52] *Sydney Gazette*, 8 and 29 June 1830 and 1 July 1830; Miles (pseud.), *Governor Darling's Refutation of the Charges of Cruelty and oppression of the Soldiers, Sudds and Thompson* (London, 1832), pp. 31-2.

calumnies would continue as long as New South Wales continued to be a receptacle of vagabonds: its character, he added, would not be altered until the present generation at least had passed away.[53] By July of 1828 he had been happy to report that only a few convict clerks remained in government service. By the end of 1830 the government offices in New South Wales had been denuded of those men who were purging their crimes by forced labour.[54]

The large settlers, believing the changes had been designed to serve their interests, began to clamour for more assigned servants. In the first half of 1831 John, William and James Macarthur submitted to Darling that the assigned servants they held were inadequate both in number and description for the extent of their flocks and the nature of the operations and improvements they wanted to carry into effect.[55] In his reply Darling reminded the Macarthurs that everyone was crying out for mechanics in New South Wales, even though the best workmen had been discharged from the service of government. In a postscript he let drop the remark that in the latest despatches from England the land question had been settled at last in a way which would add not a little to the value of the land of the Macarthurs, and that he had been written to on the subject of bringing out labourers.[56]

In a despatch of 9 January 1831 Goderich had told Darling he had come to the melancholy conclusion that the existing regulations for the disposal of land had failed. They had not prevented large tracts of land being appropriated by persons unable to improve and cultivate them. They were founded, he believed, upon an erroneous view of the true interest both of the colony and of the mother country, and exposed the colonial authorities to the suspicion of improper partiality to individuals. The existing regulations had been designed to promote the emigration of capital, considering emigration as a means of relieving the mother country. That was erroneous, because such relief could not come by the mere removal of capitalists. The real and essential service would be performed by the emigration of British labourers, who would also be the most useful for the colony, where there was extreme difficulty in obtaining labour, and competition for the service of the convicts. The existing regulations had also encouraged acquiring land which prevented the growth of a class of labourers for hire. To remedy these evils Goderich proposed a measure, simple and easy in itself, of declaring that in future no land whatever would be disposed of other than by sale by auction at a minimum price, say of 5s an acre. He also proposed to suspend all further grants of land, excepting to persons to whom Darling had already made positive promises.[57] Fourteen

[53] *Australian*, 16 October 1830; H. Dumaresq to Ann Dumaresq, 20 July 1829; Mrs H. Dumaresq to Mrs Winn, 20 February 1830 (Letters of Colonel Henry Dumaresq, MS. in M.L.); Darling to Hay, 7 August 1830, *H.R.A.*, I. xv. 659.

[54] Darling to Bathurst, 20 July 1826, *H.R.A.*, I. xii. 366-7; Bathurst to Darling, 10 March 1826, ibid., 217-18; Darling to Hay, 30 May 1827, *H.R.A.*, I. xiii. 387-9; Darling to Goderich, 2 October 1827, ibid., 534-5; Darling to Huskisson, 31 July 1828, *H.R.A.*, I. xiv. 277-8; Darling to Hay, 1 September 1828, ibid., 377.

[55] The humble memorial of John, James and William Macarthur to His Excellency Lieutenant-General Darling (1831) (Macarthur Papers, vol. 1, pp. 130-2.)

[56] R. Darling to John Macarthur, 4 July 1831 (Macarthur Papers, vol. 4, pp. 274-6.)

[57] Goderich to Darling, 9 January 1831, *H.R.A.*, I. xvi. 19-22; the story of how and why this decision was made will be told in the section on South Australia, which, it is hoped, will form a major part of the next volume in this history.

days later, Goderich discussed in some detail the methods by which it might be possible to relieve the distress prevailing among the agricultural labourers of the south of England by enabling parishes to remove to the colonies those who were without employment. He mentioned the possibility of the settlers being taxed for the use of convicts, and that revenue being used to defray their passages: he also mentioned the possibility of using the revenue from the sale of Crown lands, as proposed in the regulations.[58]

On 1 July a government notice in Sydney announced it had been determined by His Majesty's government that no land should in future be disposed of in New South Wales or Van Diemen's Land, otherwise than by public sale.[59] A month later on 1 August the procedure for bringing these regulations into effect was outlined in a government notice.[60] In the beginning the response in the colony was enthusiastic: 'Our readers', wrote the *Sydney Gazette* in July, 'will rejoice to hear, that the British government is concerting measures for the promotion of pauper emigration to these colonies, which will be the means of supplying us with abundance of cheap, honest, and industrious labourers'.[61] Some mocked at the absurd suggestion that anyone would want to buy Crown land in New South Wales. By September the grumbles, groans and apprehensions of the landowners had swollen into a roar of anxiety, and a clamour for the public meetings at which they could draw up petitions against such absurd, impractical schemes.

Then one day in October Wentworth met James Macarthur in the streets of Sydney, and found that as a landowner he had much in common with him, and agreed to put his name down together with Macarthur's on a list of those requesting a meeting to discuss the propriety of the new regulations for collecting quitrents. Divided as ever, it was not given to him to see that the power of the man against whom he had directed his most brilliant attacks had been reduced by the London decision to withdraw from the Governor the patronage over the disposal of land. Besides, as he talked then to Macarthur in that street in Sydney, one part of him was taken up with the plans of his cronies for the vilification and discomfiture of Darling when he left the colony.[62]

For that October there was more news in Sydney town than just the new land regulations. Darling had been recalled. On first receiving the news he had been dejected, haunted as he had always been by fear of failure in his relations with men ever since the stormy days at Mauritius. Now, at last in October he had been cheered a little to receive His Majesty's approbation for the zeal he had manifested, and for the great improvements which had taken place during the term he had presided over the affairs of the colony. John Macarthur, too, was suffering from the greatest sorrow of his life as he had heard from London that October that his eldest son, John, had died. Darling wrote to comfort him in his deep affliction. Eliza Darling told Elizabeth Macarthur there was but *one Comforter* in such circumstances, and all

---

[58] Goderich to Darling, 23 January 1831, *H.R.A.*, I. xvi. 34-8; in the next volume there will be a discussion on the English debate on emigration.   [59] *Sydney Herald*, 11 July 1831.
[60] *Sydney Herald*, 8 August 1831.   [61] *Sydney Gazette*, 14 July 1831.
[62] Speech of James Macarthur reported in *Sydney Gazette*, 3 December 1831.

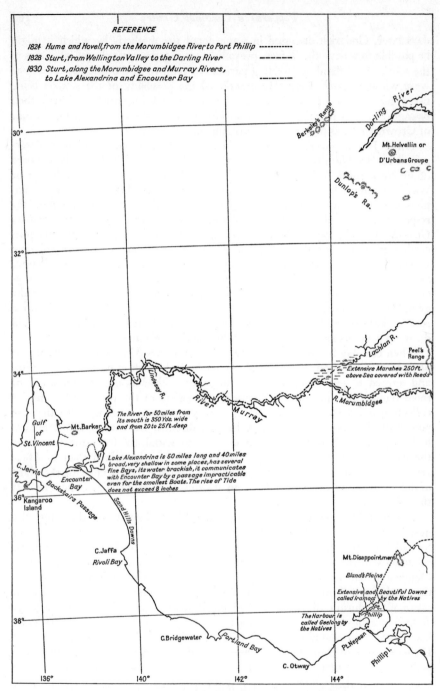

1824 Hume and Hovell, from the Morumbidgee River to Port Phillip ------------

1828 Sturt, from Wellington Valley to the Darling River --------

1830 Sturt, along the Morumbidgee and Murray Rivers,
to Lake Alexandrina and Encounter Bay ----·--·----

1 *Expedition of Hume and Hovell, 1824*
Two Expeditions of Captain Sturt, 1828-1830

Based on *Map of the Discoveries in Australia*, J. Arrowsmith, London 1832

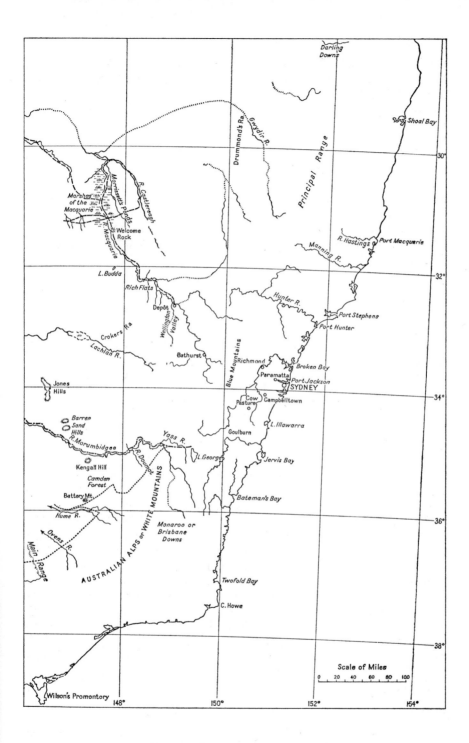

that friendship could do was to mourn with those that mourned. Broughton told Darling that the grossness and falsehood of the attacks on him passed beyond belief. So Darling, worn out by the incessant mental fatigue and application to business, but pleased a little by the praise both from the members of the Legislative Council, and one section of the press for the uprightness and utility of his administration, uttered that great hope, which had sustained him during his days in the colony— 'God's will be done', and prepared to embark on the *Hooghly* for London.[63]

On 19 October at Vaucluse an ox, and half-a-dozen sheep were roasted entire to commemorate the joyful event. Lots of Cooper's and Wright's best were poured out in libations on the joyful occasion. Men wore ribbons in their hats to add to the gaiety and the rejoicing. A band played 'Over the hills and far away'. In the evening there were splended illuminations in glass and other fancy lamps including

W (CROWN) IV.

GOD SAVE THE KING

DOWN WITH THE —

Three days later the *Monitor* printed in large capitals the expression of their joy that a disquieting and oppressive administration was at last ending:

HE'S OFF!

THE REIGN OF TERROR ENDED

That day Darling boarded the *Hooghly*, which was towed down the harbour by the *Sophia Jane*, the first steamboat in New South Wales, the old order being towed out on the high seas by the new. That night, as the General slept on, Eliza Darling was distressed to witness the terror the raging of the waters evoked in her beloved Caroline, and as she wondered whether all the coaxing in the world would get one girl's hair to curl, that shadow of failure with which she had been haunted ever since her general had had his troubles in Mauritius passed over her mind. When Ann Dumaresq heard the news that her beloved Eliza was coming back to her, she wept over the letter, and sobbed again as she ran up the street in Cheltenham to tell the news to her daughter Marianne. She was not to know then nor were any others that the drunken carousal at Vaucluse to commemorate a certain joyful event would be remembered in time as that day when they were also saying farewell to Wentworth as the leader of the radical party in New South Wales, for from that day he

63 For the letter of recall see Goderich to Darling, 15 March 1831, C.O. 201/25, p. 234; in this despatch Goderich explained that he had decided to act on the principle announced by Huskisson in May of 1828—namely, that a governor should hold office for six years; this despatch is not in the relevant volume of the *H.R.A.*; see Goderich to Darling, 23 June 1831, *H.R.A.*, I. xvi. 286; Darling to John Macarthur, 16 October 1831, and Eliza Darling to Elizabeth Macarthur, 14 October 1831 (Macarthur Papers, vol. 4, p. 305); for Broughton on the attacks on Darling see W. G. Broughton to Arthur, 16 November 1830 (Papers of Sir George Arthur, vol. 12, Letters from Bishop Broughton and from the Reverend Samuel Marsden); *Sydney Herald*, 24 October 1831; *Sydney Gazette*, 25 October 1831; *V. & P.* (L.C. N.S.W.) 14 October 1831; Journal of Eliza Darling on the *Hooghly*, 2 November 1831 (Dumaresq Papers).

began to uncover in public the great master-mistress of his passion, that aim to take the top place.[64]

[64] *Monitor*, 1, 19, and 22 October 1831; *Sydney Gazette*, 25 October 1831; J. Thompson, deputy surveyor-general of New South Wales to his father, Sydney, 5 November 1831 (Papers of John Thompson, MS. in M.L.); Journal of Eliza Darling on the *Hooghly*; the point about failure is not made implicitly in this diary which covers such points as how long Darling slept, the terrors of the children, and her hunger for news of friends. The point about failure emerges in the letters of Ann Dumaresq to Eliza Darling about the recall to England, see for example Ann Dumaresq to Eliza Darling, 5 July 1831: 'I fear General Darling will be much disappointed in this recall . . . when I reflect on the real misery we all endured' (after the return from Mauritius); see also Ann Dumaresq to Eliza Darling, 10 November 1831 (Dumaresq Papers).

6

A HIGH-MINDED GOVERNOR IN
VAN DIEMEN'S LAND

ARLY IN 1824 James Stephen told the Lieutenant-Governor elect of Van Diemen's Land, Lieutenant-Colonel George Arthur, that he had an opportunity to make that dependency of New South Wales one branch of a great and powerful nation, which must exercise a mighty influence for good or evil over a vast region of the earth. He told him of the importance of his mission to establish a Christian, virtuous and enlightened state in the centre of the eastern hemisphere and within reach of the Chinese, Hindu and Mohammedan nations which surrounded him. The problem was how to render it Christian, virtuous and enlightened.[1]

Arthur seemed to be the man to undertake such a mission. He shared with Stephen the sense of being called to live with the humble, affectionate and active followers of Jesus Christ, and to receive all those gifts and graces which adorned the Christian character. His own change had been most progressive. Born in Plymouth in June of 1784, he had joined the army as an ensign in 1804, and had seen active service in 1806 and 1809. After promotion to the rank of major in 1812 he had accepted the position of superintendent in Honduras in 1814, where he remained for the ensuing eight years, being promoted Lieutenant-Colonel in June of 1815. In 1814 he married Eliza Orde Usher, the daughter of a Lieutenant-General in the British Army. Then while reading the scriptures he had begun to be weighed down with guilt for a detestable sin against his most Holy Maker, and to know that the heart of every man was desperately wicked, and altogether in enmity with God. Happily for him in the midst of this conviction and abasement, it had pleased God to convey to his soul the most cheering reflections. In Honduras he had read of the all sufficient atonement by Christ, and had become perfectly tranquil, perfectly cheerful and perfectly happy. Through the free grace of God he had come to believe he would one day enter into eternal life.[2]

From that day he had prayed fervently to be weaned away from the amusements of this world so that he might prepare for a better. Dances, concerts, or cards were not innocent amusements: they were the work of the devil, not God's way, but the way of mammon and so must be renounced. Would

---

[1] J. Stephen to G. Arthur, 4 January 1824 (Papers of Sir George Arthur, vol. 4, Correspondence with James Stephen).

[2] G. Arthur to his sister, Honduras, n.d., probably 1819 (Letters of Sir George Arthur to his sister, photo-copy in T.S.A.).

the forerunner of Christ ever have allowed himself the madness of the quadrilles? For him the man who arrayed himself against Satan had a duty to guard others against his assaults. A soldier of God should be warned that the historian, Mr Hume, despite all his learning and elegance, was a wretched infidel: he should be warned too that at the age of eighty, Mr Young still sighed after worldly honours and amusements, and that the poet Mr Pope spuriously instilled the poison of self-righteousness into the minds of the young, the deadly effects of which were dreadful to contemplate. A man should go to the harp to sing the praises of God and not to celebrate carnal pleasures: a man should acquire the habit of speaking and praying extempore, and participate daily in family devotions. By his life he hoped to testify to his fellow-creatures that he was walking in the Gospel light, and so assist others in the way to heaven. Above all, as a soldier of God he must be free from the errors of enthusiasm and superstition.[3]

The appearance of the man reflected the faith by which he lived. He wore black clothes. He walked with a stoop, as though his shoulders were weighed down with the burden of human depravity. The pallor of the cheeks, and the tight-lipped mouth, which rarely broke into a smile, seemed a fit instrument for those passionless petitions he sent up daily to his God. Only the huge lack-lustre eyes betrayed at times those moments of hysteria, those days when the gusts of passion had swept over him, leaving that huge deposit of guilt which had been washed away by God's saving grace. His task in the world, apart from assisting others in the way to heaven, was to remove all those abominations which affronted the intentions of his heavenly father. In Honduras he had shuddered to discover that a British Act of Parliament protected brutes from the consequences of their inhumanity to their slaves.

For the most part he held a pessimistic position on the fruits of human endeavour. Was not the heart of every man too despicably wicked to be capable of anything save madness and folly? In politics he was a Tory, because the authority and rank they preached seemed to promise some mitigation of the fruits of man's folly, as well as some deterrent to his passions. Arthur was always looking for a system of discipline which would curb depravity in man without degrading him. For man was made in the image of God, and must always appear worthy of his most Holy Maker. For the rest he affected a vast indifference to what went on in the world. Yet despite his own search for ways and means to wean him from this world, and his saturating his mind and heart with every argument on the necessity for a better, he never ceased to sigh for worldly honours, and never ceased to lay up for himself treasures on earth as well as in heaven.

In London in 1823 at one moment he was sharing with James Stephen that bond of all those who lived as the humble, active and affectionate followers of Jesus Christ, and at the next moment he was pressing my lord Bathurst for an assurance that if he took up the office of Lieutenant-Governor of Van Diemen's Land, he might have the great expectation of moving on in time to New South Wales. He spent time, too, exchanging mind with James Stephen on just how long he would have to wait before Van Diemen's Land received its indepen-

[3] Ibid.; see also G. Arthur to his sister, Honduras, 8 March 1819, ibid.

dence from New South Wales. Such was the man who on 22 August of 1823 received a commission from my lord Bathurst to be Lieutenant-Governor of the settlements of Van Diemen's Land where his two predecessors had been such notorious violators of the laws of God, and where the convicts turned to drinking and whoring and fornication, not as an escape from a vale of tears but as a solace and distraction from the savagery of their gaolers.[4]

He and his family arrived on the ship *Adrian* on 11 May 1824, and landed in the government barge under a salute of seventeen guns from Mulgrave battery.[5] The day before the Honourable Chief Justice Pedder had taken his seat on the bench in the new Court House and opened the Supreme Court of civil and criminal jurisdiction, provided for in the Act of 1823 for the better Administration of Justice in New South Wales and Van Diemen's Land. John Lewes Pedder, the eldest son of a barrister of the Middle Temple, had been born in 1784, and educated at Trinity Hall, Cambridge, before being admitted to the Middle Temple in 1813, just four years before William Charles Wentworth had dreamed his great, mad dreams in Elm Court. Timorous by nature, a seeker by temperament and conviction of those harbours of life out of the swing of the sea, a man who ducked and delayed decisions by all the sophistries of the legal pedants, there was about him a tedious attention to detail calculated to irritate an Arthur who was over-hasty for the heart of every matter, and impatient with the word games of the lawyers. Yet there was about Pedder too that absence of any concern with the broader questions of the provinces of the executive and the judiciary which would bedevil the relations between Darling and Forbes in New South Wales. There was about him, too, that concern for the standards of the upright man, that eschewing evil and fearing God which drew Arthur to him with such a tender bond, that twelve years later parting from Pedder was such sweet sorrow that he embraced him and wept. All that was in the womb of time that May when Arthur first met Pedder and first met, too, the Attorney-General for Van Diemen's Land, Joseph Tice Gellibrand who, he had been warned by his fellow-soldier of God, James Stephen, had left London to run away from his creditors.[6]

There, indeed, was the irony of his situation, the source of his undying pain during his days in Van Diemen's Land—that sense of taking guard against the assault of Satan with men whose hearts were desperately wicked. From the Reverend Samuel Marsden he had heard that the inhabitants of the interior of Van Diemen's Land had no one to instruct them in the means

---

[4] Based on J. West, *The History of Tasmania* (2 vols, Launceston, 1852), vol. 1, pp. 187-8; Colonel Arthur makes an affidavit on the cruel and inhuman usage given to some of his slaves by a Mr Bowen, a magistrate in the Honduras, *The Times*, 29 September 1823; portrait of Arthur by B. Duterrau in NAT. L., J. Stephen to Arthur, 4 January 1824 (Papers of Sir George Arthur vol. 4, Correspondence with James Stephen); Letters of Sir George Arthur to his sister *passim*; Commission of Lieutenant Governor Arthur, 22 August 1823, H.R.A., III. iv. 131; for Arthur's hopes to go to the governorship of New South Wales, see the Diary of G. T. W. Boyes, 29 June 1835.

[5] *Hobart Town Gazette*, 14 May 1824.

[6] Based on *Hobart Town Gazette*, 14 May 1824; R. W. Baker, 'The Early Judges in Tasmania', T.H.R.A., *P. & P.*, vol. 8, 1959-60, pp. 71-84; J. Stephen to Arthur, 4 January 1824 (Papers of Sir George Arthur, vol. 4, Correspondence with James Stephen).

of grace.[7] The Reverend Mr Knopwood, the first Anglican chaplain, and Father Conolly, the first Catholic priest, were boon companions who were often seen going through Hobart Town arm in arm particularly after they had been loving the bottle.[8] The Wesleyan missionary, Benjamin Carvosso, had the heart of the matter in him. On first landing in Hobart Town four years earlier in 1820 he had shuddered with horror at the sight of so many men bound in chains. But was it proper to use as an improver of mankind a man who wantonly indulged in the Wesleyan error of enthusiasm?[9] The Reverend Mr Bedford, the incumbent of St David's Church since the beginning of 1823, was vain, and far too preoccupied with emoluments and fees.[10] Only the Reverend Archibald Macarthur, the minister of the Presbyterian Church, had the eloquence and the stature to lead men into the way of peace. Or so Arthur thought, for all his life he lacked that art to read the mind's construction in the face, and so detected no sign of that tempest in the blood of Macarthur which would expose him years later to public derision.[11]

To the aborigine he stood both as a protector and evangelist. The need for protection had become urgent by the time Arthur set foot in Van Diemen's Land, for from an estimated 5,000 in 1803 the numbers had shrunk to less than 500. In June of 1824 just one month after his arrival Arthur issued a proclamation warning those settlers and others who were in the habit of maliciously and wantonly firing at, injuring, and destroying the defenceless aborigines, that they would be prosecuted before the Supreme Court. All magistrates and peace officers were to enjoin the inhabitants of their districts, especially stock-keepers, not only to avoid all aggression, but to exercise great forbearance towards the aborigines, treating them on all occasions with the utmost kindness and compassion.[12]

The following month he decided to make every effort for the civilization of the aborigine, using as his medium a very acute black boy, who had been brought up by a white man's family.[13] It might have been the grain of mustard seed from which a great tree would grow. The advocates of brotherly reconciliation rejoiced and were exceedingly glad. The white man, they said, had driven families from their birthplace, and then completed their cruelty by destroying in sport and consuming for profit the principal means of subsistence for the aborigine.[14] When a group of aborigines wandered into Hobart Town in November of that year Arthur, instead of abandoning them to their corrupters and tormentors, advanced down the street to welcome them, holding out his hand in love and fellowship to them, furnished them with food and clothing, ordered fires to comfort them, and placed four constables near them at night so that their sleep might be free from interruption.

Again, the philanthropists accepted this as a sweet assurance that Christians

---

[7] S. Marsden to J. Pratt, 12 March 1823 (Marsden Papers, vol. 1, pp. 461-5); Arthur to Marsden, 24 May 1825 (Marsden Papers, vol. 1, pp. 444-7).

[8] J. W. Beattie, *Glimpses of the Lives and Times of the Early Tasmanian Governors* (Hobart, 1905), p. 36.

[9] R. D. Pretyman, 'The Early History of Methodism in Hobart, 1820-40', T.H.R.A., *P & P.*, vol. 10, 1962-3, pp. 46-62.

[10] *Sydney Gazette*, 23 January 1823.

[11] *Sydney Gazette*, 6 March 1823; *Hobart Town Gazette*, 17 September 1824.

[12] *Hobart Town Gazette*, 25 June 1824. [13] Ibid., 30 July 1824. [14] Ibid., 23 July 1824.

could conciliate the feelings and promote the welfare of the aborigines.[15] Men in high places, and as well as those in the lower ranks of the government service, were quick to respond to Arthur's concern that the white man should cease to hurt or destroy any of God's creatures throughout the length and breadth of Van Diemen's Land. In the country districts the murder of white men by the aborigines soon stirred up the ugly cry of an eye for an eye, and a tooth for a tooth. Some, too, who did not share Arthur's faith that God was the author and doer of all good things were beginning to say that the intellectual organs were not large in the native skull. And what chance did the Arthur smile of compassion have to withstand those prejudices and angers?[16]

It was the same with the convicts. Of the 12,643 people in Van Diemen's Land in the year of his arrival, 5,938 were convicts. Of these 5,467 were men, and 471 were women.[17] The convicts were there both for their punishment and reformation, and to provide labour for the settlers. But the penal discipline of convicts and the application of their services to the settlers, were in a continual state of collision in the early struggles of a new colony. He agreed too with Mr Commissioner Bigge that the gathering together of convicts did not promote their reformation. But the public works could only be carried on by convict labour, which meant having numbers of convicts collected for this purpose at the stations where their labour was required. He believed that lads capable of being reformed should be assigned to the best and most respectable proprietors. He had found to his mortification that instead of improving the character and behaviour of their servants the settlers universally encouraged the dissipated propensities of their convicts, partly out of dread and partly from a desire to prevail on their convicts to work.

He hoped that by segregating irreclaimables and worst offenders at penal settlements such as Macquarie Harbour where daily labour could be rigorously enforced and where nothing to excite their cupidity could be found, that society would be protected against their violence and their crimes, while they themselves would be saved from further degradation as well as those abominations of men driven by terror and privation in to the ways of the beast. For though God had made man lower than the angels, no man should be driven to become so loathsome as to be no longer worthy of being called the son of God.[18] Two years earlier some convicts had escaped from Macquarie Harbour, and, as food ran short, the stronger and the more cunning had killed the weaker and eaten them. Two survivors had struggled back to camp to tell their tale of horror and abomination, only to die from their privations before the law could enact its own sombre ceremony of retribution.[19]

How could he, believing God's redeeming grace to be the only deterrent to the desperate wickedness of the human heart, bear witness to his faith? For

---

[15] Ibid., 5 November 1824.

[16] W. Paton to Arthur, Woodville, River Clyde, 15 October 1824 (C.S.O. 1, 2, file no. 15, T.S.A.).

[17] Compiled from information in *H.R.A.*, III. *passim*; Report of the Select Committee on Transportation, *P.P.*, 1837, XIX, 518; R. M. Martin, *History of the Colonies of the British Empire* (London, 1843).

[18] Arthur to Bathurst, 9 June 1824, *H.R.A.*, III. iv. 143; Arthur to Bathurst, 15 August 1824, ibid., 161-3.

[19] *Hobart Town Gazette*, 9 November 1822, and 1822 *passim* for other examples.

here, indeed, men were drinking iniquity like water. The year of his arrival the journal of the cannibal Pierce was being gloated over in Hobart Town. There were stories, too, of ex-convicts purchasing women from the aborigines for the carcase of a seal or a kangaroo. If these women were not pleasing to the men, or the men came back from the hunt with great darkness in their hearts, they tied the women up and flogged them in the most cruel manner. These men lived on animal food and birds, and were scarcely a remove from the savage.[20] The only course, as he saw it, was to strengthen the hands of the more respectable and to improve, if possible, the moral character of the inferior class of settlers which, he believed, sank lower and lower from the want of those outward forms of religion to which they had been accustomed in their native country.[21]

So Arthur looked to the pious settlers for that moral improvement and discipline of the convicts which he took to be a main point in the administration of the colony.[22] There, alas, was the source of misunderstanding, anger and bitterness between him and the settlers. Ever since the British government had offered advice and encouragement to settlers to proceed to Van Diemen's Land, a steady stream had arrived in Hobart Town, and had taken up land in the Derwent valley area, or the Longford district near Launceston, but these people were often strangers to what was for Arthur the great drama of human life—that contest between God and the devil for the heart of a man. They wanted the treasures on earth. They had come, and were coming, to exploit the labour of convicts, not to save their souls. They came to cut away all that stood between them and their goal—the primeval forest, the beasts of prey, and the savages, only to find the Lieutenant-Governor of Van Diemen's Land lecturing them on their solemn duty to God to treat the aborigines on all occasions with kindness and compassion.[23]

These settlers had learned the hard way how to survive in a harsh land. The Reid family, husband, wife, and two children, had arrived at Hobart Town from Scotland in the *Castle Forbes* in March 1822. After spending six weeks in that town while Mr Reid searched for land, and Mrs Reid stocked up in the local shops, they set out for their site on the Clyde, camped, unloaded the bare necessities, built their hut, and then sent to Hobart Town for the adornments of life, the piano, the silver plate and the furniture. One night while Mrs Reid was taking her children through some points in the Shorter Catechism bushrangers occupied the hut, and began to smash open the drawers, till Mrs Reid, believing it was better to be a living dog than a dead lion threw them the keys. Then the bushrangers filled sheets with the Reid's possessions, and made off for the bush shouting out that they would be back for more. When Mr Reid returned the next day he vowed he would not stay another day in such a country, but Mrs Reid, who had that strength of a Mrs Macarthur to endure, as well as the latter's faith that all men were under the

---

[20] *Hobart Town Gazette*, 17 March 1825; *Australian*, 21 April 1825.
[21] Arthur to Bathurst, 15 August 1824, *H.R.A.*, III. iv. 161.   [22] Ibid.
[23] For the early migration of settlers to Van Diemen's Land see R. B. Madgwick, *Immigration into Eastern Australia 1788-1851* (London, 1937), pp. 25-7, 44-8, and 63-5; for Arthur's first proclamation on the settlers and the aborigines see *Hobart Town Gazette*, 25 June 1824.

J

superintendence of a benevolent Providence, inspired her husband to take courage and be of good cheer: 'I have come so far with you', she said, 'and I can go no further'.

So they stayed—and put their trust in God. But, to strengthen their divine ally, every night Mr Reid slept with loaded pistols and a drawn sword on the sea chest beside his bed just in case the bushrangers should return. They used the labour of their convict servants to make their wealth, and put up a mansion, in front of which Georgian pillars supporting a wide verandah witnessed to their ideas of comfort and grandeur, while every Sunday in the Presbyterian Church in the new town of Bothwell all the members of the family joined with other settlers from Scotland to sing the Lord's song in a strange land, for the Lord had done wondrous things, and shielded them from drunken convict servants, and bloodthirsty savages.[24]

Joseph Archer, born in Hertford in 1795, encouraged by the success of his brother Thomas in Van Diemen's Land, had entered into a partnership with one George Meredith, and chartered the ship *Emerald*, on which they sailed for Hobart Town in November of 1820. Archer, bringing with him goods and cash to the value of more than £3,250, arrived in March of 1821. He was a man of genial but not genteel manners, a man of heroic disposition who had been endowed with the courage and the drive to make the long journey over the oceans in that hope for better things, that hope that his life would acquire some purpose from success in a new land, as well as by his attachment to what he called the religion of every good man, that faith in the teaching of Jesus Christ to love his God and his neighbour without subscribing to any doctrines, let alone placing himself under the authority of the priest or the parson. Archer, too, had that gift to surround himself with beauteous things; but he was also a man of some quickness of temper. So, after selecting a site for his land near Longford in the county of Cornwall, and beginning to build that mansion of his dreams, he became more and more exasperated by the indolence and rudeness of his convict servants. One day in anger he snatched a stick and asked one of his convicts if he had a damn good hiding whether it would do him any good, and when the convict, cheeky and irreverent, said he did not know, Archer struck him four or five times with the stick, telling him in between blows that this would teach him not to let pigs into his master's garden. Two of the convict servants, having been refused a pass to proceed to Hobart Town to lodge complaints against such beatings and threats to blow their brains out, absconded.

Archer then demanded more convict servants to sow the soil on his estate at Panshanger with English grasses, and plant an Englishman's park in the sombre bush of Van Diemen's Land, but the Lieutenant-Governor had to remind him politely that the supply of such hands was limited. So Archer, who had made the long journey down to Hobart Town to join with other settlers in welcoming Arthur, and had stood in the Court House in May of 1824 and applauded with the clergy, the magistrates, and the settlers as speakers hailed Arthur as a natural vindicator of the rights of the human race,

---

[24] For the early years of the Reid family in Van Diemen's Land, see P. L. Brown (ed.), *Clyde Company Papers* (4 vols, London, 1941), vol. 1, Prologue.

began to doubt whether Arthur had any sympathy with the fires kindling in his own breast. At the same time, another darkness descended on the squire of Panshanger. Shortly before the arrival of Arthur he had gone down on his knees in St David's Church with his bride to be, Miss Elinor Binfield, a school-teacher of Hobart Town, and heard that promise of great mystery, of two becoming one flesh, for the creation of children. But with the passage of time, it was clear that there was to be no fruit from that tree, and a great sadness began to descend on Mr Joseph Archer at Panshanger.[25] In the meantime his fellow-passenger on the *Emerald*, Mr George Meredith, was beginning to have his doubts whether a man like Arthur who was so fanatically concerned with the moral improvement and discipline of the convicts, could at the same time minister to the needs of the settlers.[26]

For change was in the air. In October of 1823 a group of merchants and settlers had met in the house of Mr Edward Lord, landowner and banker, who was said to be the richest man in Van Diemen's Land.[27] A Mr Munro had started to manufacture hats from colonial fur of such quality that the *Hobart Town Gazette* claimed that from then on the head of any man or woman could be decorated with hats equal to any brought out from London.[28] At the end of the year it was reported with pride in Hobart Town that the first cloths from Van Diemen's Land wool were being displayed at London House, and praised for their superior quality.[29] The number of ships arriving from England was increasing, as were the number of breweries and distilleries.[30]

In the Cat and Fiddle, and in the Bird in the Hand, where Arthur's predecessor Lieutenant-Colonel Davey had sat in his shirt-sleeves swapping stories with the locals, and indeed in all the pot-houses of Hobart Town, the mention of Arthur's name that summer was greeted with howls of anger or ridicule. For early that summer the Lieutenant-Governor, in his zeal to improve the morals of the inhabitants, had proclaimed that no licence to retail intoxicating drinks was to be granted to any man who was living with a woman who was not his lawful, wedded wife. It so happened that Thomas Ransom, who had arrived in Sydney as long ago as 1791 and then transferred to Norfolk Island which he left for Hobart Town during the evacuation of 1814, and had held a licence for the last seven years for the commodious house he had built in Murray Street, had such an impediment. He petitioned Arthur to waive the regulation for him, but Arthur, upright and steadfast as ever, refused. So Ransom who was greatly liked was deprived of his licence to his most serious loss and injury, and obliged, if he was to continue with the woman he loved, to seek a new business at the age of seventy. Those who loved life, and those

[25] Based on *Hobart Town Gazette*, 17 March and 25 April 1821, 3 August 1822, 19 and 26 July 1823, and 6 February and 12 March 1824; for an obituary and character sketch see *Launceston Examiner*, 28 and 30 June 1853; for Arthur and his convict servants see Colonial Secretary (Arthur Period) Correspondence Files 635-675 *passim*, T.S.A.; there are references to Joseph Archer in the Franklin Papers, Scott Polar Research Institute; see also the entry under Joseph Archer in T.S.A. and the article on him in *Australian Dictionary of Biography*, vol. 1.

[26] For G. Meredith at Swan Port see Henry Melville, *The History of Van Diemen's Land From the year 1824 to 1835, inclusive*, ed. by G. Mackaness (Sydney, 1965), pp. 20-1n, 38-9n, and 65n; see also the entry under G. Meredith in T.S.A.

[27] *Hobart Town Gazette*, 1 November 1823. [28] Ibid., 17 December 1824.
[29] Ibid., 10 December 1824. [30] Ibid., 27 February and 10 December 1824.

whose humanity had not been suppressed by setting themselves up as the moral improvers of mankind, began to talk of Ransom as the victim of 'the prying eye of some persecuting hypocrite'.[31]

As the rude jokes and jests began to circulate in Hobart Town about the killjoy who had taken over in Government House where prayers and fastings and black looks had replaced the gaiety of those three friends of humanity, Collins, Davey and Sorell, the *Hobart Town Gazette* came out on 8 October 1824 with an editorial in which it described Arthur as a 'Gibeonite of Tyranny'. No one in Hobart Town was quite sure what the editor meant, except that he must have meant an especially bad form of tyranny. But Arthur knew about the Gibeonites—they hanged their enemies on the hill before the Lord—and he began to be alarmed about the effect of the editor's words on the convict population.[32]

The owner of the *Hobart Town Gazette*, Andrew Bent, represented the forces which Arthur feared would bring everything to ruin. Bent, who had been born in London in 1790, was an ex-convict who had arrived in Sydney under sentence of transportation for life in January of 1812 and was sent the following month to Hobart Town. In 1814 he had published under licence the *Van Diemen's Land Gazette and General Advertiser* the name of which he changed to the *Hobart Town Gazette and Van Diemen's Land Advertiser* on 1 January 1821. Towards the close of Sorell's administration Bent had purchased the press plant and rights of the *Gazette* from the government. Within a month of his arrival Arthur had requested Bent to refrain from all criticism of government in his paper. When Bent persisted, Arthur went one step further, and insisted that a *Gazette* which published government material was government property. Bent promptly sent his editor, Thomas, to appeal to Arthur's superior in Sydney, Sir Thomas Brisbane, who, having just made up his mind that Wardell and Wentworth could publish the *Australian* without government supervision, or censorship, could see no reason why Bent should not do the same in Hobart Town. After Thomas returned with the good news from Sydney, Bent published that famous issue on 8 October in which he told the people of Hobart Town just enough to allow them to guess at his great victory, and went on to describe Arthur as the 'Gibeonite of Tyranny', which further convinced Arthur that all the privileges so happily enjoyed in England, however gratifying to British subjects, were quite inconsistent and unsafe in penal colonies. There was, he believed, no stopping half way.[33]

Nor did his critics propose to stop half-way. On 28 January of 1825 the *Hobart Town Gazette* published a letter signed 'Colonist' which proved to be the beginning of a series of letters criticizing the administration. The first series

[31] See the petition of Thomas Ransom to His Honor, Lieutenant Governor Arthur, 4 October 1824, and the letter of Thomas Ransom to Arthur, 21 October 1824 (C.S.O. Arthur Period, Correspondence Files 1942-1966, T.S.A.); for a comment on the Ransom case see *Hobart Town Gazette*, 3 June 1825.

[32] *Hobart Town Gazette*, 8 October 1824; Arthur to Horton, 14 September 1825, *H.R.A.*, III. iv. 366-71; the words 'a Gibeonite of Tyranny' were based on the Book of Samuel 2. xxi. 9.

[33] *Hobart Town Gazette*, 8 October 1824; Arthur to Horton, 14 September 1825, *H.R.A.*, III. iv. 367; H. Heaton, 'The Early Tasmanian Press, and its Struggle for Freedom', *Papers and Proceedings* of the Royal Society of Tasmania for the year 1916.

ended in March. Then on 22 April a second series began which ended on 1 July. They were rich fare for a community which fed greedily on malice and spite against men in high places. Readers were told that Arthur had created sinecures for his friends to allow them to wax fat in the land of their adoption. They were told that the colonial revenue was being squandered on such parasites that farmers and merchants, the two pillars of colonial society, were trembling on the brink of ruin.[34]

Everyone in Hobart Town knew who that 'Colonist' was: he was Robert Lathrop Murray. In the eyes of Arthur he was a most unprincipled character of considerable talents, well-known as the head of a fictitious banking concern in London, to whom he, Arthur, had given great offence by not acceding to a most nefarious land job, which the scoundrel had attempted to pull off in Van Diemen's Land.[35] There was much in Murray's life to expose Arthur to this temptation of the upright to be censorious to, and even to hound, a man who was driven on by passions he either could not or would not control. Murray, as Arthur saw him in 1825, was a man who had the education of a gentleman and the morals of a cad. He had been born in 1777, and educated at Westminster School and Cambridge University. He had been accused of committing the crime of bigamy, for which in 1815 he had been transported for seven years to Sydney, where he became clerk to D'Arcy Wentworth, and so joined the society of a man who, like Murray, was proud of his membership of a distinguished family in the United Kingdom. What Arthur failed to see at that time was that Murray was sustained by a vision quite different from his own obsession with human vileness. Murray was reaching for the light, for the brotherhood of the Masons rather than Arthur's gloomy fatherhood of God, and that blood which washed away the guilty stains. Murray also wanted a society in which a gentleman could enjoy the comforts and refinements of civilization—and was quite untouched by Arthur's concern for the morals of convicts, or any of those hopes which a creep and a pryer wantonly paraded as the religion of that One who had come that men might have life and have it more abundantly.[36]

So both Bent and Murray saw Arthur as a menace to what they hoped to get out of life. On 20 May the *Hobart Town Gazette* came out with their summing-up. It was much better, they argued, that a few supine, ignorant and extravagantly hired public officers should be exposed for their misconduct than that a whole community should be crushed, enslaved, and subjugated. If the former administration of their colony, they argued, had been anti-commercial, anti-agricultural and anti-local in every sense, then by this time the necks of the long-suffering inhabitants of Van Diemen's Land would have been seasoned to the yoke.[37]

This cast Arthur into such a gloom that for a moment he despaired of what to do. Murray, he was convinced, was exceedingly angry because he, Arthur,

---

[34] The first series appeared between 28 January 1825 and 25 March 1825.

[35] Arthur to Horton, 14 September 1825, *H.R.A.*, III. iv. 366.

[36] For the career and character of R. L. Murray see E. Morris Miller, *Pressmen and Governors* (Sydney, 1952), pp. 12-18; see also the article on Robert William Felton Lathrop Murray in the *Australian Dictionary of Biography*, vol. 2.

[37] *Hobart Town Gazette*, 20 May 1825.

would not listen to that land-bartering transaction by which Murray would have pocketed £500. Every hour of his day was so taken up with never-ending applications and complaints from the settlers that it was impossible to think. He had come to the melancholy conclusion that he could no more himself direct the affairs of this island than he could fly. There was the rub. Business, and the never-ending abuse gobbled too much of his time. Nothing sapped or undermined his first purposes in a religious course so effectually as the hurry of public life. Still Providence had led him to Van Diemen's Land, and so in time all would be well.[38]

Within a week God had revealed to him what he must do. So Arthur offered the position of government printer to George Terry Howe, the second son of George Howe, the erstwhile owner of the *Sydney Gazette*. Howe had come to Van Diemen's Land in 1824, and began to publish the *Tasmanian and Port Dalrymple Advertiser* in Launceston on 5 January 1825. Just to make certain Howe took him seriously Arthur promised him a subsidy of £300 a year instead of the paltry £30 which had been paid to Bent, for Arthur had not wrestled with Satan in vain in those dark days of the soul in the Bermudas.[39]

Howe accepted and entered into a partnership with James Ross LL.D., with whom he produced the first edition of the *Hobart Town Gazette* on 25 June, so borrowing the title from Bent. Ross was a man dear to Arthur's heart. Born in Scotland in 1787, the son of an advocate, he had gone to the West Indies as a young man to be superintendent on a plantation, where, like Arthur, he had become an enthusiast for the abolition of slavery. In his private life he affected the piety of those who believed God's redeeming grace to be the only effectual deterrent to human depravity. After arriving in Hobart Town at the end of 1822 he had taken up land near Bothwell but had not prospered like the more worldly getters and spenders in that rich valley. So he came down to Hobart Town where at St David's Church he displayed all those outward and visible signs of the God-fearing man Arthur admired, and on the market place, and wherever two or three were gathered together, he spoke of Van Diemen's Land as a colony for the moral improvement of British criminals, a task in which government could call on the aid of pious and respectable settlers, who, for their part, had the benefit of cheap convict labour, a boon for which they must forego that other privilege of being an Englishman—that liberty of expression. In Hobart Town, he was fond of saying, a man was wise to keep a civil tongue in his head, for fear that his words might excite the convicts to rise and butcher their gaolers. There was in the face of the man a suggestion that this position of censor of the morals of the inhabitants of Van Diemen's Land was pleasing to him, because it gave him the chance to whip the weak. He saw himself as a man for whom independence of spirit was his motto, freedom was his watchword, the happines of his fellow-men his object, and the truth of his religion his buckler and his consolation. His enemies saw him as a man who had formerly been a negro-driver, and then spent the remainder of his days in advocating the cause of torture, triangles,

---

[38] Arthur to S. Marsden, 24 May 1825 (Marsden Papers, vol. 1, pp. 444-7).
[39] H. Heaton, op. cit., *passim*.

and the gallows. They loathed him, and called him a great jack-ass, a per-fidious, smiling, fawning, cringing slave, a carcase fatted on an island's spoil.[40]

When Arthur decided to prosecute Bent for imputations of tyranny, corrup-tion, and improper conduct against the government, Dr Ross obliged with words of approval in the *Hobart Town Gazette*. When Bent was sent to prison for six months Dr Ross again supported His Excellency the Lieutenant-Governor of Van Diemen's Land. That gadfly, Murray, alas, was still at large, conducting a vicious campaign of misrepresentation and vile innuendos in the new paper, the *Colonial Times*, which he began to edit for Bent on 19 August 1825.[41]

By that time Arthur realized the *malaise* had spread beyond the minds of disaffected men such as Bent or Murray who had had the effrontery to pose as advocates of the birthrights of Englishmen, just because he, Arthur, had stepped in as Murray was about to pocket £500. His Solicitor-General, Alfred Stephen, had been hinting to him that one of the senior officers of his govern-ment, the Attorney-General, Joseph Tice Gellibrand, was seeing too much of that unprincipled character Murray. Like Jehovah, Arthur was a firm believer in loyalty and obedience. But, when Stephen first planted the idea of Gelli-brand's perfidy in his head, he was reluctant to believe it. Vanity alone, if not pride, would not allow him to entertain the idea that he had been betrayed by a senior member of his government. As ever he was reluctant to believe evil of any man. Besides, he had been warned in London that Stephen was a pleasant, lively, talkative youth, who had neither thought nor read deeply upon any subject—a man, alas, not possessed of any clear and decided principles, a spendthrift who had married a woman who was neither beautiful nor rich and arrived in Van Diemen's Land on 24 January 1825 to live by the law.[42]

Early in August Stephen tendered his resignation as Solicitor-General be-cause he had found it impossible to act safely as a government officer in union with a person possessing such political feeling and acting with such professional faith as the Attorney-General. Arthur had at last to acknowledge with most distressing feeling that Mr Gellibrand was much associated with persons opposed to the government, and was living especially in constant intercourse with Mr Murray. Arthur began to look into the life of Gellibrand in which he found much to disquiet him. Gellibrand, he decided, was wholly destitute both of sincerity and good faith: he was a man of mercenary and intriguing conduct in no way fitted to participate in that unpleasant, most unpopular, but most necessary work of suppressing abuses in Van Diemen's Land. So Arthur, calling to mind that warning by that soldier of God, James Stephen, that Gellibrand had emigrated to escape his creditors, consulted Chief Justice Pedder on what power he, Arthur, had over Gellibrand. Arthur, knowing that without the law even the soldiers of God might lose their battle with this

---

[40] For the life and character of J. Ross see E. Morris Miller, op. cit., pp. 39-40; see also J. West, *The History of Tasmania* (2 vols, Launceston, 1852) vol. 1, pp. 125-7; see also the portrait of James Ross by John Gould, the original of which is in the museum at Port Arthur.

[41] *Colonial Times*, 19 August 1825; Arthur to Bathurst, 17 January 1826, *H.R.A.*, III. v. 49-53.

[42] J. Stephen to Arthur, 31 July 1824 (Papers of Sir George Arthur, vol. 4, Correspondence with James Stephen).

mercenary of Satan, announced there would be an inquiry in which Gellibrand would be called on to answer the charges of Alfred Stephen, namely that he had behaved inconsistently with the duties and dignity of his high office, that he had acted inconsistently with the purity and propriety of practice, and that, although it was his duty to protect the magistrates, he had violated that duty by advising persons to bring legal actions against the magistrates. The commission of inquiry would consist of the Chief Justice, and two of the magistrates.[43]

With Gellibrand beating his breast, and solemnly assuring Arthur that previous to leaving England he had not left one debt either legal or moral unpaid, the lovers of back-bite and slander in Hobart Town smacked their lips and prepared for their feast. For Gellibrand had his supporters in Hobart Town. He had been born in England in 1786, admitted as an attorney in London in 1816, where he practised law until he left for Van Diemen's Land as Attorney-General, arriving there in March of 1824. His friends knew him as a man who always wore his hat on an incline. In Hobart Town he was known as the man who excelled in both law and jaw: he was noted too for his retentive memory, and his skill in cross-examination. On his estate at Swanport visitors found him both entertaining and garrulous—a man who laughed much, and enjoyed life hugely. Some said that beneath the gay exterior there lurked a man who was driven on by such an eager desire for gain, such an inordinate attachment to filthy lucre, that he had at times been led into a course of practice on which the more rigid of his profession frowned, or muttered 'Tut, tut'. But Arthur wanted something more than a gentleman's tut, tut.[44]

Just as Arthur was about to have his satisfaction rumours reached Hobart Town that an event on which all could unite was about to happen—Van Diemen's Land was about to become independent of New South Wales. In the Act for the better Administration of Justice in New South Wales and Van Diemen's Land of 1823 His Majesty, his heirs and successors had been empowered at any time it seemed fit to constitute and erect the island of Van Diemen's Land into a separate colony independent of the government of New South Wales.[45] It was a subject on which Arthur, his civil and military officers, the settlers, the shopkeepers, the members of the professional class, the parsons, the priests, Ross, Bent, and Gellibrand, could all agree. All agreed that independence would promote prosperity. Nearly all agreed that the appeal from the Supreme Court of Van Diemen's Land to the Governor's Court of Appeal in Sydney was both costly and an affront to their pride. Only R. L. Murray, with what seemed like perversity at the time, argued that because of the infirmity of man's nature an appeal to Sydney, where the local circumstances of

---

[43] For the charges by Alfred Stephen against J. T. Gellibrand see *H.R.A.*, III. iv. 371-4; see also J. T. Gellibrand to Arthur, 30 August and 1 September 1825; C.O. 208/7, p. 105 and pp. 115-16, and Arthur to J. T. Gellibrand, 8 September 1825, C.O. 280/11, pp. 201-2; Arthur to Bathurst, 15 August 1826 (Van Diemen's Land Duplicate Despatches 1825-6, T.S.A.).

[44] J. T. Gellibrand to Arthur, 13 September 1825, C.O. 280/10, p. 6; for the character of J. T. Gellibrand see Simon Stukeley, 4 September 1829, in Henry Savery, *The Hermit in Van Diemen's Land*, ed. by C. Hadgraft and M. Roe (Brisbane, 1964), pp. 99-104.

[45] Section 44 of the Act to provide for the better Administration of Justice in New South Wales and Van Diemen's Land, and for the more effectual Government thereof, 4 Geo. IV, c.96, 19 July 1823, *Statutes at Large*, vol. 9.

individuals must be necessarily unfelt, formed a most protecting and valuable check. In a time of hates and animosities in Hobart Town, he wrote with a foresight time would vindicate, those Christian virtues of forbearance, forgiveness and good will to all men should be practical, but in a society such as Hobart Town, what man could be certain of justice from his fellow-men? So, for his part, he could not join in the request for an unlimited independence.[46]

The other free inhabitants swept aside the insight of this colonial Tiresias. In April of 1824 a public meeting of the landholders, merchants and other inhabitants drew up a petition humbly praying His Majesty to elevate Van Diemen's Land into a separate and independent colony.[47] By the middle of 1825 the inhabitants of Van Diemen's Land were observing with both regret and even indignation that the worst criminals who were banished by the courts of Australia as unfit any longer to blend with the society they had insulted and disgraced were sent to a penal settlement in Van Diemen's Land, where they inoculated with their venom all with whom they associated, became bushrangers, and placed the safety of all country residents at stake, and introduced the bold-faced villains of their own penal settlements to exotic vices. Why should Van Diemen's Land be transformed into a cage for the vultures of Australia?[48] On this point Arthur and Bent were as one. Down at the Cat and Fiddle where Bent was forever saying 'And I tell you another thing that is wrong with this island . . . There are too many Irish convicts', up in Government House in Macquarie Street, Arthur was also agreeing with his most bitter adversary on this point, for he, too, believed that Ireland was a breeding ground for a loathsome superstition and those human monsters, who, after a life of crime and disaffection, practised cannibalism in the sombre bush of Van Diemen's Land.[49]

Soon after the arrival in London of Arthur's predecessor, Lieutenant-Governor Sorell, with the petition of the inhabitants to the King praying for independence, my lord Bathurst transmitted to Arthur an order of His Majesty in Council, dated 14 June 1825, whereby the island of Van Diemen's Land and any island territories or places adjacent thereto were constituted into a separate colony independent of the government of New South Wales. Van Diemen's Land was to have a Legislative Council, as provided for by section 44 of the Act of 1823, composed of a number of persons not exceeding seven nor less than five. The appeal to the Governor of New South Wales from the judgments, decrees, orders and sentences of the Supreme Court of Van Diemen's Land was to cease. All instruments in writing whereby any governor or acting-governor of Van Diemen's Land remitted or shortened the term or time of transportation of any felons or other such offenders was to have the like force effect and virtue in the law as any instruments in writing to be made

---

[46] Letter of R. L. Murray to the landholders and yeomanry of Van Diemen's Land, 14 June 1824, *Hobart Town Gazette*, 18 June 1824.

[47] Public meeting of the landholders, merchants and other inhabitants of Van Diemen's Land, at the Court House, 20 April 1824, *Hobart Town Gazette*, 20 April 1824.

[48] Ibid., 17 March 1825; *Australian*, 21 April 1825.

[49] For Arthur's attitude to Irish catholics see the statement by A. McLeay in *V. & P.* (L.C. N.S.W.) 1838, p. 177, and T. P. MacQueen, *Australia as she is and as she may be* (London, 1840), p. 17; see also Russel Ward, *The Australian Legend* (Melbourne, 1958), p. 52.

by any governor or acting governor of New South Wales. The Governor of New South Wales was to have the title of Governor-in-Chief and retain the authority over such military and naval forces as were deemed appropriate to preserve law and order in both colonies and their dependent territories. The head of government in Van Diemen's Land was to continue to use the title of Lieutenant-Governor.[50]

On 3 December 1825 General Darling, who had arrived in Hobart Town at the end of November on his way to Sydney to take up the high office of Captain-General and Governor-in-Chief in and over the colony of New South Wales and its dependent territories, issued the royal proclamation erecting the island of Van Diemen's Land into a separate colony, independent of the government of New South Wales. He then administered the oaths of office to the Lieutenant-Governor and the Chief Justice; to the members of the Executive Council: the Lieutenant-Governor, the Chief Justice, the Colonial Secretary, A. W. H. Humphrey and J. Thomas; and to the members of the Legislative Council: the Lieutenant-Governor, the Chief Justice, the Colonial Secretary, E. Abbott, W. H. Hamilton, A. W. H. Humphrey and E. Curr, the agent for a new land company. Then a royal salute was fired from Mulgrave battery, and in the evening the houses of the most loyal and public-spirited inhabitants were illuminated. The *Hobart Town Gazette* hailed the day as the beginning of a glorious and an important era in their annals, a day to confirm and exalt that rank and character they were about to maintain in the eyes of the world. Henceforth, between them and Sydney, there would be no more resentment, only a feeling of generous emulation. With such sentiments of peace and good will towards all men in their hearts, some at long last began to say generous things about the Lieutenant-Governor, and nod with approval when a Sydney paper wrote that in their Colonel talent, wisdom and energy shone conspicuously. The Colonel even called for a second bottle of port after dinner at Government House—and one man went home and noted in his diary that Colonel Arthur had a heart.[51]

Such unity and good will were not to last for long. By January of 1826 the formidable J. T. Gellibrand had joined the ranks of Arthur's adversaries. As soon as Arthur had received the report of the commission of inquiry he consulted his Executive Council, who decided that Gellibrand was no longer entitled to the confidence of the government, and should therefore be suspended from office until His Majesty's pleasure could be known. He communicated their decision to Gellibrand on 8 February. Arthur decided to appoint Alfred Stephen as acting Attorney-General, his only doubt being whether the Lieutenant-Governor had the power to suspend the Attorney-General. When Stephen declined to accept the temporary position, Arthur offered the position to J. Hone who promptly accepted. Arthur, like Jehovah, judged men sternly. So Gellibrand, driven to madness by that bland rectitude

[50] Bathurst to Arthur, 28 July 1825, and Order in Council of 14 June 1825, *H.R.A.*, III. iv. 303-6.

[51] Based on the Proclamation by Lieutenant-General Ralph Darling, 3 December 1825, Encl. in Darling to Hay, 5 December 1825, *H.R.A.*, III. v. 11; *Hobart Town Gazette*, 15 December 1825; Journal of William Sorell 1823-5, in *Historical Manuscripts of Tasmania*, no. 1, 1958 (Hobart, 1958).

of his judges, which could cause them to prefer the incompetent, pompous Hone, who always reminded the locals of a duck waddling through a farm-yard, to a man of his gifts in the game of law and jaw, retaliated with such abuse and vituperation of Arthur in the *Colonial Times* that the *Sydney Gazette* compared the *Colonial Times* to the 'terrific features of a serpent's en-venomed fang'. In March of 1826, with the assistance of Andrew Bent as printer, Gellibrand published in Hobart Town a pamphlet on *The Proceedings in the case of His Majesty's Attorney-General J. T. Gellibrand Esq.*, in which he complained of the monstrous and offensive manners of the commis-sioners of inquiry, and how Arthur had prevented him from transmitting to Lord Bathurst a vindication of himself. In this way Gellibrand began to teach the people of Van Diemen's Land that a canting Puritan and vindictive tyrant was presiding over their lives, their liberties, their property and their hap-piness.[52]

In April, just as the leaves of the imported trees took the tints of the season of the sere, the yellow leaf, the members of the Turf Club asked Arthur to become a patron of their club. Arthur replied that though he highly admired a fine horse, he hoped to promote the breed of this noble animal by other means than racing, because the assembling of so many persons for purposes of amusement inevitably led to great irregularities, which would be highly injurious in a convict colony. Wretched men might become the victims of offended justice. So Arthur, mindful of that warning to the man through whom offences might come, declined. Once again in the pot-houses of Hobart Town, in the coffee rooms, drawing rooms and salons, men and women took up the cry that there was a spoil sport, a kill-joy, a bloody saint presiding over the affairs of Van Diemen's Land.[53]

Arthur, strong in the faith of Christ, waited until the storm subsided, at the end of which he rejoiced to say that he had not yielded one tittle to the noisy faction that assailed him.[54] Besides, that May he had other things of great moment to occupy his mind. Edward Curr had arrived with instructions that he be permitted to select 250,000 acres in the north-west corner of the colony for the Van Diemen's Land Company, for which he had been appointed chief agent at a salary of £800 a year. Curr, who was born in 1798, into a Catholic family, had first arrived in Van Diemen's Land in 1820, then had returned to London in 1823, where he had published his *An Account of the Colony of Van Diemen's Land, principally designed for the use of emigrants* the following year. He had then joined in London with Arthur's predecessor

---

[52] Minutes of Executive Council, 6 February 1826, Encl. no. 3, Arthur to Bathurst, 11 Febru-ary 1826, *H.R.A.*, III. v. 111-13; Arthur to J. T. Gellibrand, 8 February 1826, ibid., p. 113; *Colonial Times, passim*; Arthur to Bathurst, 15 August 1826 (Van Diemen's Land Duplicate Despatches, 1825-6, T.S.A.); J. T. Gellibrand, The Proceedings in the Case of His Majesty's Attorney General, J. T. Gellibrand Esq. . . . Hobart Town, 1826; for the sketch of Hone see Simon Stukeley, 9 October 1829 in Henry Savery, op. cit., p. 125.

[53] For the Turf Club affair see the Committee of the Tasmanian Turf Club to Arthur, 21 April 1826, and Arthur to the Committee of the Tasmanian Turf Club, 10 May 1826 (C.S.O. Arthur Period, Correspondence Files 14601-14631, T.S.A.); for comment see the *Colonial Times, passim*, for May and June 1826.

[54] Arthur to Bathurst, 15 August 1826 (Van Diemen's Land Duplicate Despatches, 1825-6, T.S.A.).

Sorell in discussions with the Colonial Office and the representatives of the money-bags of the city of London to form the Van Diemen's Land Company.

The company was floated that year with a capital of £1,000,000 under charter in the Act 6 Geo. IV c. 39. It was to have remission of quitrents on land granted to it, according to the number of convicts for whom it found employment. In April of 1825 my lord Bathurst had summed it all up in a despatch to the Colonel. It was sufficient, he said, to express the certain conviction of His Majesty's government that the introduction of capital judiciously applied could not fail to produce the most beneficial results. The gossip-mongers of Van Diemen's Land knew Curr as a man who had first arrived in the colony with a partner of great celebrity in the blackguard world, one John Raine. His family knew him as a man who reduced every one in his company to a state of vassalage which stored up resentments in the hearts of his victims. Those, too, who had known him in his first ventures in the colony had memories of a skinflint, a tight-fisted business man, excessively vain and touchy about his status in society despite his adoration of the holy mother of God, and his zeal for Catholic education. Arthur, blind as ever to these insights of the getters and the spenders, welcomed him warmly as the agent of a company which would employ convicts in an area far removed from those temptations of towns which such weak vessels could not possibly resist, and encouraged him to hurry north and survey the land.[55]

Arthur had been giving much thought to the whole problem of the disposing of land in Van Diemen's Land. As long ago as July 1825 by lord Bathurst had requested both the Governor of New South Wales and the Lieutenant-Governor of Van Diemen's Land to prepare for a system of sale of Crown land by appointing commissioners of survey to subdivide the territories of both New South Wales and Van Diemen's Land, and to value the Crown land in each settled district. Darling passed these instructions on to Arthur when Van Diemen's Land acquired its independence in December 1825.[56] After consulting his Executive Council Arthur commissioned Edward Dumaresq, Peter Murdoch and Roderic O'Connor on 9 March to make a survey of all the lands within the island of Van Diemen's Land and the dependencies thereof, to apportion the island into counties, hundreds and parishes, and to make valuation of all waste and other land within the said island and dependencies.

Edward Dumaresq, who was to be the first commissioner, was the brother of Eliza Darling, the wife of Governor Darling, and belonged by birth to a

[55] For the life of Edward Curr see article in *Australian Dictionary of Biography*, vol. 1; E. M. Curr, *Some Recollections of Squatting in Victoria* (Melbourne, 1883); A. McKay (ed.), *Journals of the Land Commissioners for Van Diemen's Land 1826-28* (Hobart, 1962), p. 11; for the formation of the Van Diemen's Land Company see an Act for Granting Certain Powers and Authorities to a Company to be incorporated by Charter, to be called *The Van Diemen's Land Company*, for the cultivation and improvement of Waste Lands in His Majesty's Settlement at Van Diemen's Land, and for other purposes relating thereto, 6 Geo. IV, c.39, 10 June 1825, *Statutes at Large*, vol. 10; Bathurst to Arthur, 2 June 1825 and Enclosures, *H.R.A.*, III. iv. 272-9; for Arthur's reaction and work for the Company see Arthur to Bathurst, 15 November 1826, *H.R.A.*, III. v. 398-400; see also Brian Fitzpatrick, *British Imperialism and Australia 1783-1833* (London, 1939), pp. 280-1, and R. M. Hartwell, *The Economic Development of Van Diemen's Land 1820-1850* (Melbourne, 1954), *passim*, and James Bischoff, *Sketch of the History of Van Diemen's Land, . . . and an account of the Van Diemen's Land Company* (London, 1832).

[56] For the instructions to Darling on this point see *H.R.A.*, I. xii. 115.

family which could trace its descent back to the twelfth century. Born in 1802 he had first taken up a career in the army, and had made his way to Van Diemen's Land where he arrived in 1825 to recover his health which had been undermined by a short service in India. Under the influence of his mother he had embraced religion with enthusiasm. There was, he believed, no book to be compared to the Bible in its beauty, sublimity, and wisdom, and sure promises. He looked forward to that time when he, his mother, his sisters and his brothers became part of the numberless family in heaven, where they would meet to worship Him, the father of all, face to face. He was a man who had put some central questions to himself: he had asked why the ungodly were in such prosperity: he had wondered whether the righteous and the wicked were all one before God. Like the psalmist he had come to the conclusion that God had placed the wicked in slippery places so that He might cast them down and destroy them. He also had an eye for the beauty of women—a beauty which he explained as God's work and God's great gift.

Peter Murdoch came from Glasgow to Sydney in 1821, and then moved to Hobart in 1824 to take up a position as commandant of the new settlement at Maria Island. Roderic O'Connor had arrived from Dublin a week before Arthur in May of 1824 with a letter from the Under-Secretary of State recommending him as a settler. He was then forty. Arthur knew him as a respectable settler, whom he had selected wholly on the ground of his character and ability for such a duty. In other respects, Arthur told London, O'Connor was a perfect stranger to him, which was probably just as well, because had Arthur listened to gossip, or gone down to the market place, he might have heard much to disquiet him in the life of this warm-hearted, eccentric, self-professed atheist for whom Voltaire was God. O'Connor had an Irishman's thirst for strong drink, an insatiable appetite for rows with his fellow-men, that flair of the adventurer to amass both acres and money, and that great stroke of luck of enjoying the regard of his fellow-men.[57]

From the journals kept by the commissioners from the day they began their survey on 19 April Arthur found much to confirm his own pessimistic view of the human situation. The commissioners wrote of a people whose innate wickedness had been swollen by living in a convict society. The commissioners wrote of vast acres of land not being cultivated. They wrote of the great men of the day reducing the small settlers to beggary, and driving them off their land to Hobart Town where they lived a miserable existence, their wives sometimes earning a little pittance by washing clothes. They wrote of a society in which the weak were oppressed, where some had taken their lives because of their misfortunes, and some were led to intoxication as the kings of the rogues grabbed their land like greedy wolves let loose in a paddock of lambs. They wrote of the great vices of the country districts, of men drinking rum to excess

[57] For the decision to appoint the land commissioners and the characters of the first three, see the introduction by P. R. Eldershaw in A. McKay (ed.), op. cit., pp. xiii-xxv; for the life and character of E. Dumaresq see E. Dumaresq to Ann Dumaresq, 9 February 1830, and Loose Pages of the Philosophical and Religious Thoughts of Edward Dumaresq (Dumaresq Papers); Arthur to Bathurst, 8 March 1826, *H.R.A.*, III. v. 120-1; for the instructions to the commissioners dated 9 March 1826, see Encl. no. 1 in the above despatch, ibid., 121-2, and for Arthur's letter to the commissioners of survey of 7 March 1826, see ibid., 123-5.

and branding cattle that did not belong to them. They wrote of improvident settlers going to merchants for a chest of tea, for bags of sugar, gallons of rum, and slops for their men, and telling the merchant: 'Sir, I have no money'. The foolish settlers, like the foolish virgins, gave warrants of attorney to the merchants for their land, took the goods at an interest rate of 100 per cent, went home happy, remained drunk as long as the rum lasted. Then the merchants seized their farms, and either sold them or used them to fulfil their own ambition of achieving that social status which the ownership of land conferred.

They wrote of how a few ex-convicts and their children had acquired vast quantities of land. They wrote of how Joseph Tice Gellibrand had used great cunning to buy and sell land at an enormous profit. On the lower orders of rural society they had an equally depressing story to tell. A system of sheep-stealing was practised to a woeful extent. A life of idleness in a stock hut was the summit of ambition for a ticket-of-leave holder. He only moved from the bed to the frying pan, except when a party was made up to rob some unfortunate settler of his sheep. Then he was all alacrity. He became like a boa constrictor who had swallowed a huge prey, and then coiled himself up until a fresh opportunity occurred of devouring another victim. To Arthur this was that human society where on the side of the oppressors there was power, where there was much evil work done under the sun, where if a man fell, he had not another to hold him up. Here indeed a man could say in his heart concerning the sons of men that they were beasts.[58]

When a numerous and respectable meeting of the free inhabitants of the colony assembled at the Court House in March of 1827 to petition the King and both Houses of Parliament for trial by jury and a house of assembly on the grounds that the colony had arrived at that period of improvement when both had become necessary, and they would not consider themselves secure or happy under any institutions which might be offered as a substitute for those which were not only the pride and birthright but the safeguard of every Briton, Arthur cast a cold, sceptical eye on the petition. It had been drafted by two at least of those wolves who had brought ruin to the small settlers in the country districts of Van Diemen's Land—J. T. Gellibrand and E. Lord. It was the work in part of Gellibrand and co. who had done their utmost to fan the flames of discontent among the prisoners. It was the work of free settlers, who were ever impatient of control, and ever ready to visit upon the local government the ruin they had brought upon themselves by their own folly and improvidence. It was, he believed, next to madness to attempt to graft the free constitution of England upon a convict colony.[59]

By way of retaliation, Gellibrand wrote to the opposition press, and filled it

[58] The generalizations and examples are taken from the Journals of the Land Commissioners of Van Diemen's Land in A. McKay (ed.), op. cit.; the passage of Arthur's reflections is based on the Book of Ecclesiastes ii, iv.

[59] *Hobart Town Gazette*, 17 March 1827; Arthur to J. Stephen, 20 April 1827 (Papers of Sir George Arthur, vol. 4, Correspondence with James Stephen); The Humble Petition of the Gentry Merchants Land Owners Housekeepers and others Free Inhabitants of His Majesty's Colony of Van Diemen's Land in Public Meeting assembled by the Sheriff of the Colony, C.O. 280/15, p. 125.

with malicious and at times seditious falsehood against Arthur and his government. Arthur wondered whether the time had come to take up Lord Bathurst's suggestion that the local legislature should impose some restraint on the local press. Happily, there had been some pleasing developments in that field. R. L. Murray had been tamed, not, alas, by any perception of his egregious folly in his early days, but by taking up a courtship with Eleanor Dixon, the daughter of a respectable settler at Ralph's Bay. That soldier of God, and worthy foe of the wickedness of the poison pen, Dr Ross, had plans to start a newspaper of his own, the *Hobart Town Courier*, in which Satan's agents would be held up to the ridicule they deserved. The first number appeared on 20 October 1827.

But when he wrote to Darling in New South Wales to see what he was doing to repress those abuses of the press which were calculated to excite the feelings of the convict population, and dispose them to a more willing submission to their discipline, he heard to his dismay of those doubts of Chief Justice Forbes about repugnancy. Well, God be praised, his own Chief Justice, Pedder, pedantic and tedious though he could be at times, was not puffed up by any of those exalted notions of the independence of the judiciary which were driving General Darling to distraction, let alone any of those temptations to play for the approval of the vulgar, convict-dominated pen-pushers in the radical press. So Arthur, after consulting the members of his Executive Council, passed through the Legislative Council on 15 October 1827 an Act to Regulate the Printing and Publishing of Newspapers, and for the Prevention of Blasphemous and Seditious Libels.[60]

Exercising the power vested in the Lieutenant-Governor by the Act Arthur, after consulting his Executive Council on 31 October, refused to grant a licence to publish a newspaper to Andrew Bent the printer and publisher of the *Colonial Times* on the grounds that he was an unsafe person to be entrusted with the direction of so great a power in a penal colony. When twenty-four inhabitants presented Arthur in November with a remonstrance praying that the act for licensing the press might be repealed, Arthur replied with that icy restraint which so maddened the red-blooded and the rum-inflamed that his Act was approved by a very large majority of the respectable part of the community. For him liberty of the press should not confer opportunities on the convict riff-raff to muddy the reputations of the upright and the respectable. Besides the remonstrance was offensive to himself, the Legislative Council and the Chief Justice, and no gentleman in the commission of the peace could have any justifiable reason for signing such a document.[61]

On 12 October 1827 the *Colonial Times* appeared as a sheet of advertisements without editorial comments. But Bent was not silent for long. On 1 May of 1828 he began to publish the *Colonial Advocate* in which he attacked

[60] Bathurst to Arthur, 2 April 1826, *H.R.A.*, III. v. 130-1; Arthur to Hay, 12 March 1827, ibid., 586-9; Arthur to Bathurst, 24 September 1827, *H.R.A.*, III. vi. 247-9; *Hobart Town Courier*, 20 October 1827.

[61] Arthur to Goderich, 27 November 1827, *H.R.A.*, III. vi. 351-2; Remonstrance of G. Meredith and others to Arthur, 21 November 1827, Encl. no. 1 in ibid., 352-6; Arthur to Mr Meredith and others, 26 November 1827, Encl. no. 2 ibid., 357-8; extract from minutes of Executive Council, 31 October 1827, ibid., 358-61.

again with spirit and passion the administration of Colonel Arthur. 'May we Tasmanians', he wrote with that eye of the patriot for the radical cause, 'ere long enjoy the privilege of Trial by Jury, Representative Government, and a Free Press; we should then be the happiest people in the world'. He asked how much longer his fellow Tasmanians would allow a false notion of pity and humanity, and singular tenderness of conscience, to expose them to the outrages of surely the most savage of all the savages in human shape. He wrote of the vindictive, oppressive, illiberal, and atrabilious spirit who presided over the affairs of Van Diemen's Land. He wrote of the prevalence of bribery: how a man could not get an assigned servant without tipping, and how a man could not get a ticket-of-leave without tipping. He said the people were enthralled: that their rights and privileges were now at the mercy of an irresponsible power: that the press, the only conservator of the public immunities, had been silenced.[62]

Arthur was not greatly troubled. In the *Tasmanian*, which had begun publication on 3 March 1827, Murray was now the most accomplished apologist Arthur had ever found for his system. The settlers, Murray explained, were the ancillaries of government for the reformation of those who had rendered themselves obnoxious to the law. In return for their land grant and aid from government stores they had a responsibility to government. That government was the prisoners' best friend. Tasmania needed harmony and united confidence. Men must see that the public good was inseparable from that of individuals. They must see also that it was not in the power of human reason to convert a penal settlement into a free country in an instant. So long as the British government continued to send convicts to this colony, it would remain a penal settlement. The end of the convict system would bring misery and despair.[63]

Arthur was pleased, though his heart was never deeply engaged in this world of politics. Even when his adversaries sneered at him as a face without a heart he was not greatly troubled, for his subject never could be any passion for the birthrights of Englishmen, and their liberties. He was concerned with that much deeper battle in the heart of a man between damnation and impassioned clay. When Dr Ross explained to his readers that though he did not approve of that stretch of sanctity which would pull down a useful notice from a church or court house door so that it might not be read on a sabbath day, he nevertheless reprobated in the strongest terms the employment of beasts of burden on a Sunday except in cases of necessity.[64] Arthur saluted a man who was talking his own language. When Dr Ross and Mr Giblin who had arrived in January of 1827 to take up duty as a school-teacher, announced in that November a plan to begin a course of elementary instruction in arithmetic and geometry at the Mechanics' Institute in Hobart Town, Arthur very handsomely promised an allotment of ground, because he shared the faith of the founders that education might promote that moral improvement he so passionately strove for for all mankind.[65]

[62] *Colonial Advocate*, 1 May 1828; *Colonial Times*, 26 December 1828.
[63] *Tasmanian*, 18 and 25 October 1827.   [64] *Hobart Town Courier*, 10 November 1827.
[65] Ibid., 17 November 1827; Arthur to Hay, 8 January 1827, *H.R.A.*, III. v. 481.

The need was urgent. In the first week of December nine men from the penal settlement at Macquarie Harbour were tried before the Supreme Court in Hobart Town for holding the head of a constable under the water until he was dead. His Honour, the Chief Justice, almost overcome by the lamentable and unexampled spectacle of nine human beings convicted of so cold-blooded a murder, passed the awful sentence of death upon them. The question was how to prevent those with hearts of men acquiring the hearts of beasts and so converting a land of great beauty into a huge cage for the vultures of mankind.[66]

Arthur answered this question confidently. The behaviour of men could be changed, not by severity of punishment, not by terror, flattery, or any appeal to their baser passions, or by changes in their political system, but by God's saving grace. When the Secretary of State asked him to forward to London suggestions to amend the constitution of Van Diemen's Land, Arthur replied with that indifferent air which pervades the language of a man concerned for salvation who has been asked to write as though any human political contrivance could minister to his high purpose. He could only repeat that despite the clamour of a Gellibrand, or a Meredith, or a Kemp, it was sheer madness to attempt to graft a free constitution on to a convict colony. He was concerned with ways and means of reforming the vicious and leading back the guilty to an upright course by the prospects of restored respectability and privilege. He was opposed to all permanent disabilities for convicts, because they only hardened, demoralized, and utterly depraved the character. For that reason, he would not favour the exclusion of ex-convicts from civil juries. All men, the bond as well as the free, should look forward to that day in Van Diemen's Land when they sat in judgment on the property, liberty, or life of their fellow-men. For this the only qualifications that mattered in his eyes were integrity, prudence and industry.[67]

For the rest, Dr Ross echoed his sentiments in some judicious articles in the *Hobart Town Courier*. The patronage of the British government ought to be reduced, because it led to the appointment of men who were not fitted for their situations. The local government should not be asked to decide on the date of the extension to the colony of those natural rights of popular representation and trial by jury. Van Diemen's Land should remain as a penal colony where the work of reformation went on among so many benighted and misguided individuals of the human race, and where honest industry with its soothing influence was gradually taking the place of idleness and misery. Dr Ross hoped to see the day when 'the march of reform' would be as fashionable a term in Van Diemen's Land as the march of intellect was in England. The grand secret of the system was the contact between prisoners and settlers. The settlers watched over, restrained, and exhibited a good example to the prisoners entrusted to their care. The prisoners embraced industrious habits, and abandoned their vicious propensities, as the only way to avoid misery or add to

[66] *Hobart Town Courier*, 15 November 1827.
[67] Arthur to Huskisson, 30 June 1828, C.O. 280/16, pp. 571-8; Arthur to Huskisson, C.O. 280/17, pp. 75-81.

K

their happiness. Van Diemen's Land offered facilities to prisoners to allow them to keep their resolution to lead a sober, honest and industrious life.[68]

In July of 1828 the Secretary of State wrote to Arthur and explained the clauses affecting Van Diemen's Land in the new Act to provide for the Administration of Justice in New South Wales and Van Diemen's Land and for the more effectual Government thereof. The Supreme Court of Van Diemen's Land was authorized, on the application of either party in a civil case, to award or to refuse a trial by jury as the justice of each particular case may seem to require, the qualification for such jurors being left to the regulations of the Governor and Legislative Council. The judges should feel themselves bound to refuse trials by jury, however much opposed such decisions might be to the current of popular feeling, in all cases where great popular excitement had been aroused, or where the dissensions arising out of the peculiar institution of society in Van Diemen's Land were involved. The Act authorized the Governor acting with the advice of the Legislative Council to extend trial by jury in pursuance of any order to be issued by His Majesty in Council. It was believed that to vest the absolute right of extending trial by jury in the Governor and Council might have exposed them to unremitting censure and hostility. In the meantime, the Legislative Council should forward to London as soon as possible a report on the merits of extending trial by jury. The right to appeal from the Supreme Court to the Lieutenant-Governor was withdrawn and replaced by an appeal direct to the King in Council.

Under the former Act of 1823 the Legislative Council was to consist of a number not exceeding seven, nor less than five. Under the new Act the highest number was to be fifteen and the lowest ten, to answer the criticism that a small body could not acquire extensive powers without arousing serious discontent and jealousy. It was hoped that a council fairly selected from the more intelligent, wealthy, and respectable members of the commercial, agricultural and professional bodies of the colony would receive a salutary influence from public opinion and at the same time exercise a wholesome control over it. The Governor was to remain a member of the Legislative Council, it being the hope of His Majesty's government that no such gentleman honoured with the King's commission would be so forgetful of his duty as to impede the full and free discussion of every question brought by him before the Council, and that the members of the Council would bear all due courtesy and respect towards the Governor. The Governor was therefore to be required to attend all meetings of the Council, at which he would exercise both an original and a casting vote.

His Majesty's government had decided to abolish the right of the Chief Justice to issue a certificate on the repugnancy or otherwise of acts passed by the colonial legislature. The provision in the Act of 1823 which enabled the Governor and His Majesty in Council in certain cases to legislate in opposition to the advice of the members of the Legislative Council was not repealed. Nor was the oath of secrecy prescribed in the previous Act for members of that Council retained. The power of the governor to issue tickets-of-leave or withdraw assigned servants from their masters was placed beyond dispute.

[68] *Hobart Town Courier*, 30 August and 6 September 1828.

Finally, the Act did not impose any restrictions on the colonial press. If abuse of the liberty of the press did really threaten peace and safety, then the right of the colonial legislature to check such a formidable mischief was indisputable, a decision they should take by disregarding alike unreasonable alarm and popular clamour. Murray, however, went on to warn Arthur that without a very grave and serious occasion the Legislative Council should not fetter a privilege, which in its legitimate exercise was so highly conducive to the welfare of society. For the rest, His Majesty's government placed every reliance on the zeal, intelligence, and industry of the members of the Legislative Council.[69]

Arthur might have been drawn by many points in these ample observations of Murray. He might have written on how Van Diemen's Land had been saved from the Darling-Forbes commotions by the common sense and wisdom of the excellent Mr Pedder, or how the press was a formidable mischief in a penal colony. But he contented himself with the briefest of replies, expressing his trust that under the provisions of the Act the prosperity of the colony would be materially promoted.[70] Time changed all things even in Van Diemen's Land. The admirable Dr Ross was writing articles every week to justify the ways of Arthur to man. Now, *mirabile dictu*, despite the reminder in the collect for the bishops and curates, that God alone worked great marvels, man could manage a few minor ones. For here was Robert Lathrop Murray so improved by his marriage to Eleanor Dixon on 1 December 1827 or, if not improved then so changed, that on 6 February 1828 he had begun to publish his new paper, *Murray's Austral-Asiatic Review*, in which Arthur was warmly praised. And Murray, who had been created senior installing officer in the Freemasons in that same year, as a recognition of his own faith in the fatherhood of God and the brotherhood of man, had to put up with the cry of Judas from those with whom he had once savaged the government of the 'saint of Hobart Town'.[71]

Arthur had other subjects on his mind which touched him more deeply. By the same mail in which he had received those ample observations, he had also received a despatch informing him that His Majesty had been advised by the law officers to disallow the Colonial Press Act of 1827 as it was repugnant to the laws of England. In this despatch Murray had gone on to repeat what he had already said in an earlier one—namely that the whole question of licensing the press had been remitted to the consideration of Arthur and the Legislative Council, which he knew, was a very arduous duty.[72] It was one from which Arthur did not flinch or duck. Ignoring alike the cries of 'Gibeonite of tyranny', and the more subtle temptation to leave well alone, to let things drift, to indulge in that masterly inactivity for which the English governing classes

---

[69] Murray to Arthur, 31 July 1828, C.O. 408/5, pp. 52-71; An Act to provide for the Administration of Justice in New South Wales and Van Diemen's Land, and for the more effectual Government thereof, 9 Geo. IV, c.83, 25 July 1828, *Statutes at Large*, vol. 11.

[70] Arthur to Murray, 14 February 1829, C.O. 280/19, p. 294.

[71] E. Morris Miller, *Pressmen and Governors* (Sydney, 1952) pp. 12-18; E. Morris Miller, 'A Historical Summary of Tasmanian Newspapers, Part I,' T.H.R.A., *P. & P.*, vol. 2, 1952-3, pp. 17-21.

[72] Murray to Arthur, 31 July 1828, C.O. 408/5.

had already won some renown, he asked his Council in December of 1828 to
pass an Act to regulate the printing and publishing of newspapers, in which the
unobjectionable provisions were included. He had been too long in the colony
to fear that the assertions in the press would be believed by the more respectable
part of the community to the serious prejudice of his administration and the
cordiality and good feeling which had existed between the local government
and the community for two years past, let alone the unanimity which prevailed
in the various departments of the government. But he was still disturbed about
the effect in the convict community of continued weekly repetition of remarks
upon the inhumanity of committing convicts to restraint, upon the wretchedness
of their condition and their treatment at penal settlements. The main advan-
age in licensing the press lay in the power to prohibit from editing or writing
in newspapers those emancipists who were driven by their experiences as convicts to hold up those in authority to ridicule or contempt. That he was sure,
was the danger of a free press in a convict colony. That was why he and every
member of his two councils sincerely regretted the disallowance of the act.[73]

For Bent the despatch from London was an occasion for rejoicing. With
great pride he announced in the *Colonial Times* on 26 December 1828 that
in the new year his paper would once again appear in the character of a newspaper, as he put it, 'Open to all, influenced by none', and added that freedom
of the press had once more been restored to the colonists of Tasmania. On 2
January his first issue contained his defence of freedom of the press. This,
he wrote, was essential to the well-being and prosperity of any nation, but in
Van Diemen's Land, where books were scarce and people lived far apart, the
people might sink into total ignorance and barbarism were it not for the press.
The liberty of the press was essential both to improve the moral condition of the
colony, and as a security against arbitrary power and invasions of the rights of
property. And he went on to call for a public meeting at which the colonists
could express their universal feeling of regret in the Act of 1828, and their
determination to follow the example of the Cape Colony and get taxation by
representation and trial by jury.[74]

While Bent was gloating over the victory for freedom of the press, other
subjects closer to Arthur's heart were engaging more and more of his attention.
In June of 1828 he had had a most uplifting visit from Archdeacon Scott who
had preached in St David's Church a most inspiring sermon on the evils of
drunkenness. There was, as Arthur saw it, far more point in a cure for
drunkenness than all this talk about liberty of the press and the birthrights of
Englishmen. Every week far too many were fined or otherwise punished for
being drunk and disorderly in Hobart Town. Drunkenness, as Dr Ross never
wearied of telling the readers of the *Hobart Town Courier*, caused nine-
tenths of crime. It induced a sort of insensibility to future events, and an inordinate hankering after present gratifications. It blunted and deadened all

73 Arthur to Murray, 2 January 1829, C.O. 280/19, pp. 5-8; An Act to regulate the Printing
and Publishing of Newspapers, 9 Geo. IV, no. 7, 24 December 1828, Acts and Ordinances of the
Legislative Council of Van Diemen's Land, C.O. 281/1.
74 *Colonial Times*, 26 December 1828, and 2 January 1829; see also *Colonial Times* of 6
January 1829 and 30 January 1830.

the best feelings of the soul. That June of 1828, with the heavens weeping too, one Thomas Pearson, a tall, athletic, comely young man from Yorkshire, had stood on the scaffold in Hobart Town, his eyes red with weeping, as, just before the drop into the silence, he told how gambling and drinking had led him into those expensive habits and dangerous company which had led him on the downward path first to forgery, then to transportation, and then to debauchery and theft in Van Diemen's Land. After the drop, those limbs which had been warm with life would become, as Dr Ross reminded his readers, loathsome with corruption and the food of worms, for that insect of sensual lust was always clamouring in Ross for the satisfaction to be gained from the use of such language.[75]

Mindful too, of that warning of the fate of those who should cause the least of the little ones to stumble, Arthur had at the beginning of his administration urged both high and low to treat the aborigines with forbearance and compassion. As he heard more and more accounts of the dreadful outrages committed by the aborigines, he began to wonder whether they were not prone by nature to enmity against the Europeans. When the aborigines obtained firearms, they had become as formidable in their descents on the settlers as the Kaffirs at the Cape of Good Hope. By the second half of 1826 he had come to the melancholy conclusion that the aborigine had acquired an implacable hatred for the white man. The least of the little ones whom Arthur had hoped in 1824 to lead into the bonds of love and ways of peace were stealing property, butchering white men, and crying out during their raids: 'Fire, you white bastards'.

Appalled by the report of the inhuman murder of seven persons in the vicinity of Penny-Royal Creek and the Macquarie River, and anxious of what those soldiers of God in Downing Street would think of him allowing Englishmen to be slaughtered by 'sooty savages', Arthur issued a proclamation in November of 1826.

> The series of outrages which have of late been perpetrated by the Aborigines of the colony, and the wanton barbarity in which they have indulged by the commission of murder in return for kindness in numerous instances shown to them by the settlers and their servants, have occasioned the greatest pain to the Lieutenant-Governor, and called for his most anxious consideration of the means to be applied for preventing the repetition of these treacherous and sanguinary acts.

The question was: what was to be done? Arthur, after an aside more in sorrow than in anger, on his earlier anxiety to inculcate a spirit of forbearance towards the aborigines, answered that if it should be apparent that there was a determination on the part of one or more of the native tribes to attack, rob, or murder the white inhabitants generally, any person might arm, and, joining themselves to the military, drive them by force to a safe distance, treating them as open enemies.[76]

---

[75] *Hobart Town Courier*, 7 June and 11 October 1828.

[76] Proclamation of 29 November 1826; for the events leading up to this proclamation see C. Turnbull, *Black War: The Extermination of the Tasmanian Aborigines* (Melbourne, 1948), pp. 72-6.

This was a declaration of war. But war, as a policy of protection, proved no more effective than compassion and forbearance. A year later Arthur announced further measures to put an end to the acts of barbarity of the aborigines against the settlers. Sufficient troops would be placed at the disposal of the magistrates and constables in every district for the common defence and protection of the community.[77] All to no avail, for each week the press of Hobart Town and Launceston carried stories of outrages committed by the blacks. In the following October at Green Ponds, as a warning of impending danger, the dogs began to bark outside the hut of a settler. With the men away working in the bush, a mother grabbed her son and daughter and fled. The savages, eager for both plunder and blood, pilfered the hut, then shrieking their blood-curdling yells, gave chase for the mother and her children, killed the son and wounded the daughter, the mother saving her own and her daughter's life by feigning death. Again the press in both towns demanded that some check be put to this horrible havoc on human life. Surely, it was argued, something must be done quickly with these people.[78]

The question was: what? Some clamoured for extermination: shoot the black bastards, and have done with it, and cut the mawkish and sentimental cackle. The *Colonial Advocate* put the case quite simply in May of 1828: 'Let them be removed, or they will be exterminated'. The *Colonial Times* had kept telling its readers all through 1826 and 1827, until the close down in October of that year, that as the settlers and stock-keepers were determined to annihilate every black who might prove hostile, the more merciful way to proceed would be to transfer them to King Island in Bass Strait to prevent the bloodshed which would otherwise inevitably ensue. Some said that as the natives had formed a systematic plan for carrying on a war of extermination against the whites, then the whites, to survive, should exterminate the aborigine.[79]

Arthur was reluctant to accept such a primitive solution. Mindful as ever of the divine command not to kill, and restraining admirably that anger which might have swayed a lesser man whose moral authority had been set at naught, he was looking for a solution which would protect the settler against such outrages without spilling the blood of the aborigines. The measure which he was inclined to accept was to attempt to settle the aborigines in some remote quarter of the island, where they could be supplied with food and clothing and afforded protection from injuries by the stock-keepers on the condition that they confined themselves peaceably to certain limits, beyond which if they passed, they should be made to understand, they would cease to be protected. The land commissioners had recommended the north-east coast of the island as being the most advantageous position for such a purpose. The one problem was how to persuade the aborigines to accept this solution.[80]

Despite all the clamour and urgent appeals for harsh measures he could not divest his mind of the consideration that all aggression originated with the

---

[77] Government Notice, Colonial Secretary's Office, 29 November 1827; *Hobart Town Courier*, 1 December 1827.

[78] *Colonial Advocate*, 1 May 1828; see also *Hobart Town Courier*, 27 September, 25 October and 1 November 1828; see also C. Turnbull, op. cit., pp. 75-7.

[79] *Colonial Advocate*, 1 May 1828; C. Turnbull, op. cit., pp. 75-7.

[80] Arthur to Goderich, 10 January 1828, C.O. 280/16, pp. 44-9.

white inhabitants, and that therefore much ought to be endured in return before the blacks were treated as an open and despised enemy by the government. In one part of him, he had never given up the idea, or rather the hope, that the aborigines would be brought to know what he had got to know in the Bermudas, to his great comfort, that God's grace alone could work the great marvel of curbing human wickedness. So, while some settlers were swearing over their pots of ale, their brandy and water, or their rum toddies, that they would shoot all the black bastards, Arthur appointed G. A. Robinson as guardian to the aborigines on Bruny Island.

Robinson, like Arthur, was devoutly religious. A builder by trade, he had been born in the year those aborigines at Port Jackson had brandished their spears and set up their horrid howl as the ships of the First Fleet moved majestically towards the shores of Sydney Cove. He had arrived at Hobart Town in January of 1824 and was joined by his wife and five children two years later. In the years between 1824 and 1829 he was active in all those societies which manifested his own faith in religion and enlightenment. He was a member of the Auxiliary Bible Society of Van Diemen's Land, and a foundation member of the Van Diemen's Land Mechanics' Institute. In the eyes of the unkind, Robinson was a booby, seeking fame, and even notoriety by telling the black men not to break any of the ten commandments. In his own eyes he was a happy instrument in the hands of God to stop the dire effusion of blood between whites and blacks by promulgating the glad tidings of the Gospel. Before leaving for Bruny he told Arthur that he proposed to instruct the aborigines in the arts of civilization, and to adore that Supreme Being by whom all things were made. Arthur, who believed there was a special providence in the fall of a sparrow, wanted desperately to believe that God, through Robinson, was about to work a great miracle.[81]

On Bruny, where he had landed on 31 March 1829, Robinson learned the language of the aborigines, talked hunting with them, and gradually gained their confidence. The aborigines were delighted to learn how to use the white man's gun: they were prepared to use the white man's medicines to cure sickness. But when Robinson told them of the danger and deformity of sin, and the never-failing retribution of an offended deity when excited by man's overwhelming depravity, the few aborigines who gathered to listen to him showed no sign that God was moving in a mysterious way to perform His wonders. When Robinson told the same few that the roar of falling waters, the sombre vegetation, the mournful cry of the birds, and the strange eerie silence by night reminded him of the utter precariousness of man's mortal pilgrimage, and his future appearance before an all-wise and omnipotent tribunal, the aborigines looked at this kind man who had taught them such useful things not with wonder, but with puzzlement—for that was not their experience of life.[82]

---

[81] *Friendly Mission: The Tasmanian Journals and Papers of George Augustus Robinson 1829-1834* ed. by N. J. B. Plomley (Hobart, 1966), pp. 11-14; G. A. Robinson, Narrative of a Mission to the Aborigines of Van Diemen's Land—undertaken March 25th 1829 (MS. in M.L.); T. F. Bride (ed.), *Letters from Victorian Pioneers* (Melbourne, 1898) p. 124.

[82] G. A. Robinson, Narrative of a Mission to the Aborigines of Van Diemen's Land.

In the meantime, while Robinson was writing in his diary that September of 1829 that he had one convert to the dread sovereign who presided over the affairs of men, in Hobart Town there was much gossip over the announcement of the new members of the Legislative Council. At long last a royal warrant under His Majesty's sign manual for the constitution of the new Legislative Council had arrived from London, nominating and appointing His Majesty's trusty and well-beloved J. L. Pedder, the Chief Justice; J. Burnett, the Colonial Secretary; T. M'Cleland, the Attorney-General; J. Thomas, the Treasurer; W. Bedford, the Senior Chaplain; R. O'Ferrall, the Collector of Customs; W. H. Hamilton, A. W. H. Humphrey, T. Anstey, T. Archer, E. Abbott, W. A. Bethune, J. Kerr and J. Cox, and declaring that in the absence of the Governor, or the officer administering the government, the Chief Justice was to preside at meetings of the Council, and adding a list of persons who should be nominated if any of the above members were dead or absent from the colony. For a season there was much talk in Hobart Town, Launceston, and the country settlements at Richmond, Sorell, Bothwell and Longford on who was in and who was out.[83]

The preceding June the gossipers of Vanity Fair in Van Diemen's Land had had a quite unexpected windfall. On 5 June the *Colonial Times* had begun to publish a series of articles on Van Diemen's Land by one Simon Stukeley who announced later that his aim was to impart information upon the state of manners and society in the colony of Van Diemen's Land, to hold up to deserved ridicule some of the vices and follies by which they were distinguished and to present a mirror wherein good qualities were exhibited. From the first number until the last on 25 December 1829, it was clear that lovers of the low-down on the life of men in high places were in for a high old time. Simon Stukeley had little, if anything, to say on the general state of the colony. His subject was people, their foibles and their airs. He wrote of greedy, rapacious lawyers: he wrote of the idle vapouring for which pert braggarts, idle coxcombs and empty-headed drivellers were ever distinguished. He wrote salaciously of women entering the critical age when an extra sentinel was required to be placed at every avenue leading to the heart. He wrote such lively character sketches of all the public figures of the day, of Arthur, Pedder, Hone, Kemp, Gellibrand, Gregson and Alfred Stephen without mentioning them by name, that for a season identification became one of the sports of Hobart Town. He wrote with envy and spite of those who put on airs, or affected social graces.

Everyone in Hobart Town knew that Simon Stukeley was Henry Savery, a convict who was once again in a debtor's prison. Savery had been born in Somerset in 1791 into a banking family of great respectability, and had prospered as a merchant in Bristol. In an evil hour he had forged bills to promote his own interests. Then, incited to terror and alarm by the fate of the forger Henry Fauntleroy who, having been seduced from the paths of righteousness into the practice of a disgusting and low sensuality, had ended his days by being launched into eternity before a crowd of 100,000 spectators outside

---

[83] A Proclamation by His Excellency Colonel George Arthur, Lieutenant Governor of Van Diemen's Land and its Dependencies, 8 August 1829, C.O. 280/21, p. 180.

Newgate Gaol, Savery bolted from Bristol to London to escape the consequences of his own act of forgery. From there he made for Cowes, planning to
board a ship for America. But with that recklessness to which his passionate
nature drove him to the end of his days, he jumped overboard when discovered
and, when rescued, impulsive as ever, dashed his head against the side of the
ship. Before his judge in Bristol he behaved as a man exposed to a great mental
agony he had neither the strength nor the choice to endure with dignity. He
professed his guilt to be as great as that of Mr Fauntleroy and was prepared,
he said, to meet the Great Judge of mankind. Man, however, was not ready to
grant him such an early reprieve from his tormentors. The judge, after
lecturing him on the enormity of his behaviour, sentenced him to death.
Twenty-four hours before the execution Savery was reprieved on condition
that he be transported for life.

He arrived at Hobart Town on the convict ship *Medway* in December of
1825. There he worked as a clerk in the Colonial Secretary's department
until he was assigned to Captain B. B. Thom for clerical work. From the
first, either because of his own search for attention, or because there was about
him that air which attracted the notice of the colonials with a taste for the
sport of holding men up to derision, Savery was much in the public eye as an
example of a favoured convict. In October of 1828 his wife had joined him,
only to find to her mortification that her husband's account of his standing in
Van Diemen's Land society did not correspond with the facts. After she
announced her intention to return to England Savery cut his throat. Once
again, men had not finished their sport with him. The doctors restored him to
health, just in time for him to be arrested for debt and clapped into prison.
There he indulged in the one sport in which he could excel—his skill in putting
down on paper his own revenge on mankind for what the gods had done to
Henry Savery.[84]

Fate too had given one other twist to the screw. All Hobart Town was
rocking with laughter that August, as Savery languished in Hobart gaol, over
the story that his wife had been the mistress of Algernon Montagu during the
long journey from England to Van Diemen's Land. Hobart Town had welcomed Montagu as a man who had relieved them from Hone, a man they
had judged to be only a few degrees removed from an idiot. Hone, it was said,
had been foisted on them by misguided charity, and that monstrous evil of
patronage. It was also said in Hobart Town that anyone who had ever seen
a duck waddling and sidling through a farm-yard, first looking on one side
and then another, casting up its eyes, all the time making a discordant noise,
could picture to himself the gait, attitude and expressions of Hone. Montagu,
by contrast, was a man of some distinction. He had been born in 1802 into a
family which frequented the society of Wordsworth, Coleridge, Lamb and
Hazlitt. His step-mother had once fascinated Robert Burns. His father had
been endowed not with those gifts of the creative imagination but rather
with that talent for gossip and malice which abound amongst those who prey

---

[84] For the English career of Henry Savery, see *The Times*, 1, 4, 13, 20 and 28 December
1824; for the life of Savery see the biographical introduction in Henry Savery, *The Hermit in
Van Diemen's Land*, ed. by C. Hadgraft and M. Roe (Brisbane, 1964).

on the men with innocent hearts. Hounded by creditors for most of his life, he had used part of his time writing, oddly enough, the standard work on the law of bankruptcy.

The son, Algernon, who had been educated for the law at Gray's Inn and Lincoln's Inn, and called to the bar early in 1826, also became so deeply indebted that he applied for the position of Attorney-General in Van Diemen's Land to James Stephen who, after recommending him, wrote off to Arthur to warn him that Montagu was a raw young man quite unaccustomed to business, and very likely to give himself up to various affectations of sentiment, romantic feeling and literary taste. There was, Stephen continued, in Montagu's manner something that looked artificial and made up, and conveyed the impression of borrowed resources—a man, alas, who was bent upon making an impression. As lawyers who had distinguished themselves in London simply would not go to Van Diemen's Land, the government had had to choose from a set of unfledged candidates.[85]

While Arthur was musing on the odd quirks of fate which had sent a Montagu, a spendthrift and a frequenter of literary salons, to appear in those law courts of Van Diemen's Land which should be engaged in the high purpose of improving the morals of British criminals, Edward Dumaresq at New Norfolk was finding in his beloved Fanny, whom he had married in 1827, a combination of beauty and loveliness in her face which he believed would endure through all time and continue into eternity. He was full that year of a glorious hope and assurance of immortal existence, for his love for Fanny was a type of that heavenly love, surpassing understanding. It was a love, he believed, reserved for those who, supremely loving God in Christ, know how to love one another to perfection. Yet, there was the rub, in heaven there was to be no giving in marriage, and men were to be as angels. What a deprivation, for, as he wrote to his dearest good mother that February to tell her how pleased he was she had sent Fanny some silk stockings because she had such a pretty foot, and it looked so well in silk stockings that he had always wished he could afford nothing else, but, alas, they were enormously expensive here.[86]

Early in 1830 Arthur discussed with his Executive and Legislative Councils the propriety of introducing trial by jury in criminal and civil cases tried in the law courts of Van Diemen's Land. With approving hints from Dr Ross in the *Hobart Town Courier* he decided to stand by his earlier opinion—namely that it would be inexpedient to introduce grand and petit juries for criminal trials in a convict colony. He and the members of his councils were happy to introduce a jury of twelve in any action at law brought before the Supreme Court if either the plaintiff or defendant so desired. The only contentious issue had been whether to permit emancipists to sit as jurors. On this the Legislative

[85] P. A. Howell, 'Of Ships and Sealing Wax: The Montagus, the Navy and the Law', T.H.R.A., *P. & P.*, vol. 13, 1965-6, pp. 101-28; Henry Savery, *The Hermit in Van Diemen's Land* (Hobart Town, 1829); J. Stephen to Arthur, 24 April 1829 (Papers of Sir George Arthur, vol. 4, Correspondence with James Stephen); for the sketch of Hone, see Henry Savery, *The Hermit in Van Diemen's Land*, ed. by C. Hadgraft and M. Roe (Brisbane, 1964), p. 125.

[86] E. Dumaresq, Loose Pages of Philosophical and Religious Thoughts (Dumaresq Papers); E. Dumaresq to Ann Dumaresq, New Norfolk, 9 February 1830, ibid.

Council had been nearly equally divided, until the opposition was reassured to learn that emancipists would be eligible to sit as jurors in England. So, relying on a high property qualification for jurors of land or real estate to the value of £40 a year, or real estate and personal estate to the value of £60 a year, or personal estate alone to the value of £80 a year, or an occupier of a house in Hobart Town to the value of £25 a year, or in other parts of the colony to the value of £50 a year, and the exclusion of all persons twice convicted of any felony or infamous crime, Arthur decided against excluding other emancipists or expirees who had one of the required property qualifications. He hoped this Act to regulate the constitution of juries, which was passed on 19 April, would meet the convenience of the public.[87]

But that April he had much more important things on his mind than the constitution of juries. The Archdeacon of New South Wales, W. G. Broughton, paid his first pastoral visit to Hobart Town. On 15 April Broughton preached in St David's Church those sentiments which always struck a chord deep in Arthur's heart. He had come amongst them, he said, to make an appeal calculated to excite admiration of the mysterious ways of Providence, and to awaken a sentiment of thankfulness to a most merciful God. Multitudes, alas, were passing their days in a state of unconcern as to their eternal destiny: multitudes, alas, were altogether living without God in the world. Many were unhappily distinguished by the practice of such daily intemperance, debauchery and profaneness as to show that all belief in God, and all apprehension of a judgment to come were obliterated from their consciences. He told them of the redoubling of efforts to scatter the dark superstition of the Hindu before the beams of divine light and truth: he told them also something that touched Arthur deeply, of the efforts to emancipate the negro from that most galling and bitter slavery which resulted from unacquaintance with the true God. He urged them to build parish churches with a school attached to them. He urged the teachers to present to the children a selection of passages from scripture in which were set forth God's hatred of sin, the especial sins God abhorred, together with His heavy punishments for the doers of those sins and His grace and favour towards the pure in heart and conduct. Above all he exhorted them to repress and discourage sin, and to extend the dominion of Christian faith, piety and holiness upon earth, so that they might present themselves blameless before the presence of His glory, with exceeding joy, through the merits and mediation of Jesus Christ. Arthur left the church lifted up by that promise that Christ would bring all manner of men unto Him. To spread the message, as well as to preserve it for posterity as a measure of the faith by which men lived, Dr Ross published the sermon in Hobart Town.[88]

At that very moment when Arthur was brimful with his God, and his yearning that all men might be granted a vision of God's throne, great madness

---

[87] *Hobart Town Courier*, 9 January and 8 May 1830; Arthur to Murray, 1 July 1830, C.O. 280/125, pp. 42-3; Arthur to Murray, 12 June 1830, C.O. 280/125, pp. 19-20; An Act to regulate the Constitution of Juries, 11 Geo. IV, no. 5, 19 April 1830, Acts of the Legislative Council of Van Diemen's Land, C.O. 281/1.

[88] W. G. Broughton, *A Charge delivered to the Clergy of Van Diemen's Land . . . 15th of April, 1830* (Hobart Town, 1830).

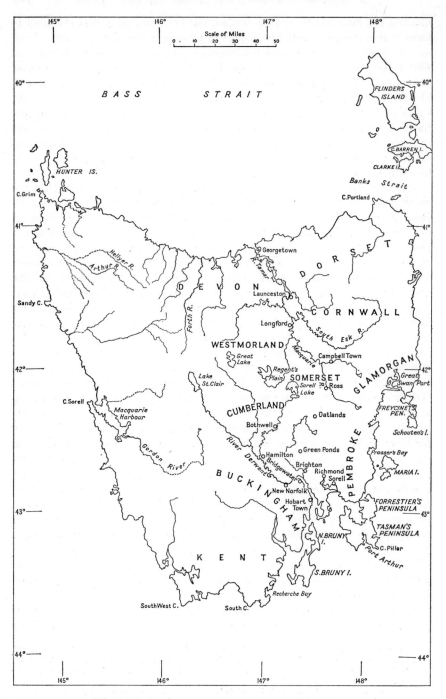

2 *The Main Settlements of Van Diemen's Land in 1835*
Based on *Map of Van Diemen's Land*, Alexander Findlay, London 1841

and folly seized men's hearts in Van Diemen's Land. In July Robinson set out on a journey of reconciliation to the aborigines. What he saw and heard filled him with compassion and understanding for the survivors amongst the aborigines. The children had witnessed the massacre of their parents and relations, and then been carried away by those merciless invaders who had taken their country from them and slaughtered their source of subsistence. Was it any wonder, Robinson asked, that they bore such hatred to the white man, and such a flame of righteous sentiment? British benevolence must prevent the race being entirely annihilated. The British should make some atonement for the wanton cruelty they had practised against the black man. But who could speak for the black man: who could understand them? In grief and shame Robinson wrote to the Reverend Mr Bedford in Hobart Town of his heart's desire that God would interfere and save the first inhabitants of this new land from total annihilation.[89]

It was too late. Four days earlier on 9 September Arthur had published his fatal proclamation. Impressed by numerous representations from the settlers, which expressed their alarm at the increasing boldness of the natives, and of the danger in which their lives and property would be placed, Arthur called on every settler to volunteer cheerfully with the police and the soldiers for one cordial and determined effort which would afford a good prospect of either capturing the whole of the hostile tribes or of permanently upsetting them from the settled districts. His Excellency cautioned all those who volunteered that it was not a matter of amusement or recreation, but a cause of the most important and serious kind, in which the lives of the whole community were more or less at stake. The island was to be divided into six districts, each under the command of a military officer. In order to give unity and vigour to the measures of the government, the direction of the whole force was placed under the command of Major Douglas. Volunteer parties should join the forces in their own districts. All ticket-of-leave holders who were capable of bearing arms were required to report themselves to the police magistrate in their district so that they might be enrolled either in one of the roving parties or otherwise employed in the public service, under the instructions of their respective employers.

The cruel murders the natives had committed with impunity on the white population had made them more bold and crafty until they had become so formidable that the strongest possible united effort of the community was necessary to subdue them. His Excellency earnestly enjoined the whites to manifest the utmost tenderness and humanity towards whatever natives might be captured. In captivity they were to be treated as beings deprived of the blessings of civilization, who had been actuated in their hostile attacks by a distressing misconception of the amicable disposition entertained towards them by the white population. His Excellency added that although no individual was to expect any specific reward, he hoped it was now well understood in the colony that a service rendered to the public was never overlooked or forgotten

[89] Field Journal of G. A. Robinson, 23 July to 13 September 1830 (MS. in M.L.); G. A. Robinson to W. Bedford, 13 September 1830 (Papers of Reverend W. Bedford, MS. in M.L.).

by the colonial government. The great round-up of the natives was to begin on 7 October.[90]

Press and public were jubilant. The long-wished for era of the complete cessation of hostilities of the blacks was, they believed, now at hand. No longer was the peace and business of the whole community to be kept for years at bay by a few defenceless, naked blacks. At long last parties of white men would scour the woods and beat the blacks from their retreats.[91] On 22 September at a public meeting at the Court of Requests in Hobart Town called to form a town guard so that a portion of the military could take part in the movement against the blacks, a surprising unanimity prevailed, as speaker after speaker dwelt on the determined hostility in the breasts of the blacks against the whites which could only be ended by a campaign such as Arthur proposed. Doubts of legality of shooting blacks or qualms of consciousness were silenced sharply by atrocity stories. Gellibrand deprecated the shooting of blacks: Mr Horne shouted him down with the case of a woman and her twin babes who had been butchered recently at the Regent Plains. For the black menace had brought Kemp, Murray, Gellibrand, Horne, and Ross at long last into such harmony with Arthur that at that meeting they could all agree that at this juncture it was peculiarly the duty of every man cheerfully to contribute to the common cause every assistance within his power.[92]

After the meeting some began to be tormented with doubt. Dr Turnbull, the secretary to Colonel Arthur, wondered why no one had cried shame upon a group of men who in cold blood could reason coldly on the propriety of consigning to extermination a whole nation. Was Van Diemen's Land to rival Mexico in scenes of carnage and unrelenting butchery? Another man spoke up for humanity and forbearance, deprecating bloodshed as equally inhuman and uncalled for. But, to reports of more atrocities by the blacks, a blacksmith offered to keep in repair the fire-arms used by the men serving in the Richmond district, adding he would join with pleasure any of the roving parties only he was tender-footed, and subject to rheumatism. Dr Ross in the *Hobart Town Courier* urged the military to use dogs. The pack was beginning to form: the hunt was on: even though one Sabbatarian, calling himself a friend of good order, morality and religion, complained of the noise created by the discharge of fire-arms on Sunday by those who were engaged in practice shots.[93]

On 25 September His Excellency published details of his plan to round up the natives of Van Diemen's Land into the county of Buckingham, and progressively drive them into Tasman Peninsula, and so prevent their escape into the remote unsettled districts to the westward and eastward. Once again he enjoined the whole community to bear in mind that the object in view was not to injure or destroy the unhappy savages, but to capture and raise them in the scale of civilization, whence they would not have it in their power to escape and molest the white inhabitants of the colony.[94] On Sunday 5 October

[90] Government Order, Colonial Secretary's Office, 9 September 1830, *Hobart Town Courier*, 11 September 1830.
[91] *Hobart Town Courier*, 11 and 18 September 1830.
[92] Ibid., 25 September 1830.   [93] Ibid., 25 September and 2 October 1830.
[94] Additional Supplement to the *Hobart Town Courier*, 25 September 1830.

in all the churches of Van Diemen's Land men and women prayed fervently to the great Author of all, the creator and guardian of the blacks as well as the whites, that success might be the result of all their efforts. In St David's Church in Hobart Town those erstwhile implacable enemies, Arthur and Gellibrand, asked their Author and Giver of all good things that this time the battle might be to the strong. Pray on, Gellibrand, for chance has in store for you a terrible fate at the hands of those savages about whom you were praying that day to the God of Battles.[95]

On 7 October the great movement began. Three thousand took to the field, including 550 from the Launceston district, and about 1600 from Hobart Town and the Derwent valley. The whole island appeared in commotion, as bugles, muskets and the cries of the chase echoed and died away in the sombre bush. Hope was in the air men breathed that spring. The number of men volunteering for service, the thoroughness of the plan, the conviction of righteousness—all seemed to promise the success they so desperately desired. There was, they said, something unspeakably animating and delightful in the sight of a whole community roused by this spirit of the purest humanity. To stories of more atrocities by the blacks to strengthen this sense of pressing need, and to much advice on avoiding lighting fires, shouting, hollooing or otherwise making noise in the bush which might give the natives prior warning, the soldiers, police, volunteers and ticket-of-leave men began their work in one general spirit of cheerful and determined perseverance on that 7 October.[96]

By the end of the month reports began to come back to Hobart Town of the fatigue and difficulty of the expedition. There were reports that between fifty and a hundred natives of the Big River and Oyster Bay tribes had been encircled. At night as the men settled down round the camp-fire, being so careful not to make a noise that no bugles were sounded except in case of alarm, the note of optimism gave way to one of doubt and even despair. The spirit of humanity, the god of battles, their own enthusiasm, their righteous indignation, their anger at the treachery and cruel abominations of the black bastards and even their fire power, had availed little so far against the cunning of the blacks, led on and directed as they were by desperate white men who had absconded from penal settlements, chain-gangs, or road parties to live with the natives in remote parts of the country and so enjoy a life of indolent sloth.[97]

By the end of October the volunteer force had occupied a line from Prosser's Bay on the east coast to Sorell, believing the natives were trapped between that line and the coast. Five scouting parties were then sent into the neck of the Tasman Peninsula to count the number of natives in the white man's cage. They moved down close to that bay where almost two hundred years earlier the Dutch navigator, Abel Jansz Tasman, hungry for 'uncommonly large profit', had come to the melancholy conclusion that here was a people with whom the white man could establish no profitable connections, and had set up a flag that those who came after them might know they had been there. They were close, too, to that spot where only fifty-eight years earlier, the

<hr>

[95] *Hobart Town Courier*, 9 October 1830.   [96] Ibid.   [97] Ibid., 30 October 1830.

French explorer, Marion du Fresne, had tried to win the natives with small
presents of mirrors, handkerchiefs, pieces of cloth, poultry and duck, but the
natives had uttered such frightening yells and hurled so many spears that the
French were forced to open fire. On that day the white man's bullets had first
spilled the black man's blood on the sands of Van Diemen's Land. Now here
they were, some of them still hoping for understanding and conciliation, and
some angry, wanting to exterminate the black men, hoping at last they could
round them up, and put them where they could neither harm nor be harmed.
In a season of turbulence, with the dogwood, the native heath, the bacon
and egg flower, and the leaves of the green trees tipped with new life, and over
all, the sombre forest, the vast dome of the sky, and the ever-knowing, ever-
complaining, ever-restless sea, that suggestion that some things were from
eternity and would not change, these men hunted down the blacks, hoping
for that miracle which would give them the happy issue out of their afflictions.

   After scouring the whole peninsula the scouting party came back to the
white man's line to tell the score: two natives had been shot and two had been
captured. It was as though the white man, like the fox, knew many things,
while the land and the black man, like the hedgehog, knew that one big thing
which was forever beyond the white man's reach. By that third week in November, the men were so chafing to attend to their private interests, to their
ploughing, their hunting, their getting and their spending, their wives and
their families, that Arthur had to accept defeat. For him, although the
expedition had not been attended with full success, yet many benefits had
resulted from it amongst which might be enumerated the cordial and unani-
mous feeling which had distinguished every class of the community in striving
for the common good. Let not any despondency descend upon the public mind:
the activity and cordiality of the community afforded sufficient proof that the
evil which had afflicted the community would be removed that summer. The
providence of God would crown their efforts in his own good time. Once
again the priests and the parsons summoned them to their churches to render
thanks to Almighty God for the great benefits they had received at His hands.
The inhabitants of Hobart Town gathered at the Court House close to
Christmas Eve, to thank His Excellency for his late anxious and personal
endeavour to relieve the colony from the scourge the blacks had inflicted upon
it, and prayed that the exertions of the Governor would continue unrelaxed.[98]

   That Christmas Eve, as Arthur's heart filled with joy over the promise of
peace on earth and good will towards men, a captain from the field of battle
was whispering to him that there was probably not a more debased race on the
face of the globe than the aborigines, which, as he put it, might almost be said
to form the connecting link between man and the monkey tribes. But Arthur
was a mighty stranger to that temptation. For him all men had been made in
the image of God. If these poor benighted creatures who were wandering in
great darkness because they had not as yet heard the glad tidings which had

---

[98] Based on Government Order, 26 November 1830, *Hobart Town Courier*, 27 November
1830; ibid., 25 December 1830; *Colonial Times*, October and November 1830 *passim*; see also
the excellent account in C. Turnbull, op. cit., pp. 118-23; for Tasman and Marion du Fresne see
vol. I of this history, pp. 32 and 186; see also Henry Melville, op. cit., p. 71.

been revealed to man in that manger at Bethlehem molested the white man, they must still be treated with forbearance and compassion. If the white man could not catch them then maybe someone such as God's fool, G. A. Robinson, might be able to persuade the aborigines to accept the white man's solution to the problem of how to allow the black man to survive. Like Arthur, Mr Robinson believed that the time had come for God to interfere and save the first inhabitants of this now agitated land from total annihilation.[99]

Besides, the aborigines were not the only ones in desperate need of God's saving grace. That September, just as the plan for the great drive to round up the blacks was beginning to mature in his mind, Arthur had much more to think about than just the wanton cruelty and treachery of the black savages of Van Diemen's Land. Charles Routley, one of the most horrid and bloodthirsty monsters that had yet disgraced the annals of humanity, escaped from Macquarie Harbour, murdered six men, sewed up the body of one of them in a bullock's skin, roasted it over a fire and ate it. After being captured he was brought up for trial in the Supreme Court in Hobart Town. He stood there in the dock, a monster in human flesh, waving his iron hook, the substitute for the hand he had lost, at his judge, and cursed God and man. Back in gaol after being sentenced to death, being suddenly overwhelmed with fears that he might be tormented in hell, he turned to the chaplain and asked 'Oh, Mr Bedford, what will become of me?' Mr Bedford told him, and Routley began to display profound contrition, and ask God fervently to forgive him. At the foot of the scaffold he implored all who could hear him to ponder the words of the gospel, and not ignore it as he had done. He beseeched all the convicts to avoid his awful end by forsaking all wicked and dissipated courses of life. With that majestic mountain as the back-drop for his last appearance on the stage of life and the blue waters of the Derwent estuary as his foreground the hangman drew the bolt, and Routley dropped into the silence, leaving behind for his contemporaries that question: 'Oh, Mr Bedford, what will become of me?' That, after all, was the question Arthur wanted all men to put to themselves, for strong soldier of God that he was, it was not given to him to take thought for the morrow when the black man had disappeared off the face of their island.[1]

---

[99] For the opinion of Captain Betts on the aborigines, see C. Turnbull, op. cit., p. 123; see also Arthur to Murray, 20 November 1830, C.O. 280/25 and G. A. Robinson to W. Bedford, 24 October 1830 (Papers of Reverend W. Bedford, MS. in M.L.); early in November, Arthur had also read this attack on the roundup in the *Australian* of 29 October 1830: 'We call the present warfare against a handful of poor, naked, despicable savages . . . a humbug . . . in every sense of the word—a farce . . . a fig for them, a fig for the whole concern'.

[1] *Hobart Town Courier*, 18 September 1830.

L

7

THE WORLD OF BETSEY BANDICOOT
AND BOLD JACK DONAHOE

IN 1828 a Devonshire farmer, who had migrated to New South Wales a few years earlier, reflected wistfully on his new way of life in a country where no holy bells knolled him to church on Sunday, where the village church evoked no serious or tender reflections in his mind, where the churchyard contained no inscription on the tombs of his family or his friends to remind him of man's great hope during his journey through life. Here all ceremonies to commemorate the cycle of birth, mating, death, the christenings, the marriages and the burials had been stripped of all their dignity and tragic grandeur. So one day in 1828 he shook his head, and summed up his despair and his nostalgia in his own way: 'It b'ant like home', he said, 'It b'ant like home'.

It was not just the absence of all the outward and visible signs of civilization, of buildings such as the venerable pile of St Paul's, or the sprawl of the Abbey, or the great houses of the gentry in town and country, or that sense of continuity and permanence, which was part of the air men breathed in older civilizations. Here the very climate and environment seemed alien or indifferent to all human endeavour. Here there was no long summer day, no long winter night, no fall of the leaf, no sudden exuberance of the flowers in the spring, no song of the birds, no continuing twilight, and no season of absolute gloom. Here there was none of that fierce contrast which in Europe had excited the imagination and the fancy to man's eternal glory, but only a dull, a medium, a plain level of uniformity.

Here there were none of those flowers which delighted the eye of the man with a lively fancy, no blue-veined violets, harebells, buttercups, daisies, soft silken primroses, none of that bloom of the heather or the hawthorn which decorated the English and Irish countryside. Here, there was no tiger burning bright in the forests of the night, no noble quadruped to fire the imagination of the poet, no challenge to immortal hand and eye to dare form such fearful symmetry, but only weird marsupials, kangaroos, wallabies and bandicoots, and huge frog-mouthed lizards—tough, coarse animals, who had acquired the strength to endure in a harsh, dry land. It was a land, Barron Field had written in 1819, which had emerged at the first sinning, and was therefore cursed, and hence its woods were barren. It was a land which had never known the paradise of the garden of Eden. Here there was none of that scenery which was either lovely or sublime—no glens, no purling streams, only rivers of mud, or dried-up creek beds, no mountains capped with snow, no towering crags, but only a flat, uniform, diminutive and sombre land. Where were the roots that would clutch in that barren land? Who would ever turn such a flint-stone into a springing well?[1]

The members of the social set of Sydney and Hobart Town were not bothered by such questions. Men had only to confine their thoughts to the interior decorations of the rooms in which the social set entertained in order to forget that they were not in the midst of the gaieties of London. It was said in Sydney that the parties there were as gay as in Montagu Square in London, and that burgundy and champagne were in abundance. In choosing the days for celebration and rejoicing they followed the calendar of the London season. Each year both in Sydney and Hobart Town they celebrated the King's birthday in a manner most worthy of the event and most gratifying to the people.

To celebrate the birthday of George IV in April of 1826 General Darling and his wife invited the various government officials, the military and naval officers, their wives, and a few of the leading colonists whose hands were happily clean from the stigma of trade, to a ball in Government House. The ball was held in the council chamber, on the left side of which was a brilliant star formed by bayonets over a royal crown, and at each end of the room was an imperial crown formed of laurel leaves which was brilliantly illuminated with lighted candles in branch candlesticks. With the women dressed in the latest London fashions, with the General and his wife making an admirable host and hostess, the ball opened with the French quadrilles, which were then very much in fashion, though as the evening advanced an occasional English country dance was introduced as a variety. The dancing was kept up to a very late hour.[2]

At Government House, Hobart Town, on St George's Day in April of 1828, there was also a gay and splendid scene. The windows of the ballroom, from which guests could hear the monotonous lap, lap of the waters of the Derwent, were beautifully decorated with transparencies, to illustrate that union of altar and throne which in Colonel Arthur's eyes was the only source of all order and true morality. In the entrance lobby to the ballroom was placed a field piece, surrounded with all the instruments of war, and surmounted with trophies of war. The guests danced on gaily and brightly to English dance tunes, in their English clothes, until they assembled in the supper room in which tables were loaded with every variety of delicacy that the range of seasons in Van Diemen's Land could afford. If the eyes of the company, it was said, had not so lately cast a glance on the hoary top of Mount Wellington, they might have fancied themselves in one of the gayest scenes of which the court of St James or the society of London's West End could boast.

In the streets, too, of Hobart Town, dandies, imitating their counterparts in the Mall in London, dressed in the very extreme of puppyism, stalked along, silly, inconsequential beings, who measured their importance by the quantity of

[1] Based on an article in the *New South Wales Register*, April 1828, no. 3, pp. 198-200, and 217-20; Barron Field, *First Fruits of Australian Poetry* (Sydney, 1819), see especially 'Kangaroo'.
[2] Based on Lady Forbes, Sydney Society in Crown Colony Days, ed. by G. Forbes, pp. 46-7 (typescript in M.L.); Commonplace Book of Rev. Thomas Comber of Buckworth, Devonshire (MS. in NAT. L.); *Australian*, 29 April 1826; for an example of the influence of British fashions, see *Australian*, 1 August 1828; *Hobart Town Courier*, 25 April 1829.

proud cloth in their trousers, by the width of their coat collars, by the position of the curl on the side of the head, by the strut and air of their walk, or by their very English dandy fal-lal-la way of replying to the most common question. Some sniffed at these ceremonials of a dull punctilious lot, and pined for the real thing: some scoffed at the local insistence that Sydney and Hobart Town society were either lively or amusing—or were not the sweetest and most delectable of all places in the world. One young man called on a lady, and suspected, horror of horrors, that her hair was in papers—pardon, papillottes.

Some complained there was too much starch and buckram at Government House both in Sydney and Hobart Town, and that the gentry were renowned for their stiffness and formality. In Sydney that fat little lady, Mrs Darling, made herself very agreeable, but try as he would, the General never could divest himself altogether of formality. In Hobart Town Mrs Arthur was plain, and homely, a dispenser of wholesome food and wholesome thoughts, while the Colonel had about him that dignity of bearing, that shrewdness and clearness of intellect of a man who had participated in the bread which came down from heaven, and had felt the goodness of the Lord in silence.[3] For the sniff of the migrant for colonial pretence had a long history—as well as their insistence that the hot sun wrinkled the faces and that colonial standards left a man more shabby.[4]

While the gentry, the civil and military officers, and the clergy of the Church of England, were attempting to reproduce in the ballrooms and drawing rooms of Sydney and Hobart Town the fashions and gaieties of the London season, out on the streets, in the tap-rooms, pot-houses, bush huts, amidst all the uproar, commotion, the lust, the thirst and the hunger, the world of Betsey Bandicoot and Bold Jack Donahoe was being fashioned. In the streets of Sydney nests of noisy, drunken and brawling women shouted at and cursed each other in such coarse and obscene language that a decent woman could not venture through the streets without having her modesty shocked by the victims of colonial depravity. Lewd words and lewd gestures greeted any lady who risked a stroll past the drunk or the sober in the streets of Sydney. In Hobart Town language and gesture were so foul that Colonel Arthur wondered whether any man with a concern for the fate of his immortal soul could walk up Campbell Street, unspotted.[5]

One night in March of 1825 soldiers in Sydney asked publicans for drink: when the publicans refused to serve them without money, this led to high words and then to scenes of outrage. The town people attacked the soldiers in York Street, and drove them with stones, brick-bats and other missiles into the barracks. Some of the stones found their way through the windows of the mess

[3] *Hobart Town Courier*, 25 April 1828; No. 30 of Simon Stukeley, 25 December 1829, *Colonial Times*, and published in Henry Savery, *The Hermit in Van Diemen's Land*, ed. by C. Hadgraft and M. Roe (Brisbane, 1964), p. 152; Extracts from a Journal kept by a country gentleman, published in *Hobart Town Courier*, 22 March 1828; W. E. Riley, Journal in New South Wales 1830-31, p. 23 (MS. in M.L.); Simon Stukeley no. 3, Hobart Town, *Colonial Times*, 19 June 1829; The Journal of James Backhouse of York, vol. 1, pp. 72-3 (MS. in M.L.).

[4] On this point see *South Asian Register*, April 1828, no. 3, p. 198.

[5] *Australian*, 16 March 1826; for Hobart Town, see, for example, Arthur to Bathurst, 15 August 1824, *H.R.A.*, III. iv. 161-3.

room of the 40th Regiment which had assembled to celebrate what the *Australian* called the 'Orgies of Saint Paddy'. It was not to be expected that the flesh and blood of soldiers could tamely brook such treatment from mere civilians. On the following night the soldiers, thirsting for a bloody revenge on their attackers, ranged the town, disguised as civilians, knocked down doors and smashed windows and hacked all who came in their way with their swords. Next day people covered with blood and bandages, their arms in slings, and their faces well sprinkled with plasters came forward to make depositions.[6] At Christmas time in Newcastle in the following year, a strong body of soldiers, inflamed by strong drink and the memory of unsettled scores with the civilians, roamed round the town swearing to cut out the entrails of any one they met. One soldier ran his bayonet through one man and killed him: another soldier ran his bayonet through the clothes of a baby, and another quietly stabbed a dog outside a door.[7]

While Sydney, Hobart Town and Launceston, Newcastle, and Parramatta, were disturbed from time to time by such brawls between soldiers and civilians, the lower orders provided their own distraction by indulging in a behaviour which provided a low comedy for the readers of the newspapers. One October night in 1831 James Tutty, who appeared to consider himself a very pretty fellow, rolled through the streets of Sydney with a horn of grog in his fist, singing most melodiously:

> Talk of the cordial that sparkled for Helen,
> Her cup was a fiction, but *this* is reality.

He was charged before a magistrate in Sydney. Two bob not being forthcoming, he was ordered, as one newspaper put it, to exhibit the symmetry of his calf in the stocks for two hours.[8]

In December of 1824 the attention of the Police Magistrate's Court was occupied with the jealousies between two married couples—Mrs Mary Whitfield, and Mrs Harriet Powers. Mrs Powers, in company with her own lawful husband, had entered the Cumberland Arms and requested permission to sit down in the public parlour. This very civil request having been most uncivilly rejected by Mrs Whitfield, Mrs Powers gave vent to her irritated feelings in a torrent of abuse in which she insinuated in quite unqualified terms that Mrs Whitfield kept the room for a certain purpose to any officer or sergeant who would tip a dollar in her favour. Mrs Whitfield, modish matron that she was, then protested feelingly that it was very shocking to be called a strumpet and a whore, and went on to taunt Mrs Powers that she had belonged to Mr Powers before Mrs Powers, and that, anyhow, Mrs Powers was not married to Mr Powers. Great and powerful was the set-to between the ladies—Mrs Whitfield remembering afterwards that those foul slurs on her character and reputation had not once excited an angry word from her husband. The magistrate ordered Mrs Whitfield to find sureties for her future good behaviour.[9]

On that stage of life in Sydney the lower orders were providing the low

[6] *Australian*, 24 March 1825.
[8] *Sydney Herald*, 19 October 1831.
[7] Ibid., 5 January and 12 February 1826.
[9] *Australian*, 30 December 1824.

comedy for the amusement and entertainment of the men and women in higher places. When a Mrs Dixon had her wig torn off her during a fight with another woman the onlookers roared with drunken laughter. The press of Sydney too found fun in her humiliation.[10] The press, too, thought it funny that a Mr Sutor, who had not arrived free in this country, had taught his parrot to sing 'My heart with love is breaking' to his intended, because he himself was so afraid of her scorn and fury that he dared not expose the view of his heart before the eyes of a woman.[11] It was as though all their pitiful efforts to cast off the chains with which they were bound to the wheel of life were but sport for those on whom the gods or chance had forged lighter chains.

One day in December of 1824 it was Mary Anne Brady, a midwife, who provided the sport. She stated to the court in a case of seduction that she never drank spirits—oh, no, your honour, she would not for the world drink a glass—at least, that is, not once oftener than once in a quarter of a year. And, of course, she should indeed tell the court nothing but the truth; for she had no idea of selling her soul to the devil for anybody.[12] One day in August of the following year a young woman about nineteen years of age, a housemaid in a respectable family in Parramatta, on being informed of the marriage of a young groom who had previously made successful addresses to her, ran down to the bottom of the garden, and threw herself into a well, but, as the *Australian* put it, sniffing amusement for their readers in a lively account of female hysteria, she disliked the situation so much that she called for assistance and so escaped with no other injury than a good ducking.[13]

In the wretched hovels at the Rocks in Sydney terrible scenes of infamy occurred. Women, determined to disgrace the society of their adopted land, became so drunk that when the police called to take away those most abandoned members of their species they were not able to remove them until the following morning.[14] The press often reported stories of women dying of drunkenness. One woman, having escaped from her husband, drank herself almost to a state of insensibility, when she committed the crime of adultery. Retribution, the *Sydney Gazette* was happy to say, struck swiftly for that very night her outraged husband murdered her. For the *Sydney Gazette* this illustrated God's vengeance upon drunkards and adulterers.[15] Priests and parsons often appeared in public as one of God's instruments for the punishment of wickedness and vice rather than the dispensers of divine love. So Margaret O'Brien was brought up before the magistrate in Sydney in April of 1826 by Father Therry for the highly reprehensible conduct of being in a public street in a state of great drunkenness. In the course of the inquiry it came out that the wretched woman had encouraged her daughter, aged thirteen, in her course of prostitution.[16]

For what they, the men in high places, the governors of the two colonies, the civil and military officers, the chaplains, the magistrates, all those charged

10 Ibid., 13 January 1825.
11 *Sydney Gazette*, 19 May 1825.
12 *Australian*, 30 December 1824.
13 *Australian*, 25 August 1825.
14 *Sydney Gazette*, 27 November 1823.
15 Ibid., 2 January 1823.
16 *Australian*, 26 April 1826.

with the high responsibility of truly and impartially administering justice for the punishment of wickedness and vice, and for the maintenance of true religion and virtue, had to contend with was that here in New South Wales and Van Diemen's Land, human depravity had been alarmingly increased by the presence of convicts, ex-convicts and their descendants. One day in April of 1823, when a Mr and Mrs Berrisford were riding in a bullock cart from Hobart Town to their home, one of the bullocks took fright, upset the cart, and threw them on to the road. While Mr Berrisford was lying unconscious an absconder rushed out of the bush, beat Mrs Berrisford most cruelly, robbed her, and disappeared again into the bush. To the reading public in Sydney and Hobart Town that was not just another example of human depravity, or the hardness of men's hearts. This was a fair example of human baseness in a convict-dominated society.[17]

Of the 36,598 white persons living in the colony of New South Wales when the first census of the population was taken in the year 1828, 20,930 were classified as free, and 15,668 as convict. But such total figures included the expirees, the emancipists, and the children of the convicts in that column to which they belonged by definition, though not necessarily by loyalty, tradition or conviction. Of 200 convict marriages registered in the colony of New South Wales for the year 1828, 105 were unions between men and women who were either serving a sentence, holders of a conditional pardon, or a ticket-of-leave. In only fifty-two of them had either party come free or been born free in the colony. Of the 387 convict marriages celebrated in 1831, 260 of them were between parties who were either ex-convict, or in some form of servitude, and in only forty-eight had one of the parties who knelt before those fatal rails come free or been born free in the colony. Of the children born before 1820, between 80 and 90 per cent were the offspring of a union of which one of the parties was a convict or an ex-convict. So in 1828, in that year of the first comprehensive counting of heads, as distinct from the early convict musters, probably over 70 per cent of the population had by birth some convict association—whatever chance or circumstance did to his mind and heart in the time of his riper years.[18] In 1828 there were 18,408 people in Van Diemen's Land, just over 40 per cent of whom, it has been estimated, were convicts.[19]

In both colonies, males greatly outnumbered females. In New South Wales in 1828 there were 27,611 males and 8,987 females.[20] In Van Diemen's Land

---

[17] *Sydney Gazette*, 22 May 1823 which took the episode from the *Hobart Town Gazette*.

[18] Return of the Population of New South Wales, according to a Census taken in November 1828 *Blue Book of Statistics Colony of New South Wales for the year 1828*, C.O. 206/69, pp. 146-7; Colonial Marriage Registers, N.S.W. S.A., 4/4508. Marriages from January 1826–April 1833 (prisoners permitted to marry) 4/4511; List of Prisoners who had been refused permission to marry commencing 20 November 1825; T. A. Coghlan, *General Report on the Eleventh Census of New South Wales* (Sydney, 1894); Ken Macnab and Russel Ward, 'The Nature and and Nurture of the First Generation of Native-born Australians', *Hist. Studies*, vol. 10, 1961-3, pp. 289-308.

[19] Arthur to Huskisson, 1 May 1828, C.O. 280/16, p. 500; W. D. Forsyth, *Governor Arthur's Convict System: Van Diemen's Land, 1824-36* (London, 1935), pp. 103-5.

[20] T. A. Coghlan, op. cit., p. 75.

in the same year there were 13,143 males, and 3,781 females.[21] The men in the lower orders, driven on by that first law of nature, practised prostitution, or the vices of the cities of Sodom and Gomorrah. The men in higher places kept concubines. From the time of Macquarie in New South Wales, and Arthur in Van Diemen's Land, the government, believing concubinage to be against religion, common decency, and the morals of society, had repeatedly declared they would not overlook the practice. Men keeping concubines were not invited to Government House, or recommended for promotion. Whenever a vigilant superintendent of police in Sydney found ticket-of-leave men guilty of keeping a concubine he either caused the parties to be married, or, failing in this, deprived them of the indulgence of the government.[22]

In Van Diemen's Land Lieutenant-Colonel Arthur took vigorous measures to root out concubinage in the lower orders, while the upper orders learned that the days when the head of society had compromised the very walls of Government House had gone for ever. Henceforth the men and women with those guilty stains were dropped from the list of invited guests.[23] From the pulpit, the parsons and the priests reminded their flocks that marriage was a state blessed by their Lord by his first miracle at Cana in Galilee. God himself, they reminded their flocks, had pronounced that it was not good for man to be alone. God had commanded men to be fruitful and multiply, and replenish the earth and subdue it. God, they reminded the people, had not created man to demoralize or degrade life. Some urged marriage to the women saying it would lift them from that state of humiliation and dependence to which the life of a concubine always reduced them.[24]

Despite the cry against existing abominations, the encouragement of marriage led to offences against God and man being committed with ten-fold enormity. Those whining hypocrites of the day, the parsons, had set up a great howl that God would not and indeed could not be mocked with impunity. Yet no sooner had they swept and garnished the houses of New South Wales and Van Diemen's Land than the parsons once again began to frown at mankind. Once again they climbed their three-deckered pulpits on Sunday mornings to call on their God to look down on a people such as had not polluted the face of the earth since the days of the great flood. That stern defender of the morals of the inhabitants of Botany Bay, the Reverend Samuel Marsden, reminded his congregation that not a week passed without the majesty of heaven being insulted by the perjuries of too many of the prisoner population. Husbands, he thundered, forsook their wives, who, finding themselves in want, became desperate, and gave themselves up to drunkenness, prostitution and theft. Parents abandoned their children who were taken into

[21] R. M. Martin, *History of Austral-Asia: Comprising New South Wales, Van Diemen's Land, Swan River, South Australia, &c.* (London, 1836), p. 303; Arthur to Huskisson, 1 May 1828, C.O. 280/16, p. 500.

[22] See, for example, the article of Mr Doran in the *Sydney Gazette*, 8 March 1827.

[23] On this point see J. T. Bigge to Bathurst, 3 February 1823, Bigge Appendix, C.O. 201/142; the reference is to Lieutenant-Governor Sorell.

[24] For an example see the article on the character of the people of New South Wales in the *South Asian Register*, April 1828, no. 3, pp. 217-20; see also the *Australian*, 7 April 1825, for a general article on the consequences of the high proportion of men to women in the colony of New South Wales.

the Female Factory where they became a charge on the government. Single women soon became a prey to the designing men who had cast off their wives.[25]

Some men sought temporary relief from the heavy dull hours in drams of alcohol, and some in occasional drams of scandal. In Sydney and Hobart Town, it was said that every man was distrustful of his neighbour. Some said that convictism bred an inordinate interest in a man's past, that fascination in picking the gap between a man's pretences and his previous record. Some said that emigrants to a new land always fixed too high a price on their own claims, and too low a price on the claims of the locals which caused tension, and a lack of reciprocal acknowledgment between people. In such a society, it was said, men became captious, discontented, and sullen, and so willingly put an ear to the idle tales of scandal current in Sydney and Hobart Town about every person. In those colonies slanderous tongues envenomed life: no man's reputation was safe from the mockers and the fault-finders.[26]

The free wantonly accused the convicts and their relatives of practising every description of vice, and plumbing new depths of human depravity in those great south seas which the high-minded in the eighteenth century had predicted would one day be peopled with beings that would be an ornament to human nature.[27] The parsons, the priests, and all the self-appointed censors and guardians of public morals went on repeating the generalization about the convicts and their relations which had been current ever since the days of Governor Hunter, namely, that a more wicked, abandoned, and irreligious set of people had never been brought together in any other part of the world, and that the children were abandoned to every kind of wretchedness and vice.[28]

Yet by the year 1822 in New South Wales, if not in Van Diemen's Land, a group of men and women were growing up who were angered by any attempts to confound them with those persons in the convict community who were said to be incurable addicts of profligacy and vice. They were the local-born, the colonial-born, the native-born, the currency lads and lasses—all those who in the words of one of the most illustrious native sons—William Charles Wentworth—had 'Australasian hearts'. Between 1821 and 1831 those born in the colony before 1810 were coming to man's estate, seeking those careers open to their talents, that access to the fruits of the land of their birth, and a life of dignity and honour, free from any stigma attached to their birth, or their group. By 1828 there were just over three and a half thousand native-born persons in New South Wales over the age of twelve. One quarter of the population of New South Wales in 1828 had been born in the colony.[29]

[25] For an article on convict marriages see the *Gleaner*, 15 September 1827; see also *Australian*, 7 April 1825; *Sydney Gazette*, 8 March 1827; S. Marsden to W. G. Broughton, 18 January 1832 (Marsden Papers, vol. 1, pp. 175-8).

[26] *South Asian Register*, April 1828, no. 3, pp. 217-20; for an example of character assassination, see John Macarthur to R. W. Horton, 16 December 1823, C.O. 201/147; for another comment on the colonial love of back-bite, see Brisbane to Bruce, 13 December 1822, (Brisbane Papers, Box 1).   [27] R. H. to J. Banks, 13 December 1786 (Banks Papers, MS. in M.L.).

[28] Hunter to Portland, 1 November 1798, *H.R.A.*, I. ii. 236-9; King to Secretaries of the Treasury, 7 July 1800, ibid., 524-6.

[29] Return of the Population of New South Wales according to the Census taken in November 1828, C.O. 206/69; R. Mansfield, *Analytical View of the Census of New South Wales for the year 1841* (Sydney, 1841), p. 10.

Observers began to notice both their appearance and their demeanour as early as 1822. Even Mr Commissioner Bigge, who cast a cold, judicial eye on all human strivings, and was no friend to the mass of men not conceived in the beds of the gentry, had a warm word for the native-born. The class of person that had been born in the colony, he wrote, afforded a remarkable exception to the moral and physical character of their parents. They were generally tall in person, and slender in their limbs, of fair complexion and small features. They were capable of undergoing more fatigue, and were less exhausted by labour than native Europeans; they were quick in their habits but remarkably awkward in their movements. In their tempers they were quick and irascible, but not vindictive. He could, he said, only repeat the testimony of persons who had had many opportunities of observing them, namely, that they neither inherited the vices nor the feelings of their parents.[30]

In their daily lives they were the victims of the insults and ridicule heaped on them by free publicists for immigrants. The upper classes objected to sending their children to any schools attended by the children of convicts lest they be contaminated by such an association, for the upper class dread of the consequences of contamination led to their demand for segregation of the children of the free from the children of the bond.[31] In the public press, the native-born were exposed from time to time to the same contumely. In March of 1827 Sterling Joe described them as a set of idle, worthless, dishonest, drunken, and unchaste animals, known by the name of Botany Bay youth, who were good for nothing beyond being the servants of their masters.[32]

Aware, too, that insult was not the only price to be paid for being native-born, aware too that they were called on to endure injuries and injustice from the mere chance of being born in the colony rather than in the British Isles, the native-born began to clamour for their rights. In January of 1826 Wentworth drew attention at a public meeting to this spirit of dissatisfaction which had grown up among the native youths of the colony, in consequence of the comparative neglect with which they had been treated, in comparison with others, in the distribution of land. Loud and prolonged hear, hears greeted these remarks, for some members of the audience were more touchy on this point than Wentworth. To the accompaniment of cheering he urged that the native youth be given that equality with immigrants they always should have possessed.[33]

The men endowed by government or the fruits of their own endeavour with much less land than a Wentworth put this grievance in much sharper language. Immigrants, they said, had been well treated on their arrival in the colony. Large tracts of land had been granted to them, and other indulgences bestowed on them. None had experienced marked neglect but the natives of the colony. The Australians were not unreasonable, they were not envious. But the land was their birthright, their legitimate inheritance. Why

---

[30] J. T. Bigge, Report of the Commissioner of Inquiry on the State of Agriculture and Trade in the Colony of New South Wales, *P.P.*, 1823, X, 136, p. 81.

[31] Archdeacon Scott to Darling, 1 September 1829, Encl. in Darling to Murray, 18 October 1829, *H.R.A.*, I. xv. 214-21.

[32] Letter by 'Sterling Joe' to the *Sydney Gazette*, 8 March 1827.

[33] *Australian*, 19 January 1826.

should they, the native-born Australians, be reduced to the status of the helots of Rome, sowers of the soil from which the immigrants would reap a rich harvest? Why were the native-born excluded from the possession of the land? Was it not a shame that English immigrants, Spaniards, Americans should be allowed the highest indulgences of a British colony, while the very natives of that colony, both those who possessed and those who did not possess capital, were entirely excluded from them? So wrote twenty young men of property— all natives of the colony—close to Anniversary Day in January of 1827.[34]

With the passions of men cheated of their expectations, and wounded by gratuitous insults to their capacity and their morals, the native youth began to brag about their powers. They boasted of many things: they boasted of how much they could eat: they were proud that a one-time convict, Samuel Terry, excelled all others in wealth, and was therefore indifferent to the little whelps of immigrants who snarled, but could not bite at their man. In July of 1827 Jack Kable, a native youth, swore he would fight anything alive for a purse of five hundred guineas. The cornstalks rose up and sprouted perceptibly, causing the 'swells' or immigrants, not to feel themselves quite at 'home'. Then a hardy chubby Scot, from the land of cakes and 'Jonny' Groats, dared to challenge this knight of the native born youth. But, how could a game chicken stand up to a native rooster?[35]

Four years earlier in October of 1823 one Fanny Flirt had written some rather disparaging remarks about Australia and Australians to the *Sydney Gazette*—saying amongst other things, that riding through rows of gum trees was not to her taste, and, as for colonial conversation, why, nothing could be so sheepish. Young Arable's wits, she let drop, had gone a-wool-gathering, ever since he began grazing. As for music, well, as Fanny Flirt put it, you only had to ask for a song in Sydney town, and young 'wholesale' would promptly chant to you, over an invoice, of course, 'Money is your friend, is it not?'[36]

This was too much for those with Australasian hearts. Two weeks later Betsey Bandicoot replied, with that magnificent, vulgar, cheeky confidence of those who loved the land they lived in:[37]

MISTER EDITOR,   . . .

every one knows their own liking; she [Fanny Flirt] might *prefar* the soft-singing notes of her Italian in his gondola (all the same as a boat, the *dictionnary* says) to the loud *coo-hee* of a currency lad riding over the blue mountains. But our Bill [a currency boy] can play the flute, hunt the wild cattle, and shoot and swim with the best in the Colony.

It would do your heart good, Mister Editor, to see how Bill tucks in, when I've fried him a pan-ful of pork, *swimming in fat*, and a smoking hot cake from the ashes. O, it would make you shine your buttons, as the saying is, to see how Bill will swig off a pot of peach-cyder; and then he lounges like any *swell*, with a nice short pipe, and smoaks and whiffs, and whiffs and smoaks, all the afternoon. But ma'aps this woud'nt be to the liking of Miss Flirt; as she is so dainty

[34] *Australian*, 20 January 1827.
[35] *Australian*, 11 July 1827; ibid., 17 May 1826; *Sydney Gazette*, 24 January 1822.
[36] Letter of 'Fanny Flirt, a Maiden Lady,' to the *Sydney Gazette*, 9 October 1823.
[37] Letter by 'Betsey Bandicoot' to the *Sydney Gazette*, 30 October 1823.

as not to be fond 'of riding through rows of gum-trees;' but, la! she should see me galloping without a saddle, a'ter Bill, when he has a mind for a bit of a frisk; and as for shoes, I never thinks of putting them on, only when I goes a shopping to Sydney, at *Mother Marr's* or *Joe Inch's* for a bonnet; or a *Little* or *Big Cooper's* for a frying-pan; and I beg a wager, I could *swim* further and faster than Miss Fanny, and *carry my clothes on my head* into the bargain, without wetting so much as my comb, which cousin Bill paid for in *'tatoes* at *Josephson's* last Christmas *hollidays*.

If Miss Fan's for a quiet life, Bill's her man; for I have made pounds, and pounds of butter, and never so such as heard Bill *out* with a word, but then he'd whistle. To tell the truth, whistling and smoaking is Bill's delight; and he likes to have a long *yarn* from the *cove*, who is sure to get a bit of tobacco, if he tells Bill a good 'un. Bill has plenty of stock, and will have a good farm, when father's off; and so Miss Fan, if she'd take a likeing to Bill, she'd find, in the long-run, Bill no such bad chop neither. But I am running on at a deuce of a rate; but Mister *Scrollam* said I could always write better than father, but I never wrote so long a job before; and shoud'nt now only for that saucy minx, Fan Flirt, whose skits about the *'dummies'* of the Colony be only sheer envy, because she has'nt the dumps; and never you go for to mind her threats about throwing you into the tanks, for there's plenty of us, who will take your part, so long as you stick up for us *currency* girls. And,

I remain, dear Mister Editor,

your unworthy humble servant,

BETSEY BANDICOOT

Warragombie Creek

P.S.—Miss Fan Flirt is very much mistaken if she thinks because she has seen the *lions* in *Lunnun Tower*, that we don't know *what's what* for all that. She'd better go for to mind her own *P*'s and *Q*'s without troubling herself about her betterers; and I suppose she conceits there's never not one like her at the *pye-anney-foart*, but its all gammon after all—*boojeree* me if its anything else; but I won't be angry, that I won't. So yours again,

B.B.

Except for this confidence that they knew what's what, and a belief in sticking up for currency lads and lasses in things both great and small, they were not committed to any political or social creed. Their public gatherings and ceremonies were not distinguished by any profession of belief. Their public speeches were not distinguished by high-minded talk of all men being created equal, let alone that all men were endowed by their creator with certain in-alienable rights, that amongst these were life, liberty, and the pursuit of happiness. They came together not as men buoyed up by any hope of better things for mankind, but rather as men determined to have a share in the fruits of their land. On 26 January 1828, the day of the anniversary of the founding of the colony, a day which those convicts who had risen to affluence and res-pectability and the native-born, such as Wentworth, celebrated with pride and hope, a royal salute was fired in Sydney. The bells of St Philip's Church kept ringing their merry peals, aided and abetted by the sonorous tonal bell of the Presbyterian Church, for Lang was not a man to allow the Anglicans to outdo him in anything. That night forty to fifty sat down to a most sumptuous dinner at Cumming's New Hotel in Macquarie Place. Mr Samuel Terry, a winder, who had once been whipped for stealing poultry, but now one of the wealthiest men in the country, was in the chair. Thomas Cooper, who had been transported as a fence, and had made a fortune by manufacturing gin from Indian corn, which the colonists lovingly knew as 'Cooper's Best', was also there. He sat down at the same table with Mr Haynes, another ex-convict, who was now a proprietor of a whole fleet of whale ships. They all joined together in toasting the King, other members of the royal family, the memory of Governor Phillip, the venerated memory of Governor Macquarie, Governor Brisbane, Governor Darling, the judges of the colony, Mrs Darling and the ladies of the colony, prosperity of the colony's agriculture and commerce, trial by jury and taxation by representation, taking care never to say what was meant by either, because that might show that people who saw eye to eye on their one big thing, might not agree on who should exercise political power. At the end of the evening, after the wine had flowed freely, they rose to their feet to drink to their one big thing—to the currency lads and lasses, adding with pride 'The land, boys, we live in'. They ended on a plea for unity, as they drank quietly to their other hope, that hope for 'Unanimity and Concord', which, in their eyes, were the sources of public prosperity.[38]

By contrast the inhabitants of Van Diemen's Land did not observe the anniversary of the founding of their colony, not just because of any difficulty in choosing the day. For this they had that embarrassment of riches: there was that day when the great Dutchman, driven by the hope of making uncommonly large profit in the great south land, had, in his day of grief and mortification, erected that flag of the Dutch East India Company, so that those who came after him might know he had been there: there was the day when Bowen had begun the first settlement at Risdon Cove: there was the day when Collins had chosen Hobart Town: there was that day in December 1825 when General Darling had proclaimed Van Diemen's Land to be independent of New South Wales. All these days passed by each year in this decade without any public recognition. For in that island they were caught up with quite different questions. They had striven to rescue the island from becoming a cage for the vultures of New South Wales: they had been caught up in a desperate struggle with the aborigines: their society had not been agitated in the previous decade, as had New South Wales, by any demands of successful or affluent ex-convicts to take a place in society, or gain public office: nor were the columns of their press filled from time to time with proud boasts by the native-born that they knew what's what, or warm-hearted appeals to stick up for currency lads and currency lasses. At their public dinners no one asked them to charge their glasses and drink to 'The land, boys, we live in'. Having been founded sixteen years after New South Wales there was not that same proportion of native-born to total population. At the end of that decade Wentworth, Australia's proudest son, turned forty, the oldest of the native-born in Van Diemen's Land was twenty-six. So, when in March of 1829 William

[38] *Sydney Gazette*, 28 January 1828; James F. O'Connell, *A Residence of Eleven Years in New Holland and the Caroline Islands*: Edited from his verbal narration (Boston, 1836), pp. 36-9.

Kimberley, William Kearney, James Lord, Thomas Lucas and fourteen other native sons of Van Diemen's Land petitioned Colonel Arthur for the first boon which a body of native colonists had ever solicited from government to enable them in their remote part of His Majesty's dominions to uphold the character of Britons, they asked for a race-course for their use and amusement.[39]

So while people in Van Diemen's Land consumed time and energy rounding up the black man, or talked of the inhuman and bloodthirsty monsters who terrorized the settlers, or were caught up in the scandal and back-bite of a small community, a few people in Sydney began to discuss the type of society that should be developed in New South Wales. Some of them argued that in a society composed of all kinds of discordant materials, with respect to both political and religious opinions, and of people of doubtful honesty and morality, a corruption of morals and general laxity of principles would ensue, unless checked by the influence of pious and upright clergymen, or gentlemen of property and honourable ideas, who should be the basis for a wealthy and high-minded aristocracy. John Macarthur, who had first presented this idea to Mr Commissioner Bigge at the very beginning of the decade, told his friends at Parramatta that if government gave nothing but small grants of land, they would not only keep the country poor and wretched, but rear up a turbulent and immoral democracy like that of America, which would in the end overturn the government, and found a licentious republic upon its ruins.[40]

Some were anxious that all creatures great and small should be taught the case for rank and order in society. To the daughter who asked her mother in Eliza Darling's wholesome pamphlet, *Simple rules for the Guidance of Persons in humble life*, if God had made all men to be born alike, how was it that there should be such a difference between people as that some should live in large houses, with carriages and servants to do everything for them, and others should be obliged to work and do for themselves, the mother replied with becoming modesty, 'this is so plainly for the good of every one, that even I can, I think, make you understand it'. She went on to explain how by the exercise of those virtues of meekness, contentment, patience, and obedience, and through the merits of their Saviour, servants would be received after death into Christ's kingdom, and hear the joyful words: 'Well done, ye good and faithful servants, enter ye into the joy of your Lord', allaying, on the way, her daughter's anxious query: are not the rich happier than the poor? Again Mary received a confident, unambiguous reply, 'I do not think so, Mary'. Mary was reminded firmly how the Saviour of man had taken upon Himself the form of a servant, and advised that whenever thoughts of discontent arose in her, she should take down her Bible and read it, as she would always find comfort there.[41]

[39] The Respectful Memorial of the Native Born, Proprietors of Land and Stock in the Colony to His Excellency Colonel George Arthur, Lieutenant Governor of Van Diemen's Land, Hobart Town, 21 March 1829 (MS. in T.S.A.).

[40] *Australian*, 3 March 1825; J. Macarthur to J. T. Bigge, 7 February 1821 (Bigge Appendix, C.O. 201/118); Memorandum by John Macarthur on 19 December 1821, quoted from S. Macarthur Onslow (ed.), *Some Early Records of the Macarthurs of Camden* (Sydney, 1914), pp. 349-50.

[41] Eliza Darling, *Simple rules for the Guidance of Persons in humble life* (Cheltenham, 1834).

In press, pulpit, pamphlet and schoolroom all through the decade the battle went on for the hearts and minds of the people of New South Wales and Van Diemen's Land. Robert Howe had taken over the editorship of the *Sydney Gazette* on the death of his father in 1821. Family ties bound Howe firmly to that ex-convict and native-born group, who resented the social stigma attached to them by the exclusives, and the more favoured treatment of the immigrants in land grants. Howe's father had arrived in the colony as a convict, so broken in health that his life had been despaired of until D'Arcy Wentworth used his charismatic powers to restore him to strength, and make him his debtor in things of the spirit for life. His son, Robert, who had been born in London in 1795 to Howe's first wife, had married a native-born woman, Ann Bird, the year he took over the *Sydney Gazette*. So the *Sydney Gazette* from time to time ridiculed the pretentious claims of the exclusives to be the ancient nobility of New South Wales, and was not above hinting to its readers that the only escutcheon to which the Macarthurs could lay claim would be a button. The *Sydney Gazette*, too, took a commendable pride in the achievements of the currency lads and lasses. When William Charles Wentworth returned to Sydney in July of 1824 they wrote 'We have no occasion to announce the latter Gentleman to be, by birth, an Australian—such being old *news*'.[42]

Howe, whose earlier life had been characterized by much drinking and venery, had been, as he put it, wonderfully and mercifully visited by God and snatched from infamy in this world and hell in the next in the year before he took over the editorship of the *Sydney Gazette*. This caused him to fill his columns with warnings of those punishments human and divine which drinkers, lechers, whore-mongers and the unseemly could expect both in this world and the next. Drunkards, for example, were held to commit crimes of the most horrid and blackest dye in direct violation of the laws laid down for man to follow by no less a personage than Almighty God. So Howe published in the *Sydney Gazette* the same message as the parsons and the priests as a deterrent to the depravity, the abominations, the tumult, the shouting, and even the sedition of a convict-dominated society.[43]

The *Sydney Gazette* had always enjoyed a close association with the government of New South Wales. In its early years George Howe had occupied a small room in Government House, until the paper moved to a humble dwelling fronting Macquarie Place erected for it by the Governor. Later George Howe had moved the office to George Street. From the first day of publication on 5 March 1803, it had carried all government announcements in return for an annual emolument to the proprietor. In the Darling period, while the *Australian* mocked at his 'Venerability', the archdeacon, and the *Monitor* slandered Darling, the *Sydney Gazette*, despite Howe's convict and native-born ties, was reluctant to take sides. With the *Australian* ridiculing each week the pretences of the 'pure merinos' the *Sydney Gazette* fulminated

---

[42] For the life of Robert Howe see R. Howe, Diary (ms. in m.l.); article on George Howe in the *Australian Dictionary of Biography*, vol. 1; see *Sydney Gazette* 22 July 1824 for the comment on Wentworth.

[43] R. Howe, Diary; *Sydney Gazette*, 2 September 1830.

against all publicists who sought to divide God's children in the colony of New South Wales. When his rivals rebuked him for his reluctance to take sides, Howe replied that he was 'neither an Emigrant nor an Emancipist'. To which his opponents replied with the withering remark: 'He certainly is not a native'. Indeed, Howe wrote with such fervour on his theme that God's grace was the only means of salvation from human depravity that Dr Redfern, who had suffered much from the slings and arrows of the 'pure merinos', publicly horse-whipped him in 1827. By that year the *Gazette* was being published on three days a week, with six hundred copies printed for each issue.[44]

From the day of its first publication on 14 October 1824, under the proprietorship of W. C. Wentworth and R. Wardell, the *Australian* refrained from any pious or sanctimonious praise for the virtuous or any censure of the wicked. They praised all human activities which brought lads and lasses to-gether: they loved all gay and lively intercourse. Not for them the black looks, the pursed lips, the tut-tuts of the parsons and the *Sydney Gazette* when they surveyed the human scene. They wrote up the behaviour of the convict com-munity, their whoring, drinking, fisticuffs and brawls as a huge joke. For them drunkenness was not the occasion for talk about hell-fire from a lugu-brious parson, but just part of the human comedy. While the parsons and Howe conjured up the fires of hell for the drinkers they, warm friends of humanity that they were, published a recipe for curing a hangover. The *Australian* despised all talk about human vileness, the unworthiness of human beings, and eternal punishment. They wrote as the true sons of the Enlighten-ment—as men who were called to lay low those infamous ones, those breast-beating sinners who begged a jealous Jehovah for his favour in the life of the world to come. The distributors of divine favours in this world, the parsons, those men whom Howe revered in the *Sydney Gazette*, were held up to ridicule as pompous asses, men puffed up with vanity and pride, and receivers of absurdly high salaries. Nor did the tone of the paper change when Went-worth withdrew from it in October of 1825: nor did it change when T. H. James became a co-proprietor and editor in March of 1828, nor in the con-fused period from July to November of the same year when a group of eight took over from Wardell and James, till 27 November when A. E. Haynes became proprietor and editor. By 1827 the *Australian* was coming out twice a week, with six hundred copies per issue.[45]

Through all these changes of owner and editor, the *Australian* maintained its support for the native-born. When there was talk of the Governor wearing a gold-bespangled coat on official occasions they wrote:

> We never were admirers of the gold-bespangled coat, which is fitted only for that race of gentry who, on some forlorn spot are invested with the consular dignity, and who dazzle the natives and wondering strangers by the splendour of their embroidery, while making their sixpenny profits on their pounds of soap or

---

[44] For this controversy see the *Gleaner*, 2 June 1827, and the *Sydney Gazette*, May 1827 *passim*; for more comments on the circulation of the *Sydney Gazette* see the *Australian*, 16 August 1826.

[45] Taken from the *Australian* imprints, 14 October 1824, 2 May 1827, 2 July to 25 November 1828, and 27 November 1828; G. B. Barton, *Literature in New South Wales* (Sydney, 1866), pp. 20-4.

quarts of milk. Let these mighty men who can add 'H.M. Consul' to their title wear the glittering gew-gaw coat to support their consequence.

The natives rocked with laughter because the *Australian* knew and so did they, that taking the mighty down from their seat was always good for a laugh with the currency lads and lasses of Sydney Town.[46]

When voices were raised in New South Wales in favour of an aristocracy the *Australian* replied in its own spirited language. The only effect of an aristocracy, they wrote, would be to raise up a servile and degraded population, a timorous and turbulent mob, which at one time would crouch under the frowns of their proud and worthless masters and at another would join in some scheme of assassination to rid themselves of their oppressors.[47] That was not their main subject of interest. In issue after issue they wrote of the virtues and achievements of the native-born. Even the number attending a funeral was used as evidence for the respectability of the native-born. The native-born, they wrote, knew more about the climate and the system of agriculture appropriate to the local soil than the immigrants. They were also more likely than the immigrants to beautify and improve the colony, not by putting up houses to meet the needs and catch the spirit of their native land, but by putting up those mansions of the gentry, and planting those nobleman's parks which delighted the eye in England and Ireland. They boasted and bragged not of any new vision of life vouchsafed to the native-born, but rather of their superior talent for the British way of life.[48]

On 19 May 1826 the first issue of the *Monitor* was on sale in Sydney. Its proprietors E. S. Hall and A. Hill belonged by conviction to that group which believed in the beneficial influences of an evangelical religion in morality and social order. Hall, who had been born in London in March of 1786, had engaged as a young man in social and religious work. By God's providence he had come to New South Wales in 1811 to preserve and strengthen the fire of vital and practical religion in the colony. His spiritual mentor in England detected in him a power of persuasion and a steady and unbending rectitude, which, with God's help, would enable him to support the government of the country and to protect injured innocence from the hand of violence. In the first issue of the *Monitor* this note of idealism and rectitude pervaded the leading article. Calling himself a friend to religion, Hall promised to preserve a freedom from personal invective, to use the language of sense and moderation, and to campaign for the law of the land.

Worldly failure, however, had left Hall with a private hell in his heart. Despite lavish land grants from Macquarie—700 acres in 1812, 390 acres in 1817, 185 acres in 1822, and 1,000 in 1821—despite association with the colonial Midas, Simeon Lord, in a company to trade with New Zealand, and his association with causes to improve the morals of the inhabitants of New South Wales, he had not prospered. The man with a vision of God's throne became tainted with the quite monstrous hatred of those who, he believed, were despitefully using their fellow-man. In exposing the oppression

[46] *Australian*, 5 January 1826.   [47] *Australian*, 3 March 1825.
[48] *Australian*, 19 January and 19 May 1826.

M

and cruelty of the convict system, the corruption of officials, their drunkenness and immorality, Hall was swept on not by any vision of a society in which men would be liberated from their gaolers and their oppressors, but more and more by that subterranean satisfaction he enjoyed when taking the mighty down from their seat. In April of 1829, by which time the *Monitor* was appearing three times a week, he appeared in the Supreme Court of New South Wales on a charge of libel against Governor Darling, and in December following for libels against Darling, F. A. Hely, J. Laidley, and A. McLeay. In the eyes of General Darling Hall was an irresponsible ill-bred fellow who had disturbed the tranquillity of the colony, and demoralized the community by treating with disrespect and contempt the clergy and the established church. In his own eyes, he was a champion of the liberties of the people. Yet to the men who viewed him with the eye of pity, Hall was the example of that destroyer who, not standing on entrenched ground, could put his talents for mockery and vilification at the service of either side.[49]

Between April and September of 1827 the *Gleaner* appeared once a week, two hundred copies of each issue being printed. Its publisher, editor, and proprietor was L. H. Halloran, D.D., a gentleman of the most respectable appearance and endeavour, who had forged a franc note in an evil hour for himself and his family, and had been transported for seven years in 1818. He was a man of many parts. By September of 1827 his wife had borne him twenty-one children. His intentions, as ever, were high-minded. The *Gleaner*, he announced, would be conducted on the proud principle, *salus populi suprema lex*, and would, in every instance, consider the public good the primary object of its labours. Disclaiming all subserviency to party feeling, he promised that his columns would never be disgraced by personality, or scurrilous attacks on individuals. He promised that he would never offend ingenuous modesty, or indulge in the levity of wit or sarcasm, at the momentary expense of another's mental peace.

Yet, being compelled, as he told his readers frankly in his first issue, 'to write for bread', because of the claims of a young family, Halloran had to find a reading public. The society of New South Wales being much too divided, much too partisan, to respond to his high-minded liberalism, Halloran attempted to appeal to all sides. He told the opponents of General Darling that he was opposed to all forms of oppression: at the same time he told the supporters of the General that he would ever advocate the necessity of subordination in society, of becoming deference, and submission to the constituted authorities. He was out of business in five months. In his last issue of 29 September, driven as ever to fish in the waters of emotional extravagance, he announced that he would give a course of theological lectures, and that as only a limited number of auditors could be accommodated, those who desired to attend were requested to favour him with an early intention of their wishes. Like Mr Micawber, he was sustained through life by an incurable optimism that one day something would turn up to bridge that gap between his getting and his spending—that even more pitiful gap between desire and capacity. He

---

[49] *Monitor*, 19 May 1826; J. A. Ferguson, 'Edward Smith Hall and the "Monitor"', R.A.H.S., *J. & P.*, vol. 17, 1931-2, pp. 163-200.

died in March of 1831, still wondering why his rectitude of intention had never conferred on him even a decent competency.[50]

By contrast, the press of Van Diemen's Land, owned and edited for the most part by ex-convicts as was the press of New South Wales, did not dwell on the slights of the immigrants towards the native-born, or ex-convicts. They published no complaints that the immigrants were robbing the native-born of their right to the land of their birth. Their columns were not filled with any boasts and brags about the achievements of the native-born. While Betsey Bandicoot was telling Fanny Flirt what was what, the press in Van Diemen's Land was urging Arthur to remove the black men before they were exterminated, or telling its readers that so long as a man swayed by uncontrollable gusts of passion and prejudice presided over their affairs, they must remain in a state of thraldom.

It was not till Dr Ross took over the editing of the *Hobart Town Gazette* on 25 June 1825 that Arthur received any commendation in the press of Hobart Town. Despite his editorial assertion that his opinions were free and uncontrolled, Ross became a stalwart supporter of the official policies, a stand he continued when he began to publish the *Hobart Town Courier* on 20 October 1827. Both the pro- and the anti-Arthur press continued to mirror the main preoccupations of that society—its concern with bushrangers, savages, and convicts, quite untouched by any division of opinion on who was to own the land, or any vision of a society different from the one they knew.[51]

By contrast in Sydney Betsey Bandicoot, the currency lass, was quite certain she could swim further and faster than Fanny Flirt, the immigrant, and carry her clothes on her head into the bargain. This pride and confidence permeated the poetry of the period. As early as 1823 Wentworth had written for all his compatriots with Australasian hearts his own passionate song of praise to the 'Land of my Birth', asking with that very proud confidence whether the blue-eyed daughters, with the flaxen hair and taper ankle, bloomed less fair in Australia than in Europe, and writing, as ever, with pride of the seed from the fathers of Australians, for was not his own father his own pride and joy—calling them

> the fathers . . . of thy new race,
> From whom each glorious feat, each deathless grace,
> Must yet proceed.

Yet he, like the *Australian*, and the *Monitor* in years to come was not touched by any vision of a new way of life—He wanted Australasia to

> float, with flag unfurl'd,
> A new Britannia in another world.[52]

---

[50] *Gleaner*, 5 April and 12 April 1827; G. B. Barton, op. cit., p. 26; for the Halloran children see *Gleaner*, 15 September 1827; K. Lumsdaine, 'Sydney College and Sydney Grammar School', R.A.H.S., *J. & P.*, vol. 31, 1945-6, pp. 5-7; *Gleaner*, 29 September 1827.

[51] The history of the press in Van Diemen's Land has been covered in part in ch. 6 of this work; the best statement of the case against Arthur is contained in the issue of Bent's *Colonial Advocate*, 1 May 1828.

[52] W. C. Wentworth, *Australasia* (London, 1823).

The *Sydney Gazette* perceived with what it called no trifling feelings of gratification that literature was making her chaste advances to enrich and dignify the mind—but what pleased them most of all was that for Anniversary Day in 1826 they could announce the publication of fifty copies of the poetical essays of Mr Tompson, 'Our young Australian bard!' they called him. 'Well, indeed', they went on, 'may we be allowed to exclaim in common with every other well-wisher of the Colony—'Advance Australia'. And that was the theme of Tompson's poetry. For the *Gazette* expected that a spirit of enterprise would be excited by the publication of the journal of those indefatigable explorers—Messrs Hovell and Hume—and everyone knew that Hume was one of Australia's native sons.[53]

That year too the venerated bard, Michael Robinson, an ex-convict, whose witty, gay and classical muse had so often been the subject of general admiration and praise amongst emancipists and native-born, read his song for Anniversary Day. He had two themes: jokes about taking strong drink, which the Reverend Samuel Marsden, and General Darling and Archdeacon Scott would not have found funny:

> In Olympus, we're told
> The celestials of old,
> > In spite of morality's lecture,
> Would steal a sly sup
> From the festival cup,
> > And sometimes get mellow with nectar.

His other theme was the future greatness of Australia:

> 'Advance' then, 'Australia,'
> By this thy proud gala,
> > Which no party *spirit* can sever;
> May thy shores and thy plains,
> Echo loyalty's strains,
> > And thy watch-word be 'FREEDOM FOR EVER!'.[54]

When Robinson died in 1827 the native-born and emancipists mourned him as the first poet laureate in the colony, and indeed as the only man whose productions had any pretensions even to the grade of mediocrity. Some said he would survive longer than Barron Field, who had insulted the locals with that line of verse in which he had prophesied that the kangaroo and not human beings would rescue Australia from the fate of failure. Barron Field, it was said, would be preserved with as much sanctity of veneration as that extraordinary relic, the paring of the toe-nail of St Peter, was guarded by those fanatical devotees who boasted its possession. For mockery, too, excited almost as much satisfaction in the hearts of the native-born and the emancipists as praise of the achievements of the currency lads and lasses.[55]

By an odd irony it was neither an emancipist, nor a native-born, nor a man who sensed that heaven and hell were priests' inventions, but an immigrant

[53] *Sydney Gazette*, 28 February 1826.
[54] *Sydney Gazette*, 1 February 1826.
[55] *Gleaner*, 5 April 1827.

and a parson who wrote of Australia as a land of hope. He was John Dunmore Lang, that fiery particle whom the members of his church associated with some lively images from the pulpit each Sunday on the torments of the damned. In 1826 he published his book of verse, *Aurora Australis; or Specimens of Sacred Poetry, for the Colonists of Australia*, in which he invoked:

> Australia! land of hope!
>
> . . .
>
> From Superstition's snare
> And Slavery's chain,
> To set the wretched free;
> 'Till Christian liberty,
> Wide o'er the Southern Sea,
> Triumphant reign![56]

No such vision was presented on the stage either in New South Wales or Van Diemen's Land. In both colonies the convicts from time to time presented a bill of fare which, they claimed, provided entertainment, but remained very toll-loll-ish, as they put it, by which they meant that their entertainment did not offend against the canons of respectability. At the convict establishment of Emu Plains in May of 1825 His Majesty's Servants, as they waggishly styled themselves, performed the tragedy of *Barissa or the Hermit Robber*; the farce of *The Mock Doctor, or the Dumb Lady Cured*, and the burlesque of *Bombastes Furioso*. Here, His Majesty's Servants claimed, were dishes in abundance, three courses, and not one coarse, to distract the audience from the miseries of exile and the agonies and humiliations of forced labour.

In Sydney and Hobart Town the theatre had languished. Some were glad of this, as in a population so singularly composed, the drama might destroy the little morality that existed in those sinks of iniquity. Some, believing the theatre could effect moral improvements, wished to revive it. The hours and nights which the convicts and their families spent in drunken revelry or at the gaming table would be exchanged for a night at the theatre, where their minds would be impressed by scenes which would teach them to hold in utter aversion what was now the object of their depraved tastes. The stage, like the press, the pulpit and the schoolroom, should hold a mirror up to life and show virtue rewarded, and vice punished. At curtain-fall, the rake, the profligate and the depraved should be exposed, and laurels of approval and reward should drape the shoulders of the honourable and the good. In this way the drama would supersede the grog shops, gambling house and brothel, thus snatching youthful and pliable minds from the very worst of snares to a place where, while amusement was the ostensible object, principles of virtue might be acquired imperceptibly.[57]

The early novel about Australia was concerned to point a moral about life and to adorn a tale. In 1830 the novel *Alfred Dudley; or, the Australian Settlers* was published in London. The Dudley family had lived in England

---

[56] Pages 147-50.

[57] *Australian*, 26 May 1825; The *Blossom*, May 1828, pp. 27-9; see also *Australian*, 24 February 1825 and for Van Diemen's Land see the exchange between 'Candor' and the editor in the *Colonial Advocate*, 1 May 1828.

in an elegant and commodious mansion, till, thanks to the machinations of a caddish business partner, they had fallen into such financial difficulties that it looked as though they would be exposed to the disgrace of not being able to send their son to a public school. The son suggested emigration to New South Wales. No, no, replies the father, my son is destined to fill a higher station than that of an Australian settler. To which the son replies, 'What are riches, what are honours compared to that interchange of affection which ennobles our nature?' So they emigrated to a farm near Sydney, where Mr Dudley, for a season, sighed every time he saw his son swing a pick, or push a shovel when his mind might have been employed reading Homer and Virgil, while men from the lower orders were yoked to the plough. Even Mr Dudley came to see that the satisfaction of converting a large mass of human misery and privation into so vast a sum of human happiness more than compensated for the renunciation of the worldly honours of the old world. Besides, there was a life of warm-hearted benevolence and hospitality for the gentry of New South Wales, free from the disasters which befell families in England, and free from those snubs and slights to which the aristocracy subjected the lesser gentry in the old world. Alfred had gained his pearl of great price. As his father told him with pride: 'you reign in the hearts of the many whom you have rendered happy. Blessed reflection! Yes, you are indeed fulfilling the end of your being, and my cherished child is the benefactor of his species'.[58]

In the same year a story on Australia was published in London which pointed the moral that both God and man punished wickedness and vice. That was 'One False Step' in J. Howison's *Tales of the Colonies*. To undertones of bourgeois censoriousness and priggishness towards a pleasure-seeking, frivolous aristocracy, the reader is introduced to Beveral Hermsdill, who wasted his inheritance in riotous living, mended his ways, but, tempted to help his mother by the ways of the wicked, makes his one false step, forges a bill, and is transported to New South Wales. So Hermsdill sailed for Botany Bay where, thanks to his genteel birth and accomplishments, he was assigned to a gentleman settler. There the daughter of the house was so comely that he hid behind the bushes in the garden on moonlight nights when the air was full of mystery and romance, and warbled to her in Italian to show her both his refinement and his tenderness. 'Why', he asked, 'why should I continue to disguise my real rank and qualifications, and unnecessarily reduce myself to a level with other convicts?' But, alas for the vanity of human wishes, the gentlemen settlers of New South Wales believed the stain of convictism could not be washed away by the purest of pure genteel blood, let alone by the gift of singing love songs in Italian by the dark and mysterious waters of the Hawkesbury. Hermsdill had committed his false step: there was no expiation which could make him welcome in the drawing rooms of the gentry of New South Wales. Some ex-convicts, coarse, vulgar and disgustingly rich, invited him to their homes, but the true gentry, and the well-bred, shunned him. As for the convicts, life with them was so wounding to his sensibilities and his pride, that he resolved to turn his back on mankind: 'Hail! earth, skies, woods,

---

[58] Anon.; the author took his information from R. Dawson, *The Present State of Australia* (London, 1830).

and waters', he cried as he took to the bush, 'you are henceforth to be my only companions'.

Rescue seems to be at hand. His mother arrives with a certificate of emancipation. But worn out by this material hardship, the outrages to his sensibilities as a gentleman, the shocks to heart and mind of living in sight and sound of the abominations of the convicts, his life slowly ebbed away as his mother took him in her arms, and poured out the hopes of a life which would make amends for past misfortunes. 'No, no, mother', he replied faintly, 'your hopes are vain, *one step in the path of crime seldom can be retrieved*'. And he expired, leaving his mother, his aunt and the woman he had loved to return to England where three unloved women rotted away their lives in genteel poverty, edified to the last by contemplating the swift retribution meted out to evil-doers by God and man.[59]

In 1830-1 the three volumes of *Quintus Servinton* by Henry Savery appeared in Hobart Town. Endowed by nature with the novelist's gifts to read the mind's construction in the face, or even heaven's decree, he had been exposed to the fate of being an object of the gossip of Hobart Town and that even more cruel fate of hearing men laughing and guffawing over the seduction of his wife by the Attorney-General of Van Diemen's Land. He had that gift to see into the heart of what was happening in a convict society, but yet lacked the strength, and the stamina to detach himself from that great net. All this might have equipped Savery to break away from the writers who wanted to adorn their tale with the moral of 'One False Step'. But Savery had lived five years in a society in which the men at the top were preaching precisely that morality, while their pupils, or their victims, had not developed an articulate morality of their own. So he wrote a tale of the sufferings endured by Quintus Servinton, of the terrible consequences that followed for him in the train of a departure from rectitude. For Savery had not known that world of Betsey Bandicoot, that new confidence and loyalty which were emerging in New South Wales of sticking up for the currency lads and lasses: nor had he known that moment of standing shoulder to shoulder with his fellow-men, and drinking to 'The land, boys, we live in'. Savery, after giving his hero an absolute and entire remission of all pains and penalties, sent him and his wife back over the oceans where the white cliffs of England once more delighted his eyes. He allowed his hero to say that God in all his chastenings was ever merciful, and then, suppressing his own humiliations from the women of snares and nets, to add that he was inclined to subscribe to the doctrine that marriages were made in Heaven. Virtue, he reminded his readers, in a final Latin tag, may increase through a wound.[60]

The first intended historian of New South Wales had hoped to point a similar moral in his proposed book 'Extracts From The Letters To My Uncle Toby, On the History of New South Wales'. He was Thomas Parmeter, a surgeon in His Majesty's forces. His purpose was to show his readers that vice

[59] J. Howison, *Tales of the Colonies* (2 vols, London, 1830) vol. 2, pp. 83-297, 'One False Step'.

[60] H. Savery, *Quintus Servinton* (3 vols, Hobart Town, 1830-1); see also Henry Savery, *Quintus Servinton* ed. by C. H. Hadgraft (Brisbane, 1962).

had a foe. Finding, however, that of writing books there was no end, and much study was a weariness of the flesh, Parmeter never published his history as a record of God's punishment of wickedness and vice. It was left to the Reverend J. Dunmore Lang in 1834 to describe on paper those occasions when it had pleased Almighty God to visit New South Wales with an afflictive drought to open the eyes of the colonists to their own folly and madness.[61]

From the pulpit, the liturgy, the psalms and the hymns the Anglican parsons created a world in which their God presided over a world of order and virtue which was sharply challenged by depraved human beings. Almighty God, the Reverend Mr Wilton told his flock at St James's Church one Sunday in September of 1827, was not a God of confusion, but rather a God of order who guarded against the inroads of anarchy and infidelity. It was God's wish that His children be taught a steady regard for morality, piety and virtue, and a firm adherence to the civil and ecclesiastical government of the colony. Let them all hope and pray, he concluded, that a Protestant crown would long flourish on the head of England's king, and let every friend to virtue and social order in every land say to their God—Amen.[62]

Every Sunday the parson and his congregation beseeched Almighty God for grace to serve him with reverence and godly fear, and asked Him to affect them with an awful apprehension of the divine majesty, and a deep sense of their own unworthiness. Every Sunday, the parson invited the congregation to repeat after him the great hope that God would destroy those who roved after other gods, while their heavenly Father had prepared a home for the good and the just who put their trust in Him and declared his wondrous works.[63]

Every Sunday the Reverend J. Dunmore Lang used his pulpit for some well-chosen images on the torments of the damned in the life of the world to come, and the bliss of God's elect. Divine providence, would, he told them, in some way or other punish all who deserted or opposed the course of God in the world. When Mr Wemyss was charged with smuggling in the *Almorah* Lang, who at other times preached of the inscrutable purposes of a loving God, pointed out that divine providence had had him arrested. It seemed to some in Sydney town that this vigilant and just ruler of the affairs of men, whose wrath Lang called down on men's heads, was always afflicting the personal enemies of the pugnacious, irascible minister of Scots Church.[64]

Yet to the dismay of the parsons, the seed they sowed fell on the stony ground of a generation of men who had not drifted into or been unconverted to unbelief, but had never known any belief. Attendance at church was one measure of the proportion in New South Wales and Van Diemen's Land who

[61] *Australian*, 14 July 1825; J. D. Lang, *An Historical and Statistical Account of New South Wales* (2 vols, London, 1834).

[62] C. P. N. Wilton, 'The Beauty of Order in the Church of England. Sermon preached in St James's Church, 6 September 1827', *Australian Quarterly of Theology, Literature and Finance*, no. 1, January 1828 (Sydney, 1828).

[63] Prayer to be used at the consecration of churches in New South Wales (Scott Papers, microfilm in NAT. L.); *Select Portions of the Psalms of David, according to the Version of Dr Brady and Mr Tate* (Sydney, 1828).

[64] *Sydney Gazette*, 12 June 1823; *John Dunmore Lang: Chiefly Autobiographical 1799 to 1878* ed. by A. Gilchrist (2 vols, Melborune, 1951) vol. 1, p. 83.

had ever heard Christ's word.[65] The parsons, confronted on the one hand by an upper class some of whom had absorbed the points made in *Candide* against that God who allowed both the good and evil to suffer from the one event, and the irony of Gibbon about that time in the history of mankind when the lame walked, the blind saw, the sick were healed, the dead were raised, demons were expelled, and the laws of Nature were frequently suspended for the benefit of the church, and by lower orders whose life was a mockery of that God who had made man, they knew, lower than the angels, but not as low as the beasts, were tempted to attribute the indifference to God to human depravity, or to savage the priests of the Catholic church. The greater the indifference the more savagely the parsons denounced from their pulpits the behaviour of a wicked and adulterous generation.

It was more than Lang's nostrils which were offended by the incense used by the priests of the Church of Rome. One morning in December of 1827, a great crowd assembled in George Street and on the heights behind the gaol in Sydney to witness the execution of four white men and an aboriginal called Tommy. Some blacks armed with woomeras, waddies and spears stood in the background, angry, yet impotent as ever to prevent the white man's infamy to one of their kind. Just before the execution launched Tommy into the silence, he vowed that his own people would avenge his death. Then the Catholic priest, Mr Power, put one of the big questions to Tommy: he asked him if he wished to be saved, and showed him a bottle of consecrated water with which he proposed to baptize him with the sign of the cross if he wished to go to heaven. Mr Lang, the madness in his blood inflamed by Mr Power's promises to Tommy, shouted to Mr Power that it would be a gross impropriety, a mockery of the rite of baptism, to sprinkle with water a man who neither understood the rite, nor would benefit from it in the life of the world to come, being entirely destitute of any knowledge of that passage in holy scripture: 'He that believeth and is baptized shall be saved'. Mr Power, quite unaffected by such biblical bluster, made the sign of the cross over Tommy's head, sprinkled him with water as he recited those words used at all times, in all places, and by all men, and baptizing him in the name of the Father, the Son, and the Holy Ghost, he told Tommy for his consolation he would go straight to heaven and be saved.

In the meantime the Irishmen who were about to suffer the same fate were beating their breasts as a sign of their great distress of mind; Mr Power showed them the crucifix and asked them if their agony could be equal to Christ's. Then the signal was given, the trap lowered, and the five men, four white and one black, dropped into that kingdom of eternal night. Robert Howe, hearty well-wisher to the Protestant religion and the birthrights of Englishmen, was deeply shocked that any man, either white or black, should, when terrified at the approach of death, throw himself into the arms of a Catholic priest, who promptly administered a course of opiates to the conscience

---

[65] Selected Examples of Reports on the State of Churches, Parsonages, etc. in New South Wales, delivered to Scott in 1827 (Broughton Papers); List of Clergy in the Archdeaconry of New South Wales and Van Diemen's Land (Papers of Archdeacon Scott in Broughton Papers).

of a willing patient, and lulled him asleep in the fatal assurance that all was well.[66]

In Protestant eyes the Catholic not only practised a vulgar superstition, he also sat, knelt, genuflected, or crossed himself each Sunday in that crowd of pantomimic gestures which in Roman Catholic worship had been substituted for intelligible words, and addressed his prayers to that multitude of saints some of whom were of doubtful and some of hateful character. He was priest-ridden. He was a constant threat to the high material civilization and liberty which distinguished the Protestant countries of Europe from their absolutist, poverty-stricken, obscurantist Catholic neighbours. In Catholic eyes the Protestant was a threat to that most precious gift of the holy faith, a threat to participation in those sacraments which could preserve him from mortal sin in this world, and so qualify him to enter the kingdom of heaven. Sydney and Hobart Town were Protestant cities in which the public buildings, the churches, and the schools were outward and visible signs of the Protestant concept of God and man. The absence of ornament and ostentation in the churches of Sydney, Hobart Town, Launceston, Bothwell, Newcastle and Parramatta, breathed the very spirit of Protestant Christianity. There, neither statue, holy picture, rich vestments, incense, or flamboyant music came between the worshipper and his god. To the native of Erin's isle there were no shrines in the fields on which he could lay his offerings of flowers, or ask the holy mother of God to pray for him in the hour of his death; there was no ringing of the angelus bell in the middle of the day; in the streets of Sydney and Hobart Town there was no tolling of the bell to remind him of that great mystery of the faith, the participation of Christ in the holy sacrifice of the mass.[67]

In addition to the absence of all those signs and wonders which comforted and uplifted him in this world, the exile from Erin had to endure some of those galling distinctions and disabilities with which the Protestant ascendancy had oppressed and humiliated him in his native land. Until the passing of an Act for the relief of His Majesty's Roman Catholic subjects by Parliament in 1829 no Catholic could hold office in either colony. Catholics had to be married by Protestant clergymen, and buried in a Protestant cemetery. The children they could not maintain were placed in an orphan school where they were baptized according to the rites of the Church of England, and educated in doctrines, which, in Catholic eyes, put their eternal salvation in jeopardy. In the orphan schools, the Catholic missal, the Douay version of the Holy Bible, and their own catechism were forbidden.

From the pulpit, from the mouths of the men and women who had lived in the dark days of the foundation of Sydney and Hobart Town, they pieced together a dark story of the sufferings of their people at the hands of the Protestant ascendancy. It was whispered in the pot-houses that that infernal hypocrite, the Reverend Samuel Marsden, that man, who had put a very literal interpretation on Christ's words: Feed my lambs, feed my sheep, and built up

[66] *Sydney Gazette*, 2 January 1828; E. Gibbon, *The Decline and Fall of the Roman Empire* (6 vols, Everyman ed., 1910), vol. 1, p. 449.

[67] *Australian*, 24 November 1825; T. B. Macaulay, *The History of England* (2 vols, London, 1899), vol. 1, p. 27.

pretty considerable treasures on earth, had had Irish Catholics flogged just because they had preferred to keep their immortal souls unspotted, even if it meant having their backsides running with blood, and the flesh torn off by the flagellator. Had not a priest been compelled to lay his hand on some members of his faith who were being flogged for rising in revolt against a power as cruel and bloodthirsty as that which had ruled Rome when St Peter was crucified and St Paul was beheaded? Had not the holy man swooned away when he saw what those barbarians were doing to men of his kind? And some Sundays the priest told them, as they listened wondrous as ever before man's inhumanity to man, that the evils from which they suffered, heresy, atheism, deism, latitudinarianism, and barefaced impiety were the consequences of a great apostasy by that man of insupportable pride, Martin Luther, who had presumed to stand against the whole church of God, and that most wicked prince, Henry VIII, who had never spared woman in his lust, nor man in his wrath.[68]

This fear of Protestant power exposed the minds and hearts of their priests to a lack of charity in their attitude to the clergy of the Protestant persuasions which contrasted sharply with the loving kindness, the pity and compassion they lavished on the faithful members of Christ's church. After a year in Sydney things rank and gross in nature rushed into the mind of Father Therry whenever he contemplated the life of the Protestant parsons. They had made their private interests, he said, instead of their public duty the object of their primary consideration. For although Therry knew that by the tenets of the Catholic Church universal charity was inculcated, and although he knew he should not labour in order to be noticed by man, as he was labouring for a higher reward than the praise of man, yet, being a man, he was troubled by what those lying tongues in Sydney made of his financial troubles.[69]

In his relations with the members of his own church he was to know something to which the Protestant clergymen were to remain strangers in relations with their own flock—that sense of having a gift to bestow which was devoutly and greedily coveted by those to whom it was freely given. 'For god sake come', one man wrote to him. No one ever used those words to the Reverend Samuel Marsden, or the Reverend William Bedford. No one wrote to a Protestant chaplain as John Chancy wrote to Therry in June of 1822:

> Yr REVce, there is no tenderness of charity or compassion reigns with grand folks here towards a poor unfortunate creature, I must be inevitably lost unles Yr. Revce. for god sake will have something done to save me from perishing in every respect as I shall be always guided by you . . . I ask God's pardon and with submission Yr. REVce. HUMble and esteemd poor sinner, John Chancy.[70]

[68] Based on W. B. Ullathorne, *The Catholic Mission in Australasia* (Liverpool, 1837), p. 5 et seq.; *A Sketch of the Rise and Progress of the Year's Mission* (Goulburn, 1861) p. 9; *An Antidote to Misrepresentation and Impiety* (Sydney, 1828).

[69] See, for example, J. J. Therry to the Attorney-General of New South Wales, n.d. (probably written in 1821); J. J. Therry to the Colonial Secretary of New South Wales, 10 June 1824; Bishop Slater to D. Power, Mauritius, 1 March 1822 (Therry Papers); S. Marsden to J. Taylor and R. Watson, Parramatta, 15 August 1822 (Bonwick Transcripts, Box 52, p. 1126).

[70] J. Chancy to J. J. Therry, 11 June 1822 (Therry Papers). This is but one example of many letters addressed to Therry for help. Read collectively they make a moving picture of the misfortunes of the Irish convicts, and their hope that he at least had a gift to bestow which would console them in their wretchedness—the very depth of which drove them to turn hopefully to his great comforter.

Men in want of a loaf of bread were drawn to intrude on his humanity: a man who had received one hundred lashes in one week, and was due to receive another asked him to intercede for him as he feared the second hundred might finish him off: those in great trouble prayed to God to put it into Therry's heart to come to them, knowing that his reverence always answered such a call: James Hardy Vaux, swindler, three times transported, an authority on flash language, after being admitted a humble member of Christ's church, asked Therry for the power of God and the good of his fellow Catholics to announce from the high altar that he had ceased to live with a woman who was not his lawful wedded wife.[71]

For the rest Therry spent his days baptizing infants, receiving adults into the church, uniting in holy matrimony those whom God had already joined together, comforting the sick, and the dying, and hearing the confessions of the penitent.[72] When E. S. Hall, great mocker that he was, accused Catholics of not knowing what they worshipped when they prostrated themselves before the blessed sacrament, Therry replied that it had been adored by the great majority of Christians, princes, kings and emperors ever since its divine institution, and would continue to be so adored until the consummation of the ages.[73]

Apart from these occasional public replies to Protestant attacks on Catholic teaching, and his zeal in protecting Catholics from attending any Protestant religious rites or ceremonies, or being exposed to subtle attempts to proselytize Catholic children in the schools, orphanages, and convict establishments of the colony of New South Wales, Therry was careful, as was Power also, and for that matter Conolly in Van Diemen's Land, to refrain from all activity which could offend the powers that be. Believing as he did that altar and throne were never so respectfully secure, as when reciprocally and eventually supported by each other, he was sure no governor of New South Wales ever contemplated by enslaving conscience to render insupportably nauseous the already bitter cup of exile and bondage.[74] Besides both he and Conolly were exhorted by their superior, Bishop Slater, to address the public authorities with great respect, using the language of deference, and avoiding interference in any of the parties, cabals or intrigues which abounded in the colonies. Above all, they were to labour without any wish to be noticed of man, and avoid as much as possible becoming the subject of public conversation. 'We labour', the bishop reminded his two priests, 'for a higher reward than the praise of man'.[75]

On one point Therry refused to be quiet. That was the education question. In both New South Wales and Van Diemen's Land the government had attempted to build a school attached to each parish church in which the schoolmaster taught the children to renounce the pomp and vanities of this wicked

---

[71] See, for example, J. Lawler to J. J. Therry, Sydney 1 June 1822; and J. H. Vaux to J. J. Therry, 19 May 1823 (Therry Papers).

[72] For evidence, see the diary Therry kept in 1822 which consists of writings by Therry on scraps of paper (Therry Papers).

[73] Draft reply by J. J. Therry to E. S. Hall (month not given) 1824 (Therry Papers).

[74] Draft of letter by J. J. Therry to the Colonial Secretary of New South Wales, 10 June 1824 (Therry Papers).

[75] Bishop Slater to Father Power, Mauritius, 1 March 1827 (Therry Papers).

world, and all the sinful lusts of the flesh. But while parson and schoolmaster laboured to explain to the children how man was made in the image of God, the utmost chaos and confusion prevailed in these schools which were condemned as seminaries of idleness and vice. At Castlereagh the gentle Reverend Henry Fulton, who had been transported for his part in the Irish rebellion of 1798, and swept briefly into a moment of prominence during the mutiny against Bligh in 1808, was grieved to find that the children had pulled the plaster off the walls, and smashed the panes of glass.[76]

It was more than the old Adam with which the critics of the education system were contending. Of just over 1,800 in the rolls of schools of New South Wales in 1829 only 1,265 ever attended a school, or about one-third the total number of children. The same was true in Van Diemen's Land.[77] Therry feared the Protestants were scheming to enslave the consciences of Catholics by proselytizing Catholics in the parish and orphan schools.[78] The Reverend J. Dunmore Lang had his own anxieties about the evils of an Anglican monopoly of education on the attitute of the children of Presbyterians to the faith of their fathers. Was it just and right, he asked, that the Scotsman alone should receive no benefit from the liberal provision which the government proposed to make for religious instruction of the colonists and for the education of their youth unless he renounced the faith of his forefathers and suffered his children to be taught this downright absurdity in the shape of ecclesiastical proselytizing theology? Why should the Scotsman be subject to a yoke in New South Wales and Van Diemen's Land which their forefathers had cast off?[79] The *Australian* had its own point of difference with education by parson and parish schoolmaster. It was, they said, too discerning an age to permit the classical fooleries of gownsmen to impede the progress of knowledge. The torrent was abroad, they said, that would sweep away all the useless rubbish that had been collecting in past ages.[80]

Amid all this babble of tongues, with the Reverend Mr Wilton talking about beauty of order, with the Reverend Samuel Marsden shouting that men drink iniquity like water, and the Reverend Mr Lang fierce, implacable and stern contrasting the bliss of the elect with the sufferings of the damned, and the Reverend Father Therry urging the faithful to obey the church of whose mandates he was the instrument, the *Australian* cheekily proclaiming that heaven and hell were priest's inventions, and Betsey Bandicoot saying that for her part she proposed to stick up for currency lads and lasses, a new voice was heard in the land. On 1 September 1830 Jack Donahoe, twenty-three years of age, low in stature, but so remarkably well-made that he reminded some of Byron's remark about those heroes who were fair in death's face, was shot dead at Bringelly. Donahoe, who had been tried in Dublin in April of 1823, arrived in Sydney on the *Ann and Amelia* as a convict in January of 1825. He was

---

[76] *Australian*, 30 June 1825.

[77] Papers concerning Clergy and School Lands, 1829 (Item 4 in Broughton Papers).

[78] Draft of a letter by J. J. Therry to the Colonial Secretary of New South Wales, 10 June 1824 (Therry Papers).

[79] See John Dunmore Lang, Episcopal Domination, in *John Dunmore Lang* ed. by A. Gilchrist (2 vols, Melbourne, 1951), vol. 1, p. 81.

[80] *Australian*, 30 June 1825.

tried again before the Supreme Court in Sydney in January of 1828, after which he took to the bush, murdered a man with whom he had lived, and burnt his body to a cinder. After Donahoe was shot in 1830 the *Sydney Gazette* and all the respectable people in the colony rejoiced that they were rid of one of the most dangerous spirits that had ever infected it, and went on to say it would be happy if those of a like disposition would take warning from the awful fate of Donahoe.

But soon in the taverns, public houses, pot-houses, and bush shanties of New South Wales, some men, using an old Irish melody, began to sing a song about a wild colonial boy, Jack Dowling [Donahoe] was his name, of poor but honest parents, a heart that knew no danger, no stranger for to fear, who had been sent across the main for seven long years to wear a convict's chain. There scorning to live in slavery bound down by iron chains, he had uttered his great cry of defiance:

> 'I'd rather roam these hills and dales, like wolf or kangaroo,
> Than work one hour for Government!' cried bold Jack Donahoo.
>   . . .
>
> He fought six rounds with the horse police until the fatal ball,
> Which pierced his heart and made him start, caused Donahoo to fall.
> And as he closed his mournful eyes, he bade this world Adieu,
> Saying, 'Convicts all, both large and small, say prayers for Donahoo!'

The song had such an evil influence that its singing was prohibited in any public house on pain of the loss of the licence. The song lived on. Bold Jack Donahoe had become part of the popular imagination of Australia.

In the public houses of New South Wales, wherever convicts, their relatives, and sympathizers came together during the decade, they sang the story of Jim Jones. This, too, was a shaking of the fist not at God, or their society, but at their floggers, and tormentors:

> For night and day the irons clang, like poor galley slaves
> We toil, and toil, and when we die must fill dishonoured graves.
> But by and by I'll break my chains: into the bush I'll go,
> And join the brave bushrangers there—Jack Donohoo and Co.;
> And some dark night when everything is silent in the town
> I'll kill the tyrants, one and all, and shoot the floggers down:
> I'll give the Law a little shock: remember what I say,
> They'll yet regret they sent Jim Jones in chains to Botany Bay.

Some also sang that moving lament of the native of Erin's isles who, having endured all the places of condemnation, had found that Moreton Bay was the worst of them all:

> For three long years I've been beastly treated; heavy irons each day
>   I wore.
> My poor back from flogging had been lacerated, and oftimes painted
>   with crimson gore.
> Like the Egyptians or ancient Hebrews, we were sorely oppressed by
>   Logan's yoke,
> Till kind Providence came to our assistance and gave this tyrant his
>   total stroke.

Yes, he was hurried from that place of bondage, where he thought he
    would gain renown;
But a native black, who lay in ambush, gave this monster his fatal wound.
Now that I've got once more to cross the ocean, and leave this place called
    Moreton Bay,
Where many a man from downright starvation lies mouldering to-day
    beneath the clay.
Fellow prisoners, be exhilarated, and your former sufferings don't bear
    in mind,
For it's when from bondage you are extricated you'll leave those tyrants
    far, far behind.

Over the waters in Van Diemen's Land, the convicts and their sympathizers
had begun to find words to express their cruel fate:

> The first day that we landed here upon the fatal shore,
> The settlers came around us, some twenty score or more;
> They ranked us up like horses and they sold us out of hand,
> And they yoked us up to ploughing-frames to plough Van
>   Diemen's Land.

They went on not to bewail their fate, but to use their experience as a
cautionary tale to the lads they had left behind in the country districts of
England:

> So all you lively poaching lads, this warning take from me:
> I'd have you quit night walking and avoid bad company,
> And throw aside your guns and snares, for let me tell you plain;
> If you knew of our misfortunes you would never poach again.

So some in their quest for a comforter to make life bearable had found it not
in the gods of their fathers, or any dreams of a new race of man, but in a
truculence towards those who had despitefully used them, or in a wail which
came close to a whine, or in a cry of anguish to others of their kind for god's
sake not to take the one false step which would lead them to suffering and
perdition.

Others found it by laughing sardonically at the fate of being a man in New
South Wales:

> The Currency Lads may fill their glasses,
> And drink to the health of the Currency Lasses;
> But the lass I adore, the lass for me,
> Is a lass in the Female Factory.
>
> O! Molly's her name, and her name is Molly,
> Although she was tried by the name of Polly;
> She was tried and was cast for death at Newry,
> But the Judge was bribed and so were the Jury.
>
> She got '*death recorded*' in Newry town,
> For stealing her mistress's watch and gown;
> Her little boy Paddy can tell you the tale,
> His father was turnkey of Newry jail.

The first time I saw the comely lass
Was at Parramatta, going to mass;
Says I, 'I'll marry you now in an hour',
Says she, 'Well, go and fetch Father Power'.

But I *got into trouble* that very same night!
Being drunk in the street I got into a fight,
A constable seized me—I gave him a box—
And was put in the watch-house and then in the stocks.

O! it's very unaisy as I may remember,
To sit in the stocks in the month of December;
With the north wind so hot, and hot sun right over,
O! sure, and it's no place at all for a lover!

'It's worse than the tread-mill', says I, Mr Dunn,
To sit here all day in the *hate* of the sun!'
'Either that or a dollar', says he, 'for your folly',—
But if I had a dollar I'd drink it with Molly.

But now I am out again, early and late
I sigh and I cry at the Factory gate,
'O! Mrs R—, late Mrs F—n,
O! won't you let Molly out very soon?'

'It it Molly McGuigan?' says she to me,
'Is it not?' says I, for she know'd it was she.
'It it her you mean that was put in the stocks
For beating her mistress, Mrs Cox?'

'O! yes and it is, madam, pray let me in,
I have brought her a half-pint of Cooper's best gin,
She likes it as well as she likes her own mother,
O! now let me in, madam, I am her brother.'

So the Currency Lads may fill their glasses,
And drink to the health of the Currency Lasses;
But the lass I adore, the lass for me,
Is a lass in the Female Factory.[81]

---

[81] For Jack Donahoe see J. Meredith, *The Wild Colonial Boy* (Sydney, 1960); see also Russel Ward, *The Australian Legend* (Melbourne, 1958), and E. Waters, Some Aspects of the Popular Arts in Australia 1880-1915, Ph.D. thesis, Australian National University, 1962; see also *H.R.A.*, I. xv. 906 for the notice prohibiting singing the song in public; *Sydney Gazette*, 5 March 1828 for an account of Donahoe's escape; for an early text of 'Bold Jack Donahoe', see A. B. Paterson, *Old Bush Songs* (Sydney, 1905), pp. 30-2; for the death of Donahoe see *Sydney Gazette*, 7 and 8 September 1828; for an early text of 'Jim Jones of Botany Bay', sung to the tune of 'Irish Mollie, Oh!' see C. MacAlister, *Old Pioneering Days in the Sunny South* (Goulburn, 1907), pp. 72-3; for the words of 'Moreton Bay' see J. Bradshaw, *Highway Robbery Under Arms* (Pyrmont, 1912), pp. 9-10; for a text of 'Van Diemen's Land' see J. Manifold (ed.), *The Penguin Australian Song Book* (Melbourne, 1964); for a text of the 'Botany Bay Courtship' see *Sydney Gazette*, 14 July 1832; see also *Old Bush Songs and Rhymes of Colonial Times*, enl. and rev. from the collection of A. B. Paterson by Douglas Stewart and Nancy Keesing (Sydney, 1957); J. S. Manifold, *Who Wrote the Ballads?* (Sydney, 1966).

8

A WHIG GOVERNOR AMIDST HIGH
TORY COUNSELLORS

EARLY IN October 1831 James Macarthur met in the streets of
Sydney his learned friend and countryman, William Charles Wentworth, to whom he communicated his opinion on the recent regulations
for the disposal of land in New South Wales, in which sale at auction at a
minimum upset price of 5s per acre had been substituted for free grants. As
Macarthur found that Wentworth's sentiments coincided with his they agreed
to mention the subject to several other influential individuals, who decided to
form a committee to endeavour to obtain the support of the whole colony on
what they believed to be the most important question ever submitted to a public
meeting in New South Wales, involving as it did the clear interests of the
community.[1]

Wentworth was then aged forty-one. Six years had passed since he had
shouted in a moment of drunken anger that he would remove the fangs of the
Macarthurs.[2] Time had not mellowed him. Chance and circumstance had
brought him nearer to that other ambition so close to his heart, that dream of
regaining for himself that access to the salons and drawing rooms of the
gentry which his father had forfeited by some deeds of folly in his past. With
the death of the father in July 1827 he had inherited a fortune. Despite gloomy
prophecies by old school friends that he was little versed in the affairs of trade,
and a great stranger to the minutiae of profit and loss, he had not only traded
successfully in bulls and horse-flesh, but had become one of the largest landowners in New South Wales. He had begun to collect at Vaucluse those outward and visible signs of worldly grandeur. In October of 1829 he had given
his hand in marriage to Sarah Cox just before she was brought to bed with his
child. Just over a year later, on 4 November 1830, Jemima Eagar, the wife
of the Edward Eagar who had helped him with the third edition of his book,
had borne him a son. A year after that he had handed out free grog at Vaucluse to all who were prepared to mock and deride General Darling on the
eve of his departure from New South Wales. Yet he was still striving to win
the regard and esteem of the members of high society, without being endowed
with the power to resist that madness in the blood which caused the very people
he was courting to shun, despise and fear him. The inner man was never
quiet.[3]

[1] Based on a speech by James Macarthur at Public Meeting reported in *Sydney Gazette*, 3
December 1831.   [2] *Australian*, 27 October 1825.
[3] W. M. Cookney to W. C. Wentworth, 5 March 1825 (Wentworth Papers, Letters to W. C.
Wentworth); W. C. Wentworth to Captain J. Piper, George Street, Sydney, 30 May 1828 (Piper
Papers, vol. 2, MS. in M.L.); W. C. Wentworth to D'Arcy Wentworth, London, 10 April 1817
(Wentworth Papers, Letters from W. C. Wentworth).

N

Like Wentworth, James Macarthur was native-born. But whereas Wentworth consumed so much of his energy in his youth fighting the consequences of exclusion from the homes of the gentry that his life assumed all the tragic grandeur of a man of stature proudly defying retribution for the sins of the fathers, Macarthur knew of a family struggle of quite a different kind. He was born at Parramatta in 1798, the fourth son of Captain John and Mrs Elizabeth Macarthur. Chance prepared the way for him to take over the leadership of the Macarthur family just as Wentworth was beginning the transition from the role of tribune of the people and irresponsible demagogue to that of Mr Money-Bags and Mr Broadacres. Like Wentworth, too, James Macarthur became in childhood and adolescence more like his mother than his father, a throw of chance which may have conferred on the former that inner turbulence, and that outer loudness of behaviour which mocked all his efforts to escape the curse of his birth, and on the latter an inner serenity, a courage and a power to endure, and a faith to sustain him when the world shook. It may even explain why Wentworth was the great unloved, and Macarthur both beloved and loving.

Fate had reserved its own turns of the screw for James Macarthur. He was 'the English gentleman Australian-born'.[4] Overshadowed in his youth by the reputation of his father for ruthlessness and reckless folly as well as the odium of supporting the extreme exclusive position, he had also inherited his father's convictions and aspirations, the dream of establishing a plantation society in Australia, led by large landholders who derived their wealth from the growing of wool by cheap convict labour. He had not inherited that satanic drive which had pushed the father into those deeds of folly which cheated him, in the autumn of his life, of the honour, the respect, the esteem, the admiration and the affection to which his great achievements entitled him. Growing up in such a shadow James Macarthur was in danger of merely handing down to posterity a claim to be one of Australia's gentlemen, one of those men of enlarged views and liberal education, who were valued in their own circle for their improvements in the breeding of stock, the tilling of the farm and garden, the making of wine, and the growth of wool.[5] These seemed to be his interests when he first began to put down on paper those remarks which would save him from the fate of returning to the dust from whence he came like all those who leave no memorial, no trace that they had been here. Chance, too, altered all that without his stir.

After being educated at Parramatta by a tutor he and his younger brother William had been taken to England by their father in 1809 when the latter was sent to England to give an account of his part in the deposition of Bligh.

[4] See the poem by Henry Parkes, 'Gone over to the Majority':

And brave Macarthur—brave in pure intent
And honest deed,—who bore, where'er he went,
Of all unworthy things a true man's scorn;
The English gentleman Australian-born.
(Macarthur Papers, vol. 32, p. 194).

[5] These points were made about James Macarthur when he died; see, for example, *The Sporting Life*, 27 April 1867 (quoted in Macarthur Papers, vol. 32, p. 195).

So James set out to acquire the accomplishments of a gentleman under the shadow of possible disgrace and humiliation for his father. When he set out on the grand tour of Europe he kept a journal which faithfully reflected what he was—a cautious young man of seventeen, who jotted down the exact cost of each meal at the end of each day in which he studied the monuments in the graveyard of European civilization. When he arrived at Vevey he noticed the pretty little room in which Madame Warens had lived, and went on characteristically to note in his diary that dinner that day had cost him 8s.[6] All his life he was to remain a stranger to that delirium of the heart which took Wentworth up into the high places and cast him down in the low. He returned to New South Wales in 1817 with his father and devoted himself to the improvement of his family's fortunes, when once again the curse of his father's stormy past haunted him. When offered the position of magistrate he declined to accept because his father was held to be unfit for public office.[7]

Chosen by his family to represent their interests on the Australian Agricultural Company, he became the senior member of the New South Wales committee of that company in 1824. When he went to England to confer with the directors in 1828 he behaved like a man whose interests seemed not to range outside the price of wool. He was delighted to report back to Parramatta his visits to a warehouse where a John Bull-looking Quaker had opened a fleece from their bale number twenty-four from which some bits of dung had dropped on the floor, and said to him in a loud voice: 'Methinks, friend, this would have enriched the soil from whence it came'. Then the Quaker had spoken of the excellence of their wool, assuring him there was no wool in the world to be compared to it.[8]

A few months later when he called on Goethe he wrote in his journal of a fine venerable old man, very courteous in his manners, who had asked many questions about New South Wales and told him that friendship was the way he learnt geography. For neither then nor at any time did James seem touched by those questions which had bothered Goethe. He was neither driven to find what held the world together in its innermost parts, nor to wonder at the burden of the mystery, let alone to laugh or shout at any cosmic irony at the heart of things. Unlike Goethe he was not bothered that a man might be overcome by sensual lust even when standing beneath a crucifix.[9] When he poured out his heart in verse he uncovered the calm, untroubled spirit of a man who could praise the gentleness of a woman's heart, and conceive of his beloved as

> Lightly pois'd on slender stem—
> Australia's dearest loveliest gem!
> At radiant morning's earliest hour,

[6] Entry for 25 September 1815 in James Macarthur, Journal of a tour in France and Switzerland, March 1815 to April 1816 (Macarthur Papers, vol. 33).

[7] James Macarthur to F. Goulburn, Parramatta, 14 October 1823 (Macarthur Papers, vol. 24, pp. 3-4).

[8] James Macarthur to William Macarthur, 57 Jermyn Street, London, 10 November 1828 (Macarthur Papers, vol. 35, pp. 66-7).

[9] Diary written by James Macarthur on a tour through Belgium and Germany with his brother Edward, 14 November 1828 to 2 January 1829 (Macarthur Papers, vol. 33).

Smiling through the dewy shower,
Thou greetest the Sun, with timid eye,

. . .

And Fancy finally pictures thee
An emblem pure of Constancy![10]

In his poetry he celebrated such simple virtues as constancy as a mirror of the goodness in his own heart. Yet chance was reserving for him the curious fate of being thrown into association with a man who knew that the imagination of man's heart was evil from the start.

Shortly after he returned to New South Wales in 1831 his father was enduring the heaviest affliction he had ever sustained in his life when his eldest son John died in London and so put his fortitude under heavy trial.[11] Soon the old man began to show unmistakable signs that for him another darkness was descending. He was beginning to become the prey of delusions that his family were taking things from him.[12] Chance was about to bestow on James a role he had never coveted, the role of leader of the Macarthur family in New South Wales. So on that day in October two victims of the sins of the fathers, two inheritors of what others had sown—the one kind and gentle in his disposition with a manner which at once inspired confidence and respect, the other coarse-grained, a prey, so his enemies said, to vulgar ambition and sensual lust—confronted each other.[13]

On one question and one question alone they could see eye to eye. That was the new regulations for the disposal of land in the Australian colonies. They were two of the largest landowners in New South Wales.[14] They agreed that a public meeting of landholders and others should be held at Parramatta to consider the expediency of petitioning the King on the subject of the land regulations. At the meeting on 6 October 1831 those present resolved that the regulations would produce ruinous consequences for the agricultural interests and the community at large, as they were injurious to the production of revenue and the progress of immigration. They appointed a committee consisting of Alexander Berry, Richard Brooks, George Bunn, William Bland, Robert Campbell sen., E. C. Close, William Cordeaux, John Coghill, William Cox, John Dickson, Sir John Jamison, Richard Jones, C. Lethbridge, John Macarthur, James Macarthur, Hannibal Macarthur, the Reverend Samuel Marsden, A. B. Spark, Robert Wardell, W. C. Wentworth and Edward Wollstonecraft to draft a petition. So exclusive and emancipist, immigrant and native-born, conservative and liberal, men such as Marsden and Wentworth

10 James Macarthur, 'Lines upon the Fringed Violet the loveliest of Australian Flowers to Miss ——' (Macarthur Papers, vol. 24, p. 365).

11 John Macarthur to R. Darling, Parramatta, 18 October 1831 (Macarthur Papers, vol. 4, pp. 307-8).

12 See, for example, John Macarthur to Edward Macarthur, 23 February 1832 (Macarthur Papers, vol. 3, pp. 202a-5b).

13 *The Sporting Life*, 27 April 1867; H. Tingcombe, *A Sermon Preached in St John's Church, Camden, on Sunday, 28th April 1867* (Sydney 1867).

14 In 1822 Macarthur held 9,600 acres at Parramatta, 3,000 acres at Toongabbe and over 14,000 acres at Camden, from S. Macarthur Onslow (ed.), *Some Early Records of the Macarthurs of Camden* (Sydney, 1914), pp. 376-88; in 1821, William Charles Wentworth held 30,000 acres at Parramatta (Bigge Appendix, C.O. 201/123, document no. D36).

who had once vowed implacable hostility to each other, were drawn together by a common interest in the laws affecting the ownership of land. The gentry and colonial bourgeoisie discovered a common interest against the policy of a British government.[15]

After the Sheriff took the chair at the public meeting at Parramatta in December 1831 to consider the petition James Macarthur summarized its contents. It prayed that, in consequence of the embarrassments which had arisen to the colony, owing, partly, to a continuance of dry seasons, and partly to a cessation of immigration, His Majesty would be pleased to direct an enquiry and such an adjustment of the claims of the Crown on arrears of quitrent as would most conduce to the true interests of the colony. He then went on to comment on that part of the petition which related to immigration and to the sale of unoccupied lands.[16] Then Hall rose to his feet and tried to sway the meeting by playing on those sentiments which had been the staff of life to the emancipists in the period of Governor Darling. He reminded them how the General had permitted old-established colonists to select the best land; he reminded them of how the native-born and recent immigrants had had to content themselves with the second best; he told them that the immigration of moral and industrious persons of both sexes who could take the place of convict servants would be the most powerful means of advancing these colonies: he told them much more on the same theme, before he sat down amidst very general applause.[17] For a moment that identity of interest between the large land-owners and the bourgeoise wavered as Hall whipped up the passions of the currency lads against the exclusives. The sense of unanimity against a British government began to slip, as differences between groups within the colony emerged once more. But before the rift could develop into recrimination, and a free display of the colonial taste for mockery and abuse, Bland moved successfully for an adjournment of the meeting. After all they had more important business at hand, the business of welcoming and ingratiating themselves with a new Governor.[18]

Two days later at twelve noon His Excellency Richard Bourke descended from the deck of the *Margaret* and stepped into the barge, accompanied by his suite. The whole of Sydney burst into rejoicing. The ship's company gave three loud and hearty cheers: the batteries and all the shipping in the harbour displayed their colours. When he set foot on shore again the guns boomed out their welcome, while a crowd of the respectable persons of Sydney assembled in the dockyard sent up a rousing cheer. As the procession wound slowly towards the Domain His Excellency was greeted with hearty cheering, which he acknowledged in the most affable and approving manner. After arriving at Government House Bourke took the oaths of office as Captain-General and Governor-in-Chief in and over the colony of New South Wales and its dependent territories. On the following Monday the towns of Sydney and Parramatta were illuminated. The gaoler at Parramatta explained to passers-by that the faces of both himself and his wife expressed a very special joy as

[15] *Sydney Gazette*, 8 October 1831.
[16] For the speech by James Macarthur, see *Sydney Gazette*, 3 December 1831.
[17] For the speech by E. S. Hall, and the text of his petition, see ibid.
[18] Based on the accounts in the *Sydney Gazette*, 6 and 10 December 1831.

Governor Bourke had been a next door neighbour of theirs in Ireland. All night long the fireworks popped and cracked, rifles discharged into the night air, and healths were drunk in punch to Governor Bourke, and his good lady and family.[19]

Bourke was no ordinary man. Endowed by nature with a rare gift of beauty of manner, he had acquired by discipline, training and experience that other great asset to men in high places, the gift of a presence which both set people at their ease and encouraged them to give of their best. Like Duncan in *Macbeth*, he remained to the end of his days an innocent not versed in the art of un-covering the cunning of the fox or the wiles of the devious and deceitful. Born in Dublin on 4 May 1777, and educated at Westminster School, London, and Oxford University where he took his B.A. in 1798, he had become an ensign in the Grenadier Guards. His jaw had been so badly shattered in the campaigns in the Low Countries in 1799 that he was forever debarred from that career in Parliament to which his talents, his tastes and even birth seemed to have prepared him. He was distantly related to Edmund Burke. After the Napoleonic Wars he retired with his beloved wife to his country estate of Thornfield near Limerick.

There his natural gentleness, his charity and reverence for all men were put to the test and not found wanting. All around him the sectarian battle raged, as Protestant slandered Catholic as morally mad, and a slave to a degrading superstition, and Catholic retaliated with slanders on the Protestant lack of both charity and the love of God. By night and day terror, outrage and violence disturbed the daily lives of people both great and small. Yet Bourke remained untouched by either fear or hatred. He imbibed the simple faith of the people, the loving kindness to each other and the faith in the life of the world to come. In the Protestant Cathedral Church of St Mary's in Limerick he read on the tablets in the church those sentiments which so simply expressed the principles by which he always guided his life. He read of that Christian holiness of life, of the law of kindness on the lips, and the love of God and man in the heart of a man, of patient continuation in well-doing until that day when he fell asleep in full assurance of a blessed and glorious resurrection to eternal life.

During his days as a gentleman farmer near Limerick he became a liberal in religion, and a supporter of reform in politics. In both religion and politics he never wavered from the upright man's faith in moderation in all things. In religion he was neither High Church nor Low: he was a liberal, but not a voluntary. In politics he belonged to the Whig interest—where he spoke for reform but never for radical measures. When straitened circumstances threatened him with that cruel fate for the Irish landed gentry of being reduced to the state of the genteel poor, he looked for preferment in public life rather than cripple his family with debt, or revive his fortunes by oppressing the long-suffering tenant farmers of Thornfield. He was offered the position of Acting Governor of the Cape Colony in South Africa. He arrived in Cape Town in February of 1826, where his days as Acting Governor were to be remembered by some as 'Bourke's wicked reign', and by others as that period when humanity and benevolence towards the coloured people, and labours to

19 *Sydney Gazette*, 3 and 10 December 1831.

rescue the lower orders of that unhappy society from the degradation of slavery bestowed on him the reputation of drafter of the Magna Charta of the Hottentots. He was back again in Thornfield in 1828, anxious as ever for service in the colonies. In March 1831 he eagerly accepted the offer to be Governor of New South Wales. He was then fifty-three.

With his hair thinning, and his wife stricken by a mortal illness, he set sail in the *Margaret*, his family, staff, and a guard of soldiers to protect them from pirates, filling the whole ship. After a rough trip, in a leaking ship, with food running short, the scanty drinking water a dirty coffee-brown, and Mrs Bourke nearly dying from the exposure to such an ordeal, they at last sailed up the placid blue-green waters of Sydney Harbour in December of 1831, out of the swing of that vast sea, and were swept away by the warmth of the welcome in Sydney. Guns boomed: people cheered: fun and joy were in the air. John Macarthur sent Bourke a cask of brandy matured from grapes grown on his estate. The Reverend Samuel Marsden told Bourke the spirit of wickedness was as great as ever in the colony. Chief Justice Forbes greeted him warmly as a fellow Whig who could also share his intellectual interests. Wentworth greeted him not just as a fellow Whig, though that was cheering enough, after the days of unleavened bread under those Tories, Darling, Scott, Macarthur and Bowman, but also as an Irishman whose family, like his own, had had a long and distinguished association with the Rockingham and Fitzwilliam Whigs. Father John Joseph Therry greeted him warmly as a man who believed in the moral and law-abiding influences of the Catholic religion. Sir Edward Parry, on behalf of the Australian Agricultural Company, waited upon the new Governor, and was received by him with much cordiality. Bourke entered very freely on the affairs of the colony and of the company. Parry was delighted.

So were the ladies of Sydney who were quick to detect a change in the atmosphere at Government House. That severity, that nervous sensibility in the system pursued on social occasions in the days of Governor Darling and his wife, which had repelled rather than promoted ease and gaiety, had happily disappeared. The pleasing familiarity of the olden days under Macquarie had come back, much to the comfort and relief of those whose station in life entitled them to break bread at the Governor's table or take a sherry and biscuit in the drawing rooms of Government House. A gentle and gracious host was now presiding in that house where an icy formality had prevailed for six years. The *Sydney Gazette* wrote of its fervent hope that His Excellency's administration might be incomparably less annoyed by the petty hostilities of party than those of his predecessors.[20]

Within three weeks of his arrival the colonial uproar had returned with all

[20] Based on *Sydney Herald*, 14 May 1832; Journal of Sir Edward Parry, vol. 1, 8 December 1831 and 5 June 1832, vol. 3, 16 May 1834 (microfilm in NAT. L.); memorial tablets in Cathedral Church of St Mary in Limerick, Ireland; R. Bourke to John Macarthur, n.d. (Macarthur Papers, vol. 4, p. 309); Margaret Kiddle, *Men of Yesterday* (Melbourne, 1961), p. 37; Hazel King, *Richard Bourke* (Melbourne, 1963); *Australian Dictionary of Biography*, vol. 1; R. Therry, *Reminiscences of Thirty Years' Residence in New South Wales and Victoria* (London, 1863), pp. 129-41; *Sydney Gazette*, 6 December 1831; J. D. Lang, *An Historical and Statistical Account of New South Wales* (2 vols, London, 1834), vol. 1, pp. 226-7; *Sydney Herald*, 2 January 1832.

its old fury. On 18 December some free inhabitants attended a public meeting at the Court House in Sydney to prepare an address of welcome to the new Governor. This time no member of the Macarthur family attended the meeting: the clergy of the Church of England, in deference to Bathurst's orders to keep out of politics, stayed away: the Reverend Mr Lang and Father Dowling were present. The Court House was stacked with all those men who for good or ill had savaged the late Governor, and shouted in drunken joy over the rum, the punch and the beer at Vaucluse three days before Darling had left Sydney for ever. Mr Francis Stephen began by reminding them they had not come together to agree to a mere unmeaning piece of flattery. Bourke was a man, he said, to whom much had been given: a man educated in liberal principles, and they would expect much from him. He went on to read out the text of the address—underlining with his accent the past inveterate system of misgovernment, and that they not only welcomed the end of a reign of discord and terror, but greeted the arrival of His Excellency as the dawn of a happier era. From Bourke all that they required was the birthright of Englishmen, justice and impartiality in the distribution of public patronage, a more efficient administration and the end of the press law. They wanted instead, he continued to roars of applause, laws to attract a tide of immigration to counteract the evils arising from an increase in the prisoner population, and to diminish the alarming disproportion between the sexes. What they wanted to encourage in the colony was free discussion and the free institutions of Great Britain, and to foster agriculture, manufacturing and fisheries. Once again the colonial bourgeoisie were clamouring for those conditions which would bring them that large profit and that measure of liberty to which they had first committed themselves as long ago as 1819 in the 'Rag and Bob-tail' petition of that year.

After the address was seconded Garling, a solicitor with a lawyer's love of the absence of all fuss and popular tumult, tried to get a word in edgeways in the name of moderation and, possibly, human decency. He implored them to delete such offensive phrases as 'the inveterate system of misgovernment', only to be shouted down by the men with the loud voices. Standing his ground he suggested amid the uproar, the curses, the hisses, and the abuse reserved for any man who dared to dissent at a public meeting in New South Wales, that the words 'the reign of discord and terror' were highly objectionable. But Hall and Stephen called out they could not agree to expunge a single word. Then, to deafening and enthusiastic shouts, Wentworth rose to his feet and explained briefly there was no need for him to speak unless some one put forward a forcible objection. He suggested they vote forthwith—which they did, the address being carried with acclamation. Only Garling stood out against the tide.[21] For several days there was much shaking of heads in the drawing rooms of the ancient nobility of New South Wales, much gloomy talk about demos and their levelling, tyrannical and conformist tendencies.[22]

But no such doubts or inhibitions restrained the moving spirits of the public

[21] *Sydney Gazette*, 24 December 1831.

[22] *Australian*, 13 May and 17 June 1826; John Macarthur to Edward Macarthur, 5 June 1832 (Macarthur Papers, vol. 3, pp. 129-31); John Macarthur to J. D. Lang, 17 November 1831 (Lang Papers, vol. 6).

meeting. On 26 December a delegation appointed at the meeting met Bourke at their request. When he told them of his pleasure in reading of their attachment to the mother country, and how the free institutions of the mother country had created and preserved its happiness and glory, and how he had no doubt that the legislature of the United Kingdom would introduce into the colony institutions of a similar character, they were delighted. Once again they compared the warmth of the new man with the cold, off-putting exterior of his predecessor, from whom no advocate of free institutions had ever received an approving hand. A Whig might undo all the evil influences of the Tories in Downing Street over the past decade. So they went back to the trivial round and the common task buoyed by the hope that at long last the tide towards free institutions would soon be in full flood. They were not to know then that John Macarthur had already made his usual present of brandy to the governor, and Bourke had already flattered him as a skilful and spirited horticulturist. While some were wrangling over political institutions some were taking more interest in how to cure smut in wheat or scab in sheep, and others were taking interest in the salvation of their immortal souls.[23]

All through December and January of that summer of 1831-2, Whigs, liberals, emancipists, and currency lads went on hoping for much from Bourke's liberality and benevolence. When he met the Legislative Council for the first time on 19 January 1832 he spoke of his hopes of laying before them a bill for the further extension of the jury system. He told them of the decision of the British government to use that part of colonial revenue raised from the sale of Crown land to introduce free labourers from the United Kingdom into the colony. He spoke too of his hopes to improve the morals, augment the wealth and procure the comfort and convenience of all classes by encouraging the development of public schools, places of religious worship, the formation and improvement of roads, and the repair and erection of public buildings.[24] The *Sydney Herald* was delighted. They compared the state of political peace they enjoyed under the mild sway of Governor Bourke with the upheavals in Europe: a revolution in France, and England in a violent state bordering on revolution because of the introduction of machinery. A few cargoes of immigrants would, they hoped, inspire moral propriety amongst their own working classes, and enable them to convert the surrounding oceans into a source of national wealth and industry.

Under the ownership of W. Stephens, F. M. Stokes and W. McGarvie the *Sydney Herald* had begun publication on 18 April 1831. Taking as its motto the couplet from Pope:

> In Moderation placing all my Glory,
> While Tories call me Whig, and Whigs a Tory.

it had boasted from the beginning 'Sworn to no Master, of no Sect am I' and had announced with pride its intention to remain independent in thought and speech. It had gone on to promise that it would only employ sound argument to convince, and not ribaldry to confound. It promised its readers plain,

---

[23] John Macarthur to Edward Macarthur, Camden, 23 February 1832 (Macarthur Papers, vol. 3, pp. 202a-22). [24] *Sydney Herald*, 2 and 23 January 1832.

useful and substantial knowledge, for there was about it from the beginning an air of moral earnestness, religious dissent and of political conservatism. William McGarvie, a stationer and bookseller who had arrived in New South Wales in 1828, abandoned his interest in the *Herald* after six weeks, but his brother, the Reverend John McGarvie, D.D., wrote its early leading articles, in which that hatred of the pretensions of Anglicans blended strangely with a defence of all that love of order and station in society which Scott, Broughton and Eliza Darling had been recommending as an urgently needed ideology for the noisy, disrespectful wine-bibbers and gluttons coming to man's estate in New South Wales. Stephens, the senior partner in the firm, was a recent arrival in Sydney where he joined the staff of the *Sydney Gazette* till he decided to publish the *Sydney Herald*. He was then just over twenty-five.[25] The colonial bourgeoisie were beginning to dream their dreams.

The day before Bourke first met the Legislative Council, the adjourned meeting to prepare a petition on the subject of the land regulations was held in Walker's large room at Parramatta. Wentworth moved that, as Bourke had announced in a public notice a further extension of time of three years for those indebted to the Crown for the purchase of land, they should drop the petition. Wentworth was speaking in public as an apologist for a Whig governor. Sensing some need to explain his new role, he pointed out that he had not abandoned his belief in the principles of the petition: the urgency of it had just disappeared. By political astuteness Bourke had dissolved the combination of gentry and large landowners of New South Wales against the land policy of the British government. The way was now clear for the differences between immigrant and emancipist and conservative and liberal on trial by jury and a house of assembly to resume their position as central issues in the politics of New South Wales.[26]

When Bourke introduced a bill for the extension of trial by jury into the Legislative Council five of its seven nominated members opposed it, because they objected to the proposed admission of any person as a juror who did not arrive free in the colony. As for their motives Bourke reported to London in February it was the envy of wealth which was at the root of this struggle. Only those free settlers with large grants of land—and not the small free settlers—were implacably opposed to the emancipists.[27] So, behind the sound and the fury Bourke detected the class differences between the antagonists. By March he was putting it more strongly. Gentlemen who came out free, he reported to London, did not refuse to associate with emancipists in the direction of a gainful concern, but deemed it a contamination to sit in the same jury box with them. He was happy to report that after some debate the prejudice had been overcome and the bill for the extension of trial by jury had become law on 3 February 1832.

The Act for regulating the Constitution of Juries, and for the Trial of

[25] *Sydney Herald*, 30 January 1832; the first issue of the *Sydney Herald* 18 April 1831; for the early history of the *Sydney Herald* see *A Century of Journalism: The Sydney Morning Herald and its Record of Australian Life 1831-1931* (Sydney, 1931).

[26] *Sydney Gazette*, 30 January 1832.

[27] Bourke to Goderich, 6 February 1832, *H.R.A.*, I. xvi. 515-17; Bourke to Howick, 28 February 1832, ibid., 542-5.

Issues in Certain Cases in the Supreme Court of New South Wales, prescribed that in all actions at law in which the Supreme Court awarded a trial by jury, that jury was to be composed of men between the ages of twenty-one and sixty years who possessed a clear income arising out of lands, houses, or other real estate of at least £30 per annum, or a clear personal estate of the value of at least £300. Every man attainted of treason or felony or convicted of any crime that was infamous, who had not received a pardon for such crime, or the full term of his sentence of transportation not having expired, every man of bad fame, or of dishonest life or conduct, or of immoral character or repute, and every man who either while serving a sentence, or after the expiration of such a sentence was convicted of any treason, felony, or other infamous offence was excluded from jury service. The *Sydney Gazette* was delighted that the Governor had taken on this most weighty and important topic. Trial by jury was the bulwark of their liberties, their property, and their lives. They wanted him to go further and extend it to trials of criminals. There had been a time, they admitted, when the public mind had been so poisoned and inflamed by prejudice that it was unfit for the sober functions of a court of justice. Happily those days were past. Writing in a paper with a long record of sympathy with the emancipist, the Reverend Mr Mansfield ended with a promise: 'We hold out the hand of reconciliation and hope to meet with a cordial grasp'.[28]

But it was just that hand of reconciliation which John Macarthur was not prepared to meet with any grasp. That February he was by no means happy about the drift of events. No property, he believed, could be safe, and no industry could be pursued in security, unless the accursed radicals were suppressed. He was worried about the intimacy that was growing up between Forbes and Bourke, who had decided on the text of the Jury Act without consulting the other members of the Council. He had had a private interview with Bourke before the Council met but could not get him off commonplace subjects. He had also had a debate with the Chief Justice who became warm in response to all his bluster. He had hoped that McLeay, sound Tory that he was and no friend to the accursed radicals, would vote with him, but, alas, he and the other officers came to the decisive meeting with long faces, having been given pretty broad hints the day before that if they expected to retain their seats then they must oppose the Macarthur motion against the Act. It all went to show that the new Governor was a passionate and despotic man, with whom he had no desire to sit down to table. Mrs Bourke and Miss Bourke had seen no ladies since their arrival and had returned no calls. So the Sydney ladies were ready to rebel. For himself he did not intend to meddle in government affairs any more than he could help. He hoped to live cheerfully on his estate at Camden, and turn his back on the Botany Bay worthies.[29]

28 Bourke to Goderich, 19 March 1832, *H.R.A.*, I. xvi. 564; An Act for regulating the Constitution of Juries, and for the Trial of Issues in Certain Cases in the Supreme Court of New South Wales, 2 Will. IV, no. 3, 3 February 1832, in T. Callaghan (ed.), *Acts and Ordinances of the Governor & Council of New South Wales, and Acts of Parliament enacted for and applied to, the Colony* (2 vols, Sydney, 1844-5), vol. 1, pp. 644-50; *Sydney Gazette*, 21 January 1832.

29 John Macarthur to Edward Macarthur, Elizabeth Farm, 26 March 1832 (Macarthur Papers, vol. 3, p. 209a).

While John Macarthur was confiding to his son Edward that in spite of all his philosophy, melancholy thoughts prompted by the death of his son bore so heavily upon him that when alone he indulged in a bitterness of grief no language could describe, his political foe was called on to endure the same dark, undying pain of the deprived. Ever since her arrival in the colony Mrs Bourke had suffered from an incurable disease, and had witnessed the approach of the hour of separation from husband and family with a pious resignation to the will of the Supreme Disposer of events. At the end on 7 May she had enjoyed that peace of mind, that happy serenity which came from her undisturbed confidence of hope that she would reach the temple of eternity. It was the duty of survivors, said the *Sydney Herald*, to submit to the dispensation since in the moral, as well as in the physical world, as far as events were under the control of Providence, 'Whatever is, is right'. They committed the remains of this lamented lady to the tomb at Parramatta on 10 May in a solemn and impressive ceremony—His Excellency, his family, the clergy, the judges, the heads of government departments and most of the respectable civil and military officers of the colony following in the train to the graveside where Broughton committed her body to the dust from whence she came.[30] A few months later Bourke put up on the walls of St John's Church in Parramatta a plaque which testified both to his love and his faith:

> Reader,
> she was the most affectionate and gentle of God's creatures . . . He who places this marble to her memory would be the most wretched of mankind, did he not feel the Christian hope of meeting in a better world her whom he has lost in this.

In his grief Bourke turned more and more to Forbes for comfort in his great affliction, and the Chief Justice, sensing the strength of the bonds between two men who shared a common vision of the world, responded with all the warmth and tenderness at his command.[31]

By that time it was not within the power of John Macarthur to say anything to Bourke to comfort him in his great agony. As Bourke, with that dignity which nature had conferred on him, turned again to the affairs of men, Elizabeth Macarthur was telling her beloved Edward about the pang she felt whenever she saw her husband, who had begun to behave in such a queer way, that he was accusing his son-in-law of poisoning him. 'Let us be thankful to the Almighty', she added, 'that a wholesome restraint was placed upon your beloved father before his malady had induced him to acts of greater violence'.[32]

The Reverend Samuel Marsden was beginning to show signs of the great ordeal he had endured ever since that day in March 1794 when he had first set foot in New South Wales. Early in 1832 he suffered a severe illness during

---

[30] *Sydney Gazette*, 8 and 12 May 1832; *Sydney Herald*, 14 May 1832.

[31] Plaque in St John's Church, Parramatta; for examples of the growing intimacy between Forbes and Bourke, see F. Forbes to R. Bourke, n.d. but probably immediately after the death of Bourke's wife (Bourke Papers, vol. 11); see also F. Forbes to R. Bourke, 12 April 1832, ibid.

[32] John Macarthur to Edward Macarthur, Parramatta, 5 June 1832 (Macarthur Papers, vol. 3, p. 219 et seq.); Elizabeth Macarthur to Edward Macarthur, 30 June 1832 (Macarthur Papers, vol. 10); Elizabeth Macarthur to Edward Macarthur, 23 March 1832, ibid.

which those close to him feared for his life. Believing in his heart that those who died in the Lord were blest, he was beginning to look forward to that eternal rest where the wicked ceased from troubling the righteous. To prepare himself for that journey from which no traveller had returned, save Christ, he was beginning to retire more and more from the world where there must be tribulation. He sat much by himself—his lips were often seen to move in prayer: he paid visits to the Macarthurs at Camden, and told them of what God had provided for those who believed in his Son. He had begun to withdraw from the world of affairs, from all that uproar, clamour, sound and fury which had caused him such disquiet, and such deep damnation. He was preparing to praise the dead, to long for what they enjoyed, their peace, their perfect peace.[33]

Just as Marsden began to retire from the world of men, the Archdeacon, W. G. Broughton, seemed driven to snare himself in the world's great net. From time to time in 1831 and 1832 he wrote to Bourke and asked him to transmit requests to London about his salary, and about his position in the order of precedence in the colony. 'I beg leave to dislaim', he wrote to Bourke as early as December 1831 on the question of precedence, 'any personal consideration in respectfully submitting my objections on this deprivation of a precedency, which was Conferred not for the benefit of the Individual, but for the credit of the Established Church of which His Majesty is the earthly head'.[34]

This concern for the prestige and power of the Church of England soon drove him down into that pit of public controversy, where men contended not for charity or love of God, but for pomp and circumstance and power. For Broughton believed passionately that the Church of England should be the established church in the colony, both as a divine instrument of truth and in recognition of her historic role in England as the vessel of catholic tradition, and as Protestant opposition to the errors and superstitions of the Roman Church. Before the end of 1831 he had joined issue with the Reverend J. D. Lang on whether the Church and School Corporation had encouraged the clergy of the Church of England in secular pursuits and so was responsible for the lowering of morals. When the British government announced its intention to send Wesleyan missionaries to the aborigines Broughton again protested that the Church of England, not he, had been slighted, because it was the divine mission of the Church to advise the government on all questions concerning education. Goderich, disturbed by reports of the reluctance of the aborigines to embrace the Christian religion, had understandably not been concerned with questions of divine favour, but with the more earthly question of who would bring the blessings of Christianity to the aborigines.[35]

This profound belief in the Church of England as the repository of all

[33] S. Marsden to D. Coates, 3 August 1827 (Bonwick Transcripts, Box 53, p. 1764); S. Marsden to T. Hassall, Parramatta, 10 February 1834 (Marsden Papers, Miscellaneous, p. 179); Elizabeth Macarthur to Edward Macarthur, Parramatta, 23 March 1832 (Macarthur Papers, vol. 10).
[34] W. G. Broughton to Bourke, 22 December 1831, Encl. in Bourke to Goderich, 2 January 1832, *H.R.A.*, I. xvi. 500-1.
[35] W. G. Broughton to Goderich, 19 November 1831, Encl. in Acting Governor Lindesay to Goderich, 18 November 1831, *H.R.A.*, I. xvi. 451-2.

truths both human and divine soon drove Broughton down into the murky waters of the sectarian controversy. On 2 April 1832 Roger Therry, a prominent Catholic layman, had written to Sir Edward Parry asking him to sign a memorial to the Governor, returning thanks for past favours, soliciting additional means of providing religious instruction and education for the present and rising generation, and to secure the reappointment of the Reverend John Joseph Therry to his former position as chaplain. Parry refused on the grounds that such assistance would be inconsistent with his Protestant profession of faith—Rome, he added, practised an increasing disregard of all scriptural and vital religion. Roger Therry then replied to Parry in a speech in the Roman Catholic chapel in Sydney on 29 July. In August Broughton entered the controversy by publishing a pamphlet, *A Letter, in Vindication of the Principles of the Reformation.* Like his forbears in England, he explained, he was a Protestant, because he entertained the conviction that the truth of God and the purity of the Gospel could not be maintained under the system which the Church of Rome had tried to force upon them. Believing as he did that holy scripture contained all things necessary to salvation, he urged his fellow Protestants not to fail to remember that all the corruptions of the pure doctrines of God had arisen from a desertion of His word. Protestants, therefore, were not justified in lending active aid to strengthen and extend a system which they must regard as the parent of error and opposed to the truth of God. He reminded his readers that Roman Catholicism was not an equally acceptable mode of worshipping the same God: 'I do not expect to be immediately or generally believed, but time will prove that I am right. To its decision I appeal . . . earnestly desiring that all men may know and embrace the truth'.[36] Once again Broughton had shown that he would follow his truth even if it cost him the respect and affection of his fellow-men.

For a brief season the *Sydney Gazette*, under the editorship of Ralph Mansfield dedicated as formerly under George and Robert Howe to the cause of liberty and the Protestant religion, wrote with pride of the role of the Protestants in bringing liberty, light and truth to England.[37] But this concern of the *Sydney Gazette* and the *Sydney Herald* for the men of heroic ingredients, and with the claim of the Catholic Church to be the sole possessor of the keys to open the door to eternal salvation, did not occupy the public stage for long. Leaving Broughton on his lonely eminence, not understanding the vision that sustained him, sensing possibly that he loved God and truth so passionately because he was never able to love his fellow-man, they rushed on to those things which touched them more deeply—the ownership of wealth, the political institutions best suited to serve the classes who owned that wealth, and the quest for a sober, industrious and obedient working class sufficient in numbers to produce such wealth.

By May and June of 1832 the inhabitants of Sydney town had much more lively things to talk over than the intellectual pranks of their parsons and their

---

[36] E. Parry to R. Therry, Port Stephens, 5 May 1832, quoted in R. Therry, *An Appeal on behalf of the Roman Catholics of New South Wales, in A Letter to Edward Blount, Esquire* (Sydney, 1833); W. G. Broughton, *A Letter, in Vindication of the Principles of the Reformation* (Sydney, 1832); *Sydney Gazette*, 18 August 1832; for the Roman Catholic Memorial to Bourke, see *Sydney Gazette*, 21 August 1832. [37] *Sydney Gazette*, 18 August 1832.

priests. News had reached Sydney that His Majesty's government had decided to assist the migration of females to New South Wales to supplement the supply of labour, and assist in reducing the high proportion of men. Some said they would only get married, an error, they said, which would only lead on to errors of much more serious character. Mr Secretary McLeay, using that energetic language he always employed when lecturing his contemporaries on the laws of Christian marriage, retorted: 'The sooner they commit such errors the better'. In June of 1831 His Majesty's government had appointed the Duke of Richmond, Viscount Howick, F. T. Baring, H. Ellis and R. W. Hay as commissioners of emigration, with T. F. Elliot as secretary, to collect and diffuse information on the subject of emigration to British possessions abroad, and to render any such assistance in their power to persons who wished to emigrate. In October of 1831 the commissioners had issued their first regulations. Government would pay £8 towards the passage of selected females between the ages of fifteen and thirty years of age who wished to emigrate to New South Wales or Van Diemen's Land. All women between the ages of fifteen and eighteen must be accompanied by their parents. Preference was to be given to women travelling with their families, to those qualified to act as servants in agricultural districts, and to those who were prepared to pay a larger proportion of the passage money.[38]

The *Sydney Herald* donned the mantle of the prophet. These individuals, they said, would be the parents of future legislators, statesmen and heroes. They would be for New South Wales what the immigrants had been for America—the patriarchal predecessors of the Washingtons and the Franklins. They would swell the numbers of the industrious and the virtuous.[39] The *Red Rover* arrived in August with women from charitable institutions in Dublin and Cork. The *Sydney Gazette*, after praising their neat and respectable appearance, went on to express the hope that they would be able to effect that important amelioration in the moral condition of the working population which the measure was intended to accomplish, for the young ladies, dressed in their neat bonnets, looked to be just the vessels to rescue the men of Sydney from Sodom and Gomorrah. The *Sydney Gazette* had not observed that some of these ladies were not really ladies at all, but women of the streets, wolves who had put on grandmama's bonnet. Time would show whether they were the virtuous, frugal females the parsons and respectable matrons of Sydney town were looking to as solvents for their 'motley society'.[40]

At the same time the *Sydney Herald* began a spirited discussion of the use of convicts, in which they argued that the system should be judged not by its success or failure in punishing or reforming criminals, but by its contribution to the wealth of the colony. They complained that at the penal settlement of Moreton Bay the labour of one thousand prisoners was wasted at an enormous expense. For their part Norfolk Island could be sunk in the sea tomorrow and no memorial of its utility or productiveness would remain. Incorrigible prisoners

---

[38] *Sydney Gazette*, 17 May 1832; Goderich to the Commissioners of Emigration, 1 July 1831, C.O. 384/27; The Commissioners of Emigration to Goderich, 10 October 1831, C.O. 385/12; see also R. B. Madgwick, *Immigration into Eastern Australia 1788-1851* (London, 1937), pp. 92-3.
[39] *Sydney Herald*, 14 June 1832.   [40] *Sydney Gazette*, 17 May and 14 August 1832.

should be employed building roads, rather than in useless labour at penal settlements, as roads were more important to get produce to market than all the reforms in church and state. Women, they argued, should not be incarcerated in the Female Factory at Parramatta, but should be offered to the settlers to make use of their labour. When government announced in July the sale of goods possessed by the convict commissariat, they asked whether this could be taken as a harbinger of an alteration in the penal system of this colony. 'We pause', they wrote, 'for a reply'.[41]

They were not as deeply concerned with the moral evils of the existing order. From time to time they drew attention to the horrors inseparable from that system. When a man was executed for highway robbery in August he said on the scaffold he would rather resign himself to that fate, as the will of God, than go for life to a penal settlement.[42] The colonists were not deeply disturbed: this moral fastidiousness over the convulsive struggles of a man who chose to be ushered into eternity rather than endure the sufferings at Norfolk Island was not for them, but rather for the 'Saints' in London, those evangelicals, humanitarians, and moral improvers who were appalled by what the convict system did, not only to its victims, but to all members of society. The *Sydney Herald* reported most of the outrages, and the abominations to the sensibilities of the victims, as though they were a huge joke. Some things moved them to indignation. They were indignant with the constables who pummelled female convicts in the ribs with their staves, when the women did not move as smartly as the constables demanded.[43] But when a woman was sent to the Female Factory for three months for telling lies to the injury of the good name of her mistress, they were troubled not by the sufferings of the victim of such terror, but by the loss of labour to the mistress. The inequality of punishment between bond and free touched them not at all: being drunk might cost a convict seven days at the mill, or a flogging: it might cost a free man a reproof from his master.[44]

When the convicts sought oblivion by means of that comforter which has sustained men down the ages through all the changing scenes of life, they had to endure the humiliating experience of having their behaviour held up to public ridicule, followed by a punishment designed to terrorize them against doing likewise when freed from their gaolers. Sometimes the press report of such behaviour was brief:

John Cochrane, *morally* drunk, 1 hour stocks.
Mary White, *allegorically*—ditto, hours ditto.
Charles Osborne, *literally*—ditto, 3 hours ditto.
and Ann Davidson, *theologically*—ditto, 4 hours ditto.[45]

Bench, lawyers, police, press and reading public seemed driven by some dark force to find pleasure and amusement in the discomfiture of a fellow human being, to mock rather than look with pity on those who could not stop.

[41] *Sydney Herald*, 17 May and 7 June 1832.   [42] Ibid., 21 August 1832.
[43] Ibid., 9 January 1832.
[44] Ibid., 19 November 1831; see also J. Bingle, *Letter to the Right Honorable His Majesty's Principal Secretary of State for the Colonies* (Sydney, 1832); and J. Bingle, *A Letter to the Right Honorable Lord Viscount Glenelg* (London, 1837).
[45] *Sydney Herald*, 6 September 1832.

ALEXANDER McLEAY

Portrait by an unknown artist in the Mitchell Gallery, Sydney

RICHARD BOURKE

Portrait by Archer Shee in the Dixson Gallery, Sydney

In July William Harrison and Jane Holmes were charged with being found like babes in the wood, fast asleep in each other's arms, on their master's premises. Mr Harrison, by way of defence, alleged that the fascinating charms of Jane had caused him to go astray. Jane, on the other hand, maintained that the seductive powers of the irresistible William had been the cause. She felt very sorry, but their worships must be aware that accidents would happen in the best regulated families. The bench of magistrates, not perfectly comprehending this doctrine, sent her to Mrs Gordon's sheering establishment and William to a cell for ten days.[46] Even the ravings of the mad were considered fit subjects for humour. When the bench of magistrates decided in December 1832, as they put it, that the upper story of Bridget Leon might be out of order, they sent her to Gordon's bedlam for a month. The *Sydney Herald* reported this, too, as good for a laugh.[47]

They were all quite happy to reduce unnecessary cruelties and abominations, provided such gestures of humanity did not decrease the productive power of the convict, or increase the cost of administering the system. Their prescription for the material and social progress of New South Wales was social utility and humanity, which man should never allow to come into conflict. Somewhere between severity of punishment and leniency, there was a happy mean which it was the duty of all liberal men of good will to follow. For fifteen years John Bingle had worked on his estate of Puen Buen at Scone on the Upper Hunter where he had built a reputation for himself as an explorer and landholder, a generous supporter of the church and charity, and a somewhat impetuous pursuer of bushrangers. Before Bourke had arrived in the colony a dispute had broken out between Bingle and H. C. Sempill, another settler in the district. When Bingle and Sempill vilified each other to Bourke in January of 1832 the latter informed the Colonial Secretary in writing that another magistrate, Captain Pike, had heard complaints by Bingle against Bingle's convict servants in Bingle's own parlour, and there and then had sentenced them to receive a punishment of one hundred stripes each. After some delay Bourke ordered the police magistrate at Maitland to take depositions from Bingle and Sempill, and forward them to Sydney. After reading these Bourke decided to censure both Bingle and Pike. Bingle then arranged with Stephens and Stokes, the proprietors of the *Sydney Herald*, to publish his pamphlet, *Letter to the . . . Secretary of State for the Colonies*. By August of 1832 Bourke was wondering whether Bingle had acted under the direction of persons of more talent and worse meaning than himself. He even wondered whether Bingle was perhaps a tool in a little plot to arouse the sympathy of the public, and the proportionate degree of ill-will towards his own measures. He was not to know then that the proprietors of the *Sydney Herald* were about to acquire a material interest in Bingle's estate at Puen Buen, which would give the *Sydney Herald* a worldly motive for rousing the sympathy of the public for the settlers of the Hunter River.[48]

---

[46] Ibid., 30 July 1832.   [47] Ibid., 27 December 1832.

[48] Bourke to Goderich, 24 August 1832, *H.R.A.*, I. xvi. 719-23; see also J. Bingle, *A Letter to the Right Honorable Lord Viscount Glenelg* (London, 1837); *Sydney Herald* 15 and 18 May 1837; Papers of J. Bingle (MS. in M.L.); article on J. Bingle in *Australian Dictionary of Biography*, vol. 1.

O

Bourke's motive was to check abuse of the power exercised by settlers and magistrates over convicts, not to challenge or call in question the fundamentals of the system. He wanted efficiency, humanity, and equal punishment for the same offences, all those principles of Whigs and utilitarians which he shared with the Chief Justice, to apply to the punishment and reformation of criminals in New South Wales. A few months after he had censured Bingle and Pike for their abuse of power, he told Sir Edward Parry, the manager of the Australian Agricultural Company, that he could not conceive how any parents could be induced to send their children to a school of which the master was a convicted felon. He also told Sir Edward he thought there was a great deal of absurd sensibility about the treatment of the female convicts, who, if they were riotous and disorderly, ought to be handcuffed like the men.[49]

The same motives pervaded the Act to consolidate and amend the Laws for Transportation and Punishment of Offenders in New South Wales, which the Legislative Council passed in August of that year. The Council, Bourke explained, had attempted to reduce the confused state of the law on transportation, and make a few alterations in some of its provisions. The Act reduced the number of offences for which men could be sent to penal settlements, and substituted labour in irons on the roads and public works of the colony—which was what the press and settlers had been clamouring for. The Act removed the power of two justices to send a convict to a penal settlement for three years, and confined the power to justices in Quarter Sessions. It enacted that no person born free or arriving free could be transported to a penal settlement for a first offence. In general, except for some mitigation of the severity of corporal punishment, the law was little more than a clearer arrangement of the former statutes for which he was under much obligation to the Chief Justice for the great attention he had given to the subject.[50]

In the interests of that precision and enlightenment to which he and the Chief Justice were so passionately committed he published, for general information, a summary of the regulations for the assignment of convict servants. After stating clearly that convicts of notoriously bad character in road parties were to be removed from party to party at least once a quarter to break up their connections, and explaining that assignment implied a temporary appropriation of their services, such convicts being liable to be withdrawn at any time at the pleasure of the Governor, he announced that preference would be given to new settlers, to persons residing in the country, and to those of good moral character who paid due attention to the conduct of their servants. No convict was to be assigned to any settler that did not employ a free or ticket-of-leave overseer of good character: no convict was to be assigned to a master who frequently returned convict servants especially for trifling offences, without making endeavours to reform them, to such as could not give them constant employment, or were known to treat them with inhumanity,

---

[49] Journal of Sir Edward Parry, vol. 2, 15 April 1833 (microfilm in NAT. L.).

[50] An Act to consolidate and amend the Laws for the Transportation and Punishment of Offenders in New South Wales, 3 Will. IV, no. 3, 24 August 1832, in T. Callaghan, op. cit.; see also Bourke to Goderich, 30 October 1832, *H.R.A.*, I. xvi. 780-2.

or who did not supply them with proper food or clothing.[51] Again Bourke and Forbes were reaching for that mean point between clarity of the law, humanity, reformation, and due punishment.

So when Bourke received from London the text of an imperial Act to abolish punishment by death in certain cases, which restrained the power of the governors of colonies to grant tickets-of-leave or exemptions to convicts until after certain specified terms of servitude, and disabled convicts from acquiring property or maintaining suits in courts of justice before they were pardoned, he protested. This, he said, would not only impose on the ticket-of-leave holder a disability, but would deprive him of any certainty of obtaining the fruits of his labour. As such it might expose a number of sober, honest and industrious men to return to their former paths of profligacy simply because the law had taken away from them the opportunity to protect their savings.[52] For in the spring of 1832 there was a promise in the very air that Bourke, ably aided by Forbes, and prodded by Wentworth, could achieve in New South Wales a part of that liberal dream of material progress, equality before the law, and the abolition of barbarisms of the past, which would pave the way for free institutions. Everything that spring was going happily and prosperously in the colony: the Governor was much liked, the seasons were favourable for crops and stock, and the people in good humour. The *Sydney Herald* was carried away by optimism and goodwill. Bourke had introduced improvements in the post office and in the building of roads, and there were rumours that the act of travelling by steam on common roads at the rate of ten miles per hour might be introduced, in spite of hills and dales and inequalities of ground. The *Sydney Herald* hailed Bourke as the friend of Australia and told him it was his great good fortune to confer a lasting benefit on the colony by convincing their masters in London that the people of New South Wales were now fit for British institutions.[53]

Believing a Whig Governor, ably supported as he was by his fellow Whig, the Chief Justice, could achieve what none of his predecessors had even attempted, a group of citizens asked the Sheriff to call a public meeting for Anniversary Day, 26 January 1833, at the Court House at twelve noon to petition His Most Gracious Majesty and the House of Commons for a Legislative Assembly for the colony. Sir John Jamison began the proceedings by rebuking Howick for saying the colony was not ripe for free institutions. Just as he was about to read the petition James Macarthur rose to explain that though he did not oppose the abstract right of the inhabitants to have the institutions they desired, yet he must put in a word for Howick. The chairman smartly chipped in to express a wish that speakers would not allude to Howick. Whereupon Wentworth insisted upon the right of every free-born Englishman to make any observation he thought fit upon the conduct of any public officer. He would not be intimidated, and if the chairman tried any such tricks with

[51] Regulations respecting assigned servants, 17 November 1832, in *New South Wales Calendar and General Post Office Directory* (Sydney, 1834).

[52] Bourke to Goderich, 20 November 1832, *H.R.A.*, I. xvi. 802-5.

[53] *Sydney Herald*, 28 May and 31 May, 25 June and 16 August 1832.

him he would ask the meeting to throw him out of the chair. Then the chairman explained timidly he had only wanted to make a suggestion. Francis Stephen then moved the petition to the King, taking the opportunity to ask the meeting whether the assertion by Howick that party animosity existed in the colony between immigrants and emancipists were not false. They shouted their 'hear, hears'. But when a Mr Chambers moved some minor amendments he was greeted with hisses and ridicule. The petition was carried unanimously.

Then Wentworth rose to propose a similar petition to the House of Commons. He began by saying he was convinced the boons now prayed for would be refused while the Under-Secretary of State was allowed to consider the colony as his patrimony. That functionary had fingered the colonists' money for so long that he would never give it up, unless the colonists made strenuous efforts, for honesty and money never went together. As for the members of their own Legislative Council, they were the most subservient creatures that could be found; all they were engaged in was voting money into their own or their neighbour's pocket. After speeches by Sir John Jamison, James Macarthur, Dr Bland, Edward Smith Hall and Sydney Stephen, this petition too was put and carried unanimously.[54]

The petition to the House of Commons began by thanking those in the United Kingdom responsible for the extension of trial by jury in the colony. It went on to assert the inalienable rights of Britons, in whatever colony they might have fixed their abode, to the constitution of the mother country. It rebutted the charge of party spirit and rancour: it rebutted too the charge that the emancipists would acquire an overwhelming influence over all other classes in a house of assembly. Emancipists and immigrants worked together harmoniously in banks, colleges, and charitable societies. They would behave in the same cordial spirit in the discussions of a house of assembly. As for the Legislative Council, that was not only nominated, and irresponsible, but possessed no points of contact with the people. What was needed was a representative assembly founded upon the basis of property and population. So, happy to rely on the wisdom of the House of Commons, and knowing that it could not be the desire of that House to alienate the attachment of the rising colony by any longer withholding that inherent right of the British constitution of levying and appropriating their own taxes, which followed English subjects wherever they resided, the petitioners concluded that as in duty bound they would ever pray.[55]

Outside the public meeting some misgivings were expressed. The *Sydney Herald* reported that a great portion of the community was disgusted with the illiberal, overbearing, and unstatesmanlike manner of the proceedings.[56] From far away in Whitfield, in Northumberland, the Reverend Thomas Hobbes Scott wrote of his misgivings to James Macarthur. He wished New South Wales had a better 'Social Compact'. He hold him it was the fate of all new societies to be almost destitute of families of distinction: that New

[54] *Sydney Herald*, 28 January 1833.
[55] The humble petition of the free inhabitants of New South Wales, *Sydney Herald*, 31 January 1831.   [56] *Sydney Herald*, 31 January 1831.

South Wales had to put up with the increased disadvantage of being peopled with those who were habituated from their birth to a life of crime. No wonder the rabble was in the ascendant. What pained him was that the Governor should invite to his table an irresponsible demagogue such as Wentworth.[57]

At the end of that summer, as the humid weather changed from time to time into a blistering westerly blowing over the hot interior, or a southerly buster swept in to refresh jaded nerves, it looked as though the future lay with Wentworth and his magnificent oratory on the birthrights of Englishmen. On that Anniversary Day in Sydney Wentworth convulsed his audience with his jokes about placemen, about that placeman, Busby, who was, he said, soon to strut about in a gold-laced coat for the savages in New Zealand to gape at, and perhaps the next day be turned into a roast meal for the savages to eat. Those who guffawed and stamped and clapped him were not to know then that it was the gold lace and the salons of the Government House group which Wentworth secretly craved just as passionately as those birthrights of Englishmen.

That autumn news reached Sydney that the pension of £750 a year which the Colonial Secretary received was to be paid out of colonial revenue. So here was another opportunity for Wentworth to savage a placeman—an opportunity with an appeal too to the dark side of Wentworth's heart, for McLeay was not only just a little absurd—a man talking high Toryism in the accents of a Scottish dialect—but he was intimate in the circles hostile to Bourke, intimate with Macarthur and Bowman. Besides McLeay had a soft effeminate face, and there was about him that suggestion of a man who drank tea with the ladies. When Wentworth heard that McLeay was to take the chair at a meeting of the Benevolent Society, he could not resist that drive to savage a placeman, a Tory, and a tea-drinker.

One evening in June the Benevolent Society met in the Court House in Sydney, with the Colonial Secretary McLeay in the chair, the Reverend Mr Cowper and all the quality and respectability in the floor of the house. William Bland had just delicately suggested that he should receive an honorarium for his work as secretary to the society when Wentworth entered the room. Up to that point there had been peace and harmony, but from the moment Wentworth entered, that calm was turned into a tempest. Wentworth spoke with anger of how in New South Wales £750 was paid every year to a bloated pensioner. As the object of this abuse, McLeay, was in the chair, universal hooting and hissing broke out. The ladies began to retire from the court-room. The gentle Reverend Mr Cowper, faithful as ever to his Master's teaching that men should agree with their adversaries quickly, whispered to Mr Wentworth he had better desist as he was driving away the ladies. But with a look of ineffable fierceness Wentworth called out 'Let them go! Those who carry their senses in their heads will remain. Those who carry their senses in their heels will be off'. He then repeated some of his stronger sayings. Once again the hissing began: 'Hiss again', Wentworth

[57] T. H. Scott to James Macarthur, Whitfield Rectory, 22 July 1833 (Macarthur Papers, vol. 59, pp. 165-6).

cried truculently. The hisses redoubled. 'Hiss again', he called out at the top of his voice, and the hisses became deafening. Over the uproar and the clamour Wentworth shouted that appeals to private benevolence were a mere mockery of charity. The chairman then rose and said with dignity that he had come to the meeting to do all in his power to promote the interests of the Benevolent Society, but not to be grossly insulted, and he thought it best to retire. As he left the chair and walked to the door Wentworth, as though suddenly realizing the social standing of the object of his vulgar abuse, began to plead with McLeay to remain: 'Mr President, Mr President', he cried in a desperate appeal to a man he had so recklessly savaged, but the groans and hisses drowned his voice as McLeay walked into the night. When his political cronies tries to address the meeting their voices too were drowned by the hisses and the groans of the respectable. Far away in Cheltenham in England Eliza Darling was delighted to hear that that odious man Wentworth had been hissed and hooted by the good people of Sydney till he could say no more.[58]

At the same time an unseemly sectarian row broke out in Sydney, when Broughton selected what Catholic apologists called a moment of adversity to tell his fellow Protestants they could not subscribe to a fund to build a Catholic chapel without guilt. Roger Therry replied for the Catholics by deploring the harsh note in that decision, calling it something uncongenial to the spirit of enlarged benevolence, something so little reconcilable with that meek precept of divine charity to 'love one another'. Therry, who had been born in Ireland in 1800, had come to the colony at the end of 1829 as commissioner of the Court of Requests, and had soon won a reputation with his fellow Catholics for his zeal in promoting their material welfare.[59]

The Reverend Henry Fulton, who had been convicted at Tipperary in August of 1799 for seditious practices, and had lived through the stormy days of Bligh and Macquarie without a stain on his reputation for charity, joined in with a pamphlet in which he repeated the Protestant view of the past, namely, that for centuries the Church of Rome had been idolatrous and a synagogue of Satan. The Reverend W. B. Ullathorne promptly replied that if the Protestants were to destroy the Catholic church then that little, comfortable modern church which Fulton and the Archdeacon called their own, and which was built out of the old materials on a ruined corner of those huge foundations, would tumble with them. Ullathorne, who had been appointed Vicar-General of the Catholic church in New South Wales, had arrived in Sydney on 18 February 1833. He was then of such boyish appearance that a member of the Irish Catholic laity dismissed him as a young cub. But behind the youthful appearance there was growing into manhood a youth with such confidence in his own powers and his vocation as one of Christ's representatives that men dubbed him *ego solus*. He was born in Yorkshire in

[58] *Sydney Herald*, 6 June 1833; Eliza Darling to Marianne Boissier, 11 December 1833 (Dumaresq Papers).

[59] R. Therry, *An Appeal on behalf of the Roman Catholics of New South Wales, in A Letter to Edward Blount, Esquire* (Sydney, 1833), p. 4; for Therry as a man see R. Therry, *Reminiscences of Thirty Years' Residence in New South Wales and Victoria* (London, 1863); for these improvements see *Sydney Herald*, 28 and 31 May and 25 June 1832.

May of 1806, into a Catholic family which was proud of its descent from Sir Thomas More. After a carefree life at sea he experienced a religious conversion at Memel, and came back to England to study at the Benedictine school of St Gregory at Downside where he imbibed the Christian humanism of his illustrious ancestor, as well as the Benedictine teachings on the role of the church as the handmaiden of the élite in society. This put a great gulf between him and the Irish priests who grew up in that atmosphere in which priests learned they must swim with the popular wave or sink in the mighty deep. He was ordained priest in September of 1831, and sailed for Sydney in the *Sir Thomas Munro* on 16 September 1832.[60]

While the leaders of the various Christian denominations were exposing each other to public derision another group of men, spurred on by the hope that the spread of Enlightenment would promote that peace on earth and good will to all men which the leaders of the Christian churches professed but so singularly failed to observe, came together to found a Mechanics' Institute in Sydney. As the *Stirling Castle* sailed to Sydney from Scotland in 1831, a group of Scottish mechanics on board had attended classes under the leadership of Mr Henry Carmichael, in singular contrast with the drunkenness and lechery with which the bond and the free generally passed the time on that long and tedious voyage over the oceans. Carmichael, a schoolmaster and theorist in education by profession, had taken his degree at St Andrew's in Scotland, and then worked as a tutor in London, when Lang engaged him as a teacher for the projected Australian College in Sydney. The mechanics found the shipboard experience so edifying that at journey's end they resolved to found a Mechanics' Institute in Sydney.[61]

On 19 January 1833 three men and a boy walked up Church Hill in Sydney and entered a brick building near Scots Church. The men were John Reilly, saddler, a native of Ireland; William Hipkiss, a bootmaker, native of England; and David Taylor, builder, a native of Scotland. The boy was J. R. Fenwick. There on three empty brandy cases, using a copy of the rules of an English School of Arts, they began to draft a constitution for a Mechanics' Institute. When a strange noise was heard outside the building the boy was sent to investigate. Soon he came back and told them it was a hubbub of two to three hundred men working in irons, and Mr Reilly turned to him and said that the work they were engaged in that day would assist to unrivet those chains and allow those men to become men again, and not remain beasts of burden.

They were aiming high. Their great hope was that through a judicious blend of such useful subjects as landscape gardening, hydraulics, the strength of colonial timbers, and subjects of moral enlightenment such as lectures on intemperance, men would become both better and happier. Science and useful knowledge were to be the instruments of those better things for mankind which the teachers of the Enlightenment had predicted would follow man's

---

[60] H. Fulton, *A Letter to the Rev. W. B. Ullathorne, C.V.G.* (Sydney, 1833), p. 4; W. B. Ullathorne, *A Few Words, to the Rev. Henry Fulton, and his readers; with a glance at the Archdeacon* (Sydney, 1833), p. 55; for the life of Ullathorne see Dom Cuthbert Butler, *The Life and Times of Bishop Ullathorne, 1806-1889* (2 vols, London, 1926).

[61] For the life of H. Carmichael see *Australian Dictionary of Biography*, vol. 1.

liberation from the promises of religion, and its vile stress on the depravity of man. In the beginning the founders hoped they would substitute a life of earnest happiness for that vale of tears taught by the priests, parsons, and rabbis of the various religious denominations. Bourke, the first patron of the institution, hoped it would promote a taste for mental cultivation among persons in the middle ranks, thereby greatly tending to check the coarser pursuits unhappily too common in the colony.[62]

So when those of like mind came together at the Court House on 22 March to found a branch of the Mechanics' Institute, Carmichael took up the theme of the benefits of the diffusion of scientific and other useful knowledge. He told them the white man owed his superiority over the aborigine not to any difference of physiology, but to his different degree of knowledge. He told them how theoretical knowledge was advantageous to the practical mechanic. He told them how the Institute hoped to supply those deficiencies in early education for those from the mother country and for those born in the colony. He told them of his hope to give mechanics, after the routine of their daily toil had been run, habits of intellectual intercourse and scientific investigation. He told them of his hope that the Institute would promote the best interests of the colonial youth. They already had a reputation for skill in athletic and gymnastic exercises. It was his hope that regattas, cricket matches, boxing and jockeyship which now occupied so high a place in their minds, just as kangaroo dances and mock fights did with the aborigines, as to preclude entirely the cultivation of the intellectual powers, would soon lose their hold over the native-born youths, as they saw the tangible advantages of knowledge over ignorance. He looked to the day when the native-born Australians would be proud of their conquests in the arena of intellectual gladiatorship as they were now of boasting of their prowess in gymnastics of mere 'bone and muscle'. Finally the Institute would offer an alternative to that existence between the pot-house and the workshop. The youths no longer need be the slaves of gross and grovelling appetites, a disgrace to human nature, and absolute pests to the peace and welfare of society. A ticket to the rooms of the Institute would be a passport to the society of honourable men.[63] The *Sydney Herald*, in the more sober language of the men of respectability, hoped the school would be conducive both to the happiness and prosperity of the community.[64]

While the Christians wrangled over who was Christ's vicar on earth, and a few took up this promise of the fruits of moral enlightenment, a great storm was brewing in the public life of the colony. All through the first half of 1833 the publicists accepted the proposition that until such time as a sufficiently large body of free labourers came to the colony, notwithstanding the moral evils of the convict system, they must still prefer such an evil to the great evil of having no servants or labourers.[65] All that was required, the

---

[62] Report of the Sydney School of Arts, 1886, quoted in D. C. Griffiths (ed.), *Documents on the Establishment of Education in New South Wales 1789-1880* (Melbourne, 1957), pp. 199-200; Bourke to Stanley, 24 October 1833, *H.R.A.*, I. xvii. 248.

[63] H. Carmichael, Introductory Lecture to School of Arts, *New South Wales Magazine 1833*, p. 68 et seq.

[64] *Sydney Herald*, 25 March 1833.   [65] Ibid., 17 June 1833.

3 *The Main Settlements of New South Wales in 1835,*
excluding Port Phillip and Moreton Bay

publicists believed, was a system of penal discipline which would effectually suppress insubordination on the part of convict servants, and so render the greater proportion of them at least useful labourers.[66] By August some of the settlers on the Hunter River believed that Bourke's Transportation Act had had a most mischievous effect on the convicts. Those two dangerous Whigs, Bourke and Forbes, had been actuated by a mistaken policy of leniency rather than severity, and had caused an alarming increase in crime and insubordination in the Hunter River district. The authority of the master had been set at naught, and the punishment inflicted by the magistrates publicly and contemptuously derided, accompanied by a vague persuasion amongst the convicts that their offences would no longer be visited with proportionate punishments.[67]

In the whole colony of New South Wales there was no more exasperated critic of this policy of leniency than 'Major' Mudie. Mudie had arrived in Sydney in July of 1822 to take up a grant of 2,500 acres at Patrick's Plains on land on which he conferred the name of Castle Forbes in honour of Sir Charles Forbes. There from November 1822 to November 1832 he had endured the hardships, the privations, and the loneliness of the pioneer. By 1832 he was intensely proud of his achievement of creating civilization where hitherto barbarism had prevailed. He was proud too that neither the convicts nor the aborigines had perpetrated any outrage or violence of any kind during his first ten years.

Soon after the arrival of Bourke he had noticed a change in the manners of the men on the farm. Restlessness, rudeness, idleness, insolence, turbulence and impatience of all control had replaced the sullen subordination of the earlier days. Mudie believed this new spirit of insubordination, hurtful as it was to both his pride and his pocket, for carelessness meant loss of sheep, was caused by Bourke's Transportation Act. These tendencies were aggravated by rumours that all convicts would find favour in Bourke's eyes, and, horror of horrors, it was said Bourke had even issued instructions that in future convicts could choose their own masters, and, if they suffered under hardship, they could write a letter to him.

Mudie decided to crush this spirit of insubordination by a policy of severity. He decided that he would confront the Governor's leniency with a settler's severity. Between August and November of 1833 Poole, Hitchcock, Riley, Nagle, James Brown, Henry Brown, Harvey, Perry and Ryan, all assigned servants on his estate, were flogged so regularly that by November there were symptoms of a crisis at Castle Forbes. In an exchange with Mudie Poole swore profanely: three others joined in. Mudie took them to the neighbouring magistrate, who being swept on by the general hysteria in the district, obliged Mudie by sentencing Poole to be flogged, and sent the three others to the iron gang. Poole then took to the bush, released the other three, and descended on Castle Forbes to seek vengeance on all who had

[66] Ibid., 27 May 1833.
[67] See, for example, The Humble Petition of the undersigned Landholders and other Free Inhabitants of the District of Newcastle and Port Stephens, 22 August 1833, and The Humble Petition of the undersigned Landholders and Free Inhabitants of the District of Hunter's River, *V. & P.* (L.C. N.S.W.) 28 August 1833.

practised the abomination of trying to flog convicts into servility and obedience.

They pillaged the stores, threatened the women and shouted to Mrs Larnach, the wife of Mudie's partner John Larnach, that they would bring her husband's bloody head and stick it on the chimney, and if her father had been at home, they would have stuck his head on the other. They then rushed down to the water-hole where Larnach and nine men were washing sheep. Hitchcock shouted at Larnach 'Stand still you b—— b——, or I'll blow out your brains'. When Larnach dashed for safety, Hitchcock fired at him and missed. Then the whole mob of them rushed on to the estate of a Mr Sparke, one of those floggers on whom they had sworn to take vengeance, stripped him, tied him to a post, and flogged him with a cat-o'-nine-tails while Ryan kept asking him whether he would get another man flogged. But it was their last act of revenge, for soon after they left Sparke bleeding on those lonely plains the mounted police caught up with them and arrested them.

They were brought to Sydney and tried before Chief Justice Forbes and a military jury in December. When asked whether they had anything to say in their defence they pleaded that their employers had treated them so harshly that they had been driven to dark deeds of desperation. In the awful hour of their impending death a dignity and a majesty began to descend on Hitchcock and Poole. Hitchcock asked that as they had but a short time to live he hoped they would be granted a few hours in the cell to prepare themselves for a future world. His Honour, the drafter of the Act which, in Mudie's eyes, had induced these poor helpless victims to embrace ideas which swept them on to their destruction, then addressed the prisoners in a most solemn and feeling manner. After remarking on the enormity of their offence he proceeded to pass the awful sentence of death upon them.

Perry, Riley and Ryan were executed in Sydney on 21 December. But Hitchcock and Poole still had one other ghastly function to perform for their fellow prisoners. They were to be an example to the districts swept by the evil winds of insubordination, that such enormities as they had wantonly practised could only end in a cruel death. Their unhappy fate was to deter other misguided men from such desperate crimes. They were taken from Sydney to the Hunter River by sea, and then placed on their coffins in a horse-cart in which they proceeded to Castle Forbes under a military escort in the hope that this awful exhibition would act as a warning to the convict servants of the Hunter River Valley. Poole distributed religious tracts to the spectators of that melancholy procession. Hitchcock seemed much affected and spoke but little.

That night they bivouacked in the bush and then proceeded on their mournful way to Castle Forbes, only to find no one there who could knock off their irons, and no clergyman of any persuasion who could hear their last confessions and prepare them for that other journey on which they were about to start. Again they set off to find a blacksmith and came back to the foot of the drop too exhausted to heed the words of comfort from a local schoolmaster, too exhausted even to say those last words of penitence and warning to the other servants who gathered there to say farewell. All passed off quietly as Hitchcock and Poole were launched into eternity. The gallows remained for months as a warning to evil-doers in that district, presenting an eerie spectable to lonely travellers who passed by during the night.[68]

The sound and the fury stirred up by these events did not die down till the British government abolished the transportation of convicts to eastern Australia. All supporters of the Bourke-Forbes policy, who believed in mitigation of severity, were appalled by the story of the brutality which had been practised at Patrick's Plains. Humanity, it was said, was outraged. The supporters of severity, such as Mudie and Larnach, retorted that it was the only way to extract value from the labour of the convict, and prevent society from sinking into anarchy, as the conduct of the convict servants was still extremely bad. Bourke sent the Solicitor-General and the principal superintendent of convicts to Patrick's Plains to inquire into the conduct of Mudie and Larnach towards their convict servants. They reported in January that the complaints were for the most part unfounded. Henry Dumaresq for one was not happy about this. He shared with his sister, Eliza Darling, the idea that it would be possible to transplant 'merry England' to New South Wales, and in place of the wilderness, to plant there the verdant lawn, the village church, and the cultivated park with the gentleman's seat rising above the village. When gentlemen complained against their convicts, he said, Bourke did nothing. But no sooner did convicted felons complain against their masters than Bourke appointed a commission of inquiry. All this was very bad, he thought, and people were beginning to complain.[69]

But the clamour could not be quietened by judicial inquiry, for by that January in 1834 what was up for discussion was not just the behaviour of two angry men, who, under the great dome of the sky, had tried to subdue men of their kind with the lash and leg-irons, but the whole future of transportation to New South Wales. After the Mudie affair a note of hysterical denunciation entered the public discussion of the convict system. The *Sydney Herald* that January told its readers the colony of New South Wales was deluged with principles of disorganization. They told them that the conduct of the prisoners in the employment of government was bad beyond description. They told them that as a sentry at Bathurst was taking out a gang of men to work them in irons, they rushed him, unarmed him, and proceeded to a station and robbed the place of everything.[70]

All through the months of January, February, March, April, May and June in every issue of the paper, they reminded their readers of the evils and absurdities of the convict system. One day they published a story to illustrate what they called penal laziness. With the heavy sarcasm fashionable in the press of

---

[68] Based on J. Mudie, *Vindication of James Mudie and John Larnach* (Sydney, 1834); *Sydney Herald*, 16 December, 23 and 30 December 1833, and 31 March 1834; *H.R.A.*, I. xvii. 409-10 and 542-3; *Sydney Gazette* for December 1833 and January 1834.

[69] The Colonial Secretary of New South Wales to James Mudie and John Larnach, 13 January 1834, quoted in J. Mudie, *Vindication of James Mudie and John Larnach* (Sydney, 1834), pp. 50-1; see also *Sydney Gazette*, 10 April 1834; Eliza Darling to Edward Dumaresq, 24 October 1833, and Henry Dumaresq to Edward Dumaresq, 4 February 1834 (Dumaresq Papers).

[70] *Sydney Herald*, 9 January 1834.

the day they told their readers that any person who wished to see the severity of penal discipline should watch gangs engaged in drawing earth from the Domain. Here were four donkey-carts each drawn by five strapping fellows, and loaded with about as much earth as an Irish labourer could carry in three pods. Other people, the *Herald* continued, must work in a different manner to supply the groats to pay for the maintenance of convicts in absolute idleness.[71] Early in February they regaled their readers with a story of how a justice of the peace, one John Lamb, had endeavoured to quell a riot of convicts in the employment of government in Sydney, only to be knocked down and assaulted in a most savage and brutal manner. The villains, they added, were encouraged by some distilled rascals. Again they suggested the story should be sent home to England as an additional proof of the workings of the convict system.[72]

At the same time, as they never wearied of telling their readers, not even the rudiments of civilization were present in the country districts of New South Wales. From Newcastle to Liverpool, a distance of 160 miles, there was neither a place of worship nor a school-house. Children were growing up in ignorance: parents and children were living in a state of heathen barbarism. In the country districts there was insubordination and barbarism: in the towns there was material and moral filth.[73] In Sydney in the month of April not a spade or a pick had been used on the roads of that town for a month, although the late rains had gouged out sufficient pot-holes to break the necks of half the inhabitants of Sydney. What, asked the *Sydney Herald* in a tone of righteous indignation, were the convicts about in the Barracks? What were those loafers up to who, sponging on the patrimony of government, outraged the ears of the respectable females of Sydney by repeating obscene and insulting language?[74]

Nor were idleness, insolence, insubordination and depravity the sum total of their crimes against humanity. The convicts and their families were guilty of a crime of even greater infamy. They, and their families, proposed to drag all people down to their own degraded level. They were tainted, in the eyes of the *Sydney Herald* and others, as much by their levelling and egalitarian tendencies as by their tendency to debauch the morals of all with whom they came into contact. For these reasons as early as January of 1834 the *Sydney Herald* was calling for an inquiry by the English government into the whole system, an inquiry which would banish the frightful system then in existence in New South Wales, and lay the foundations in the colony of the principles of purity and justice. The abolition of transportation would be the prelude to that revolution in morals and politics, to the creation of indispensable conditions for the way of life of a colonial bourgeoisie, for the respectability and moral rectitude of the free rather than the present corruption and levelling of the bond. Why, they asked, should the colonists of New South Wales and their children be continually demoralized for the benefit of English criminals? Why should the free community be degraded? The penal farce must be brought quickly to an end. Or so they demanded on 13 February 1834.[75]

In March news reached Sydney that in future the British government pro-

---

[71] Ibid., 23 January 1834. [72] Ibid., 6 February 1834. [73] Ibid., 31 March 1834.
[74] Ibid., 14 and 24 April 1834. [75] Ibid., 20 January and 13 February 1834.

posed to purchase in the colony the stores for the convicts. The *Herald* saw this as a source of gain to Britain, and of profit to New South Wales, but warned the colonists that this was the first step towards the colonists paying for the stores. It was ominous, they argued, of coming events. Why should they be saddled with the maintenance of British culprits out of colonial revenue, especially when they had no effective voice in the raising or spending of that revenue?[76]

By the second half of the year this debate on the convict system had moved into the centre of the stage of the public life of New South Wales. People, wrote the *Sydney Herald* in July, were now calculating whether it was not more advantageous to employ free men at wages, than a set of idle, insolent, and insubordinate ruffians. Was the immigrant to be kept in subjection and slavery to a body of convicts? Were the children of the free to run the risk of convict contamination and depravity for a difference of £5 per head between the expense of the respective classes. The profession of convict-driver, they insisted to their readers, was neither honourable nor lucrative.[77] So they demanded two things: the removal of the taint of convict labour, and granting this country that voice in her legislature, which would remove the stigma of convictism.[78]

The editor of the *Monitor* did not share these views. A great change had come over the opinions of its editor, E. S. Hall. The hothead of the convict party in the stormy days of Governor Darling was now writing week after week in the *Monitor* on the advantages of the convict system. It was rumoured in Sydney that the price for financial help from 'Major' Mudie had been to prostitute his talents to the services of the supporters of severity. Hall's earlier sympathy with the victims of a master's cruelty or a governor's oppression were, it was said, but a balm with which to soothe his own outraged pride and thwarted ambition. Whatever the reason, week after week, the *Monitor* kept telling its readers that prisoners sent from the counties of England were on the whole a more useful set of men than any class of immigrants whom the British government would be able, and the parishes of the county towns in England willing, to part with.[79]

With stories pouring in from the inflammable district of the Hunter that convict ruffians had attacked and plundered the premises of Captain Dumaresq, that July a group of landholders, employers of convict labour and other free inhabitants, had come together to petition His Majesty on the convict question. They complained they were suffering in their property and peace of mind from the insubordinate state of the convict population. They argued that the only answer to such insubordination was the policy of severity.[80] In 1834 W. A. Watt, a ticket-of-leave holder working as a journalist on the *Sydney*

[76] Ibid., 24 March 1834.   [77] Ibid., 17 July 1834.   [78] Ibid., 31 July 1834.
[79] *Monitor*, quoted in *Sydney Gazette*, 14 August 1834.
[80] An Dulpume of 1001, Pury Pollolu Dupered, in a Letter addressed to the Right Honourable *The Secretary of State for the Colonies*; signed at end, 'Humanitas' (Sydney, 1834), pp. 70-2; The humble Petition of the undersigned Landholders, Employers of Convict Labour, and other Free Inhabitants of the District of Hunter's River, in the Colony of New South Wales, July 1834, quoted in An Unpaid Magistrate (R. Therry), *Observations on the 'Hole and Corner Petition'*, *in a Letter to the Right Honorable Edward G. Stanley Principal Secretary of State for the Colonial Department* (Sydney, 1834), pp. 7-8; *Sydney Gazette*, 3 July 1834.

Gazette, using the pen-name 'An Emigrant of 1821', published the pamphlet *Party Politics Exposed*. He wrote in the defence of his persecuted fellow-convicts who were, he believed, languishing in the bitterest bonds of slavery, condemning those who advocated that degree of severity which only nourished despair. He called them the Hole and Corner men, the men who crept into holes and corners like rats rather than stand up before their fellow-men in the full light of day. He warned men of his kind in London that transportation was legalized abomination and savagery—warned the gay dogs of the Mall, and the exquisite loungers of Regent Street that they would be exchanging the reins of the sporting tandem for the bullock's bridle. The great aims of penal legislation as means of leading to the suppression of crime were wholly defeated by blind severity.[81]

The *Herald* was disgusted. They denounced the pamphlet as a specimen of colonial literature. It had, they said, excited indignation, surprise and consternation in the minds of the immigrant population. It was, they said, a choice effort of the Convict School of Philanthropy, a regular Newgate production, which would be utterly unworthy of notice, were it not for the fact that this nest of 'Gentlemen Convicts' was supported by persons who ought to be ashamed of the connection, assuming it were possible to bring a blush to their criminal cheeks. The *Herald* had begun to hint that Bourke and Forbes were sympathetic with the convict levellers. But they were not greatly troubled. As one of their letter writers put it: 'Let the leprosied, diseased reptile, crawl to the recess of some cavern and slough in silence, nor dare to raise its branded head and taint Heaven's pure air with its foetid breathings'.[82]

With tempers rising and the bile flowing freely 'Major' Mudie took up his pen to defend the cause of severity. In September he published his pamphlet, *Vindication of James Mudie and John Larnach*. The root of the evil, as he saw it, was probably the notion that Governor Bourke was the friend of poor prisoners. That, he believed, was the tap-root of those other wide spreading evils, the great lateral roots of idleness, insolence and disobedience. That was why a convict had sworn to his master: 'By the Holy J—— I'll have you punished for this'. That was why convicts thought of road parties as the elysium of the prisoners, the ultimate aim and object of the restless, the idle, and the drunken. That was why settlers were deprived of labour, and convicts were able to debauch with impunity all with whom they associated.[83]

In the same month Roger Therry, calling himself an Unpaid Magistrate,

[81] An Emigrant of 1821, *Party Politics Exposed, in a Letter addressed to The Right Honorable The Secretary of State for the Colonies*; signed at end, 'Humanitas' (Sydney, 1834); the authorship is disclosed in the *Sydney Herald*, 27 July 1835: 'This specimen of colonial literature was readily attributed to the classic pen of a convict, named William Watt, a ticket-of-leave holder, and editor of the *Sydney Gazette* . . . We are to receive a copy of this celebrated work this day, which we will be enabled to prove to be written by Watt and published at the *Gazette* office', from J. A. Ferguson, *Bibliography of Australia*, vol. 2, 1831-1838 (Sydney, 1945).

[82] *Sydney Herald*, 27 and 21 July, and 11 August 1834.

[83] J. Mudie, *Vindication of James Mudie and John Larnach* (Sydney, 1834), pp. xviii-xx; Bourke was puzzled by the hostility to him on the Hunter River. He was inclined to explain the antagonism of the settlers by personal slights which he had unwittingly administered to them. As for Mudie's pamphlet, he said nobody reads it and described Mudie and his friends as 'the poor faction, which talked big for a while'; see Bourke to his son, 26 September and 10 October 1834 (Bourke Papers, vol. 6, Letters to his son).

replied to the so-called Hole and Corner—the advocates of severity—men in his pamphlet, *Observations on the 'Hole and Corner' Petition*. The Hole and Corner men had detected insubordination and anarchy: he, in contrast, wrote of the general tranquillity of the colony. They had written of lax discipline in government establishments: he refuted the charge. They had seen themselves as the defenders of law and order: he saw them as a small faction, who were disappointed that the Bourke government preferred to rule by law, and to consult the general interests of the colony: he saw them, too, in a harsher moment, as individuals who wanted to arrogate to themselves all the wisdom, and all the virtue, just as, he believed, they wanted to engross all the wealth of the community.[84] The *Herald*, after accusing him ungraciously of contradiction and inconsistency, went on to sneer at him as a man in a semi-official position who had used his influence and talents to promote the interests of convicts.[85]

All through these angry exchanges the voices of two men of prominence had been silent.

Wentworth had contributed nothing to the debate because the arguments about severity and leniency touched him not at all. The days when he was bothered by that 'early blot', the convicts' clanking chains deforming the wilds and stigmatizing the plains of the land of his birth, belonged to the past. Never again would the tribune of the people use the language of the leveller. Never at ease with those titles of tribune of the people or 'Australian Counsellor' which the press had conferred on him, events were forcing him more and more to define his position in politics. More and more he was finding it right and proper that he should be known as a Whig. At Camden one other voice, which had always spoken up when radicals, levellers, and Botany Bay worthies were working great mischief, was now still for ever.

Two years earlier John Macarthur had begun to rave round the house at Parramatta with pistols and swords in his hands. His wife asked the Supreme Ruler of the universe to give her the strength to bear it with dignity, and enable her to do her duty. By the middle of 1833 she had tried to place him under restraint at Parramatta, but to her great grief and shame he slipped out from time to time and chatted inanely in the streets with those who came to mock and those who came to mourn. One day in May, as he shouted madly in those streets in which he had stormed and raged and dreamed a great dream to his everlasting glory, in the days when his heart was hot within him, they bustled him into a carriage and hurried him off to the seclusion of Camden.[86] There he died on 11 April 1834 and was buried at Camden Park on a spot selected by himself where in his later years he used to enjoy the cool breezes, and watch contented groups of sheep, cows and horses grazing. For the Camden estate, sheep and his family were his glory and his love, and it may be doubted whether outside the family he had ever loved any man, or any man had loved

[84] An Unpaid Magistrate (R. Therry), *Observations on the 'Hole and Corner Petition', in a Letter to the Right Honorable Edward G. Stanley Principal Secretary of State for the Colonial Department* (Sydney, 1834), especially pp. 9-10 and 35-7.

[85] *Sydney Herald*, 8 September 1834.

[86] Elizabeth Macarthur to Edward Macarthur, 30 June and 2 November 1831 and 26 May 1832 (Macarthur Papers, vol. 10); *Australian*, 17 and 24 May 1833.

VAUCLUSE, PORT JACKSON

W. C. Wentworth's house is on the left

Drawing by E. B. Boulton in the Mitchell Library, Sydney

PANSHANGER, THE SEAT OF JOSEPH ARCHER

Lithograph by George Frankland in the Mitchell Library, Sydney

him. Official Sydney wrote formal letters of condolence to the family. Colonel
Lindesay wrote to his son James Macarthur from India to offer condolences
on the death of his inestimable and excellent father. The press was cold and
formal. The *Australian* announced the death without comment. The *Sydney
Gazette* praised him in language they had never had the grace to use while
Macarthur stormed and strutted on the stage of public life. He was, they said, a
gentleman who in political life had advocated the imperious principle of confining all offices and civic honours to immigrants. In private society on the
other hand he had united the highest qualities. His prisoner servants had
never had occasion to complain of deficient sustenance: 'It was', they concluded, 'much to be regretted that strong political prejudices should have so
much sullied the otherwise excellent disposition of such a man'.[87]

In spite of the lonely madness of the last year which brought grief and
anguish to his wife, the achievement lived on. He had built his plantation; he
had pioneered the life of the gentry in New South Wales; he, with others, had
pioneered the growth of fine wool from sheep grazing on the grasses of New
South Wales; he had risen from comparative obscurity to an eminence of
tragic grandeur in a country which had rewarded all his dreams and ambitions
with unending mockery. His son James became the squire of Camden. Unlike
the master of Vaucluse James Macarthur devoted all his energies not to those
deeds of madness and folly which cheated Wentworth of some of the prizes of
this world, but to a creative use of his talents and his resources. He had plans
for the more active and efficient management and control of the extensive
Macarthur concerns which would make them more productive as well as less
expensive than they had hitherto been. He had plans for the welfare, comfort
and respectability of his family. He hoped his beloved mother and sister would
soon take courage and come to live with him at Camden, where he would
cultivate what had always been his ideal—the life of the English gentleman
who happened to be Australian born, hoping here that one day he might be
truly styled one of Australia's gentlemen.[88]

While the attempt by the flogging 'Major' at Patrick's Plains to achieve
tranquillity by severity led inexorably from a story of outrage on the frontiers
of human civilization into a debate on the future of New South Wales, the
high-minded Bourke was pushing on with changes which eroded away other
corner-stones in the foundations of that society of plantation owners and wool
kings, who had been exploiting cheap labour to create the wealth which was
to be the foundation of honour and glory for them and their remotest posterity.
In the second half of 1833 and early in 1834 Bourke had disturbed them not
merely by saying to all and sundry that the manners and morals of the people
would be much improved, and ultimately their wealth and happiness would be
much augmented by a gradual relinquishment of the services of convicts, but
by his other measures against privilege in society. When he had introduced into
the Legislative Council in August of 1833 a bill to continue the Jury Act of

[87] James Macarthur to R. Therry, 25 February 1859 (Macarthur Papers, vol. 1, pp. 179-81);
P. Lindesay to James Macarthur, 6 August 1834 (Macarthur Papers, vol. 2, p. 56); *Australian*,
14 April 1834.
[88] James Macarthur to Edward Macarthur, 17 October 1834 (Macarthur Papers, vol. 35, pp.
264a-7).

P

1832, and to make further provision for trial by jury in criminal cases, the news quickly went round Sydney that Bourke and Forbes were proposing that all and every issue of fact before the Supreme Court against any person or persons for any crime, misdemeanour, or offence was to be tried by a jury of twelve of the inhabitants of the said colony, provided any person or persons so arraigned expressed his desire to be so tried. Once again the Tories in the council had their doubts. Robert Campbell, a merchant who had used his wealth to build up large pastoral interests on the Limestone Plains where convicts and the breeding of ewes were the means to his family's glory, had objected vehemently to exposing his children to the degradation of being brought in association, day after day in the jury box, with the refuse of the gaols and hulks of the mother country. The *Australian* promptly denounced the members of the old guard who, having to choose between contamination and lack of their birthright, preferred to dispense with their birthright. The *Sydney Gazette* came out in defence of trial by military officers, to which they claimed there could be no objection except in political cases. For themselves they feared gross corruption and ignorance from the introduction of juries in criminal cases. But Bourke, committed as he was to a policy of finding for his jurymen men who were not of bad fame, or of immoral character and repute, and ably supported again by Forbes, refused to exclude ex-convicts, being convinced that Campbell's motives were as much the defence of landed wealth and privilege as concern for the morals of the people of New South Wales.[89]

In March of 1834 he had turned his mind to the problem of education in New South Wales. Feeling as he did a deep interest in the education of the rising generation in the colony, and believing that in education the schools should conform as closely as possible with the principle of equality of opportunity, he saw that in the colony of New South Wales there were glaring inconsistencies between these ideals and the existing system. One was the privileged position of The King's School at Parramatta, conceived by Archdeacon Broughton as a school where the sons of landholders, professional people and merchants would be steeped in Christian apologetics, and in a study of those classical texts which had been found in the mother country to be an excellent schooling for a governing class. Why, Bourke asked, should government subsidize a school for the sons of the wealthy colonists and civil servants of the government when the children of the poor were being educated in mere hovels under convict schoolmasters? Besides, he continued, the exclusive nature of the institution was another objection as none but members of the Church of England could attend it. So by March of 1834 Bourke was beginning to move towards some general system of education provided by the government upon an extensive scale and conducted by able teachers.[90]

In the meantime the number of free immigrants arriving each year was

---

[89] Bourke to Stanley, 2 October 1833, *H.R.A.*, I. xvii. 236-8; R. Campbell to Bourke, 11 September 1833, Encl. in above, ibid., 238-9; An Act to continue for a limited time an Act of the Governor and Council of New South Wales . . . and to make further provision for Trial by Jury in Criminal Cases in the said Colony, 4 Will. IV, no. 12, 28 August 1833, in T. Callaghan, op. cit., vol. 1, pp. 653-8; *Australian*, 16 August 1833; *Sydney Gazette*, 17 August 1833.

[90] Bourke to Stanley, 3 March 1834, *H.R.A.*, I. xvii. 382; Bourke to Stanley, 10 March 1834, ibid., 390-4; Bourke to Stanley, 11 March 1834, ibid., 394-5.

beginning gradually to change the composition of the population. In 1833, 8,000 people had arrived, of whom 2,500 were free. The *Sydney Herald* began to write of a distinguished era in the annals of the colony, in the not too distant future, when the disparity in numbers between the free and the bond would disappear. Then at last, they wrote, that much wanted, thrifty, industrious middle class of society would take its place between the planters and placemen at the top and the bond and emancipist workers at the bottom of society. As they saw it, the country could not prosper in its moral and political relations until that day occurred. For they knew that in all societies which used slave or semi-slave labour the middle class tended to be both weak and cowardly. The question, as they saw it, was just how quickly the colony could move from a convict-planter authoritarian type of society into a middle class, bourgeois liberal type of society in which the bourgeoisie were free to worship their gods of wealth and respectability, and the lower orders were sober and industrious, and content with their humble station in life.[91]

In July a group which believed that the wealth and resources of New South Wales should be exploited for the benefit of those 'boys who lived in the land' rather than of their kinsmen in the United Kingdom petitioned the Sheriff to summon a public meeting. When the Sheriff refused, on the grounds that no officer of the government should serve the interests of any party, they then asked Wentworth to preside. He agreed. On 29 July a huge crowd gathered at the Royal Hotel to agree to summon a public meeting for 28 August, the object of such a meeting being to address the House of Commons upon the subject of the intended mal-appropriation of the proceeds of the sale of the waste lands and also to remonstrate against the estimates, and for other purposes connected with the above matters.[92] The bourgeoisie were beginning to see that if immigration, land laws and education were to be administered in their interests, they they must take over the government, and run it as a committee controlling their own affairs. The path to such a simple conclusion was not straight: nor was visibility very clear as faction fights and personality problems muddied the waters.

When they met again on 28 August at the Court House John Mackaness, who was voted into the chair, expressed the hope that any member who had any sentiment to express would be heard with a becoming patience. Wentworth then rose to his feet and told them to resounding cheers that they had gathered together that day to answer the question whether the whole produce of the soil should be swept away from the colony and handed over to placemen and men who could dip into ministers' pockets. It was, he thundered, a question of tribute. After a side-swipe at Hall, whose physical composition, he told them, was well known to be mixed up with a great deal of corruption, they laughed, and jeered and leered, displaying as ever what one observer later called that brutal love of any species of slander, scandal and quarrelling which was inherent in the mass of that barbarous population.[93] He went on to say that the rapacity of ministers had caused them to throw a sheep's eye at the revenues from land sales. And again they laughed. The people of New South Wales, he

[91] *Sydney Herald*, 13 January and 24 March 1834.
[92] Ibid., 31 July 1834.   [93] Ibid., 21 April 1836.

continued, would know all the misery and degradation incident to the conditions of a tributary state, unless they had the energy to resist it. They would be treated as they deserved to be treated—like dogs. He had, however, nothing constructive to offer to the audience he had so worked up with his brilliant oratory. All that he could offer was a lame resolution: 'That it is the opinion of this Meeting, that the proceeds derived from the lands of the Colony, whether by sale, lease, or other reservation of quitrents or grants, are part of the public revenue'.

The Reverend Mr Mansfield at least had some constructive ideas on how the public revenue should be used. He wanted it to be used to improve the shameful state of the streets and roads, and the contemptible mockery of street lighting. He wanted better immigrants than the *Red Rover* girls: he wanted useful and discreet servants and young men of respectability with respectable and virtuous wives. Other speakers stuck to the theme that the revenues from land sales should be used for the benefit of the colony. One after another accused British ministers of dipping their hands into the pockets of the people, and being merciless encroachers on the civil rights of the people. When one solitary speaker defended the Secretary of State, Lord Stanley, he was swept aside by the meeting, which once again roared with laughter when Captain Biddulph called out he thought Lord Stanley might with propriety be called the authorized bushranger. After passing a vote of thanks to the chairman, the meeting broke up savouring the joke against the Englishman, determined to win their rights by constitutional means, for they were British too, though they never asked themselves then which institutions they would create supposing they were to take over the management of their own affairs.[94]

Just before Wentworth and Mansfield pounded the rostrum at the Court House Forbes joined Bourke in his carriage for a journey and chat from Sydney to Parramatta. Bourke told him that as he saw it there were two political groups in the colony—the immigrants and the emancipists. But Forbes would have none of this. As he saw it, the two parties in the colony resembled in principle and in many particulars the political divisions which had existed for many years in the parent country. Some were liberals, and some were what at home would be denominated Tories or conservatives. It was, he believed, just as much an accident that the liberals should support the emancipists as that in England the Whigs had supported Catholic emancipation. The liberals could not see why an emancipist should not be restored to his rights in New South Wales, in the same way as he would be restored in England. They deprecated distinctions which were calculated to sow the seeds of dissension and so separate the colonists into castes.

One other point he must add. As for two generations all power and patronage had been exclusively exercised by the Tories, it was not to be wondered at that the colony had been filled with 'red hot Tories'. Nor was it surprising that His Excellency was the only one of liberal principles in his government. All his counsellors, especially the Colonial Secretary McLeay, would have voted in England for Wellington, the Tory, rather than Grey the Whig and reformer. In short, he must tell him, His Excellency was a Whig Governor in the

[94] Ibid., Supplement, 1 September 1834.

midst of High Tory counsellors. He, Forbes, was not quarrelling with any political creed. He was simply stating a fact. The politics of England were and must be for many years to come the politics of New South Wales. This colony, as Forbes saw it, was but in the cradle. It had no local population, for it was not given to Forbes to respond to, or possibly even know of those hopes and aspirations in the minds of the currency lads. Two years earlier the *Currency Lad* had begun publication in New South Wales, with a noisy and cheeky demand that the currency lads should fill the main positions in New South Wales, but that was something to which the Chief Justice remained a mighty stranger in his adopted land.[95]

While Forbes was still musing on political groups in New South Wales the news reached Sydney, late in September, that thirteen of the men who had taken part in the mutiny on Norfolk Island in the preceding January had been launched into eternity after remarkable displays of penitence. On the morning of 15 January 1834 thirty convicts of the worst character had made a rush on the guard, as another group who had feigned sickness overpowered the attendants at the hospital. In the meantime another party of convicts from Long-ridge had broken into the tool-house, and were rushing to join their confederates. But, thanks to the energetic measures taken by Foster Fyans, the captain of the guard, the soldiers soon had the situation in hand. All told 162 convicts had joined in the mutiny. Of these two were killed, and seven died later from their wounds. At a special session of the Supreme Court held on Norfolk Island in July, twenty-nine of the mutineers were capitally convicted. Of these sixteen were reprieved, and thirteen executed on 22 and 23 September in the presence of the convicts and two chaplains, the Reverend H. T. Stiles and the Reverend W. B. Ullathorne, who stood at Gallow's Gate, from where the condemned men could take their last look at that very vast sea, and then followed them on the last journey to that beautiful spot where they were given back the earth from which they had come. So Walter Burke, a native of the county of Tipperary, aged twenty-one years, and J. S. Nell, aged twenty-two, and eleven others were laid there. Above some of them, their friends cut words into the stone to express their hope: 'Lord have mercy on his soul'. Some of them had no memorial. Thomas York, aged twenty-two years, a private in the 4th or King's Own Regiment had also been laid there in that kingdom of perpetual night after being killed during the fighting whilst in pursuit of mutineers engaged with others in a disgraceful attempt against the peace of the settlement.[96]

Foster Fyans solicited the Secretary of State to appoint him to a police magistracy and make him a grant of land in consideration of his exertions in quelling the disturbance. By contrast, Ullathorne, unable to stop being haunted by the terrible experience of seeing comely young men nipped by death's untimely frost, of seeing God's creatures acquire the heart of a beast in that hell of

[95] F. Forbes to R. Bourke, 19 August 1834 (Bourke Papers, vol. 11); for the opinion of Forbes that the judges of New South Wales were also divided between the liberals and conservatives see F. Forbes to R. Bourke, n.d. but probably written in March of 1834 (Bourke Papers, vol. 11).

[96] *Sydney Herald*, 16 October 1834; Bourke to Spring Rice, 15 January 1835, *H.R.A.*, I. xvii. 638-9; headstones of tombs in the cemetery at Norfolk Island.

the Pacific, was never quiet again until he found the words in which to express his horror. He told his fellow-men that they had been doing an ungracious and an ungodly thing: that they had taken a portion of God's earth and had made it a cesspool, and that the removal of such a plague concerned the whole human race.[97]

Like Ullathorne, Broughton, too, had his worries that September, though they were of a different kind. He was worried by the influence of the press in fostering a disregard for religion in general: he was worried too by the extreme activity of the Catholics in perverting those who had no true discernment of what Protestantism was. He was alarmed by something much deeper. Each year, he told a friend in London, thousands of convicts were cast upon the shores of New South Wales and Van Diemen's Land without any effort being made to prevent them instantly becoming pagans or heathens. This deadly infection, he feared, would be propagated even to their remotest descendants. The question the English had to answer was whether they were prepared to lay the foundation of a vast community of infidels, and whether collectively or individually they could answer to Almighty God for conniving at such an execution of the transportation laws as would infallibly lead to that result.[98]

Those who eyed the passing show in New South Wales through a conservative window found much to alarm and disgust them in the behaviour of the lower orders of society. They found it a drunken part of the world, where the habit of dram-drinking was so universal that even the poor aborigines were found dead in the streets, having too faithfully copied the pernicious habits of the more civilized 'white fellow'.[99] Vagabonds who frequented the theatre used vile language to the annoyance of every respectable person present.[1] The various spots of vacant land round Sydney were generally resorted to by blackguards of the worst description who indulged in the diabolical and pernicious vice of gambling.[2] Funerals of the lower orders degenerated invariably into grotesque bacchanalian orgies, in the course of which sorrow, wrote the *Sydney Herald*, was liquidated—indeed absolutely drowned.[3] Women daily held a clatter-clatter in the streets of Sydney to the great amusement of the lookers-on, as in the eyes of the conservatives the convict system encouraged all that coarse, loud-mouthed vulgar behaviour, all extravagance of speech, dress and behaviour which so disgusted them.[4] The conservatives heard the sound and the fury, and missed the laughter and the gaiety, the bounce and the gusto, and never paused to ponder over the silence and the emptiness which would descend when these men were tamed. The conservative fear was that convictism would bring all men down to its own degraded level of drunkenness, beastly sexual play, and coarse, vulgar amusements. Far away in Cheltenham, busy as ever for the cause of true religion and virtue, Eliza Darling added her mite to the fund for the education of the lower orders by publishing her pamphlet *Simple*

---

[97] Bourke to Spring Rice, 23 March 1835, *H.R.A.*, I. xvii. 702; for the life of Foster Fyans see *Australian Dictionary of Biography*, vol. 1; W. B. Ullathorne, *The Catholic Mission in Australasia* (Liverpool, 1837), pp. iv-v.

[98] W. G. Broughton to A. M. Campbell, London, 9 December 1834 (Bonwick Transcripts, Box 54, p. 1935).   [99] *Sydney Herald*, 16 June 1834.   [1] Ibid., 10 July 1834.
    [2] Ibid., 13 January 1834.   [3] Ibid., 2 January 1834.   [4] *Sydney Gazette*, 12 August 1834.

rules for the Guidance of Persons in humble life; more particularly for young girls going out to service, and with her usual thoroughness, arranged for a number of copies to be distributed in Sydney in places where they could do most good.[5]

As though to confirm these fears of what convictism was doing to humanity in New South Wales, Robert Wardell left his house astride a white horse one day in September, and came upon two prisoners of the Crown, John Jenkins, a runaway from the iron gang, and Thomas Tattersdale, an assigned servant, whom he questioned, not knowing that Jenkins was seeking revenge for the floggings he had received at Wardell's instigation. Wardell asked superciliously: 'Who are you?' to which Jenkins replied: 'I am a man', and then shot him dead. Wardell was then forty-one. By the splendour of his talents the lamented gentleman had, in the course of his professional career, amassed the handsome fortune of £30,000. He had about him that air of distinction and achievement which excited the envy of the convicts. He had that erect posture, the well proportioned head, the Roman nose, the tight narrow lips, and the eyes stern and unsmiling, with which he seemed to look down on the world coldly and relentlessly.

Wentworth, overwhelmed with grief at the loss of a man with whom he had shared not just the pleasures of the bottle, but a vision of life, a man to whom he had given his heart, announced with a becoming dignity that the funeral procession would leave from Wardell's home. With the *Sydney Herald* writing that in the present state of the country the sooner a respectable man made his will the better, as he had no security that he might not be the next victim of the outlaw's bullet, Wardell's body was committed to the earth. Two months later on 7 November John Jenkins and Thomas Tattersdale stood before the Chief Justice and a jury of civil inhabitants indicted for that they, not having the fear of God before their eyes, but being moved and instigated by the devil, did on 7 September murder Robert Wardell. They were found guilty. Just before Forbes passed the awful sentence of the law, Jenkins knocked out Tattersdale, and looked for a moment as though he would kill Forbes had he not been deterred by the sword of the officer standing by his side. Two days later, before they were hanged, Jenkins spoke from the scaffold: 'Goodbye, my lads', he said, for he too had his bonds in life, 'I shot the Doctor not for gain, but because he was a Tyrant . . . If any of you take to the bush shoot every tyrant you come across . . . I have not time to say any more lads, but I hope you will all pray for me'. He still refused to shake hands with Tattersdale: 'Let every villain', he shouted as the hangman let him drop, 'Let every villain shake hands with himself'.[6]

From such episodes the conservatives drew the somewhat hysterical conclusion that the spirit of convictism threatened annihilation to every person who should dare to question the character of any of its votaries. That September some were whispering in the salons and pot-houses of Sydney town and

[5] Ibid., 22 May 1834; Eliza Darling, *Simple rules for the Guidance of Persons in humble life* (Cheltenham, 1834).
[6] Based on *Sydney Herald*, 7 and 11 September, 10 and 13 November 1834; *Australian*, 11 November 1834; tablet to Robert Wardell, St James's Church, Sydney.

Parramatta, and out on Patrick's Plains, and down south in the Monaro, that were it not for the infatuated delusions of those two Whigs, Bourke and Forbes, about mitigating the severity of punishment, ladies and gentlemen would not have to walk in fear of their lives, or having their morals contaminated by the Tambourine Sals who now presided at the tables of society, quite forgetful of their true place in society with gypsies, strumpets, and serving girls.[7]

Not everyone was tempted to give way to despair, or throw up their hands in disgust. Just as one order of society was dying, giving off its own smell of decay, and impressing some minds with the impotence of men in the face of human evil, others were responding to a promise of better things from the spread of Enlightenment. On Christmas Day of 1834, the anniversary of the coming of the Christ child, Carmichael announced his intention to begin a normal school in Sydney for the education of teachers. In that school no one would be taught religious opinions: no attempt would be made to pledge a man to any creed. On the contrary every encouragement would be given to the pupils to form opinions of their own. They would be taught the duties of morality and rectitude of intercourse with each other. They would be taught to be amiable and benevolent to each other. They would be taught to be able and honourable. For Carmichael believed that if men were taught to practise from the heart their duties to each other, they would not be likely to be found deficient in their duties to God. He saw himself as a man professed to labour for mankind. So a new note of hope for mankind was sounded in New South Wales at the end of a year in which the men of the older faiths had prophesied doom and disaster, or shaken their heads about the life of man in the coming age of unbelief in Australia. By contrast Carmichael did not cry out to his God to give him strength to endure a vaudeville of devils. He believed that with Enlightenment men would have life and have it more abundantly. Enlightenment would free men from their slavery to gross and grovelling appetites, destroy the pests to the peace and welfare of society, and give everyone a passport to the society of honourable men.[8]

---

[7] *Sydney Herald*, 16 October 1834.   [8] Ibid., 18 and 25 December 1834.

9

BOTANY BAY WHIGS AND
BOTANY BAY TORIES

EARLY IN the new year of 1835 the Reverend Samuel Marsden read to his mortification in Lang's *An Historical and Statistical Account of New South Wales* the charge that he was guilty of episcopal intolerance towards Presbyterians. He sat down in his study at the parsonage in Parramatta, and wrote a letter to the *Sydney Herald* in which he reminded its readers of his generosity towards the Presbyterians in 1826 when he had lent them £750 to build a church. Then a voice from his past came back to remind him of the day as long ago as 1810 when, disregarding the divine exhortation that he that humbled himself would be exalted, and with a haughtiness which it now pained him to recall, he had told the lay missionary William Pascoe Crook that he was not authorized by either God or man to celebrate the Lord's supper in the colony of New South Wales.[1]

This time he showed little fight, as he had neither energy nor inclination left to vindicate his name and honour in the eyes of his fellow-men. A spirit of resignation and withdrawal had descended on the parsonage at Parramatta. 'Greatheart' Marsden was beginning to yearn for his eternal rest. His wife, Elizabeth, was so filled with the same longing to escape from this vale of tears that while she remained alive in this world she spent her time in prayer to prepare herself for that which was to come. Her release from the wheel of life came that same year. In October she died, and her body was committed to the dust in St John's graveyard. On a memorial tablet to her in St John's the Reverend Samuel Marsden asked a mason to cut these words in the stone 'The blood of Jesus Christ His son cleanseth us from all sin'.[2] His favourite daughter, Martha, was yearning too for that peace which the world could not give, that peace which passed all understanding and the joy that was unspeakable and full of glory. God's faithful servant and his family were beginning to turn their backs on the world.[3]

While Marsden was raising hungry, beseeching eyes to heaven, hoping God was just even if man was vile, Bourke was beginning to take unto himself that delight of living in a land of great natural beauty, a land of warm sun, of ripening fruit, and bright coloured flowers and shrubs. As the summer of 1834 began to wax, and the sun and air seemed to be calling all and sundry to

---

[1] *Sydney Herald*, 19 and 23 February 1835.

[2] Elizabeth Marsden to Thomas Hassall, n.d., written probably between 1832 and 1835 (Hassall Papers, vol. 3, pp. 6069-71); memorial tablet to Elizabeth Marsden in St John's Church, Parramatta.

[3] W. B. Marshall to Martha Marsden, 1 January 1835 (Marsden Papers, vol. 1, pp. 569-76).

a life of gaiety and pleasure, and with the promise of a fine wool season, and everything in New South Wales very prosperous, Bourke, who had recovered from his private grief, and had his own personal consolation in a beloved son and daughter, began to confront the future with a quiet confidence.[4] Some vision of what he could achieve in New South Wales was beginning to take shape in his mind. He was beginning to entertain the hope that it was to be his good fortune to preside over the introduction of British political institutions, to introduce trial by jury, and create that house of assembly for which radicals, liberals, and emancipists had clamoured ever since the days of Governor Brisbane with an intemperance of language quite alien to his own gentle nature.[5] He was beginning to hope too that he might see the end of the evil inflicted on this fair portion of the globe by the constant influx of immoral and debased individuals.[6]

The difficulty was, as Forbes had put it to him that August day in 1834, he was a Whig amidst high Tory counsellors. McLeay the Colonial Secretary, was deeply and implacably committed to the protection of the gentry of New South Wales against affronts from the convict party, the shopkeepers, and the men soiled by engaging in trade. Kinchela, the Attorney-General, was a Tory whom he had to watch very carefully in Council, and so was C. D. Riddell. The Tories, too, had their supporters on the bench of the Supreme Court, where the brave Forbes took his seat with Tories such as Mr Justice Burton, who had been spouting Tory sentiments ever since he took his seat on the bench in December of 1832. McLeay, exasperated by Bourke's pressure on him to support in the Legislative Council jury bills concerning which he shared the reservations of the local Tories, had somewhat indiscreetly told some of his fellow councillors that if things went on that way much longer, he would resign. Happily for Bourke, Forbes was more than a match for McLeay, Kinchela and Riddell in debate. The one man who might have discomfited the Chief Justice, who believed that open enmity with Forbes was preferable to friendship, Henry Dumaresq, had retired to his estate at St Heliers, having found public life hateful, heartless, and irritating in all countries and in all times, but more especially in New South Wales. Bourke found Thomson very sensible, very steady, and very honourable. He took great pleasure in his company, and derived great benefit from his assistance.

Henry Dumaresq, who had rather a wicked tongue when encouraged to perform on the Botany Bay Whigs, thought Thomson looked very sad and very seedy after his marriage to Bourke's daughter. As Thomson had first arrived in New South Wales in December of 1828 to take up the position of clerk to the Legislative and Executive Councils which Dumaresq had been obliged to relinquish, Dumaresq was not a very reliable witness. Thomson belonged by birth to those professional classes in the British Isles who were superseding the army officer families such as the Dumaresqs in the government of the colonies. Born in Edinburgh on 1 June 1800 to a civil servant of great distinction, and educated in Edinburgh and at Harrow, he had had some

---

[4] R. Bourke to his son, 24 November 1834 (Bourke Papers, vol. 6).

[5] R. Bourke to his son, 30 July, 26 September, 10 October and 26 October 1834, 11 March and 11 April 1835, ibid.   [6] Bourke to Aberdeen, 12 August 1835, *H.R.A.*, I. xviii. 71-4.

experience in the United States and Canada before accepting the offer of the clerkship in Sydney.[7]

At the same time Bourke was drawing closer to Wentworth. Unlike the rapport of Bourke and Forbes this was not that coming together of two men who held identical opinions on the world of politics and the life of the world to come. To Bourke's Christian hope of meeting in a better world those whom he had lost in this, Wentworth was a stranger. But in the here and now they seemed to have much in common. They were both Protestant Irish and both, on their own confession, Whigs by political conviction. That alone prepared the way to an understanding. There was even more to it than a vague agreement on political principle. Wentworth belonged by birth to the Fitzwilliam family, who had been patrons of Edmund Burke, to whom Richard Bourke was not only distantly related, but with whom he felt such a bond that he was using his leisure moments in Sydney to put down on paper notes for a life of that statesman. Chance, too, had drawn Bourke and Wentworth closer together in the politics of the colony. By the beginning of 1835 Bourke had become quite exasperated by the opposition from McLeay to the extension of trial by jury and the introduction of a house of assembly, on which Bourke had set his mind. Wentworth had already savaged McLeay as a bloated pensioner at that ill-fated meeting of the Benevolent Society, where he had also held him up to ridicule as the defender of a dying order of society. Bourke deplored the intemperate language, the vulgar abuse, and the ranting, but he had much sympathy with the political convictions which had induced the attack. As for the stories that the proprietor of Vaucluse was living it up in his private life in ways to which the gentle mild-mannered Bourke was a stranger, that could not touch their relationship because Bourke had never set himself up as a judge of other men.[8] Others in Sydney were not so reticent in their references as this strange friendship and regard blossomed between two such mighty opposites. The *Herald*, that self-appointed defender of the morals of the free, rebuked Bourke for associating with a man who they mistakenly believed was the spokesman for the pro-convict group in New South Wales and who, they inferred, had the politics of the rabble, and the morals of all those who had been tainted by associating with ex-convicts.[9]

When Bourke met the Legislative Council on 18 May there was a sense of impending change in the air. Ever since 20 April there had been rumours that the colony would be called on to pay for the upkeep of the convicts. All through the long hot summer the *Sydney Herald* had thundered on the cost of the convict system to the settlers, on the lawlessness of the convicts, and on some mobs of ex-convicts in Sydney who were aping the worst actions of a Westminster mob. The *Sydney Herald*, too, had campaigned against the new system of trial by jury in criminal cases in which, as they put it, cattle-stealers tried their comrades, and the receivers of stolen goods tried the thieves, and

---

[7] R. Bourke to his son, 11 April 1835 (Bourke Papers, vol. 6); H. Dumaresq to W. Dumaresq, 6 March 1832; H. Dumaresq to Eliza Darling, 20 September 1832, and extracts from the letter of H. Dumaresq to General Darling, 3 July 1833 (Letters of Colonel Henry Dumaresq, 1825-38, MS. in M.L.).

[8] R. Bourke to his son, 11 March 1835 (Bourke Papers, vol. 6).   [9] Ibid.

consequently acquitted them.[10] In the Legislative Council there were men who agreed with their attacks. McLeay, like the poor, Bourke had still with him. Kinchela, deaf to anything except the high Toryism of the *Sydney Herald*, was still there. Robert Campbell was as anxious as ever to protect his family from the convict contamination which, he believed, followed from the Bourke policies as night from day. Richard Jones, the founder of the merchant firm of Jones and Riley in the days of Macquarie, which some remembered with pride as Sydney's solitary mercantile firm, and some called 'this sordid rapacious house', had taken up 10,000 acres in the Hunter River district in the year he first became a member of the Legislative Council. Like Campbell, he had become a critic of the Bourke policies. So Bourke was still a Whig amidst Tory counsellors, who were appalled by the evil influence of the Chief Justice on the Governor. Up in the Hunter and down in the Limestone Plains, on the Monaro, and at Camden, where that English gentleman Australian-born, James Macarthur, resided, these Botany Bay Tories were faced with an insoluble dilemma: how to transfer power over land and immigration from the Governor in a nominated council to their own group without increasing the power of the bourgeoisie, the Botany Bay Whigs, and their sinister supporters amongst the emancipists and mobs of Sydney.[11]

When Bourke met the Legislative Council and told them that the revenues of the Crown now placed at the disposal of the Council were sufficient, at least, to provide for the police and gaol establishments, and the expense of bringing immigrants to this colony, some members murmured their dissent. On 25 August and 4 September, W. Lithgow, A. Berry, E. C. Close, R. Jones, H. H. Macarthur, J. Blaxland, A. Bell and R. Campbell had put down in writing their opposition to charging police and gaols to colonial revenue. They urged that the colony would have less money to import that free labour which would improve the moral condition of the inhabitants. They argued, too, that this abstraction of a large portion of colonial revenue could only serve to perpetuate the evil of the transportation system which would mean that New South Wales would never rise to a very high rank among British colonies, but continue to be the principal receptacle of convicts from all parts of the empire.

To draw up a more permanent record of their misgivings Council proceeded to appoint a Select Committee on Police and Gaols, with that sound Tory McLeay in the chair. They brought down a report which presented in more measured language the ideas put in currency by the conservative press in New South Wales. They had much to say on the evil and corrupting influences of the convicts. They recommended religious instruction and enforcement of a proper observance of the sabbath as moral restraints. In their opinion, the tranquillity and happiness of a colony were often directly in proportion to observances of religion. They recommended the discontinuance of road parties becaues their loose discipline was, they believed, the cause of great

10 *Sydney Herald*, 15 January, 12 and 19 February and 5 March 1835.

11 For the life of R. Jones see *Australian Dictionary of Biography*, vol. 2; *Sydney Morning Herald*, 8 December 1852; E. Jones, Early Reminiscences (MS. in M.L.); R. Bourke to his son, 13 August 1835 (Bourke Papers, vol. 6): 'From McLeay, Atty. Genl. I receive no assistance in Council, and the leader of His Majesty's Opposition says foolish things without being much ashamed of them. He is more silly than ever ... I hold my ground out of doors.'

evil. They had much to say about another great evil—the contamination of the interior of the colony by gangs of cattle-dealers and other disorderly persons, who were either freed men, or long-term men holding tickets-of-leave. These men raised a property by committing depredations on the neighbouring flocks and herds, or sold spirits and so provided other inducements for thieving, gaming, and every species of debauchery, including the seduction of the servants of established settlers. For their part the committee would not permit ticket-of-leave men to purchase, rent or take possession of land, or reside in any place other than a township, except as the hired servants of some free person of character approved by the magistrates. The Tories of Botany Bay had begun to collect the evidence which would convince the men in black in London that in the penal colony of New South Wales there had been a moral corruption of the free by the criminal portion of the community: that in the world of Betsey Bandicoot and Bold Jack Donahoe there was that monstrous evil of a society most thoroughly depraved in its vicious propensities.[12]

Not all the Tories were prepared to commit themselves to such a slander. James Macarthur was too proud as an Australian to besmirch his fellow-countrymen. Bourke and Forbes were looking for a solution to the labour problem which would graft virtuous migrants on to the sober and industrious amongst the currency lads. When he published his new regulations for the assignment of male convict servants Bourke had hoped that by substituting an intelligible qualification and a strict routine of business, instead of vesting a discretionary power in the superintendent of convicts, he would be able to dispose both equitably and productively of the services of the convicts. He had also appointed G. M. Slade as commissioner for the assignment of convict servants. With help from Forbes he had drafted, he believed, sound regulations based on the utilitarian principles of the law reformers of the day.[13] Some of the larger landholders, the Hole and Corner men of the Hunter River district, the Macarthurs at Camden, and Campbell on the Limestone Plains, detected something quite sinister in the new regulations. Worked on by the *Sydney Herald*, they entertained the idea that Bourke was encouraging the small settlers, the ones who admitted convicts to their tables and their rum drinking parties, at the expense of the large landowners. So, when the *Sydney Herald* went on to argue that New South Wales was a gaol yard, that their Governor and Council were but a standing committee to regulate a prison, that all the inhabitants were prisoners, and that the early answer to their situation was to abolish penal servitude, and establish a free system of labour, some of the large landowners shouted a loud 'Amen'.[14]

The doubt was whether they could obtain an adequate supply of free labour,

[12] *V. & P.* (L.C. N.S.W.) 4 September 1835; R. Campbell wrote his dissent on 25 August; see also the opinions of W. Lithgow, R. Jones, H. H. Macarthur and A. Bell, ibid.; Evidence to the Final Report of the Select Committee on Police and Gaols, ibid., 9 October 1835.
[13] Bourke to the Secretary of State, 26 June 1835, *H.R.A.*, I. xvii. 750-1; see also *New South Wales Calendar and General Post Office Directory 1835*; see also Glenelg to Bourke, 1 February 1836, *H.R.A.*, I. xviii. 283-4.
[14] *Sydney Herald*, 25 May and 9 July 1835; for an example of the opposition of the large holders of land to the new regulations, see the letter written by J. Smith to Glenelg on behalf of the Australian Agricultural Company on 30 November 1835, Encl. in Glenelg to Bourke, 1 February 1836, *H.R.A.*, I. xviii. 285-6.

which would have some of the advantages of the bond—cheapness, and obedience. To resolve that doubt the Legislative Council appointed in June a select committee under the chairmanship of Forbes to collect evidence and report back to Council. As they began to collect evidence news reached Sydney that the chains on convicts in road parties were to be struck off, partly because judges lacked legal power to sentence convicts to work in chains, and partly because it was held imprudent to push punishment beyond that point of suffering where it ceased to produce any salutary effect, and induced absolute despair. So the chains on the men in the stone quarries on Goat Island were knocked off, and the chains on the men in the road party in the Illawarra district were knocked off, to their deep undying gratitude, just as James Macarthur's cousin, Hannibal Macarthur, the man whom E. S. Hall had exposed as an advocate of severity in the Darling period, told the members of the select committee on immigration that as there were no effective restraints for the vicious propensities of convicts, he had come to the conclusion the colony should attract free men at liberal wages who would curb the vicious practices of the depraved by their example of virtuous and industrious habits.[15]

Forbes was chairman of the committee, and after hearing evidence from the Colonial Secretary, the Treasurer, the Reverend J. D. Lang, unofficial members of the Legislative Council, landowners and other employers of labour, he presented the report on 18 September. In it he traced briefly the history of migration into the colony from the appointment of the first commission in June of 1831, to the last immigrant ship from Ireland, during which period 2,848 had received assistance to migrate. Having presented an account of the original policy of appropriating the proceeds of Crown lands sales to immigration, and the general character of the immigrants who had arrived, he went on to consider the best means of extending and promoting the introduction of a moral and industrious class of migrant. He had no hesitation in saying that a great number of the female migrants were quite unsuited to the wants of the colonists. The problem, as he saw it, was a simple one. The colony had been made the receptacle for the outcasts of the United Kingdom, and was consequently loaded with a vast disproportion of immoral people, who could only be counteracted by an extensive introduction of free and virtuous inhabitants. One possible way to do this was for the colony to send an agent to England to represent the true wants of the inhabitants, and to give accurate information to possible migrants. He should supervise the whole of immigration from the first advertisement to final embarkation. Finally Forbes recommended, after consulting the wishes of the inhabitants of New South Wales, that the agent should press for married mechanics with wives and children, for married mechanics without children, for married farm servants without children, for unmarried farm servants, and unmarried women.[16]

Bourke knew from Mr McLeay and the general tittle-tattle in society that the ladies of delicacy in Sydney had drawn the line at acting as patronesses to

[15] Bourke to Aberdeen, 24 July 1835, *H.R.A.*, I. xviii. 47; Aberdeen to Bourke, 4 March 1835, *H.R.A.*, I. xvii. 685-7; Evidence of H. H. Macarthur to Select Committee on Immigration, 11 June 1845, *V. & P.* (L.C. N.S.W.) 1835, p. 315.

[16] Report of the Select Committee on Immigration, 18 September 1835, *V. & P.* (L.C. N.S.W.) 1835.

the prostitutes of *Red Rover* fame. Sharing as he did the views of the Chief Justice that the land fund of New South Wales should be used to encourage the migration of the sober and the virtuous rather than common prostitutes who by their abandoned and outrageous conduct kept migrant ships in a constant state of alarm, he announced in October that he proposed to accept some of the recommendations of the committee to promote the introduction of men and women of good moral character and industrious habits. He proposed to send an agent or agents to the British Isles to pick out such migrants. He also proposed to offer to those settlers who had the means and would prefer to engage mechanics or agricultural labourers by their own agents, a bounty equal or nearly equal to the expense of such persons, being married couples under the age of thirty years, and unmarried females between the ages of fifteen and thirty years, and single men between the ages of eighteen and twenty-five. This would be another means of supplying the deficiency of labour in New South Wales. On 28 October these bounty regulations were published in Sydney.[17]

In the meantime, outside the Legislative Council the landholders and bourgeoisie who were excluded from that select circle had already demanded a more sweeping solution to their problems. As they saw it, it was not just a problem of their getting power over this or that subject of legislation, but of how to acquire self-government for New South Wales. In April 1835 Sir John Jamison, the chairman of the committee which had forwarded the public petition of 1833 to London, had received a letter from Henry Lytton Bulwer, author and member of the House of Commons with a rather quaint, and indeed eccentric passion for colonial affairs, in which he had offered to act free of charge in the capacity of parliamentary advocate for the colony. When seventy-five magistrates, gentlemen and other respectable householders of the colony had requested the sheriff to call a public meeting to discuss the Bulwer proposal and he had declined they decided to call a public meeting themselves at the Court House on 29 May.

On that 29 May in a rather lukewarm atmosphere, the chairman, John Mackaness, asked John Stephen to read aloud the letter from Bulwer which suggested the colonists should form a permanent committee which, he believed, would give them weight with the minister and the press. At the moment in England he warned them no one cared, no one thought of New South Wales. 'You', Bulwer wrote 'will become a matter of English interest, when you blend yourself with England's daily affairs'. Whereupon Sir John Jamison, moved, seconded by Wentworth, that the meeting coinciding in the measures proposed by Bulwer, did pledge themselves to carry the same into effect, and to that end did cordially accept the disinterested and friendly offer by Bulwer to act as their colonial parliamentary advocate. Jamison explained that he saw the committee as one which would relieve them from their present closed council and establish a council of a superior description by including all the men of superior intelligence in the colony.[18]

---

[17] Bourke to Glenelg, 14 October 1835, *H.R.A.*, I. xviii. 161-3; for an extract from the regulations of 28 October 1835, see ibid., 828.

[18] *Report of the Provisional Committee of the Australian Patriotic Association*, pp. 1-5 (Sydney, 1835); *Sydney Herald*, 1 June 1835.

Wentworth went further. He raised immediately the system for the disposal of Crown lands. The colony, he reminded them, had received a pledge that the revenue from the sale of lands would be devoted exclusively to immigration, but so far of the £100,000 raised only £10,000 had been spent on immigration. Some of it had been given to a person for services performed in England. But this, he warned them, was a mere nibble, and away he went to raise with them the question of the enormous police establishment which must now be paid for by the colonists. They were being asked to pay the salary of a judge for Norfolk Island. In time the colonists might even be asked to pay the salaries of judges who tried and condemned the convicts sent to these shores. He agreed there was need for a talented advocate in the British Parliament, but they must first establish an extended colonial legislature because without that their agent in the House of Commons could do but little good. He for one warmly supported the creation of a committee, as the forerunner of that house of assembly on which he had set his heart ever since he returned to the colony in 1824. Every man who had a grain of public spirit in his composition would stand forward with his mite. He felt bound to be a liberal subscriber. There were many persons in the colony who were better qualified as to pecuniary means, but, humble as his resources were, he felt no hesitation in putting his name down for £50 a year.

The question was who would have the right to elect such a committee. Wentworth suggested all those who contributed £5 a year. Richard Hipkiss, one-time member of the Birmingham Political Union who had migrated to New South Wales in May of 1832, and a believer in self-help and self-improvement through co-operation, was known in the colony amongst the Botany Bay Tories as a leveller and a chartist. He thought £5 was too high, as it would tend to represent property alone. Intelligence also should be represented. Then Wentworth rose to his feet, and in a brief speech revealed at last where he stood on the question of who should exercise political power in New South Wales. He poured scorn on the suggestion of Hipkiss. As he saw it, the important measures which they had under consideration were more likely to be forwarded by the united talent and intelligence which property naturally combined with itself than by adopting a measure which would leave their council open to an undue proportion of colonists of humble talent and pretension, to the exclusion of men of education and local experience. He then turned characteristically to savage the Sheriff for being so lily-livered that he would not preside at a public meeting, so that the gulf between Wentworth and the Hipkiss supporters was closed over by his brilliant mockery and wit. He was now using in public the language of the Whigs, and dissociating himself from radicals, and those pro-convict groups who wanted to reduce the whole of society to one common level.[19]

On 10 June the subscribers to the establishment of a colonial political agency in London met at the Royal Hotel where, under the chairmanship of Sir John Jamison, a provisional committee of some sixty individuals was appointed. The following day at the first meeting of the provisional committee a correspon-

---

[19] *Sydney Herald*, 1 June 1835; for the beliefs of R. Hipkiss see Michael Roe, *Quest for Authority in Eastern Australia 1835-1851* (Melbourne, 1965), pp. 90-6, 187 and 194.

dence committee consisting of Wentworth, Henry Carmichael, Francis Stephen and Doctor Bland were appointed. When the provisional committee met again on 17 June they decided that the future name of the association should be the Australian Patriotic Association. At their next meeting on 8 July they got round to the question which would bedevil them all through their history, the election of a directing committee. In this debate on how that committee was to be elected that difference of opinion between Wentworth and Hipkiss, between the Whig view of political power as reflecting the interests of property, and the liberal view that political power should reflect intelligence and population, was once again to divide them. By December when the members had got round to drafting a constitution for New South Wales they were so divided on the qualification of electors that they were tempted to leave that space blank, and ask the British Parliament to fill it in. Bland wanted the most extensive franchise possible. Wentworth, sensing a ground-swell amongst his erstwhile supporters against his Whiggish principles, astutely suggested they should rely on the liberality of the members of the British Parliament, knowing full well that in that excellent club for the gentry and Mr Money-Bags, the interests of the men of property would not lack effective advocates.[20]

By that time Wentworth had moved further away from that section of the Australian Patriotic Association which was sympathetic to liberal principles and emancipist interests. When William Watt, a prisoner of the Crown holding a ticket-of-leave, who was known to the Tories as a perpetual firebrand, a degraded person who had been allowed to annoy men of standing because of Bourke's mistaken policy of lenity, had been charged in August with stealing a printed slip from the *Sydney Herald*, Wentworth had led the prosecution against Watt.[21] In September, when one of his convict servants whom he had charged with insolence to members of his family was sentenced to twenty-five lashes, Wentworth shouted at the Sydney bench of magistrates that this was but a mockery of punishment.[22] In the following month, when five of his convict servants at Vaucluse and some others had stolen his ketch and attempted to escape, he had told the bench he had no doubt the ringleader had planned to poison him as an act of revenge as six weeks earlier he had had the man flogged for drunkenness and intolerable insolence.[23]

So Bourke and Forbes celebrated knocking off the iron chains of the convicts in the second division of punishment as a great step forward; that young cub, Ullathorne shuddered whenever those scenes at Gallows Gate in that hell island of the Pacific haunted him; the *Herald* went on writing of the Female Factory as an emporium of vice, and the convict as disgusting and filthy trash; and Wentworth said not a word.[24] When the *Herald* wound up the year by asking their readers to say whether England was justified in persisting to deluge the colony with her criminals, once again the squire of Vau-

---

[20] *Report of the Provisional Committee of the Australian Patriotic Association*, p. 7 et seq.; *Sydney Herald*, 10 and 17 December 1835.

[21] *Sydney Herald*, 3, 7, 10, and 17 September 1835; in the issue of 17 September 1835, Watt had written a letter in which he had stated that his 'character was as good as yours'. The *Sydney Herald* referred to the 'feverish hand of that frenetic felon William Watt'; see also the letter of Watt to *The Times*, 1 September 1836. [22] *Sydney Herald*, 28 September 1835.

[23] Ibid., 2 November 1835. [24] Ibid., 5 October and 24 September 1835.

cluse said not a word. In such a change of face he was not alone. In that year Edward O'Shaughnessy, an Irish poet who had been transported in 1824 for offences probably committed while in liquor, and had written as an apologist for the emancipists, transferred to the *Sydney Herald* where he was soon denouncing 'convict trash' with all the gusto with which he had belaboured the Tories in his days on the *Sydney Gazette*. It was said in Sydney town that the proprietors of the *Sydney Herald* had paid his debts.[25]

The range of subjects that bothered men then, as ever, was immense. While Wentworth was concerned with political solutions to the problems of life, Broughton was telling Colonel Arthur in Van Diemen's Land that the Protestant character of his community would give it peculiar advantages above its neighbours. If the heart of any community was sound it would support the Church of England against popery, for the Church of England was, he believed, the only ark of refuge against the deluge of fanaticism and infidelity which was now pouring in upon their world. There was, he believed, no contending with the madness of the people. As for the people of Van Diemen's Land he had in his heart a sad foreboding about the effect popery would one day have on them.[26] At the same time J. Händt, who had been sent by the Church Missionary Society to bring the glad tidings of the gospel to the aborigines in the Wellington district, was bothered because aboriginal women who had been lent by their husbands to the white stockmen were dying in the full bloom of life from a loathsome disease. He wanted to know how he could handle a monster of iniquity who was living with three or four aboriginal girls of eight or nine years of age. Sickened by the moral wretchedness surrounding him, he sat down to tell his mentors in London how his spirit almost fainted in that inhospitable wilderness, wondering, as he did, how his Redeemer could be popular with such devoted servants of the prince of darkness.[27]

Bourke had quite different things on his mind. In politics he believed he was holding his own outside the Legislative Council against McLeay who was more silly than ever. He had been deeply pleased to hear of his creation as a Knight Commander of the Most Honourable Order of the Bath on 26 January of 1835. The country desperately needed rain. But soon after the rains came in October to refresh the grass a judge of the Supreme Court started a great commotion. Mr Justice Burton, who was endowed by nature with one of those temperaments which seeks to avoid the sound and the fury of life by being ingratiating to the men in black, and seeking not to provoke them to that derision or contempt they lacked the strength to endure, had surprised him by brewing a great political storm in the colony. William Westbrooke Burton, fifth son of a solicitor, had been born in England in 1794, had seen naval service during the Napoleonic Wars, and had been called to the bar

[25] Ibid., 31 December 1835; for E. O'Shaughnessy see *Australian Dictionary of Biography*, vol. 2; see ms. cat. under E. O'Shaughnessy in M.L.; see also *A Century of Journalism: The Sydney Morning Herald and its Record of Australian Life 1831-1931* (Sydney, 1931), *passim*.

[26] W. G. Broughton to Arthur, 27 July 1835 (Papers of Sir George Arthur, vol. 12, Letters from Bishop Broughton and from the Reverend S. Marsden).

[27] Journal of J. Händt, 28 May, 30 June and 6 October 1835; see also the letter of W. Watson to W. Jowett, Wellington Valley, 1837; (both ms. in archives of Church Missionary Society, London).

in 1824 in the days of peace. He had served with such distinction on the Supreme Court at the Cape of Good Hope that Bourke had warmly welcomed him when he arrived in Sydney in December of 1832 to take up his position on the bench of the Supreme Court of New South Wales. In private Burton was in sympathy with the Botany Bay Tories, and a believer in the social utility of religion, especially that Pauline charge to servants to obey their masters. Somewhat to the surprise of Bourke this timid man had addressed a petit jury, on discharging them from attendance at the close of the last criminal session of the Supreme Court for 1835, on the degraded state of the colony, as witnessed by the prevalence of crime and the immorality of the population. Masters of convicts were not sufficiently attentive to the morals of their men: overseers were careless: the men in road parties lived by plunder: improper persons held licences for public houses. The grand cause of all this profligacy and crime was an overwhelming defect of religious principle, the polar star to guide a man in all his conduct. So lamentable a circumstance must seriously retard the establishing, in the colony, of those free institutions which were the pride and the boast of the parent country.[28]

Bourke construed his remarks as an insinuation that his government was not employing due means for the punishment and prevention of crime. So did sections of the public press. The *Herald* used the judge's remarks as proof of their contention that the policy of leniency had deluged New South Wales with crime, and needled Bourke by holding him up to public contempt as the leader of what they wantonly described as the 'court and convict faction'.[29] Despite protestations by Burton that he had not sought to muddy the waters of party controversy, that his concern had been with the higher matters of law and order, and eternal salvation, and leading men to that polar star of religion, the party opposed to Bourke snatched greedily at the prize he had thrown into their lap with such pomp and yet with such innocence. Hall published the charge in full in the *Monitor* on 21 November.[30]

Behind Hall in the *Monitor* Bourke knew, and so did all the political gossips and pundits of Parramatta and Sydney town, there lurked the figure of Mudie of Hole and Corner fame. Bourke knew too that Mudie was friendly with those members of the Legislative Council who had opposed all his measures for liberal reform. Mudie was probably in collusion with McLeay, who was in politics a bosom crony of Riddell, the Colonial Treasurer—the Frondeur of the Government, as Bourke called him. When Roger Therry put himself forward as a candidate for election as Chairman of the Quarter Sessions, these persons of wealth, and some of the magistrates who had shown themselves hostile to Bourke's administration, promptly turned the election into a party issue and put forward Riddell as their candidate. Bourke, after an exchange of letters, sent for him and told him he had decided that he could no longer place

---

[28] Bourke to his son, 19 July, 13 August, 12 September and 24 October 1835 (Bourke Papers, vol. 6); *H.R.A.*, I. xvii. 785; Bourke to Glenelg, 18 December 1835, *H.R.A.*, I. xviii. 228-32; for the text of this charge to the jury see James Macarthur (ed.), *New South Wales: its present State and future Prospects* (London, 1837), Appendix 3; see also K. G. Allars, 'Sir William Westbrooke Burton', R.A.H.S., *J. & P.*, vol. 37, 1950-1, pp. 257-94; Deas Thomson Papers (MS. in M.L.). [29] *Sydney Herald*, 4 February 1836.

[30] *Monitor*, 21 November 1835; see also James Macarthur (ed.), op. cit., pp. 34-44.

any confidence in the sincerity of his intentions or his advice. He had, therefore, decided to suspend him as an executive councillor. That was in December. In the same month he wrote to London requesting that, as he could
no longer with due regard for His Majesty's service and his own honour sit in
the Executive Council with Mr Riddell, if contrary to his expectation His
Majesty restored Mr Riddell to that body then he, Bourke, might receive
His Majesty's gracious permission to return immediately to Europe.[31]

As soon as the news spread round Sydney town, the *Sydney Herald* immediately sharpened up its language against the 'court and convict faction'.
The *Monitor*, having degenerated in the eyes of the liberals and the emancipists into the role of paid hireling of the Hole and Corner men, sneered at
Bourke as a defender of publicans and sinners.[32] With such ridicule and
mockery ringing in his ears Bourke began to see more and more of Wentworth. In January of 1836 he finally commissioned Wentworth as a justice of
the peace. Again the *Herald*, with a singular blindness to the true affections of
Wentworth's heart, and a total ignorance of that Fitzwilliam interest and
background which had always driven Wentworth to seek the society and
esteem of the landed gentry, wrote of this as pandering to the mob. The news
from London that January had contained at least one item that was not
pleasing to Wentworth. On 30 July 1835 Maurice O'Connell, anxious to
expose the savagery and cruelty of the English governing classes, had moved
for a select committee to inquire into the conduct of General Darling while
Governor of New South Wales, particularly with reference to the grant of
Crown lands made by him, his treatment of the public press, the case of
Captain Robison and the New South Wales veteran companies, and the alleged
instances of cruelty towards the soldiers Sudds and Thompson and other free
persons. The committee reported Darling to be entirely free from blame and
that he had done nothing inconsistent with his duty as a public functionary, or
with his honour as an officer and a gentleman. Eliza Darling was delighted
that her General had had a fair inquiry. Critical though she was of Bourke and
that odious Wentworth, she was most anxious that her dear brother Henry
Dumaresq should remember his duty to reverence the powers that be, and
refrain from writing anything against the Governor. For herself she was
delighted to say the King had shown his appreciation of her General by
conferring on him the title of Knight Grand Cross of the Royal Hanoverian
Guelphic Order on 2 September, a day after the committee had announced its
report. Back in Sydney a group of Darling's supporters came together to con-
gratulate him on being set at rest forever from his persecutors who had so
pertinaciously and unjustly assailed him.[33]

[31] Bourke to Glenelg, 2 December 1835, and Encls, *H.R.A.*, I. xviii. 216-17; Bourke to
Glenelg, 2 December 1835, ibid., 223-4; R. Bourke to his son, 7 November and 30 November
1835 (Bourke Papers, vol. 6).

[32] *Sydney Herald*, 4 February 1836; *Monitor, passim*, February and March 1836.

[33] R. Bourke to his son, 17 January 1836 (Bourke Papers, vol. 6); *New South Wales Government Gazette*, 6 January 1836; *Sydney Herald*, 11 February 1836; Letters relative to the punishment and death of Joseph Sudds, also portions of Mr Wentworth's letter of impeachment omitted
in former returns, *P.P.*, 1831-2, XXXII, 620; Report of the Select Committee to inquire into
the conduct of General Darling, *P.P.*, 1835, VI, 580; Robison Papers (MS. in M.L.); *P.D.*, 3rd
series, vol. 29, p. 1254, and the debate on 10 September of 1835 in vol. 30; The Address of the

Bourke, never a man to waver when the Tories rocked his little world, went on to rescue this man of large possessions and acknowledged ability from official neglect and contumely. He knew Wentworth as a man who had uniformly expressed his full confidence in his own administration. He believed Wentworth's support to be valuable because of his influence on a large body of wealthy people. He had only placed him in a position to which his large possessions and acknowledged ability entitled him. Wentworth, Bourke knew, was then buying the estates of Windermere and Luskinyre in the Hunter District. And Wentworth, he knew, was opposed in party and personality to McLeay, who had no doubt represented him as ill-disposed. Such was not the case. For his part he enjoyed the company of this supporter of a liberal government. That was why he had called on Wentworth at Vaucluse, to the alarm of the editor of the *Sydney Herald* who wanted to see something sinister in two Irishmen, both belonging by birth to families of ancient lineage, and sharing a common political creed, sipping a friendly cup of tea beside the placid waters of Sydney Harbour.[34]

For the new commission of the peace contained more than a friendly bow towards the master of Vaucluse. It contained a stern rebuke to all those magistrates who had actively opposed Bourke's administration. The names of Bingle, Mudie, Lamb, and others were dropped from the list. Bourke had acted because these men had used the seat of justice to display factious feeling against the government as well as what he called other improper conduct.[35] Riddell was suspended, the Hole and Corner magistrates had been dropped, Bulwer was representing the Patriots in London, and Wentworth, rather than Berry, Jones, Robert Campbell, Blaxland, or James Macarthur, had the ear of Bourke. The Tories of Botany Bay needed to act quickly if they were to have any say in drafting the future constitution of New South Wales.

In March Richard Jones, a member of the Legislative Council, one-time merchant, and now very much Mr Broadacres of the Hunter River Tories, but not a stooper to the ways of the mocker, the slanderer, or the overstater, invited members of Council, magistrates, clergy, landholders, merchants and other free inhabitants of like mind to his town house in Sydney to discuss what ought to be done. The hotheads Mudie and Bingle turned up: so did men such as Robert Campbell, who in a charming old-fashioned way went on believing that *the* question in the politics of New South Wales was how to prevent the members of one's family being obliged to rub shoulders with the descendants of convicts. So did James Macarthur, who deplored all violent and intemperate language, and wanted power to be exercised by the gentle spirits amongst the landed gentry, a race of men as rare in New South Wales as green grass in summer.[36]

undersigned civil officers, magistrates, landholders, merchants, and other free inhabitants of the colony of New South Wales to Lieutenant General Sir Ralph Darling, 23 January 1836, *Colonist*, 11 May 1837; H. Dumaresq to Edward and Fanny Dumaresq, 22 January 1836 (Dumaresq Papers); Eliza Darling to her daughter Cornelia, 7 August 1835, ibid.

[34] R. Bourke to his son, 17 January and 1 March 1836 (Bourke Papers, vol. 6); *Sydney Herald*, 11 February and 3 March 1836; *Sydney Gazette*, 7 May 1836.

[35] *New South Wales Government Gazette*, 6 January 1836; Bourke to Glenelg, 24 January 1836, *H.R.A.*, I. xviii. 264-5.   [36] Bourke to Glenelg, 13 April 1836, *H.R.A.*, I. xviii. 391-2.

From the discussion in the house of Richard Jones two petitions emerged. In the first of these, which was addressed to the King, they submitted that the flourishing condition of affairs in New South Wales was unhappily counterbalanced by a lamentable depravity of manners, and by the fearful prevalence of crime, caused partly by insufficient police, partly by the relaxation of convict discipline, and partly by the inadequacy of means of religious and moral instruction, and more than all from the continued influx of transported criminals. For their part they looked forward to that day when they received the inestimable boon of free institutions in the stainless lustre of their constitutional purity, and transmitted them to their children, but they wanted a rational and well-founded freedom quite distinct from the disorganizing doctrines which under the name of liberty would subvert the landmarks of social order, and, confounding all just distinctions, sap the foundations of society. They drew up a petition in similar terms to the House of Commons, in which they pressed the House to appoint a committee to inquire whether the transportation system should be continued, the capabilities of the colony as a free settlement, and how far it would be wise to change the constitution of the Legislative Council.[37]

On 2 April the *Sydney Herald* published the text of the two petitions in their advertisement columns, and called for signatures. Immediately anger and uproar broke out in Sydney and Parramatta, amongst the native-born, the emancipists, liberals, and all those common people not distinguished for their wealth or their pretensions, who bitterly resented the Tory insult to their reputations and their honour.[38] The *Sydney Gazette* wrote with restraint of the most mischievous tendency of the petitions.[39] It was this note of 'I am not worthy yet, my Lord' which stung many into bewildered anger, and gave them that sense of being insulted and mocked by men who had added offence to injury by electing themselves as the defenders of order and morality. To add further insult the *Sydney Herald* dismissed such a reaction as 'the alarm of the UNWASHED'.[40] With rumours flying round Sydney that James Macarthur and Mudie were planning to sail for London to lobby for the old order, and that Forbes was also sailing, though everyone knew he was a sick man, and, so the uncharitable whispered, much keener on getting a knighthood for himself than getting the inestimable boon of constitutional purity out of those men dressed in black in Whitehall, the opponents of the *Sydney Herald* petitions decided to take action.

On 29 March 1836 Sir John Jamison, Wentworth, Sydney Stephen, Dr Bland and eight others announced there would be a public meeting at the Royal Hotel on 12 April to consider the two petitions drafted in Richard Jones' house. Among the crowd spilling over into the streets were those who had come for the high-minded purpose of putting down on paper their ideas on the future of New South Wales, those who had come to vindicate their name and honour against the insults by the Botany Bay Tories, and those who had come to enjoy a display of colonial back-bite and slander. All had their satisfaction

---

[37] For the text of this petition, see Encl. A.1 in Bourke to Glenelg, 13 April 1836, *H.R.A.*, I. xviii. 392-5; for the text of the similar petition to the House of Commons see Encl. A.2 in ibid., 395-9.
[38] *Sydney Herald*, 2 April 1836.
[39] *Sydney Gazette*, 2 April 1836.
[40] *Sydney Herald*, 28 April 1836.

on that day. They began by voting the veteran Sir John Jamison into the chair, who, after declaring the meeting open for free discussion, called for calmness and gentlemanly demeanour, and mentioned his wish that speakers should be encouraged to express their opinions freely, but temperately, for, after all, they were driven by their circumstances into the role of defenders of freedom, as well as being put on trial by their rivals for behaviour worthy of free men.

Then Wentworth rose to his feet. It was a more mature, a more secure Wentworth, a man who had achieved at last a measure of the recognition he craved. He began by telling them he agreed with parts of the *Herald* petitions. He agreed, for example, that the land fund should be appropriated for the purposes of immigration. He did not agree with their acceptance of the Burton charge to the jury on the increase in crime, and proceeded to a lengthy, indeed long-winded, though restrained, refutation of that charge. Then he began to warm up. He rejected their proposal for a Legislative Council nominated in Downing Street. What an excellent plum pudding this would be for them—a sirloin of beef from which they could cut and come again almost to eternity. He then turned to a defence of Bourke, the head of a government which had invaded no man's property, violated no man's liberty, and wantonly sacrificed no man's life. Then he let slip his pride in Bourke—'We've now got a Whig governor', he shouted, 'and being myself a Whig', he went on, 'I am well pleased'. Darling, he added, was a Tory: Bourke was a Whig. 'Show Whitehall', he cried, left hand on hip, and with that characteristic sweep of the right hand, as though he were defying the world, and with the eye no longer of the angry man, but rather of the man who had began to view the human comedy with disdain, if not with contempt, 'show Whitehall', he shouted, 'that you know the difference between a Titus and a Nero'. In his moment of triumph he was making it plain for all who had ears to hear, that if he were to draft the constitution of New South Wales, then it would be a constitution based on the Whig principle that political power should be exercised by those with some stake in the country.[41]

He went on to move the adoption of a counter-petition, which asserted that the only safe and effective remedy for the admitted defects of the present Legislative Council was in the establishment of a representative legislature upon a wide and liberal basis. It went on to refute in detail the charge about the alarming increase of crime, about the general want of discipline among the convicts, and the inefficiency of transportation as a means of secondary punishment. All these charges had been grossly exaggerated. It went on to record an entire and cordial approval of the wise, disinterested, liberal, just, paternal and constitutional policy which had marked the government of Bourke. As for the other petitions they were got up by a small illiberal party, who wanted to induce His Majesty further to delay the granting of free institutions. They were a factious oligarchy who trusted in their secret influence in the mother country to acquire that undisputed preponderance which would place at their disposal the whole power and revenue of the colony. The petition therefore humbly prayed that the honourable House of Commons, on the expiration of

[41] *Australian*, 15 April 1836.

the present Act providing for the government of the colony, would be pleased to address His Majesty for a representative assembly upon a wide and liberal basis.[42]

Outside the public meeting men shook their heads, or snorted in disgust, or went about their business indifferent to the fate of victors and losers in the lottery of politics. The *Sydney Herald* sneered at what they called this howling violence of patriotic rage. They wrote in a language of near hysteria about the rabble opposition, blind to what was plain by then for all to see—that the leaders of both groups had at least one thing in common—a determination to keep the rabble out of politics. The *Sydney Herald* wrote more in sorrow than in anger that Wentworth wanted to be the idol of the Jew pedlars of Sydney, that he was attempting to influence the British Parliament with the signatures of transported Jews, keepers of public houses in Botany Bay, and the felonious frequenters of the tap-rooms. The 'native champion', they prophesied, would soon be more closely viewed, and what folly had mistaken for a comet, inquiry would find to be only a meteor formed by vapours of putrefying democracy, which would plunge their followers into a bog. His day, they concluded, had gone by. This, they predicted, would be the Patriot's last speech.[43] The *Sydney Gazette* also had its misgivings about Wentworth. Why must he go on, they asked, reiterating the charge that Darling was a murderer and a tyrant? What dark, subterranean passions drove him on to seek satisfaction in such savagery? It was neither commonly tolerable, commonly rational, nor commonly decent. Yet, they added ruefully, more in sorrow than in anger, for such arrant foolery Mr Wentworth had been applauded. They did not go on to ask whether this reflected just on his supporters or on mankind in general.[44]

At that time they were all caught up in the sound and fury of the day. Even Bourke, sheltering from the buffets of those gales of public ridicule behind the walls of Government House, sat down to write to his son in England, and told him of the scheme of the Botany Bay Tories to keep up the old Council, and how they, the Tories, were vilifying the country generally so that they might pose as the only honest men in it. As for Wentworth, he had made a very able speech, which, he must admit, might have been even better with less vituperation. But the point was, the friends of a liberal system of government had at last spoken out, and he for one was deeply pleased.[45]

Stung to further demonstrations of their sentiments by the sneers, the ridicule, and the insults in the *Sydney Herald* the supporters of the Royal Hotel petition gathered to say farewell to Forbes. In April the barristers of New South Wales and the proprietors of Sydney College had fulsomely praised him at farewell functions.[46] Still the *Sydney Herald* was not impressed. To them Forbes was a vain man who, under the garb of a professed love of humanity and hatred of oppression, had propagated in New South Wales the

---

[42] For the text of the petition see Encl.B. in Bourke to Glenelg, 13 April 1836, *H.R.A.*, I. xviii. 399-403.

[43] *Sydney Herald*, 18 April and 5 May 1836.   [44] *Sydney Gazette*, 14 April 1836.

[45] R. Bourke to his son, 2 and 15 April 1836 (Bourke Papers, vol. 6).

[46] Address from New South Wales barristers on his departure for England, April 1836 (Forbes Papers); Address from the proprietors of Sydney College, ibid., p. 133.

pestiferous doctrine of the equality of all men. He was a man who would pander to the mob to earn that flattery of his vanity which was the very staff of life to him. On 16 April a crowd gathered at the racecourse to present Forbes with a farewell address. A camera obscura was advertised at sixpence a peep; free beer was distributed to all and sundry, and a huge mob sent forth clouds of smoke from their short pipes. Despite the number of black-guards who wandered about on the fringe of the crowd, a strict decorum pre-vailed. Mr Thomas Stubbs read the address to Forbes who replied with feelings of respect and thankfulness.

When Forbes sailed at last on 21 April the road gangs, gaol gangs and iron-gang men swelled the cheers of the respectable men who gathered at Sydney Harbour to wish him God-speed. Forbes, according to the *Sydney Herald*, had sailed out on the high seas cheered by convict clamour, and a host of transported Jews, but they added, those immigrants who wished to protect their families from convict contamination would go down on their knees that night, and pray that Forbes might at long last throw overboard the principles of his convict friends, and not play the role of apologist for the unwashed in the corridors of power in London. They were not to know then that Forbes carried with him a letter from Bourke recommending him for a knighthood. And who could ever know what went on in the heart of that judge as he stood at the rail of the ship, the roars of popular approval were ringing in his ears, and voices calling out to him their gratitude because he had delivered men from their chains, freed the press, and laboured long for the coming of free institutions; yet he also carried in his papers that letter which might set the seal on his life's ambition, and at the same time he had unmistakable intima-tions that his life was drawing to a close, and with them a quite new sensation, the thought perhaps he should now prepare for another prize—the prize of life everlasting.[47]

In the meantime both the Botany Bay Tories and the Botany Bay Whigs began to collect signatures for their respective petitions. The *Sydney Herald* urged all the respectable, all the men of property, and all free immigrants to affix their signatures to the two petitions in their office. A committee consisting of Jamison, Wentworth, Blaxland, Lawson, Dutton, Bland and the two Coxes, Major Druitt, S. Stephen and others—all good Whigs, and no supporters of the old convict party—was appointed to collect signatures for the opposition petition. They went for numbers as well as property and respectability. And when one paper urged the publicans of Sydney to show their gratitude to Bourke by collecting signatures, the *Herald* wrote gleefully that this was appropriate because, after all, the opposition petition was the work of people with the mind and values of publicans.[48] By July the *Herald* petitions had collected four hundred signatures: the counter-petition had collected nearly six thousand. In that month Bourke forwarded the copies of all three to London with the simple statement that the counter-petition must be declared to speak the sentiments of the people of New South Wales, adding it was clear

---

[47] Based on *Sydney Herald*, 11, 18, 21, and 28 April 1836; for Bourke's letter on the knight-hood, see R. Bourke to his son, 2 April 1836 (Bourke Papers, vol. 6).
[48] *Sydney Herald*, 15 April 1836.

that a vast majority of the colonists, capable of forming sound opinions, desired the establishment of trial by jury and a legislature either wholly or in part representative. Privately, Bourke let his family know that the proposals had his concurrence. For his part he rejoiced that the friends of a liberal system of government had at last spoken out.[49]

James Macarthur went on board the *Abel Gower* to sail for London in the same month, taking with him the originals of the two *Herald* petitions. He did not see it in the same light as Bourke—for him it was not a question of numbers, but rather of what the men of property thought. He boarded the ship and sailed out on to the high seas firm in his faith that Whitehall would uphold the select few against the many. Those men in London who made the decision would pay more attention to the representations of a moderate number of the wealth, respectability and intelligence of the colony than to the representations of a convict rabble. The *Sydney Herald* thought it would be a pretty thing if he were to entertain the House of Commons with a full and true account of the life and adventures of some of the 'patriots'.[50] They were not to know that the man in whom they had put their trust was not capable of puddling in those muddy waters of colonial back-bite and scandal. He had the milk of human kindness. He was a gentleman who built an absolute trust in other men; he was both blessed and cursed with the innocent man's unwillingness to believe that the imagination of the hearts of some men was evil from the start. Bourke, with whom he had much in common, apart from the great difference in political opinions, wrote to his son in London that even though Macarthur was a Tory, he was not violent in his politics. He was happy to say the two of them had always been on the best of terms and had insisted that all words of abuse should be removed from the Tory or *Herald* petitions.[51]

James Mudie had also left at the end of March, to present extravagantly and wantonly his denunciation of that wicked and adulterous generation in New South Wales, taking with him a swag of testimonials from those who had responded to his own pathetic requests for character sketches with which to impress the discerning Stephen and the indifferent Glenelg. He hoped that at least in London he would not be hooted and assailed on the streets as he had been many times and oft in Sydney town by the supporters of Bourke. Forbes had sailed in April, the mental strain through which he had passed leaving him desperately in need of freedom from work and worry. The uncharitable said his real concern was not his own health but the health of the colonial government, and others, with even less charity, said he wanted to make that knighthood a certainty.[52] Lang boarded the *Abel Gower* with James Macarthur, believing that the welfare of the Presbyterian Church required him to take another voyage to England, but with one eye firmly fixed on Whitehall and the impending inquiry into the future of transportation. Lang, too, had his own

[49] Bourke to Glenelg, 25 July 1836, *H.R.A.*, I. xviii. 456-7; R. Bourke to his son, 2 and 15 April 1836 (Bourke Papers, vol. 6).   [50] *Sydney Herald*, 22 August 1836.

[51] Ibid., 25 April 1836, Compliments to James Macarthur at the St George's Day dinner in Sydney; W. Shakespeare, *Macbeth*, I. iv. 12-14; R. Bourke to his son, 21 July 1836 (Bourke Papers, vol. 6).

[52] J. Mudie to Glenelg, 1 February 1837, C.O. 201/267, pp. 551-4; James Mudie, *The Felonry of New South Wales*, ed. by W. Stone (Melbourne, 1964), p. x.

source of confidence. That May he had written to his mother that divine providence had chosen him to preserve New South Wales for the things of
Jesus Christ, just as earlier divine providence had chosen Paul for work in
Asia. Just before boarding the ship, again like the apostle, he had with all his
moral ferocity chastised his fellow clergy for adultery and drunkenness. Lang
was never a man to heed that warning about casting the first stone. As ever he
thrived in a time of 'dark nights and stormy seas'. Ever since the beginning of
1835 he had been using mediums other than the pulpit and the pamphlet
with which to address the people of New South Wales. On 1 January of that
year he had begun to publish the newspaper the *Colonist*. Of the two persons
that lived in Lang—the millenarian who looked to the day which he expected
to come quite quickly when men would neither hurt nor destroy in God's holy
mountain, and the controversialist who was inwardly a ravening wolf, the
latter seemed to pervade his newspaper. For despite his professed intention to
diffuse useful knowledge, and inculcate right principles in regard to the means
of promoting the moral welfare and the general advancement of the colony
of New South Wales, and despite his professions of faith to God's people each
Sunday at Scots Church, there was no hint in his newspaper of the spirit of his
divine master who had once walked beside the waters of Galilee, plucking the
ears of corn, and asking his disciples to consider the lilies of the field. Week in,
week out, Lang had savaged his rivals in the convict-dominated *Sydney Gazette*
as levellers and men who wanted an early escape from the convict taint. In
1836 he began with a most unseemly relish to chastise all God's children who
had strayed from His ways like lost sheep.[53]

Then in June William Bernard Ullathorne, after a trip to Van Diemen's
Land which only served to convince him that more men were required to tend
Christ's vineyard in Australia, and still haunted by that ghastly experience in
Norfolk Island, boarded the *Eldon* in Hobart Town and sailed for London.
He was looking for priests, but wanting too to say his big thing about that
nation of crime where men stole, murdered, committed adultery, and swore
falsely. Somewhat to his mortification *ego solus* found himself sailing those
seas for the greater glory of his God in a heavy tub, with an uncultured
captain.[54]

At the same time life went on in Sydney, Parramatta, Windsor, and the
outlying districts of New South Wales. Women gathered for their never
ending clatter-clatter in the streets of Sydney. Convicts who broke the laws of
God or the laws of man, men and women who sought a temporary relief
from their sufferings in drink, or in each other's arms, were held up to public
ridicule. The *Sydney Herald* told the story of a man who made his child aged
two intoxicated with gin, and then sat down to enjoy the convulsions from
which the child suffered. On the same day they described the great solemnity
which pervaded the singing of high mass at St Mary's Cathedral. So while one

[53] J. D. Lang to his mother, sister and brother, 16 May 1836, quoted in *John Dunmore Lang:
Chiefly Autobiographical* ed. by A. Gilchrist (2 vols, Melbourne, 1951), vol. 1, pp. 216-17;
Colonist, 21 April, 19 and 26 May 1836; see also *Colonist*, 1 January 1835 and 1835 *passim*.
[54] W. B. Ullathorne, *Autobiography* (London, n.d. probably 1891-2), pp. 116-17; *Hobart Town
Courier*, 20 May and 10 June 1836; Bourke to Glenelg, 24 July 1836, *H.R.A.*, I. xviii. 453.

man tortured a little child, others asked Christ to take pity on all men.[55] There were those moments of grief, which prompted some to cut into stone a statement of the faith by which they lived, so that posterity would know their great comforters. When the vicar of St James's Church, the Reverend Mr Hill, suddenly died in May, the parishioners placed on the walls of that church a tablet to his memory in which they praised him for imbuing the young with a deep reverence for the words of everlasting salvation. When the Reverend Samuel Marsden heard the news of the death of Mr Hill he wrote off to London: 'The death of the revd. Mr Hill was almost too much for me. I am not now so strong in Body or in mind as I was formerly.'[56]

While the factions and groups in New South Wales were contending for the prizes of this world, the Secretary of State was making up his mind on questions affecting their spiritual welfare. In November of the previous year he had accepted Bourke's suggestion that the archdeaconry of New South Wales should be erected into a bishropric. The zeal and energy displayed by Mr Broughton as archdeacon, and the strong interest he had taken in the spiritual welfare of the colony, had pointed him out as the fittest person to be invested with the episcopal office.[57] So in an impressive ceremony at Lambeth Palace chapel on 14 February 1836 the bishops of London, Winchester and Gloucester presented William Grant Broughton to the Archbishop of Canterbury, as this godly and well-learned man to be ordained and consecrated Bishop of Australia. Broughton vowed that day that he would show himself gentle and be merciful for Christ's sake to poor and needy people, and to all strangers destitute of help.[58]

All through February Broughton had taken up with Glenelg in London the things closest to his heart. He was worried, he told him, whether his insurance policies would cover the new boundaries of his diocese: he was worried by the number of people growing up in Australia strangers to the message of salvation: he was troubled by the extent of responsibility he would incur before God if he were to fail to plant some seed in such barren soil. For, like all the other faithful members of Christ's church, he was concerned with both God and Mammon: concerned with the pomps and vanities of his position as Christ's representative on earth, as well as with that hard saying that the meek would be comforted, the mourners, those who were sorry for what had happened at Calvary, would be rewarded, and the mockers condemned to everlasting fire, that those who sold all they had and gave to the poor would enter into that other kingdom he so passionately coveted. For Broughton suffered all his life from the pangs of one aspect of the vice of avarice—the avarice of seeking a heavenly reward for choosing the path of virtue.[59]

When he arrived back in the colony he was met at the landing stage on 4

---

[55] *Sydney Herald*, 5 April 1836.

[56] Tablet for the Reverend Mr Hill in St James's Church, 30 May 1836; S. Marsden to D. Coates, 3 August 1837 (Bonwick Transcripts, Missionary, vol. 6, p. 1885).

[57] Glenelg to Bourke, 30 November 1836, *H.R.A.*, I. xviii. 204.

[58] F. T. Whitington, *William Grant Broughton, Bishop of Australia* (Sydney, 1936), pp. 63-5; The Form of Ordaining or Consecrating of an Archbishop or Bishop, *Book of Common Prayer*.

[59] See W. G. Broughton to Glenelg, 20 February 1836, Encl. in Glenelg to Bourke, 12 May 1836, *H.R.A.*, I. xviii. 419-21.

June not by the poor and the needy and all strangers destitute of help, to whom he had solemnly vowed to show himself gentle and merciful for Christ's sake, but by the high and mighty in the society of New South Wales—the acting Chief Justice, the Colonial Secretary, the assistant judges, the Colonial Treasurer, and some members of the Legislative Council. They greeted him as a man who would uphold in the colony those sacred principles to which England owed under providence the pure and devoted tone of her morality, her civil freedom, her domestic peace, and her pre-eminence among the nations of the earth. They hailed his lordship with confidence as a man sent by God to ensure that their own community might ever reflect the brightest features of that favoured people from whom they had sprung.[60] For it was not given to the exclusives at that time to dream the dream of a vigorous culture created by the native-born.

Outside that tiny group of men before whose eyes there floated a vision of recreating in Australia the English society of squire and parson, other voices were being heard in the colony of New South Wales. Within a week or so of the return of Broughton some were saying that freedom's battle against the swaddling bands of political and religious orthodoxy was being won.[61] Two days before the defenders of the old order had hailed Broughton as God's gift to the gentry of New South Wales Bourke had unfolded to the Legislative Council his dream for the future of that society. He had told them how it was fitting that in the wake of her ever-increasing prosperity her children should not only justly claim to participate in British institutions, but should satisfy their desire for knowledge. To encourage and satisfy that prevailing desire of obtaining knowledge, and to extend the blessings of wholesome education to the poorer classes of society, it was necessary, he told the members of the Council, to introduce a system of general instruction for the people of the colony.[62]

By one of those odd ironies in human affairs, while Broughton was making his long journey over the oceans, driven on by the vain hope of rescuing generations unborn from the evils of unbelief by nurturing them in the wholesome teachings of the Church of England, another ship, the *Henry Tanner*, had sailed over the oceans bearing a despatch from Glenelg in which he had written in his prayer-book prose the death-knell to an Anglican-dominated education system in New South Wales. He reminded Bourke that in no part of the world was education a more sacred and necessary duty of the government than in New South Wales. He reminded him, too, of the effect of education on higher interests, on good order and social improvement, and how it elevated the human character, and offered the firmest obstacle to crime and immorality. The only question was that of the most effective mode of attaining that end. He had decided to commit to the Governor and the Legislative Council the task of suggesting and enacting such laws and regulations for the distribution and appropriation of the funds applicable to the general purposes of religion and

[60] Address to the Lord Bishop of Australia by Members of Council, Clergymen, Civil Officers, Magistrates, and other Free Inhabitants of New South Wales, 4 June 1836, *Sydney Herald*, 13 June 1836.   [61] *Sydney Herald*, 16 June 1836.
[62] *V. & P.* (L.C. N.S.W.) 2 June 1836.

education. He went on to propose that some plan should be adopted for the establishment of schools for the general education of youth in the colony, unconnected with any particular church or denomination of Christians, in which children of every religious persuasion might receive instruction.[63]

On 25 July Bourke formally moved in the Legislative Council that a sum of £3,000 be appropriated towards establishing National schools, similar to those in the Irish system of education. In 1833 Bourke had first set out what he hoped to achieve in education. He proposed two things. Believing that in a new country in which there were persons of all religious persuasions it was impossible to establish a dominant and endowed church without much hostility, and believing that the inclination of the colonists, which was keeping pace with the spirit of the age, was decidedly adverse to such an institution, he was suggesting that support should be given to the three great divisions of Christianity—the Anglicans, the Catholics and the Presbyterians. Believing also that in a thinly scattered population it would be foolish to have a multiplicity of schools he suggested government should create National schools for the general education of colonial youth after the manner of the Irish schools which had been established in that country by Stanley when he was Chief Secretary for Ireland in 1831. In such schools the children would have their religion in text books which were Christian in context but free of dogma.[64]

Ever since Bourke had spoken with both charity and the tongue of an angel on the education question the *Sydney Herald* had kept up a running fire of criticism—'Being Englishmen', they wrote early in July, 'we do not like the name Irish system of education . . . [we] also have an objection to theoretic governors, and lawless Irish convicts'. Then they let slip their real objection to the proposal. The children of the respectable, they thundered, should not have to associate at school with those who would corrupt and destroy their morals. They wound up with the traditional sectarian argument that the Protestant creed must be presented in the schools.[65]

Broughton, too, took fright, being fearful that the bill would prevent the education of Anglicans in the principles of their distinct polity. That was in the middle of July 1836.[66] By the end of the month darker fears overwhelmed him: he began to be afraid that the whole Protestant position was endangered —that that great blessing of the Protestant ascendancy, which, in his mind, was the origin both of their liberty and their pre-eminence, was in mortal danger. On 22 July he formally asked permission to be heard by the Legislative Council as he entertained conscientious objections to the principle upon which it was proposed to impart religious instruction to the children frequenting such schools. In a petition of protest of 25 July he wrote rather wildly that the necessary effect of the system would be to dash the Bible out of the hands of the people, and to place it again under lock and key. He went on to beg the Council in the sight of God not to sanction a measure so fraught with danger, and even with

[63] Glenelg to Bourke, 30 November 1835, *H.R.A.*, I. xviii. 201-7.
[64] *V. & P.* (L.C. N.S.W.) 25 July 1836; Bourke to Stanley, 30 September 1833, *H.R.A.*, I. xviii. 466-70; A. G. Austin, *Australian Education, 1788-1900* (Melbourne, 1961), pp. 32-3.
[65] *Sydney Herald*, 4 July 1836.
[66] W. G. Broughton to Bourke, 13 July 1836 (Broughton Correspondence, MS. in M.L.).

certain destruction to the prevalence and salutary influence of the reformed religion.[67]

Then on 3 August he agreed to address a meeting summoned by a committee of Protestants to protest against the National schools. On that night, to roars of applause from those Baptists, Presbyterians, Methodists, Congregationalists and Jews whom in calmer moments he had denounced as wreckers of that order and stability in which he so passionately believed, Broughton shouted that Protestantism rested upon the principle that holy scripture contained all things necessary to salvation: that the use of it should be free to every man who had a soul to be saved: that if they yielded to an interdict upon the use of the scriptures in one place, the same power might one day prohibit the free use of them at any time and in all places. The Roman Catholics supported the bill: the Protestants opposed it. In the heat and passion of the moment Broughton was inflaming sectarian sentiment against Bourke.[68]

The *Monitor* wrote that this would prove the beginning in the colony of the dreadful pestilence of Orangeism. They castigated Broughton for his bigotry and accused him of kindling the flames of religious fanaticism and persecution. Broughton, who had entertained the vision of a bishop presiding over a church both catholic and universal, was degraded in the eyes of some to the role of a tout for the men of the Orange Lodge.[69] Early in August one of his clergy, the Reverend Mr Rusden, his face clouded by that great Protestant source of darkness, that terror of the whore of Babylon, stood outside his church one Sunday morning not long after he had spoken those words of comfort about all those who were in love and fellowship with their neighbour, and told the convicts, as they filed past, that the Catholics were about to take over the land, and that none of them should leave the church grounds until they had signed the Protestant petition against National schools drawn up at the meeting of 3 August.[70]

The petitioners agreed with Bourke that the colony needed schools which would inculcate in the rising generation sound principles of religion and morality, together with such useful knowledge as would best qualify them to discharge the duties of life. They urged him to follow the wise and benevolent principle of allowing to each of the three leading branches of the Christian faith a sum from the public revenue for the purpose of education. In Ireland the Catholics were in the majority: in New South Wales the Protestants were in the majority. Besides, they asserted, the greater proportion of the free inhabitants opposed the introduction of the Irish system.[71]

[67] Petition by W. G. Broughton to the Legislative Council of New South Wales, 22 July 1836, *Sydney Herald*, 28 July 1836; The Humble Petition of William Grant Broughton, Doctor in Divinity, Bishop and Ordinary Pastor in the Diocese of Australia, 25 July 1836, *Sydney Herald*, 4 August 1836.

[68] W. G. Broughton, *A Speech delivered at the General Committee of Protestants, on Wednesday, August 3, 1836* (Sydney, 1836).

[69] See the *Monitor*, August, September and October 1836.

[70] P. L. Campbell to Colonial Secretary, 3 September 1836, Encl. in Bourke to Glenelg, 7 October 1836, *H.R.A.*, I. xviii. 566-8.

[71] The Petition of the Undersigned Inhabitants of the Colony to His Excellency the Governor and the Honorable the Legislative Council of New South Wales, August 1836, Sub.Encl. in Bourke to Glenelg, 7 October 1836, *H.R.A.*, I. xviii. 568-9.

In public Bourke replied with dignity to the arguments used by the opponents. He explained that by the use of scripture lessons in the ordinary business of the schools, the children would become familiar with the leading truths and practical duties of Christianity. He explained carefully that the use of the scriptures would not be forbidden at the National schools, and that such schools would not subvert the fundamental principles of Protestantism.[72] Privately he was irritated and exasperated by the public performances of Broughton. By 25 July he was writing to Glenelg in London that Broughton's opposition afforded additional reasons against placing that prelate in any of the colonial councils.[73] By early August he had come to the melancholy conclusion that Broughton was not only cursed with the vice of intolerance, but was also, alas, an exclusive in politics. He had also decided that his lordship, being as exclusive in politics as he was in religion, was collaborating for the defence of the old order in society with McLeay and all the other high Tory counsellors with whom he was plagued.[74] It had become more and more clear that those who saw the education controversy as part of the never-ending sectarian brawl in New South Wales between Catholic and Protestant were living in a dream; that behind all the talk about subverting the Protestant ascendancy and behind the Catholic fear that if the scriptures alone were taught, instead of the gospel of Christ, the children would soon be taught the gospel of men and, later still, the gospel of the devil,[75] there lay the much more fundamental question of who was to exercise power in New South Wales. In private Broughton saw himself as a crusader who had sacrificed everything he held dear—his mother, his brethren, his kinsfolk and friends and country—to set himself in the front of the battle against the forces of popery and infidelity, which threatened both New South Wales and the whole world. It was a satisfaction to know that in attaching himself to the cause of the Church of England, a cause which he saw every day more and more reason to identify with the continued maintenance of the pure and true profession of the gospel, he could not be suspected of interested motives. He was fighting against that unholy league between the old superstition and the miscalled modern liberalism which had sworn to destroy the Church of England. He proposed to build a citadel in New South Wales against the devastating ravages of that power. It grieved him to find that the pursuit of political objects and that desire to stand well with the world for their accomplishment could so blind the sagacious judgment of Bourke that he could not see his duty to stand firm against the revival of the ancient tyranny. As for this charming scheme of placing all sects on an equal footing, and this anxiety to live peaceably with all men, did not Bourke remember what his blessed Lord had said to the Scribes and the Pharisees?[76]

By October the sectarian dog-fight had become tangled up with the faction fight between the Botany Bay Whigs and the Botany Bay Tories. With that

[72] See, for example, the Minute of His Excellency the Governor to the Legislative Council, 22 July 1836, *Sydney Herald*, 4 August 1836.

[73] Bourke to Glenelg, 25 July 1836, *H.R.A.*, I. xviii. 457.

[74] Bourke to Glenelg, 8 August 1836, *H.R.A.*, I. xviii. 474-8.

[75] See, for example, the *Sydney Herald*, 12 September 1836.

[76] W. G. Broughton to Arthur, 21 September 1836 (Papers of Sir George Arthur, vol. 12, Letters from Bishop Broughton and from the Reverend S. Marsden).

extravagance of language which characterized the political controversies of the day the *Sydney Herald* informed its readers that on the one side there was their bishop, all the clergy save one, the High Churchmen and all the Tories. On the other side there was one of the clergy, some of the clergy of the other persuasions, all the Catholics (and just so that their readers would not miss the point they used two exclamation marks), all the Hebrews (they scored three exclamation marks) and all the Whigs. Why, asked the *Herald*, should the immigrant Protestants (they meant the wealthy and the respectable ones) be plundered for the support of convict papists, under the guise of general education? This, they thundered, was the wish of Botany Bay Whigs and convict papists.[77]

Bourke decided that McLeay at least must go. As long ago as August 1835 he had overheard McLeay telling his political cronies that he was so disgusted by the drift of events in New South Wales that he did not propose to hold office for another session of the Council. But despite this evidence of McLeay's constant intercourse and intimacy with the enemies of the government, when Bourke called on McLeay to resign, the latter replied that he had no intention of doing so. In August of 1836, at the height of the education controversy, he told his cronies in a tone of complaint and anger that many persons were looking for his appointment, but they would look in vain.[78] So in September Bourke sent for McLeay and told him it was quite evident from their differences of opinion upon important matters of policy that they could not act together, and that either the Colonial Secretary or the Governor ought to withdraw.

Once again McLeay refused to budge. So Bourke gave him till January to make up his mind, adding that if a resignation was not forthcoming by that time he proposed to act on his instructions from London and commission his son-in-law Edward Deas Thomson as Colonial Secretary to the colony of New South Wales and its dependent territories. Thomson and his beloved daughter were a constant source of delight and strength to him as the year drew to a close. He had a new task on his hands with the occupation of Port Phillip. The colony was tranquil and prosperous, wool was realizing high prices, trade was brisk, the price of labour high, provisions abundant—if only the colonial politics could be freed of their endless fatigue, and back-bite, and mockery and slander.[79]

On 2 January 1837 Bourke, acting on instructions from London, formally commissioned Edward Deas Thomson as Colonial Secretary of New South Wales.[80] The *Sydney Herald* promptly protested that the colony was to be thrown bound at the feet of the Bourke family, that the government of the colony was to be handed over to a family compact, and the influence of the respectable immigrant families was to be still further reduced in the public life of the colony of New South Wales.[81] All through January the *Herald* continued its vendetta against Bourke and his political friends. They sneered at

[77] *Sydney Herald*, 6 October 1836.
[78] Bourke to Glenelg, 8 August 1836, *H.R.A.*, I. xviii. 477-8.
[79] Bourke to Glenelg, 16 September 1836, *H.R.A.*, I. xviii. 542-4; R. Bourke to his son, 7 October and 30 December 1836 (Bourke Papers, vol. 6).
[80] Bourke to Glenelg, 3 January 1837, *H.R.A.*, I. xviii. 637-9.
[81] *Sydney Herald*, 5 January 1837.

R

the Jesuitism of the 'Honourable Francis', and held him up to public ridicule as a judge tainted with filthy political principles.[82] They accused Bourke of a shameful relaxation of convict discipline, of shameful pluralities, of appointing political partisans to public office, and of supporting the convict faction against the immigrant colonists.[83]

Later in that month of January 1837 the *Sydney Herald* defined the two main political groups. In this part of the world, they wrote, a Tory signified a respectable person who had immigrated to this colony and brought with him virtuous principles: he abominated convict principles, and even looked with suspicion on any man who had been a convict until he was convinced of his reformation. A Tory was no drunkard—no gambler: a Tory associated with moral and respectable men, not with the dissolute and worthless: he was not a concubine-keeper: he was a kind father, and an affectionate husband: he owed no man a penny: an independent man was the Botany Bay Tory. By contrast, they continued, Whig principles and convict principles were synonymous terms in Botany Bay. The Tories were the most respectable, moral, and intelligent men in the colony: the Whigs were the most dissolute and unprincipled men who had filled the female factory with bastards—which everyone knew was a dig at Wentworth, and, by implication, a rebuke to Bourke for inviting such men to break bread with him at Government House.[84]

Three months later all the self-styled respectable members of that provincial society—six members of the Legislative Council, eighty-one magistrates, and upwards of five hundred of the most respectable colonists—gathered in Sydney to present an address to McLeay, in which they praised him for his efficiency and urbanity and spoke of their pleasure that he had decided to spend his years in retirement contributing to the advancement of science, religion, morals and the arts. As though to give an additional twist to the knife with which they were tormenting Bourke, Broughton, Riddell, Burton and other civil officers suggested that a portrait of McLeay should be hung in a prominent place in Sydney as a lasting memorial to the regard and esteem in which he was held.[85]

By then it looked as though the men in London had come down on the side of the Botany Bay Tories. Towards the end of January, to his great mortification, Bourke read in a despatch from London that Riddell was to be restored to the Executive Council. The despatch went on to say that no reflection whatever was cast on his conduct or his judgment. He was praised in language which no Secretary of State had bestowed on a Governor of an Australian colony since Grenville had touched Phillip so deeply by telling him that His Majesty was graciously pleased to approve of his conduct in the execution of the arduous and important service which had been committed to his care. Glenelg told Burke that he entertained the fullest confidence that he would have the satisfaction of learning that Bourke would not hesitate to continue in the discharge of those duties which he had hitherto performed with so much credit to himself and so much advantage to His Majesty's service.[86]

[82] Ibid., 16 January 1837.   [83] Ibid., 5 January 1837.
[84] Ibid., 19 January 1837.   [85] Ibid., 4 May 1837.
[86] Glenelg to Bourke, 11 August 1836, *H.R.A.*, I. xviii. 483-4; for Grenville's praise of Phillip, see Grenville to Phillip, 19 June 1790, *H.R.A.*, I. i. 120.

But what consolation was that for the mortification of having to work with a man between whom and himself there was a great gulf set? What comfort was it to be told that he had been right to remove certain names from the list of magistrates? Besides, the *Sydney Herald* was not slow to whoop with delight—'AT LAST!' was their way of telling their readers with glee about the restoration of Riddell, and predicting that the respectable immigrants would soon be emancipated from Bourke and his measures.[87] In public Bourke bore the affront to his pride with dignity: in private he wrote to his son in London of his grief and his anguish and told him that he could not sit in Council with Riddell without prejudice to his honour.[88]

In the meantime Wentworth was being seen less and less in the society of the Patriots, a move he made not with dignity and urbanity, to which he remained a stranger until his life's end, but with all the uproar, all the raging at his enemies, all that disquiet of heart and mind which had accompanied all the major events of his life. In January he had been invited to take the chair at the dinner to commemorate the anniversary of the founding of the colony. He had at first agreed but, finding only the native-born were to be invited, he declined, justifying himself with one of those grand summaries of his life. The current of his life, he said, had been opposed to exclusiveness and intolerance, and now in his old age, he could not adopt a different tone in politics. The *Sydney Herald*, great hounder that it was of Botany Bay Whigs and the dissolute, held him up to public gaze as the golden boy of Governor Bourke, who could get convict servants more quickly than less favoured mortals.[89] The popular press, sensing some betrayal, began to attack him with all that vituperation of men who believed one of their number had been seduced into deserting his erstwhile mates by vulgar ambition. They called him the Ursa Major of the Australian political hemisphere, who sometimes roared like a bull of Bashan, and sometimes howled and frothed like a rabid bulldog. They asked him to tell them all when he intended to redeem his pledge to request that Darling be impeached.[90] When the *Sydney Gazette* rebuked him in March for letting down his one-time friends he wrote in anger to the editor 'Let my name be erased from the list of subscribers to your pestilent publication'.[91] So an implacable hatred for the rabble and the mob began to settle deep in that heart which in previous decades had spoken with such recklessness and daring of its implacable hatred of all exclusives in general and the Macarthurs in particular. The way was being prepared for Wentworth to say sixteen years later, remembering this vulgar abuse from the rabble: 'I shall die a Conservative'.[92]

While Wentworth was storming and raging another man was widening the

[87] *Sydney Herald*, 26 January 1837; see also *Australian*, 27 January 1837.

[88] Bourke to his son, 28 January 1837 (Bourke Papers, vol. 6); R. Bourke to Lord Monteagle, 28 January 1837 (Bourke Papers, vol. 9).

[89] *Sydney Herald*, 30 January 1837.

[90] Ibid., 2 February 1837; for Wentworth's reply to this charge see ibid., 9 February 1837; see also the *Sydney Herald*, 13 February 1837; *Colonist*, 13 July 1837.

[91] *Sydney Gazette* and *Australian*, March 1837 *passim*; *Australian*, 13 January and 4 April 1837; *Monitor*, 27 January 1837; *Sydney Gazette*, 25 March and 4 April 1837.

[92] Speech by W. C. Wentworth on the New South Wales Constitution Bill; printed in E. K. Silvester, *Speeches in the Legislative Council of New South Wales on the Second Reading of the Bill for Framing a New Constitution for the Colony* (Sydney, 1853), p. 230.

gap between desire and capacity. With the Bishop of Australia the desire for the spiritual welfare of all men committed to his charge had always been infinite, but the capacity had become more and more limited. In the summer of 1836-7 he had made a tour of his vast diocese. From Patrick's Plains on the Hunter River to Goulburn, almost the southern extremity of the occupied parts of New South Wales, he had told the men and women who had gathered on those hot plains to hear the Lord's song in a strange land that he had come amongst them to promote genuine devotion, to lead men to their eternal happiness, and to fight for the adherence to the principles of the Protestant faith, which must, he believed, form the basis of any system of education under which they could place their children with a safe conscience. In rude bush huts, under the shade of gum trees and in the parlours of the squatters he had called on men to remain faithful in the new world to the creeds of the old. In the country there was some reality to this hope of re-creating in Australia that society of squire, parson, and peasant which he had known at Farnham in England.[93]

In the towns of New South Wales the very spirit of the age mocked his vision and exposed him as a man desperately trying to force the practices of a dying faith and a decaying social order on the rude, egalitarian, noisy, vulgar, but magnificently alive society of Sydney. Soon after his return to Sydney from the mission to the heathen of New South Wales, and with the rural gentry's words of good cheer and faith and confidence still ringing in his ears, he accepted an invitation from Bourke to attend a levee at Government House. He entered the reception room proudly dressed in the clothes befitting his high station in the colony of New South Wales, seeing the men and women in the room as dedicated to the same high mission as he was, namely, to bring that great, creative civilization of Europe to the barbarians of the new world. He entered with that demeanour of all men who see themselves as the vessels of higher civilization—and in his moment of triumph suffered a pang of inner pain. For there in the same room was John Bede Polding, wearing the canonical dress of a bishop of the Church of Rome.

Exercising that authority which they believed had been committed to them from 'on high', the Holy See, zealous to direct the people of New South Wales in the way of God's commandments and to procure their eternal salvation, had decided on 3 June 1834 to set up the Vicariate-Apostolic of New Holland, with Polding as the first bishop. Polding had in abundance those qualities which Broughton chased all his life in vain. Like Broughton he had a good head, and an overflowing zeal, but nature or his calling had conferred on him that sweetness of temperament, that sociableness of appearance which only served to expose more harshly the worldly hopes and ties in Broughton. Born in Liverpool in 1794, orphaned early, Polding was steeped in the two strands of Catholicism in Australia. He knew and loved the Liverpool Irish: he had been trained for the priesthood as a Benedictine. Reaching Sydney in September of 1835 he had quickly won his way to the hearts of the people he served. Seeing they were indifferent to everything except money and drink, he

93 *Sydney Herald*, 30 January 1837.

brought them to a sense of the great mystery not by chiding them, but by that mixture of humour and firmness, and by bearing witness in his own person to all the honour and glory of those for whom Christ was King.[94]

So Broughton, proud and sensitive of his station as Bishop of Australia, confronted a man who he believed represented that old superstition which in alliance with modern liberalism had sworn to destroy the Church of England. Affronted that a Romish priest should presume an equality with him, overcome for a moment too with the terror that Bourke had perhaps succumbed to that great lie that the minions of Rome had their mandate from 'on high', Broughton turned his back on the gathering and went home. There he sat down to write a protest to Bourke, pointing out that he could not recognize Polding because he had sworn that no foreign state had or ought to have jurisdiction within this realm, and adding for his part that he would appeal to His Majesty and Parliament to protect his dignity and his honour, as though such deep matters could be settled by an earthly tribunal. With a becoming dignity Bourke replied that he had not foreseen that Polding would appear in the habit of a bishop of the Church of Rome. Broughton was not to know then that Bourke had just received from Glenelg a despatch in which he had expressed his deep regret that an attempt to diffuse among the rapidly increasing population of New South Wales the blessings of education on a scale commensurate with the growing wants of the colony should become the source of discord and division among those who ought to be united in the bonds of Christian charity.[95] But that was precisely what Broughton could not bring himself to do—not for him that charming scheme to place all sects on an equal footing, nor indeed that false liberalism of the age which asked men to live peaceably with those with whom they disagreed on great questions.

By allowing others to see that the high-minded Broughton suffered from all the weaknesses of those who allowed themselves to put on proud looks, he forfeited not only his influence over Bourke, but a central place in the councils of New South Wales at a time when it was entering a decisive period in its history. By one of those ironies in human affairs Broughton squandered his right to be heeded in the colony just at a time when he had begun to see clearly one great tendency of his day and age—the withdrawal of the state from the support of religion. At no distant date, he told Bourke, the state would be removed from all concern about and all concern with the interests and affairs of religion. 'We', he told Bourke in a letter, 'have the taste only of the first fruits, our successors will have the full harvest'. He looked with black despair to the coming age of unbelief, seeing it, not like Newman as a winter which would soon be over, followed by a spring of bright promise and budding hopes, of keen blasts, and cold showers, and sudden storms, heralding the return of life. Broughton was terrified that men would descend to the life of the goat

[94] For the life and character of J. B. Polding see T. L. Suttor, *Hierarchy and Democracy in Australia 1788-1870* (Melbourne, 1965); for the decision to permit Polding to exercise ecclesiastical authority to give him greater influence over the clergy in the colony see Aberdeen to Bourke, 20 February 1835, *H.R.A.*, I. xvii 682-3; see also *Australian Dictionary of Biography*, vol. 2.

[95] Based on W. G. Broughton to Bourke, 1 and 5 June 1837, and R. Bourke to W. G. Broughton, 3 June 1837 (Broughton Correspondence, MS. in M.L.); Glenelg to Bourke, 27 February 1837, *H.R.A.*, I. xviii. 695-8.

and the monkey, would cease to be those angels to whom God had given a vision of His throne, and become like the worm to whom God had given sensual lust.[96]

At the same time another man of God, the Reverend Samuel Marsden, made one last desperate attempt to persuade a wicked man to forsake his way, and an unrighteous man his thoughts, and to return to the Lord who would have mercy upon him and would abundantly pardon him. With the passage of time he had become very weak and feeble: his eyes were dim with age: he wrote with difficulty. Yet decay neither of mind nor of body dimmed his awareness of what he called the spirit of wickedness, or that conviction that he had been sent by God to urge his generation to seek the Lord while He might be found.[97] When rumours reached Sydney at the beginning of 1837 that the Reverend Mr Yate was practising unspeakable abominations with Maori boys at Waimate, a mission station close to that Bay of Islands where in 1814 Marsden had first told the Maoris of those tidings of great joy, he did not hesitate for one moment to respond to that call. Reckless as ever of his personal comfort or safety, or the affection, admiration and respect of his fellow-men when the ways of the wicked were reported to him; old and feeble, dreading sea-sickness as much as ever, aware in his heart only of a painful sense of duty towards his God and the true interests of religion, and quite prepared to leave any judgment of what he was doing to the supreme governor of all events; knowing too that the thoughts of man were not the thoughts of God, nor man's ways the ways of God, he embarked on the *Pyramus* on 7 February 1837, with his beloved daughter Martha, and sailed out on to the high seas for Hokianga on the west coast of the north island of New Zealand. Every morning and every night she read prayers to her father as his sight would not permit him to read. When the weather permitted she read to Papa from Washington Irving's *History of Columbus*. For Martha Marsden believed that to pray to Jesus and to read edifying books was all men needed for their eternal salvation, and had no notion of what was consuming Papa, and leading him on to his destruction.[98]

For a time after they entered the estuary of Hokianga they were in much danger of being overwhelmed by the heavy violent waves which constantly broke against the sides of their vessel, and rolled over the deck. When no such disaster befell them, once again Marsden thanked divine providence for rescuing them from a watery grave. As they made their way along the estuary he mused again on how everything God had created—the earth and sky, trees, birds, beasts, flowers—was pleasing in his sight, and everything man had created was vile. It was the same at Waimate. There God had clothed the earth with a pleasing mantle, while man practised drunkenness, adultery and murder. As there were no laws, judges or magistrates, Satan was maintaining

[96] W. G. Broughton to R. Bourke, n.d., written probably in 1836 or 1837 (Broughton Correspondence, ms. in m.l.); J. H. Newman, *The Second Spring: A Sermon Preached on 13 July in St Mary's College* (repr., London, 1954).

[97] Based on S. Marsden to W. G. Broughton, 10 November 1837 (Marsden Papers, vol. 2, pp. 128-9); S. Marsden to M. Jowett, 10 August 1837 (Bonwick Transcripts, Box 54, p. 1999); Journal of Martha Marsden, (ms. in m.l.); *Isaiah* 1v. 6-13.

[98] Martha Marsden to D. Coates, February 1837 (Bonwick Transcripts, Box 54, p. 1988).

his dominion without molestation. Such a body of European drunkards and riotous blasphemers must be placed as quickly as possible under some civil government. His beloved Maori chiefs, he was happy to say, were as hungry as ever for stories about the Saviour.

As for Yate, he called on him and told him what charges had been made against his moral character, and told him that he, Marsden, would defend him if he were innocent, but that if he were guilty, he, Yate, must go to England. To which Yate replied that he was guilty. So Marsden bade him farewell and saw him no more, and turned to his beloved Maoris who carried him on a hammock down to the sea where he went on board the *Rattlesnake* and sailed for New South Wales, being so grieved for Yate that all through the journey home he hung down his head, and humbled himself before God. In this mood of humility and contrition Greatheart Marsden returned to Sydney in July hoping that this time at long last his deeds would be pleasing not only in the sight of God but also of man, only to find a nest of enemies were up against him on account of Mr Yate. Weak in body and ill able to bear the anxiety of mind he was in, and knowing that he had acted from a painful sense of duty towards his God, he turned once again to the supreme governor for that wisdom, power and goodness for which he had scanned the face of his fellow-man in vain. There were other things to disquiet him. That very wise and prudent man, the Bishop, was at variance with Governor. On this too Marsden, remembering his own trials with all the governors of New South Wales, save Bourke, went down on his knees at Parramatta, and asked the great head of the church to protect them all from error and violence, and to deliver Broughton from what he had been through. He knew that zeal in the service of his God had alienated him from the world of men. He knew that a man of great heart in the sight of God would be a leper in the eyes of man. Had they not all been told of old: 'For my thoughts are not your thoughts, neither are your ways my ways, saith the Lord'. Then just as forces in the world outside him were sweeping away that material setting which had given birth to his harsh belief that only severity and strictness, but not cruelty, could restrain human depravity, the kingdom of perpetual night began to claim him for its own.[99]

Bourke, too, had his problems. All through the first part of 1837 while the *Sydney Herald* hounded him as the evil genius of the court and convict faction, a friend to drunkards and the fathers of bastards, a foe to the upright and the respectable, he went down on his knees and prayed fervently that Almighty God would smooth the passage of his mother to the grave and give her eternal happiness through Christ. While the *Sydney Herald* shrieked resign, resign, resign, Bourke was wrestling with the greatest grief in his life. In May the news of the death of his mother reached Sydney. With dignity and confidence he turned to his faith for strength to sustain him in his days of grief and anguish. He trusted in God's mercy to permit him to see her in the next world. He humbly hoped that his affections would survive in the next life with a fervency

[99] Based on S. Marsden to W. G. Broughton, 10 November 1837 (Marsden Papers, vol. 2, pp. 128-9); S. Marsden to D. Coates, 26 (no month given) 1837 (Bonwick Transcripts, Box 54, p. 1884).

and purity much exceeding what was known in this world, and that without diminution of his love of God who, he believed, would then be 'all in all' he would know again and love those whom he had loved here.[1]

Characteristically he neither indulged in any extravagant displays of grief, nor whined to those who were near and dear to him about the cruelty and indignity to which he was exposed by the *Sydney Herald* and their faction. A simple, straightforward man, he was always at work. He was among his papers by six every morning and did not leave them except for prayers till three in the afternoon, after which he took a ride, had dinner, and then went back to his papers. Even on his rides he mostly visited the public works which were in progress. During the sessions of the Legislative Council in Sydney his work was even heavier. In between official business, and presiding as head of society, he made excursions to the remote settlements. He was known in the colony as a capital campaigner—sleeping in the bush frequently for nights together in a tent after taking his tea out of a tin can, always, it was said, with meek resignation.[2]

The Legislative Council met on 30 May for its first session for 1837. His son-in-law Edward Deas Thomson, the new Colonial Secretary, and Sir John Jamison, an old campaigner for the Whig cause, were sworn in as new members. Bourke then rose to his feet and spoke with pride of the unexampled prosperity with which it had pleased providence to bless the land, of the flourishing state of the revenue, and the large profits derived from pastoral and commercial pursuits. He spoke too of the uniform tranquillity and the rapidly increasing prosperity: 'Gentlemen', he concluded with commendable pride, 'it has been often and truly observed that the happiest ages of the world afford the scantiest materials for the historian'.[3] The *Sydney Herald* snorted at such complacency, but the other papers, the *Australian* and the *Sydney Gazette*, celebrated the coming of more spacious and less dark days, with eulogies for Bourke.[4]

The main task, as Bourke saw it, was to procure or aid the introduction into the colony of useful labourers of various descriptions, as the supply was still below the demand.[5] A week before the session of Council began he had received a memorandum from John Mackay stressing the necessity for introducing as speedily as practicable Indian labourers who, Mackay hold him, ate little rice, but many snakes, lizards, rats and mice. They were clothed in a simple and scanty way, were unacquainted with the luxury of a bed, and had that patient disposition and tractable habits which should make them excellent shepherds.[6] Two days later, on 24 May, a group of flock-owners reminded him that the want of labour was felt to such an alarming extent throughout the colony that in many cases the plough remained idle and stock were being lost through lack of hands.[7]

[1] R. Bourke to his son, 25 May 1837 (Bourke Papers, vol. 6).
[2] H. F. Gisborne, private secretary to Bourke, to his father, 16 October 1837 (Correspondence of H. F. Gisborne, MS. in M.L.).   [3] *V. & P.* (L.C. N.S.W.) 30 May 1837.
[4] *Sydney Herald, Australian, Colonist* and *Sydney Gazette*, June 1837 *passim*.
[5] The Address of Sir Richard Bourke to the Legislative Council, *V. & P.* (L.C. N.S.W.) 30 May 1837.
[6] Additional Memoranda by John Mackay, 22 May 1837, ibid.; the first memorandum by Mackay to Bourke was presented in October 1836.   [7] Ibid., 24 May 1837.

Bourke's solution was to ask Council again to appoint a committee to consider the problems of immigration. J. R. Mayo told them the great advantage of the Indian over the European was that those degrading pests, the public houses, could not seduce such labourers. Wentworth told them he could not approve of the introduction of Indians, because it would be impossible to prevent an intermixture of races, which, he believed, it would be highly desirable to avoid. He looked to the United Kingdom for a future supply, and of those he preferred Irish labourers to any other, because a good word went a long way with an Irishman. Hannibal Macarthur also preferred Europeans to Asians. Sir John Jamison, Alexander Berry, and James Bowman were prepared to take the Indian hill-coolies, partly because the need was desperate, and partly because they could not see how any immigration scheme could get them the ten thousand labourers they needed from the United Kingdom.[8] The committee in its first report on 25 August contented itself with a statement of the problem: the want of shepherds, stockmen, agricultural labourers in general, and of mechanics in a smaller proportion had become so alarming and necessitous.[9]

Bourke spent much of his time during the next few months summing up his opinions on the future. In one despatch he discussed the minimum upset price of land, in which he took the opportunity to warn the men in London of the evil effects of land-sharks and land-jobbers.[10] In another he put down his opinions on the future of the convict system, in which he explained that though he had come to the melancholy conclusion that no real reformation of heart was efficiently assisted by the system of management pursued at Norfolk Island, he also believed there would always remain a remnant of unhappy men who could not with propriety be restored to society. For this reason he advised against abolition of the penal settlement on Norfolk Island, while at the same time recommending that the number there should be reduced. He agreed that assignment was attended with great evils, and accepted the opinion that inasmuch as it had some of the features of slavery it must go. But, realizing that the sudden withdrawal of assigned servants from the settlers would occasion much distress, he took the liberty to suggest that the assignment system should be abolished gradually.[11]

By that time there was about all this an air of unreality, simply because the centre of interest had shifted away from Sydney to London. All through the latter half of the year all the public men of New South Wales cocked an anxious eye over the water for news from London. While Bourke was composing his passionless prose on the minimum upset price of land or the future of the convict system, at the same time he was instructing his son in words of some passion on the appearance of Mudie's book in London, calling the author a great ruffian and a blockhead, and later warned his son of the false and

---

[8] Evidence of J. R. Mayo, W. C. Wentworth, H. H. Macarthur, Sir John Jamison and A. Berry to the Committee of Immigration of Indian and British Labourers into New South Wales, Interim Report of Committee, 11 May 1837, *V. & P.* (L.C. N.S.W.) 1837.

[9] Report of the Committee of Immigration of Indian and British Labourers into New South Wales, 25 August 1837, *V. & P.* (L.C. N.S.W.) 1837.

[10] Bourke to Glenelg, 6 September 1837, *H.R.A.*, I. xix. 75-9.

[11] Bourke to Glenelg, 22 November 1837, *H.R.A.*, I. xix. 187-8.

scandalous character of Mudie's book, *The Felonry of New South Wales*.[12] The *Sydney Herald* welcomed the book because it would provide any committee appointed by the House of Commons to inquire into the future of the convict system with some useful hints, and tell them the truth about the activities of the low convict clique in the colony.[13] The *Australian*, after rebuking Mudie for his shocking recklessness, his odious effrontery, and his revolting hardness of heart, accused him of being instigated by ingratitude, ferocity and revenge, of gratifying his malice and his spleen by a publication of such infamy and viciousness that they could not find one redeeming quality in it.[14] By contrast the *Sydney Gazette*, after deploring the feelings of rancorous malignity against the present Governor, felt bound to express their opinion that in publishing the *Felonry* the 'Major' had done the state some service.[15]

When rumours reached Sydney that Forbes had changed his mind in London, and that he now agreed with Colonel Arthur of Van Diemen's Land that crime and vice were on the increase in the penal colonies, both to a most lamentable extent, once again the deep division in the colony came out in the public comments. With a malicious glee the *Sydney Herald* told their readers that their reporter had lately seen posted on some of the trees on the Forbes estate on the Hunter River the awful word 'scab'.[16] When the news of the publication of Macarthur's book—*New South Wales; its present State and future Prospects*—arrived, the *Sydney Herald* hailed it as the work of a gentleman. The *Australian* denounced him as the champion of Toryism and exclusiveness, adding in anger that Macarthur was a man who wanted to stamp with an indelible brand of infamy the emancipist portion of the colonists, and deprive them perpetually of political and civil rights. How different, they argued, from Wentworth who had once written with passion of man's duty to chase the black reign of barbarism and cruelty from every region of the earth.[17]

On 27 October 1837 a great concourse of people gathered outside Government House in Sydney to hear the Sheriff read the proclamation which had been signed by the Governor, the judges, other officers and gentlemen and one native black calling Victoria their only lawful and rightful liege lady, by the grace of God, Queen of the United Kingdom and Ireland, Defender of the Faith, and Supreme Lady of the territory of New South Wales and its dependecies to whom they did acknowledge all faith and constant obedience. The assembled crowd gave three hearty cheers for the Queen: a *feu de joie* was fired: the band played 'God save the Queen'.[18]

This harmony did not last for long. When all the respectable people gathered again to vote an address to the Queen, a row broke out over who was to take the chair. The conservatives wanted McLeay: others, led by Wentworth, wanted a man outside the political dog-fights. This time the conservatives had their way, as McLeay was loudly called for, and enthusiastically received into the chair. The *Sydney Herald* was delighted with this defeat of

---

[12] R. Bourke to his son, 20 May and 7 September 1837 (Bourke Papers, vol. 6); J. Mudie, *The Felonry of New South Wales* (London, 1837). [13] *Sydney Herald*, 28 August 1837.
[14] *Australian*, 8 September 1837. [15] *Sydney Gazette*, 31 August 1837.
[16] *Sydney Herald*, 7 August 1837. [17] Quoted in ibid., 27 November 1837.
[18] Ibid., 9 and 30 October 1837; this scene is included here because in the next volume an attempt will be made to describe the impact of the Victorian age on the Australian colonies.

the Botany Bay 'Patriots', adding with supercilious disdain that a few of the 'unwashed' had crept into the extreme back seats, towards the close of the proceedings, and had been heard to make some ignorant and impertinent remarks.[19]

The victory was short lived. While the conservatives were sneering at their opponents as the unwashed, or denouncing the *Australian* as an organ of transported thieves which vomited its filthy abuse on the respectable members of New South Wales society,[20] or holding Wentworth up to public ridicule for his exuberant displays of frothy eloquence and abuse, and labelling him as the man of bull-feast notoriety,[21] Bourke opened a despatch from England in which Glenelg accepted his resignation and went on to tell him he could not let the occasion pass without expressing the high sense which Her Majesty's government entertained of the zeal, energy, and enlightened views which had distinguished his administration.[22] The *Australian* bestowed very high praise on Bourke by declaring him to be 'perfect in his generation'.[23] The *Sydney Herald* rejoiced that the colony was to be at long last liberated from a man who was popular with 'shoeless and shirtless rascals'.[24] The *Sydney Gazette* was not surprised that the most influential and reputable portion of the colonists were arrayed against the Governor. This, they said, was the price Bourke paid for being 'the convicts' friend', and his obstinate determination to enforce the Irish system of education down Protestant throats.[25]

Spurred on by such abuse the friends of Bourke gathered in public meeting at the School of Arts to vote an address to His Excellency and present him with some lasting memorial of the general respect and esteem which the colonists entertained for his public and private virtues. After John Blaxland was voted into the chair Wentworth presented himself to the meeting to loud and sustained applause. In the overflow of his passionate heart he paid a moving tribute to the man to whom he owed so much. He began by saying that on the arrival of Bourke the colony was almost a universal scene of rapine, violence, and disorder. But now, warming to his theme and that thunderous applause which caused his mind to soar, there was universal peace and quietness. Before there was poverty: now there was prosperity, all thanks to the wise and vigorous administration of Sir Richard Bourke. Once again the applause was loud and prolonged. Bourke, Wentworth went on, had got rid of a paid press, had given up the assignment of convicts into other hands, had stopped hunting down men as though they were savage beasts, had introduced trial by jury on a more extensive scale, had restored religious equality among all classes of the community, and had behaved magnanimously towards those who had launched gross and truculent attacks on his government. He spoke for an hour and a half, eloquently, energetically, and was frequently greeted with loud applause and vehement cheering. For he, too, was having his moment of triumph, his moment as the apologist for a great governor and a great man. With confidence and pride he then read the address, which covered in more detail the points in his speech. Sir John Jamison proposed the erection

[19] *Sydney Herald*, 20 November 1837.   [20] Ibid., 30 November 1837.
[21] Ibid., 21 November 1837.   [22] Glenelg to Bourke, 3 July 1837, *H.R.A.*, I. xix. 4.
[23] *Australian*, 28 November 1837.   [24] *Sydney Herald*, 4 December 1837.
[25] *Sydney Gazette*, 29 October 1836 and 7 December 1837.

of a statue to Bourke. Roger Therry spoke of him as a man who had resisted oppression, who, rather than see all power and all wealth possessed by a few, had preferred to consult the interests of the whole community. When J. E. Manning summed him up as a great and good man, the applause was deafening.

But at the last levee held by Bourke in Government House to give the public at large an opportunity of testifying their loyalty and affection for the Queen's representative, Bourke, because of his reputation as the convicts' friend, felt obliged to shake the hand of a most disreputable character, who was not visited by any person of standing in the community, in front of all the higher classes of society. When another man, held to be of low repute by 'the few', held out his hand, Bourke refused and turned away indignant from such over-familiarity by the low-born in one of those Botany Bay assemblies when the higher classes snubbed the disreputable. As His Excellency left Government House on 5 December to embark on the *Samuel Winter* one continual cheer followed him all the way to the water's edge. But it was said that those were not the cheers of the higher and respectable classes, but rather the cheers of that felon mob whose popularity Bourke had courted. The shirtless and shoeless, they waved their hats, and gave off shouts that rent the sky, and followed him till at long last the sea delivered Bourke from their filthy adulation. In 1831 the convicts and their families had sung that song of joy 'Over the hills and far away', three days before the steamboat slowly drew the *Hooghly* and General Darling down that majestic sheet of water. This time, the same people were lamenting the departure of the convicts' friend. Swept on by that great gust of popular passion they were all unwittingly contributing to the Tory thesis that convictism, both as a corrupter and leveller of mankind, had rendered New South Wales unfit for the institutions of the free.[26]

[26] *Australian*, 5 December 1837; *Sydney Gazette*, 7 December 1837; the following is the text used on the statue erected for Bourke:

This Statue
of
Lieutenant General
Sir Richard Bourke, K.C.B.
is erected by the people of New South Wales to record his able, honest, and benevolent administration from 1831 to 1837.

Selected for the government at a period of singular difficulty, his judgment, urbanity, and firmness justified the choice. Comprehending at once the vast resources peculiar to this colony, he applied them, for the first time, systematically to its benefit. He voluntarily divested himself of the prodigious influence arising from the assignment of penal labour, and enacted just and salutary laws for the amelioration of penal discipline. He was the first governor, who published satisfactory accounts of the public receipts and expenditure. Without oppression, or detriment to any interest, he raised the revenue to a vast amount, and, from its surplus, realized extensive plans of immigration. He established religious equality on a just and firm basis, and sought to provide for all, without public works of permanent utility. He founded the flourishing settlement of Port Phillip, and threw open the unlimited wilds of Australia to pastoral enterprize. He established savings' banks, and was the patron of the first mechanics' institute. He created an equitable tribunal for determining upon claims to grants of lands. He was the warm friend of the liberty of the press. He extended trial by jury after its almost total suspension for many years. By these and numerous other measures for the moral, religious, and general improvement of all classes, he raised the colony to unexampled prosperity; and retired amid the reverent and affectionate regret of the people; having won their confidence by his integrity, their gratitude by his services, their admiration by his public talents, and their esteem by his private worth.

10

THE SAINT OF HOBART TOWN

AT THE BEGINNING of the year 1831 the Lieutenant-Governor of Van Diemen's Land continued as great an enigma as ever to all the observers of the human comedy in that harsh land. Some who took tea with him in Government House, and stayed on for the evening devotions of the family, testified that on such occasions they were favoured with comfort from their Lord. By contrast Dr Scott, who had devoted great care and a considerable portion of his time tending Mrs Arthur when she was in a most alarming way, was never asked to take a glass of wine or other refreshment. And when he announced to the little great man that the patient was restored he was dismissed with thanks so cold that it chilled his heart to receive them. Others again saw him as a canting Puritan, a man who under the cold mask of piety, and much bending of the knees, had quietly feathered his own nest with thousands of acres of the best land in the Derwent Valley, and pots of money in the bank.[1]

There was about him that air of bloodless majesty, that air of mingled awe and bewilderment which surrounds God's vessels, who believe they have been allotted a chosen place in the divine plan for the salvation of man, but consume their energies fighting a losing battle against the tendencies of their age. Knowing that the hearts of the sons of man were filled with evil he began the year determined to shield the surviving aborigines of Van Diemen's Land from human wickedness. He was driven on as ever by that lofty ideal of displaying to those least of the little ones the same forbearance and compassion which his Saviour had lavished on the multitude during those days when he had walked beside the waters of Galilee. He also sensed the worldly wisdom of protecting the survivors of the long unequal war between black and white and had accepted the suggestion of that great booby, that fool in Christ, G. A. Robinson, that those whom the white man could catch as well as those whom the white man could talk into accepting civilization should be moved to an island in Bass Strait. Like Arthur, Robinson saw the aborigine as another manifestation, if a rather surprising manifestation, of the glory of God, who might be converted from barbarism to civilization. But if they could not or would not be converted, should the seed of Christian civilization fall on the stony ground of their innate and incredible savagery, then at least on an island in Bass Strait they could inflict no further harm. Even if they were to

---

[1] See, for example, J. Backhouse, *A Narrative of a Visit to the Australian Colonies* (London, 1843), p. 16; Diary of G. T. W. Boyes, 20 July 1831; E. Markham, Voyage to Van Diemen's Land (MS. in M.L.).

rot and pine away on a lonely, wind-swept island, it was better that they should meet their death in that way, whilst every act of kindness was being manifested towards them, than that they should fall a sacrifice to the inevitable consequences of their continued acts of outrage upon the white inhabitants.[2]

In February thirty-four aborigines were uprooted from the land of their birth and transported to an island where they were taught things they did not wish to learn by a man who saw himself as the instrument of divine providence to bring the message of salvation to these least of the little ones. Not being endowed with the gift of tongues, and lacking even the crudest means to hand on to posterity memorials of their grief and their rage they pined away their time, while Robinson spent his days either instructing this band of survivors or trying to persuade others to accept the white man's plan of conciliation for that wretched people.[3] When the aborigines from the wild, inaccessible country on the west coast put to death two white men with peculiar cruelty, again the settlers clamoured for protection and revenge, shouting their own piece of savagery, that ancient cry of an eye for an eye and a tooth for a tooth, and dismissing with anger and contempt the policy of the Saint of Hobart Town with his mealy-mouthed words of forbearance and compassion.[4]

Discarding those sentiments of exultation he had experienced when he and Robinson had sought comfort and guidance from their Lord, Arthur turned for a solution to the men of this world who advised him to appoint a committee of the Legislative Council to look into the matter. These men believed the kindness and forbearance of the previous year's great round-up had more than atoned for the injuries sustained by the natives in the earlier period of British occupation. They held the aborigines to be the treacherous ones, the wanton aggressors and thirsters after plunder, whose path was marked by fire, rapine and the most dreadful atrocities, and believing the aborigines to be insensible to kindness, devoid of generous feelings, bent on revenge, and determined to pursue their murderous course, they urged Arthur, in the name of God, to protect the white man from such savages. The solution as they saw it was to speed up the removal of the remaining aborigines to an island in Bass Strait where there was abundance of yams, and where every effort should be made to wean them from their barbarous habits. Then, reminding themselves of the teachings of their holy faith, they wound up with the lofty sentiment that as Christians they could have but one feeling of compassion towards their frightened fellow creatures. Thirsting for revenge but, at the same time, hungry for that reward of the men who do God's will, they recommended Arthur to encourage Robinson to use the arts of persuasion rather than round-ups or gunpowder, and get the survivors on to that island out of harm's way.[5]

He was just as anxious to get the convicts out of harm's way. Their thieving,

---

[2] Arthur to Murray, 1 January 1831, C.O. 280/28, pp. 17-20; Extract from Minutes of the Executive Council on Aborigines, 12 February 1831, Encl. in Arthur to Murray, 4 April 1831, C.O. 280/28, p. 416.   [3] Arthur to Murray, 4 April 1831, ibid., pp. 416-24.

[4] See, for example, *Hobart Town Courier*, 9 April 1831 and May 1831 *passim*.

[5] Report of Committee of the Legislative Council of Van Diemen's Land on Aborigines, 24 October 1831, C.O. 280/30, pp. 154-70.

whoring, drunkenness, treachery, blackmail, bullying, deeds of savage violence, and even cannibalism demonstrated that aboriginal calamity in which all men had been implicated ever since Adam's fall. Like the aborigines the convicts were to be pitied, and shielded from the temptations which they lacked the will and power to resist, which would cause them great wretchedness in this world, and prepare them for the eternal bonfire in the life of the world to come. It was the duty of God's elect to provide them with both incentives for virtue and deterrents against transgression.

As soon as the newly arrived convicts could be mustered in the penitentiary at Hobart Town, Arthur addressed them on their future prospects. He spoke with certainty of the degraded state into which they had brought themselves. It was, he said, a state which could justly be likened to that of slavery. On their future he gave them good counsel: he warned them against the evils of bad company and drunkenness, telling them they might with profit to themselves regard the door of a public house, through which many of them had come into their present situation, as the entrance to a gaol. He reminded them that he and all those in authority under him would watch their conduct most minutely, that if their conduct was bad they would be severely punished, put to work in a chain-gang or sent to a penal settlement, or they might end their days on that scaffold from which malefactors were launched into eternity. If they behaved well, they would in the course of time earn a ticket-of-leave which would permit them to reap the fruits of their labour. By persevering in good conduct they might earn first a conditional pardon and later a full pardon which would enable those so disposed to return to their native land.[6] To encourage them to turn from their wickedness he assigned all but the incorrigible to masters who provided them with food, clothing and bedding.

The more he watched the behaviour of the convicts the more convinced he became that they were not deterred from crime by the fear of punishment, but rather by the removal of every opportunity for indulgence. Ticket-of-leave men, for example, enjoyed such an extravagant supply of food and clothing and such high wages that they were tempted to squander it in riotous living and dissipation. Why, he went on, should the convicts who were free by servitude be enabled to indulge in debauchery out of their surplus wages while innocent men lived and starved in their native country? He wanted to diminish the opportunities for all convicts, ticket-of-leave men and expirees to indulge in such drunkenness. Unaided, men were too weak to resist temptation. Terror might deter, but it would also degrade. The only way, consistent with dignity, to save men from greater wretchedness in this world and from God's wrath when they appeared at the judgment seat was to remove all temptations and opportunity. Like most of the self-appointed improvers of mankind it was outside his range of mind to think for one moment of the anger and rage aroused by such forcible deprivation in the hearts and minds of the victims of his high-minded concern.[7]

[6] Based on Arthur's speech to the convicts who arrived in the *Elizabeth*, 20 February 1832; see J. Backhouse, op. cit., pp. 19-20.

[7] For the mind of Arthur on this point in 1831, see Arthur to Goderich, 9 July 1831, C.O. 280/29, pp. 168-73.

In the month that he wrote to Goderich at such length about the deplorable effects of high wages Edward Broughton, a prisoner of the Crown at Macquarie Harbour, felled a tree on top of a constable for no other reason than because he was a constable, and the unwilling or passive instrument of flogging the men. He therefore hated him. In company with four others, including one Macavoy, Broughton absconded into the bush, where, driven to desperation by hunger, the demon of evil, as Dr Ross put it in the *Hobart Town Courier*, walked in the middle of them to such effect that four of them agreed to kill the luckless fifth and ate heartily of his flesh. Hunger drove Broughton and Macavoy to kill the other two and eat them too. But then with the folly of men who had given way to such madness, or may be driven to seek expiation for their crimes, as though their guilt were stronger than their hunger, they gave themselves up, were tried for their horrid crimes, and sentenced to be hanged at Hobart Town in August. Dr Ross shuddered to think that such crimes should have been committed in the face of the serene and eloquent beauties of nature. Maybe divine providence would sink into the fathomless ocean this insular spot of earth in which such unspeakable wickedness had crawled. Drinking, dissipation, the company of abandoned women, and races and fairs had first led these men into their wicked practices. The only safety from such abominations was to persevere in perfect rectitude to the end—and keep away from pleasure. As ever there was about the language of Ross the atmosphere of a man who was deriving some quite perverse satisfaction from reproving mankind. There was about him always that air of a man for whom the affectation of piety had a dark attraction for his sensual cruelty.[8]

For Arthur the sovereign remedy for all human depravity was to encourage the spread of that religious feeling which would tend to counteract the baneful effect of the example of the wretched outcasts. He proposed to build schools and churches: he proposed to bring out more persons to teach the young and such as were of riper years of the great battle raging in the human heart between Jehovah and Beelzebub. The drunkenness and other vicious habits of these men which it would defile his pen to name, would then decrease. Unlike Bourke in New South Wales, he never looked forward to that time when the convict system had withered away. As he saw it Van Diemen's Land was a gaol for the punishment and reformation of British criminals: his task was to make it an efficient instrument for that purpose.[9]

His rôle as an improver of mankind exposed him to the undying hatred of some of the convicts: the rôle of Lieutenant-Governor of a penal colony for the improvement of the morals of gaol-birds also exposed him to the wrath of those settlers for whom the presence of convicts was simply a temporary expedient for their own aggrandisement. As long ago as March of 1827 the gap between the settlers and Arthur had first appeared. Some of them had then prepared a petition to the King and both Houses of Parliament for trial by jury and legislation by representation. Arthur, believing their conduct had struck at all subordination in a colony such as Van Diemen's Land, advised my

[8] *Hobart Town Courier*, 13 August 1831.
[9] Based on Report of the Lieutenant Governor of Van Diemen's Land for the Year 1830, C.O. 280/30, p. 31 et seq.

lord Bathurst that if he granted such characters their petition, they would revolutionize the colony in five years. In July of 1830 he had again told the Secretary of State that the introduction of grand and petit juries in criminal trials would be highly inexpedient in a penal colony.[10]

By chance the reply from London arrived at a time when the behaviour of some of the free settlers had stiffened his opposition to their demands. On 23 May 1831 the Sheriff convened a meeting of the inhabitants of Hobart Town to address His Majesty on the occasion of his accession to the throne. Under the influence of Gellibrand, Horne, and Kemp the meeting changed from a gathering to express platitudes into one making an angry statement of grievances. They began by talking about the need to secure a legal title to their lands, about the iniquitous quitrents, the inefficiencies of the survey department, and the Colonial Usury Act which threatened to concentrate landed property in the hands of the comparatively few. Soon they began to discuss those things which offended them as free men. One man complained that under the Harbouring Act a convict constable could break into the home of any colonist in the middle of the night on the mere suspicion that he was harbouring a convict. Another man alleged that to collect information against a man who was not *comme il faut* with the Saint of Hobart Town, the convict police even intruded on the family circle round the fireside: another shouted that police spies were stationed under windows, that they had their ears and eyes on the keyholes of the free. Convictism, it was said, had exposed the free population to frightful indignities and terror. Then one man asked a simple question: seeing, he said, there were men that night in the Court House who by their education, their talent, their industry, and their respectability were entitled to be commissioned as magistrates, why then, he would ask, was the bench of magistrates swamped with men who had been appointed by the Saint? Was not the time ripe for the colony to have a legislature of its own, composed of representatives elected by the colonists? Was not the time ripe for them to have in London an agent of their own who could present their grievances? They put all this down in a series of resolutions, which were to be printed in the *Courier*, the *Colonial Times*, the *Tasmanian*, and the *Launceston Advertiser*. From then on, whenever they gathered together to exchange words on the canting Puritan of Hobart Town and his felon police, they referred to this day as the 'glorious twenty-third of May'.[11]

Flushed with success, they sought a meeting with the Lieutenant-Colonel who received them with that chilly dignity which only served to turn their enthusiasm for the institutions of the free into anger and rage. Arthur too was nettled inwardly by the insinuation that he, a soldier of Christ in God's unending battle with Satan, would use the methods of the peeping Toms to serve his high purposes. He told them he would forward their resolutions to London in due course. All the members of the opposition knew that he allowed

[10] Arthur to Bathurst, 23 March 1827, *H.R.A.*, III. v. 653-5; Goderich to Arthur, 25 January 1830, C.O. 408/7, pp. 97-8.
[11] *Hobart Town Courier*, 11 March and 28 May 1831; Henry Melville, *The History of Van Diemen's Land: From the Year 1824 to 1835, inclusive*; ed. by G. Mackaness (Sydney, 1965), *passim*; for the following resolutions passed at the meeting see *Hobart Town Courier*, 28 May 1831.

S

several months to elapse before sending the resolutions to London. They took this as just another proof of Arthur's indifference to their interests. For his part, the Lieutenant-Governor was not convinced that their support for free institutions was other than lukewarm. Like Dr Ross of the *Hobart Town Courier*, he had yet to hear a full-throated colonial roar of approval for these proposed changes from the respectable members of the society of Hobart Town.[12]

When it was announced in Hobart Town on 11 June 1831 that in future all land in Van Diemen's Land was to be disposed of not by grant but by sale at a minimum upset price of 5s per acre, and that the proceeds from such sales would be used to pay passages of female migrants, again a gap yawned between the response of the Governor and the response of the settlers. For his part he heartily rejoiced that as Governor he had been relieved from the duty of making grants of land which though sometimes gratifying, was often exceedingly distressing. He only wanted to add that government was not likely to sell thousands of acres of scrubby and unprofitable land at 5s an acre. By contrast, the settlers greeted the new regulations with a roar of disapproval. They had come to the colony expecting a land grant and convict labour in return for their investment of capital. Now government was not honouring an essential part of the contract. As for migrant labour, the settlers feared the colony would be saturated with a class of persons worse than convicts, because they would be far less under control. Government, they believed, had been seduced by the example of America where soil and climate were favourable for a society of settlers each toiling on his own plot of land. In Van Diemen's Land the worker, being a convict, could not be expected to be as industrious. So estates must be so large that no man could acquire them at the ruinous price of 5s an acre.[13] But the disappointment of the settlers at being cheated of their expectations did not touch Arthur deeply.

He had other subjects to ponder much more important than the material well-being of the free settlers of Van Diemen's Land. On 25 May 1831, 224 of the men who had been transported for participating in the agricultural riots of 1830-1 arrived in Hobart Town in the *Eliza*. On 4 August ninety-eight of them arrived in the *Proteus*. On both occasions Arthur spoke to those men with the 'calfless legs and sloping shoulders' of his great hope to achieve their reformation by Christian principles. He told them he was not there to wreak vengeance on them: that was the province of Almighty God. His divine master had taught him that if a man was thirsty, he should give him drink. He reminded them that they stood convicted before a human tribunal: he exhorted them not to be found guilty in the sight of God before whose judgment seat they must one day stand. He told them of the degraded state to which they had been reduced by their folly, and that good conduct would open the way to a free pardon, and enable them to return to their native land.[14]

[12] Arthur to Howick, 14 January 1832, C.O. 280/33, pp. 136-47.

[13] Arthur to Goderich, 11 July 1831, C.O. 280/29, p. 274; Arthur to Goderich, 27 October 1831, C.O. 280/30, pp. 224-8; *Hobart Town Courier*, 11 June 1831.

[14] For an excellent account of the arrival of the agricultural labourers transported for burning hay-ricks and threshing machines, see G. Rudé, ' "Captain Swing" and Van Diemen's Land', T.H.R.A., *P. & P.*, vol. 12, 1964-5, pp. 6-24; *Hobart Town Courier*, 4 June and 6 August 1831; for Arthur and the arrival of convict ships, see J. Backhouse, op. cit., pp. 17-20 and 137-8.

The same sense of high purpose side by side with worldly shrewdness continued to shape his policy to the aborigines. One part of him still hoped for a general conciliation of the natives and all through the second half of 1831 he exhorted all and sundry to refrain from any act of hostility. Another part of him believed that it was impossible to place any dependence upon the conduct of savages. He hoped and prayed fervently that Christmas of 1831 that that booby, that fool in Christ Robinson, would bring the aborigines in quickly so that they could get the survivors on to an island in Bass Strait, and have done with it. So when Robinson triumphantly entered Hobart Town one Saturday early in January of 1832 with a party of some forty blacks from the Oyster Bay and Big River tribes whom he had persuaded to live on an island, Arthur and the inhabitants received their entry into town with the most lively curiosity and delight. Outside Government House the band struck up a merry tune and the natives evinced once again the susceptibility of the savage beast to the white man's music. Excited by the music into a mood of great good humour and a desire to make themselves agreeable, they displayed their feats of wonderful dexterity on the lawns of Government House. Then, still laughing and joking and gambolling down the street like little children they boarded the boat in which they were to proceed to Great Island in the Furneaux Group. Swept on by the white man's benevolence and compassion, and their own fatal love of fun and games, and the promise of better things to come, some forty more left the land on which their people had moved and had their being since time immemorial. They left not in grief and rage but in high good humour.[15]

The following day, being a Sunday, the Lieutenant-Governor attended divine service at St David's Church where he went down on his knees and with more than his usual fervour rendered his thanks to Almighty God for the great benefits he had received at his hands. He thanked his God for ending the sufferings of the settlers from the bitter scourge from which the colony had so severely suffered for many years. Although it was impossible to reflect without sorrow upon the indiscriminate vengeance which these savages had taken on the white man, their wrongs had been many and great. He could only ask for the divine blessing on his scheme to treat them with the utmost compassion and continue to extend both protection and kindness towards them in their asylum on Great Island. On that first day when the bitter scourge had been at long last removed, Arthur bowed before his God, and said in secret: thine be the glory, believing that his Father who saw him in secret would reward him in secret.[16]

While he was still singing praises to his God for the happy issue out of the affliction caused by the aborigine a despatch arrived from London with instructions that all public works should be done by contract, and that the convicts whom this measure would relieve from government employment should be distributed amongst the free settlers. They should be placed under such strict discipline in government employment that they would prefer assignment to a settler to work in a government gang. In this way the cost to government of the transportation of convicts would be reduced. Never a man to be swayed

[15] *Hobart Town Courier*, 14 January 1832.
[16] Arthur to Goderich, 7 January 1832, C.O. 280/33, pp. 9-11.

by ledger sheet arguments, he proceeded to look in detail at what he was interested in—namely, whether the suggested change would promote the moral reform of the convicts.

The simple fact was that the situation of the convict was greatly improved by being removed from a state of destitution in England to a country where labour was scarce, and the labourer consequently in great demand. What disturbed Arthur was not the effect on the dread of transportation of such a high standard of life, for he was never greatly interested in deterrents against crime. Even less was he interested in employing severity from which he recoiled in horror, for he was a sensitive man, and indeed a most compassionate man. Had not his Saviour had compassion on the multitude? What disturbed him was that any material indulgence might encourage the natural tendency of the convict to depravity. What he liked about the system for convicts employed in government service was that they had few opportunities of making money. They were also locked up at night, and so deterred from the opportunity of indulging in excess, or gratifying their implacable desire to be mischievous. He wanted the convicts in assignment to be deprived of all those indulgences which enabled them to participate with vicious companions in their debaucheries. If convicts were indulged they would commit offences, as all indulgences must, he believed, feed that total depravity of mankind to which the convicts bore such ample testimony. In his evangelical zeal he planned to deprive the convicts of the few pleasures they knew, all unaware of the anger and hatred he was stirring up in their hearts by his high-minded attempts to improve them.

It was the same with the women. Their riotous and disorderly conduct when confined in the House of Correction in Hobart Town made it absolutely necessary that another yard should be added with cells for separating the women. To confine one hundred women together tended to destroy all subordination, he had found. So once again he displayed that concern for their reformation, that drive to remove from them all causes of any private hell in their hearts, so that they might be humble, and lowly and obedient in this world to prepare themselves to face their judge on the resurrection morning with confidence. It never occurred to him that in taking such action he was depriving the women of one of the few pleasures they could enjoy in Van Diemen's Land, and stirring up in their hearts an implacable anger against a soldier of Christ, who believed so fervently that the hearts of the sons of men were desperately wicked. In any case, Arthur believed it was despicable for a man not to stand by that which was right just because it made him unpopular.[17]

Arthur, too, had the usual temptation of the upright to assume that all those who disagreed with him were either publicans or sinners. Though he did not esteem himself to be an exception from the feeling common to all men of being influenced more or less by prejudice, yet when anyone expressed dissatisfaction with his administration he was always tempted to say to himself, and to his superiors in London, one could not expect anything else from a liar, a fornicator, or a drunkard. Edward Abbott was a one-time military officer who had served in the New South Wales Corps, and served with distinction as Deputy Judge Advocate of Van Diemen's Land from 1815 until

---

[17] Arthur to Goderich, 18 February 1832, ibid., pp. 368-81.

1824, and was then offered the position of civil commandant at Port Dal-rymple and a grant of 3,210 acres. He had so displeased Arthur that when it became known that he had not improved his land Arthur tried to take it from him. So in 1832 Abbott, being then sixty-six years of age, angered by Arthur standing between him and his deserts, opened his mouth wide in Hobart Town and hinted that the Lieutenant-Governor had been somewhat partial in granting land. Abundance of green acres, he said, had been lavished on saints and supporters, while sinners and opponents had not received a single acre. Arthur explained his decision in this particular case as due to the habits and propensities of Mr Abbott during his administration.[18]

By March rumours began reaching him that all was not well with the police magistrate of Richmond, Mr James Gordon. Gordon's father had served as steward on the estates of the Duke of Northumberland. He himself had emigrated to New South Wales in 1806 where, thanks to his influence in high places in England, he obtained the position of Naval Officer at Hobart Town. In 1826, impressed by his success as a farmer at Sorell, Arthur had raised him to the bench of magistrates. Between 1826 and 1830 he had held various offices until Arthur offered him the position of police magistrate at Richmond. By then Arthur was beginning to have his doubts about Gordon. There were stories in Hobart Town that Van Diemen's Land's most progressive farmer was a wine-bibber and a drunkard. In offering him the position Arthur took the opportunity to lecture him for his intemperate habits, and reminded him that every officer concerned with administering justice should himself be free from reproach. He warned him that if he was not temperate he would cer-tainly be dismissed.[19] All through 1831 the rumour-mongers and tell-tale-tits, who enjoyed an inflated currency in a society in which convictism and the evangelical piety of the tenants of Government House had intensified the human fear of exposure, kept pouring into Arthur's ear stories of most im-proper and intemperate carousals indulged in by Gordon and the chief constable of the district, Mr Gilbert Robertson, a person who was possessed of a certain cleverness as a writer. Arthur was deeply shocked, not just by the never-ending drinking parties, though they were bad enough, but also by an intimacy be-tween the two men which was quite inconsistent with their relative situations in the society of Van Diemen's Land. Gordon was a civil officer and a gentle-man: Robertson was a servant of government, and believed to have sufficient negro blood in his veins to explain to the respectable his being a prey to the baser passions of drunkenness and lechery.

When the collector of internal revenue reported in February 1832 that once again he had received no fees from the police magistrate at Richmond, Arthur instructed the Colonial Secretary to inform Gordon that he proposed to hold an investigation. The members of this commission of inquiry reached Rich-mond early in March to find Gordon in bed suffering, so he claimed, from the after-effects of a fall from a horse, though the righteous, the creeps and the

---

[18] Arthur to Goderich, 21 January 1832, ibid., pp. 249-52; R. W. Giblin, *The Early History of Tasmania* (2 vols, London, 1928 and Melbourne, 1939), vol. 2; entry for E. Abbott in T.S.A.

[19] Arthur to J. Gordon, 18 September 1829, Encl. in Arthur to Goderich, 8 September 1832, C.O. 280/35, pp. 57-94; E. M. Miller, *Pressmen and Governors* (Sydney, 1952); material on J. Gordon in T.S.A.

pryers were not slow to snigger when they pounced on the story, for in their eyes the inefficiency and incompetence of Gordon were all the fruits of over-indulgence. Within a week the members of the commission sent back to Arthur their report on the irregularities of the unhappy Gordon, who was by then quite exhausted from his attempts to impress the respectable while succumbing in private to drives he had neither the power nor the inclination to control. On 10 March Arthur presented the report of this commission to his Executive Council who recommended that because of his long service Gordon might be given the opportunity to resign. Three days later Gordon wrote to thank Arthur for the kind manner in which he had conducted the inquiry, and offered to resign. So matters stood when Gordon returned to Richmond at the end of March after exposing himself to the judgments of the Saint of Hobart Town.[20]

Once he got back to Richmond he began to have second thoughts. There he talked things over with Gilbert Robertson and other boon companions of like mind. He began to see himself not as a victim of his own folly, but as a martyr of a pernicious system of human discipline. The tone of apology and indeed all tendency to crook the knee before authority, and say he was very sorry he had sinned against Arthur and with Arthur's help he would try to sin no more, disappeared from his correspondence. Instead he became truculent and defiant. He refused to resign his seat on the Legislative Council. He accused Arthur of oppressing him and turning him out of office for the sole purpose of making a vacancy for the gentleman who lately filled the situation of private secretary to the Lieutenant-Governor. He published his correspondence with Arthur as a pamphlet. When Henry Savery wrote an unfavourable review of his work in the *Tasmanian* Gordon wrote to London to protest against the use of convicts to besmirch the reputation and honour of the free.[21]

He frequented more and more the company of those who were disaffected towards the government, especially Gilbert Robertson who, like himself, had been dismissed from office as a wine-bibber, and had his own score to settle with Arthur. On 6 July Robertson began the publication of an opposition paper, *The Colonist*, in which he cited Gordon as a victim of oppression. On 30 July Robertson wrote a long letter to the Secretary of State, the purpose of which was to give him and other members of the British government and legislature a correct account of the state of the colony, and of the interests of its inhabitants. He began with examples of Colonel Arthur's treatment of individuals. He ended on questions of public policy. The sale of Crown lands, he told the Secretary of State, was the most impolitic measure that could have been adopted, both as regards the colony and the mother country. Incalculable advantage, he concluded, would occur by placing not only colonial affairs, but the control of convict labour and expenditure in the hands of an elective legislature on the principle of the British constitution. The man whom Arthur

[20] C.O. 280/35, pp. 95-142; see especially Extracts from the Minutes of the Executive Council for Van Diemen's Land, 10 March 1832 and Arthur to J. Gordon, 16 March 1832 and J. Gordon to Arthur, 19 March 1832; J. Gordon, *The correspondence relating to the resignation of Mr Gordon as Police Magistrate at Richmond* (Hobart Town, 1832).

[21] See Colonial Secretary of Van Diemen's Land to J. Gordon, 16 August 1832, C.O. 280/35, p. 46; J. Gordon, op. cit.; Arthur to Stanley, 4 January 1834, C.O. 280/46, pp. 7-11.

had denounced as a low-born drunkard who was of no account in society had
raised the battle cry of freedom in Hobart Town.[22]

At the same time landholders whose private lives lacked the public notoriety
and scandal of Gordon and Robertson were beginning to grumble and groan.
Their grievance was Arthur's insistence that they should pay to government
the arrears of quitrent. Quitrents had been imposed first in November 1823
in the time of Sorell, and confirmed in November 1824 in the early years of
Arthur's administration. All persons receiving grants of land were to be free
of quitrent for the first seven years. After that time a quitrent of 5 per cent
per annum was to be paid upon the estimated value of the land. In the redemption of his quitrent the grantee was to have credit for one-fifth part of
the sums he might have saved to government by the employment and maintenance of convicts.[23] When Arthur informed the landholders of Van
Diemen's Land that government proposed to collect arrears of quitrent, they
responded in that extravagant language of the man on the land when asked to
pay tribute to Caesar. At meetings at Hamilton, Bothwell and Swan Port in
1832 they drew up petitions which thundered against the tax as unequal,
unjust, intolerable. Its collection, they said, would in one fell swoop absorb the
labour of years. Payment of quitrent would involve in ruin the prosperity and
happiness of every landowner in the colony. They had left a country suffering
from the imposition of heavy starvation to essay their fortune in a wilderness.
As compensation for rending asunder all their dearest ties, and risking their
persons and means in an unknown distant and savage part of the globe, they
had expected a free gift of land equal in extent to the amount of capital they
had severally imported. They had expected to pay a modest quitrent, and to
earn a comfortable subsistence despite the heavy losses sustained by the pillage
and roguery of convict servants and the enormous wages they had to pay to
free labourers. What they had not expected was this severe oppressive, grinding
rack-rent, which they were wholly unable to pay.[24]

Once again Arthur failed to respond with any human warmth or sympathy
for their plight. To men who believed that the fruits of all their labour and
their suffering were about to be stolen from them by soft-handed men who
had not broken their backs ploughing Van Diemen's Land, he chose the most
maddening language. He wrote to them of his duty. He told them, high-
minded as ever, that he had no grounds whatever to entertain the slightest
expectation that the instructions which had been conveyed to his government
to exact the quitrents would be relaxed. Similar replies to the landholders of the
other districts of Van Diemen's Land planted the suspicion in their minds that
their welfare and sufferings, the hardships they had endured, and the blight-
ing of their hopes did not trouble the mind or conscience of the Saint of
Hobart Town. In grief and rage they began to speak of him as a man who was

---

[22] For the text of this letter see the *Colonist*, 3 August 1832.

[23] Regulations for Grants of Land in New South Wales and Van Diemen's Land, Colonial
Office, November 1824; Printed in Appendix to Report from Select Committee on the Disposal
of Lands in the British Colonies, *P.P.*, 1836, XI, 512, pp. 499-502; Bathurst to Brisbane, 1
January 1825, *H.R.A.*, I. xi. 443-4.

[24] For the texts of these petitions see the advertisement columns of the *Hobart Town Courier*
for 1 June 1832; see also Arthur to Goderich, 28 July 1832, C.O. 280/34, p. 294.

so puffed up with compassion for the murderous, plundering savages of Van Diemen's Land or so preoccupied with the reformation of their wretched convict servants that he could not spare a thought for the long-suffering land-holders of Van Diemen's Land. The hot-headed amongst them subscribed to the *Colonist*, where they could read that July and August weekly hints that from the earliest days to the present time Arthur had a long record of oppressing individuals and treating the sacred birthright of Englishmen with indifference and contempt.[25]

At the end of July 1832 the *Colonial Times* told its readers that a legis-lative assembly was a measure of much importance to the real and continuing prosperity of both New South Wales and Van Diemen's Land because it would put the control of both revenue and expenditure in the hands of those who paid the taxes. Those miserable loungers with which the streets of Hobart Town and Launceston were crowded would speedily learn that the spade or the grubbing hoe was their best occupation. This colony wanted no cats that caught no mice. There was very little satisfaction to the honest industrious settler paying taxation which was spent upon a parcel of Do-littles and Ne'er-do-wells, the holders of sinecures, and the convict toss-pots of Hobart Town. The voice of the bourgeoisie, shouting the gospel of work, was beginning to be heard in a land which hitherto had heard only the monotonous chants and the laughter of the aborigine, or the swish of the flagellator's lash, and the howls of its victims.[26]

The difficulty for the *Colonist* and the *Colonial Times* and those of like mind was to bring the people to that point where they would take some action to achieve their birthrights. It was difficult enough to bring them together in any public meeting. Like most colonial communities they were cursed with the evils of apathy, fault-finding, and family feuds. The minds of the settlers in the interior were entirely occupied in the improvement of their lands, and the management of their flocks and herds. Few of them could spare the time or expense necessary to make a journey to Hobart Town. Alarmists were pro-phesying the consequences of servile submission to authority, and predicting the day would come when the inhabitants of Van Diemen's Land acquired the degraded character of the subjects of long-established despotisms. The *Colonist* predicted the day might come when the people would be driven to wrest their liberties by physical force, when future inhabitants renewed those dreadful scenes which South America had exhibited since she had shaken off the yoke of the unjust and unnatural parent.[27]

That August, gentlemen poured in in such numbers from all parts of the interior to Hobart Town for a meeting to pray for the accession of their rights as Britons that there was not even a vacant spot at the whole of the chairman's table. Good will and unity pervaded the meeting. Gellibrand, wearing his hat on the incline as usual, had come to the meeting to take the chair. Kemp, who was said never to be happy unless he was talking, took the floor early for his traditional long-winded speech on the rights of Englishmen. Captain Hunter,

---

[25] Arthur to the landed proprietors of the Sorell, Ouse, and Macquarie Districts, 26 May 1832, *Hobart Town Courier*, 1 June 1832; see columns of *Colonist* July and August 1832 *passim*.
[26] *Colonial Times*, 31 July 1832.   [27] *Colonist*, 17 August 1832.

Mr Gregson and Mr Murray spoke as Britons and colonists with that warmth of feeling which the occasion demanded. Mr Horne struck the only discordant note by shouting above the uproar provoked in all colonial meetings by any expression of dissent, that the thirty selected by the meeting to present the petition were not to be trusted and lacked the power to bind the people to anything. But he was quickly silenced. With one voice they went on to pray His Majesty to grant full and ample enforcement of their birthright by extending to this colony legislation by representation. Glorying as they did in the institutions of their mother country, they felt that pride which swelled the hearts of every Briton in the enforcement of those rights which belonged to a British constitution.[28]

When the day came to present the petition to the Lieutenant-Governor and ask him respectfully, though firmly, to forward it to His Majesty again they were met with that icy indifference with which Arthur greeted all those strivings which they identified with their pride and their glory. Gaining the regard of men was not his concern. While these landholders, shopkeepers, lawyers, and press proprietors were showing their view to Arthur, he was pondering over a different problem. He was asking himself what must be the human condition of a country first colonized from Newgate before those convicts, the emancipists, the expirees, and their families came under the wholesome influence of religious belief. Without religion there must be drunkenness, fornication, outrage, and unspeakable abominations. So while Gellibrand, Kemp, Horne, Bent and others were attempting to persuade His Majesty to grant them legislation by representation, Arthur was telling the Secretary of State that as without religion there could be no morality and no subordination, but only drunkenness, fornication and outrage, for his part he believed what Van Diemen's Land wanted most of all was nine pious and enlightened chaplains.[29]

On the night of 24 August, in thick and hazy weather with a great gale blowing up from the South Pole, news reached Hobart Town that the *Princess Royal* with the first assisted unmarried female migrants on board had run aground in the estuary of the Derwent. Arthur was in a quandary. He wondered how he could save their lives without endangering their virtue. He doubted whether there was any able-bodied civil officer whom he could trust in the company of unmarried women. In desperation, deciding that at least he and the Chief Police Magistrate could be trusted, he set off with him in a small boat, and rode the waves with a single-minded concern for the morals of those women, and supervised their conveyance in small vessels to Hobart Town where they were lodged in the Female Orphan School. In the weeks that followed he continued to fuss and fret over their moral welfare. He appointed a ladies' committee of forty-two respectable and virtuous matrons, and charged them to find suitable employment for the women. As a result of their benevolent exertions seventy-two were provided for as milliners and dressmakers or placed in the most respectable service. But alas, the remaining

---

[28] For an account of the meeting see the *Colonist*, 17 August 1832; for the text of the petition, see Henry Melville, op. cit., pp. 135-6n.
[29] Arthur to Howick, 9 May 1832, C.O. 280/34, pp. 140-2.

females were too abandoned to allow them to live with reputable families. So he sat down and wrote to London and urged them to send women who could marry tradesmen or who could be domestic servants, but, for God's sake, to send no more of that most abandoned class which had recently disgraced the streets of Hobart Town. Once again, the Saint of Hobart Town found himself strangely out of sympathy with the temper of his people. In the pothouses of Hobart Town the mockers quickly brought these women to derision. Some, as in New South Wales, hoped that these women would become in time the worthy mothers of future Tasmanians—a term coming into use among those who saw a non-convict future for their colony. Others lamented the arrival of so many of the outcasts of society from the dregs and lowest quarters of the metropolis of London. Others again, with that colonial eye for the heart of the matter, shouted that once again the colonists were not getting their money's worth.[30]

So while Arthur asked his God each night to give him that thing most necessary and requisite—namely, the wisdom and strength necessary to reform convicts, they were beginning to dream of future Tasmanians. When one of the 'Royals' was charged a third time with drunkenness in the magistrate's court in Hobart Town the *Colonial Times* wrote more in sorrow than in anger that they already had enough candidates for reformation. They wanted, they said, good, useful, and virtuous females who would marry industrious ticket-of-leave men, expirees and pardoned men, build them comfortable homes, and so restrain them from following evil propensities. They wanted women who could tame the old Adam, not Magdalenes. With the *Colonist* and even the *Hobart Town Courier* they welcomed all those improvements which were preparing the way for the future when men were no longer bowed down by iron chains. They welcomed the work of the temperance societies which were making the scenes of drunkenness as rare as they were formerly disgusting. They welcomed the lectures by Dr Ross to the Mechanics' Institute, because they were designed to elevate the minds of the listeners above things material. They hoped that by the labours of the clergy, the press, and the schoolmaster the day would come when an irreligious and dissolute person was both rare and shameful to the community at large. They welcomed the introduction of street lighting in Hobart Town in May not only because it conferred a lively appearance on their town, and even clothed it with beauty, but because it would act as yet another wholesome check to night offences. The bourgeoisie were beginning to sketch their ideal of a society of order and decorum, where the virtuous and the respectable reaped their rewards, and the ungodly were left struggling on that slippery slope down which they would slide to everlasting damnation.[31]

One Thursday evening in September 1832 as the moon rose in serene majesty over the dark waters of the Derwent a company of three hundred

---

[30] Arthur to Goderich, 8 September 1832, C.O. 280/35, pp. 9-10; for opinions in Hobart Town see *Colonist*, 31 August 1832; the *Colonial Times*, 4 September 1832; *Hobart Town Courier*, 31 August 1832 and September 1832 *passim*.
[31] *Colonial Times*, 18 September 1832; *Hobart Town Courier*, 10 March, 28 April, 12 and 26 May 1832.

assembled at Government House for a grand ball and supper. The ball was opened by Mrs Arthur and Captain Forster and kept up with great spirit. There were quadrilles, dances, sets and waltzes to the music provided by the band of the 63rd Regiment. When the health of the King was proposed the bursts of applause were deafening. Then Arthur raised his glass and asked them to drink the toast: 'May true British feeling never be wanting among British subjects throughout the world'. They knew what he meant. Then he asked them to charge their glasses again and drink to the toast: 'May the love of old England never be extinguished in the colony she has planted in Van Dieman's Land'. Eyes moistened: lumps formed in throats. For that was their great dream—that they could transplant English society to the antipodes. Then the dancing began again, and was kept up till a late hour, when the revellers returned to their homes, flushed, gay and happy, and sustained by the conviction that what was civilization for them could be re-created in their new environment.[32]

A fortnight earlier Henry Hellyer, an architect and surveyor for the Van Diemen's Land Company, put a pistol against his head and blew his brains out. Hellyer, who was born in 1790, had played a part with Edward Curr in exploring and mapping the rugged country of the north-west in the neighbour-hood of that Cape Grim where Curr, after some heated differences with Arthur, had finally chosen the site for the company's activities. He had had the courage and the strength to endure the gloomy weather, and the dreary state of the surrounding country, and to enjoy the savage grandeur in that sublime solitude. He had triumphed over nature only to be defeated by man. For in the headquarters of the company that winter of 1832 lying tongues brought him to his destruction. A convict spread a story that he, Hellyer, had had him flogged and stopped his ticket-of-leave because the convict knew Hellyer's wounds were that very old disease in the annals of mankind. And Hellyer began to be morose: he prayed to his God to deliver him from such false tongues: he asked his God what was he to do if he should lose his reason and rush on into madness. Then, impatient as ever, not willing to wait for human or divine aid he asked God to forgive his enemies, persecutors, slan-derers, and blew his brains out. Curr, who loved him, reported the event to Arthur as a mental delusion, amounting to insanity. Arthur agreed: 'I have no doubt', he minuted on Curr's report, 'the unhappy Gentleman met with his death in the manner stated by Mr. Curr', never allowing the question to cross his mind whether the society of Van Diemen's Land had so played on the unfortunate Hellyer as to drive him to the desperate remedy of using death as a happy issue out of that stricken society of slander, backbite, and the everlasting mock.[33]

Arthur continued to behave as he always had behaved, namely, in con-sistency with that teaching of his Saviour who had commanded men that they

[32] *Hobart Town Courier*, 21 September 1832.

[33] For the suicide of Henry Hellyer see E. Curr to G. Arthur, 15 September 1832, and minute by Arthur of 26 September 1832 (Colonial Secretary's File, Arthur Period, t.s.a.); H. Hellyer, 'Descriptions of the Forth Gateway' in J. Ross (ed.), *The Hobart Town Almanack for the year 1832* (Hobart Town, 1832).

resist not evil. In November seven soldiers drank rum in a public house till, elevated by their pot-courage, they rushed out in the street hunting in packs for sport, seized a helpless civilian, and belaboured him with their bayonets till the people came to his assistance. A riot then began, as soldiers and constables walloped the defenceless pedestrians of Hobart Town. The editors of the *Courier* and the *Colonist*, Dr Ross and Mr Robertson, who had been ill-treated by the soldiers with the rest, fetched Arthur who halted close to the scene, thinking it prudent, as he put it, not to mix openly with the people. A whaler, thinking His Excellency should see for himself the sufferings of the people at the hands of soldiers and police, showed Arthur his wounds but Arthur, compassionate man that he was, could not or would not unbend. Some colonists raised a feeble huzza to mark his presence: the fighting stopped: the house-master of Van Diemen's Land retired to his study.[34]

At a reform dinner at the Ship Inn in Hobart Town that October, the greatest cordiality and good humour had prevailed throughout the evening until the toast-master called: 'Gentlemen I give you the toast of His Majesty's representative'. He was greeted with silence. These men who were caught up in the utilitarian, reforming, and indeed ameliorating mood of the day had come to the conclusion that Arthur and his retainers at Government House did not share their hopes or their enthusiasms. The diners regaled the people outside with a hogshead of porter. When they too were called on to drink to the health of the Lieutenant-Governor they greeted the proposal with groans, which changed to cheers when a man shouted 'Let's drink the health of Governor Bourke'. But that, after all, was the way in which Arthur expected the 'swinish multitude' to behave, as it was not given to him to see that the groaners and the drinkers would fashion the future of that society over which it was his high honour to preside.[35]

Besides, there were few in high places on whom he could rely, or who could confer distinction or evoke approval, let alone enthusiasm for his administration. John Burnett, who had arrived in November of 1826 to take office as the first Colonial Secretary, was far from well, the victim of a dropsy and his own extravagant nature which had driven him to spend far beyond his means at a time when his health precluded him from saving the family from financial ruin. At first, Arthur had found him inexperienced in business but a man of integrity. Soon rumours began to fly round Hobart Town that Burnett had been in collusion with Roderic O'Connor in a land deal. But when Arthur taxed him with it, and pressed him for more diligent attention to his duties, Burnett explained he was a man of such a sensitive nervous system that everything which agitated his mind immediately affected his bodily health and brought on illness. Pedder, the Chief Justice, was faithful but far too fond of legal pedantry to be close in all things to one of Christ's soldiers. Algernon Montagu, the Attorney-General, was a spendthrift, and, according to rumour, the seducer of the unhappy Savery's wife. But that was the trouble. Arthur knew so little of the conduct even of his own servants, because he was never

[34] Letter by 'Quarter-Staff' to *Colonial Times*, 20 November 1832.
[35] *Colonist*, 26 October 1832.

brought into contact with them, and so judged them by the partial and often exaggerated representations of others. Besides, according to the wits of Hobart Town, he was far too dependent on the optical apparatus of Captain Matthew Forster, who had taken up his duties as Chief Police Magistrate in December of 1831.[36]

Bedford, the principal chaplain, was so incredibly vain and puffed up with his own importance that he spent his time flirting with the new-fangled notions of the Tractarians which inflated the parson into a priest rather than a preacher of the wholesome evangelical doctrine of how man's depravity could only be redeemed by faith in that One who had hung on that tree for the comfort and redemption of all sinners. The Colonial Treasurer, Jocelyn Thomas, had dipped his fingers deeply into the colonial treasury. O'Ferrall, the collector of customs, was guilty of disgraceful, cruel and most immoral conduct. Though a married man he had seduced an unfortunate woman with a promise of marriage which caused the woman to destroy herself as soon as his perfidy was exposed. Then when the *Princess Royal* had arrived in August of 1832 he had approached Mary Anne Porter, and persuaded her to live with him, notorious evil-doer that he was, to his own delight and to Arthur's great pain. When rumours began to circulate in Hobart Town that O'Ferrall had been sharing the takings from the treasury with Thomas, Arthur seized the chance to show that evil-doers were snared in the net of their own wickedness, and suspended him from the office of collector of customs.[37]

Early in March 1833 when all Hobart Town seemed to have gone to the races, one person who had quite a high reputation on the island for his ability to sit a horse, was auspiciously absent from the national amusement. He was Lieutenant-Colonel George Arthur, who stayed at Government House in a high-minded demonstration that it was better, as he was fond of putting it, to be moral than to pursue pleasure. The worldly-wise men shook their heads in dismay: would it not be better, they asked, for the Lieutenant-Governor to mix among the people, and so procure a better feeling towards him personally than he had unfortunately hitherto obtained. Others argued that the Lieutenant-Governor had just as much right to stay away from the races if he thought proper, as to go to them. Others again retorted angrily that the man was so caught up with this fever to appear moral that he had lost the art of appearing as a mortal to those driven on by the great hungers of mankind.[38]

But Arthur carried on quite oblivious of this gathering storm of human anger and outrage stirred up by such single-minded dedication to virtue. Popularity was not his aim: nor did the judgments of his peers, let alone the fickle likes and dislikes of the multitude, touch him at all. Men judged each other harshly. What mattered was the judgment of God, with whom there was mercy and plenteous redemption. Had not the psalmist said, that if God marked

[36] For J. Burnett, see entry in T.S.A. and *Australian Dictionary of Biography*, vol. 1; for the comment on Arthur see Diary of G. T. W. Boyes, 16 March 1836; for M. Forster, see J. Franklin, *Narrative of some passages in the history of Van Diemen's Land* (London, 1845).

[37] Arthur to Goderich, 1 February 1833, C.O. 280/39, pp. 3-4; Arthur to Goderich, 5 February 1833, C.O. 280/39, p. 214; Arthur to Goderich, 22 February 1833, ibid., pp. 199-206; see also the editorial comment in the *Colonist*, 1 March 1833, on this suspension.

[38] *Colonial Times*, 19 March 1833; see also the *Launceston Advertiser*, March 1833 *passim*.

all that men did amiss, none could endure it? Arthur's eye was single, his whole concern was for a life in accord with God's precepts, yet those who had lacked all charity were even saying at tea parties and tradesmen's balls that the Colonel was so much in the habit of telling lies that he had already lost all sense of distinction between truth and falsehood.[39]

So matters stood when an item of news from London started up a debate on the convict system. That March the news reached Hobart Town that in future the expenses for the penal settlement at Port Arthur were to be paid out of the colonial fund instead of being defrayed by the mother country. The opposition press was incensed. This dipping the hands *ad libitum* into their pockets for purposes over which they had no control was, they argued, an additional reason for a legislative assembly chosen by themselves, which would at least protect their property from being wrested from them in order to put into operation some new-fangled doctrines of convict discipline. If the men had been set to the roads, so as to enable farmers to bring their produce to market, there would be some reason for it. But no, their money was to be used to put to hard labour a number of strong, able-bodied fellows who would be driven to perform heavy and laborious work of no benefit to the colony as a punishment and a means of reforming their morals. This, indeed, was a wild-goose scheme—for which the industrious, thriving settlers of Van Diemen's Land had to pay. The *Colonial Times* went on to tell its readers that anyone who saw the wretched outcasts dragged from ships would be left in no doubt that transportation was slavery.[40]

This was a conclusion which Arthur was never prepared to accept. Believing passionately as he did that transportation should be neither a boon to evil-doers, nor the cause of their greater degradation or slavery, he put down on paper his ideas on punishment and the convict system. The *Colonial Times* and the *Colonist* began their discussion in this world: Arthur began his in heaven. As he saw it, punishment of wickedness in its true sense and meaning was the prerogative of the Almighty. Man endeavoured to prevent by penal laws those acts which were adverse to the interests or supposed interests of society, and to reform the perpetrators of those crimes.[41] The penal system of Van Diemen's Land was designed to achieve those ends. The convicts in assignment in Van Diemen's Land at the beginning of 1833 lived in conditions calculated to arouse that desired dread of transportation in the breasts of their fellow criminals, to provide adequate punishment for their transgression against the laws of society, and effective incentive for their reformation and future law-abiding life. They were assigned generally to settlers in the interior where they were employed clearing and cultivating forest land. They were sufficiently fed, and decently clothed, but were allowed no wages. Idleness and insolence of expression or even of looks—indeed anything betraying the insurgent spirit—subjected them to the chain-gang or the triangle, or to hard labour on the roads. The assigned convicts were deprived of liberty, were exposed to all the

---

[39] Diary of G. T. W. Boyes, 23 November 1835.
[40] *Colonial Times*, 19 March and 2 April 1833.
[41] Arthur to Goderich, 8 February 1833, C.O. 280/39, pp. 44-6; Arthur to Goderich, 15 February 1833, ibid., pp. 151-8.

caprice of the family to whose services they might happen to be assigned, and subjected to the most summary laws. The condition of the convicts in no way differed from that of slaves except that their masters could not apply corporal punishment, and had a property in their labour for a limited period only. They were in one respect worse off than the West Indian negro, for they suffered the additional misery of knowing they had been their own tormentors. Or so Arthur thought, for Arthur was a deeply religious man, who conceived of the whole world as a stage on which the players were taking part in that drama of good and evil, the first act of which had begun when Eve was tempted by the serpent and did eat of the fruit of the tree of the knowledge of good and evil. Arthur knew more of what God had planted in men, than of man himself.[42]

The same high-mindedness and detachment pervaded his rules for the discipline and labour of the convicts employed on public works. They were kept in barracks, with the exception of a very few well conducted men as overseers, and men with wives and families, who were not allowed this indulgence without an ample probation. They were called for labour at break of day, shortly after which they were mustered to their respective places of labour by the overseers, who were appointed for good conduct. On no account were they permitted to labour for themselves. For good behaviour convicts employed on public works could be lent to settlers who would, should they so desire, make a voluntary gift to the convicts for their good conduct.[43]

The roads of the colony were formed and kept in repair by the convicts who were sentenced to their labour by the magistrates of Van Diemen's Land, if their offences were not of such magnitude as to sentence them to labour in the chain-gang. At the beginning of 1833 the convicts employed on the roads in the colony worked in parties and lived in huts as near their work as possible. Many gangs were supervised by free overseers, who were generally expirees, but a few of them by prisoners of well-known good character who received such a position as an indulgence for their good conduct. By day, from sun-up to sun-down, they laboured so severely with pick, spade and harrow that many of them applied to be sent to private service. Returns were made at regular intervals, stating the behaviour of each man while in the gang, and the committee before whom these returns were made fully satisfied themselves that an amendment had occurred before recommending reassignment to the Lieutenant-Governor, who, in his turn, had to be duly satisfied for Arthur was both just and stern.[44]

The convicts working in chains, of whom there were 545 at the beginning of 1833, laboured by day in gangs: by night they were lodged in a hulk, double-ironed, lying down to sleep in fetters: their food was coarse and scant; the work was incessant and monotonous, consisting as it did of breaking and wheeling stones for repairing the roads. The most depraved were put to the heaviest and severest labour. To be relieved from this wretched state required the utmost good conduct. Every fresh offence prolonged the servitude and rendered the offender less chance of relief. They were constantly guarded by the military and denied the smallest indulgence. Arthur, who was no supporter of severity, spent many an anxious moment, pondering how such a harsh punishment could stop short at the point where the victim was irretrievably hardened by the experience.[45]

Nowhere was this problem of a severity of punishment for the hardened and the incorrigible which would not degrade, or cause despair, or cause a man to curse his creator more apparent than in the penal settlements. In October of 1832, having been instructed to reduce the number confined in such settlements, and to assign the corrigible to more productive labour, Arthur had closed down the settlements at Maria Island and Macquarie Harbour and housed all the convicts sentenced to penal settlements at Port Arthur, which he hoped to make into a model penal settlement where the convicts would experience both severity and certainty of punishment. There were 475 convicts there at the beginning of 1833. They consisted of those sentenced to servitude in a penal settlement for an offence committed in the colony, men whose offences before coming to the colony were of an atrocious nature, men whose offences on the voyage required a marked example, and such educated convicts whose irregularities compelled the government to administer to them a most rigid course of correction.[46] Even at Port Arthur, where the convicts were incessantly occupied in the most painful work, under close supervision, without even the smallest indulgence, and debarred from communicating with any friend or companion outside the settlement, Arthur had formed a gang of those who had conducted themselves to the satisfaction of the commandant from whom the most fitting and deserving were chosen to fill the more subordinate offices. As he saw it, the man without hope had lost all incentive to amendment. By contrast the perpetrators of the most atrocious crimes and those guilty of misconduct at the penal settlement, were consigned to the penal settlement chain-gang, in which the work was incessant and most galling, the rations of the sparest, and any disobedience of orders, turbulence or other misconduct was instantaneously punished by the lash.[47]

This same principle of reward for good conduct and punishment and increasing physical hardship for bad conduct could be traced through the whole system. The indulgence of a ticket-of-leave could be obtained by a convict conducting himself in such manner as to convince the authorities that he was so far reclaimed from his evil course that it became no longer dangerous to society to entrust him partially with his liberty, as he was bidding fair to make an atonement for his former misdeeds. A man sentenced to seven years transportation could apply after four, a man to fourteen after six and a man to life after eight years. The condition of holding such a ticket was that the very first conviction of any offence before a magistrate rendered the possessor liable to forfeit his indulgence. His place of residence was noted, and he could not move without the permission of the police magistrate of his district. So once again tried good conduct procured this precarious liberty until the original sentence of servitude

[45] Ibid.   [46] Ibid.   [47] Ibid.

GEORGE ARTHUR

Portrait by Benjamin Duterrau in the National Library, Canberra

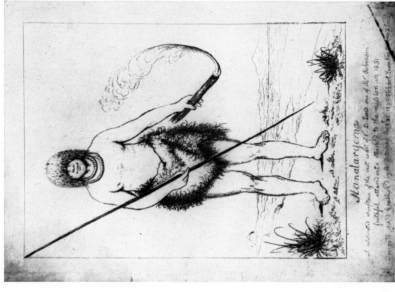

MANNALARGENNA

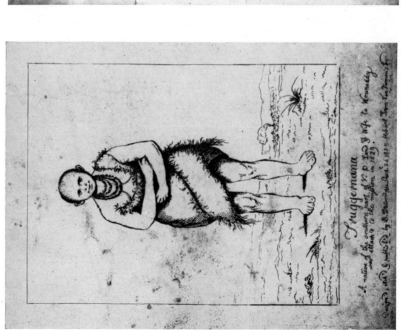

TRUGANINI

Aborigines of Van Diemen's Land

Etchings by Benjamin Duterrau in the Mitchell Library, Sydney

expired, while the slightest lapse returned him to that state of bondage from which the ticket had relieved him.[48]

Throughout the whole system the same principle prevailed. The indulgence for tried good conduct did not consist in any increase in such creature comforts as tobacco, alcohol, higher wages, or better clothes, for all those in Arthur's eyes were the means by which men had fed their vanity as well as their vices from time immemorial. The Saint of Hobart Town was concerned to make men virtuous rather than happy. The Saint also believed that men would be less likely to wander from the path of virtue if they were deprived of all such comforters as alcohol to which they might turn to distract them from their wretchedness or even, at a deeper level, to make their life bearable.

The Saint also held that men should remain in that station in society which God had ordained for them. At the beginning of 1833 he decided to round up the educated convicts in Hobart Town and Launceston and send them to Port Arthur. In that penal settlement they would not be able to walk about the town filling up the gulf which should separate the bond from the free. As he saw it, the educated convicts were like the half-blacks in the slave colonies. In Van Diemen's Land there should be no mingling between the bond and the free. Besides, he went on, at Port Arthur their degradation would not excite consideration, neither would it tend to eliminate the respect of the lower for the higher classes of society. At Port Arthur they would be compelled to substitute habits of sobriety, industry and exertion for those of drunkenness, sloth and indolence. At Port Arthur they would acquire the virtues of unqualified submission and patient endurance.

It was as though Arthur had seized a whip and driven these men out of Hobart Town for their sins of pride and covetousness, and sloth and drunkenness and fornication, and lying and hypocrisy and treachery to each other as well as to themselves, and condemned them to earn their bread in the sweat of their brow rather than by their wits. Like others who gathered for prayers and reading of the psalms in the privacy of their houses, he thought a spell in the solitary confinement cells for drunkenness, if administered every fortnight, must be attended with much benefit to the moral and physical health of the convicts. He believed that he was doing it all for their own good, that his motive was of the highest, being no less than that of their eternal salvation. It never occurred to him to ask whether he was receiving some dark subterranean satisfaction from such behaviour. The heart of man might be deceitful above all things, and no one could know it. He might confess to prejudice but on God's business no doubt ever crossed his mind. It never bothered him that when he visited one of the convict gangs of Van Diemen's Land he was greeted with neither affection nor enthusiasm. He was never hailed as their saviour, their protector or their friend. No man wept for joy to see the man who had saved him from some inner torment, some private hell in his heart. No man wrote to him as the convicts had written to Father Therry in Sydney 'for God's sake come'. Between Arthur's high-mindedness and convict behaviour there was a great gulf fixed. He saw their life as a hideous struggle

[48] Ibid.

T

between salvation and damnation. They saw themselves as engaged in an un-equal struggle against their gaolers and tormentors.[49]

For being found standing in the mess room with his cap on during divine service a convict had his sentence in the chain-gang extended for fourteen days; for stealing tobacco from a fellow prisoner one was sentenced to fifty lashes; for being found in bed with his master's convict female servant, for being absent from his master's service for two nights, for repeated insolence to his master, gross neglect of duty, and violently assaulting another man, one was sentenced to twelve months in the chain-gang; for being drunk and ex-posing his person in the street one was sentenced to fifty lashes and chain-gang during the remainder of his sentence; for being in a state of intoxication at muster one was reproved; for repeated neglect of duty and being absent from lodgings at night one was sentenced to twenty-five lashes, while for being drunk a second time and being absent from his master's lodgings and being insolent to his master the same man was sentenced to fifty lashes; for being found in town without a pass and trafficking for his own benefit, one was admonished and ordered to return home; for repeated drunkenness and neglect of duty one was confined to the cells on bread and water; for absconding one was sentenced to fifty lashes; for improper conduct to-wards a female convict one was admonished; for disobeying the overseer's orders, and harbouring a female convict, one was sentenced to labour for two months in the chain-gang; for being in a public house after hours one was sentenced to two months hard labour in a road party; for being in a dis-orderly house after hours one was admonished; for being in a disorderly house after hours one was given six days at the tread-wheel; for spoiling 450 feet of wood by cutting it crooked, one was ordered to make up 450 feet in fourteen days; for mutinously refusing with others of the chain-gang to work one morning because their breakfasts were not ready at the normal hour, one was given fifty lashes; for introducing tobacco and smoking it contrary to the rules of the chain-gang, another was given twenty-five lashes; for repeatedly abus-ing his overseer and being insolent to his master yet another was given fifty lashes; for leaving his master's house without leave, one was reproved; for attending church muster in a dirty state another was given three hours in the stocks.[50]

Arthur's system, which had been designed to provide labour to government and settler, to reform the corrigible, and to put the incorrigible out of harm's way, produced a bewildering variety of responses amongst the convicts. There was Mc Jas. Eurow or McEurows transportee for life who arrived in Van Diemen's Land in the *Minerva* in 1818. After receiving his ticket-of-leave, he was charged with violently assaulting Jane Pyers on the highway. For this he had to forfeit his ticket-of-leave. From that time until 1839 he was charged every two or three months before a magistrate with drunkenness and for such

[49] Arthur to Goderich, 15 February 1833, C.O. 280/39, pp. 158-9; Arthur to Goderich, 27 February 1833, ibid., pp. 250-77; Diary of G. T. W. Boyes, 15 January 1836.
[50] Examples taken from the Convicts' Conduct Register, Male. A. 1809-29, 13. 1807-30 (T.S.A.).

offences as striking a woman, neglect of duty, being absent without leave and returning in a state of intoxication, and with being insolent to the surgeon. For these offences he was flogged, worked in the tread-mill, given twenty-fours hours solitary confinement, confined to his cell on bread and water, and withdrawn from the list of convicts who could be assigned to private settlers. On 24 May 1839, twenty-one years after his arrival in Van Diemen's Land, he received his conditional pardon, and disappeared from the pages of history into that anonymous mass of people in the island who nursed that memory of an ancient wrong: that their labour, their blood, their agony and their suffering was the price for creating civilization and the wealth of the gentry.[51]

There was Ino Douglas, a transportee for life who arrived in Van Diemen's Land in 1825. On 10 October 1825, for raising false reports respecting the treatment of prisoners at Maria Island, he was reproved. On 14 November 1826 for repeatedly abusing the overseer on the property of Joseph Archer at Panshanger and being insolent to his master he was sentenced to fifty lashes. On 2 July 1827 for disobedience to orders and injuring a mare, the property of his master, he was sentenced to one hundred lashes. On 6 October 1828 for quitting the premises of his master on a Sunday without leave, and for tippling in the house of J. King, he was punished with twenty-five lashes and returned to his master's service. On 25 March 1835 he was discharged from the service of Joseph Archer by a decision of the Lieutenant-Governor. By that time he had received 390 lashes and had served a period in road parties and chain-gangs.[52] He, too, was one of those victims of an ancient wrong.

The experiences of the women were just as varied. Elinor Brady was sentenced in Dublin to transportation for seven years and arrived in Van Diemen's Land in 1817. By the end of the year she was up before a magistrate for disobeying the orders of the Lieutenant-Governor and confined in a solitary cell on bread and water for one week. One week later she was again charged with disobeying orders and confined in a solitary cell on bread and water for fourteen days. Early in 1818 she was charged with being drunk and disorderly and sentenced to one week's hard labour in gaol. On 7 December 1818 she was again charged with being drunk and disorderly, for which she forfeited her ticket-of-leave and endured hard labour in gaol until assigned. On 24 April 1819 she was charged with being drunk and disorderly and sentenced to three months' hard labour in gaol. On 9 March 1820 she was charged with being drunk and disorderly and disguising herself in man's clothes, and was sentenced to hard labour in gaol. But at that point her convict record ceased. Perhaps she mended her ways; perhaps she married and raised a family and handed on to them her picture of an Irish wrong and English perfidy; or perhaps she sank into her grave without reproach to either the potter who had so fashioned her clay as to expose her to sufferings beyond her power to endure or understand, or to the officials who in their zeal to maintain law and order and subordination had so despitefully used her. For she too dropped back into

[51] Mc. JAs Eurow or McEurows. Arrived in *Minerva* 1818, Convicts' Conduct Register, M. 1809-29 (t.s.a.).

[52] Ino Douglas. Life 1825, Convicts' Conduct Register, D. 1809-29 (t.s.a.).

anonymity, and left no lasting memorial, except possibly in the collective consciousness of those who came after her.[53]

Esther Barker, who was transported for seven years, arrived in Van Diemen's Land in 1823. On 9 June of that year she was accused of insolence to her master, and put on bread and water in a cell for one week. Twice in July 1825 she was accused of being drunk and disorderly, for which she was reproved the first time and sentenced to a session on bread and water for the second offence. In March of the following year she complained to the magistrate of her master and mistress for abusing her, for which she was ordered to be placed in the Female Factory until she could again be assigned. But in January 1827 she was again in trouble. This time she was accused of absenting herself from her master's house on Sunday afternoon and remaining absent until the morning. For this she was confined to her cell on bread and water for seven days, after which she was to be assigned to country service. Being away from the tempting sounds and the sights that dazzle did not help her to mend her ways, for she was put on bread and water for seven days, and in the stocks for one hour for absconding from her master. All through 1829, 1830, 1831 and 1832 she was frequently fined 5s for drunkenness. In the latter year she was freed from servitude, after which she passed into such anonymity that a man with the eye of pity could only hazard a guess whether her gaolers tormented her to the end of her days for her inability to stop, or whether once out of their reach and power she found peace.[54]

Not all were tormented by their gaolers. Sarah McKenzie, who was transported for fourteen years for receiving stolen goods, arrived in Hobart Town in the *Mary* in 1823. She had a good husband and one child. She was tried before a magistrate in October 1825 for being absent from divine service,. and reproved. In November of the following year she was charged with being drunk and again reproved. She did not appear before the magistrates again. Perhaps chance helped her, perhaps circumstance, or perhaps she just changed with the passage of time.[55] Mary King, who was transported for fourteen years from Edinburgh for an unspecified crime, arrived in Van Diemen's Land in the *Mary Ann* in 1822. In May of that year she was up before the magistrate for being absent from her master's premises and being drunk and disobedient. The price of her folly was one week in Hobart Gaol on hard labour. In March of the following year she was before the magistrate again for disobeying the orders of Dr Garrett, and enticing six females from the hospital, for which she was confined to a cell till the next day. For the next nine years of her servitude she was not touched by her gaolers, and died on 28 January 1834 on the eve of her emancipation.[56]

The *Hobart Town Courier* had greeted the rioters, incendiaries and machine-breakers of 1830-1 who had been transported to Van Diemen's Land as able-bodied, hard-working country men who should prove to be good farming men. Most of them adopted that docile, law-abiding behaviour recommended to them by the Lieutenant-Governor. William Dove, an agricultural

---

[53] Elinor Brady. Dublin 7 years. 1817. Principal Superintendent of Convicts, Alphabetical book of female convicts arriving in Van Diemen's Land, B. 1803-35 (T.S.A.).
[54] Esther Barker, ibid.   [55] Ibid., M. 1803-35.   [56] Ibid., K. 1803-35.

rioter who arrived in the *Proteus* on 4 August 1831 was charged on 15 August 1833 with being out after hours and being found under suspicious circumstances. For this he was reprimanded. On 3 March 1835 he was charged with being drunk and furiously riding his master's horse. For this he was sent to the tread-wheel for ten days, after which he was returned to government for distribution in the interior as a ploughman or a groom. On 21 January 1836, he was again before a magistrate for insolence to his master, for which he went to the cells for fourteen days on bread and water, and was returned to gaol. The following year on 3 February he received his free pardon. One Samuel Draper who also arrived in the *Proteus* in August of 1831 spent part of his days in hard labour, in the chain-gang, or being tied to the triangles for neglect of duty, for insolence, for feigned illness, and not being able to keep a civil tongue in his head,[57] until October of 1836 when a free pardon delivered him from his tormentors. For the most part Arthur had not spoken to these men in vain, for by their labour and their good conduct most of them went on to their emancipation without knowing that abomination of flogging, or that degradation of the chain-gang which had been designed as a terror to evil-doers. On 1 August 1835, 264 of them were pardoned, 86 in October of 1836 and in 1837 the Lieutenant-Governor was instructed to serve conditional pardons to the remainder provided they were not serving current sentences.[58]

Arthur was proud of the achievement. He was proud of the fact that of the seventeen thousand convicts who had been transported to Van Diemen's Land since 1804, five thousand had never had any complaint brought against them before a magistrate. He was proud of what his system had fashioned out of the accumulated refuse of the whole population of a country like Great Britain. Just as a horse that had been strictly trained became quite subdued and docile, so the convict of Van Diemen's Land would in time become likewise through the performance of compulsory labour. It was his proud conviction that Van Diemen's Land might be made a terror to evil-doers for the next quarter of a century at least. Free institutions would quickly work the subversion of his whole intention of keeping Van Diemen's Land a penal colony. His great aim was to give those with vicious minds a new direction. Like most men who were indifferent to man's regard he never seemed even to tell himself that Van Diemen's Land as a terror to evil-doers was not an ideal to which many would respond in an age when the trumpets had already heralded that day when all men were at long last to be freed from their chains.[59]

[57] *Hobart Town Courier*, 4 June and 6 August 1831; Case of William Dove, alias Dow, transported for seven years for machine-breaking, Norfolk, 5 January 1831; Case of Samuel Draper, transported for seven years for machine-breaking, Essex, 4 January 1831 (Principal Superintendent of Convicts, Convicts' Conduct Register, T.S.A.).

[58] G. Rudé, ' "Captain Swing" and Van Diemen's Land,' T.H.R.A., P. & P., vol. 12, 1964-5, pp. 6-24.

[59] Arthur to Goderich, 1 July 1833, C.O. 280/42, pp. 3-14; Arthur to Hay, 31 January 1834 C.O. 280/46, p. 156.

THE SOLE DISTINCT CAUSE OF
ALL THE MISCHIEF

WHILE THE COLONEL was preparing his plans to make Van Diemen's Land a terror to evil-doers for the next quarter of a century, some of the settlers and some of the intellectuals in Hobart Town had come to the conclusion that Arthur's government was becoming every day more and more a terror to the free. One of these was Gilbert Robertson. In February of 1832 a mischief-making servant had whispered in Arthur's ears that at harvest time on the Robertson estates at Richmond things had been done which Arthur would scarcely believe. When asked for an explanation Robertson had laughed it off as just part of the festivity and merriment with which men had always celebrated bringing in the harvest. Arthur was so shocked that he deprived Robertson of the right to have assigned servants. Whereupon Robertson solemnly warned Arthur the day might come when he would find redress for his wrongs.[1]

In March of 1833 he saw his chance. On the first day of that month Henry Savery, who already enjoyed a reputation as a trafficker in writings on low subjects, had written an article in the *Tasmanian* in which he had reviewed James Gordon's pamphlet on his correspondence with Arthur over the former's enforced resignation from the office of police magistrate at Richmond. Gordon was already well-known in Hobart Town as an opponent of Colonel Arthur. Day after day he was to be seen standing, or rather swaying, outside the doorway of Government House, telling all and sundry that he was excluded from taking his rightful place as a member of the Legislative Council by the infamy and oppression of Colonel Arthur. Now Robertson threw open to Gordon the columns of the *Colonist* to tell the reading public of Van Diemen's Land that the man who had done him great evil had recently stooped to even greater depths to blacken the reputation of the free: Arthur had used that unsavoury gossipmonger Henry Savery to hold Gordon up to ridicule in the eye of the public.[2]

In April Gordon began a lively and somewhat disrespectful correspondence with the Colonial Secretary who suggested that if Gordon had a grievance he should seek redress in the ordinary tribunals. So Gordon charged the luckless Savery before the Chief Police Magistrate in Hobart Town with writing an article in the *Tasmanian* tending to blacken his, Gordon's, character contrary

[1] J. Montagu to Arthur, 16 June 1832; G. Robertson to J. Montagu, 18 June 1832; G. Robertson to Arthur, 22 June 1832, Encl. in Arthur to Hay, 1 March 1834, C.O. 280/47, pp. 2-16.
[2] *Tasmanian*, 1 March 1833; these events are described in Arthur to Goderich, 20 June 1833, C.O. 280/41, pp. 261-86; for the text of the order of 9 July 1828, see ibid., p. 286; for Gordon's behaviour in Hobart Town, see Arthur to Stanley, 4 January 1834, C.O. 280/46, p. 7.

to a government order of 9 July 1828 which forbade holders of tickets-of-leave to write in the public press, on pain of being transported to a penal settlement. For a moment that May it looked as though once again Savery was to be scapegoat for all the mischief-makers of Hobart Town. But on 10 June the Executive Council, after recommending that Savery's ticket-of-leave be restored, went on to point an accusing finger at Gordon, who, they said, had proved himself unworthy to serve His Majesty either as a Legislative Councillor or as a magistrate. Four days later the Colonial Secretary wrote to Gordon in that censorious, reproving language in which Colonel Arthur had such fluency, that he, Gordon, had aimed a blow at the authority of government, and had attempted to bring it into disrepute. This only served to sharpen up the language of Robertson in the *Colonist*. He began to write of the condition of free-born Englishmen who were held in the most abject and degrading subjection to the will and caprice of the chief authority of Van Diemen's Land. But no such language could strike Arthur. He told the Secretary of State a man such as Robertson was bound to sink to the bottom of society unless he was kept floating on its surface by being made an object of importance by those in authority.[3]

Within a month another settler floated to the surface because of the activity of the chief authority in Van Diemen's Land. That August Arthur heard that Hogarth, a convict servant in the police office at Waterloo, had taken a bribe from Mr Meredith, a settler at Oyster Bay, to get him more assigned servants. Everyone knew that at those levels such bribery went on: everyone knew that, thanks to Arthur, it had become much less prevalent than before his arrival. But Arthur, remembering that command to be perfect, referred the matter to his Executive Council who resolved that a man who stooped to bribery was not fit to have assigned servants. Mr Meredith, who already had a reputation as a violent opponent of Arthur's measures, was incensed both by the affront to his pride as a free man, and by the loss he would sustain, because convict labour for all its inconvenience was cheaper than free labour. He began to warn fellow settlers to take warning from what had happened to him. 'What is the fate of one may be the fate of many', he said in a moment of anger, dropping a phrase which was to become a battle cry of the opposition against Arthur in the coming struggle between the settlers and the chief authority. The *Colonist* went further. Meredith's association with an opposition paper, they said, had provoked Arthur into this abuse of his power to withdraw assigned servants to silence a political antagonist, as the withdrawal of assigned servants could bring ruin to a man. Arthur, it was said, was not only an upright man: he was vindictive and ruthless to all who opposed him.[4]

Then in November William Bryan, an Irish Protestant gentleman as old as the century, who had amassed 11,000 acres of land on the west Tamar since his

[3] Extracts of the meeting of the Executive Council, 10 June 1833, C.O. 280/41, pp. 336-56; Arthur to J. Gordon, 14 June 1833, ibid., pp. 356-60; Arthur to Goderich, 20 June 1833, ibid., pp. 278-81; *Colonist*, 14 May and 6 August 1833.

[4] *Colonist*, 6 August 1833; Arthur to Stanley, 6 January 1834, C.O. 280/46, p. 33; *Colonist*, 17 December 1833 for the Meredith battle cry, 'what is the fate of one man may be the fate of many'; for the vindictiveness of Arthur, see J. West, *The History of Tasmania* (2 vols, Launceston, 1852), vol. 1, p. 187.

arrival in the colony in May 1824, was mentioned in two cases before a magistrate in Launceston which suggested he, Bryan, had had the most improper transactions with his assigned servants. Arthur, concluding that a man who had given facilities to his convict servants to prey on the whole neighbourhood was unworthy of the honour and privileges bestowed on settlers, erased Bryan's name from the Commission of the Peace, and withdrew his assigned servants. Bryan, angered both by the financial loss and the injury to his name, set out for Hobart Town to hold himself up to public view as proof of Meredith's warning: the fate of one had begun to be the fate of many. On 7 November he offered to resign as a magistrate, but Arthur, believing Bryan's conduct warranted a stern course, refused to accept the resignation, and stuck by his decision to erase Bryan's name from the Commission of the Peace. So on 30 November Bryan wrote in anger to Arthur to express his abhorrence of the system of Secret Inquiries and Free Pardons which had been used to procure evidence from convicts to the injury of a free man, a process so subversive of all security, peace and welfare that for his part he proposed to appeal to the courts of law to protect him against such arbitrary abuse of power, by declaring the withdrawal of his assigned servants to be illegal. For Arthur, by a stroke of the pen, had deprived him of thirty convict servants.[5]

In the meantime, Gilbert Robertson, an early victim of Arthur's high-mindedness, or vindictiveness, was hitting all the harder in the columns of the *Colonist*. The chief authority, he wrote, was guilty of crimes against the people of Van Diemen's Land. He was guilty of jobbery and corruption: he was guilty of using magistrates to spy on free men. The only solution was for the colonists to petition and petition and petition until the mother country granted their birthrights, because such importunity would obtain what the justice of Arthur denied.[6] At the same time, with more restraint and a trained eye for the forces of their day, the *Colonial Times* and the *Tasmanian* were telling their readers that with the coming of free labour, the convicts would only be employed on the commonest work, or soon might not be required at all—that when that day dawned the colony might get those institutions all Englishmen coveted and admired.[7] But again Arthur remained unmoved. The free institutions of England could not be introduced unchecked into a penal colony. He never wavered from that stand. Besides, he went on, the free population had emigrated knowing it was a convict colony. They could complain neither with reason nor with justice against measures designed to punish convict culprits. With the passage of time a new note began to enter the Colonel's discussion of this system. He began to speak with the pride of a man who had created the system: 'my natural desire', he wrote, 'is to protect the system which I have established in the colony with indescribable labour from being demolished by those who know nothing of its situation'.[8]

[5] For the correspondence between William Bryan and Arthur see the *Colonist*, 3 December 1833; see also Arthur to Stanley, 1 December 1833, C.O. 280/43, pp. 404-5; *H.R.A.*, III. iv. 47; Hay to Arthur, 28 October 1825, ibid., 384-5.

[6] See, for example, the *Colonist*, October to December 1833.

[7] See, for example, the *Colonial Times*, 29 October 1833.

[8] In, for example, Arthur to Goderich, 1 July 1833, C.O. 280/42, pp. 13-16, and Arthur to Goderich, 12 August 1833, ibid., p. 241.

Chance had added its own great stir to the muddy waters of the public life of Van Diemen's Land. In October 1833 William Lyttleton, the magistrate who had presided in the court during the case against the servants of William Bryan and who was well-known to be a loud-mouthed defender of the Colonel's policy of assigning convicts to the virtuous and the respectable, had shouted to passers-by in a public street in Launceston expressions highly derogatory to the character and honour of William Bryan, winding up with the menacing remark that, my God, the man had been lucky not to be hanged. T. Lewis, one of those men born with a strength not to bend the knee to the powers that be, stood there in the street in Launceston, a pace or two apart, as Lyttleton gave out his slander, and his idle boasts. Lewis rushed to Bryan, who selected him as a proper person to ask for an explanation and apology from Lyttleton, failing which he was to mention that as a gentleman Bryan would demand that other form of satisfaction known amongst gentlemen.[9] Bryan sat down to write a letter to the *Colonist* in which he gave free rein to his outraged pride. He had submitted, he wrote, to the foulest calumnies that inveterate malice could invent. Search warrants against him had been obtained through corrupt swearing. His lands and paddocks had been scoured by armed men, some of whom, he hastened to add, were felons. He had borne all this indignity patiently in the full confidence that the law would give him ample redress. Now he had found to his mortification that the laws were openly outraged by the First Magistrate in the colony who had illegally deprived him of his convict servants. For his part he trembled for the state of degradation to which all were exposed by the vassalage of the press.[10]

William Bryan's elder brother Samuel, who had arrived as long ago as 1822 and acquired 2,000 acres on the South Esk near Launceston and a reputation for his skill in draining low-lying land, had confirmed his membership of the colonial gentry by marrying in October of 1832 Jane Henty, the daughter of that Thomas Henty who had migrated because he believed that in Van Diemen's Land he and his family would be placed in the first rank in society. Samuel Bryan now began to be disquieted. Outraged by the indignities and injustices inflicted on his irascible brother, he went to Arthur to say he had decided to hand back his own convict servants rather than run the risk of their being withdrawn on the report of any minion of the government.[11] To which Arthur's A.D.C. and nephew, Charles Arthur, with that rashness of the young puppy in his uncle's pack, replied that the Assistant Principal Superintendent of Convicts at Launceston had instructions to re-assign them forthwith to the 'service of respectable settlers'. Once again the opposition forces raised the cry of insult and outrage, as William Bryan came down into Hobart Town

---

[9] For this version of the episode in the Launceston street, see the petition of T. Lewis to Lieutenant Governor Arthur, 7 June 1834, Hobart Town Gaol, Encl. in Arthur to Hay, 2 March 1835, C.O. 280/56, pp. 5-12.

[10] Letter of William Bryan to the *Colonist*, Launceston, 11 January 1834; ibid., 14 January 1834.

[11] Samuel Bryan to Lieutenant Governor Arthur, Launceston, 14 February 1834, *Colonist*, 25 February 1834; Charles Arthur, A.D.C., to Samuel Bryan, Launceston, Government Cottage, 15 February 1834, ibid. 15 March 1834; for comments on this letter, see ibid., March 1834 *passim*; for Samuel Bryan, see also M. Bassett, *The Hentys: An Australian Colonial Tapestry* (London, 1954), pp. 35-6 and 238-9; see also *Australian Dictionary of Biography*, vol. 1.

breathing fire and brimstone, and all the language of vengeance, but never asking himself whether by combination with men who had suffered a similar plight he might achieve more. Bryan wanted redress from the First Magistrate, and saw himself as the victim of a vindictive man, and not of a corrupt or immoral system. He wanted his servants and his honour.[12]

The *Colonist* was prepared to take the discussion a stage further. It began by writing wildly of a reign of terror and repeated week in week out the warning of Meredith: 'what is the fate of one may be the fate of all'. Entreating the colonists to look to their own interests—to recollect that they no longer resembled children in a go-cart, but were now mature adults who possessed the power and the ability to succeed in the performance of any undertaking that their interests might urge them to, it went on to ask whether William Bryan could get justice from the Supreme Court of Van Diemen's Land. Pedder, the Chief Justice, was a member of the Executive Council and well-known to be an Arthur man. Would a jury have the courage to stand up to the 'system'? Would the government permit a jury? By April 1834 the *Colonist* was writing with the righteous indignation of the prophets of the Old Testament. Merit, it told his readers, was in rags: vice was in gilded cages. Happily this would not last for long. When oppression would no longer find food for its insatiate maw it would perish, having starved itself by greedily devouring the goose which supplied the golden eggs. The crisis was at hand, and the evil must, sooner or later, work its own cure.[13]

To add fuel to the flames of public excitement an unfortunate wretch by the name of Greenwood, much given to absconding, drinking and gambling, escaped from the hulks in Hobart Town in March, and attended the racecourse at New Town. On being recognized, once again he bolted, only to be collared by a constable whom Greenwood, as a last desperate act, cut and maimed. On 18 March he appeared before Mr Mason and Mr Spode in the Magistrate's Court in Hobart Town. Mason, who had caught Arthur's eye for the zeal with which he performed his duties as a muster master of convicts and been promoted to the bench of magistrates, was already the butt for the low comedians of Hobart Town who branded him as 'the boy' and 'Mr Muster Master Mason'. He could not resist the opportunity to torment Greenwood for his crimes against society: 'You will first receive a hundred lashes, then be handed over to the Supreme Court, where you will be found guilty, and I have no doubt be hung'. Mr Spode, a milder man, who was not driven to taunt the weak, concurred in the decision, but said not a word either of rebuke or encouragement.

Greenwood was then flogged. After his back had healed he was arraigned before the Supreme Court on the capital charge of cutting and maiming, found guilty and sentenced to be hanged. Arthur, doubting whether a man should suffer a second penalty for an offence for which he had already received

[12] Based on *Independent*, 25 January and 1 March 1834; *Colonist*, 28 January, 4 February, 4 March, 1 and 15 April 1834.

[13] See Henry Melville, *The History of Van Diemen's Land: From the year 1824 to 1835, inclusive*, ed. by G. Mackaness (Sydney, 1965), pp. 50-7; for Arthur's point of view, see Arthur to Aberdeen, 13 July 1835, C.O. 280/58, pp. 71-81; for the press, see the *Colonist*, 22 April and 27 May 1834, and *Tasmanian*, April 1834 *passim*.

a heavy punishment, asked the Executive Council to advise him on whether to carry out the death penalty. It so happened he was looking for an opportunity to provide a lesson to the convict population. Some time previously three men in a chain-gang, who had been sentenced to be flogged, attacked the flagellator and cut his throat. Another flagellator promptly flogged the men, who were later tried, convicted and executed. Arthur, fearful lest mercy be an incitement to more convict insubordination, and yearning with compassion for Greenwood, signed the death warrant and Greenwood was hanged on 16 April at Hobart Town gaol. Immediately some of the press, blind as ever to the anguish and the stature of the object of their vulgar abuse, wrote of him as a cold tyrant who had sent poor Greenwood to his great account with his master, with his lacerated back still unhealed. Arthur, they said, had stained the annals of their fair island.[14]

No sooner had the body of Greenwood been cut down than the opposition press battened on to the case of Thomas Lewis. On 9 May he appeared in the Supreme Curt before Mr Justice Montagu and a jury of seven military officers on a criminal information of inciting William Bryan and William Lyttleton to fight a duel. Lewis conducted his own defence. Throughout the trial His Honour betrayed a regrettable lack of impartiality towards Lewis, interrupting him, reproving him, and at one time saying sternly that for every question Lewis put, unconnected with the present case, he would fine him £5. Everyone knew Montagu was bent on making an impression: everyone knew he was a man of borrowed resources. The opposition, sensing Montagu knew that a verdict of guilty would be pleasing to Arthur, immediately saw Lewis as another victim of arbitrary power—another one about to suffer the fate of many. When Lewis took his stand on the plea that he was being persecuted, not prosecuted, again the opposition hailed him as one of their men. Montagu, it was clear, had savaged Lewis, because he, Lewis, had been disrespectful to a magistrate, and so challenged that principle of subordination. After the jury had brought in its verdict of guilty, Lewis was fined £150, and imprisoned for eighteen months and further until such fine be paid. People who met in the streets lifted up their hands with astonishment to say: 'To what are the people at length reduced?' William Bryan told all who were still willing to listen to him that if Lewis died, because his body was too frail to endure the rigours of Hobart Town gaol, then Arthur would be his murderer.[15]

With Lewis feverishly petitioning Arthur not for mercy, but for justice, and the hotheads branding God's soldier as a murderer, William Bryan prepared to go into the law courts to regain those convict servants, the loss of whom, he maintained, had already cost him £6,575. Bryan was in a quandary. Everyone knew he had said that Arthur's system of government had no parallel save in

[14] *Colonist*, 22 April and 27 May 1834; Arthur to Aberdeen, 13 July 1835, C.O. 280/58, pp. 71-81.

[15] For the report of the trial, see the *Colonist*, 13 May 1834; for the petition of T. Lewis to Lieutenant Governor Arthur, 7 June 1834, Hobart Town Gaol, C.O. 280/56, p. 5 et seq.; for Arthur's account of these events, see Arthur to Hay, 2 March 1835, ibid. pp 3-4; *Colonial Times*, 13 and 20 May 1834; *Hobart Town Courier*, 16 May 1834: see the advertisement columns in the *Colonial Times*, 15 July 1834, for the correspondence between the Colonial Secretary and T. Lewis.

some province of the Ottoman empire. How then could he expect justice from the minions of that system? His one chance, he believed, was that the government would permit the case in which he was raising the question of the power of the Governor to withdraw assigned servants to go before a judge and jury.[16]

When the case began on 20 June before the Supreme Court, the Solicitor-General, Edward McDowall, acting on instructions from the Attorney-General, rose to his feet and said that the case was intended chiefly to determine the right of the Lieutenant-Governor as to the revocation of assignment of offenders under sentence of transportation. He went on to say that as the case had roused considerable popular excitement and as articles published in the *Colonist* newspaper, in which Bryan had an interest, had materially prejudiced opinion, the Crown was not prepared to allow the case to go before a jury. He therefore moved to postpone the trial of the case to the sitting after next term. Bryan, after consulting his legal adviser, J. T. Gellibrand, another man a cubit or two short in moral stature in the eyes of the chief authority, gave notice that he would abandon his cases. He had been refused a jury of his peers and he would be tried by no other tribunal.[17] Within an hour of announcing this decision on 1 July 123 of his friends and supporters, including Gellibrand, Horne, Kemp, Glover and Melville, viewing with alarm the power vested in the Supreme Court of refusing trial by jury, requested the Sheriff to convene a public meeting of the free inhabitants of the colony for the purpose of addressing His Excellency the Lieutenant-Governor. The *Colonial Times* rather rashly predicted that this latest outrage to Bryan would waken the drowsy inhabitants of the colony to a just sense of their own degradation. The *Trumpeter* cheekily asked for the jury—the whole jury—and nothing but the jury. The *Colonist* solemnly told the people their fate was in their own hands, and that they must triumph if they did not sacrifice themselves by slavish fear on the one hand, or offensive personality on the other.[18]

Well before the meeting began at twelve noon on 14 July 1834 the Hobart Court House had been crammed full. This day was memorable to all who entertained hopes of better things for mankind, but not because they were concerned with how to protect their material interests against further encroachments by government. After the Sheriff had taken the chair the Attorney-General explained at some length his own attitude to the introduction of trial by jury, for in Hobart Town every man felt called on to speak in public as though he were conducting his own defence against a charge of treachery. He felt called on to explain why he who was known to speak up for trial by jury, had opposed a jury in the Bryan case. Then Gellibrand rose to his feet, and spoke too at great length on the subject that touched them. The recent acts,

[16] For Bryan's point of view, see W. Bryan to Spring Rice, 18 October 1834, Encl. in Arthur to Stanley, 23 December 1834, C.O. 280/52, pp. 249-58; see also W. Bryan to Spring Rice, 2 December 1834, ibid., p. 263, 'I hasten to England to meet the volume of slander'.

[17] Report of the proceedings in the Supreme Court, 20 June 1834, *Colonist*, 1 July 1834; for the reports of the proceedings in the other two cases, see *Colonial Times*, 19 July 1834; for Bryan's decision to abandon his legal cases, see *Trumpeter*, 1 July 1834.

[18] This request to the Sheriff and his reply are printed in the *Trumpeter*, 1 July 1834; *Colonial Times*, 8 July 1834 and *Colonist*, 8 July 1834.

he said, had so infringed upon their rights and liberties, and upon the appearance of justice itself, that it had become the duty of every man to resist them constitutionally. To loud cheers from the audience, to cat-calls, and whistles of approval, he read the first resolution: 'That we consider Trial by Jury the indisputable right of all free subjects of the Crown, and that it is essentially necessary to the preservation of our liberties, that this right should be as fully enjoyed in Van Diemen's Land as in Great Britain, especially when it is considered, that in Van Diemen's Land we have no Representative Assembly, and consequently no barrier between the people and the power of the Crown'.

Then Mr Kemp, another man with a distinguished history of fighting the struggle of the free for their rights in a convict colony, moved a second resolution: 'that we view with feelings of alarm the power exercised by the Supreme Court of refusing, in its discretion, Trial by Jury in any case, but more especially in cases where it is openly avowed that the Crown is substantially a party to the suit'. Then Mr Hackett put himself at the mercy of the meeting. He regretted, he said, that the third resolution upon this glorious day should be trusted to so weak a vessel as himself. But Mr Hackett found the words to match the hour. Miserable indeed, he told them, was the remnant left to them of those sacred institutions to which they had been accustomed. He thanked Mr Kemp for so bravely sounding the tocsin of alarm and went on, amidst roars of applause, to move the third resolution: 'that being impressed with the conviction that the King has transmitted instructions to the Local Government to introduce generally the inestimable privilege of full Trial by Jury, an Address embodying these sentiments be presented to His Excellency the Governor'.

Then they turned their attention to that address in which, once again, they put their case for a jury of twelve as a barrier between the extraordinary powers of the Crown in the colony and the people's rights. No one raised awkward questions about the qualifications of jurors. They were not divided as Sydney had been between emancipists and immigrants: they were not divided, as Sydney had been, between Whig and Tory, liberal and conservative. Here, there was no Hipkiss, or Mansfield, to talk of self-help and enlightenment as a passport to respectability, no Wentworth to tell them that power belonged to those with a stake in the colony. They were driven on by something quite elemental. They were driven, as the garrulous Mr Horne let slip in seconding the address, by a sense of threat to their possessions, to their pockets as well as their pride, to ask the fundamental question: by whom are we governed? As Horne shouted to them, when a man realized that the answer to that question was: not even by the King, but by a Secretary of State sixteen thousand miles distant, then, he said, he felt warm, and his words ran hot. Liberty had made England what she was. It had been said that the air of England was too pure to be breathed by a slave. He wished he could say the same of Van Diemen's Land. Let them petition again and again: let them get trial by jury first, then they would get representation and all the other blessings.[19]

Arthur was not the man to yield to the clamour of the multitude. Government, as he saw it, must enjoy privileges in a convict society. In an earlier

[19] For the report of the public meeting, see the *Colonial Times*, 15 July 1834.

exchange in June with Mr Kemp on the question whether all cases touching government should be tried by a judge and jury Arthur had put the question: was the government to be protected? To which Kemp had replied: 'Surely Your Excellency, if the Government cannot rely upon the decision of twelve citizens, upon whom can it rely?' But that was just the point at which Arthur stopped in his thinking. For a government which did not enjoy the consent or approval of the propertied classes must fall back on force and use informers; this meant using convicts to spy on the free. So when the deputation had met him on 1 July he had read to them with all the voice of rectitude, that he would not fail to keep in view the sentiments which had been expressed by so numerous and so respectable a body of men, adding, pointedly, that he could not refrain from expressing his concern that the jury question should have been again brought forward by them before the government had had time to develop its thoughts on the subject. As a good Tory, he believed it was the task of the few to put forward ideas, and for the many to follow: it was the task of the few to command, and the duty of the many to obey.

The members of the deputation had been struck dumb. Arthur, in a dignified attempt to break the silence, had added that he would be happy to hear any gentleman's sentiments on the subject, for, according to one eyewitness, all the members of the delegation were still so astonished that they remained silent, and bowed their heads and withdrew. But no sooner were they out of the room than a wave of disappointment and anger swept over them. They proceeded to the Ship Inn where over a glass and away from those chilly formalities of the house up the hill, and that bloodless face of rectitude, they talked freely on what was to be done. The whole thirty-seven of them, including Kemp, Gellibrand, Horne and Melville, petitioned the Sheriff to summon another public meeting, so that this time, Arthur's reply being so dismally unsatisfactory, they might make application to the British Parliament for the redress of their grievances.[20]

But Arthur's response after the second meeting was just as disappointing and unsatisfactory as after the first. Deciding this time not to meet them face to face he sent them one of those off-putting replies through the Colonial Secretary. He told them that anxious as he had always been to balance the interests of the state and the liberties of the free people of Van Diemen's Land, it was his desire to introduce, in some degree at least, the privileges of trial by jury but that it would be imprudent for the inhabitants to urge on the Lieutenant-Governor to announce upon his own responsibility a decision upon a subject vitally involving the interests of every class of the community. Once again words chosen to conciliate only fanned their anger. They wanted action. The passions of the moment had left them strangers to all appeals to moderation or warnings about the dangers of a decision. They found Arthur's attitude extraordinary, told him so in no uncertain words, and summoned the people once again to a public meeting on 2 August.[21]

[20] On the exchange between Arthur and A. F. Kemp, see the *Colonial Times*, 17 June 1834; for the interview with Arthur, its aftermath and the petition to the Sheriff, see ibid., 22 July 1834.

[21] J. Burnett to the Members of the Deputation to Arthur, 23 July 1834, *Colonial Times*, 29 July 1834; the members of the Deputation met and applied as a group of fifty to Arthur; for their reply, see ibid., 29 July 1834.

After the Sheriff took the chair in a crowded Court House, Thomas Gregson rose to his feet and quickly established the tone of the meeting. Gregson was a man who saw Arthur as a menace to that life of ease and pleasure to which he had devoted his energies ever since he had arrived in Van Diemen's Land in 1821. On his estates at Jericho and Risdon, amounting in all to 3,500 acres, he had cultivated his taste for horse-racing and hunting which gave Arthur such pain. In July of 1832, in collaboration with G. Meredith, another gentleman who had failed to conform to the Arthur standards of rectitude, he had begun to publish the *Colonist*, with the sensual, jolly and gay Gilbert Robertson as his editor. Gregson and Robertson were both revolted by all this cant about sinners losing all their guilty stains in the blood of the lamb, when preached by a man who was vindictive and spiteful to those who did not grovel before a jealous Jehovah. Gregson wanted a society in which a man could enjoy the fruits of his labour—a society in which the men with a stake in the country ran it properly. So he told them they should limit themselves to the great end they had in view, taxation by representation. With a house of assembly, he went on, they would have not only a mediator between the government and the people, but also a public guardian of their rights. They roared their applause: they whistled, hooted, and shouted, as one of their leaders taught them that the only way to protect their interests and their rights was to make the state into a committee of management for the affairs of the bourgeoisie. They could not, Gregson continued, look to the local government for the restitution of their rights—nor to Downing Street for then they would be black-balled by the official faction here. They must look to a reformed Parliament in London and the British public to procure for them a British constitution. He then moved the first resolution: 'That the Colony of Van Diemen's Land, being purely and essentially British, possesses an undoubted right to enjoy the blessing of the British Constitution'.

Mr Fenton then rose to his feet, and after explaining that this was his first public meeting, he went on to tell them that he did not agree that the Governor did not go hand in hand with the people, as the Governor himself had too great a stake in the colony to be indifferent to its prosperity. He then went back to the heart of the matter and said that as he hoped to hand down his property intact to future generations of his family accompanied with the free institutions of the mother country, he had much pleasure in moving: 'that the free population amounts to 18,000—the annual exports £200,000—and the revenue raised by direct and indirect taxation, exceeds the annual sum of £90,000, over which the colonists possess no control, and therefore it is our duty to petition His Majesty and also both Houses of Parliament to grant us legislation by representation'. After this Kemp moved the third resolution: 'that this and the sister colony of New South Wales are the only colonies of British origin under the British Crown, in which the people have not the advantage of a Legislative Assembly of their own election'. Thomson moved a fourth resolution that the very information given to the Legislative Council by Arthur in August 1833 afforded abundant proof of their fitness for the right. After which J. T. Gellibrand, who by a combination of charm and rapacity had begun to wax fat in the land, moved the adoption of the address which prayed for legislation by means of a full and fair representation. The time had come, he said, for a searching of hearts. The recent public meeting and its aftermath had produced almost a revolution in men's minds. For his part, he was on the side of moderation. In the words of the Lieutenant-Governor, a strange model for Gellibrand to use, let them prove their fitness for a House of Assembly and then the Lieutenant-Governor must join them in their petition to the King and the British Parliament. He had begun to grope towards some sort of marriage between the government and the bourgeoisie. It was as though he had heard those shouts of the people outside the Ship Inn the night they refused to drink the toast to Arthur, and had taken fright.

Other speakers were anxious, like Gellibrand, to dissociate the respectable members of the meeting from any contamination by the people. The gallant Captain Glover, who had danced with his wife on the boards of Government House when the walls resounded with gaiety and laughter, eyes had moistened, and lumps formed in throats when the Lieutenant-Governor had drunk that toast to England, told them how that morning, coming along Macquarie Street, he had met a friend, who, of course, he need hardly add, was favoured with a peep behind the screen (ha, ha, ha, for the gallant Captain was very English, and thought that in the great moments of life it was good to laugh heartily) and this friend had warned him the government thought the meeting was rank radical. So the Captain made some inquiries and found it was not: so, here he was addressing the meeting of the respectable, just as determined as any of them that their hard earnings should not go to support those who lent their money upon usury and the convict loafers of Van Diemen's Land. The bourgeoisie was beginning to show where it really stood. On 4 August they met again at the Court House to discuss the question of titles to their lands. Again Gellibrand spoke first, and explained how the tenure of their land came home to their pockets. Once again believing that their possessions were at stake, some took the opportunity to make a profession of faith. 'Gentlemen', Mr Kemp began, 'I believe you know, that I am what is usually denominated a "Liberal"—an enemy to arbitrary power—an enemy to restrictions, which in any way check agricultural or any other property'. There, indeed, was the sense of the meeting: the political institutions of Van Diemen's Land were not serving the agricultural and commercial interests of the men of property.[22]

At that time, not so much from a failure of nerve, but rather from the novelty of their situation, they had no clear ideas on what to do about it, except vague faith in trial by jury and a house of assembly as a barrier between government and people. With Arthur adamant that free institutions were incompatible with a convict colony, they were caught on the horns of a dilemma. They were enemies to any restrictions which checked their material interests. Yet one of their great material interests was convict labour. Then in the middle of this sound and fury the editor of the *Colonist* put forward a novel idea on 1 July. If, he argued, settlers dreaded the withdrawal of their convict servants, if they trembled lest the fate of one became the fate of all, the

[22] Based on report of both meetings in *Colonial Times*, 5 August 1834; for T. G. Gregson, see L. L. Robson, Press and Politics, M.A. thesis in Library of University of Tasmania; C.O. 280/51, pp. 136-40, and 146-8.

Mr. G. A. Robinson (in his bush dress)
who was appointed by His Majesty's colonial government missionary to the
aboriginal tribes of V. D. Land for removing them which he effected without
force or bloodshed
Design'd, etch'd & publish'd by B. Duterrau Aug. 24 1835 Hobart Town Van Diemen's Land

GEORGE AUGUSTUS ROBINSON

Etching by Benjamin Duterrau in the Mitchell Library, Sydney

JOSEPH TICE GELLIBRAND

Copy in Mitchell Library, Sydney, of a miniature by an unknown artist

remedy was simple: hand back the convicts to the government. That, he went on, would remove the millstones from their necks by removing all occasion for the terror of power. The extraordinary powers exercised by the Lieutenant-Governor would be shaken to their very centre foundations as soon as the settlers were relieved of their dependence upon the local government in respect of their servants. He then named the greatest advantage of all in his eyes: the removal of the stigma of their being a penal colony would remove from them the reproach, as well as the misery, of being called, and being in reality, the gaolers and executioners of the mother country's felons, and made to pay, and pay dearly for the honour of being so. The horrid system, so repugnant to every feeling mind, of compulsory labour would be at an end. A free and happy peasantry would take the place of the miserable and heartless bondsmen. 'People of Tasmania', he concluded, 'the power is in your hands'.[23]

But these were not so much voices crying in the wilderness, as voices speaking to a people who gained their daily bread by the sweat of convict labour, and a people who could see no immediate prospect of receiving a sufficient supply of cheap free labour to replace their convict servants. This impotence of the bourgeoisie during the great uproar in the winter of 1834 sprang as much from their way of life in Van Diemen's Land as from this deep division between sentiment and interest. Apart from the public meetings they had neither practice nor experience in the art of co-operation. In part the prisoners of their own ideal of individualism, the bourgeoisie in the towns felt neither the occasion nor the desire to co-operate for their own purposes. Government, by using convict labour, provided the essential services of communication and transport which might have otherwise produced such coming together, but had not created institutions of local government as nursery schools for initiation of settlers into political life. In the country districts the settlers had no tradition of combining to achieve common objectives. They had combined under the direction of the paternal government in Hobart Town to meet the challenge of the aborigine, but that emergency had ended by December of 1830. As for the bushrangers the settlers had made their own individual arrangements for the defence of their property and their lives. They had turned up to meetings in 1832 and 1833 in their own districts to growl about quitrent. But for the rest, they lived in isolation, exiles from the country of their birth, exiles from each other, caught up in the struggle to wrest a living from a harsh land, driven on by some vision of building up for themselves treasures on earth and planting a family. But by 1834 they had neither that surplus wealth to afford them the leisure to live more graciously, nor indeed the time to respond to the appeals of those hotheads and radicals in Hobart Town with their mad schemes of settlers handing back the servants who ploughed their land, tilled their soil, watched their sheep, and cleaned their houses. So when Arthur, with a becoming pride, had mentioned to London in April that he had not the slightest reason to apprehend a combined insurgent spirit amongst the convicts, he might well have added that he had even less reason to fear sustained combination by the free for any purpose.[24]

---

[23] *Colonist*, 1 and 8 July 1834.   [24] Arthur to Stanley, 4 April 1834, C.O. 280/47, p. 398.

U

So while Robertson, Gellibrand, Gregson, Horne and a few others were telling the people of Tasmania they had the power in their own hands to replace the miserable and heartless bondsmen with a free and happy peasantry, Arthur was writing to London to say that Van Diemen's Land should continue to fulfil all the purposes of an immense gaol, and that those who had become its willing inmates should abide cheerfully by the rules and customs of the prison. Convict discipline, he went on, was to be regarded as the grand consideration to which every other in the colony must be subservient when coming into collision with it.[25]

As for those displays of public passion at the meetings of 9 June and 12 July designed to force him to concede trial by jury, he thought of them as examples of those ebullitions of excitement to which all small communities were prone. He had waited for those passions to calm down, and then passed through the Legislative Council an Act for the extension of trial by jury and to regulate the institution of juries under which, happily, the men to be summoned for jury service would be very respectable, and not swamped by men whose sentences had expired. This Act prescribed that in all actions at law all issues of fact and all damages recoverable were to be assessed by a jury consisting of four duly qualified persons. The Act also provided that either plaintiff or defendant could apply to the said court for the trial to proceed before a jury of twelve persons. Section six enacted that in any case before the Supreme Court or any of the Courts of General Quarter Sessions in which the Lieutenant-Governor or other officer administering the government, or any member of the Legislative or Executive Council or any military or naval officer was the prosecutor then the case was to be tried before a jury of twelve persons selected from the class of special jurors. Arthur was happy to say he had thus been able to extend trial by jury without encroaching on the principles of convict discipline announced in earlier despatches.[26]

That year he had much to distress him. Earlier in the year he had received a despatch from my lord Stanley who had told him that while the condition of the convict in the penal settlements was doubtless irksome and painful, yet the condition of far the greater number of prisoners who were assigned to settlers, and the comparative ease and freedom from restraint which they enjoyed was producing little effect upon their companions in crime in England. He was aware of the importance of convict labour to the prosperity of the Australian provinces, but he was also deeply aware of the serious effects of assignment on the efficacy of transportation. He went on to instruct Arthur to employ a 'degree of rigour' in the punishment of the convicts committed to his charge.[27] The *Tasmanian*, believing that cruelty produced desperation, and so perpetual crime and perpetual executions, labelled the new policy 'worse than death'.[28] Arthur was shocked. He knew there was a point beyond which

[25] Ibid., pp. 394-7.
[26] Arthur to Stanley, 18 November 1834, C.O. 280/51, pp. 122-33; An Act for the Extension of Trial by Jury and to regulate the constitution of Juries, 5 Will. IV, no. 11, 15 November 1834, Acts and Ordinances of the Legislative Council of Van Diemen's Land, C.O. 281/1; see also Minute of Arthur to the Legislative Council of Van Diemen's Land, 25 August 1834, C.O. 280/49, pp. 418-19. [27] Stanley to Arthur, 26 August 1833, C.O. 408/9, p. 406 et seq.
[28] *Tasmanian*, 24 and 31 January 1834.

severity ceased to be effective—a point where the mere animal in man was allowed to exist, and hope and fear were usually subdued, and neither correction nor prevention would be the result.[29]

Sick at heart he had gone down early in the year to speak to a shipload of convict boys. At first sight he had recoiled in horror and disgust. It was impossible to imagine, he wrote, a more corrupt fraternity of depraved little felons, who had been trained to a vicious course by being thrown upon the world totally destitute, and then tutored in crime by their dissolute parents. But he had suppressed the horror and disgust, and had allowed his high-mindedness to take over. As all human beings were objects of compassion, he went on, he had decided to send the boys to Point Puer, near Port Arthur, where under the supervision of the Commandant of Port Arthur, a kind and humane man, they would be introduced to a way of life which would at least give them the chance to rise out of the mire and moral filth of life which was all they had known up to that time.[30]

With my lord Stanley badgering him to employ a degree of rigour, and some of the opposition likening his system to a fate worse than death, the stature of the man grew in adversity. Believing the pollution in the convicts' minds to be the necessary result of the unbridled wickedness in which so large a proportion of them rioted habitually, the only means to counteract this that he knew was to get the priests and the parsons to teach those men and women the source of such wickedness. The priests and the parsons must teach them concerning the natural proneness of the human heart to evil. They must teach them by faith and works, for Arthur believed too in the efficacy of that sacramental bread and wine he received from the Reverend William Bedford each Sunday meekly upon his knees to rescue men not only from the flames of hell in the world to come but from evil and crime in this world.[31]

But this side of his nature he was not prepared to expose to the vulgar gaze in Van Diemen's Land. All through the uproar of the Bryan case, the Greenwood case, and the Lewis case, and the consternation roused by the policy of 'worse than death', he kept a distance between himself and the leaders of the people in Hobart Town. They saw the bloodless face, the large lustreless eyes, behind which they were not invited to intrude. When His Excellency joined some of his people in prayer on Sunday in St David's Church the curtains in his pew were drawn. Yet there on his knees in prayer, or taking the sacrament, he received the strength to confront a hostile world with dignity, and a deepening of his faith in God's saving grace for the whole of mankind, for the 'sooty savages', the filthy, ragged convict boys, a human monster such as Routley, as well as for the dandies and puppies of Hobart Town—yes, and even for the men who cheated at cards.[32]

While Arthur was communing with his God behind those drawn curtains in that full and sure conviction of the equal significance of all men in the sight of God, those who observed him as the chief authority of Van Diemen's Land

[29] Arthur to Stanley, 4 February 1834, C.O. 280/46, p. 90.
[30] Arthur to Hay, 8 February 1834, ibid., p. 286.
[31] Arthur to Stanley, 15 October 1834, C.O. 280/50, pp. 148-71.
[32] See, for example, the letter by a Settler to the *Colonist*, 3 June 1834.

were just as convinced that His Excellency was more concerned with the welfare of the bond than the free. When the *Strathfieldsaye* arrived at Hobart Town in August 1834 with over 280 female servants on board, a mob of over two thousand gathered on the Saturday afternoon to watch the landing. As the women landed blackguards jeered at them, used vile and brutal language, and some, more direct than others, put propositions to the women which shocked and scandalized the members of the Ladies' Committee. Some of the women began to show unmistakable signs of distress. One young girl threw herself on the ground and begged that they would let her die because she had seen enough of the colony. By nightfall the girls were lodged at the Bellevue hostel. There they fared no better, as all the next day, a Sunday, convicts, ex-convicts and all the ruffians of Hobart Town pestered them with rude jests, gestures, and propositions, like dogs outside the kennels of bitches. The press asked where were the scrupulous, conscientious psalm-singers to protect these virtuous girls from insult, infamy and destruction. Mrs Arthur and one or two ladies did all they could, but that was little enough to prevent the scenes of infamy. It so happened that on the same Sunday 320 convicts were landed. They were immediately supplied with rations: their clothing was good. His Excellency arrived and addressed them. They received no insult. It was plain for all to see, it was argued, that His Excellency was more interested in convicts than in free men.[33]

That September he also reported to London on one unexpected result of the introduction of land sales at a minimum upset price of 5s per acre. Fewer gentlemen migrants who used convict labour were taking up farms in the interior. He had also noticed that the increase in the number of free immigrants had already been enough to lead to a decline in the demand for convict labour. Yet, faced with this prospect of the disappearance of the material framework for his system, Arthur, unlike Bourke in New South Wales, did not lend his influence to those forces working to liberate Van Diemen's Land from the stigma of convictism, but rather used his talents and his energies to postpone the coming of that day.[34]

That same month, on 4 September 1834, the ship carrying George Loveless who had been transported for seven years for participating in a conspiracy to raise wages at Tolpuddle, near Dorchester, dropped anchor in Hobart Town. The following day, in the gaol-yard at Hobart Town, within the confines of those forbidding walls, Arthur told Loveless what a fool he must have been for having anything to do with such things. To which Loveless replied with dignity: 'The motives by which we were influenced were to prevent our wives and families from being utterly degraded and starved'. Arthur, who believed the heart of man to be desperately wicked, assumed that Loveless must have been the victim of more artful men. As he saw it, Loveless could be won back to a life of docility by a knowledge of God's saving grace, and the fear of damnation rather than by the deterrents of severe

---

[33] For the comments of the press, see the *Colonial Times*, 19 August 1834 and *True Colonist*, 19 August 1834; see also Henry Melville, op. cit., pp. 137-9; for the reactions of Arthur, see Arthur to Stanley, 26 September 1834, C.O. 280/49, pp. 364-6.

[34] Arthur to Stanley, 27 September 1834, C.O. 280/49, pp. 392-4.

punishment. His was a vision of tamed and shrunken men. He would train a race of the docile to go forth and multiply and replenish the earth of Van Diemen's Land and subdue not only it, but also their own innate vicious propensities. Loveless had quite a different dream of what men could be once they liberated themselves from their oppressors. He had that dream of the day when all men were brothers. Arthur had the vision of that day when God had tamed all men. It was Jehovah who stilled the raging of waters, and the madness of the people. So two men with different visions of the future of mankind confronted each other that day in the gaol-yard at Hobart Town. To achieve the vision of Loveless, men had to combine, but because of their isolation and the convict system, his seed fell on stony ground in Van Diemen's Land. And Loveless would leave Van Diemen's Land on 30 January 1837 without scratching the surface of that vast apathy and indifference.[35]

In the meantime all those in Van Diemen's Land who believed that the Arthur policy of using the settlers as materials for his own system of convict discipline had inflicted nothing but ruin on themselves petitioned the Sheriff to convene a public meeting for 20 February 1835 so that they might strike a blow at the very root of the tree.[36] But on this question of the future of the convict system the groups opposing Arthur were bitterly divided. The *Colonial Times* asked its readers whether the British colonists of Van Diemen's Land were to become white slaves when in other parts of the world negroes were being emancipated. A different view was put in Gilbert Robertson's *True Colonist*. He had taken over the *Colonist* and republished it as the *True Colonist* on 5 August 1834, arguing that the abolitionist view of the subject was too absurd to admit of argument. In the *Hobart Town Courier* Dr Ross went on telling his readers that the convict system in Van Diemen's Land was the best form of secondary punishment known to man.[37]

At the meeting in the Court House on 28 February, called to discuss the future of the convict system in Van Diemen's Land, the note of righteous anger was not heard. No one told them that they had been engaged in an ungracious and unlovely thing: no one told them that they had taken God's oceans and converted them into a sewer: no one told them that the removal of such a plague concerned the whole human race. It was not given to Father Conolly to be lifted up into the rôle of one of God's prophets. The Reverend William Bedford, and the Reverend Philip Palmer passed them all by on the other side. The Reverend Archibald Macarthur, who had so often moved the

---

[35] G. Loveless, *The Victims of Whiggery*, ed. by D. A. Davie (Hobart, 1946), pp. 22-4; Arthur to Le Fevre, 20 December 1834, C.O. 280/52, pp. 230-4. On 19 March 1834 George Loveless, James Loveless, Thomas Stanfield, John Stanfield, James Hammett and Joseph Brine were sentenced to seven years' transportation for administering unlawful oaths. All of them were transported to New South Wales on the *Surrey* which reached Sydney on 17 August 1834. George Loveless sailed on the *William Metcalfe* which reached Hobart Town on 4 September 1834. George Loveless was pardoned on 10 March 1836. When he heard that his wife was not to join him in Van Diemen's Land, he left Hobart Town on 30 January 1837 and arrived in England on 13 June 1837. Four of the others reached England on 17 March 1838, but it was not until August 1839 that James Hammett arrived there. The pamphlet by George Loveless was first published in August 1837.

[36] *Colonial Times*, 17 and 24 February 1835.

[37] Ibid., 24 February 1835; *True Colonist*, 10 and 14 February 1835; *Hobart Town Courier*, February 1835 *passim*; E. M. Miller, *Pressmen and Governors* (Sydney, 1952), p. 179.

ladies of Scots Church to tears with his account of how much Christ had suffered when He hung there on that rude, red tree, said not a word. The speakers quietly got on to the issue which all could understand: could the colony dispense with convict labour? On this the abolitionists did not have it all their own way. Some doubted whether the colony had reached a stage where it could afford to dispense with convict labour. They were told it was true that if the whole of the convict population were taken away, then their imports would be diminished and the ostentatious luxuriance of the settlers would be checked. The settler would have to employ his sons on his sheep, or the plough, and his daughters in the dairy, but, in return for this the laziness which living among a slave population bred in masters would be unknown. The poor working man of England would have a chance to become the rich working farmer of Van Diemen's Land. Gellibrand, never a man to take lightly any sacrifice of income, pointed out in language very strong and energetic the degradation the young generation suffered from their parents migrating to this great gaol, and added that free men would always work harder than the bond. They were not concerned with the effect of transportation on crime in the United Kingdom. Their concern was with 'the land we live in'. They agreed. And when Hackett told them 'let England feed her starving population, and there would be less crime' they clapped him as a just and righteous man, and went on to pass their resolutions urging the abolition of the transportation of convicts to Van Diemen's Land.[38]

Outside the meeting those with a stake in the convict system quickly rallied to its defence. Some settlers in the Launceston district, all large employers of convict labour, were moved to forget for a day the problems of the autumn ploughing, the never-ending grumbles against the incompetence and sullenness of their servants, and came together in Launceston on 6 March to pass resolutions in which they utterly denied that those of 28 February were carried with the sanction or approval, or had any right to be considered as the address, of the inhabitants of Van Diemen's Land.[39] Arthur took the opportunity to lecture the British government on the conditions under which the settlers of Van Diemen's Land would be contented with convict labour. He had no doubt the settlers would prefer free labour if the immigration system could procure enough to reduce wages to their natural level. He warned them that opposition to transportation would begin in earnest if part of the colonial revenue had to be spent to pay for the convicts. He warned them that if the settlers surrendered the convicts then in assignment to government, that it would cost government at least £100,000. He warned them too that any cause which increased political activity in the colony was bound to encourage the demand for free institutions as well as the desire to organize against transportation. But for himself he had no intention to lend his support to those forces of the future by working for the day when Van Diemen's Land was free of the convict stigma, and its inhabitants were enjoying their birthrights as Englishmen. He proposed to go on stressing to the settlers the advantages which they derived from the use of convict labour because that, as he saw it, was the stronghold upon which the

---

[38] Based on *Colonial Times*, 3 and 10 March 1835.
[39] The resolutions of 6 March 1835 are in C.O. 280/56, pp. 212-13.

government must rely as a means of maintaining an economic as well as beneficial system of convict labour. He saw no reason to change his mind in response to the changes of the little world over which it was his high honour to preside.

Arthur's task remained the same as ever: to administer his system of transportation as a severe punishment, to reform the convicts, and to ground the rising generation in religion and morals. He wanted more schools and churches, not more migrants and political progress. In his view this agitation for political progress was the work of 'unquiet spirits' who very mischievously discussed convict questions in the public press to the peril of good order and discipline, and tranquillity.[40]

In June 1835 news reached Hobart Town of the loss of life on the ship *Neva*, which had struck a reef off King Island in Bass Strait on 13 May. Of the one hundred and fifty female prisoners, fifty-nine children, nine other women, officers and guard, only twelve women managed to swim ashore. Some of them drank greedily from casks of spirits and died, victims, it was said, of their own depravity. Here was much food for thought for those who believed, with the author of the Book of Job, that men drank iniquity like water.[41] In June of 1835 they gathered in St David's Church to ask God's forgiveness for their sins. By raising his eyes from his pew Arthur could see the faces of both the principal chaplain, Mr Bedford, and the Rural Dean, Mr Palmer. To Mr Bedford's great errors Arthur was by no means blind. He knew that Bedford had been delighted by Broughton's idea of the clergy as priests not out of any profound conviction about the catholic heritage of the Church of England, but because such talk fed his vanity and his overweening ambition. Arthur knew too that Broughton had in private been strengthening Bedford's stiff-necked opposition to state aid to the Wesleyans by once again inflating Bedford's ego with talk of the Anglican Church as God's instrument to save the world from Rome and unbelief. Arthur knew too that between Bedford and Palmer there was a great gulf fixed. Palmer had arrived in June of 1835 to take up the position of Rural Dean, and ever since then these two clerics had engaged in a most unseemly argument as to which of them was the colonial 'great man' in the church. Bedford had accused Palmer of prying into his affairs, and, horror of horrors, of putting a gown on a layman, and asking this layman to go up into the pulpit and preach. Palmer had told Arthur that Bedford's word was not to be relied upon, and that his financial embarrassments, the product of reckless folly and pride, had led him into meanness in money matters which were of public notoriety. So these two members of Christ's church consumed time and energy pointing out the motes in each other's eyes.[42]

As for the Catholic chaplain, Father Conolly, it was said of him that his eyes

[40] Arthur to Spring Rice, 21 April 1835, C.O. 280/56, pp. 241-53; this despatch was written as a comment on the resolutions passed at the public meeting of 28 February 1835; Arthur to Spring Rice, 14 May 1835, C.O. 280/57, pp. 108-20; Arthur to Glenelg, 26 January 1836, C.O. 280/64, pp. 347-59.

[41] For the details, see *H.R.A.*, I. xviii. 135-50; see also *Hobart Town Courier*, 3 July 1835; their figures of the numbers on board differ slightly from the figures in the account in *H.R.A.*

[42] Arthur to Hay, 30 September 1835, C.O. 280/59, pp. 238-45; for Bedford as a gossip in Hobart Town, see Diary of G. T. W. Boyes, 7 September 1835.

were so misted over with strong drink during the celebration of the holy mass that he was not able to see clearly who was in the chapel, let alone inspire his superstitious, illiterate, unwashed flock to turn to God rather than man for the means of grace and the hope of glory. Happily in September the saintly Polding called in for a month at Hobart Town on his way to Sydney. He had about him a dignity of bearing, and enough of that gentleness of spirit and cultivation of mind to convince Arthur there might be something in the man's claim that his spiritual authority had been committed to him 'from on high'.[43]

As for the Wesleyans he was anxious to give them all the support he could because, thanks to them, at least the outward conduct of many of the convicts had been reformed. For himself he was not all that happy about their vulgar talk of a change of heart, when all that had happened in reality was that under the influence of the music and the preaching, the persons concerned had experienced a strong feeling of excitement. But he had to admit that their system of instruction had won some of the lower classes from their degrading vices. Although strongly attached himself to the Church of England, he had always been an advocate of maintaining the most conciliatory and liberal spirit towards other communions who were not opposed to her doctrines. For this he had incurred the wrath of the Bishop of Australia who had lectured him in writing and face to face on the miserable expedient of being betrayed into that affectation of being thought liberal. He knew, too, the Lord Bishop's view on the Church of England as God's instrument to preserve the world from the great evils of Rome and unbelief. The Bishop had indeed warned him of the danger of being led away by the specious liberal theories then afloat. He knew, too, that Broughton had been talking to Bedford and Pedder to urge them to do their duty as Anglicans, and defend Christ's church against the authoritarianism of Rome, and the liberalism of the Methodists and the Presbyterians. Nevertheless he decided to ignore the jeremiads of the Bishop of Australia, lamenting with Bourke his intolerance, and his stand as an exclusive. Like Bourke he determined to move with the spirit of the age, which was against privilege in things ecclesiastical as well as things secular, and to recommend the Legislative Council to make grants in aid to Anglicans, Catholics, Presbyterians and Methodists in proportion to their numbers. His aim was the religious and moral improvement of all classes of the community: his aim was to remove the convict taint from the rising generation, by increasing and establishing the spiritual church of Christ. To promote the interests of religion in the colony the depraved and the poor must be sought after, a task in which the Wesleyan missionaries and the Catholic chaplains had a distinguished record. That was in September and October of 1835.[44]

In the last week of that October all the wits of Hobart Town were rolling with laughter because one of these men to whom Arthur looked to remove the convict taint from the rising generation had been making free with the wife

[43] Arthur to Stanley, 6 February 1834, C.O. 280/46, p. 235; T. L. Suttor, *Hierarchy and Democracy in Australia 1788-1870* (Melbourne, 1965), p. 29.
[44] Arthur to Glenelg, 26 January 1836, C.O. 280/64, pp. 347-59; W. G. Broughton to Arthur, 24 January 1834 (Papers of Sir George Arthur, Correspondence with Bishop Broughton and the Reverend Samuel Marsden); A. G. Austin, *Australian Education, 1788-1900* (Melbourne, 1961), pp. 68-70.

of Dr Turnbull. Everyone in Hobart Town soon knew that when Mrs Turnbull, the wife of the private secretary to the Lieutenant-Governor, had visited the dying Mrs Macarthur, the Reverend Archibald Macarthur, the minister of Scots Church, had attempted to kiss her, and when repulsed, had said with all the desperation of a man whose calling had placed out of reach what he so desperately needed to still the uproar in his heart, 'You cannot mistake me, you must often have observed how I looked down upon you from the pulpit'. When questioned by the Elders, Macarthur said he had only tried to introduce that 'holy kissing' which had distinguished the life of the early Christians. But when during examination another woman testified Macarthur had seized her with his teeth by the back of the neck, the Elders realized their minister had peculiar ways of manifesting his holiness. With the public censors of morals shouting there was a crying iniquity in the land, that a minister was prostituting sacred things to the unhallowed purpose of vice and immorality, the Elders of the Kirk held a special service at which J. D. Lang, who had arrived by chance from Sydney, demanded and even obtained the resignation of Macarthur. The *True Colonist* expressed their delight that the property of the church was no longer subservient to a 'kissing and cuddling religion'. Macarthur, who had arrived in Hobart Town at the end of 1822 to become the first Presbyterian minister in Van Diemen's Land, had a most gentle, kindly face, and was filled to overflowing with that command of the Galilean fisherman that men should love one another. He had none of that drive to hound mankind which drove Lang on to the end of his days and he watched his wife die while the Pharisees howled that their God would not be mocked. Arthur who, unlike Lang, had become like one of those elderly ones who walked away first when the one without sin was invited to cast the first stone, wrung his hands in despair, that one so fair, and so promising to remove the convict taint, should have done something so desperately wicked.[45]

Macarthur was not the only one that October to be wounded by the gap between his own desires and what his fellow man would allow. George Stephen, a relative of Alfred Stephen, had cheated at cards. Alfred said that having made his bed George must lie in it. Gilbert Robertson used the story in the *True Colonist* to illustrate the behaviour of the men who had the ear of Arthur. George Stephen somewhat rashly promised the Lieutenant-Governor that if he were received back into society, he would not play cards again. So Arthur, who was prepared on this as on other questions of forgiveness to be a seventy times seven man, received George back, only to find it was a promise George would keep until he had the first opportunity of breaking it.

That October the rumours began to fly round Hobart Town. Mr Bedford, never a close friend to the Colonel, gave it out that Arthur was soon to be replaced. Captain Wentworth, the bearer of an illustrious name in the colony, became so excited in the streets of Hobart Town about the conduct of Colonel Arthur that another man was obliged to interfere for the honour and dignity of vice-royalty. Some were saying that it was all very well to talk of the free

[45] *Hobart Town Gazette*, 11 January 1823; Diary of G. T. W. Boyes, 27 and 29 October 1835; *Hobart Town Courier*, 8 January 1836; *True Colonist*, 18 March and 15 April 1836; *Hobart Town Courier*, 29 May 1847; Arthur to Hay, 11 May 1835, C.O. 280/57, p. 145.

labourers replacing the bond, but the paupers who had arrived so far were worse than either of the plagues inflicted upon the Egyptian idolaters.[46]

While men were thus showing their view at Hobart Town, at New Norfolk Edward Dumaresq was giving thanks to Almighty God that his wife's uncommon beauty of person was accompanied by both piety and virtue, and wondering whether he would enjoy her beauty and loveliness through all eternity. At the same time, too, Joseph Archer, who had recently returned from a grand tour of Europe, despairing of his wife ever bearing him a child, raised up at Panshanger a manor house of lasting beauty and splendour.[47]

In the meantime in the *Colonial Times* Henry Melville kept on insisting week in week out that the only possible way to rescue the convicts from low disgusting vices, and the whole of society from contamination by convicts, was to abolish the whole convict system. Melville had taken over the *Colonial Times* from Bent on 5 March 1830. In Hobart Town he was known as a wayward eccentric. Arthur, who had a boundless compassion for all men, looked on him with the eye of pity, though not with respect. He was prepared to forgive the ways of the foolish provided they did not incite unquiet spirits to riot or low vices. Dr Ross, the editor of the *Hobart Town Courier*, seemed to be rubbing his hands with glee when he told his readers on 26 June of 1835 that, though it distressed him to mention it, Mr Henry Melville had unhappily lost his reason.[48]

Melville was a man who had always shrouded himself in mystery. He had kept the date of his birth a secret: he had kept the date of his arrival in Hobart Town on the *Cape Packet* in 1828 a secret: he changed his name to Henry Melville, for reasons which he was not prepared to confide to any man. It was said in Hobart Town that he was a member of a sect of Freemasons who were notorious enemies of godliness: it was said that the man was a necromancer who held secret communion with the dead. Some laughed that anyone so queer should pose as the defender of public morals: some whispered that the reason for all the queerness was that the man had taken leave of his senses. When he was married by special licence at New Norfolk on 6 February 1832 to Eliza Romney, the only daughter of the late Joseph Fisher of Philadelphia, Henry Savery was one of the witnesses, for Melville befriended and was drawn to men of talent who had become vagabonds on the face of the earth.[49]

Yet, like Savery, he was strangely unaware of the consequences of tossing the weak into the world's great net. In the middle of 1833, discovering that his

---

[46] Entries in Diary of G. T. W. Boyes for 22 September, 19 and 24 November and 16 December 1835.

[47] Reminiscences of Edward Dumaresq; Loose Pages of the Philosophical and Religious Thoughts of Edward Dumaresq (Dumaresq Papers); for Joseph Archer, see *Hobart Town Courier*, 15 April 1854; *Launceston Examiner*, 28 and 30 June 1853; Letters of Joseph Archer in C.S.O. Arthur Period Correspondence Files 636-675, T.S.A.

[48] *Hobart Town Courier*, 26 June 1835.

[49] Ibid., 11 February 1832; the phrase used by J. T. Macdougall after he had bought the *Colonial Times* from Melville at the beginning of 1839; see *Colonial Times*, 5 February 1839; see the comment by Chief Justice Pedder on Melville's Petition to the Queen's Most Excellent Majesty praying for compensation for injury sustained in consequence of an illegal judgment passed upon him by the judges of the Supreme Court, 26 March 1840 (C.S.O. 5/235/5983, T.S.A.).

assigned servant Frederick Smith was guilty of 'filthy habits', he took the servant to the Police Office, hoping that a reprimand might have a salutary influence on his future behaviour, only to find to his horror that the Police Magistrate, Mr Muster Master Mason, was not, like himself, a censor and an improver, but a hounder and a punisher of the weak. Mason sentenced Smith to twelve months in a road party. Melville then appealed to Arthur in the name of humanity to reduce such a harsh sentence, but he, Arthur, could see no reason why the law should not take its course.[50]

From that time Melville's comments on the transportation system became more and more hysterical. By the middle of 1835 he was writing of Van Diemen's Land as a gaol on a large scale, where beardless boys, ignorant old men, and transported felons insulted, assaulted, and robbed free men. Van Diemen's Land was like a bundle of twigs, which, in their collective strength, could stand great resistance, but which, when taken separately, might be easily broken. The bundle of twigs for Van Diemen's Land, their future source of strength must, he argued, be a house of assembly.[51] So when the letter in which Lytton Bulwer suggested the foundation of a political association in Van Diemen's Land arrived in Hobart Town in September, Melville seized on it as an opportunity to promote his own policy that a house of assembly would end transportation to Van Diemen's Land.[52]

Five hundred of like mind came together in the Argyle rooms on the night of 17 September 1835 to form such an association. All the old campaigners for trial by jury and a house of assembly turned up in force. To much cheering Thomas Horne told them the meeting clearly showed they were now determined to do something for themselves, but let them not give their enemies cause to say that they had met as rebellious spirits. A lawyer by profession, Horne had been born in England in 1800, educated at Westminster School and Oxford University, and had been admitted to the Bar in February of 1827. He had arrived in Hobart Town with his wife and child in February of 1830, and had been admitted into the Supreme Court to practise as a barrister. In 1833 he had become the Worshipful Master of the Operative Lodge of Tasmania. There was about him a homeliness amounting almost to gaucherie, for he was a plain, plodding, straightforward lawyer, reckless and generous to the victims of poverty. It was said in Hobart Town that he carried opposition to Arthur and charity to excess—that in all else he was a prudent, exemplary family man. By nature he was a timid spirit, a man who was anxious to find the appropriate institutions to serve the interests of the bourgeoisie and then return to a quiet life, a snowy dove, as it were, who was driven by circumstances to play briefly the role of an eagle.[53]

As the meeting listened in their dark suits, cravats, and high collars, those outward and visible signs of their aspirations at least for a life of virtue and respectability, Horne moved the first resolution:

[50] H. Melville to R. Lang, Private Secretary to Arthur, 6 June 1833 (C.S.O. Arthur Period, 1/506/11092, T.S.A.).

[51] *Colonial Times*, 2 and 16 June, 25 August and 8 and 15 September 1835.

[52] Ibid., 8 and 15 September 1835.

[53] *Launceston Advertiser*, 14 September 1844; file on Thomas Horne in T.S.A.

Considering—That the people of Van Diemen's Land are not represented by the Legislative Council, consisting of fourteen individuals, seven of whom are Government Officers, the others nominated by the Governor, and appointed by the Crown, and not a *single individual elected by the people.*

That the people have no confidence in the Council:

That the laws passed by the Council are not for the benefit of the Colony, being in principle a constant assumption of power over the people on the one hand, and a loss of constitutional liberty on the other:

That the power of taxing the people is not in the people themselves, by their Representatives:

That the interest of the people cannot be consulted as it ought to be, so long as the present system of forming the Legislative Council exists:

That there is no medium between the people and the power that governs them—

Therefore it is expedient that a *Political Association* be formed, for all purposes not forbidden by Law, until the Elective Franchise be obtained by the people of Van Diemen's Land.

This was seconded by Mr David Lord, an emancipist's son, who had himself become so wealthy as a landowner, banker and trader, that no one knew the extent of his riches. It was carried unanimously for on such questions the local bourgeoisie had very little to argue about.[54]

Then Gellibrand rose to his feet: a big man, big bones, chubby face, large wondrous eyes, a suggestion perhaps of effeminacy, certainly of delicacy of feeling, and perhaps of some spiritual refinement which fitted ill with his reputation for rapacity. Now he stood there a tribune, not so much of the people, but of the bourgeoisie of Hobart Town, and told them, as he had told them so many times before, that they must struggle for their rights as Englishmen, not as radicals, or anarchists, or opponents of all government, but as men who wanted to protect their best interests. He moved:

That the Association consist of free British subjects, and that the object of the Association be to watch over and support the interests of the Colonists, and that such persons as are present who may be willing to join the Association register their names on the roll, attaching to their signatures the amount each Member may please to subscribe for the furtherance of the object of the Association; and that no Member be allowed to subscribe more than one shilling weekly.

After which Mr Kemp, another veteran of the struggle, told them at great length, for he was never happy unless he was talking, that they were without the slightest security, that they were trifled with, that a Council had no advantage so long as the Governor considered himself at liberty to do as he pleased. So he moved:

That the Members pledge themselves to assist the Colonial Authorities in enforcing British Laws and administering British justice; and that the Colonists being in no wise represented in the Legislature, this Association do (as far as it is practicable) represent the Colonists to the Local Government.

[54] First Session of the Political Association held at the Argyle Rooms, 17 September 1835, *Colonial Times*, 22 September 1835.

Then after agreeing that at the first general meeting of the Association a committee should be elected, and until that time, Mr Henry Melville be solicited to act as secretary *pro tempore*, they adjourned until 5 October.[55]

When they met again on the agreed day the room was more crowded than on the previous occasion. To rapturous applause Gellibrand congratulated the colony on its impending emancipation, for they were, he believed, about to possess that great desideratum, legislation by a full, free, and unbiased representation. In an atmosphere of confidence, even of gaiety, they agreed to form a Political Association, the first object of which was to obtain by every just and loyal means, a real and effective representation of the people of Van Diemen's Land, and went on to proclaim with pride that the constitution of their society was essentially popular, as it admitted as equal members all free persons whatever, and, winding up with a glance towards high-mindedness, and a reassurance for timid souls, they said they would look chiefly to the obtaining and preservation of the rights and interests of the people of this colony, taking care never to sanction any measures which were calculated to circumscribe or endanger any just rights or immunities of the privileged orders.[56]

Excitement was running high when news reached Hobart Town that Robert Bryan, the nephew of William Bryan, and James Stewart were to be charged at Launceston with feloniously stealing one heifer, and Michael Fogerty with receiving 50 lb. of meat, being the carcass of the said heifer. Sensing victimization of the Bryan family by the men in high places, Gellibrand agreed to act as counsel for Bryan, and applied to have the trial moved from Launceston to Hobart Town away from the atmosphere of a court dominated by the settlers of the district. These settlers were thirsting for the blood of the cattle-stealers and supported such odious things as felon police because they accepted them as part of a system from which they obtained their cheap convict labour. All to no avail, for the trial went on at Launceston on 23 October 1835 before Chief Justice Pedder and a military jury of seven officers who found Bryan and Stewart guilty, and acquitted Michael Fogerty. Pedder then sentenced Bryan and Stewart to death.[57]

With that recklessness which he displayed throughout his public life in Van Diemen's Land whenever the actions of the government collided with the life of the people, Gilbert Robertson wrote of it in the *True Colonist*, as a 'GOT UP CASE', calling it the most frightful of all the frightful proceedings that had yet been perpetrated by their most frightful government. The jury, he went on, had been picked by Colonel Arthur. A charge of wilful and corrupt perjury had been preferred against the four constables who had given evidence against Bryan. Three of these witnesses were convicts. Robertson was back on his great theme of the iniquity of using felon police to spy at the keyholes of the free.[58]

On 3 November Melville, careless of the precise facts like most men of feeling, gave vent to his indignation in the *Colonial Times*: Felon police had perjured themselves, hoping to obtain free pardons or other indulgences; the oaths of felons had been believed; Arthur had been so keen on a successful

[55] Ibid., 22 September 1835.
[57] Ibid., 3 November 1835.
[56] Ibid., 6 October 1835.
[58] *True Colonist*, 30 October 1835.

prosecution that he had driven the Chief Justice to Launceston in his own coach—sure proof of evil collusion between the executive and the judiciary; the day after the trial Arthur had dined with Mr Lyttleton, the magistrate of Launceston who had slandered William Bryan in the streets of that town; Pedder was both a judge and a counsellor of the executive; there were hundreds of felons in Van Diemen's Land ready to swear any man guilty of any unnatural crime, felony or murder in return for a glass of rum.[59]

This time Arthur decided to take a stand. At the sitting of the Supreme Court on 6 November the Attorney-General, Alfred Stephen, announced he wished to call the attention of the judges to certain observations in the *Colonial Times* of 3 November which, he said, reflected on the Court and its officers, as well as on the administration of justice. Unless such publications were punished by the Court they were calculated to bring that same Court into disrepute. He therefore applied for a writ of attachment against Mr Henry Melville, the printer and publisher of the *Colonial Times*.[60] The Court began to hear the case on 13 November, and adjourned to 17 November when they assembled again to hear legal argument, and the judgment. The Chief Justice allowed himself to speak with some passion. Any man, he said, who insinuated that the Court was base enough to lend itself to the government for the purpose of injustice had uttered a contempt. Melville had been guilty of even baser charges: he had insinuated that because the Chief Justice had expressed an opinion in the Legislative Council he could not do justice in the Court. He had insinuated that the jury lent themselves through wickedness or weakness to the government, and had been bribed by a dinner from the Governor. As it was absolutely necessary to punish such a publication, especially because of the repeated outrageous attcaks upon the government and every person connected with it in the press, it was his duty to sentence Melville to be imprisoned in His Majesty's gaol in Hobart Town for twelve calendar months; to pay a fine to the King of two hundred pounds; to enter into recognizance for good behaviour for two years, and that Melville should be imprisoned till the fine was paid. Melville was then removed to the gaol.[61]

Immediately a portion of the press vented their anger and their horror. The *Colonial Times*, after dwelling on the general alarm amongst the depressed colonists, denounced Pedder as the man who had destroyed public liberty as well as the liberty of the press.[62] The *Cornwall Chronicle* in Launceston wrote of a reign of terror. Bearing in mind the cruel fate of their brother editor in Hobart Town, they added that if fate should ordain their incarceration, they would suffer with pleasure because they would be doing their duty 'the Attorney General', they concluded, '*may* inflict upon us his engine of bodily torture —but our soul is our own—it is out of *his* reach!!!'[63] The *True Colonist* denounced the gilded slave guarding power, adding that now no man of

[59] *Colonial Times*, 3 November 1835.

[60] Supreme Court Sittings in Banco, Friday 6 November 1835, *Colonial Times*, 10 November 1835.

[61] For the report of the trial on 13 November, see *Hobart Town Courier*, 20 November 1835; for the report of the proceedings on 17 November, see *Colonial Times*, 24 November 1835.

[62] *Colonial Times*, 24 November 1835.

[63] *Cornwall Chronicle*, 21 and 28 November 1835.

independence was safe. They accused Arthur of being the cause of all the mischief and the misery. Arthur, they said, had ruined the colony, and degraded the people to the level of convicts. He had sunk the colony in a morass of moral depravity: he had enriched himself, but had ruined the colony.[64] Gilbert Robertson, who had been clapped into gaol for libel, again asked Arthur to look with the eye of pity on both Melville and himself, and release them from their sufferings. In the vain hope that the sight of the unprotected innocents would move the obdurate heart of their oppressor he had sent his five little girls to Government House to beg His Excellency the indulgence of a separate apartment for his wife, but His Excellency had refused to see them.[65]

With Melville, on the other hand, Arthur believed there was room for grace. Through his Colonial Secretary he instructed the Sheriff to discharge Melville from prison in that season of peace on earth and good will to all men. He was willing to hope that the release might incite in Melville better feelings, and awaken a higher sense of duty, leading Melville in future, by the influence of a better motive than fear of punishment, to abstain from a system of detraction which was not more injurious to the interests of his own family, than it was subversive of all peace and order, and ruinous to the welfare of society.[66] He was not to know then that Melville had just finished in gaol *The History of Van Diemen's Land* in which he lamented that Arthur's system of government had 'reduced the Settlement to misery, and brought five-and-twenty thousand free British and loyal subjects to so low an ebb of poverty'. He was not to know that Melville had just written in so many words that the greatest boon they were all praying for was 'an enlightened generous Governor'. For that matter Melville was not to know either that because he had accepted Arthur's act of grace, those friends who had hailed him as the 'martyr to independence' would soon abuse him as a truckler to those in power.[67]

While the white players were strutting on their stage, the surviving aborigines were setting up a wail of lamentation on Flinders Island. On 4 December Mannalargenna, a celebrated native chieftain of Van Diemen's Land, became numbered with the dead. On the following day upwards of one hundred aborigines followed the body to the grave. G. A. Robinson, loving and tender as ever to a people whom he saw as victims of some purpose which God would undoubtedly uncover in His own good time, preached to them on the meaning of that death. He told them to rejoice for without that mercy of God they might have been born of heathen parents. Before the white man the black man had been guided solely by the light of creation. Now he had the knowledge of salvation. When a good white man or a good black man died, God told his angel spirits to take them to heaven where they never would be

---

[64] *True Colonist*, 13 November 1835.   [65] Ibid., 4 December 1835.

[66] The text of Melville's petition to the House of Commons of 21 December is published in the *Colonial Times*, 29 December 1835; Henry Melville to tne Lieutenant Governor of Van Diemen's Land, Hobart Town Gaol, *Launceston Advertiser*, 31 December 1835 and 14 January 1836; John Montagu, Colonial Secretary of Van Diemen's Land, to Henry Melville, 29 December, *Colonial Times*, 29 December 1835.

[67] *Launceston Advertiser*, 14 January 1836; *Colonial Times*, 5 January 1836; Henry Melville, op. cit., pp. 185-6; Melville finished the work on 18 December 1835.

sick any more, never be hungry any more, never be cold any more, but they would be happy forever. There was no music like heavenly music. If they did everything according to God's word, they would certainly know that bliss. While Arthur was hoping to awaken in Melville a higher sense of duty, Robinson was holding out to the aborigines the hope of a release beyond the grave from all those hurts which they had endured in this world because of the pitiful equipment with which their Creator had endowed them.[68]

In the meantime the drift against Arthur gathered momentum in the minds of the free. There was a persistent rumour that he was about to be appointed governor of New South Wales, and the catty were beginning to whisper to each other 'the sooner the better'. Robert Lathrop Murray, always a man for extravagance of language, told the Public Auditor in the streets of Hobart Town: 'I beg to say that I do not consider it would add to my respectability if I visited Government House'.[69] Week in week out, a section of the press reminded their readers of all the abominations and disgraceful cruelties which had occurred at Hobart Town under the administration of Colonel Arthur of Honduras notoriety.[70] In January of 1836, E. Abbott, T. Hewitt, T. A. Lascelles, G. Gatehouse, T. G. Gregson, T. Y. Lowes, G. Robertson, W. A. Brodribb, C. T. Smith, T. Horne, J. T. Gellibrand and H. Melville recommended a public meeting to consider what was to be done. At the meeting Gilbert Robertson moved this resolution:

> That this meeting is of opinion that the interests of the Colony require that the Colonists do petition His Majesty that he will be graciously pleased to remove Colonel George Arthur from the Government of this Island, and also do petition the Commons House of Parliament, praying that they would take the state of this Colony into consideration, and address His Majesty for the removal of Colonel Arthur.

That night the speakers had much to say against the Lieutenant-Governor. Robertson said the Colonel had acted as if it had been his object to destroy agriculture and bring the colony under the grasp of the money-lenders and Indian adventurers—that the object nearest His Excellency's heart was filching money from the people. He spoke of the Americans as sons of freedom, who were not liked by the Colonel, though an East Indian huckster or soldier was certain to be caressed and invited to Government House. Another speaker said that after all they were Britons, although Arthur tried to misrepresent them in London as a factious and disaffected people.[71]

Melville, cheeky as ever when Robertson was driven by some dark malice, suggested that while they were at it they may as well ask for the recall of the Chief Justice and the Attorney-General, who had rendered themselves so exceedingly unpopular. Besides by their removal a death blow would be given

---

[68] 'Posthumous Testimony to Mannalargenna, A celebrated Native Chieftain of Van Diemen's Land who departed this life, Friday, DECr. 4th, ANNO DOMINI 1835', written by G. A. Robinson (Papers of Sir George Arthur, vol. 28, Aborigines, 1825-37).

[69] Diary of G. T. W. Boyes, 29 June 1835, and 4 April 1836.

[70] Letter in *Sunday Herald*, 19 October 1834 and comments on this letter in *True Colonist*, 24 June and 1 July 1836, and *Colonial Times*, 2 February 1836.

[71] *True Colonist*, 22 January 1836.

ABORIGINES IN THE STREETS OF SYDNEY

From Augustus Earle's 'Views in New South Wales and Van Diemen's Land'

A GOVERNMENT GAOL GANG IN SYDNEY

From Augustus Earle's 'Views in New South Wales and Van Diemen's Land'

to the monstrous ruinous law charges of the Supreme Court.[72] The gap between the opposition and the chief authority was ever widening: as Robertson was telling the audience at the public meeting that any member of the privileged class with experience in oppressing the enslaved occupiers of the soil was held by Arthur to be a valuable acquisition for the magistracy of the colony, Arthur was sitting down in Government House writing to the Secretary of State in London that by the encouragement of temperance societies, and of every other possible means of moral improvement, as well as by the extension of instruction in religion to every district, his government would not fail to exert every effort to elevate the desires of the people above low debauchery and sensual gratification.[73]

Arthur removed Pedder from the Legislative Council in April on instructions from London, it being deemed imprudent for a man to sit as a judge of cases arising from laws he had helped to draft, and announced that Pedder's place would be taken by the Chief Police Magistrate, the pleasure-loving Matthew Forster. Once again the opposition press saw this as a sinister attempt to strengthen the rôle of the police in the public life of Van Diemen's Land.[74] But while they roared and bellowed, Arthur went about that great business of his life. He went down to a female prison ship to hear Mr Bedford read prayers and develop a most appropriate discourse to the prisoners: he visited that most noble of colonial establishments, the King's Orphan School: he visited Port Arthur on 23 April and stood with commendable pride while the foundation stone of the church designed by the convict architect Blackburn was laid to the glory of that God whom he believed could alone work the great marvel of cleansing the human heart of its desperate wickedness. He was pleased, too, to hear of the excellent system of signals on the Tasman Peninsula.

He was even more pleased to hear that only forty-three had died at the penal settlement in six years. He came back to Hobart Town late in April in time to tell the Legislative Council that the main aim of transportation was being answered—that convicts were being punished and reformed, and agriculture and commerce were almost everywhere rapidly extending.[75]

Then on 25 May Arthur opened a despatch from London which had been brought by the *Elphinstone*. Within an hour the news was all over the town that Arthur had been recalled. That night the news seemed to diffuse a general joy through Hobart Town. On Tower Hill Mr Kermode lit a huge pile to celebrate the event. George Meredith spoke with glee to his friends of their approaching emancipation. The timid Mr Boyes, for whom the streets of Hobart Town had become a nightmare where the respectable were insulted and attacked, rejoiced that they were about to be delivered from their frightful position. Colonel Arthur stood guilty: he had taken the part of butchers who

---

[72] *Colonial Times*, 5 January 1836.

[73] Arthur to Grey, 27 January 1836, C.O. 280/64, p. 395.

[74] For the instructions to remove Pedder from the Legislative Council, see Glenelg to Arthur, 14 October 1835, C.O. 408/12, pp. 31-2; for the attitude of Arthur, see Arthur to Glenelg, 18 April 1836, C.O. 280/65, pp. 361-7; see ibid., for the exchange of letters between Arthur and Pedder; *True Colonist* and *Colonial Times*, April and May 1836 *passim*.

[75] *Hobart Town Courier*, 8, 23 and 29 April and 6 May 1836.

V

excited bulldogs to madness and set them on to tear each other to pieces. He was the cause, the sole, distinct cause of all the mischief.[76]

It was some comfort to Arthur to read the words of praise from his masters in London for his long career of distinguished public service. It was some comfort to him to know that he had not disquieted himself as a soldier of God in vain, as he had earned the gratitude of the colonists at large. It was some comfort to read the words of praise of Dr Ross in the *Hobart Town Courier*, who called him the father of his people. It was some comfort to know that his friends proposed to present him with an address and some silver plate in recognition of his claim to be the most faithful servant the British Crown had ever possessed.[77] But such comfort was short-lived. For stories soon began to circulate about the motives for signing the address of 'extreme regret'. Old Mrs Leake, it was said, had told her son that if he did not sign he would never get another bit of bread in her house. Boyes, who had been telling people for weeks that Arthur was the sole, chief cause of all the mischief, had also signed, and so testified in public to an 'extreme regret', when in private he was telling people that Arthur's son was a 'footstool of tyranny'.

That June Arthur heard that Joseph Tice Gellibrand, a stranger as ever to decency and decorum, was walking round the streets of Hobart Town like some vulgar mountebank, attempting to fasten to the walls of the town a most wicked and libellous placard. This notice cautioned the public against those crawling creatures who under the still existing system of intimidation were employed in getting up money to pay for a plate for Colonel Arthur, the father of usury, the author of the impounding law, the supporter of Mason, the withholder of grants, the partial distributor of Crown lands and convict labour, the founder of an Act to authorize felon constables to break into houses, the persecutor of Gordon, Gellibrand, Lawrence, Meredith, Kirkwood, Abbott, Youl, Welsh, Burnett, Bryan, Douglas, Lowes, R. Bryan and innumerable others. The colonists were urged to laugh at Arthur's supporters, and to thank His Majesty for the mercy he had manifested in the recall of Colonel Arthur.[78]

At the end of June the opposition announced their intention to hold a dinner to commemorate the downfall of the system. Only upwards of thirty turned up to that public dinner at the Macquarie Hotel. But what they lacked in numbers, they made up for in the strength of their abuse. Flushed with food and drink and glad tidings of the recall they gave tongue freely to their anger and their indignation. Gregson, who delivered a lecture on the liberty of the press, took the chair. Over the port and the nuts they began to giggle about the skill of some of Colonel Arthur's magistrates as leg-lifters till the time came for them all to leave for the theatre, where a crowded audience roared with

76 Diary of G. T. W. Boyes, 25 May and 7 August 1836; Diary of C. H. Leake, 29 May 1836 (T.S.A.); Cartwright to G. Meredith, 6 July 1836 (Meredith Papers).

77 Glenelg to Arthur, 10 January 1836, C.O. 408/12, pp. 58-9; *Hobart Town Courier*, 27 May 1836.

78 Arthur to Glenelg, 4 June 1836, C.O. 280/66, pp. 130-8; for the text of the placard, see *Hobart Town Courier*, 10 June 1836 and the *True Colonist*, 13 July 1836; for the story about Mrs Leake, see the Diary of C. H. Leake (T.S.A.); Diary of G. T. W. Boyes, 26 May and 20 September 1836.

laughter at the specially selected pieces—*The Hypocrite* and *More Blunders than One*. All night the people discharged fireworks in the streets: houses were illuminated: toasts were drunk in all the pot-houses in Hobart Town to commemorate the end of the system, coupled with the name of Lord Glenelg who, it was said, was the first Englishman in a high place to pay the slightest attention to the wishes of the colonists. When Arthur and his friends took comfort from the small numbers who had attended, his opponents retorted that there were only thirty in the whole of Van Diemen's Land who enjoyed the independence to free them from the terror of oppression and intimidation. Even that night some miserable, contemptible, wretched, overbearing, tyrannical, crawling creature of Colonel Arthur's had ordered a strong force of felon constables to keep the people away from the paddock in which the recall was being celebrated.[79]

While the few were drinking and carousing and dancing in the streets, members of the Executive Council were urging Arthur to take legal action against Gellibrand as an example to the swinish multitude of the consequences of such cruel buffoonery, and insubordination. Arthur was not prepared to stoop so low. Deeply impressed by the divine command that all men should live in love and fellowship with each other, he had been looking for some time for the appropriate occasion to be reconciled with Mr Gellibrand. Besides, he knew too of the warning of the divine founder of his religion to agree with his adversary quickly. At a more mundane level he knew too that any action for libel would be used by Gellibrand and his followers to attack his character. Why should he give Gellibrand the opportunity to use the Supreme Court as a tribunal for the investigation and vilification of his character? With a becoming dignity he refrained and turned to those details of administration over which he had always exercised such masterly control, and prepared for his departure, knowing full well that the enemies of his government as well as his person would once again despitefully use them, just as that odious man Wentworth and his drunken friends had hounded Darling three days before his boat moved down the waters of Sydney Harbour.[80]

There was still much to be done. In August he suggested to the Legislative Council some modification of the educational system. He suggested that district committees consisting of persons of different denominations should undertake the superintendence of the schools within their area, and report to a central board of education in Hobart Town, also representing the different denominations. As the community was largely composed of Protestants he proposed to adopt a scheme of education founded on that of the British and Foreign Bible Society. The reading of the entire scriptures would be the basis of instruction, for on that alone, as he saw it, could be based any system of education that would stand the test of time. He was aware it could scarcely be hoped that the Roman Catholics would send their children to such schools, but he proposed

---

[79] For an account of the Public Dinner, see the *True Colonist*, 24 June and 1 July 1836.

[80] For the extract of the Minutes of the Executive Council on 13 June, when Arthur consulted them on the appropriate action to take against Gellibrand, see Encl. in Arthur to Glenelg, 9 July 1836, C.O. 280/66, pp. 340-9; for Arthur's opinion, see Arthur to Glenelg, 13 July 1836, ibid., pp. 411-14.

to meet that difficulty by granting aid to such schools as their congregation or indeed any other congregation might desire to maintain separately. Broughton kept warning him he was in danger of being led away by specious theories. But he had made up his mind that the intolerance of the Bishop was the greatest menace of all.[81]

In the few moments of leisure he allowed himself from his labours he sat for his portrait by Benjamin Duterrau, an artist of French descent who had migrated to Van Diemen's Land in the early 1830s to take up a position as art master in a school. Probably at about the same time the same artist painted Truganini, daughter of the chief of Bruny Island, and one of the last aboriginal women of Van Diemen's Land. Duterrau thus had a chance to put on canvas the faces of two representatives of a doomed way of life: Arthur, an apologist for a religious view of the world, who wanted Van Diemen's Land to be a terror to evil-doers for the next quarter of a century; and Truganini, who was attempting to preserve on Flinders Island the way of life of the aborigines. But Duterrau did not risk a guess at what was going on behind those masks which they both presented to the outside world. Arthur looked at Duterrau with that inner calm of a man who believed one day he would render his account in a higher place. Truganini looked at him not with grief or anger, but with that expressionless, timeless face with which the physically weak confront their conquerors and masters.[82]

As the time for his departure approached Arthur began to survey the scene with a becoming pride. He had encouraged the state to adopt the role it had adopted in heathen Sparta and assume a responsibility for the education of youth. He had induced the children of every class and creed except the Roman Catholics to assemble in each parish under one schoolmaster. By promoting such conciliation now schisms and sectarian bitterness might be avoided in the future. Crime was on the decrease. He was happy to report an increase in the demand for convict servants. The colony had derived great benefit from convict labour. The men in the road-gangs had constructed the indispensable public works by the labour of their hands. Thanks to convict labour some of the settlers now had that surplus wealth which would enable them to retire from active exertion, and aspire to the possession of every luxury. Convicts, parsons, school teachers, settlers, and civil and military officers had laboured under the superintendence of a benevolent providence to create a civilization in thirty-two years in a savage wilderness.[83]

In the middle of October he said good-bye to the people in the country districts. At Launceston, Campbell Town and Ross the settlers who had received the great benefits of cheap, docile convict labour at his hands gathered to express their gratitude. At Ross in an area of great natural beauty, with the hawthorn in bloom, the rich green English grasses, and the solid stone buildings breathing that beauty and orderliness he had striven to create in this strange land, they thanked him for transforming a trackless inhospitable land that had

---

[81] Arthur to Glenelg, 20 September 1836, C.O. 280/67, pp. 421-7; R. Bourke to Arthur, 27 September 1836 (Papers of Sir George Arthur, vol. 8).

[82] See the portraits of Arthur and Truganini by B. Duterrau in NAT. L.; Duterrau spelt the name Trucaninni.   [83] Arthur to Glenelg, 4 May 1836, C.O. 280/66, pp. 3-41.

a few years ago acknowledged no other lord but the wily savage into a park land which yielded to the industry of civilized man. The unsightly sod hut, the emblem of their infancy, had everywhere vanished to make room for substantial comfortable dwellings. Where lately the dusky native held his corroboree, rising turrets now invited the Christian to offer up his prayers. They enjoyed a degree of prosperity in perfect security. Such things could not flow from blind chance. To Arthur they owed their thanks. To which Arthur replied that they owed their deliverance not to man but to God. God, not man, could replenish the earth and subdue it. To Him they should give all the glory and the honour that the time when the native was a terror by day and the bushranger a terror by night, was now over. They should praise God, too, for that bond of sympathy and kind feeling which was growing up amongst them.[84]

On his return to Hobart Town he met the members of the Legislative Council for the last time. He received from them an address which testified with such eloquence to the fruits of his labours amongst them that when the time came for his reply, he was so overwhelmed and touched that he wept. On his last Sunday in Hobart Town, before he knelt at the altar rail to receive the gifts of divine love, he held out the hand of reconciliation to Gellibrand, who, thinking His Excellency was reaching for a prayer book, promptly placed one in the outstretched hand. But Arthur, no empty believer in the pessimists' despair about human communication, made plain his desire, and they went down on their knees together in that spirit which the divine founder of his religion had recommended to all men who intended to follow the commandments of God.

On the following Saturday, 29 October, an immense body of settlers from all parts of the colony gathered at Government House to bid him farewell. They had to wait an hour or so for His Excellency to appear, for Arthur, driving himself as hard as ever, was busy writing a long letter to his successor. Near four o'clock in the afternoon Arthur entered, deeply affected by the trying occasion, and shook them all by the hand, the whole five hundred of them, including Clancy the tailor and Farell the butcher, and then, leaning on the arm of the faithful Pedder for support, and weeping copiously he walked slowly down Murray Street to the New Wharf followed by all the public officers and military and by several hundred of the Town's people, and embarked on the *Elphinstone* in the midst of cheers and under a salute from ships in the harbour.

Down at the landing stage at the bottom of Murray Street the vilifiers and the praisers gathered to take their last farewell. There were those who had come to think of Arthur as one of the greatest curses that had ever befallen a community of Englishmen, those who thought of him as the man who had created that infamous system of police where no free man was safe for one moment, or as a canting Puritan who had feathered his nest so well that the appropriate coat of arms for the man would be a cuckoo sitting on a nest of other bird's eggs. Those for whom he was a man who had scourged the

---

[84] See the account in the *Hobart Town Courier*, 28 October 1836.

country for twelve years, drowned with shouts of laughter the hurrahs of the Arthur supporters. Mr Muster Master Mason was in a boat by himself because, it was said, no one would even sit in a boat with him. Henry Jellicoe, loyal to the end to the Colonel, rather rashly mingled in the crowd wearing a placard in which he called Gregson a liar, bully, and dastardly coward—a demonstration which provoked Gregson to thrash Henry Jellicoe with a stick. Boyes, who had gleefully filled his diary with anti-Arthur gossip, took his tender farewell with all the other weepers. One convict said out aloud he hoped the time was not far distant when the emancipists drove out of the island every one who besmirched the good name of the convicts. Melville and Robertson spread stories that the felon police had instructions to arrest any man who rejoiced that Van Diemen's Land had at last been liberated from her oppressor. Some were heard to say that as they were getting rid of Arthur they might as well also get rid of Forster, Pedder, Montagu and Mason, and all other crawlers, sycophants and creatures of Colonel Arthur's misrule. So on a sunny day the *Elphinstone* put out to sea, as the inhabitants of Hobart Town went on with their back-biting. The opponents of Arthur dispersed believing they had taken part in a glorious day, on which they had been delivered from a despot. They hooted as the ship moved majestically down those lovely waters: the friends cheered and called out tender words of farewell to the father of their people.[85]

As the *Elphinstone* made the long haul home Arthur looked for a meaning in what had happened to him in Van Diemen's Land. He decided that had it not been for that merciful God who ruled his life for good he might have been struck down by his enemies. He decided that in London he would cast himself on the providence of God, rather than trust in man, for though, unworthy creature that he was, he deserved nothing but wrath, God's mercy and goodness had always protected him against the persecution of his bitter enemies. Strong in this faith he arrived in Plymouth in March of 1837, to find that his enemies, like his adversary the devil, were prowling round London town seeking to devour him. Unlike his illustrious predecessor from New South Wales, Lachlan Macquarie, he resisted the temptation to usurp the function of the deity, by trying to repay those who like that blackguard Bryan had spread all manner of things against him falsely. Despite uphill work he was happy to say by November the Secretary of State had expressed himself fully and perfectly satisfied upon every subject. As an outward and visible sign of his achievement a grateful government conferred on him a knighthood for his work in Van Diemen's Land, and appointed him to the position of Governor of Upper Canada. Later he served with distinction as Governor of Bombay from 1842 to 1846, after which he returned to England where, as another mark of esteem, the University of Oxford conferred on him the degree of Doctor of Civil Laws for his long and distinguished public service. The world

---

[85] Account based on Arthur to Glenelg, 29 October 1836, and Arthur to Franklin, 29 October 1836, C.O. 280/66, pp. 155-71; Arthur to R. Bourke, 6 October 1836 (Papers of Sir George Arthur, vol. 5, Letters from Sir George Arthur, 1822-50); *True Colonist*, 4 November 1836; *Tasmanian and Austral-Asiatic Review*, 28 October and 4 November 1836; *Launceston Advertiser*, 3 November 1836; *Cornwall Chronicle*, 29 October 1836; *Colonial Times*, 1 November 1836; *Hobart Town Courier*, 4 November 1836; *Trumpeter*, 28 October 1836; J. Bell to G. Meredith, 28 October 1826 (Meredith Papers); Diary of G. T. W. Boyes, 29 October 1836.

seemed to be treating Arthur well. He died on 19 September 1854 and was buried with full honours.[86]

Fate was to reserve its own turn of the screw for his reputation with posterity. Nearly three years after Arthur left Van Diemen's Land the Lord Bishop of Australia, William Grant Broughton, sat down over tea and cakes for a cosy chat in Sydney town with the wife of Arthur's successor. They began to compare Arthur and Bourke. The Bishop told her Arthur was cunning and mysterious in a much worse way than Bourke: Sir Richard, he said, was a good scholar: Colonel Arthur was very ignorant, ignorant he believed even of the history of England. Arthur, the Bishop continued, laid himself out for compliments. So, over the tea and cakes, posterity in the Australian colonies began their sport with Arthur.[87]

Nor did the historians treat him any more kindly. The first history of Van Diemen's Land to cover the years of his administration was written by Henry Melville, a man who had been placed in a felon's gaol for attacks on Arthur's system of administration. His was a story of how Arthur had reduced the gem of the southern ocean to a most lamentable condition.[88] The Reverend Mr West, the next historian, was equivocal. Writing in 1852 in the heat and passion of the campaign against transportation, it was not easy for West to look with a kindly detachment on the man who had wanted Tasmania to remain a terror to evil-doers for at least the next quarter of a century. So though like Arthur a Tory in politics and an evangelist in religion, West was grudging in his praise. Sir George, he wrote in his magnificent language, could not be withdrawn from the ranks of eminent functionaries, and his administration was on the whole entitled to something more than respectful remembrance. After rejecting with scorn the suggestion that Arthur had acquired his wealth improperly, West went on to regret that the manners of the man were formal, and his temper vindictive. Despite this West detected in Arthur 'the moral grandeur of a forgiving spirit'.[89]

Fenton, writing in 1884 for a generation which was smugly assuming that they owed their liberal institutions and material progress to their emancipation from a convict society, found something repellent in Arthur's manner which checked the reciprocity of feeling so desirable between the governor and the governed. Arthur had patronized the Bible and Benevolent Societies, those groups obsessed with sin and depravity, but not the Turf Club which stood for pleasure. Arthur had favoured some individuals and oppressed others. He had bestowed grants of land on his friends with a liberal hand, and removed convict servants from others according to his exclusive will and pleasure. He had promoted close relatives to important positions in the colonial government.[90]

[86] Arthur to Pedder, Montagu, Forster and Gregory, St Helena, 17 January 1837; Arthur to Montagu, St Helena, 17 January 1837; Arthur to Spring Rice, Monmouth, 8 March 1837; Abstract of letter of Arthur to Mr F., 2 November 1837; Arthur to J. Gregory, 9 November 1837 (Papers of Sir George Arthur, vol. 5, Letters from Sir George Arthur, 1822-50).

[87] Lady Franklin to Sir John Franklin, 20 June 1839, in *Some Private Correspondence of Sir John and Lady Franklin*, ed. by G. Mackaness (Sydney, 1947), pp. 92-3.

[88] Henry Melville, op. cit., pp. 184-6.   [89] J. West, op. cit., vol. 1, pp. 185-8.

[90] J. Fenton, *A History of Tasmania from its discovery in 1642 to the present time* (Hobart, 1884), pp. 135-41.

So the man who had lived for the day when he would appear before the throne of grace became sport for the fault-finders. A man with a forgiving spirit and a deep compassion had paid that terrible price men exact from those who seem to resist the march of humanity from the darkness towards the light.[91]

[91] Perhaps the most discerning comment on Arthur was made by R. W. Giblin in *The Early History of Tasmania* (vol. 2, Melbourne, 1939), p. xxix, 'Capable and useful in domestic government, in the political arena he seemed to suffer from a kind of paralysis or complete incapacity to read the signs of the times and to adapt himself to changing conditions'. See also pp. xxviii, 560-1, and 570 et seq. For some other opinions on Arthur see Kathleen Fitzpatrick, *Sir John Franklin in Tasmania 1837-1843* (Melbourne, 1949), pp. 14-16; W. D. Forsyth, *Governor Arthur's Convict System* (London, 1935), pp. 5-12, 167-8; R. M. Hartwell, *The Economic Development of Van Diemen's Land 1820-1860* (Melbourne, 1954), pp. 209 and 251; Brian Fitzpatrick, *The British Empire in Australia* (Melbourne, 1941), pp. 67-8; M. C. I. Levy, *Governor George Arthur* (Melbourne, 1953), pp. 6-9 and 351; G. W. Rusden, *History of Australia* (3 vols, Melbourne, 1897), vol. 1, pp. 552-6 and 574-8.

TOWARDS THE LIGHT

NIGHT AFTER NIGHT in the early 1830s a young man sat in the rear row of the strangers' gallery of the House of Commons in London recording predictions that never came to pass, promises that were never fulfilled, but were only meant to mystify. He wallowed there in words. As he mused over the state of England he found much to startle and enrage him. One man soaked up pineapple brandy while he extolled the virtues of tea and temperance with his fellow members of the United Grand Junction Ebenezer Temperance Association. The loyal freemen of one town expressed loudly their Christian hatred of negro slavery in heathen lands afar, while remaining devoted to the factory system in their own country. The learned members of the legal profession loudly defended all the ingenious machinery for the torture and torment of their fellow human beings, because they ministered to their pecuniary advantage. He was Charles Dickens.[1] These men he described, these provokers of his horror and his rage, his pity and his tenderness, had to make up their minds on many things of great moment to the future of mankind. One of these was the future of transportation to the Australian colonies.

As long ago as 1817 Bathurst had expressed a doubt whether transportation was either a source of terror in the United Kingdom or the means of reformation in the colonies.[2] Ever since that day desultory exchanges had occurred between abolitionists and reformers in London. Mr Commissioner Bigge had recommended changes in the system to improve its efficacy as a punishment and a means of reformation.[3] Wakefield, while languishing in Newgate Gaol for his deed of folly, had written a startling picture of indolence and vice in the Australian colonies, and of criminals hailing transportation as a happy issue out of their afflictions in the United Kingdom.[4] In 1831 and 1832 a committee of the House of Commons on secondary punishment had brought down two reports in the second of which they had expressed the hope that in future transportation would be clothed with sufficient terror to deter from the commission of crime many whom no virtuous motives would influence. The members of the committee went on to express the hope that criminals would learn that

---

[1] Based on Charles Dickens, *David Copperfield* (Oxford ed., 1948), ch. 43; see also Charles Dickens, *Pickwick Papers* (Oxford ed., 1948), ch. 32, 33 and 35; see also E. Johnson, *Charles Dickens: His Tragedy and Triumph* (2 vols, London, 1953), vol. 1, p. 173.

[2] Bathurst to Sidmouth, 23 April 1817, note 5, *H.R.A.*, I. x. 807-8.

[3] See vol. I of this history, pp. 369-72.

[4] E. G. Wakefield, *A Letter from Sydney, the principal Town of Australasia*. Edited by Robert Gouger (London, 1829). The story of the publication of this work in a series of articles in the *Morning Chronicle* will be told in the next volume of this history.

whatever advantages might eventually be acquired by banishment from the land of their birth could be obtained only by the painful endurance of a severe and protracted servitude.[5]

That was a point on which one Richard Whately, by the grace of God and the rites of the Church of England, Archbishop of Dublin, had grave doubts. He had been born in London in the year in which the First Fleet had set sail for Botany Bay. By nature he was so frail that he compensated for physical weakness by poring over his books. At Oxford he was distinguished both for his brusque manner and for his power to shine in society by scoring off his opponents. He formed friendships with Thomas Arnold, Nassau Senior and John Henry Newman but, though driven just as desperately as the latter to find the means of grace, he drew back from the journey of the soul which Newman was then beginning. He took orders, wrote pamphlets on emigration, lectured on political economy, and recommended to the students at Oxford the *via media* in things of the soul between indifference and intolerance. In 1831 he was consecrated Archbishop of Dublin.

By then he had decided to awaken the public to the futility and mischievous results of transportation, which had failed to excite a salutary terror in offenders. In his *Thoughts on Secondary Punishments, in a letter to Earl Grey*, published in London in 1832, he warned the faithful to beware of misplaced compassion, but also of that admiration and emulation which was excited in many by declarations of penitence at public executions in the United Kingdom and the Australian colonies. What was the advantage, Whately asked, in holding out to associates in crime this triumphant departure from life, and the hope of a like happy end, with rewards in heaven, for a life spent in crime? He wanted transportation to be both formidable and humane, to occasion as little as possible of useless suffering, to be alike a corrective, and at the same time cheap and profitable to the community, or at least not excessively costly.[6]

Far away in Van Diemen's Land Lieutenant-Governor Arthur was deeply disturbed to find that a Christian and a gentleman should hold such erroneous opinions on the efficacy of transportation as a punishment and as a means of reformation. He dashed off thousands of words to the Secretary of State to prove that transportation was the best secondary punishment ever invented by the mind of man. To address a wider public he composed there and then a pamphlet entitled *Observations upon Secondary Punishments*, had it printed in Hobart Town, and sent copies off to London to join in the debate in which Whately had intervened. In the same year his *alter ego* in the colony, his never-failing claqeur and sycophant Dr Ross, published *An Essay on Prison Discipline*, and duly sent off copies to London.

Arthur argued that transportation was both formidable as a punishment and a means of reforming convicts. He added that he did not for one moment mean to imply that it was possible to suppress crime by punishment alone. He hoped

---

[5] Report of the Select Committee appointed to inquire into the best mode of giving efficiency to Secondary Punishments, *P.P.*, 1831, VII, 276, p. 521 and *P.P.*, 1831-2, VII, 547, p. 559.
[6] For the life of R. Whately, see *Dictionary of National Biography*, vol. 60; R. Whately, *Thoughts on Secondary Punishments, in a letter to Earl Grey* (London, 1832).

that he and Whately could find common ground that God's saving grace was the only weapon against the wickedness in the human heart. He appended to his pamphlet a letter by Broughton in which the latter argued that crime was increasing, not because of the inefficiency of any particular mode of punishment, but from a diminished prevalence of the fear of God. As soon as the barricades of the law were exposed to the whole rush and pressure of men's unruly appetites, those barriers would inevitably bend and give way. Broughton recommended the fear of God rather than the fear of the lash or the rope, as the most effective antidote to the old Adam in man.[7] The debate was beginning to embrace the whole range of human life and experience.

A babble of voices began to be heard in London. Some spoke up for the end of all punishments of blood. Some likened Whately to Judas Iscariot. Some praised him for keeping general principles in view.[8] Undismayed by either the abuse or the flattery Whately turned to score off his opponents with that same ridicule and scorn with which he had shone in the common rooms and drawing rooms of Oxford when he and Thomas Arnold and John Henry Newman were pondering how a man could best prepare for the life of the world to come. In his pamphlet *Remarks on Transportation*, published in London in 1834, he retorted that transportation had two objects essentially at variance with one another—the efficiency of the penalty and the prosperity of the colony. The most obvious way of making the labour of the convicts as advantageous as possible to the colony was to make them as unlike slaves as possible, or, in other words, to put them in the comfortable situation which free labourers enjoyed. The very reverse of this was suitable in a place of punishment. The plain fact was the settlers in the Australian colonies had an interest in the convict, because such labour contributed to the profits of his farm. Because of this the settlers spread the stories about effective punishment and reformation, as it was in their vulgar material interests to do so. They showed it as a place of considerable comfort, where convicts full of cheering confidence were speedily restored to a respectable place in society. But when the settlers wanted to talk of its utility as a punishment, they reversed the picture, and showed the convict undergoing the most galling and degrading slavery. God, he reminded his readers, had sent these men a strong delusion so that they might live with their lie. For Whately knew his Bible, even if he did not know Australia.

He also dropped another point into the debate. With one of those literary flourishes in which he took such pride, he wrote that in the Antipodes there were people among whom everything was reversed. He meant that transportation had corrupted the morals of the free. Small wonder, at Oxford, men had said of Whately that his limitations were as conspicuous as his powers. He had the gifts of the publicist to put into words an idea which was in the air in his day: a fear that transportation, like the system of slavery in Africa, the

[7] G. Arthur, *Observations upon Secondary Punishments . . . to which is added a letter upon the same Subject, by the Archdeacon of New South Wales* (Hobart Town, 1833); J. Ross, *An Essay on Prison Discipline, in which is detailed the system pursued in Van Diemen's Land* (Hobart Town, 1833).

[8] Report of the Society for Diffusing Information on Capital Punishments, London, 21 November 1832 (broadsheet in NAT. L.); *Frazer's Magazine*, vol. 6, 1832, pp. 566-75.

United States, and the West Indies, was creating a society thoroughly depraved and corrupt in its vicious propensities. Just as some members of Council, magistrates, clergy, landholders, merchants and other free inhabitants of New South Wales were to argue that the flourishing condition of affairs in New South Wales was unhappily counterbalanced by a lamentable depravity of manners and a fearful prevalence of crime, and that His Majesty should institute an inquiry into the state of the colony, so Whately ended his pamphlet with a request for an inquiry into the nature, apparent effects, and all other circumstances of the various modes of prevailing crime. That seed would not fall on stony ground, because there was rich soil both in the colonies and London for its germination.[9]

In his book *England and America*, published in London in 1834, Wakefield argued that assignment was slavery in a disguise, and that convicts and their descendants were breeding a thoroughly corrupt and vicious race of men.[10] The reviews and periodicals in London tried to preserve the note of moderation which Whately and Wakefield seemed so bent on destroying. They discussed at length the reports of the Select Committee on Secondary Punishments, and the book by Beaumont and de Tocqueville on the penitentiary system in the United States. They asked the sensible questions: would a penitentiary be preferable to transportation: were criminals apprehensive of transportation: was assignment slavery: had the convicts corrupted and degraded the whole of Australian society?[11] Early in 1835 Arthur replied to Whately's extravagances, patiently explaining to his readers that in Van Diemen's Land the master had not been brutalized by having convicts under his control, and the convict had not been hardened. As for augmenting the terrors of punishment to increase the degree of apprehension amongst criminals in the United Kingdom, he could only repeat that the Protestant religion alone could plant in the human heart an armoury of weapons with which to oppose every dishonest solicitation in its beginnings.[12]

From far-away Australia the evidence on the lamentable depravity of manners and the prevalence of crime began to pour into the Colonial Office. John Thompson, the Deputy Inspector General of Hospitals in Sydney, sat down in June of 1836, to write a letter to Glenelg in which he told him it was truly frightful to contemplate the state of society in New South Wales, that it was, if he might put it this way, a tainted flock, or a perfect earthly pandemonium. Stephen, at the Colonial Office, not a man to be influenced by the inflaters and exaggerators of this world, noted in the margin: 'This is not a letter to be answered, but neither is it to be laid aside'.[13] A great tide of opinion

---

[9] R. Whately, *Remarks on Transportation, and on a recent defence of the System; in a Second Letter to Earl Grey* (London, 1834); The Petition of the undersigned Members of Council, Magistrates, Clergy, Landholders, Merchants and other Free Inhabitants of New South Wales, *H.R.A.*, I. xviii. 392-5.

[10] E. G. Wakefield, *England and America* (2 vols, London, 1833-4), vol. 1, 1833.

[11] See, for example, the review article in the *Edinburgh Review*, January 1834, vol. 58, pp. 336-61, of G. de Beaumont et A. de Tocqueville, *Du Système Pénitentiaire aux Etats Unis*.

[12] G. Arthur, *Defence of Transportation, in reply to the remarks of the Archbishop of Dublin, in his Second Letter to Earl Grey* (London, 1835).

[13] J. Thompson, Deputy Inspector of Hospitals to Lord Glenelg, Sydney, 16 June 1836, C.O. 201/258, pp. 599-601; see also Minute by James Stephen on above, ibid., pp. 601-2.

had begun to lap against the walls of the Colonial Office in Downing Street. The members of the best families had begun to tell them they ought to do something about the pernicious effects of the convicts on the morals of Australians. On 21 March 1836 Edward Macarthur, Elizabeth's beloved Edward of those rude pioneer days, now grown to man's estate, a veteran of Waterloo and other military campaigns, sat down in the very waiting room of the Colonial Office to tell them that although he knew it had been said that the practical benefits of convict labour more than counterbalanced the moral objection, yet, for his part, he could not be of that opinion. Indeed he was quite grieved about it, after all the pains his family had taken to render New South Wales a place for men of honourable connection. This time Stephen, ever a man to defer to the opinions of the quality, minuted that Sir George Grey himself would probably want to reply to Mr Edward Macarthur.[14]

Towards the end of that year Stephen was poring over the words of Mr Justice Burton that it was as though the whole business of the people of New South Wales was the commission of crime. He was reading of a society in which, according to the learned judge, there was a plethora of crimes of violence, murders, manslaughters in drunken revels, perjuries, and false witnesses from motives of revenge or reward. When they calmly looked at the vast amount of crime amongst them, Burton had said, could they feel otherwise than convinced that so lamentable a circumstance must seriously retard the establishment in this colony of those free institutions which were the pride and boast of the parent country? For himself he had an English heart. But could there be free institutions without moral improvement? So the idea was planted that transportation had so corrupted and depraved the free that the introduction of these birthrights must be postponed. Glenelg, in commenting that October on the Burton charge, had dropped the significant words that anyone who tried to describe the condition of the colony as to crimes must not leave out of view the peculiar character of its population.[15]

Knowing that the Act to provide for the Administration of Justice in New South Wales and Van Diemen's Land was to expire in 1837, and that talk of an inquiry on the future of transportation was in the air, men from the Antipodes began to invade London at the end of 1836. They had been preceded in 1835 by William Bryan, who dreamed of a horrible revenge on Lieutenant-Colonel Arthur for depriving him of the use of his convict servants, and thus causing him great mortification, and pecuniary loss. For a season Bryan swaggered and strutted round the salons and coffee houses of London boasting that the talented, the powerful and the liberal would help him to cause Arthur, like Humpty Dumpty, to have a great fall. But Stephen cast a cold eye on all talk about revenge, which Bryan uncovered with such vehemence that Stephen began to have doubts about Bryan's sanity. Such a

[14] E. Macarthur to Sir George Grey, Waiting Room of Colonial Office, 21 April 1836, C.O. 201/258, pp. 138-40; see also Minute of James Stephen on above, ibid., p. 140.

[15] Charge delivered by His Honor Judge Burton to the Jury, at the close of the Sessions of the Supreme Court of New South Wales for the year 1835, Sydney, 18 November, 1835, in James Macarthur (ed.), *New South Wales; its present State and future Prospects* (London, 1837), Appendix, pp. 34-53; Glenelg to Bourke, 21 October 1836, *H.R.A.*, I. xviii. 576.

man could not help the men in Downing Street to answer their problems of great moment.[16]

With James Mudie the case was different. Like Bryan he had come to London thirsting for revenge for all the hurts to his pride, and the pecuniary losses he had suffered at the hands of a colonial governor. By chance he had arrived in London in July at a time when the Colonial Office was beginning to take an interest in the idea that convictism had produced a lamentable depravity of morals and a fearful prevalence of crime in the penal colonies. Mudie's aim was to arraign Governor Bourke at the bar of public opinion for the state of society in New South Wales. To do this early in 1837 he published a book *The Felonry of New South Wales*, dedicating it to all members of both Houses of Parliament, of upright and honourable feelings and principles. To blacken Bourke's name he developed two themes. The first was that so far from being regarded as a severe punishment, transportation took the convict to a land of promise, where he was assured of abundant subsistence with or without the exertion of easy toil, and where he could obtain great wealth. The second was that the convicts and their descendants had become so profligate, treacherous, dishonest and mutinous, that they had corrupted the whole of society, a large portion of which consisted of rottenness. As for the women convicts they were the pest and gangrene of colonial society, and lower than the brutes, a disgrace to all animal existence. But Mudie had his uses. To the delight of men in London who were strangers to the dark passions pounding away in his breast, he had touched on subjects which interested them deeply. Here was a reckless man, saying wildly and extravagantly something they wanted to hear, namely, that the convicts had corrupted the whole of society in New South Wales. Could the saints of Exeter Hall, the men with a Christian hatred of negro slavery, and the men of affairs who believed migration to the Australian colonies would do more than transportation to solve the problems of redundant population in the United Kingdom, use for their own high purposes the opinions of a man tainted with naughtiness of heart?[17]

In November of 1836 the Reverend John Dunmore Lang had arrived in London after an arduous voyage in the *Abel Gower*. The stories of how he had enforced strict moral standards among the clergy had gone before him. The man had no pity for those whom God had created morally lame or blind. When a standard-bearer fell by his own sinful act under the temptations of the devil, he felt a spirit of desolation, as though glory had departed. But such incidents provided him with the occasion not for compassion but to berate those who had not fallen so far: 'Let everyone who thinketh he standeth', he used to tell them, 'take heed lest he fall'. E. O'Shaughnessy, a person of dissi-

---

[16] For William Bryan in London, see Arthur to Glenelg, 7 April 1836, C.O. 280/76, pp. 93-5; W. Bryan to Glenelg, 16 October 1835, C.O. 280/92, p. 144; W. Bryan to James Hackett, 12 January 1836, C.O. 280/76, pp. 654-5; The Memorial of W. Bryan to Glenelg, received at the C.O., 23 June 1836, C.O. 280/92, p. 9; Article on W. Bryan in *Australian Dictionary of Biography*, vol. 1; see also G. Arthur to James Stephen, 12 January 1837 and J. Stephen to G. Arthur, 16 March 1837 (Papers of Sir George Arthur, vol. 4, Correspondence with James Stephen).

[17] For James Mudie in London, see James Mudie, *The Felonry of New South Wales*, ed. by W. Stone (Melbourne, 1964), especially pp. 2-5, 52, 107-13, 114, 118 and 142-4.

pated habits, used W. Watt, a ticket-of-leave holder who was living notoriously with a concubine right under the very nose of the colonial police who were required to prevent such affronts to lovers of decorum, to fill the pages of the *Sydney Gazette* with observations on colonial politics and morals. Lang retorted in the *Colonist* that it was the aim of the convicts to reduce the respectable to the same level as themselves, to abolish all distinctions which God and man had established between right and wrong, and to emancipate the convict community from all sense of degradation and guilt. Against convict levelling Lang set the laws of God: against convict corruption, Lang set that great drama between man and the devil. With that boundless energy which had characterized all his days in the colony, he had used his leisure hours on the *Abel Gower* to write fifty thousand odd words for a book *Transportation and Colonization*, the main object of which was to point out to His Majesty's government, to members of Parliament, and to the British people, the absolute necessity of some immediate and extensive change in the regulation and management of the transportation system in the Australian colonies. New South Wales, he believed, stood peculiarly in need of a free immigrant population of such a character as to counteract, and not to increase and aggravate, the peculiar tendencies and characteristics of the south of Ireland population. For Lang, too, had other nightmares. One of these was that the Protestants of New South Wales would be swamped by sweepings of popish peasants, prostitutes and prisoners from Ireland.

In his pamphlet he also took up two themes which the Christian haters of negro slavery, radicals, and moral reformers were discussing that year. Assignment, he wrote, sometimes entailed a state of hardship and punishment to a degree almost intolerable to human nature, or one of idleness and indulgence. Educated convicts had raised up a formidable party in the colony for the countenance and protection of vice and villainy. He was not saying that assignment was slavery or that convictism entailed the moral depravity of all, but he was close to it. He also touched on the other subject set for discussion in that year—the propriety and wisdom of conferring the birthrights of Englishmen on societies with a lamentable depravity of morals, and a frightful prevalence of crime. On this Lang had his doubts. Why trust such a frail and corrupt vessel as man with the shaping of his own destiny? Insofar as liberals and radicals entertained such hopes for man, he shrank from them. Men were foul and vile, and only God could cleanse them. He saw himself as a voice from the wilderness, who had come to tell them that because of the intolerable expense and the moral abominations, His Majesty's ministers must cease forthwith to treat New South Wales and Van Diemen's Land as the dunghills of the Empire. It never occurred to Lang to speculate on what His Majesty's ministers might consider appropriate for such a society, nor did he concern himself with the pain and anger aroused in the native-born and in all those with Australian hearts by calling 'the land, boys, we live in', a dunghill.[18]

18 For J. D. Lang in London, see J. D. Lang, *Transportation and Colonization; or, the Causes of the comparative failure of the transportation system in the Australian Colonies* (London, 1837); *John Dunmore Lang: Chiefly Autobiographical 1799-1878*, ed. by A. Gilchrist (2 vols, Melbourne, 1951), vol. 1, pp. 194-204 and 218-20; see also *Australian Dictionary of Biography*, vol. 2.

By contrast James Macarthur, after his arrival in London in November of 1836, attached importance to not being at a loss for friends with influence in high places. Mr Commissioner Bigge, now an old man, but still capable of making heads turn when he walked down the corridors of power in Downing Street, still remembered kindly that white Arab horse which John Macarthur senior had placed at his disposal in New South Wales as long ago as 1819. Sir George Grey in the Colonial Office gave James Macarthur a most flattering interview. Conservative feeling was now manifesting itself so firmly through England and Scotland that Chief Justice Forbes had quitted London in alarm.[19] By 14 December Macarthur was certain that he and the powerful men in Downing Street talked the same language. On that day he had talked with Stephen and Glenelg, finding them both of his own opinion on the future of transportation, emigration, and the constitution of New South Wales. Stephen told him transportation must be done away with, and emigration substituted for it, and as for convicts and radicals, well, he, Stephen, wished he could send them to Canada as a free gift to Mr Radical Papineau. Sensing he was with men of like mind he handed in that day the text of the petition, and told Glenelg that the best thing to do was to give New South Wales a Legislative Council with more members from men of all parties, provided they had never been convicts. He was so excited by it all that he decided to skip church that Sunday and write to his dear brother William, sending Edward to church to pray for all of them, their dearest and their best. By chance that 15 December when he exchanged mind with Stephen and Glenelg was his birthday. He had just completed his thirty-eighth year. He had, he believed, just ground to hope he had spent the day not to the disadvantage of his native land. He ended it, characteristically, by asking God to bless his dearest sister as for him the welfare of his family, the welfare of New South Wales, and the intentions of the deity were all part of some cosmic harmony. It was given to him to confront his destiny with an easy, quiet, unassuming confidence, to believe that in the forthcoming year he would be called on both to shape the future destiny of his native land, and to take to himself a wife, so that he and his seed would come into that rich inheritance for which his father and mother had so magnificently prepared the way.[20]

To enable his opinions to reach a wider audience he had commissioned Edward Edwards, known as a young Nonconformist nobody from nowhere, who was earning a living by researching and writing for others, to prepare a book setting out his ideas. He handed over to Edwards the texts of the petitions, the Burton charge to the jury, and presumably uncovered the drift of his own mind. On the transportation system the book took up very much the same position as Mudie and Lang. The prosperity of the colony, the author wrote, was unhappily counterbalanced by a lamentable depravity of manners, and by the fearful prevalence of crime, which proceeded either from the convicts or

[19] James Macarthur to William Macarthur, 28 November 1836 (Macarthur Papers, vol. 35, pp. 268-70); James Macarthur to William Macarthur, 9 December 1836, ibid., pp. 272-3.

[20] Based on James Macarthur to Glenelg, 15 December 1836 (Macarthur Papers, vol. 35, pp. 281-2); James Macarthur to Private Secretary to Glenelg, 15 December 1836, ibid., p. 283; James Macarthur to his sister Elizabeth, 15 December 1836, ibid., pp. 284-6; James Macarthur to William Macarthur, 18 December 1836, ibid., pp. 288-90.

WILLIAM MOLESWORTH

Portrait by J. Watson-Gordon in the National Portrait Gallery, London

JAMES MACARTHUR

Portrait by an unknown artist at Camden Park

the ex-convicts. On the remedy for this state of affairs Macarthur was both dignified and quaint. His recommendations were a blend of gentility and self-interest, of mildness of manner and anxiety not to give offence wedded to the promotion of the material well-being of his family and his class. Assignment in towns, he urged, should cease. But, he went on, so long as convicts were assigned, they should be confined as much as possible to laborious employments such as tending of sheep which was reformatory, but not to the tending of cattle, which engendered a reckless disposition and lawless habits, and led to much disorder and crime. He was prepared to entertain the idea that assignment might cease altogether, as soon as the demand for labour in the colony was met with free immigrants.

He was anxious to communicate what it was like for an English gentleman who happened to be born in Australia to live in a convict society. Gently and without the malice and recklessness of Mudie he revealed the loathing of the gentry for the successful ex-convicts, and those who went in for the vulgar display of wealth. He described the convicts he approved of, those with a retiring disposition, men anxious to avoid the public gaze, who displayed a feeling of contrition which arose from virtuous shame for past transactions. He loved those passages in the liturgy in which the dictates of his own heart seemed to receive divine approval, 'a contrite heart, O God, thou shalt not despise'.

In the book he went on to uncover his distaste for all vulgarians, all people, great and small, who threatened to dispute his and the divine sense of the natural fitness of things. Educated convicts were in the highest degree mischievous. The immoderate use of spirits was another cause of the disorder and crime prevalent in New South Wales, because it changed men fashioned in the divine image into coarse and vulgar beasts. The book uncovered too a division in his own mind. On the one hand, self-interest as an employer of rural labour attracted him towards a defence of assignment. On the other hand, as a gentleman, he recoiled at the taint the convict system left on both men and society. He ended this section by stating his conviction of the urgent necessity, as well as the obvious utility, of instituting an inquiry into the whole subject of transportation to New South Wales—not knowing then that in such an inquiry the contradictions deep in his own mind, symptomatic as they were of the contradictions in the minds of the landowners of New South Wales, would be held up for all to see.[21]

On the future constitution of New South Wales he knew no such division between self-interest and his own sensibilities as a man. On this subject he wrote with firmness, a stranger alike to doubt and prevarication. He wrote as a man who was not prepared to allow ex-convicts to sit on a jury. This repugnance to be associated with persons who had been convicted of crime, he said, had a deep foundation in the best feelings of the human breast. He was just as unhappy with the number of publicans who sat on each jury in Sydney,

[21] For the collaboration between Edward Edwards and James Macarthur, see J. Metcalfe, 'Edward Edwards: His Association with "New South Wales; Its Present State and Future Prospects" ', R.A.H.S., *J. & P.*, vol. 38, 1952-3, pp. 153-80; James Macarthur (ed.), op. cit., see especially pp. 33, 41-7, 54-9, 60-8; for Macarthur's opinions on the prevalence of crime in New South Wales before he gave evidence to the Transportation Committee, see James Macarthur to Sir George Grey, 9 February 1837, C.O. 201/267, pp. 512-23.

W

for on this point Macarthur's quarrel was as much with the spirit of the age, as with the convict influences on New South Wales society, He was, on his own confession, just as anxious to exclude from the jury box persons of bad repute and low standing in society as ex-convicts. On the Legislative Council he took the same stand. He wanted a part-nominated and a part-elected Council, but above all he wanted a Council composed of men of standing in society. As he told Lord Glenelg when he presented the petitions of his group in December, he and his fellow petitioners represented a large majority of the character, property and intelligence of the colony.

In politics Macarthur was a Botany Bay Tory. Like de Tocqueville he believed that to enjoy liberty was to do that which was good and just. On the ruins of this old liberty of doing what was good and just, the Botany Bay Whigs, he feared, wanted to establish that liberty for corrupt natures, and allow men to do what they liked. As he saw it, the advocates for the abolition of all restraints, the 'everything is allowable' men were the men with dirty collars, the publicans, the loud-mouthed, the coarse and the vulgar who were clamouring to take over the government of New South Wales. To check the lamentable depravity of manners, and the frightful prevalence of crime he recommended a sound religious education. Sensing like de Tocqueville that the great mass of mankind had a 'depraved taste' for equality, and fearful of the levelling tendencies of convictism, Macarthur hoped to plant in the land he lived in the giant oaks of gentry in whose ample shade the weak and the gullible could shelter from the vulgar glare of that equality of conditions and licentiousness which threatened to bring everything to ruin.

He was a man of vision—a man with a mission to perform before he fell asleep like his father, and was gathered into the fold. In London he behaved with the quiet confidence of a man who believed in his power to influence the shape of things to come. On first arriving in London he was glad to hear that Forbes had quitted the corridors of power in London, and sought refuge in the country, for Forbes had seemed all too anxious to buy the approval of convict upstarts by heady talk about the liberty of the press and the birthrights of Englishmen. From that implacable foe of the democratic rabble, Colonel Henry Dumaresq, he had heard that the casuistry and sophistry of Forbes did not stand on entrenched ground, that the secret hopes of the man's heart left him open to persuasion on the great question of the future constitution of New South Wales.[22]

Forbes was sensitive as ever to the drift of opinion in Downing Street and Westminster, and in the salons and drawing rooms of those Whig aristocrats and intellectuals on whose approval he relied for the fulfilment of the secret ambitions of his heart. He was not slow to take the hint from Stephen and Grey that he should stop thinking as a provincial and see the problem of New South Wales as part of a much wider problem. He coveted a knighthood as a

[22] James Macarthur to Sir George Grey, 2 January 1837, C.O. 201/267, pp. 500-6; James Macarthur to William Macarthur, 9 December 1836 (Macarthur Papers, vol. 35, pp. 272-3); see also James Macarthur (ed.), op. cit., pp. 79-106, 132-6, 272-80; see the inscriptions on the tombstone of John and James Macarthur, Camden Park Estate; extracts from Henry Dumaresq's letter to General Darling, 3 July 1833, 'I had come to the conclusion that his [i.e. Forbes'] enmity was safer than his friendship'. (Letters of Colonel Henry Dumaresq, MS. in M.L.).

reward for his long, distinguished and faithful services to the Crown in Bermuda, Newfoundland and New South Wales. He was not prepared to buy such a title by becoming servile for he had his pride, and there was always about him a dignity of bearing, a high conception of honour which he was not prepared to compromise for the sake of satisfying worldly ambition. On 8 September 1836 he apologized for troubling Lord Glenelg during the usual season of relaxation from official fatigues, but hoped he would not intrude himself unnecessarily on his Lordship's attention if he took the liberty of saying that he, Forbes, already knew of Sir Richard Bourke's favourable mention of his long services.[23]

All through the autumn and winter of 1836-7 he put down on paper his ideas on the future constitution of New South Wales, and on the future of transportation. On both he wrote as an attendant judge, and not as a politician. He wrote as a man reluctant to take sides. In analysis and prediction he was superb: in recommendation he was weak and vacillating. He saw the convicts as men employed as pioneers to subdue the wilderness and prepare the way for future emigration and new colonies in the East. He saw that it would be desirable for the social welfare of the colonies that the whole population should be pure and uncontaminated. But when it came to the point of saying whether transportation should be discontinued, all that Forbes could say was that for the reciprocal interests of the mother country and the colony such discontinuance should be prospective and gradual. He was a stranger to the passions of those men with a material stake in the system, or the moral passions of those who saw it all as an ungracious and an unlovely thing, the removal of which concerned the whole human race.[24]

Wracked by influenza all through a winter spent in damp, swirling mists of Cambridge, disappointed at the long delay in replying to his request for a mark of His Majesty's favour, a lesser man might well have given way to despair, or consumed himself in the sports of the envious and the malicious. But he had about him not that patience of the saints to endure to the end, but the stamina of the man waiting for the call he knew would one day be his. He was not Prince Hamlet, nor was meant to be. He was an attendant judge, a man who would do to swell a progress, to start a scene or two, advise the Governor, advise the Secretary of State, advise Stephen, or advise any man who bore the burden he himself could never shoulder. He was deferential, glad to be of use, politic, cautious and meticulous, and full of high sentiments. Perhaps at times he was almost ridiculous. Perhaps at times as he waited in those chancelleries for the others to come out, he might have exposed himself to derision, had not some inner strength, some iron control over the gusts of vulgar ambition left his face a map on which few men could read those secret hopes of the heart.

---

[23] F. Forbes to Glenelg, 8 September 1836, C.O. 201/257, p. 581; S. Walpole, *Life of Lord John Russell* (2 vols, London, 1889), vol. 1, pp. 279-80; G. Nash, *Reaction and Reconstruction in English Politics 1832-1862* (Oxford, 1965), p. 21; for Forbes in London, see A.C.V. Melbourne, *Early Constitutional Development in Australia* (2nd ed. by R. B. Joyce, Brisbane, 1963), pp. 231-6; article on Forbes in *Australian Dictionary of Biography*, vol. 1.

[24] F. Forbes to J. Stephen, 18 October 1836, C.O. 201/257, pp. 583-6; F. Forbes to J. Stephen, 28 November 1836, and enclosing a memorandum on the expediency of continuing transportation to the Australian colonies, ibid., pp. 592-609.

Nature had conferred on him a dignity of bearing, which prevented him chasing after the Glenelgs and Stephens of this world down those corridors in Downing Street, and plucking their sleeves and asking them, with a note of desperation, for news of that mark of His Majesty's favour. Forbes was never the lackey, and never the fool.[25]

On the days when his health permitted it, he enjoyed some unrestrained conversation with James Macarthur upon the subject of forming a local legislature, and found to his delight that the differences between them were minimal. On 31 March 1837 he wrote for James Stephen the fruits of his thinking. The hero of the Botany Bay Whigs, radicals, liberals, publicans, and convicts had come round to the Macarthur position that the Legislative Council should be part nominated, and part elected by all who possessed a prescribed property qualification. Emancipists with that qualification should be eligible to vote, but not to sit as members. Early in April, with the crocuses and daffodils in bloom, and the buds of new life swelling on the trees, he was told that his name had been submitted to the King for the honour of a knighthood. But just as honours and worldly fame were being showered on him intimations of impending death cheated him of the enjoyment of his prize. Sensing that the illness from which he had suffered all through the winter at Cambridge was mortal, he turned to the sacred scriptures to solace him in his hours of suffering, poring over them to find the path for the heavenly prize. For he was eager for that too, and began to prepare for it with all the zeal, the industry, and the single-mindedness with which he had pursued the honour William IV conferred on him that spring morning in April the same year.[26]

In January Lieutenant-Governor Arthur had come up to London town to find as had so many of his predecessors that he was being despitefully used by the men he had antagonized during his long years of service in the colonies. William Bryan was grossly calumniating him. In the House of Commons he was being exposed to a persecution quite unparalleled during the whole of his absence from England, as one speaker had suggested slanderously that he, Arthur, had been guilty of sadism during his period in Honduras. Stephen counselled him not to let his heart be troubled. The Colonial Office had doubts about the sanity of Bryan. But that, after all, was not the heart of the matter. Arthur, he said, must cease to be a colonist and take a metropolitan view of such strange people as William Bryan. It was the task of the metropolitans not to concern themselves in petty schemes of revenge, or in vulgar preoccupation with the distribution of prizes in the human lottery, but to address themselves to the more serious questions of whether crime was on the increase in the penal colonies, whether assignment was a form of slavery, whether the convict system was corrupting the whole of society, whether the colonies of New South Wales and Van Diemen's Land could afford to dispense with convict labour,

25 F. Forbes to J. Stephen, 31 March 1837, C.O. 201/266, p. 468; for the character sketch see 'The Love Song of J. Alfred Prufrock' in T. S. Eliot, *Collected Poems 1909-1962* (London, 1963).

26 F. Forbes to Glenelg, 27 March 1837, C.O. 201/266, p. 465; F. Forbes to J. Stephen, 31 March 1837, enclosing a memorandum on the two petitions, ibid., pp. 468-507; G. Grey to F. Forbes, 8 April 1837, ibid., p. 507; G. Grey to F. Forbes, 3 April 1837, ibid., p. 466; Forbes Papers, p. 167; *Bermuda Royal Gazette*, 17 May 1842.

and whether emancipists should be excluded from juries and voting and membership of the future legislatures in the penal colonies. On these questions opinion within the Colonial Office and amongst those public men either interested in or responsible for the decision was divided.[27]

James Stephen was an abolitionist. Born in 1789 into a family with a long association with the anti-slavery movement, he had grown up in the atmosphere of the Clapham Sect, deeply imbued with their faith in the fatherhood of God and the brotherhood of man. For although he was austere, and looked down with disdain and indeed disapproval on men who were corrupted by careless amusements, and knew that in the world he could only expect tribulation and sorrow, he remained firmly in that world. From the despatches pouring in from Sydney and Hobart Town he came to the conclusion that assignment was a form of slavery, and that convicts and their descendants were corrupting, degrading, and tormenting the least of God's creatures—the Australian aborigine. That was enough to put him with those who believed that the removal of such a plague concerned the whole human race.[28]

By chance a turn in the wheel of political fortunes gave Stephen the opportunity for which he had been waiting. In April 1835 the government of Lord Melbourne took office. Charles Grant kissed hands for the Colonial Office and was raised to the peerage in the forthcoming month as Lord Glenelg, and Lord John Russell took over the Home Office. Stephen had an immense admiration for Glenelg, calling him the most laborious, and the most enlightened minister of the public, not sensing that Glenelg was an incurable procrastinator.

Glenelg was born in Bengal in 1788, matriculated at Magdalene College Cambridge as a pensioner in 1795 where, like the Reverend Richard Johnson and the Reverend Samuel Marsden, he came under the influence of the evangelical revival, and thus acquired that high spiritual seriousness which, when united with high intellectual powers, endeared him to Stephen. After serving in the Treasury and in Ireland he had worked with Stephen on the Act to abolish slavery. When he took over the Colonial Office in April of 1835 it looked like a coming together of men of like mind. Events were about to try Glenelg and find him wanting. The systematic colonizers were pestering him to permit them to colonize South Australia: men were illegally trespassing in the district of Port Phillip: Mudie, Lang, Macarthur and Ullathorne were pestering him about New South Wales: Bryan, Gellibrand, Meredith, Melville and Kemp were pestering him about Van Diemen's Land. The Canadas were seething with rebellion. Glenelg had all the qualities—the industry, the zeal, and the high-mindedness to rise to the occasion. Only one

[27] Arthur to W. G. Broughton, 28 June 1836 (Papers of Sir George Arthur, vol. 12, Letters from Bishop Broughton and from the Reverend Samuel Marsden); Arthur to J. Stephen, 12 January 1837 (Papers of Sir George Arthur, vol. 4, Correspondence with James Stephen); Arthur to the Rt. Honble the Judge Advocate General, 29 September 1836, and Arthur to Spring Rice, 11 and 19 March 1837 (ibid., vol. 5, Letters from Sir George Arthur, 1822-50).

[28] L. Stephen, *The Life of Sir James Fitzjames Stephen* (London, 1895), pp. 31-65; C. E. Stephen, *The Right Honourable Sir James Stephen* (London, 1906); P. Knaplund, *James Stephen and the British Colonial System 1813-1847* (Madison, 1953); E. Dowden (ed.), *Correspondence of Henry Taylor* (London, 1888), p. 49; A. Mozley (ed.), *Letters and Correspondence of John Henry Newman* (2 vols, London, 1890), vol. 2, pp. 138-9.

thing was lacking. He could not make up his mind: he became the butt of the coffee house wits. A scholar and a man of God, he was brought to derision till Melbourne, in desperation, called for his resignation and Glenelg returned to his books, with a sense of ill-usage and a mortified spirit, but not before he had made one decision of great moment for the future of Australia.[29]

Like Stephen, Lord John Russell had been a figure of fun in his schooldays because of an oddity with which his Maker had endowed him. For he was tiny. Born in 1792 the third son of the Duke of Bedford, a seven-months baby, he had inherited his mother's delicacy of constitution. Almost smothered in childhood by his mother's love, he had gone to school in London where he fagged for his brother, who beat him mercilessly, not knowing that, fortunately for posterity, he was imprinting on a delicate mind and innocent heart a profound horror of such cruelty, and making a lifelong crusader to rescue humanity from tortures similar to those he had suffered as a boy. For the rest of his schooldays the Bedford family home was his classroom till he attended the University of Edinburgh, and travelled in the Peninsula in the wake of Wellington's army as an observer, for his height and his sickly digestion militated against shouldering arms in that sea of troubles. In 1813 he had been elected as member for Tavistock in the Whig interest. By 1830 he had identified himself with the reforming wing of that party.

Opponents ridiculed him as that tiny, quiet, fragile, modest, almost insignificant-looking man, so neat, so plain, and formal in his black coat and snow-white neckcloth. The caricaturists drew him as a boy, who marched out in front in the age of little men, the days of the pygmies after the giants who lived in the land before the days of parliamentary reform. Some, with characteristic cruelty, drew him as a girl—for they were not to know that among those who were privileged to be shown the view, as it were, behind the cold and reserved mask, he was known as Don Giovanni. By great self-discipline, he had overcome all the handicaps of birth—the height, and the tone of voice that smacked of aristocratic affectation. He had acquired a self-possession, a tact, a skill, a parliamentary know-how, and a felicity of diction surpassed by few of the distinguished men of his day. Charles Dickens, who had observed with mounting anger the chatter of the men in the House of Commons and, like the prophets of old, had exposed the great gap between their professions on the floor of the House and their performance, excepted Lord John Russell from his condemnation.[30]

There was about Lord John a sense of a divine mission to reduce the area and scope in which His Majesty's liege subjects could exploit the law in order to torment each other. So, while the cynics, scoffers and mockers shouted from the house-tops that the aim of the Whigs was to remain in office, and put down

[29] Charles Grant, Lord Glenelg, *Dictionary of National Biography*, vol. 8; see also C. C. F. Greville, *Memoirs. A Journal of the Reigns of King George IV and King William IV* (4th ed., 3 vols, London, 1875), vol. 3, pp. 256 and 276.

[30] For Lord John Russell see *Dictionary of National Biography*, vol. 17; S. Walpole, *The Life of Lord John Russell* (2 vols, London, 1889); *Frazer's Magazine*, June 1845; R. Russell (ed.), *Early Correspondence of Lord John Russell* (2 vols, London, 1913); D. Cecil, *Lord Melbourne* (repr., London, 1945), p. 202; E. Johnson, op. cit., vol. 1, p. 88; C. C. F. Greville, *A Journal of the Reign of Queen Victoria, from 1837 to 1852* (3 vols, London, 1885), vol. 1, p. 5.

the radicals and radicalism so that they and their descendants could live surrounded by pomp and splendour for ever, and taunted Russell as 'Finality
Jack', Russell went on gradually reforming. After the great Reform Act of
Parliament in 1832 he had turned to those questions within the parish of
the Home Office—to tithes, church rates, and the church in Ireland. By
September 1836 he was ready to turn his mind towards the reform of the
criminal law, that vast empire not only for the punishment of wickedness and
vice, but also for the promotion of human cruelty and suffering. In that month
he told the Commissioners for the Reform of the Criminal Law that government might well deem it expedient to propose to Parliament a bill specifying on
which subjects capital punishment should be retained. He also asked them to
consider in what cases the punishment of transportation should be retained, and
whether it should be applicable at all in cases of larceny. Within a month he
had made up his own mind on this latter point. Transportation, he believed,
might be kept as a punishment for grave offences. But, as for the present
system of transporting a numerous array of thieves and poachers into New
South Wales and Van Diemen's Land, that appeared to him to be fraught
with bad and even dangerous consequences, because it meant sending an
immense body of criminals to two colonies which were already overloaded with
a criminal and immoral population. Of the 3,025 sentenced to transportation
in 1835, 1,505 had been sentenced for simple larceny alone. If the penalty of
transportation was taken away from simple larceny, they could diminish by at
least one-half the total number of persons sentenced to transportation, which
would be a good thing because, in his view of the subject, much of the evil in
the penal colonies arose from the excess of numbers sent there. They became,
instead of penal colonies, the territory of a depraved community. Convicts
could not be kept in order: they abandoned or defrauded their masters: they
destroyed all regularity of local government: they sowed the seeds of future
insubordination which might, if allowed to take its course, place the colonies
in the hands of convicts and murderers.[31]

So when he introduced his proposal for the reform of the criminal law to the
House of Commons on 23 March 1837, he told them that he entertained considerable doubts whether the system of transportation ought to be continued
as it had been carried on of late years. From the evidence before him he had
come to the conclusion that the four or five thousand persons who were sent
out every year to New South Wales were not absorbed in the general population, but formed a large and vicious separate mass. He reminded them that
New South Wales was a colony containing 100,000 persons (the current
figure being 85,267) and that by sending out four to five thousand convicts
every year the obvious consequence must be to make that colony the most
depraved community that had ever been seen in the world. For himself, he
did not propose to abolish transportation altogether—for 'Finality Jack' was
always the reformer and never the radical. What he proposed was to restrict
transportation to certain classes of criminals and to certain offences.[32]

---

[31] The correspondence between Lord John Russell and the Criminal Law Commissioners on 19
September and 20 October 1836 is reprinted in *The Times*, 1 April 1837.
[32] *P.D.*, 3rd series, vol. 37, 23 March 1837, col. 709-10.

Amongst the few members who listened to Lord John that night was a young radical who wanted that 'unclean thing' not to be reformed but to receive its death warrant. He was Sir William Molesworth. He had been born in London in 1810. Like Stephen and Russell Molesworth had been cursed at birth with an oddity which so disfigured him that boys teased him unmercifully all through his days at boarding school. The gods or chance seemed to have cursed him with such an easy surrender to passion, such a spirit of recklessness that he bade fair to become a vagabond on the face of the earth. He was expelled from Cambridge for challenging his tutor to a duel. He became an unbeliever, and flaunted his atheism in a society whose masters and rulers were only too happy to exploit for their own purposes the social utility of the Christian religion. Belonging by birth to the Whig interest, he became a radical—a utilitarian and an unbeliever who on his own confession preferred to be disliked rather than compromise his beliefs. Other men of passion were drawn to him. Carlyle, who found another radical, Roebuck, not at all to his taste, calling him Roebuck Robespierre and an acrid character out of whom very little would ever come, nevertheless warmed to Sir William as a man who had the air of a good roistering schoolboy. For Molesworth believed a man should plunge, a man should draw his inspiration from Byron's vision of judgment and Keats' battle between damnation and impassioned clay, rather than from that innocent one who had told men to resist not evil. In these things he was poles apart from Stephen, Lord John Russell and the saints of Exeter Hall. He was a strange mixture of the playboy and the intellectually earnest, a man who believed men should behave as though some one was watching and caring, even though they knew there was no such person. In 1835 he took over the *London Review* and rather shocked Mill by devoting space to a long article on the poems of the young Tennyson. For that Greek quest for beauty lived in Molesworth, as well as more than a hint that like the men whom the Gods loved he would die young, though not before he had reduced the area of darkness in the human heart by spreading sweetness and light. As member for East Cornwall between 1832 and 1834 he gave, it was said, an immense shove to the ballot and other radical measures—all very salutary but not that grand gesture for the emancipation of mankind which he was seeking.[33]

In March of 1834 chance gave him that great opportunity. In that month six agricultural labourers from Tolpuddle in Dorsetshire were sentenced to transportation for seven years. By probing the iniquity of the sentence passed on six simple and deluded farm-labourers of Dorsetshire he found his life's work. He found that transportation was attended by what he called moral evils of the most appalling character. The boy with a natural desire to improve himself had found the opportunity to improve a section of mankind. On 23 February of the following year he told the House of Commons that the Duke of Cumberland and his clique ought not to be spared because they were rich

[33] For Molesworth see *Dictionary of National Biography*, vol. 38, and Mrs Fawcett, *Life of the Right Hon. Sir William Molesworth Bart. M.P. F.R.S.* (London, 1901); Harriet Grote, *The Philosophical Radicals of 1832, comprising the life of Sir William Molesworth* (printed privately, London, 1866).

and well educated, whilst the poor, ignorant Dorsetshire labourers were suffering for the infringement of those laws the purpose of which they could not understand. Then he went to Bellamy's Kitchen where he and his friends put away sundry mutton chops, and Welsh rarebits, washed down with copious draughts of bottled porter and sherry, for the roistering schoolboy lived on in the breast of this man who had dedicated himself to destroy that unclean and unlovely thing—the transportation system.

Wakefield was also campaigning hard for abolition; Mr Over-Secretary Stephen, who, alas, was not a man for the pleasures Molesworth loved so madly, was also on his side; the saints of Exeter Hall, and the clergy and laity of the Clapham Sect were strange allies in the campaign, together with the political economists, the measurers, and the utilitarians who argued that assisted emigration could do more to solve the surplus labour problem than the transportation of convicts. Molesworth now began a correspondence with Lord John Russell on what was to be done. To his delight Lord John told him on 5 April 1837 that if transportation were to continue, it would create the most depraved community that had ever existed in the world.[34]

Perhaps Molesworth inferred too rashly that Russell was in the bag, and that he with his usual bland self-confidence would carry Melbourne and even that notorious procrastinator Glenelg who, according to the coffee house wits, had reduced the art of doing nothing to a system. After midnight on 8 April, a fruitful time for minority men, Molesworth rose in the House of Commons and proposed that a select committee be appointed to inquire into the system of transportation, its efficacy as a punishment, its influence on the moral state of society in the penal colonies, and how far it was susceptible of improvement. He was hoping for a committee of men of like mind. He himself was appointed chairman, Lord John Russell was one of the members, but, alas, so were Sir George Grey and Lord Howick, both committed to reform rather than abolition, and a long list of uncommitted men—Mr Leader, Mr Ward, Mr Hawes, Mr William Ord, Mr Fowell Buxton, Sir Thomas Fremantle, Mr Francis Baring, Sir Robert Peel, Mr Lennard, Mr Ridly Colborne; Mr Charles Buller was a sound systematic colonizer, and, as such, committed to abolition. On 24 April Mr Fowell Buxton was discharged from any further attendance on the select committee, and the name of Mr Hutt added to the members. On 9 May Mr Henry Lytton Bulwer, the agent in London for the Australian Patriotic Association, was added to the committee.[35]

Almost exactly fifty years after that golden Sunday on 13 May 1787 when the First Fleet had weighed anchor off Portsmouth, and that clergyman had gone down on his knees to ask God to forgive all of them, the Transportation Committee began to take evidence in a room in the old House of Commons at Westminster. Outside that room the sound and the fury of life went on very much as it had gone on when the First Fleet had set out on that journey

[34] Mrs Fawcett, op. cit., pp. 137-41; Molesworth appears to have taken Mrs Grote, the wife of the historian of Greece, into his confidence about his 'potations'. From Mrs Fawcett's account at pp. 137-41 of her life of Molesworth it appears that Mrs Grote wrote an account of this in her memoir of Molesworth, but a copy of Mrs Grote's work could not be found.

[35] *Journals of the House of Commons*, vol. 92, 8 April 1837, pp. 217-18; ibid., 24 April 1837, p. 292, and 9 May 1837, p. 345.

across the oceans to begin European civilization in a harsh and barren land inhabited by a handful of exceedingly black, barbarian savages.

The temper of life in the British Isles was very much as it had been fifty years earlier. At Aylesbury in March 1837 the mind of the murderer of a gamekeeper was greatly eased by the spiritual consolation he received from the chaplain who read to him portions of scripture, which held out to him the hope of a pardon in the world to come.[36] At Liverpool a man had knocked down his drunken wife, and stamped on her three times till she expired. The learned judge addressed him on the awful nature of his crime, and threatened to send him to the bar of his God as a warning to all to abstain from intoxicating liquor, but sentenced him instead to be transported for life beyond the seas where he was to be worked in chains.[37] On 6 April two women were charged, as had been so many of those who boarded those ships outside Portsmouth in 1787, with keeping a house of ill fame. On the same day a young woman, decently dressed, fell under a coal wagon when intoxicated and expired.[38] The Protestants sustained themselves with the same theological fare with which their predecessors had been nourished, believing that their eternal happiness and their temporal welfare depended upon a proper cultivation of true Protestant sentiment—that popery meant enslavement of the mind, and uncleannesses which it would defile their pens to describe.[39]

In Ireland, in the county of Tipperary, four armed men, with their faces blackened, went to the house of a farmer and swore they would not allow any man to live in the neighbourhood who had taken blood-money. Irish men and women still shrieked and wailed when the judges sentenced those found guilty of violent protests against the laws of man. They still cursed their melancholy history, treasured their holy faith as a happy issue out of all their afflictions, and by tenderness and loving kindness to each other showed that they had preserved the image of Christ, which the English had sullied with their Protestant apostasy, and their laying up for themselves treasures on earth. At Cork that April amid scenes of riot and uproar Catholics shouted at Protestants as bullies, braggarts, liars, and cowards, while the Protestants nursed their own delusion that all Catholics lacked the elementary virtue of honesty—that, as they put it, they never look you in the eyes.[40]

In England and Scotland there were reports of business failures, and of workers losing their employment through technological changes in industry. Early in April there were two thousand eight hundred handloom weavers idle in Glasgow and its neighbourhood.[41] Eight thousand weavers were out of employment at Spitalfields, and in want of the necessaries of life. To relieve their distress the young Queen donated one hundred guineas.[42] From pulpit, press and pamphlet the improvers of mankind hounded the weak for their transgressions and held out promises of change to those who heeded their counsel. One gave warning: Take heed, and do not covet, and a rector's wife added this warning to emigrants:

[36] *The Times*, 1 April 1837.   [37] Ibid., 3 April 1837.   [38] Ibid., 6 April 1837.
[39] See, for example, the Reverend Mr Lang's Speech to the London Protestant Association, and the Resolutions of that Association, *The Times*, 1 April and 13 May 1837.
[40] *The Times*, 10 April 1837; see also G. de Beaumont, *Ireland, Social, Political and Religious* (2 vols, London, 1839).   [41] *The Times*, 4 April 1837.   [42] Ibid., 12 April 1837.

[Nor] seek in white robed innocence to dress
The earth-born daughters of licentiousness;
Or e'er attempt in polished lines to prove
That sensuality or vice,—is love![43]

Domestics of all grades were told that their station properly and honourably filled was too respectable to need the aid of fine clothes. They were reminded that they could not touch pitch, and remain undefiled.[44] A moralizing broadsheet illustrated Christmas in the drunkard's family: no pudding for the poor little children, no play and no home but the pot-house. By contrast, at the teetotaller's Christmas all was plenty and peace, 'such as all men might win, with a blessing from God by abstaining from gin'.[45] Radicals held out their own promise of better things for mankind, to be achieved by changing political institutions. While Christians protested their unworthiness, and their taints, the radicals celebrated with their brother democrats the feast of reason and the flow of soul.[46] *The Times*, speaking for all conservatives, countered that the aim of radicals was to break down each and all of the public institutions of the country—military, civil, and religious—always deviating from common sense and decency.[47]

At the declarations of the polls that May, Tories and conservatives complained that voters had been driven to the poll like swine to a market under the lash and power of the liberal borough-manager, while radicals complained that polling had been carried on under the awe of the sabres of the British army. Angry men shouted against these base, bloody and brutal Whigs. Mobs at Huddersfield and Westminster called loudly the names of their heroes— Roebuck and Molesworth.[48] It was nothing to them that just fifty years earlier the First Fleet had sailed for Botany Bay. They were not to know that Molesworth had other things on his mind that day than the feast of reason and the flow of soul. By then the committee which he had the honour to chair had been taking evidence for one month.

On a lively day in spring, just as the countryside was beginning to celebrate the annual miracle of rebirth, Sir Francis Forbes came to the committee fresh from the royal levee, hoping that the intimation of decay in his body was but a bad dream, that he too, like nature, could share in the rebirth; confident and full of good will towards these men who had at last singled him out for distinction; humble, yet vain enough to savour the new honour about to be conferred on him—the honour of being the first witness before the select committee to inquire into the system of transportation. To his surprise, and possibly also to his delight, he was able to begin by correcting the chairman, Sir William Molesworth, on a question of fact. For Molesworth, possibly in the

---

[43] The Rector's Wife, *The Emigrants; A Tale of Truth* (Eton, 1835).

[44] A Looker On, *A Short Letter To The Servants in Great Britain; From A Friend* (London, 1852).

[45] The Drunkard's Christmas (London, n.d., broadsheet in British Museum); for an attack on the temperance clergy, see Charles Dickens, *Pickwick Papers* (Oxford ed., 1948), ch. 33 and 52.

[46] *The Times*, 13 May 1837.   [47] Ibid., 8 April 1837.

[48] *The Times*, 10 and 13 May 1837; for a description of the elections, see also Charles Dickens, op. cit., ch. 13, Some Account of Eatanswill; of the State of the Parties therein; and of the Election of a Member to Serve in Parliament for that ancient, loyal and patriotic Borough.

nervous excitement of a young man of twenty-seven years taking the chair of a committee which might influence the future course of European civilization in the south seas, possibly in the deep ignorance of all things Australian common to some men in public life in England, began by asking Forbes: You are Chief Justice of Australia? And Forbes replied: New South Wales. But if Forbes hoped that this was to be one of those inquiries he loved so passionately, fact-finding and looking at a question from all angles without committing oneself to anything, he was doomed to disappointment. The chairman quickly showed that for his part he was anxious to collect the evidence for the abolition of transportation.

So Sir Francis had to spend much time on subjects where he felt least happy. He had to discuss the wealth of emancipists; he had to tell them all he knew about convicts living with aboriginal women; he had to tell them about the number of houses of ill fame in Sydney; he had to tell them whether convict men and women, or ex-convicts, sometimes occupied the best places in the theatre in Sydney; he had to tell them whether there was sodomy in New South Wales. Sir Francis was a little put out by this prying of the chairman into examples of depravity in New South Wales: no voyeur he, nor a secret sharer of such wickedness and vice. It was as though Molesworth were implying that he, Sir Francis, the Chief Justice of New South Wales and its dependent territories, a man who hoped to pass one day through the gate leading to everlasting life, had spent his days with his eye to the keyholes of the brothels of New South Wales. He could only tell Molesworth that New South Wales had been called a Sodom in the newspapers, adding, sound lawyer that he was, that he knew this only on mere supposition and belief.

On the subject of crime and punishment he was on more familiar ground. He agreed in general with Mr Justice Burton about the frightful prevalence of crime, that the main business of New South Wales seemed to be the commission of crime and the punishment of it. For Sir Francis had begun to drift with that current of opinion he had detected in high places and to see the world more and more through the eyes of James Macarthur and Mr Justice Burton. As for that other charge, 'the total corruption of them all', he just could not undertake to say what Burton meant by the sentence. He agreed with it generally, which was clearly what Molesworth wanted him to say, but added, as an afterthought, that it was too sweeping, and was certainly not true of the free population or the native-born. For Sir Francis was a stranger to any prompting to be treacherous to those who had given him their respect, their admiration and their affection. In general, he told the committee, he did not favour a sudden end of transportation—knowing how deeply the chairman was committed to abolishing the unclean thing. As for the suffering at the penal settlements, all he could say was that human nature could endure a great deal.[49]

On 21 April James Mudie testified like a man who had put a hand on a Holy Bible, and swore that he would tell them the truth, the whole truth and

[49] Evidence of Sir Francis Forbes to the Select Committee on Transportation, 14 and 18 April and 2 May 1837, Report of the Select Committee on Transportation, *P.P.* 1837, XIX, 518; G. Grey to F. Forbes, 3 April 1837 (Forbes Papers); see the paper, Statement re unnatural crimes 1831-5, committed in New South Wales, for evidence that Forbes had collected information on unnatural crime before leaving for London.

nothing but the truth, so help him God. But by the truth the 'Major' meant anything which would blacken the reputation of Bourke, a point on which he could be used by Molesworth, because Mudie was only too happy to give examples of how Bourke's convict system had corrupted and degraded the whole of society. He told them of how the wives of convicts prostituted themselves to other workers in the country districts of New South Wales, who paid in sugar and tea; he told them how husbands boasted that they put two bags behind the door, one for the sugar, and one for the tea, and if the bags were full when they returned from their work at the end of the day, they did not complain. He told them of how the convicts slept with aboriginal women, and then told their men when a pale-face child was born that their women had been eating too much white bread. All this encouraged Molesworth to ask Mudie about unnatural crimes. On this the 'Major' was most accommodating; he told them how the convict boys of New South Wales answered to the names of Kitty and Nancy, and how the men who went in for that sort of thing were known as sods. When the chairman asked whether other convicts did not look on such conduct with abhorrence and detestation, the 'Major' said 'No', thus conceding the point the chairman was anxious to establish— namely, that here were the germs of a nation so thoroughly depraved in their vicious propensities that they did not even loathe such abominations. So Molesworth, who was well known to exercise an irresistible attraction for aristocratic ladies, because he had the ideas and the morals of an infidel, collected the evidence with which to damn a whole society for moral depravity.

As for the society of New South Wales, Mudie painted an equally lurid picture. Tambourine Sal, a convict woman who had played the tambourine about the streets of London like a gypsy, a coarse vulgar woman of the lowest grade, now presided at the head of a table in one of the wealthiest houses of Sydney. He must say, he added, in all fairness, no concubine had ever been invited to a Government House ball or any official entertainment. As for the native-born, they spent their leisure at such blood sports as boxing, bull-baiting, and dog-fighting. Emancipists were so partisan as jurors that they seldom convicted one of their kind. So when Charles Buller, political economist, systematic colonizer, member of Parliament, tall and burly, very fetching, it was said, to the ladies of the Whig and radical salons because of a strong wit, an indefinable but unmistakable charm, and a broken nose which spoke of deeds of daring and possibly of conquest, asked him whether the root of the evil consisted in having a convict population, Mudie replied with his usual brashness that there was no question about it, never pausing for one moment to reflect that he was insulting the descendants of those men and women who just fifty years earlier had essayed the seemingly impossible with their pitiable equipment and laid the foundations of civilization in Australia. It never occurred to Mudie to wonder what the 'Betsey Bandicoots' of New South Wales, the ones who were proud of knowing what was what and prouder still of 'the land, boys, we life in' would think of a man who had likened them to goats and monkeys in their low sensuality.[50]

---

[50] Evidence of J. Mudie to the Select Committee on Transportation, 21 April, 5 and 9 May 1837, op. cit. No attempt is being made to summarize all the evidence, or to name all the witnesses; the intention is to take the witnesses who were either principal characters in the history of

The next witness was a man who was a stranger to such darkness. With the confidence of the man who knew he had won the esteem of men such as Stephen, Grey, Russell and Glenelg, and the confidence of a man who knew that the woman of fortune to whom he had opened his heart was by no means indifferent to his advances, James Macarthur entered the committee room on 19 May, and was confronted with a question which went to the heart of his experience of life. 'I believe', said Molesworth, 'your father was a great landed proprietor in New South Wales'. And dear, kind James replied with simple dignity: 'He was; the late Mr John Macarthur'. Molesworth knew nothing of the tragic history of that great giant of a man who had fallen asleep just three years earlier, unloved and unhonoured in the country in which he had dreamed his great dream. He wanted James Macarthur to tell the committee whether the landowners of New South Wales would be prepared to dispense with convict labour on their estates. He wanted to know whether the abolition of assignment would ruin the colony. James, not haunted or tormented by family guilt, but remembering with pride and affection the quick and generous impulses of his father, the readiness to take arms against oppression or injustice, and the calm philosophy which made him a delightful and most instructive companion, replied with a becoming pride, no, it would not have the effect of ruining the colony, and went on to say that the system of selling lands and using the proceeds as an immigration fund afforded a means of doing away with the convict system. When Molesworth pressed him to disown the native-born, James had nothing but such praise for their moral quality that Molesworth, possibly nettled at being confronted by a non-stooper from the colonies asked: 'Are you native-born yourself?' And James answered: 'Yes, I am'. As he told his brother his Australian blood was up at such an imputation upon the character of the 'Currency'. So when Molesworth pressed him again for an instance of disorderly conduct on the part of the native-born, James sparred and added: '*a Republican spirit* might be very disorderly', which so amused the non-radicals on the committee that they set up a shout. And James confessed to his brother that he was not a little pleased because it all went to show what a footing he was on with those men who were about to decide the future of New South Wales.

As the exchange continued James, divided as ever on the future of the convict system, was at pains to stress how assignment reformed the convict, being careful to add, he only meant assignment as a shepherd because that gave them habits of regularity, and was, he believed, most successful when the employers enforced cleanly habits and regular attendance at divine service on the sabbath day. On 26 May, the second day on which he gave evidence, Molesworth asked him whether the whole number of convicts now in the colony could be employed at government expense on public works with advantage to the colony. James replied, cautiously, probably not the whole number. For he was neither a malleable nor an obliging witness. He was asked

Australia or who contributed to the conclusions of the Committee; for the additional points on Molesworth and Buller, see P. Bloomfield, *Edward Gibbon Wakefield* (London, 1961), pp. 111-113.

whether there were peculiar temptations to drunkenness in New South Wales, and replied simply 'Perhaps there are', and added later that in his view human nature must be the same in all parts of the world.

That concern with what was in man never was his subject. What touched him deeply was the behaviour, and demands of the emancipists. For a brief moment before the committee he let fly, gave out his own cry of pain, and spoke with disgust, and horror, and loathing of those emancipists who wallowed in licentiousness, those emancipists who had amassed their wealth by dishonest means, those proprietors of grog shops, gambling houses, and those receivers of stolen goods, only to add, when the storm within subsided, that he knew exceptions, emancipists of property who were free from this prevalent depravity, but they were rare indeed. For his part he would exclude them from jury lists unless they could produce sufficient proof of good conduct. But when the chairman put it to him, giving him a chance to bring his evidence to a close, that every shipload of criminals sent from England tended to decrease the facility of remedying the social evils of transportation, Macarthur replied, yes, of course it did, and paused, and added, that other considerations might again counterbalance that tendency. For it was not given to him to see clearly whether it was in the interests of his class to accept without qualification the abolition of the convict system.[51]

By chance on the second day of Macarthur's evidence the man who had raised doing nothing into an art seemed at last to have made up his mind. On that 26 May when James Macarthur was being pressed by the chairman to say that New South Wales could dispense with assignment without serious pecuniary consequences, Glenelg signed a despatch to Bourke in which he told him that, being strongly impressed with the evils which appeared to him inherent in the system of assignment, he trusted that the measures in progress for the increase of free emigration to the Australian colonies, could adequately supply the future demand for labour without continuing a practice which was open to so many objections. He wanted Bourke to favour him with any suggestions with a view to the discontinuance, at the earliest practicable period, of the assignment of convicts to individual settlers. He also told Bourke to take such measures as would induce the settlers to look to immigration rather than assignment as the source from which they might obtain the requisite labour for the cultivation of their lands and for other purposes.[52]

Four days later the Reverend J. Dunmore Lang began his evidence. With that smooth and oily manner, that rubbing of the hands, and much laughter which concealed his sense of man's creation of a human dunghill in New South Wales, he began with a generalization for the historian. Transportation, he told them, as a species of punishment, was likely under proper management to prove very efficient in the attainment of the great ends of punishment, the reformation of criminals, and the prevention of crime. Then he donned, with

---

[51] Evidence of James Macarthur to the Select Committee on Transportation, 19 and 26 May and 9 June 1837, op. cit.; James Macarthur to William Macarthur, 18 March 1837 (Macarthur Papers, vol. 35, pp. 310-12); James Macarthur to William Macarthur, 7 June 1837, ibid., pp. 318-20; James Macarthur to R. Therry, 24 February 1859, ibid., vol. 1, p. 229-31.

[52] Glenelg to Bourke, 26 May 1837, *H.R.A.*, I. xviii. 763.

his usual glee, the mantle of one of those Old Testament prophets who had denounced a wicked and adulterous nation who preferred to dwell in the tents of the ungodly. Molesworth, who secretly loathed the clergy precisely because of their attitude to human depravity, was deeply pleased as Lang went on to tell them he would abolish assignment because it was a great moral evil. He told them he would abolish assignment of women, because the pain inflicted was generally speaking insufficient. Molesworth, who was a radical first and foremost to reduce the degree of pain and torture human beings inflicted on each other, had to let that pass. For Lang went on, in response to the questions of the chairman, to say the right thing: to say that convicts were contaminating the whole of society: to say that transportation occasioned a large portion of the population to think lightly of crime: to paint a picture of vice, degradation and immorality in those lurid colours some members of the committee were so anxious to hear. He told them of the amount of perjury in the law courts, how prosperity had encouraged gaiety (a bad thing, as he saw it) in the upper classes, and the practice and prevalence of the lower vices attendant upon dissipation among the lower classes, and how this was not to be explained by the body being heated by the warm climate but by the original character of the individuals, and how the convicts had taught the aborigines the European vices of drinking, and poxed their women. It was a picture of humanity rendered hideous by vice and dissipation. But Molesworth, who was disgusted and angered by the parsons who insulted humanity by their weekly pulpit ravings about the imagination of man's heart being evil from the start, nodded gravely to it all—because, after all, that was what he wanted to hear. But it was not quite what Lang wanted to say, believing as he did that the discontinuance of transportation would be calamitous in the extreme. The roistering schoolboy had got such strange things out of the mouth of a man of prayer and divine hope that Lang left the room, as he put it later, 'altered and humbled'.[53]

Towards the end of June, the man who had described transportation as the best secondary punishment known to man entered the room to give evidence. Arthur the Tory and believer in the resurrection of the dead faced Molesworth the radical and the infidel. The members of the committee began by asking him about his years of office, and some statistics, and Arthur answered promptly for he knew his Van Diemen's Land. Then they probed him about the ticket-of-leave men, and Arthur was away to his first generalization, describing their life as the most advantageous that a convict could be placed in. Molesworth, hungry for evidence that assignment was but another form of slavery, asked him whether a cruel master could ill-treat his servants, only to be told by Arthur that the ill-treated could always apply to the nearest police station. But Molesworth was not to be brushed aside. He put it to Arthur that the convict was as much at the mercy of his master as the slave was, except that his master could not apply corporal punishment to him except by order of a magistrate. To which Arthur, the one-time apologist for assignment, replied, yes, he was. Molesworth then pressed him more closely, and asked him whether an assigned

[53] Evidence of J. D. Lang to the Select Committee on Transportation, 30 May, 2 and 6 June 1837, op. cit.; *Colonist*, 17 January 1838; *Monitor*, 5 January 1838; *John Dunmore Lang*, ed. by A. Gilchrist, vol. 1, p. 220.

servant was not haunted with a continual sense of degradation, and a vehement desire to escape from it. Again Arthur said, yes, he was. Well then, Molesworth asked: if assignment destroyed self-respect, how then could it reform? To which Arthur could only reply with one of his favourite generalizations: 'I think', he said, 'it affords a better prospect of reformation than any other species of punishment that I am aware of'.

Then after Arthur had agreed that the degradation of the penal settlements could only harden a man, that marriage was the best means of reforming the female convicts, and had assured Molesworth that unnatural crime was not common amongst the free settlers, he was ready to add the weight of his own opinion to that other point on which Molesworth was so anxious for all and sundry to agree, namely, the effect of the convicts on the morals of the free inhabitants of Van Diemen's Land. Molesworth put it to him that on the whole the continuation of the system tended to the demoralization of the community. Arthur agreed. 'I think', he replied, 'it is impossible that such a class of persons can be residents in any community without the most polluting consequences. If the advantages of transportation could not clearly be made out as beneficial to this country, certainly, I think, as regards the colony itself, it should be put a stop to', which was what Molesworth wanted to hear, and, incidentally, what Arthur was not saying when he crossed swords with the Archbishop of Dublin. So, after agreeing with Molesworth that nothing would justify the evils of transportation except the paramount importance of such a settlement to the mother country, Arthur left the room.[54]

On 13 July with Molesworth in the chair, and Lord John Russell, W. Ord, C. Buller, Hawes, and R. Colborne also in attendance, the committee agreed to report to the House of Commons, which was about to rise for the summer recess, that they had received evidence but were unable to conclude their inquiries, and prepare a complete report. They recommended to the House that their evidence be printed, that as what they had done so far set in the strongest light the importance of the inquiry, and the urgent necessity of further and serious investigation into the efficacy of transportation as a punishment, and of its bearing on the welfare and morality of that country as a means of colonization, the committee be reappointed in the next session of Parliament. On 14 July the House of Commons granted them power to report to the House their observations together with the evidence taken before them so far.[55]

On 24 November, in the new session of the House, the committee was reappointed and charged once again to inquire into the system of transportation, its efficacy as a punishment, its influence on the moral state of society in the penal colonies, and how far it was susceptible of improvement. Molesworth was once again in the chair, with Lord John Russell, Sir George Grey, Mr Leader, Mr Ward, Mr Hawes, Mr Ord, Viscount Howick, Sir Thomas Fremantle, Mr F. Baring, Sir Robert Peel, Mr Charles Buller, Viscount Ebrington, Sir Charles Lemon and Mr French as his fellow members. On 29

[54] Evidence of G. Arthur to the Select Committee on Transportation, 27 and 30 June 1837, op. cit.

[55] Report of the Select Committee on Transportation, *P.P.*, 1837, XIX, 518, p. 1.

November they held a business meeting of the committee, with Molesworth in the chair, and five members attending, including Russell who was just as dedicated to the abolition of the 'unclean thing' as Molesworth. They met again on 29 January 1838 when they decided to inquire more closely into the economic consequences in the penal colonies of the abolition of transportation, and the influence of convicts and ex-convicts on the moral state of that society.[56]

On the first point they called on James Macarthur once again to guide them. They wanted to know whether, in his opinion, immigrant labour would be cheaper in the end than slave or forced labour. He was most helpful. He told them on 5 February that the colony would be in the highest degree benefited. He told them also that, if he had his way, then the whole of the land fund would be used for immigration. He told them also much of what they wanted to hear about the reluctance of the free to work with the bond. But when the chairman put it to him that free workers would surely be better than thieves, doubt and indecision crept back into Macarthur, and he said, yes, they would, only to add that the free, alas, could not be put under restraint. Then they asked him whether he thought the use of Indians or Chinese in the penal colonies would be a most serious evil, and he said yes—for that, too, was what Stephen, and Molesworth, and Buller and all men of heroic ingredients believed in London—namely, that Australia should not be freed from the taint of convictism at the price of all the evils of miscegenation.

They then questioned him on the future constitution of New South Wales. Buller, sound systematic colonizer that he was, asked him whether New South Wales should have a British type of constitution. On this Macarthur urged them to hasten slowly: 'You mean that', Buller put it to him, 'looking at the state of society caused by the existence of transportation for so many years, you think that certain modifications of the usual forms of representative government ought to be adopted in any plan brought into execution in that colony?' 'Yes,' replied Macarthur, 'that is precisely what I want to say'. And when Molesworth asked him why he, Macarthur, would not favour the free Canadian constitution of 1791 for New South Wales, he replied he would not because a large number of the free inhabitants of New South Wales were persons who were formerly convicts and had become free. So James Macarthur had his opportunity to teach Lord John Russell that it was possible to abolish transportation without surrendering to the reckless demands of the Botany Bay Whigs, the liberals, radicals, publicans, wealthy emancipists, and all those with what he called social peculiarities.[57]

With this assurance from Macarthur that New South Wales at least would be greatly benefited by the abolition of transportation, the members of the committee turned their minds once again to the evidence for moral pollution. On 8 February W. B. Ullathorne, the Vicar-General, gave evidence. He had never forgotten that day in September 1834 at Norfolk Island when he, a young priest in the Catholic Church, believing that God had made men lower than the angels, but not as low as the beasts, had entered a room in the gaol,

[56] Ibid., *P.P.*, 1837-8, XXII, 669, p. 1.

[57] Evidence of James Macarthur to the Select Committee on Transportation, 5 February 1838, *P.P.*, 1837-8, XXII, 669.

and, as he mentioned the names of the men who were to die by hanging, they dropped on their knees and thanked God that they were to be delivered from that horrible place, while the others, the reprieved, remained standing mute and weeping. He had come to England to persuade priests to return with him to prevent such abominations. In Liverpool in 1837 he had published a pamphlet in which he had expressed his own anguish at what man had done to God's creatures in the penal colonies of Australia:

> We have been doing an ungracious and ungodly thing. We have taken a vast portion of God's earth, and have made it a cess-pool; we have taken the oceans, which, with their wonders, gird the globe, and have made them the channels of a sink; we have poured down scum upon scum, and dregs upon dregs, of the off-scourings of mankind, and, as these harden and become consistent together, we are building up with them a nation of crime, to be, unless something be speedily done, a curse and a plague, and a by-word to all the people of the earth.
>
> The eye of God looks down upon a people, such as, since the deluge, has not been. Where they marry in haste, without affection; where each one lives to his senses alone. A community without the feelings of community; whose men are very wicked, whose women are very shameless, and whose children are very irreverent. Whose occupation has been, and is, as that described by the prophet of sorrow, '*to steal, to murder, to commit adultery, to swear falsely*'.
>
> The naked savage, who wanders through those endless forests, knew of nothing monstrous in crime, except cannibalism, until England schooled him in horrors through her prisoners. The removal of such a plague from the earth concerns the whole human race.[58]

So now on this cold bleak day in February William Bernard Ullathorne, this young cub, the priest saved from the vanities of *ego solus* by that command of his divine master to have compassion on even the least of the little ones, told them what he had seen in New South Wales and Van Diemen's Land. He told them that the huddling of boys together in a convict ship was always accompanied with a great deal of moral pollution: he told them that through the association of the men with the boys the moral contamination was very great indeed: he told them that he knew of convict shepherds who spent a great portion of their time in prayer, but most of them were very vicious, and indulged in a great deal of evil: he told them he knew one convict who was blind who used to thank God for his blindness because it shut out the scenes of iniquity in the barracks: he told them of the evil effects of the convicts on the children of the colony, who had not, as a consequence, that spirit of reverence either for their parents or any superior authority, and how the convicts created amongst their children an insolence of feeling and of bearing towards their elders: he told them unnatural crime was so prevalent it had caused him such pain and torture of mind that for his part he would even deliberately give his life if that would contribute towards the removal of that evil. As for the penal settlements, there a man lost the heart of a man, and was fashioned in the shape of a beast: there evil was distinguished by the convicts as good, and good as evil, to which coercion was no answer, for that only gave a man the heart

[58] Evidence of W. B. Ullathorne to the Select Committee on Transportation, 8 and 12 February 1838, op. cit.; W. B. Ullathorne, *The Catholic Mission in Australasia* (Liverpool, 1837), pp. iv-v.
X2

of a beast. The man of God, who believed that the life of man was not intended to end like that of the beasts, who went back to the dust from whence they came, and left not a trace that they had been here,[59] was on common ground with an infidel.

So was Sir Richard Bourke. In January of 1837, exhausted and weary, he had shown his heart to his friend, Spring Rice, 'I must go home', he had written from Sydney. Now here he was just over a year later in London, determined to work hard, which, he believed, was the perfection of wisdom, but troubled by the false and scandalous attacks on him in Mudie's book, anxious lest all the letters which McLeay and his son had written to the Colonial Office might have sullied his reputation and his honour with those men whom he had served to the best of his ability for the last seven years. He was worried, too, lest in the exchange of letters between his own son and his enemies in *The Times* and the *Morning Chronicle*, some of that mud would besmirch his own honour and his own reputation. But his heart was not troubled for long. Stephen greeted him as a man of stature, and told him that Molesworth was making effective use of his despatches in drafting his report for the Transportation Committee. As for the reckless charges of the flogging 'Major' he had talked so wildly before the committee that even the chairman had thought of asking him to withdraw. No one in London believed Bourke's policy had anything to do with the alleged lamentable depravity of manners or the frightful prevalence of crime. On the contrary everyone who mattered believed Bourke had acted with wisdom, justice and humanity.[60]

By that time Molesworth made no attempt to suppress his opinions as an abolitionist. On 6 March he told the House of Commons his committee would spare no pains to discover by what means the productive and commercial prosperity of the penal colonies might be preserved when the main cause of that prosperity, a constant and increasing supply of convict labour, would be abolished for very shame at the continuance of the moral horrors of transportation. He told them, too, that he could hardly conceive a greater absurdity than the proposal to set up democratic institutions in colonies amongst the ignorant and superstitious millions of India, or the convict and once-convict inhabitants of New South Wales. Macarthur had not spoken to the radical in vain. He told them, too, that it was their duty to take care that the office of Secretary of State for the Colonies was not filled by one of the most incompetent members of the government. But not even Molesworth's oratory and

[59] Evidence of W. B. Ullathorne to the Select Committee on Transportation, 8 and 12 February 1838, op. cit., p. 14 et seq.

[60] R. Bourke to Lord Monteagle, Sydney, 28 January 1837 (Bourke Papers, vol. 9); R. Bourke to his son, Sydney, 5 May 1837 (Bourke Papers, vol. 6); for Molesworth on Bourke, see the Report of the Select Committee on Transportation *P.P.*, 1837-8, XXII, 669, p. xxix; for the exchanges in the London Press about Bourke, see the letter of Dudley Perceval to the *Morning Chronicle* written 10 October 1837; see also *Sydney Herald*, 30 March 1837; see also *The Times*, 27 September 1836 for an article on Bourke's administration; for a defence of Bourke, see the letter of R. Bourke jr to the *Morning Chronicle*, 14 December 1836, reproduced in the *Sydney Herald*, 17 April 1837; for the correspondence of A. McLeay and his son with the Colonial Office over the former's resignation, see C.O. 201/258, pp. 176-91; see for example, W. J. Macleay to Glenelg, Soho Square, 1 September 1836, and the marginal minute by James Stephen; neither the father nor the son seemed to realize they had written to a man who had raised doing nothing into an art.

wit and passion could persuade Melbourne to dispense with Glenelg. So Glenelg stayed, unlikely as ever to say anything definite on the future of transportation or the future constitution of the colonies, and Molesworth turned back to his committee hoping to persuade them to abolish the unclean thing.[61]

Molesworth collected further evidence on the failure of transportation to excite an appropriate degree of apprehension in the minds of the criminal classes of the United Kingdom. He also read the report submitted by Captain Maconochie, a young man with some years of experience in Van Diemen's Land, and a sense of mission to rid punishment of all that degraded a man and lowered him to the level of a beast, who had suggested a different system of penal discipline. He also re-read with care that part of Macarthur's evidence in which the latter had suggested how the convicts formerly in assignment could be employed in road parties to the profit of the colony, and the improvement of the morals of those undergoing punishment.[62] On 2 April the last witness completed his evidence. He was Major Thomas Wright who had served in the army on Norfolk Island. The last word came from a man who had served on that island where the committee had been told a man's heart was taken from him, and there was given to him the heart of a beast. Although Wright emphasized that he could only state matters to the best of his recollection, Molesworth never had entertained any doubts from the start that it was the convict system and not innate depravity which had taken men's hearts from them and given them those hearts of beasts. They met again on 6 April and 30 May to discuss the nature and scope of their report.[63]

On 20 July Molesworth submitted his draft to eight members of the committee, including Lord John Russell, but not Sir George Grey or Viscount Howick—those two sceptics on the case for abolition. To plant a colony, and to form a new society, Molesworth wrote, had ever been an arduous task. In New South Wales the community had been composed of the very dregs of society, the consequences of which were vice, immorality, frightful disease, hunger, dreadful mortality, and the most hideous cruelty practised towards the unfortunate natives. Transportation did not produce apprehension in the minds of criminals. The great and yearly emigration to all the British colonies, even to the penal ones, would soon deprive exile to Australia of all its imaginary terrors. Transportation, though chiefly dreaded as exile, was undoubtedly much more than exile: it was slavery as well. The question was: as the extraordinary commercial prosperity of those colonies was occasioned by the constant supply of convict labour, would the colonies be ruined if that supply were cut off? Happily the committee did not need to weigh the economic advantages of transportation against its moral evils, for, on the evidence before them, and thanks especially to Macarthur, it was clear that if the colonies were to depend

---

[61] Speech by W. Molesworth on Lord Glenelg's Colonial Administration, 6 March 1838, reproduced in H. E. Egerton (ed.), *Selected Speeches of Sir William Molesworth on Questions Relating to Colonial Policy* (London, 1903), pp. 1-53; see also C. C. F. Greville, *Memoirs. A Journal of the Reigns of King George IV and King William IV, passim.*

[62] A. Maconochie, *Report on the State of Prison Discipline in Van Diemen's Land* (London, 1838); for evidence of use made of this report, see Report of Select Committee on Transportation, *P.P.*, 1837-8, XXII, 669.

[63] Evidence of Major T. Wright to the Select Committee on Transportation, 2 April 1838, op. cit.

on the gaols for their labour their prosperity had reached its climax, and must soon begin to decline.[64] Nothing, Molesworth wrote, could be better demonstrated than that labour must be supplied from other sources than that of transportation, if New South Wales and Van Diemen's Land were to continue to flourish. But, he insisted, the Australian colonies would be ill-advised to supply their want of labour by importing Hindus, for that would be just another form of slavery to which colonists might have recourse when suffering from a want of labour. Besides if the Hindus remained and multiplied, they would form a separate and probably a slave caste. No statesman familiar with the difficulties arising from the use of slaves in the southern states of the United States of America would consent to curse Australia with such an evil.

Having dispensed with the argument of economic security, Molesworth returned with all the more confidence to sum up the case against transportation. Its two main characteristics were, he wrote, inefficiency in deterring from crime, and remarkable efficiency, not in reforming, but in still further corrupting those who underwent the punishment. These qualities of inefficiency for good and efficiency for evil were inherent in the system, which therefore was not susceptible of any satisfactory improvement. Lastly, there belonged to the system, extrinsically from its strange character as a punishment, the yet more curious and monstrous evil of calling into existence, and continually extending, societies, or the germs of nations most thoroughly depraved. The committee, therefore, was of the opinion that the present system of transportation should be abolished—or, as they put it in their specific recommendations: transportation to New South Wales, and to the settled districts of Van Diemen's Land, should be discontinued as soon as practicable.[65]

So, by one of those odd ironies in human affairs a radical and an infidel used the ideas of a Tory from Botany Bay, James Macarthur, of a young cub who believed his authority had been committed to him from 'on High', William Bernard Ullathorne, of the bizarre 'Major' Mudie, and of a clergyman who believed New South Wales had been used as a dunghill of the Empire, to condemn not only the convict system, but all creatures great and small born to man's estate in New South Wales and Van Diemen's Land. A committee of the House of Commons had branded a generation of men with an intense pride in the land they lived in, who believed no immigrant could stand up to a 'native rooster', who were beginning to prefer the loud cooee of a currency lad riding over the blue mountains to the soft singing notes of an Italian in a gondola, men who were certain they knew what was what—this committee had called them 'the germs of nations most thoroughly depraved as respects both the character and degree of their vicious propensities'. With that indifference of the improvers of mankind to the outrages they inflict on the sensibilities of their victims Molesworth presented the report to the House of Commons on 3 August, and then blandly told his constituents at Leeds, whom in an impulsive moment he had called the dirtiest looking dogs he had ever beheld, how inefficient, cruel and demoralizing transportation was; how

[64] For the influence of Macarthur on this point, see the Report of the Select Committee on Transportation, *P.P.*, 1837-8, XXII, 669, pp. xxxviii-xxxix; Mrs Fawcett, op. cit., pp. 143-4.

[65] Report of the Select Committee on Transportation, op. cit., pp. iv, xix, xx, xxxiii-v, xli, xlvi.

utterly it failed in attaining the two grand objects of penal legislation, the prevention of crime by means of terror, and the reformation of offenders; and how deplorable was the moral state of the communities to which it had given birth. He wanted humanity to walk towards that chink of light at the end of a long, dark corridor in their history. As he saw it the 'unclean thing' had received its death warrant.[66]

The other actors in the drama continued to receive the prizes and the blanks in the human lottery. Bourke, after writing a memorandum for 'Finality Jack' Russell on the transportation and assignment of convicts, retired to his beloved Thornfield where, in the season of the sere, the yellow leaf, he found that honour, love, troops of friends, and recognition, to which all men aspire and which few achieve. He died in 1855 knowing that the 'unclean thing' had ended, and Whiggism had triumphed in New South Wales.[67]

Ullathorne was to know a prize of a different kind. After a brief return to New South Wales he left for England at the end of 1840, and was consecrated Bishop of Hethluna in 1846. In September 1850, with the re-establishment of the Catholic hierarchy in England, he was appointed Bishop of Birmingham. There with that grace and insight which had enabled him to see into the heart of the matter about transportation, he perceived the genius in a priest in his diocese, and encouraged him to answer the question 'What does Dr Newman mean?' The result was one of those lofty peaks in the mountains of human achievement, when in 1864 John Henry Newman published the *Apologia pro Vita Sua*.[68]

By contrast the gods or chance were preparing a cruel fate for Sir Francis Forbes. Just as he gained the worldly prize of his knighthood, sickness broke him. Impatient for a time, he cursed but then faith conferred on him a dignity and strength with which to confront the malice of his enemies. Compelled by ill-health to retire from the office of Chief Justice on 1 July 1837 on a pension of £700 a year, he returned to New South Wales. There the press mocked him as a man who had sold the birthrights of Englishmen for a mess of potage in a royal palace. The *Sydney Herald* urged him to enjoy his *otium cum dignitate*, and eat his mutton chop at his splendid station in the Hunter River district where his one-time friends, the convict levellers of New South

---

[66] Ibid., p. xlvii; Molesworth's report to his constituents at Leeds, Pencarrow, 1 October 1838, quoted in Mrs Fawcett, op. cit., pp. 143-4; Molesworth dedicated the report to his constituents at Leeds, see Mrs Fawcett, op. cit., p. 143. The reception of the committee's report in London was rather mixed. *The Times* of 12 September 1838 thought their idea of an occasional confinement in prison for a thief would be an agreeable variety in their profligate and reckless career. Blackwood's *Edinburgh Magazine* of November 1838 believed England was determined to confer the largest share of moral and physical advantages upon her remote and struggling offspring. The English juries had shaped a new dominance in the south seas. The *Quarterly Review*, vol. 62, 1838, agreed with the committee that the time had come when the practice of transportation could no longer be continued on its present scale.

[67] For the life of W. B. Ullathorne and his association with Newman after leaving New South Wales see Dom Cuthbert Butler, *The Life and Times of Bishop Ullathorne, 1806-1889* (2 vols, London, 1926); for the writing of the *Apologia pro Vita Sua*, see the excellent introduction by Basil Willey to the World's Classics ed. (London, 1964).

[68] Correspondence with Sir Richard Bourke, on the state of Convict Discipline, *P.P.*, 1837, XIX, 550.

Wales, enraged by the great apostasy, had posted the word 'scab' on one of
his trees. But a great darkness had begun to descend for Sir Francis. With
limbs lame and brain diseased by debility he prayed then not for worldly
favours, but that God's will be done quickly so that he might know that peace
of God passing all understanding. He died at Newtown on 8 November 1841.
The *Australian* mourned him as a most upright and impartial judge, a fearless
asserter, in evil times, of the liberty of the press and the people, and an
enlightened friend to national education. Wentworth, to whom his poverty-
stricken widow appealed for assistance, passed her by, but Dr Bland offered
help in memory of the man who at the pinnacle of his power had rejoiced
when the felons' chains had been struck off.[69]

Though rumour had it that Lang had left that committee room in London
in 1837 an altered and humbled man, he was not prepared to endure in
unmurmuring silence and patient resignation the suspicious glances and
averted looks of men who, he believed, had been poisoned in secret by the
slanderous effusions of a heartless traitor, and had wounded and betrayed the
cause of Christ's church. Within a month of that humbling experience he was
berating his enemies with all the reckless extravagance which had caused him to
brand God's creatures in New South Wales a dunghill of the Empire.[70] For
the flogging 'Major' of Castle Forbes man's judgment was equally harsh. On
his return to Sydney, the son of Kinchela whipped him in the streets of Sydney
for slandering his father in *The Felonry of New South Wales*, after which he
was shunned as the man who, in an evil hour of seeking revenge on the
beloved Bourke, had contributed to that wicked lie that convictism had
germinated a vicious and depraved nation in the south seas.[71]

On one man at least the gods smiled. With the wool market slowly recover-
ing, successful talks with Bourke's successor, and intercourse with Downing
Street of a very satisfactory character, James Macarthur began to write as a
man who was about to enter into his kingdom. Beloved and respected by all
who knew him, in that spring of 1838 he had offered his hand in marriage to
a young woman of fortune, Amelia (Emily) Stone, the daughter of a Lom-
bard Street banker, who had been born in Calcutta on 26 February 1806.
They were married that June by his old friend, Thomas Hobbes Scott, who
wrote to Elizabeth Macarthur to tell her that James and Emily would afford
her in the evening of her life all the comfort and joys she so richly deserved.
James was so carried away by his great good fortune that he gave Scott a
present so magnificent that the latter was overcome and wanted to hand it
back and would have done so, had he not known how affluent James was, and
how offensive it would be to refuse. With the *Sydney Herald* waxing enthusiastic over him as a gentleman, and the *Australian* branding him as the champion of Toryism and exclusivism, who would stamp emancipists with an
indelible brand of infamy, James prepared to bring his bride back to Camden

---

[69] *Australian*, 11 November 1841; Lady Forbes to James Macarthur, 4 November 1852 (Macarthur Papers, vol. 27, p. 124).

[70] *Colonist*, 17 January 1838; *Sydney Herald*, 7 August and 30 October 1837; *Monitor*, 5
January 1838; *John Dunmore Lang* ed. by A. Gilchrist, vol. 1, p. 222.

[71] *Sydney Herald*, 28 May 1838.

Park. For, as had been said of old, men hold some things wrong and some right, but to God all things are fair and good and right.[72]

[72] James Macarthur to William Macarthur, 18 March 1837, 6 July 1837, 4 October 1837 and 7 June 1838 (Macarthur Papers, vol. 35, pp. 310-79); T. H. Scott to Elizabeth Macarthur, 14 June 1838 (Macarthur Papers, vol. 59, pp. 191-4); *Sydney Herald*, 9 November 1837; *Australian*, 27 November 1837; the passage from Heraclitus is quoted in J. and J. M. Todd (eds.), *Voices From The Past* (London, 1955), p. 109.

EPILOGUE

B Y APRIL OF 1838 the eyes of the Reverend Samuel Marsden were very dim with age. For just on forty-five years he had gone through many toils and hardships, and had often had to contend with unreasonable and wicked men in power. He had gone through many dangers by land and water both amongst the heathen and amongst his own countrymen. But the Lord in His mercy had delivered him at all times from the snares of his enemies. God willing, he hoped that year to have again the great gratification to see the poor heathen in New Zealand, and give them again the hope of immortal glory. But such was not to be. In the parsonage of St Matthew's at Windsor, in that district where twenty years earlier he had taken his stand against Andrew Thompson's lapse from rectitude, his hour of need struck on 12 May. Repeating the word 'precious' over and over again in a vain attempt to say that a good hope in Christ was precious in a man's hour of need, death closed his earthly career as he struggled to tell his fellow-men of the Saviour whom he had served through his life.

Three days later a very large and most respectable group gathered at St John's Church in Parramatta to pay their last tribute to a man who was endeared to them by many of the noblest virtues that adorned mankind. After the majestic words of the service for the burial of the dead, with its reminder that man was full of misery, that he came up, and was cut down like a flower, they committed his body to the dust. Five days later, on 20 May, the Reverend Henry Stiles, the rector of St Matthew's, Windsor, preached a panegyric at St John's, Parramatta. He told the congregation that just as Luther had been sent by the Head of the church to Germany, John Knox to Scotland and Cranmer to England to unfold His glorious gospel, when those countries were almost hidden in Romish darkness, so no less truly was Samuel Marsden raised up to diffuse the light of the same gospel upon the darkness of heathen sin in New Zealand, and upon the darkness of human depravity in early Australia. Marsden had represented man as in a condemned and helpless state, lying in all the pollution and filthiness of his sin and totally unable to justify himself wholly or in part by any works of righteousness. God alone could redeem man from the bondage to sin and death. In Marsden's eyes God was the only author of the little that was good in man.[1]

[1] S. Marsden to D. Coates, Parramatta, 10 February and 26 April 1838 (Bonwick Transcripts, Box 54, pp. 2000-4); *Sydney Gazette*, 15 and 17 May 1838; Diary of George Suttor, 15 May 1838 (MS. in M.L.); H. Stiles, *A Sermon, preached in St John's Church, Parramatta, May 20th, 1838, on the occasion of the death of The Rev. Samuel Marsden, of Parramatta* (Sydney, 1838). There are memorials to Marsden in St John's Church, Parramatta, St Matthew's Church,

Some months later Henry Dowling, the son of a Baptist minister in England, who had arrived in Van Diemen's Land in 1830, and begun to publish the *Launceston Advertiser* in 1831, because he wanted the world to have more light, published an edition of the *Pickwick Papers* in Launceston. Like Mr Pickwick, Dowling knew there were dark shadows on the earth, but the lights, he believed, were all the stronger in contrast. Like Mr Pickwick he believed that some men, like bats or owls, had better eyes for the darkness than for the light, but again like Mr Pickwick he preferred to look at his fellow-men when the brief sunshine of the world was blazing full on them. No longer need men flying from the darkness and dissensions of Europe seek America as the one country where man had lit up the wilderness. Men might have it better, too, in Australia. There something of an extraordinary nature might turn up one day on that shore when men liberated themselves from the curse of Adam's fall. There men, freed at last from the stain of the Old World, freed too from the convict's clanking chain, might see that heaven and hell were priests' inventions, and come to trust the brotherhood of man.[2]

Windsor, at Farsley in Yorkshire, England, and at The Bay of Islands and Waimate, North Island of New Zealand. The tone for the judgments by the historians on Marsden was set by L. Macquarie in his *A Letter to the Right Honourable Viscount Sidmouth* (London, 1821) and W. C. Wentworth in *A Statistical Account of the British Settlements in Australasia; including the Colonies of New South Wales and Van Diemen's Land* (3rd ed., 2 vols, London, 1824). Apart from the words of praise by the clergy and the missionaries, this unfavourable tone pervaded most comments from that day to the present. See, for example, Eris O'Brien, *The Foundation of Australia (1786-1800)* (London, 1937), p. 65: 'Marsden in particular was noted for the severity of his sentences, and his position was summed up succinctly by the convicts, who said that though he prayed for mercy on their souls on Sundays, he had little mercy on their bodies on weekdays'. This opinion has been taken up by the poets and painters. See, for example, 'Vesper-Song of the Reverend Samuel Marsden' in K. Slessor, *One Hundred Poems 1919-1939* (Sydney, 1944), *e.g.*

> O, souls that leak with holes of sin,
> Shall I not let God's leather in,
> Or hit with sacramental knout
> Your twice-convicted vileness out?

See also the painting of the Reverend Samuel Marsden by Donald Friend which portrays a man who believed he could welt souls into heaven or hell. The New Zealand estimate of Marsden has always differed from the estimates in Australia; from the Maori encomium of 'Greatheart' to J. R. Elder's monumental work, *The Letters and Journals of Samuel Marsden 1765-1838* (Dunedin, 1932) the praise has been maintained.

[2] For Henry Dowling see entry in T.S.A.; see also Charles Dickens, *Pickwick Papers* (Henry Dowling, Launceston, Van Diemen's Land, 1839), ch. 57; for America as a promised land see D. J. Boorstin, *The Americans*, vol. 1, The Colonial Experience (New York, 1958); for the idea that America had it better than the Old World, see Goethe's poem 'Den Vereinigten Staaten':

> Amerika, du hast es besser
> Als unser Kontinent, das alte,

For the strength of this idea in Europe in the second half of the nineteenth century, see, for example, the effect on Shatov and Kirilov of being too close to each other in America in F. M. Dostoevsky, *The Devils* Part Two, *Night* (Penguin ed., London, 1953) and F. Kafka, *America* (with an introduction by Edwin Muir, London, 1949); for the idea that something extraordinary would turn up in Australia, see Charles Dickens, *David Copperfield* (Oxford ed., 1948), ch. 52. This idea will be taken up in the next volume of this history.

A NOTE ON SOURCES

A select bibliography of the period 1822 down to the gold decade will be included in the third volume. For the bibliography of this period readers should consult J. A. Ferguson, *Bibliography of Australia*, vol. I: 1784-1830 (Sydney, 1941), vol. II: 1831-1838 (Sydney, 1945). There is also an excellent select bibliography in M. Roe, *Quest for Authority in Eastern Australia 1835-1851* (Melbourne, 1965).

The following are the main guides to the material:
Guide to Collections of Manuscripts relating to Australia (National Library of Australia, Canberra, 1965).
Newspapers in Australian Libraries: A Union List—Newspapers Published in Australia (2nd ed., Canberra, 1967).
Ann Mozley, *A Guide to the Manuscript Records of Australian Science* (Canberra, 1966).
M. I. Adam, J. Ewing and J. Munro, *Guide to the Principal Parliamentary Papers Relating to the Dominions 1812-1911* (Edinburgh, 1913).
General Index to the Accounts and Papers, Reports of Commissioners, Estimates &c. &c. 1801-1852. P.P., 1854, LXVIII, 159.
General Index to the Reports of Select Committees 1801-1852. P. P., 1854, LXX, 509.
Guide to Manuscripts in the British Isles relating to Australia, New Zealand and the Pacific Islands (in preparation). Sponsors, The Australian National University and the National Library of Australia, Canberra.

The material published in the *Historical Records of Australia*, Series I, III, and IV, should be supplemented by using the following Colonial Office Papers:

201. Papers concerning New South Wales. They include enclosures often not in the relevant despatch in *H.R.A.*, minutes in the margin, and draft replies.
202. Despatches to the Governors and Administrators of New South Wales.
204. Blue Books or Annual Statistics for New South Wales.
280. Papers concerning Van Diemen's Land, including extracts from proceedings of the Legislative Council and Executive Council.
408. Despatches to the Lieutenant-Governors and Administrators of Van Diemen's Land.
282. Papers of the Executive Council of Van Diemen's Land.
284. Blue Books or Annual Statistics for Van Diemen's Land.
281. The Acts and Ordinances of the Legislative Council of Van Diemen's Land.

The Acts and Ordinances of the Legislative Council of New South Wales can be read most conveniently in T. Callaghan (ed.), *Acts and Ordinances of the Governor & Council of New South Wales, and Acts of Parliament enacted for, and applied to, the Colony* (2 vols, Sydney, 1844-5).

Votes and Proceedings of the Legislative Council of New South Wales 1825-38.

For a list of the extant proceedings of the Legislative Council of Van Diemen's Land, see J. A. Ferguson, *Bibliography of Australia*, vols I and II.

The main holdings of printed books, official material, newspapers, pamphlets and manuscripts for New South Wales and Van Diemen's Land are in the National Library of Australia, Canberra; the Mitchell Library, Sydney; The State Archives of New South Wales, now housed in the Public Library of New South Wales, Sydney; and the Tasmanian State Archives in the State Library of Tasmania in Hobart. Most newspapers of the United Kingdom for the period 1821-38, other than *The Times*, are in the branch of the British Museum at Colindale. Other Irish and Scottish papers may be seen in the National Library of Ireland in Dublin and in the National Library of Scotland in Edinburgh.

The location of the principal manuscript sources is as follows:

Mitchell Library, Sydney

Papers of Sir George Arthur	Lang Papers
Bonwick Transcripts	Macarthur Papers
Bourke Papers	Marsden Papers
Forbes Papers	D'Arcy Wentworth Papers
Hassall Papers	Wentworth Papers

National Library of Australia, Canberra
Brisbane Papers
Broughton Papers (microfilm)

Tasmanian State Archives
Meredith Papers

Library of the Royal Society, Hobart
Diary of G. T. W. Boyes

Private Collections
Dumaresq Papers. Mount Ireh, Longford, Tasmania
Therry Papers. Canisius College, Sydney

The location of all other manuscript material is given in the relevant footnote.

Y

INDEX